Handbook of Research on Strategic Communication, Leadership, and Conflict Management in Modern Organizations

Anthony Normore
California State University - Dominguez Hills, USA

Mitch Javidi
International Academy of Public Safety (IAPS), USA

Larry Long
Illinois State University, USA

A volume in the Advances in Human Resources Management and Organizational Development (AHRMOD) Book Series

IGI Global
DISSEMINATOR OF KNOWLEDGE

Published in the United States of America by
IGI Global
Business Science Reference (an imprint of IGI Global)
701 E. Chocolate Avenue
Hershey PA, USA 17033
Tel: 717-533-8845
Fax: 717-533-8661
E-mail: cust@igi-global.com
Web site: http://www.igi-global.com

Library of Congress Cataloging-in-Publication Data

Names: Normore, Anthony H., editor. | Javidi, Mitch, 1958- editor. | Long, Larry W., editor.
Title: Handbook of research on strategic communication, leadership, and conflict management in modern organizations / Anthony Normore, Mitch Javidi, and Larry Long, editors.
Description: Hershey, PA : Business Science Reference, [2019]
Identifiers: LCCN 2018055820| ISBN 9781522585169 (hardcover) | ISBN 9781522585176 (ebook)
Subjects: LCSH: Conflict management. | Communication in organizations. | Communication in management. | Leadership. | Organizational effectiveness.
Classification: LCC HD42 .H3663 2019 | DDC 658.4--dc23 LC record available at https://lccn.loc.gov/2018055820

This book is published in the IGI Global book series Advances in Human Resources Management and Organizational Development (AHRMOD) (ISSN: 2327-3372; eISSN: 2327-3380)

British Cataloguing in Publication Data
A Cataloguing in Publication record for this book is available from the British Library.

Advances in Human Resources Management and Organizational Development (AHRMOD) Book Series

Patricia Ordóñez de Pablos
Universidad de Oviedo, Spain

ISSN:2327-3372
EISSN:2327-3380

Mission

A solid foundation is essential to the development and success of any organization and can be accomplished through the effective and careful management of an organization's human capital. Research in human resources management and organizational development is necessary in providing business leaders with the tools and methodologies which will assist in the development and maintenance of their organizational structure.

The **Advances in Human Resources Management and Organizational Development (AHRMOD) Book Series** aims to publish the latest research on all aspects of human resources as well as the latest methodologies, tools, and theories regarding organizational development and sustainability. The **AHRMOD Book Series** intends to provide business professionals, managers, researchers, and students with the necessary resources to effectively develop and implement organizational strategies.

Coverage

- Process Improvement
- Employee Relations
- Workplace Discrimination
- Collaborative Method
- Compliance
- Change Management
- E-Human Resources Management
- Entrepreneurialism
- Organizational Learning
- Corporate Governance

IGI Global is currently accepting manuscripts for publication within this series. To submit a proposal for a volume in this series, please contact our Acquisition Editors at Acquisitions@igi-global.com or visit: http://www.igi-global.com/publish/.

The Advances in Human Resources Management and Organizational Development (AHRMOD) Book Series (ISSN 2327-3372) is published by IGI Global, 701 E. Chocolate Avenue, Hershey, PA 17033-1240, USA, www.igi-global.com. This series is composed of titles available for purchase individually; each title is edited to be contextually exclusive from any other title within the series. For pricing and ordering information please visit http://www.igi-global.com/book-series/advances-human-resources-management-organizational/73670. Postmaster: Send all address changes to above address.

Titles in this Series

For a list of additional titles in this series, please visit: www.igi-global.com/book-series

Management Techniques for Employee Engagement in Contemporary Organizations
Naman Sharma (Entrepreneurship Development Institute of India, India) Narendra Chaudhary (Symbiosis International University, India) and Vinod Kumar Singh (Gurukul Kangri Vishwavidyalaya, India)
Business Science Reference • copyright 2019 • 339pp • H/C (ISBN: 9781522577997) • US $225.00 (our price)

Emotion-Based Approaches to Personnel Management Emerging Research and Opportunities
Sara Fazzin (Niccolò Cusano Italian University in London, UK)
Business Science Reference • copyright 2019 • 235pp • H/C (ISBN: 9781522583981) • US $165.00 (our price)

Corporate Social Responsibility and Opportunities for Sustainable Financial Success
Julia Margarete Puaschunder (Columbia University, USA & The New School, USA)
Business Science Reference • copyright 2019 • 300pp • H/C (ISBN: 9781522576198) • US $200.00 (our price)

Contemporary Human Resources Management in the Tourism Industry
Demet Tüzünkan (Okan University, Turkey) and Volkan Altıntaş (Izmir Katip Celebi University, Turkey)
Business Science Reference • copyright 2019 • 405pp • H/C (ISBN: 9781522557609) • US $205.00 (our price)

Managing Diversity, Innovation, and Infrastructure in Digital Business
Nilanjan Ray (Adamas University, India)
Business Science Reference • copyright 2019 • 287pp • H/C (ISBN: 9781522559931) • US $195.00 (our price)

Managerial Competencies for Multinational Businesses
Macarena López-Fernández (University of Cádiz, Spain) and Pedro M. Romero-Fernández (University of Cádiz, Spain)
Business Science Reference • copyright 2019 • 364pp • H/C (ISBN: 9781522557814) • US $215.00 (our price)

Organizational Culture and Behavioral Shifts in the Green Economy
Violeta Sima (Petroleum-Gas University of Ploiesti, Romania)
Business Science Reference • copyright 2018 • 334pp • H/C (ISBN: 9781522529651) • US $205.00 (our price)

Disruptive Technologies for Business Development and Strategic Advantage
Anatoly V. Zhuplev (Loyola Marymount University, USA)
Business Science Reference • copyright 2018 • 364pp • H/C (ISBN: 9781522541486) • US $195.00 (our price)

IGI Global
DISSEMINATOR OF KNOWLEDGE

701 East Chocolate Avenue, Hershey, PA 17033, USA
Tel: 717-533-8845 x100 • Fax: 717-533-8661
E-Mail: cust@igi-global.com • www.igi-global.com

List of Contributors

Table of Contents

Section 2
Leadership and Communication in K-16 Education

Section 3
Identifying Challenges and Opportunities in Public Safety Leadership and Management

Detailed Table of Contents

Section 2
Leadership and Communication in K-16 Education

Web 2.0 technologies have progressively transformed social interactions among people. In addition, there is plenty of evidence of a positive influence of social relationships on work-related attitudes and behaviors. Within these frameworks, the purpose is to evaluate the effect of using online social networks on the workers' attitudes and behaviors, particularly in the context of higher education. The authors used an online survey to evaluate the attitudes and behavior of 157 faculty members. To assess the use of OSNs, they used a dichotomous variable. The t-student test and the PLS method were used to analyze the data. They conclude that the use of OSNs influences the workers' performance, but not job satisfaction, organizational commitment, or organizational citizenship behaviors (extra-role performance). The relationships they propose in what concerns the workers' attitudes are all empirically supported. Lastly, they describe the study limitations and we suggest some perspectives for future research.

There is a significant lack of documented research on Australian school improvement that is contextualized within business improvement model settings. This is the case even though Australian schools have been operating within a business environment for a while now. This chapter aims at addressing this gap by discussing what educational quality is within schools. It will present an adapted version for continuous school improvement within school systems in Australia. This adapted version of continuous school improvement provides a theoretical framework on how schools operating as self-managed business systems can ensure that the delivery of educational quality is strategically sustained at the organizational level and that focus remains on the important core business of student learning. This adapted version has been described as strategic TQM and a case is made for its use in Australian schools through five transformations that are brought about through the SCOPE cycle for school improvement.

This chapter explores concerns and challenges associated with the transition to online graduate instruction from the traditional face-to-face format. The author discusses several catalysts for the transition to virtual teaching, the ethics of being present, impediments to learning and communication online, and participant concerns. The chapter also considers online knowledge and meaning-making, online communities, and associated uncertainties. Finally, new financial decisions and considerations leading to hardships for faculty and their families as well as trends for leadership and communication moving forward are addressed.

need information fast, and any delay between the decision and the action taken could cause medical errors. One suggested solution for this problem is to implement wireless phone systems. However, psychological theory and empirical evidence, both suggest that wireless phones have the potential of creating additional problems related to interruptions. The fact that hospital workers prefer interruptive communication methods before non-interruptive methods, amplifies the risk of overloading staff. The key is how to handle the balance between increased availability and increased interruptions. In this chapter, the authors present solutions and possibilities based on context aware communication systems that aim to reduce interruptions and thereby also alarm fatigue.

This completed action research utilizes the conceptual framework of quantum mechanics in action science field studies for bias-free behavioral data collection and quantification. The research question tied to experimental verification if action research field studies can practically utilize the theory of communicative action and the theory of quantum mechanics to contextualize the quantification with pathological and distorted behavioral pattern. The result is a quantum-like formalism that provides intermediary conceptuality for organizational intervening initiatives. This process of contextualization behavior in projects via quantum probability experimentally evidenced. The chapter concludes by reviewing the results of two experiments that the hypotheses that the theory of quantum mechanics and the theory of communicative action qualifies as a building block for a planned methodological approach to intervene and steer problematic social structures in the desired direction.

When faced with crises, organizational leaders must identify, prioritize, and communicate with organizational stakeholders. Increasingly, organizational leaders find themselves responding to crises made by persons that represent or are associated with the organization in some way. However, most case studies of image repair campaigns focus on the individual that has transgressed rather than on the often-simultaneous campaigns undertaken by the organizations with which they are associated. To study these issues more closely, this chapter uses The Ohio State University's (OSU's) tattoos for memorabilia scandal as exemplar and offers meaningful insight and pragmatic considerations for practitioners dealing with similar situational constraints.

Higher education leaders need to identify differences among generations of employees and students and develop a strategic plan for managing and motivating across the generations. This case study addresses the following question: "How do higher education leaders lead and motivate multigenerational employees

Preface

INTRODUCTION

For the purposes of this volume, *Handbook of Research on Strategic Communication, Leadership, and Conflict Management in Modern Organizations*, we continue to focus on organizations and the intricate dynamics that make organizations tick. Among those dynamics and prevalent throughout the content are pivotal features that can either serve as catalysts for organizational success or as a cancer that can cause an organization to crumble: leadership, management, communication, and conflict. These concepts are crucial to all organizations. How they are utilized generally determines the sustainability and fate of the organization. These concepts will be defined as broadly as possible to encompass not only ethnic, cultural, and gender difference but all the differences protected and promoted by professional and philosophical difference. Organizations today must somehow find ways to effectively bridge, blend and lead all to be their most productive. We have searched far and wide to solicit authors who study or researched leadership, organizational health and development, or who have first-hand experiences in dealing with ways to improve organizations including communication and conflict mediation, management and orchestration. This collection of chapters is the result of numerous contributors who live and work in various non-profit and for-profit organizations throughout the world.

As editors of this volume we realized long ago having worked globally on development, environmental, education, and other organizational projects that professionals often work at odds and in silos focused only on their restrictive professional mandate and traditional style. We have witnessed professional and organizational biases, acknowledge our own, and have at times framed issues accordingly. From our individual and collective professional experiences and multi-pronged research, we have further encountered a potpourri of professionals (e.g., economists, engineers, scientists, educators, criminal justice personnel, corporate CEOs, etc.,) who communicated the significance of individual achievement and failed to effectively partner with the communities and clientele they served. At their worst, they fight over "turf" rather than collaborate for the common good (Erbe, 2014).

Among the litany of lessons learned from our experiences we see the need to deliberately and intentionally change communication approaches. Being aware of cultural differences is critical for any organization to be successful. We believe it is equally critical to honor and respect the integrity of cultural differences (Normore, 2009). We further believe this is best demonstrated in organizations in the way layers of leaders communicate their organizational goals and intentions. People sometimes express and communicate their particular concern that their cultural knowledge and practices are not being maintained to the extent that they would like. This concern is especially common for populations under pressure to change from forces which are seen as controlled by a dominant group.

Throughout this collection of chapters, communication will be defined broadly as well as simply to include any time and the myriad ways organizational constituencies are able to effectively bridge differences for reaching a shared goal. Consistent with our perspective, the National Communication Association (2015) succinctly and clearly defined the discipline of communication as a focus on how people use messages to generate meanings within and across various contexts, cultures, channels, and media. Within this framework, organizational communication is concerned with the symbolic act through which organizations adapt to, alter, or maintain their environment for the purpose of achieving organizational goals (Cummings, Long, & Lewis, 1987). We believe it is important to differentiate between the terms "communication" and "communications." Communication is concerned with an exchange of symbols/messages/meanings among humans and is a most common method for exercising leadership. In contrast, communications is concerned with the means, technologies, channels, and media people use when communicating. Communication is a strategic message creation activity; communications is a focus on the methods and channels selected for transmitting the message. Communication, along with leadership and conflict management, are inextricably intertwined elements within organizational processes that impact on outcomes.

Although leadership has been widely studied, there is a persistent lack of agreement about what constitutes the most effective leadership styles. For example, some authors understand an effective leader as somebody who people follow, or as someone who communicates well and guides people. Others define leadership as more collaborative and include team facilitation: strong communication skills coupled with the ability to organize in order to achieve a common goal. Recent scholars in educational leadership have paid considerable attention to practices and policies that have marginalized special populations (e.g., disabilities, race, socio-economics, ethnicity, gender, aged, sexual orientation, mentally ill, homelessness, etc.,) and pose challenging questions to leaders, scholars, and the broader community to engage in discussions about leadership for social justice, global cultural literacy, and intercultural, multicultural, and cross-cultural proficiency (Erbe & Normore, 2015; Normore & Brooks, 2014; Normore & Erbe, 2013). Leadership theory and leadership practice are responding to societal changes by shifting focus from what leaders do, and how they do it, to the purpose of leadership. For our purposes, effective leadership is broadly operationalized as a process of cultural and social influence in which various people enlist the help and support of others in the accomplishment of a common task. Leadership is not to be confused with management which by and large focuses on tasks-orientation and efficiency rather than influence and effectiveness.

The *Handbook of Research on Strategic Communication, Leadership, and Conflict Management in Modern Organizations* is inherently and potently transformative for organizational leaders and managers who encourage the most innovative form of managing and solving conflict, and who foster the most effective forms of internal and external communication, in support of the local, national and global communities served. If organizations lack even the basics of what is being advocated throughout this book, they may benefit from investigating the contemporary role of organizational leadership. Such organizational conflict resolution experts are prepared to coach leadership in impartial inclusive process, mediate across difference and otherwise assist all members of organizations develop the skills and consciousness needed to effectively communicate, negotiate, and collaborate across differences.

THE STRUCTURE OF THIS VOLUME

This volume is comprised of 22 chapters organized into five sections: "Mediating and Negotiating Organizational Conflict," "Leadership and Communication in K-16 Education," "Leadership Challenges and Opportunities in Public Safety Leadership and Management," "Strategies for Improved Communication," and "Collaboration and Improved Engagement."

Section 1: Mediating and Negotiating Organizational Conflict

This section features five chapters. In Chapter 1, "Fixing the SIC: Preventing and Managing Self-Inflicted Crises," Andrew S Pyle (Clemson University, South Carolina), explores three cases of organizational conflict resulting from self-inflicted crisis events. The author examines the social media-based communication practices of three organizations and draws lessons from both successes and failures for how organizations should respond to self-inflicted crises. In Chapter 2, "Alternative and Indigenous Dispute Resolution: A Legal Perspective," Saleem Gul, (Institute of Management Sciences, Peshawar, Pakistan) provides a detailed discussion on the concepts surrounding the terms 'conflict' and 'dispute'. The chapter provides a detailed discussion, based on contemporary literature, to differentiate between disputes and conflicts. The author discusses dispute resolution in tribal and indigenous societies and what locally derived methods are practiced. Brian Jarrett and Kara Dellacioppa (California State University Dominguez Hills) of Chapter 3, "Negotiating Moral Reasoning in Mediation," examine the importance of understanding moral reasoning processes in individuals involved in mediation. They discuss Lawrence Kohlberg's model of moral reasoning and applies it to a case study of a workplace dispute. They also present care ethic versus justice ethic debate put forth by feminist psychologists challenging mainstream theories of moral reasoning. Chapter 4, "Collaboration and Conflict in Three Workplace Teams' Projects," Tom Cockburn, Peter A.C. Smith, The Leadership Alliance Inc., and Gordon A. Cockburn, GA Consulting Ltd., looks at micro level details of conflict and collaboration in three organizations as well as the observed socioemotional dynamics. Chapter 5 shifts the focus to "MAGNUS Leadership: Using Principled Negotiation to Improve International Negotiation." Authors Alexander Javidi, Larry Long, Mitch Javidi, L. Brooks Hill, Anthony H. Normore, and James Klopovic (National Command and Staff College, and International Academy of Public Safety), examine how leadership connects to principled and international negotiation and offer a few practical tips for beginning the journey of becoming MAGNUS. Recommendation for international MAGNUS negotiators are offered.

Section 2: Leadership and Communication in K-16 Education

This section features four chapters. In Chapter 6, "The Use of Online Social Networks and Its Influence on Job-Related Behavior: The Higher Education Context," authors Vera Silva Carlos (University of Aveiro, Campus Universitário de Santiago) and Ricardo Gouveia Rodrigues, (Universidade da Beira Interior, Portugal), evaluate the effect of using online social networks on the worker's attitudes and behaviors, particularly in the context of Higher Education. In chapter 7, "The Case for Effectively Using Existing Business Improvement Models in Australian Schools," Venesser Fernandes (Monash University, Australia) presents an adapted version for continuous school improvement within school systems in Australia. This adapted version of continuous school improvement provides a theoretical framework on how schools operating as self-managed business systems can ensure that the delivery of educational quality is strategically sustained at the organizational level and that focus remains on the important core business of student learning. In Chapter 8, "The Role of Leadership and Communication Challenges: Re-Conceptualizing Graduate Instruction," Heather M. Rintoul (Nipissing University, Ontario, Canada) explores concerns and challenges associated with the transition to online graduate instruction from the traditional face-to-face format. The author discusses several catalysts for the transition to virtual teaching; the ethics of being present; impediments to learning and communication online; and participant concerns. Chapter 9, "Leading Teacher Professional Learning: Shared Language for Shared Goals," Doron Zinger, Jenell Krishnan, Nicole Gilbertson (University of California, Irvine) and Kate Harris, (Pittsburgh CAPA 6-12) present one aspect of communication in teacher professional development, building shared understanding of key terminology and ideas. The authors present three case studies of professional development program from across English, history, and science and highlight professional development design and implementation approaches that produced varying degrees of success.

Section 3: Identifying Challenges and Opportunities in Public Safety Leadership and Management

This section features four chapters. In Chapter 10, "Identifying Blind Spots in Leadership Development," authors Timothy W. Turner (Federal Bureau of Investigation), and Richard J. Conroy (Dallas Baptist University) examine 360-degree assessments in terms of leadership development, training, and coaching. Multi-rater assessment use is reviewed in the context of emotional intelligence competencies. Chapter 11, "Finding Star Performer Leaders: The Secret to Running Successful Organizations," Reuven Bar-On (National Command & Staff College), describe an innovative and valuable method for creating predictive models designed to assist in hiring high performing leaders – "star performers" – as well as to continue to enhance their ability to perform on an even higher level. This approach – "Star Performance Modelling" – is described in detail including the process involved and how best to apply the star performer models that are created. Chapter 12, "First-Line Police Supervisory Leadership: A Pivotal Role in Effective Communication and Engagement," Brian Ellis (Sacramento Police Department and National Command and Staff College), and Anthony H. Normore (California State University and National Command and Staff College) highlight the extant literature on organizational leadership and its pivotal role in effective communication and engagement processes. The authors focus on first-line supervisors and the impact of communication and engagement on officers under their supervision. Employee trait, state, and behavioral constructs coupled with the culture of emotional connection between police officers and the police organization are explored. In Chapter 13, "Dynamic Presence rather than Command Presence: How Communicative Intelligence Influences Police/Citizen Interactions," Renée J. Mitchell (University of Cambridge) and Kendall Zoller (Sierra Training Associates) assert that police-citizen interactions are a complex process where verbal and nonverbal interactions are occurring simultaneously and interpreted immediately, leading to multiple chances for misunderstanding or misinterpretation of the officer's intent. With little research on the actual techniques to create the perception of police legitimacy, these authors link communicative intelligence to the verbal and physical behaviors officers should engage in to enhance procedural justice and improve police legitimacy.

Section 4: Strategies for Improved Communication

The section features five chapters. In Chapter 14, "Mobile Communication in Hospitals: Problems, Possibilities, and Solutions," Terje Solvoll (Norwegian Centre of E-Health Research and University Hospital of North Norway) argues that mobile communication for health care workers are a critical part of hospitals infrastructure. Many of these systems do not work well together, leading to difficulties regarding multiple communication devices with different usage area, unavailable or missing equipment, and alarm fatigue. In this chapter, the author presents solutions and possibilities based on context aware communication systems which aims to reduce interruptions and thereby also alarm fatigue. In Chapter 15, "Complex Action Methodology for Enterprise Systems (CAMES): A System to Contextualize the Behavioral Management Issue as Quantum Mechanical Variable," Olaf Cames (University of Liverpool, UK) examines the results of two experiments that the hypotheses that the theory of quantum mechanics and the theory of communicative action qualify as a building block for a planned methodological approach to intervene and steer problematic social structures in the desired direction. Chapter 16, "Strategic Communication in Crisis: Winning May (Not) Be Everything," authors Lauren J Keil (Optum Consulting), and Angela M Jerome (Western Kentucky University) use The Ohio State University's (OSU's) tattoos for memorabilia scandal as exemplar and offers meaningful insight and pragmatic considerations for practitioners dealing with similar situational constraints. In Chapter 17, "Help Me Understand: Effectively Communicating Across Generations," Carolyn N. Stevenson (Purdue University Global) asserts that higher education leaders need to identify differences among generations of employees and students and develop a strategic plan for managing and motivating across the generations. In a case study format, the author shares that implications for higher education leaders lie in establishing an organizational culture that promotes satisfaction for all individuals in the higher education setting. In Chapter 18, "Strategic Managerial Communication in the Digital Era: Implications for Ethical and Unethical Behavior," Isabell Carolina Camillo (Niagara University, New York) and Angelo A. A Camillo (Sonoma State University) discuss the topic of communication with emphasis on ethical managerial communication within the global context.

Section 5: Collaboration and Improved Engagement

The final section contains four chapters. In Chapter 19, "Dataveillance in the Workplace: Moving Beyond Divergent Perspectives," Regina Connolly and Cliona McParland (Dublin City University), outline emerging issues relating to use of employee monitoring, and summarize both management rationale for monitoring as well as employee privacy concerns and proposes an ethical framework that is useful for balancing these differing perspectives. In Chapter 20, "Improving Virtual Team Effectiveness," Edward T. Chen (University of Massachusetts Lowell) addresses the virtual workplace and teleworking. The author introduces communication systems that are on the rise to make virtual teams more effective. Performance of virtual teams are explained, and ways to enhance the virtual team effectiveness. In Chapter 21, "Collaborative Learning Strategies in Organizations," Sandra Sanz Martos (Universitat Oberta de Catalunya), and Mario Pérez-Montoro (University of Barcelona) aims to define, identify and characterize communities of practice and differentiate them from other organizational structures which are not such communities. It establishes a comparison among them and observes the benefits obtained from each structure, indicating which strategy to apply depending on the goal or challenge. In the final chapter, Chapter 22, "Using Innovative Internal Communication to Enhance Employee Engagement," Karen Mishra (Campbell University, North Carolina) Aneil K Mishra (East Carolina University) and Khaner Walker (Lenovo Consulting) examine how one $45 billion Fortune Global 500 technology company uses internal communication to promote collaboration and engagement across dispersed employees' teams. The authors describe how the company has developed both its intranet and its new mobile app and how innovative internal communication can promote engagement and collaboration.

Anthony Normore
California State University – Dominguez Hills, USA

Mitch Javidi
International Academy of Public Safety (IAPS), USA

Larry Long
Illinois State University, USA

REFERENCES

Cummings, H., Long, L., & Lewis, M. (1987). *Managing communication in organizations* (2nd ed.). Scottsdale, AZ: Gorsuch Scarisbrick Publishers.

Erbe, N. (2014). *Approaches to managing organizational diversity and innovation*. Hershey, PA: IGI Global Publishers. doi:10.4018/978-1-4666-6006-9

Erbe, N., & Normore, A. H. (2015). *Cross-cultural collaboration and leadership in modern organizations*. Hershey, PA: IGI Global Publishers.

National Communication Association. (2015). *What is communication?* Retrieved from https://www.natcom.org/discipline/

Normore, A., & Erbe, N. (2013). *Collective efficacy: interdisciplinary perspectives on international leadership*. Bingley, UK: Emerald Group Publishing. doi:10.1108/S1479-3660(2013)20

Normore, A. H. (2009). Culturally relevant leadership for social justice: Honoring the integrity of First Nations communities in Northeast Canada. In J. Collard & A. H. Normore (Eds.), *Leadership and intercultural dynamics* (pp. 47–68). Charlotte, NC: Information Age Publishing.

Normore, A. H., & Brooks, J. S. (2014). *Educational leadership for social justice: Views from the social sciences*. Charlotte, NC: Information Age Publishing.

Normore, A. H., Javidi, M., Anderson, T., Normand, N., Hoina, C., & Scott, W. (2014). *Moral compass for law enforcement professionals*. Holly Springs, NC: International Academy of Public Safety.

Northouse, P. G. (2012). *Leadership: Theory and practice*. Thousand Oaks, CA: SAGE.

Parks, S. D. (2005). *Leadership can be taught: A bold approach for a complex world*. Boston, MA: Harvard Business Review Press.

Acknowledgment

As editors and authors we continue in our aspiration to courageously examine issues that deal with a plethora of challenges in our appreciation of the pivotal role of leadership and management in organizations and its essential role in communication and conflict management. The contributors push the reader to tackle these issues found in organizations and their impact on our global society as a whole. They challenge us to consider the changes we need to make, conduct personal examination of how we lead and pose difficult questions about why we engage the ways we do. Our hope is that these chapters will serve as catalysts for further discourse and research on collaboration within and across disciplines so these disciplines can appreciate of what each brings to table in support of organizational health and success. We wish to acknowledge a myriad of people who have influenced our lives and our professional work. Our sincere gratitude goes to our families and friends, and to IGI Global Publishers, particularly Courtney Tychinski and the other staff who supported us, for the opportunity to disseminate our work, and to all the contributing authors and to reviewers who reviewed the original manuscripts. In particular we wish to acknowledge Renee Mitchell, Kendall Zoller, Andrew Pyle, Heather Rintool, Doron Zinger, Daniel Davis, Brian Ellis, Christopher Hoina, Angela Jerome, Chris Hoina, and James Klopovic who willingly gave their time to review chapters in volume 1 and provide feedback accordingly. They share in our passion for organizational leadership, horizontal, vertical, and lateral communication, and the importance of understanding and appreciating how best to mediate, negotiate, manage, and resolve various forms of conflict.

Section 1

Mediating and Negotiating Organizational Conflict

Chapter 1
Fixing the SIC:
Preventing and Managing Self-Inflicted Crises

Andrew S. Pyle
Clemson University, USA

ABSTRACT

Social media platforms provide channels for both individuals and organizations to engage with global audiences. A successful social media message can reach millions and shape the way the public views a particular person, group, or cause. As organizations become more engaged with the public through social media platforms, a new area of organizational risk has also developed. It is possible for an organization to create a self-inflicted crisis through the unintentional transmission of a poorly worded or ill-conceived social media message. This type of self-induced crisis event creates organizational conflict that must be managed quickly. This chapter explores three cases of organizational conflict resulting from self-inflicted crisis events. All three events caused major conversations to erupt on social media platforms. The author examines the social media-based communication practices of three organizations and draws lessons from both successes and failures for how organizations should respond to self-inflicted crises.

INTRODUCTION

It is an unfortunate truth that the internet can be a dark, dangerous place. Some of the worst aspects of humanity thrive in the fetid currents of deviance that flow unimpeded online. Yet, at the same time, the world of the internet can be a rich, wondrous place. Over the past few years, there have developed heart-warming stories, hope-inspiring anecdotes, and memes and GIFs to make even the most cold-hearted curmudgeon crack a grin. The same internet that gave us Gamergate (Valenti, 2017), an internet movement of predominantly white men attempting to force female developers out of the world of video games, also gave us Lachlan Lever, the seven-week old baby boy with moderate-to-severe hearing loss who smiled when he heard his parents' voices for the first time (Waxman, 2014). It is in the capacity for viral growth of a story, concept, or movement, that we see the incredible power of the internet – both for heartwarming stories and for digital disaster.

DOI: 10.4018/978-1-5225-8516-9.ch001

A compelling example of both the positive and the negative potential for the internet to shape a conversation is the "Accidentally social viral 4x" Ben Tobias (https://twitter.com/GPDBenTobias), public information officer for the Gainesville, Florida police department. On the negative side, Tobias's department became known for the "Hot Cop" incident following Hurricane Irma. Gainesville police were helping residents following the storm, and a selfie of three officers went viral with messages ranging from, "Do a calendar fundraiser!" to marriage propositions, and even some salacious suggestions from Facebook users (O'Kane, 2017). What seemed like excellent publicity for the Gainesville police turned sour when Facebook users found one of the three officers posting racist, anti-Semitic content on his personal Facebook page (Twedt, 2017). Tobias had to quickly respond and manage what had become a social media crisis. The officer was suspended, and the potential benefit to the community was tarnished by the officer's comments.

In contrast to the "Hot Cop" incident, Tobias also had a video become a viral hit following a noise complaint. In an era when viral police videos conjure images of Walter Scott in North Charleston (Blinder, 2017) and Alton Sterling in Baton Rouge (Berman & Lowery, 2018), the Gainesville video came as a breath of fresh air. An officer who responded to the noise complaint found a group of children playing basketball outside of their home. Rather than shutting down the game or offering a warning or citation, the officer joined the game (Shortell, 2016). The video, posted to the Gainesville police Facebook page, rapidly went viral and became a spotlight of positive police interaction in a community at a time when such interactions seemed rare. While Tobias's viral messages are anomalous for a single individual (who is not already a super-star celebrity), they are representative of the power and potential impact of digital content in the modern era.

Considering the potential for the viral spread of digital messages, no one who has used social media in the past few years will be surprised that individuals and organizations regularly place themselves in self-inflicted crises (SIC). Since the first piece looking at this phenomenon was published (Pyle, 2016), there have been numerous instances of the SIC phenomenon. This chapter explores some of those cases and offers practical implications for scholars and practitioners. The chapter consists of three parts. First, the author reviews relevant literature. Next, the author conducts a comparative case study of four distinct self-inflicted crises: the Dove ad featuring a color-changing woman (Slawson, 2017); the cascading crisis of Urban Outfitters' apparent art theft (BBC News, 2018); the 2017 Pepsi commercial in the style of a Black Lives Matter march (Victor, 2017); and lastly a re-examination of the 2014 DiGiorno "#WhyIStayed" crisis (Griner, 2014). Finally, the author presents a set of lessons learned from the case studies, as well as principles to inform organizational communication for organizations facing SIC.

REVIEW OF LITERATURE

Social Networking Sites

Social Network Sites (SNSs) such as Facebook, Instagram, or Twitter, are (boyd & Ellison, 2007):

web-based services that allow individuals to (1) construct a public or semi-public profile within a bounded system, (2) articulate a list of other users with whom they share a connection, and (3) view and traverse their list of connections and those made by others within the system (p. 211).

These sites exist to serve a variety of functions, from maintaining connections with existing friendship networks, to finding other individuals who share a particular interest (boyd & Ellison, 2007). In addition to these functions, SNSs have led to the creation of dynamic communities of engagement. These communities create the space for rapid messaging to vast audiences. At the same time, these communities allow for the development of contentious, conflict-ridden environments.

Organizational Conflict

Conflict is part of all relationships. Organizations exist as networks of interconnected relationships. As Tjosvold (2008) asserts, "to work in an organization is to be in conflict" (p. 19). Roloff (1987) defines organizational conflict as "activities that are incompatible with those of colleagues within their network, members of other collectivities, or unaffiliated individuals who utilize the services or products of the organization" (p. 496). Rahim (2002) adds that conflict is "an interactive process" (p. 207). Accepting that conflict is a regular and accepted part of life in an organization, there are perhaps two ways that organizational members can approach and respond to conflict as it arises. On the one hand, people can view conflict as a debilitating, overwhelming, or detrimental event, or series of events. Taking this view can lead to the deterioration of the organization (Aula & Siira, 2010). More specifically, a negative view of conflict can result in accidents, absenteeism, and a general decrease in overall health and well-being (De Dreu, C.K.W., van Dierendonck, D., & Dijkstra, M.T.M., 2004; Meyer, 2004).

From another perspective, conflict can be viewed as an opportunity for growth or renewal. Rather than thinking of the negative, organizational members can move toward a conflict-positive perspective (Tjosvold, 2008). From this perspective individuals can see conflict as an opportunity for improvement and positive change in the organization, seeking to grow from conflicting perspectives and ideas. With this concept of conflict, organizational members should pursue three key goals for effective conflict management: pursue organizational learning, meet the needs of organizational stakeholders, and communicate ethically throughout the process (Mitroff, 1998; Rahim, 2002; Tompkins, 1995). By seeking to learn from the events that led up to the conflict, the conflict itself, and how it was resolved (whether successfully or not), organizational members can help the organization function more effectively and avoid similar conflict in the future. By meeting the needs of stakeholders, organizations can help those in conflict to feel heard. Organizations can also foster environments where stakeholders shape the organization by assessing and potentially revising outdated policies and unclear organizational goals. Lastly, while pursuing ethical communication practices, both organizational members and organizational leaders are more likely to make decisions and perform actions that will benefit the organization and the larger community. This also benefits stakeholders and helps those in conflict trust the organization and its leaders.

While conflict in organizations is a regular occurrence, there are times when it can escalate to the level of crisis. In the current social media context, social-mediated communication has created a context where conflict can become a crisis in moments.

Organizational Crisis

An organizational crisis is defined "as a specific, unexpected, and non-routine event or series of events that create high levels of uncertainty and simultaneously present an organization with both opportunities for and threats to its high priority goals" (Ulmer, Sellnow, & Seeger, 2019, p. 7). This definition is good for the cases evaluated in this chapter, with one small caveat. The crises that develop because of social media errors or misstatements are generally self-inflicted crises (Pyle, 2016). These crises, therefore, should be preventable events. Although they should be preventable, it does not alter how organizations should respond to and manage these crises.

While many organizational leaders, and most legal teams, will immediately want to save face and engage in reputation management following a crisis, this may not be the best option for the organization. Much of the extant literature on crisis communication indicates that engaging in open, honest communication and developing strong stakeholder relationships is a healthier option that will lead to renewal and to stronger organizational relationships in the future (Botan, 1993, 1997; Olaniran, Scholl, Williams, & Boyer, 2012; Olaniran & Williams, 2001; Ulmer, et al., 2015, 2009, 2007). A theoretical perspective that captures this concept is the discourse of renewal (Ulmer et al., 2019).

The discourse of renewal argues for organizations to pursue four key communication goals before, during, and after crisis. First, organizational learning is vital. Organizations should learn from past successes and failures and from those of other organizations (Ulmer et al., 2019). Second is effective organizational rhetoric. Organizational leaders should communicate early and often during a crisis and should help key stakeholders look toward a "new normal," rather than trying to get "back to normal" (Ulmer et al., 2019). The third communication goal is ethical communication. Organizational members and leaders should strive to communicate ethically in crisis situations. This is perhaps best represented by Nilsen's (1974) concept of significant choice. Nilsen argues that stakeholders must be provided with the information they need so that they can be equipped to make choices based on all available, relevant information, rather than on partial or cherry-picked information. Ulmer et al. (2019) apply the concept of significant choice to crisis response situations. The final goal is for organizational members to maintain a prospective vision, looking forward for ways to achieve renewal after the crisis, rather than dwelling on the past and fixating on what might have been done differently (Ulmer et al., 2019).

The tenets of the discourse of renewal align well with the recommendations found in the literature on organizational conflict management. Both bodies of literature argue for the value of open, honest, ethical communication. There is also a call for key stakeholders to be involved in the process of managing the event. Importantly, both call for a focus on renewal, growth, and vision for the future, rather than dwelling on who is to blame and what might have been done differently leading up to the conflict or crisis. While it is useful to learn from past mistakes, it is detrimental to allow those mistakes to be the sole focus, preventing growth and forward movement. There are several recent cases that support these perspectives.

CASE DESCRIPTIONS AND ANALYSES

This chapter is built around a comparative case study of four self-induced crises that required some level of conflict management. A comparative case study is useful as a tool for analyzing individual, organizational, social, and group dynamics (Flick, 2004; Yin, 2014). The following cases were chosen because they are recent exemplars of organizations that either effectively or ineffectively managed conflict after a self-induced crisis. The cases were selected as part of a purposeful maximal sample, as they demonstrate different perspectives on the problem the author wishes to study and address (Creswell, 2013). Data for the cases were gathered from organizational websites, reports from news media, and from Twitter using Salesforce Social Studio social media listening software.

Dove

In 2017, Dove released a full-length advertisement that featured a series of women changing their shirt, and as one shirt was removed, another appeared beneath as the woman changed to a new woman. When the advertisement was released it was well-received as an interesting and creative video. Unfortunately, when people think of the clothes-changing Dove advertisement they do not remember the full-length ad, people tend to remember a much shorter clip that Dove posted to Facebook as a follow-up to the original advertisement (Slawson, 2017).

This pared-down clip features a woman of color changing her shirt and turning into a white woman. The clip in question came at a time when multiple organizations were facing backlash related to questionable content dealing with representations of race. For example, in early 2017 the German skincare company Nivea launched an ad campaign targeting customers in the Middle East, a region known for selling skin-lightening cosmetics. The advertisement read, "White is Purity," and ran with the tag "Keep it clean, keep bright. Don't let anything ruin it" (BBC News, 2017). In addition to being a problematic message in a global context, the alt-right movement and other similar white-supremacist groups picked up the advertisement with commentary along the lines of, "Nivea has chosen our side." The company had to respond quickly to pull down the ad and issue an apology.

Or consider, just a few months earlier, the Chinese laundry detergent Qiaobi posted a video advertisement of a Chinese woman shoving a detergent gel pack in a paint-covered Black man's mouth and shoving him into a washing machine (Graham-Harrison, 2016). When he emerges from the machine, he has turned into a Chinese man and he and his clothes are sparkling white. The company insisted that the ad content was not problematic, and that people with concerns of racism were overreacting to the video's content. On the tail end of several events like this, Dove's social media team stepped in with their three-second clip of a color-changing woman.

As often occurs, the background story on this case is unfortunate because of how avoidable this SIC was. As mentioned previously, the three-second clip was pulled from a much longer advertisement that ran earlier in the same year (the full advertisement is unfortunately not available online, it was pulled after criticism of the three-second clip). The official response to the event was a clear apology and a claim that the video "missed the mark" for what Dove was intending to showcase (Slawson, 2017). While this response is generally in line with best practices, the reality is that the situation was completely avoidable. It is common practice in the social media world for a person or small team to put together content and post it directly to a social media page. For social content, there is often not a gatekeeper or an additional set of checks to vet and approve posts. It seems this was the situation in this case. On the one hand, an extra set of vetting would slow down posting and make it challenging to post in a timely fashion. On the other hand, an extra set of eyes on this video could have prevented the entire event from occurring. To avoid SIC, organizations must have key checkpoints to prevent unnecessary content recalls.

Urban Outfitters

If you have read Pyle's (2016) piece on SIC, Urban Outfitters will feel like a very familiar case. Urban Outfitters was in trouble in 2014 because of a "vintage sweatshirt" line that included a Kent State sweatshirt with what appeared to be bloodstains and bullet holes, an allusion to the 1970 campus shootings which resulted in the deaths of four students (Winchel, 2014). Urban Outfitters offered no apology and responded simply that people had misunderstood the purpose of the sweatshirt (Wilson, 2014). Urban

Outfitters has demonstrated a strong track record of producing offensive materials without a clear and convincing apology after the fact. In this instance, rather than engaging with key publics to address their concerns, Urban Outfitters remained silent and ignored the conversation. This repeated SIC mismanagement led to discontent with the company (Huddleston, 2014).

Fast-forward to 2018 and Urban Outfitters has come under fire for what appears to be a recurring, cascading SIC – theft. As early as 2008, Urban Outfitters was credibly accused of stealing art or proprietary content from small-scale artists and selling it as original content without attribution to the artist or owner (Kamer, 2010). The first widely-reported instance of this occurred in 2010, when Urban Outfitters sold gothic style jewelry featuring bones and skulls. The item in question was clearly taken from a concept developed by Lillian Crowe, a small-scale artist whose work was predominantly sold to local markets in New York.

This would have perhaps been the end of the discussion for Urban Outfitters, if there had not been a series of similar events that unfolded over the ensuing eight years. In 2011, Urban Outfitters was accused of stealing Stevie Koerner's "A World of Love" concept (Linkins, 2011). Koerner is another small-scale artist who does most of her sales on Etsy, an online sales platform for artists and artisans. This was soon followed by theft of a fashion line sold by Tumblr user "Glam-Trash," whose T-shirt design was lifted by Urban Outfitters in 2013 (Brooks, 2013). Just a couple of years later, Urban Outfitters was sued by the Navajo Nation for using the name "Navajo" without permission in multiple products ina fashion line (Woolf, 2016). In less than a ten-year span, Urban Outfitters had more than a half-dozen instances of credible theft claims or of misappropriation of protected, licensed material. Most recently, in May of 2018, a small-scale sculptor from Bristol was shocked to discover that a design she developed for a special line of pottery had been ripped off by Urban Outfitters and sold in mass quantities online (BBC News, 2018). The artist, Sarah Wilton, learned about the theft when her friend saw the pottery style in the local Urban Outfitters shop and sent her a photo of the pottery.

With each of these accusations of theft, Urban Outfitters has pulled the content from their online and physical stores and issued an apology along the lines of the following:

We take matters such as this very seriously and removed the product as soon as this was brought to our attention. Urban Outfitters has worked with [artist] since [year] to help bring awareness and sales to their creative network of artists. As long-time supporters of [artist] and independent creatives, we would never intentionally appropriate their work. The origin of the design is still being investigated with the designers at [company]. We appreciate your patience while we work to resolve this issue.

This type of apology for a single, isolated incident would seem like a genuine, heartfelt apology. Unfortunately for Urban Outfitters, these events have not occurred in isolation.

None of these theft accusations, independently, is a major crisis for an organization of this size. However, with the number of events that have occurred in the past ten years, Urban Outfitters has completely depleted any reservoir of goodwill (Ulmer et al., 2019) they might have developed with their stakeholders or with the general public. As a result of unethical product development and long-term, repeated theft of independent artists' work, no amount of insistence that the organization is innocent seems believable to an external audience. The organization has demonstrated a pattern of unethical behavior that has tarnished its reputation, perhaps irrevocably.

Pepsi

In the fall of 2017 mass protests had become the norm across most major cities in the U.S., and police brutality had become a topic of conversation and the focus of organized resistance at a scale that has not been seen in the U.S. since the height of the Civil Rights Movement. It was during this national conversation that Pepsi aired their now infamous advertisement that was an apparent homage to the Black Lives Matter movement (Victor, 2017). This advertisement was well-made, well-funded, and spurred a national conversation. Unfortunately for Pepsi, the conversation was not one that framed Pepsi in a positive light.

In Pepsi's advertisement, several key pieces became the focus of criticism from both sides of the U.S. political spectrum. First, there were representations of members of various cultural groups that were problematic because of the blatant stereotypes they portrayed. For example, the ad features a man of south-east Asian descent who is playing a cello and a group of Black men doing "hip hop style" dances. These characters are portrayed alongside a mass protest march clearly intended to represent the Black Lives Matter movement, among other advocacy groups. On the other side of this narrative stand serious, disapproving police officers – all of whom appear to be white men. As the ad proceeds, Kendall Jenner sees the protest while she is in the middle of a professional photo-shoot. Jenner leaves the shoot, removes a wig and her makeup thereby becoming a "regular person," and joins the parade of protesters. The ad comes to a head when the protesters run into the wall of police, and Jenner breaks the tension by handing one of the officers a Pepsi to drink. He accepts it, and everyone begins celebrating – Pepsi had solved racism.

The backlash to this ad came from multiple perspectives. On one side, Pepsi was criticized for its use of over-worked stereotypes to represent various groups in their ad. On the other side, Pepsi was criticized for the framing of the message, which occurred on three fronts. First, a white woman needed to step in and save the day for the protesters. Second, the suggestion was that Pepsi was going to be the key to solving all the societal problems that were laid out in the advertisement, which is an obviously absurd proposition. Lastly, the ad frames the protesters as heroes and frames the police as the enemy. While police brutality has clearly been an issue that needs to be addressed, framing police at a protest as the enemy to be appeased is problematic framing.

The most widely publicized criticism of the ad was probably a skit performed on Saturday Night Live shortly after the ad was aired (Saturday Night Live, 2017). The ad focuses on the problematic representations of various cultural groups, the homage to Black Lives Matter, and the framing of Jenner coming in to "stop the police from shooting Black people by handing them a Pepsi" (Saturday Night Live, 2017). Following the backlash, Pepsi released an apology which included the following (Victor, 2017):

Pepsi was trying to project a global message of unity, peace and understanding. Clearly, we missed the mark and apologize. We did not intend to make light of any serious issue. We are pulling the content and halting any further rollout.

The response on social media was fierce and ranged from serious criticism to a range of trending memes. People compared the image of Jenner handing a Pepsi to a Police officer to the image of Ieshia Evans being arrested by police during a protest in Baton Rouge following the death of Alton Sterling (Victor, 2017). In several protests following the release of the ad, protesters recorded themselves attempting to offer cans of Pepsi to officers and then lamented the failure of the beverage to act as a miraculous peace offering.

The Pepsi case is a clear example of an organization attempting to latch on to a national or global conversation and make their product relevant. In the political and cultural landscape of 2017, Pepsi's attempt to be part of the protest conversation was a resounding failure. An advertisement that was intended to "[capture] the spirit and actions" of people involved in protest and activism (Victor, 2017) instead captured corporate capacity to mis-read the broader cultural context it was attempting to join.

DiGiorno

Note: This final case was the final example in Pyle's (2016) SIC study and has been re-published in this chapter. The DiGiorno case remains one of the most successful SIC responses the author has seen to date and stands out as an exemplar for other organizations to examine and learn from.

In modern society, secrets are increasingly difficult to keep. People are under surveillance most of the time, especially in urban areas where businesses have security cameras, traffic lights have cameras, and almost every person walking down the street has a phone with a built in high-quality camera. It should have been no surprise to Ray Rice, then, that video of his assault on his then-fiancée (now wife) Janay Palmer would eventually be released. In February of 2014 Rice and Palmer were arrested on assault charges as the two had a public physical altercation (Bien, 2014). What was not known until September of 2014 was that while in an elevator, before they were arrested, Rice knocked Palmer unconscious then dragged her by her hair from the elevator (Bien, 2014). The video of the assault was shared widely over social media and traditional media outlets. Quickly, the conversation around the assault began to focus around the question, "Why did she [Palmer] stay?" (Kaplan, 2014). This message was troubling to Beverly Gooden, a woman who survived and eventually escaped from an abusive relationship (Kaplan, 2014). On September 8, the day the video of Rice's assault in the elevator was released, Gooden was so frustrated by the rhetoric suggesting Palmer "should have just left" that she went to Twitter and started sharing her own story using the hashtag "#WhyIStayed" (Kaplan, 2014). Gooden's tweets were as follows (@bevtgooden, 2014, September 8):

Domestic violence victims often find it difficult to leave abusers http://www.blueridgenow.com/article/20120108/ARTICLES/120109857 ... #WhyIStayed

All these folks trashing women for staying in abusive situations have NO clue what happens the moment you reach for a door handle.

I tried to leave the house once after an abusive episode, and he blocked me. He slept in front of the door that entire night. #WhyIStayed

Gooden went on to list more than a dozen reasons why she stayed in the relationship, including "he said he would change," and "my pastor told me God hates divorce" (@bevtgooden, 2014; Kaplan, 2014). Once Gooden began sharing her experiences, other people began to share their own stories using "#WhyIStayed." Over the time that the hashtag was trending, thousands of abused individuals shared their stories of why they stayed in abusive relationships, offering support and encouragement to one another and to those similarly trapped.

Late in the day on September 8, someone on the DiGiorno Pizza social media team noticed that "Why I Stayed" was a trending topic. DiGiorno runs a humorous twitter account (@DiGiornoPizza) and often tweets about trending topics in order to connect with new Twitter users. In this instance, someone on the DiGiorno team jumped on board without first researching the purpose of the hashtag. They tweeted "#WhyIStayed you had pizza" (@DiGiorno, 2014, September 8 [tweet has been removed from the account]). Within a few minutes there were dozens of angry tweets targeting DiGiorno and the company's apparent decision to try to sell pizza by capitalizing on a tragic event. A hashtag that was developed to support individuals in abusive relationships was now being coopted for free advertising.

Except, it seems that DiGiorno was not intentionally making light of the event. Four minutes after the #WhyIStayed tweet went out it was deleted and this follow up was broadcast: "A million apologies. Did not read what the hashtag was about before posting" (@DiGiornoPizza, 2014, September 8). Their response might seem disingenuous, but the apology did not stop at one tweet. Over the course of 24 hours there were hundreds of tweets. DiGiorno's social media team went into high gear, apologizing by name to each person who tweeted about DiGiorno's mistake. Each apology was both personalized and targeted. The apology tweets did not use a copy-and-paste template or the same repeated verbiage. The apologies seemed heartfelt:

@Posietron I'm so sorry - I made the mistake of not investigating before posting. I saw it trending and participated. Never again.

@Starkman88 @Stareagle agreed. I made a mistake and couldn't be more embarrassed or sorry.

@AllisonRockey Me either. It was a terrible lapse in judgment to not investigate the conversation before participating. I'm so sorry Allison

@ejbrooks @jordanbks It was. And I couldn't be more sorry about it, Emma. Please accept my deepest apologies.

The apologies continued at the rate of a couple of apologies per minute from 11:15 pm until after one o'clock the following morning. Six hours later the apologies picked back up and continued all day on September 9. The DiGiorno account would apologize when someone tweeted about the offensive tweet, and then would apologize a second time if the person expressed further anger, dismay, disappointment, or concern.

Perhaps the most fascinating aspect of the DiGiorno #WhyIStayed case is that within a few hours of the initial apology, individuals who were the first to criticize DiGiorno became DiGiorno's champions, defending them against attacks by individuals who learned about the tweet well after the fact. One individual indicated they have made the same kind of mistake and appreciated DiGiorno owning their mistake: "@DiGiornoPizza apology ACCEPTED, #digiornopizza ! I never check hashtags before using them. #ApologyAccepted others need to #GetOverIt" (@allychat, 2014, September 11). Another person applauded the personalized apologies: "Props to @DiGiornoPizza on personally apologize (sic) for a mistake. adweek.com/adfreak/digior…" (@The_Raheel, 2014, September 9). Other users went directly to countering attacks from other users: "@emitoms @DiGiornoPizza seriously? It's the most apologetic acct ever. Never seen such remorse over an honest mistake. Leave the pizza alone" (@RealMikeWelch, 2014, September 9). Although this situation developed because of an insensitive and thoughtless action,

Digiorno's leadership and social media team seems to have grasped the value of building social capital in the wake of the social media fallout.

The discussion on social media continued in this way for several days. While DiGiorno's apologies to users who expressed their anger consisted of a few hundred tweets, the larger conversation over three days comprised more than 8,000 tweets. Much of the tweet traffic over that time was from users defending DiGiorno for their personalized apologies. By September 11, many outlets had published stories about the event with titles such as: *3 Ways DiGiorno Reacted Well to Their Twitter Crisis*; and *The Perfect Response to Social Media Crisis*. In this instance, DiGiorno's self-inflicted crisis turned into an opportunity for effective communication and growth. The social media team was able to manage the ongoing conflict with upset Twitter users, all potential consumers of DiGiorno's products, and was able to come through the event in a healthy and respectable position.

LESSONS FROM SUCCESS AND FAILURE

There is much to be learned from studying prior successes and failures, so that organizations can communicate more effectively in the future. As social media use spreads and consumers expect information more quickly, organizations will continue to create self-induced crisis events. By learning from organizations that have weathered such events, both successfully and unsuccessfully, other organizations can prevent SIC – and manage them more effectively when they occur. By drawing on the four case studies presented in this chapter, the author draws four major lessons from which organizations can learn and adapt. First, when a problem arises, organizations should respond quickly and openly. Second, organizations should acknowledge when they have done something wrong. Last, it is important for organizations to be part of the conversation when a conflict or crisis is ongoing, rather than ignoring the conversation and attempting to remain aloof.

Respond Quickly and Openly

When organizations encounter conflict with stakeholders during self-induced crisis events, the first lesson they should apply for managing the conflict is to respond quickly and openly. As Ulmer et al. (2019) demonstrate, stakeholders respond positively to being provided with relevant information in the midst of an uncertain situation. By responding quickly and providing the information stakeholders are seeking, organizations can maintain their credibility with their publics. Dove seems to have achieved success via their quick and open apology, as did DiGiorno. Pepsi also seems to have pivoted away from the conversation around its abysmal advertisement. Urban Outfitters faces a challenge in that its apologies are not viewed as genuine because it is so regularly in the midst of crisis.

Acknowledge Mistakes

The initial tendency when faced with an unexpected challenge or organizational error is often for the organization to distance itself from the event and seek firm footing for legal defense. Urban Outfitters attempted to distance itself from public outrage over many of the thefts by claiming they were not truly thefts, while also pulling down the products that had been on sale. Dove, Pepsi, and DiGiorno's approach of quickly acknowledging their mistake and working for several days to express their regrets is an effective model for responding to this type of event. One need only look to past crisis events to see that this approach has proven effective.

Consider the oil spill that took place off the coast of Huntington Beach, California, in 1990. The spill happened a few months after the Exxon Valdez spill at a time when "oil spill fervor was at its height" (Sandman, 2012). The ship was leased by British Petroleum, but was operated by a contract shipper. The CEO of BP America was asked in a press conference whether the spill was BP's fault. The CEO responded, "Our lawyers tell us it is not our fault. But we feel like it is our fault, and we are going to act like it is our fault" (Sandman, 2012, p. 67). As a result of their forthright response and quick cleanup "BP's image in the vicinity of the spill is higher today than it was before the spill" (Sandman, 2012, p. 67). The response by BP was so successful that the Huntington Beach spill has nearly disappeared from popular memory, while the Exxon Valdez spill the year before remains a well-known and oft-discussed piece of history. Acknowledging mistakes on the front end creates time and space for organizations to rebuild credibility and allows key publics time to forgive the mistake and move on.

Participate in Relevant Conversations

In an increasingly high-speed communication environment, one of the most damaging moves an organization can make is to simply avoid being part of the conversation. For example, airline customers use Twitter and Facebook to express complaints or to get up-to-date information on arrival times and gate changes. Airline representatives acknowledge that social media platforms, such as Twitter, are becoming more and more relevant (Carrington, 2013).

DiGiorno remains an exemplar in this context. Following a major social media gaffe, the company moved quickly to take part in the rapidly developing conversation around its message. DiGiorno's decision to remain engaged in the conversation resulted in acceptance from a large portion of the individuals who were angered by their tweet, as well as eventual positive press for how they handled the event.

Organizations using social media to connect with stakeholders must remember the power of social-media messaging to benefit as well as to damage credibility and organizational relationships. Organizations should utilize social media platforms to engage with stakeholders in meaningful ways. Specifically, social media platforms should be used to engage in effective conflict management with internal and external stakeholders. The flexibility and unprecedented reach of social media can be used to connect with key publics at an incredible pace. Engaging in productive dialogue that once would have required town hall meetings or similar face-to-face interactions can now, in part, be managed in an online forum. While press releases, email Listservs, and newsletters allow for only one-way communication, social media platforms now allow organizational members to effectively engage in dialogue with key publics.

FUTURE RESEARCH DIRECTIONS

This chapter explores how organizations can prepare for, respond to, and manage the conflict of self-induced crisis events. This study is far from exhaustive and should serve as a launching point for research in related areas. First, further studies should be conducted of other organizations that have undergone similar events and faced similar crises. Studying a larger sample of organizations will enhance the understanding researchers have of these phenomena and how they can be managed effectively. Additionally, it would be helpful to connect with social media users who have taken part in the conversation around social-media based responses to organizational conflict and self-induced crises. By surveying users who have been involved in these events researchers can determine whether preliminary findings are consistent over a much larger population than can be determined in an interview or case study. Future research should seek to expand both the breadth and depth of the current study.

CONCLUSION

This chapter consisted of three parts. First, the author reviewed relevant literature. Next, the author conducted a comparative case study of four distinct self-inflicted crisis events: first, the Dove ad featuring a color-changing woman (Slawson, 2017); second, the cascading crisis of Urban Outfitters' apparent art theft (BBC News, 2018); third, the 2017 Pepsi commercial in the style of a Black Lives Matter march (Victor, 2017); and lastly a re-examination of the 2014 DiGiorno "#WhyIStayed" crisis (Griner, 2014). Lastly, the chapter concluded with lessons learned from the case studies, a set of principles to inform organizations managing this type of organizational conflict, and proposed directions for future research.

A new area of organizational risk has developed as a direct result of increased organizational engagement on social media platforms. The possibility for organizations to create a self-inflicted crisis through the unintentional transmission of a poorly worded or ill-conceived social media message is one that should not be ignored or minimized. Self-induced crisis events create organizational conflict that must be managed quickly. It is vital that organizations not leave a communication void. When there is a void it will tend to be filled, and in the midst of a developing crisis that void could be filled by misinformation and speculation. It is important for organizations to steer the conversation as much as possible. By adopting the practices suggested in this chapter, organizations can pursue a more engaged, connected relationship with key stakeholders.

REFERENCES

BBC News. (2017, April 4). *Nivea removes 'white is purity' deodorant advert branded 'racist.'* Retrieved from https://www.bbc.com/news/world-europe-39489967

BBC News. (2018, May 22). *Urban Outfitters removes vases 'ripped-off' from Bristol artist.* Retrieved from https://www.bbc.com/news/uk-england-bristol-44189267

Berman, M., & Lowery, W. (2018, March 30). Baton Rouge police release video showing fatal shooting of Alton Sterling, plan to fire one officer. *The Washington Post.* Retrieved from https://www.washingtonpost.com/news/post-nation/wp/2018/03/30/baton-rouge-police-will-fire-officer-who-shot-and-killed-alton-sterling/?utm_term=.f817ac12c1fd

Bien, L. (2014, November). A complete timeline of the Ray Rice assault case. *SB Nation.* Retrieved from http://www.sbnation.com/nfl/2014/5/23/5744964/ray-rice-arrest-assault-statement-apology-ravens

Blinder, A. (2017, May 2). Ex-officer who shot Walter Scott pleads guilty in Charleston, *NY Times.* Retrieved from https://www.nytimes.com/2017/05/02/us/michael-slager-walter-scott-north-charleston-shooting.html

Botan, C. (1993). A human nature approach to image and ethics in international public relations. *Journal of Public Relations Research*, *5*(2), 71–81. doi:10.12071532754xjprr0502_02

Botan, C. (1997). Ethics in strategic communication campaigns: The case for a new approach to public relations. *Journal of Business Communication*, *34*(2), 188–202. doi:10.1177/002194369703400205

boyd, d. m., & Ellison, N. B. (2007). Social network sites: Definition, history, and scholarship. *Journal of Computer-Mediated Communication, 13*(1), 210-230.

Brooks, R. (2013, November 7). Is Urban Outfitters stealing work from independent designers AGAIN? *The Village Voice*. Retrieved from https://www.villagevoice.com/2013/11/07/is-urban-outfitters-stealing-work-from-independent-designers-again/

Creswell, J. W. (2013). *Qualitative inquiry & research design: Choosing among five approaches* (3rd ed.). Thousand Oaks, CA: Sage.

Feldman, J. (2014, May 28). Urban Outfitters accused of ripping off artist's design, sparks Tumblr fury. *Life*. Retrieved from https://www.huffpost.com/entry/urban-outfitters-spires-copyright-infringement_n_5403244

Flick, U. (2004). Design and process in qualitative research. In U. Flick, E. von Kardorff, & I. Steinke (Eds.), *A companion to qualitative research* (pp. 146–152). Thousand Oaks, CA: Sage.

Fonseca, F. (2012, February). Navajo nation sues Urban Outfitters over goods. *Associated Press*. Retrieved from http://www.nbcnews.com/id/46574519/ns/business-retail/t/navajo-nation-sues-urban-outfitters-over-goods/#.Vd-wTLS_uTA

Graham-Harrison, E. (2016, May 28). Black man is washed whiter in China's racist detergent advert. *The Guardian*. Retrieved from https://www.theguardian.com/world/2016/may/28/china-racist-detergent-advert-outrage

Granshaw, L. (2014, May 24). Did Urban Outfitters sell an artist's work without permission – again? *The Daily Dot*. Retrieved from https://www.dailydot.com/business/urban-outfitters-steal-artists-work/

Huddleston, T. (2014, November). Urban Outfitters' profits and shares tumble. *Fortune*. Retrieved from http://fortune.com/2014/11/17/urban-outfitters-shares-dip-as-namesake-brand-weighs-down-same-store-sales/

Kamer, F. (2010, May 27). Are Brooklyn fashion designers being ripped off by Urban Outfitters? *The Village Voice*. Retrieved from https://www.villagevoice.com/2010/05/27/are-brooklyn-fashion-designers-being-ripped-off-by-urban-outfitters/

Kaplan, A. M., & Haenlein, M. (2011). The early bird catches the news: Nine things you should know about micro-blogging. *Business Horizons*, *54*(2), 105–113. doi:10.1016/j.bushor.2010.09.004

Kaplan, S. (2014, September). #WhyIStayed: She saw herself in Ray Rice's wife, Janay, and tweeted about it. So did thousands of others. *The Washington Post*. Retrieved from http://www.washingtonpost.com/news/morning-mix/wp/2014/09/09/whyistayed-she-saw-herself-in-ray-rices-wife-janay-and-tweeted-about-it-so-did-thousands-of-others/

Linkins, J. (2011, May 26). Urban Outfitters continues their grand tradition of ripping off designers. *Life*. Retrieved from https://www.huffpost.com/entry/urban-outfitters-steal_n_867604

Mitroff, I. I. (1998). *Smart thinking for crazy times: The art of solving the right problems*. San Francisco: Berrett-Koehler.

Nilsen, T. R. (1974). *Ethics of speech communication* (2nd ed.). Indianapolis, IN: Bobbs-Merrill.

O'Kane, C. (2017, September 13). Viral photo of Florida "hot cops" leads to calendar fundraiser for Irma. *CBS News*. Retrieved from https://www.cbsnews.com/news/hot-cops-gainesville-florida-viral-photo-hurricane-irma-calendar-fundraiser/

Olaniran, B., & Williams, D. (2001). Anticipatory model of crisis management. In R. Heath (Ed.), *Handbook of public relations* (pp. 487–500). Thousand Oaks, CA: Sage. doi:10.4135/9781452220727.n41

Olaniran, B. A., Scholl, J. C., Williams, D. E., & Boyer, L. (2012). Johnson and Johnson phantom recall: A fall from grace or a re-visit of the ghost of the past. *Public Relations Review*, *38*(1), 153–155. doi:10.1016/j.pubrev.2011.08.001

Park, H., & Reber, B. (2008). Relationship building and the use of Websites: How Fortune 500 companies use their Websites to build relationships. *Public Relations Review*, *34*(4), 409–411. doi:10.1016/j.pubrev.2008.06.006

Rahim, M. A. (2002). Toward a theory of managing organizational conflict. *International Journal of Conflict Management*, *13*(3), 206–235. doi:10.1108/eb022874

Sandman, P. (2012). *Responding to community outrage: Strategies for effective risk communication*. American Industrial Hygiene Association.

Saturday Night Live. (2017, April 9). Pepsi Commercial – SNL. *YouTube video*. Retrieved from https://www.youtube.com/watch?v=Pn8pwoNWseM

Shortell, D. (2016, April 18). 'Basketball cop' turns noise complaint into national project. *CNN*. Retrieved from https://www.cnn.com/2016/04/18/us/beyond-the-call-of-duty-basketball-cop/index.html

Slawson, N. (2017, October 8). Dove apologises for ad showing black woman turning into white one. *The Guardian*. Retrieved from https://www.theguardian.com/world/2017/oct/08/dove-apologises-for-ad-showing-black-woman-turning-into-white-one

Tjosvold, D. (2008). The conflict-positive organization: It depends upon us. *Journal of Organizational Behavior*, *29*(1), 19–28. doi:10.1002/job.473

Tompkins, T. C. (1995). Role of diffusion in collective learning. *The International Journal of Organizational Analysis*, *3*(1), 69–85. doi:10.1108/eb028824

Twedt, C. (2017, September 20). 'Hot cop' in hot water as anti-Semitic posts surface. *Ragan's PR Daily*. Retrieved from https://www.prdaily.com/crisiscommunications/Articles/Hot_cop_in_hot_water_as_antiSemitic_posts_surface_23267.aspx

Ulmer, R. R., Seeger, M. W., & Sellnow, T. L. (2007). Post-crisis communication and renewal: Expanding the parameters of post-crisis discourse. *Public Relations Review*, *33*(2), 130–134. doi:10.1016/j.pubrev.2006.11.015

Ulmer, R. R., Sellnow, T. L., & Seeger, M. W. (2009). Post-crisis communication and renewal: Understanding the potential for positive outcomes in crisis communication. In R. L. Heath & D. H. O'Hair (Eds.), *Handbook of Risk and Crisis Communication*. New York: Routledge.

Ulmer, R. R., Sellnow, T. L., & Seeger, M. W. (2019). *Effective crisis communication: Moving from crisis to opportunity* (4th ed.). Thousand Oaks, CA: Sage.

Valenti, J. (2017, September 24). Zoe Quinn: after Gamergate, don't 'cede the internet to whoever screams the loudest. *The Guardian*. Retrieved from https://www.theguardian.com/technology/2017/sep/24/zoe-quinn-gamergate-online-abuse

Victor, D. (2017, April 5). Pepsi pulls ad accused of trivializing Black Lives Matter. *NY Times*. Retrieved from https://www.nytimes.com/2017/04/05/business/kendall-jenner-pepsi-ad.html

Waxman, O. B. (2014, December 15). 10 times social media made the world better in 2014. *TIME*. Retrieved from http://time.com/3633786/heartwarming-stories-2014/

Wilson, M. (2014, September). Urban Outfitters CEO to employees: Kent State sweatshirt sale an 'unfortunate occurrence'. *PR Daily*. Retrieved from http://www.prdaily.com/Main/Articles/Urban_Outfitters_CEO_to_employees_Kent_State_sweat_17280.aspx

Winchel, B. (2014, September). Urban Outfitters offends with red-stained 'vintage' Kent State sweatshirt. *PR Daily*. Retrieved from http://www.prdaily.com/Main/Articles/17261.aspx

Woolf, N. (2016, November 18). Urban Outfitters settles with Navajo Nation after illegally using tribe's name. *The Guardian*. Retrieved from https://www.theguardian.com/us-news/2016/nov/18/urban-outfitters-navajo-nation-settlement

Yin, R. K. (2014). *Case study research: Design and methods* (5th ed.). Thousand Oaks, CA: Sage.

ADDITIONAL READING

Levine, R., Locke, C., & Searls, D. (2009). *The cluetrain manifesto*. Basic books.

Seeger, M. W. (2006). Best practices in crisis communication: An expert panel process. *Journal of Applied Communication Research*, *34*(3), 232–244. doi:10.1080/00909880600769944

Sellnow, T. L., & Seeger, M. W. (2013). *Theorizing crisis communication*. Malden, MA: Wiley-Blackwell.

Senge, P. M. (2006). *The fifth discipline: The art and practice of the learning organization*. Broadway Business.

Ulmer, R. R., Sellnow, T. L., & Seeger, M. W. (2015). *Effective crisis communication: Moving from crisis to opportunity* (3rd ed.). Thousand Oaks, CA: Sage.

Van den Hurk, A. M. (2013). *Social Media Crisis Communications: Surviving a Public Relations Fail.* UK: Pearson Education.

White, C. M. (2011). *Social media, crisis communication, and emergency management: Leveraging Web 2.0 technologies.* CRC press. doi:10.1201/b11251

KEY TERMS AND DEFINITIONS

Conflict: A state of discord caused by the actual or perceived opposition of needs, values, and interests between people working together.

Crisis: A specific, unexpected, and non-routine event or series of events that create high levels of uncertainty and simultaneously present an organization with both opportunities for and threats to its high priority goals.

Hashtag: (On social media sites such as Twitter) A word or phrase preceded by a hash or pound sign (#) and used to identify messages on a specific topic.

Micro-Blog: Social networking sites that allow users to exchange small elements of content such as short sentences, individual images, or video links.

Social Media: Websites and applications that enable users to create and share content or to participate in social networking.

Social Networking Sites: Web-based services that allow individuals to (1) construct a public or semi-public profile within a bounded system, (2) articulate a list of other users with whom they share a connection, and (3) view and traverse their list of connections and those made by others within the system.

Twitter: The largest micro-blogging site on the internet, with over 302 million active monthly users.

Chapter 2
Alternative and Indigenous Dispute Resolution:
A Legal Perspective

Saleem Gul
Institute of Management Sciences, Pakistan

ABSTRACT

This chapter provides a detailed discussion on the concepts surrounding the terms conflict and dispute. After establishing the necessary grounding, the chapter then moves into exploring (in significant detail) the concepts framing the idea of alternative dispute resolution (ADR). The chapter provides a detailed discussion, based on contemporary literature, to differentiate between disputes and conflicts. Then the discussion will focus on removing commonly found confusions related to the vocabulary of conflict and ADR. Following this, various key government acts and reports that shape the state of ADR are discussed. In an effort to ensure brevity, only those concerns that relate directly to ADR or directly address ADR are discussed. This follows with a discussion on dispute resolution in tribal and indigenous societies and what locally derived methods are practiced.

1. INTRODUCTION

Disputes are common amongst today's organizations. It is therefore important to understand how to resolve them and to appreciate the law and regulations framing the canvas of dispute resolution. This chapter focuses on disputes in general and Alternative Dispute Resolution mechanisms and processes in particular. We begin with a background discussion on dispute resolution and make the case for studying this topic further. Then the discussion presents a critical review of the literature pertaining to disputes. The purpose of this is to arrive at a common understanding and definition of a dispute and to differentiate between disputes and conflicts. Although, this chapter is about the alternative methods of resolving organizational conflicts and disputes. However, because of the close relationship of Alternative Dispute Resolution (ADR) to conventional dispute resolution and to establish the context for further discussion on ADR some of the discussion focuses on the conventional methods of resolving disputes.

DOI: 10.4018/978-1-5225-8516-9.ch002

After providing a background to dispute resolution and differentiating between disputes and conflicts and defining disputes the chapter then follows with a discussion detailing the processes of mediation and arbitration. In this section the focus is on the ADR techniques, however because of ADR's close association with the litigation process some elements of the legal system (as it relates to ADR) are also discussion. For all, purposes the adjudication process seems to be an anomaly process because it resides on the boundary of the standard legal system and the alternative system. The process of mediation, adjudication, and arbitration are discussed, and the reader is provided with an overview of the process. Then our focus turns to alleviating common misunderstandings between the various methods used in ADR. This includes a discussion comparing: mediation with arbitration and arbitration with adjudication. The discussion then focuses on various acts passed by the UK government and other important acts and reports that have had a significant impact in forming the state of ADR as we know it today. Areas where the UK legal system differs from that of the USA are also pointed out. The documents and acts covered in this chapter include: The Housing Grants, Construction and Regeneration Act (HGCRA) and the Right to Adjudication, Admissibility of hearsay Evidence and the Civil Evidence Act of 1995, The Human Rights Act of 1998 and its Relevance to Adjudication, The Arbitration Act of 1996, United Nations Commission International Trade Law (UNCITRAL) Model Law on International Commercial Arbitration, Alternative Dispute Resolution and the Civil Procedures Rules 1998 (including the new legal terminology that replaced the one in effect prior to 1999), and the Access to Justice Act of 1999. These were chosen for inclusion in the chapter because of their explicit relevance to the topic of discussion and the significant impact that they have had on ADR. In this discussion the genesis of ADR is outlined, and the present state of ADR is clarified. To bring completeness to the topic, the chapter then focuses on exploring indigenous and tribal methods of dispute resolution. Finally, future research directions are provided before the chapter is concluded.

2. BACKGROUND

Conflicts and disputes are nothing new, we as humankind have been experiencing conflicts and disputes from the onset. The oldest conflicts that we read or hear about are mostly biblical, some examples include the conflicts between God and the devil, followed by conflicts between brothers Caine and Abel, and between God and the Babylonians. Needless to state, the cause, nature, and durations of conflicts have varied over the times and so have their outcomes. Conflicts and disputes if managed or resolved lead to stronger and longer-lasting relationships (Jehn, 1994), to an expedited and judicious conclusion (Fenn, 2006), and to a greater readiness to work together in the future (Rahim, 2001). Conversely, if not managed properly, they can wreak havoc and may lead to actions causing impairment or death, and destruction as seen in the case of wars.

Although, in general usage the terms conflict and dispute are used interchangeably, however they are two markedly distinct concepts. Each consisting of its own unique life-cycle, management and resolution mechanisms, tools of analysis, etc. (Fenn, 2006). It is therefore important to differentiate between them. The term conflict, it so happens, is in wider use compared to the term dispute (Fenn, Lowe, & Speck, 1997). Conflicts are interest driven (Burton, 1993), and as interests often vary conflicts therefore are pandemic. Disputes on the other hand are distinctly associated with issues of justice, and although not as prevalent as conflicts, require immediate and serious efforts to achieve resolve (Fenn, Lowe, & Speck, 1997). These concepts will be discussed in more detail in section 3.

The terms management and resolution may be used as suffixes to both conflict and resolutions. However, the intent of management and resolution would vary depending on whether it is associated with a conflict or a dispute. In the case of conflict management, the concern is the management of the interests of the parties involved and ensuring that agreed interests continue to be maintained (Rahim, 2001). Whereas, conflict resolution is concerned with resolving concerns arising from any perceived or actual disparity of interests (Fenn, 2006). In the case of dispute management, the focus is on ensuring that injustices do not arise (Fenn, Lowe & Speck, 1997). While, in dispute resolution the concern is the provision of expedient and equitable justice (ibid), as and when lapses occur (although, this is easier said than done). Conflicts may be, and often are, resolved by the parties involved in the conflict. Disputes on the other hand require the intervention of a neutral third party (Moffitt & Bordone, 2005).

Some conflicts and disputes are short-run, lasting perhaps hours or days, whereas more serious breaches of interest or injustice can be extremely protracted (Fenn, 2006). For example, cases dealing with small claims are resolved quickly but property disputes can take a long time to settle. Various thoughts exist on how to deal with such issues. We can classify these into two categories: the preventive and the corrective (Rahim, 2001). In the preventive mode the focus is on managing the situation so that it does not escalate, become protracted, or lead to a loss of property or life. While, in the corrective mode the focus is on de-escalating an escalated scenario and on achieving some sort of resolution that may be amicable or not (as in the case of lose-lose negotiation techniques, see Blake and Mouton (1964)). And at times when a resolution is not possible to leave the negotiation table in such a state that future deliberations and negotiations may eventually be possible (e.g. when the 'withdrawing' style is adopted).

It should be clear from the discussion so far that conflict and dispute are two very interesting but distinct concepts. However, focusing on both in a single chapter would only lead to a topical discussion of both and would be unfair. Therefore, to do justice to the topic and to provide a detailed discussion this chapter focuses only on disputes and their resolution. We will, revisit disputes in contrast to conflicts and disagreements in section 3, to begin to comprehend the concept of a dispute more fully.

Over the years many alternatives to resolving disputes have emerged. Although, the nomenclatures of these mechanisms vary, they may essentially be classified into two broad categories: the formal and the informal (Fenn, 2006). The informal category of dispute resolution is also termed Alternate Dispute Resolution (ADR). The formal mechanisms of resolving disputes would include any legally available remedies, these include: litigation and adjudication. The informal mechanisms of resolving conflicts include mediation and arbitration. Mediations and arbitration pervade all sorts of disputes from the commercial and contracts to the personal. As discussed above, the underlying factor binding the formal and ADR methods of dispute resolution is a struggle for rights. ADR also extends to personal or tribal involvements such as a dispute between a couple (Rands, Levinger, & Mellinger, 1981) or a dispute between a tribe and one of its members.

In certain places the ADR dispute resolutions mechanism however, are used as 'the' formal mechanism. This is because certain geographic regions are provided unique constitutional statuses. Case in point would be the tribal belt in the North West of Pakistan. Here, the 'jirga' [lit. a gather of elders] (or more formally an 'administrative jirga') is the only legally available remedy for disputes between the tribes and the government. In the same spirit, an example of an informal dispute resolution method would be the 'panchayat' [lit. gathering of five], which prevails in the provinces of the Punjab across the Indian-subcontinent. The 'panchayat' is a mechanism akin to a 'jirga' but used solely for disputes between families, neighbors, and at times communities i.e. in a non-administrative manner. An administrative jirga may be classifiable as a method of arbitration. However, the non-administrative 'jirga' and the 'panchayat' are open to public attendance and therefore violate the confidentiality requirement of arbitration. Although interesting, this chapter purposefully does not discuss the jirga or panchayat system any further, this is because these are localized methods of dispute resolution that exist in a specific community. Rather, the chapter focuses on providing a more general exploration on indigenous and tribal methods of dispute resolution. A detailed discussion on these and other informal dispute resolution methods is presented in section 7.

The next section, section 3, presents a discussion aimed at differentiating between the concepts of a conflict, dispute, and a disagreement. This will enable us to have a common understanding of the concept of a dispute and will aide in forwarding the discussion towards dispute resolution processes.

3. DIFFERENTIATING BETWEEN CONFLICTS, DISPUTES, AND DISAGREEMENTS

As indicated in the introduction section of this chapter, the conflict body of literature provides evidence of an entanglement between the notions of: conflict, dispute, and disagreement. The discussion contained in this section therefore, seeks to differentiate between the three.

Burton (1993) envisions conflicts and disputes to be different temporally. For him, conflicts are long-term, while disputes are short-term. Burton (1993) goes on to argue that conflicts are unavoidable, yet manageable (Kolb & Bartunek, 1992; Lax & Sebenius, 1986). While disputes are avoidable, occurring only when conflicts are not managed and resolved. Fenn's (2006) definition of a conflict takes a similar stance and envisages disputes as existing within larger, long-term conflicts.

On the other hand, a disagreement is a bargaining impasse, which in Schelling's (1957) view is a struggle between bargainers to commit themselves to their preferred bargaining positions. Thus, disagreements or bargaining impasses are resolved through a process of negotiation. If such impasses are not overcome, the disagreements become protracted. Frustrations run high during such cases, many examples exist from around the world where loss of human life occurred because of the pain and suffering experienced by the parties involved. Similarly, Carneval and Pruitt (1992) identify the resolution of disagreements as an occurrence of mediation. Such agreements could be explicit (where both parties actively participate in reaching a decision) or 'tacit' (where both parties move towards a decision without discussion) (Carneval & Pruitt, 1992). Explicit agreements are normally written down so that the parties involved do not back out. The existence of disagreements is a positive phenomenon as it generates reasoning and alternatives (Jehn & Mannix, 2001). Interestingly, disagreements vanish as soon as full-disclosure is made by both parties (Sosa, 2010), perhaps because there is no longer any hidden agenda or imperfect information left.

In further clarifying the difference between conflicts and disputes, Burton (1990, 1997) considers a conflict as a serious challenge to existing norms, relationships, and rules of decision-making, and a dispute as the control of discontent stemming from the implementation of specific policies. Later, Burton (1998) categorizes disputes as occurring over material and physical resources, whereas conflicts occur over human needs and aspirations. Examples of conflicts include the conflict between Israel and Palestine and between India and Pakistan regarding Kashmir. While Fenn et al. (1997) consider a conflict as an incompatibility of interest and a dispute as associated with distinct justiciable issues (such as injury or claims for equitable relief). Hence, both disputes and conflicts are 'affective' i.e. relational in nature but have different causes. It is important to note that conflicts have both positive and negative aspects, while disputes are solely afflictive (Fenn et al., 1997).

Interestingly, disputes are classified into two categories 'litigated' (i.e. where a court's verdict is reached) and 'settled' i.e. those that settle prior to trial or prior to verdict pronouncement during a trial (Priest & Klein, 1984). Although, litigation is not the only mechanism for dispute resolution, it is not favored because a trial is considered to be a failure of reaching a decision socially (Gross & Syverud, 1992). Furthermore, litigations involving trial by jury, also referred to as a 'legal lottery' for their inconsistent outcomes, are favored even less than those involving trial by judge. Additionally, within the legal circles, there are arguments that too many disputes are settled out-of-court (either pre-trial or pre-verdict) and mediated or arbitrated. Whereas, the focus in case of litigation should be on adjudication and not settlement.

Disputes emerge and are transformed through a process in which 'unperceived injurious experiences are, or are not, perceived (naming), do or do not become grievances (blaming), and ultimately emerge as disputes (claiming)' (Felstiner, Abel, & Sarat, 1980). Work by Harrisson (2003) identifies seven different categorizations of disputants: information seekers, exception seekers, victims, enforcers, protectors, targets, and destroyers. These differences point at the motivation of the disputants involved and explains why each dispute is unique and is resolved differently.

Conflict too has been envisioned as forming a continuum, ranging from conflict avoidance to violence (C. Moore, 1989). Alternatively, Fenn at al., (1997) proposes a continuum ranging from conflicts to disputes, where the former requires conflict management and the latter dispute resolution (Fenn, 2006) i.e. arbitration or litigation. Moreover, conflict management usually makes use of non-binding techniques, while dispute resolution makes use of a combination of binding and non-binding methods (ibid).

Envisioning conflict, settlement, and lack of conflict or peace as disjoined events is certainly valid in many contexts and can aid our understanding. For example, knowing what state a party is in could signal their intent or commitment and could also serve as a deterrent to the other party (Kahn, 1964; Schelling, 1957). However, contending parties are simultaneously 'in conflict' or 'at peace' i.e. the intensity of the conflict varies along a spectrum. Conditions of absolute conflict or absolute peace do not exist. These moments can be explained as productive and 'appropriative activities', where the former is concerned with doing productive work and the latter focused on seizing resources controlled by other defending against invasions. Interestingly, appropriative activities may also include profiteering through robbery, confiscation, redistribution, or coercive encroachment.

To avoid any confusion between a conflict and a dispute, we accept Fenn's (2006) differentiation and consider conflicts to be longer lasting, having both positive and negative aspects, whereas disputes are short-term, afflictive, and arising within conflictual conditions. Etiologically, therefore conflict management is accepted as a means of preventing the occurrence of disputes (i.e. a preventive measure), while dispute resolution is considered as a corrective measure. In agreeing with Burton (1990) we accept conflicts to be related to issues of human needs and aspirations, while disputes are related to material and physical resources. Conflicts are managed throughout the period where two parties are engaged, while disputes require resolution through external input in the form of mediation, arbitration, judge, or jury. Several disputes could arise during a conflict, while the intensity of conflict during the period of engagement between parties varies.

Now that we have a clearer understanding of the difference between conflicts, disputes, and disagreements it would aide our understanding further to say a few words about the choice of methods available for resolving disputes.

Table 1. Dispute triggers, adapted from Fenn (1997)

Triggers of Disputes	Focus	Identified by
Unrealistic expectation, contract documents, communications, lack of team spirit, and changes	Construction general	Bristow and Vasilopoulous (1995)
Payments, performance, delay, negligence, quality, and administration	Construction procurement and contracts	Conlin, Langford, and Kennedy (1996)
People, process, and product	Construction contracts	Diekmann, Girard, and Abdul-Hadi (1994)
Contract terms, payment, variation, time, nomination, re-nomination, and information	Construction general	Heath, Hills, and Berry (1994)
Root causes and proximate causes	Construction general	Kumaraswamy (1997)
Management, culture, communications, design, economics, tendering pressures, law, unrealistic expectation, contracts, and workmanship	Construction law	Rhys Jones (1994)
Acceleration, access, weather, and changes	Construction claims	Semple, Hartman, and Jergas (1994)
Misunderstanding and unpredictability	Construction claims	Sykes (1996)

4. PATHWAYS TO RESOLVING DISPUTES

As mentioned earlier there are two distinct pathways to resolving a dispute: the formal and the informal (Fenn, 2006). First let us have a look at the formal path. The origin of the formal methods of resolving disputes lies in the concept of a 'sovereign', where a hereditary leader (or one gaining power over the people after deposing a sovereign) would wield powers of resolving disputes between their subjects. As societies progressed and the power of the sovereigns were culled, and in many countries replaced by elected governments, that power was transferred to the legislative bodies. Presently, the formal methods of resolving disputes fall under the domain of such bodies. Where, disputes between the subjects of a nation are resolved using litigation (Rahim, 1986).

However, the legislative bodies have been slow to respond in providing expeditious justice, perhaps because of a lack of competence, resources or will. Some possible arguments for the lethargy prevailing in the legislative systems include the ever-increasing population (which puts a sever burden on the legislative bodies) and the inherent complexity found in society that is giving rise to an ever increasing number of unexplored issues (Semple et al., 1994). As an example, the Internet and World Wide Web have given rise to a diverse set of issues that have required major changes in the legislative process e.g. see (Blavin & Cohen, 2002). The intricate and changing nature of society and business is also a cause of many disputes that burdens the legislative systems further (Forst, 1984), for example: disputes related to discrimination, gender, racism, etc. have been instrumental in laying the foundation for previously unseen types of disputes. The process of litigation is costly and many perceive that the judgments that are issued often are one-sided and do not cater to the mutual benefit of the parties involved (Hylton, 1990). Lastly, some countries, such as those in the Third World, face the added dynamic of corruption that further complexify's the litigation process (E. Buscaglia, 1996).

There are various types of costs associated with litigation, such as: court fees, retainer fees payable to the lawyer, and the cost of the judgment in case of losing the case (Kritzer, Sarat, Trubek, Bumiller, & McNichol, 1984). Because of the exorbitant cost of the litigation process and unpredictability of outcomes, and the emotional drain it places on those involved this mode of dispute resolution has been termed a "legal lottery" (Bowers, 1996). Interestingly, in some industries both the formal and the informal methods of disputes resolution are problematic, e.g. according to Lord Denning (in "Dawnays Ltd v FG Minter Ltd," 1971) "One of the greatest threats to cash flow is the incidence of disputes. Resolving them by litigation is frequently lengthy and expensive. Arbitration in the construction industry is often as bad or worse".

Alternatively, disputes may be resolved using informal methods. These methods perhaps predate the formal mechanism and are more prevalent because of their accessibility, discretion, and swiftness in resolution. Such methods are regaining popularity owing to the issues plaguing the formal mechanism and are increasingly being used as an alternative to litigation, see as an example (E. Buscaglia & Stephan, 2005). In very simple terms, the informal methods to dispute resolution, also known as alternative dispute resolution (ADR), consist of three key parties: the disputants and a mediator or an arbitrator (Fenn, 2006). Both parties in a dispute are provided equal opportunity to present their case (including providing testimony and evidence) and the arbitrator or mediator is tasked with playing their role in the dispute (Cheung, Suen, & Lam, 2002). The mediator's role is that of a facilitator, while the arbitrator's role is that of a judge and jury. Alternative Dispute Resolution (ADR) is now increasingly being used as the favored method of dispute resolution (Cheung, Suen & Lam, 2002). Additionally, the Construction Round Table, a group of main contractors and major sub-contractors, in their voluntary Code of Conduct commit themselves, *inter alia*, to: fair dealings with subcontractors, taking the team lead in the interest of the project, and accepting prompt third party dispute resolution – thus, paving the ground for ADR.

Mediation, arbitration, and adjudication are terms used in the law, to refer to the process of alternative dispute resolution that aims to resolve a dispute between two parties with concrete effects. The role of the mediator or arbitrator is of a third party, who facilitates the disputants to negotiate a settlement (Smith, 1962). This is in contrast to the role of a 'conciliator', who is an expert in the subject area surrounding the dispute and may offer advice during the dispute resolution process (Wenying, 2005). It may be argued that all conciliators take the role of mediators, but not all mediators are conciliators.

The terms mediator, arbitrator, and adjudicator are broad references to instances where a third party helps others reach a settlement. When used in the context of business, the process of mediation has a structure, timetable, and dynamics that 'ordinary' negotiations do not (Bühring-Uhle, Kirchhoff, & Scherer, 2006). The law ensures privacy and confidentiality during ADR and participation is voluntary. It should be noted that mediators facilitate rather than direct the mediation process using a variety of techniques during an ADR to open or improve dialogue and empathy between the disputants (McGovern, 1996).

The cost of using a mediator includes a retainer fee comparable to that of an attorney. However, the time required to complete the mediation process is significantly less than the time it takes to resolve a dispute in litigation. Additionally, mediation increases the control that the disputants have over the resolution process (McGovern, 1996). Whereas, control in the case of litigation or adjudication, resides with a judge or the jury. Therefore, mediation is likely to produce a result that both parties accept. To ensure that the agreements reached because of the mediation process are not violated, the mediated agreement is fully enforceable in a court of law. For mediation to be successful, both the parties must be willing to work together towards a resolution. By the fact, that if the parties agree to mediation we get a sense that they are willing to negotiate.

Mediation is one of the key techniques in ADR and will therefore be discussed in some detail. For those interested in knowing more about Mediation, please see C. W. Moore (2014). The mediation process may have disclosure requirements if stipulated by the courts. Disclosure pertains to documents, reports or other material. In litigations the disputants are required to exchange such material gathered through a process of discovery or disclosure and the same is true in the case of arbitration or mitigation (Ponte, 2001). The mitigation clauses may require the parties to attend in person; participation at one stage may compensate for the absence in another. Parties choosing to go into mitigation may be required by a judge to make a summary of the dispute and then bring the summary to the mitigation table. Although there are no formal compulsory elements to a mitigation process, the following elements are found in most mitigation scenarios: ground rules of the mitigation process, parties detailing their stories, identification officials, clarifying and indicating respective interests and objectives, search for objective criteria, identification of options, discussion and analysis of solutions, adjustment and refinement of proposed solutions, and a record of the agreement in writing.

The process of ratification provides safeguards for mediating parties. This could alleviate any opportunities for a third party to undermine the mediation result. As an example, in some cases the court must explicitly endorse the mediation agreement. A mediator at his discretion may refer a party to a dispute to specialist for further assistance at the end of the mediation, such as to: psychologists, counselors, social workers, etc. There are special codes of conduct binding the mediator, common elements of which consist of: informing participants of the process, adopting a neutral stance, explicating potential conflicts of interest, maintaining confidentiality, ensuring wellbeing, directing participants to appropriate sources for legal advice, and practicing within their fields of experience. The parties involved in a dispute may choose mediation through consensus, or it may be stipulated by contract. At times the mediator may be liable for misleading the parties or for breaching confidentiality. However, follow-on court action is rare.

Mediator liabilities can arise in several forms including:

- Liability of contract
- Liability and tort
- Liability for breach of fiduciary obligations

Liability in contract arises if the mediator breaches the contract, written or verbal, between the parties. The two most common forms of breach are *failure to perform* and *anticipatory breach*. The limitation of liability includes a requirement to show actual cause. Liability in tort arises when a mediator influences a party (thereby, compromising the integrity of the decision), defames a party, breaches confidentiality, or is negligent. To claim damages, the party must show actual damage, and must exhibit that the mediator's action was the direct cause of the damage. Liability of breach of fiduciary obligations arises if the parties misconceive their relationship with the mediator as anything other than that of neutrality. Court action in such cases is unlikely to succeed since such liability relies on misconception.

There are varieties of mediation, including:

1. Evaluative mediation
2. Facilitative mediation
3. Transformative mediation
4. Narrative mediation
5. Mediation with arbitration
6. Online mediation, and
7. Biased mediation

These are explained in brief next. In the evaluative mediation process the mediator evaluates the fortitude of the arguments presented by both parties and predicts the outcome of a court decision if litigation were to take place. During a facilitative mediation, the mediator is concerned with the mediation process and not its outcome. The mediator as facilitator helps the parties find resolution to their dispute. In the transformative mediation, the mediator as a transformer is concerned with encouraging some sort of transformation to occur during the mediation process. Transformations may include: a change is perspective of a party, improved communication, arriving at a mutually defined agreement, etc. The mediator in the narrative mediation seeks to extract examples and stories constituting a lived experience of the disputants. These allow the parties to see the problem(s) a new and to come up with new and unique solutions. The mediator's role here is to emphasize on helping the party realize that the dispute is not people centric, rather it is problem centric (Winslade & Monk, 2000). In mediation with arbitration, preference is towards reaching settlement through mediation but if that fails the process of arbitration is employed. The arbitration results are binding on the parties. Online mediation simply refers to medium of technology used during mediation. Lastly, biased mediation would be one where the mediator takes the side of one party against another.

5. ADR TERMS IN COMMON USE

The term ADR is an umbrella term encompassing four popular processes that sound quite similar. In an order to alleviate any confusion between these concepts each is compared against its closest rival below.

5.1. Mediation vs. Arbitration

The terms mediation and arbitration are used synonymously, but they are slightly different. Although, mediation and arbitration are alternatives to litigation, they are sometimes used in conjunction with litigation. Both mediation and arbitration necessitate the involvement of an independent third party to oversee the process, and they both may be binding. However, it is common practice to use mediation in a non-binding manner and arbitration as a binding process. Binding arbitration leads to the replacement of the trial process with arbitration.

Moving from mediation to arbitration is not a thoughtless process. Although, mediation may cause some anxiety in that a party or both the parties may feel that mediation is slow, or they may not be happy with its outcome. However, in the *The Channel Tunnel Group Ltd. V. Balfour Beatty Construction Ltd* ("The Channel Tunnel Group Ltd v. Balfour Beatty Construction Ltd," 1993) the House of Lords held that the courts have the jurisdiction to refuse to hear proceedings brought into breach of an agreed dispute resolution. The court ruled that "… those who make agreements for the resolution of disputes must show good reasons for departing from them…". It was beside the point that a party seeking payment found their "… chosen method too slow to suit their purpose."

Arbitration can involve a single arbitrator or consists of a panel of arbitrators who act as judge(s). In case panel-arbitration is used, the panel consists of an arbitrator chosen by each party and a third arbitrator chosen by both the parties together. Decisions in such a case are made by majority vote. In the case of construction disputes the third member of the arbitration panel is chosen from the International Chamber of Commerce (following industry rules). Alternatively, a single mediator (whose role is that of a facilitator rather than a judge) generally conducts mediation.

Over the years ADR in the form of mediation and arbitration has gained some favor. As an example, taking cues from the access to justice movement in the UK, the Philippines have served as a role-model for many countries in establishing mobile courts. These courts travel around the country resolving disputes using mediation and arbitration. However, success of the mobile courts has been hindered by the lack of proper law making. In that, parties to mediation had the option to pursue litigation if they were not content with the decision rendered by the mobile courts. Later changes in the laws have resolved this issue, whereby once the parties choose to go to mediation they cannot exercise litigation. Another pathway to justice has also made significant ground, such as the Federal Ombudsman office in Pakistan that allow for non-litigious resolution of disputes between civil citizens and federal and provincial offices.

5.2. Arbitration vs. Adjudication

Although, arbitration and adjudication are different processes for resolving disputes, they are similar in a few respects. They both are:

1. Alternatives to the litigation process
2. Confidential processes, and
3. Binding (although to different degrees)

Arbitration is a more generally used process spanning disputes falling in the domain of employment law, international trade, contracts, construction, intellectual property, and sports. The process of arbitration has already been explained in sub-section (A) above.

Adjudication is a process used mostly in the construction industry. The use of adjudication is provisioned as a right during construction disputes through the HGCRA (discussed in section 6.1). It is also used as a process to resolve tenant disputes.

Adjudication is a legal process in which an arbiter or judge listens to arguments, views evidence, and comes to a decision determining the rights and obligations between the parties involved. The process of adjudication is also described as a 'mini-trial' that results in a fairly quick decision, as compared to a full-trial that tend to be protracted (Washington State Office of Administrative Hearings, 2015). In the case of construction disputes the time allowed for adjudication to reach a decision is 28 days.

Adjudication can go severely wrong. As an example, in the case of *Bouygues UK Ltd v. Dahl Jensen UK Ltd (In Liquidation) ("Bouygues UK Ltd v. Dahl Jensen UK Ltd," 1999)* £250,000 were patently awarded to the wrong party. When Bouygues failed to honor the decision, Jensen won an enforcement order from the court. Bouygues had contended that the figures did not add up, and that if the adjudicator was correct it could only be because he was releasing the final moiety of retention, which neither party had requested. Thus, the adjudicator had exceeded his authority and the decision was null and void. Jensen on the other had argued that it was part of his remit, but because he had made a mistake, thus the decision was valid. The adjudicator invited both claimants to reconsider but to no avail. Eventually, a decision was passed in favor of Jensen with the argument by the adjudicator that he "… was doing precisely what he had been asked to do, and was answering the right question, but he was doing it in the wrong way".

6. ADR: A LEGAL PERSPECTIVE

This section presents the key Acts and Model Laws that shape the ADR landscape. Specific sections of the acts that are relevant to the topic of ADR are reproduced, where necessary, or discussed in detail. This section is meant to bring to fore the key developments founding the basic constructs of ADR and the boundary within which it is enacted. Understanding these constructs will enable the reader to not only understand the landscape of ADR as it is now but also to develop the necessary comprehension of where it is headed. Although, the topics discussed below may not on their surface seem to relate with each other. However, each deal with a specific but essential element of ADR.

6.1. The Housing Grants, Construction and Regeneration Act (HGCRA), and the Right to Adjudication

The HGCRA is an omnibus act that extends to housing grants, laws pertaining to construction contracts and architects, regeneration of sites, energy efficient construction, and dissolution or formulation of new townships. In simpler terms, it could be considered as the defining act pertaining to construction. This section focuses on the HCGRA's implication in ADR.

Adjudication is a statutory right of any party involved in a contract dispute falling in the domain of the HGCRA (Housing Grants, 1996). The key sections of the act are 108(1) to (5). These are reproduced below:

1. A party to a construction contract has the right to refer a dispute arising under the contract for adjudication under a procedure complying with this section. For this purpose, 'dispute' includes any difference.
2. The contract shall:
    a. Enable a party to give notice at any time of his intention to refer a dispute to adjudication.
    b. Provide a timetable with the object of securing the appointment of the adjudicator and referral of the dispute to him within 7 days of such notice.
    c. Require the adjudicator to read a decision within 28 days of referral or such longer period as agreed by the parties after the dispute has been referred.
    d. Allow the adjudicator to extend the period of 28 days by up to 14 days, with the consent of the party by whom the dispute was referred.
    e. Impose a duty on the adjudicator to act impartially.
    f. Enable the adjudicator to take the initiative in ascertaining the facts and the law.
4. The contract shall provide that the decision of the adjudicator is binding until the dispute is finally determined by legal proceedings, by arbitration... or by agreement.
5. The contract shall also provide that the adjudicator is not liable for anything done or omitted in the discharge or purported discharge of his functions as adjudicator unless the act or omission is in bad faith, and that any employee or agent of the adjudicator is similarly protected for liability.
6. If the contract does not comply with the requirements of subsection (I) to (4), the adjudication provisions of the Scheme for Contraction Contracts apply.

Clause 5 above, of the HGCRA resulted in the Joint Contracts Tribunal (JCT) to reconstitute their form JCT SFBC 98 by including some of the recommendations of the Latham Report and by making it compliant to the HGCRA via the introduction of Cause 41(A) (Pickavance, 2007).

Adjudication is increasingly being suggested as a binding or non-binding method of potentially unlocking disputes. Aside from the jurisdiction of the HGCRA, adjudication is finding its way into activities that fall outside the domain of construction.

6.2. Admissibility of Hearsay Evidence and the Civil Evidence Act of 1995

Before the introduction of the Civil Evidence Act of ("Civil Evidence Act," 1995) 'hearsay' evidence was inadmissible in the cases of litigation and arbitration. The only way to include key evidence was to call in a hostile witness. This caused significant issues in the case of Rent Review disputes, where the key witness could not participate as they would either be bound by confidentiality agreement or ineligible because of conflict of interest (Hackett, 2000). A somewhat similar problem often arises in construction disputes as well. Where, a sub-contractor X pursuing a main contractor would obtain evidence from another sub-contractor Y in an informal and free manner. However, sub-contractor Y may be hopeful for a favorable outcome of the case, or is expectant of future business and therefore may not be willing to provide testimony, or appear on behalf of sub-contractor X.

The Civil Evidence Act of 1995 relaxes the previous position on 'hearsay' evidence, and gives discretionary powers to judges and arbitrators, contingent on six tests (Hackett, 2000):

1. Is it really unrealistic to include the original source of the evidence now being relied upon?
2. Was the original statement made contemporaneously?
3. Does the evidence involve multiple 'hearsay'?
4. Do the parties involved have motive to conceal or misrepresent matters?
5. Was the original statement an edited account, made in collusion or made for a particular purpose?
6. Do the circumstances, in which the 'hearsay' evidence is mentioned, suggest an attempt to prevent proper evaluation of its importance?

It is recommended that 'hearsay' evidence be accepted with care keeping in mind the motives and credibility of the person of source. The best type of evidence would be actual factual accounts presented by either of the parties.

6.3. The Human Rights Act 1998 and Its Relevance to Adjudication

The Human Rights Act of 1998 came about as a result of acceding to the European Convention on Human Rights. This act seeks to provision individuals with the right of protection against the state or its system lead (alleged) oppressions. The act mandates 'public authorities' to provide a fair and public hearing for those with grievances. The term 'public authorities' is an umbrella term that encompasses both: (1) a court of tribunal or (2) any person who is a public functionary.

This act is relevant to dispute resolution as arbitration falls under the concept of a 'tribunal'. However, arbitration is not a public hearing, thus the consequences of this act are significant. Latter interpretations of the act led to the conclusion that this act applies directly in the cases of forced arbitration. However, the courts determined that 'voluntary arbitration' does not fall under the term 'tribunal' and thus arbitration in such a case does not have to be public. However, it should be noted that voluntary arbitration is subject indirectly to the act by the following (a) the general duty of arbitrators to apply English Law and (b) it is obligatory for the Commercial Court under the Act to apply Convention rights albeit to the extent required of an appellate court (Robinson, 2002)

6.4. The Arbitration Act of 1996

Arbitrations (local and domestic) in the UK and Great Britain are governed by the Arbitration Act 1996, which is a successor of three acts dating back to the 1950. As discussed earlier in this chapter arbitration is the preferred mechanism of dispute resolution over litigation. The key reason for this, courtesy of Lord Woolf, is that arbitration offers better case management and early trial dates. However, arbitration is under threat from section 9 of the Arbitration Act 1996, which allows for the courts to retain action where an arbitration clause exists. As many solicitors are amending construction contracts in favor of litigation, arbitration may possibly be completely replaced with adjudication. However, this does not imply that arbitration is losing favor as a dispute resolution process involving other types of disputes. In fact, a survey by Price Waterhouse Coopers (2013) reveals that arbitration was still the preferred mode of dispute resolution in the construction sector.

Although, the Arbitration Act 1996 takes influence from the UNCITRAL Model Law (discussed in section 6.5), the UK government's refusal to adopt it has been a cause of some criticism. The Arbitration Act 1996 applies to disputes both domestic and international, outlines the principles underlying the legislation (e.g. fairness, anonymity, and bounding court intervention), and provides for appeals in the case of point of law.

6.5. UNCITRAL Model Law on International Commercial Arbitration

The United Nations Commission on International Trade Law (UNCITRAL) adopted the Model Law on International Commercial Arbitration in 1985. Last amendments to the Model Law were made in 2006. The UNCITRAL Model Law is a detailed guideline for legislators for adoption, or for formulating arbitration acts of their own pertaining to disputes in light of the particular needs of international arbitrations. The model law has been adopted by 66 countries in 99 different jurisdictions (United Nations Commission on International Trade Law, 2015).

There are two key parts to the UNCITRAL, the Model Law and the Arbitration Rule. The arbitration rules are a comprehensive set of procedures that disputing parties may agree to follow during an arbitration. There are three versions of the UNCITRAL Arbitration Rules, the latest of which was introduced in 2013 and includes transparency clauses pertaining to investor-state arbitrations (United Nations Commission on International Trade Law, 2015).

6.6. Alternative Dispute Resolution and the Civil Procedure Rules 1998

Civil procedures in the UK went through major reforms as a result of Lord Woolf's (the then Lord Chief Justice) Access to Justice reports of 1995 and 1996 (Lord Woolf, 1998). Problems haunting the legal system as identified in the Woolf Report that necessitated the reforms include: high expense, slowness, and complexity. Since its introduction all court procedures in the UK now follow the Civil Procedure Rules 1998.

ADR is not mentioned in the 1995 Woolf Report but features prominently in the 1996 report. This is not to say that Alternative Dispute Resolution (ADR) was not a part of the legal framework prior to the Woolf reports. On the contrary, ADR was being encouraged since the early 1990s by the Commercial Courts that went on to issue its *Practice Note: Commercial Courts; Alternative Dispute Resolution* in 1994. This note mandates that legal advisors' council their clients to resolve disputes using mediation, conciliation, or otherwise; and to inform the parties of the most cost-effective modes of resolving disputes. These recommendations were adopted by the High Courts in 1995 through the issuance of a *Practical Note: Civil Litigation; Case Management.*

The Civil Procedure Rules in sections 1.4(2) encourages cooperative behavior from both parties and *inter alia* encourages the use of ADR procedures (in para 1.4(2)(e)) whenever deemed appropriate by the courts. Since its introduction the Civil Procedure Rules has been amended 60 times with the last major amendment occurring in 2013. Further, as of 2009 the pre-action protocols also formally began encouraging ADR via the letter of claim, mandating that it should 'state (if this is so) that the claimant wishes to enter into mediation or another alternative method of dispute resolution, and draw attention to the court's power to impose sanctions for failure to comply with this practice direction'. This gave rise to a reciprocal requirement in the letter of response, which states '...Both the Claimant and Defendant may be required by the Court to provide evidence that alternative means of resolving their disputes were considered. The Courts take the view that litigation should be a last resort...' (41st amendment to the CPR). It is quite confusing to note that ADR is recommended but not compulsory (i.e. other methods may also be used) as specified in the *Practice Direction: Pre-action Conduct* issued April 2009. Other methods would include: mediation, arbitration, early neutral evaluation, and ombudsmen schemes.

The Woolf Report and amended Civil Procedure Rules have given rise to a New Legal Dictionary. A comparison of the 'old' vs. 'new' legal terms is provided in table 2. Terminology specific to arbitration is identified in parenthesis.

Table 2. Glossary of new vs. old legal terminology

New Terms	Old Terms
Claimant	Plaintiff (Litigations)
Claimant	Claimant (Arbitration)
Defendant	Defendant (Litigation)
Respondent	Respondent (Arbitration)
Claim Form	Summons or Writ
Defence	Defence
Application Notice	Interlocutory Summons
Statement of Case	Pleadings
Disclosure	Discovery
Further Information	Further and Better / Particulars & Interrogatories
Permission	Leave
Assessment	Taxation of Costs

6.7. Access to Justice Act 1999

The Access to Justice Act 1999 goes beyond the recommendations of Lord Woolf's Report *Access to Justice* that addressed how civil procedures could be made more user friendly. The Access to Justice Act 1999 sets out to update procedures for obtaining financial assistance in bringing or defending legal actions in civil or criminal courts. Further, it reviews the procedures for challenging decisions passed by the lower courts and allowing cases that touch on particular points of law focusing on public policy to go all the way to the House of Lords. Although the Access to Justice Act 1999 does not make any direct references to ADR in the context of commercial disputes, it does mention in Section 8(3) that mediation is appropriate for many family disputes than court proceedings. However, impact of the Access to Justice Act pervades the legal system.

One of the concerns of the Access to Justice Act 1999 (AJA) is Conditional Fee Arrangements (CFA). Prior to 1990 the general rule that prevailed prevented anyone from acting on other than full fee basis. Since, the introduction of the Access to Justice Act 1999 CFA is now allowed. It is important to note that the CFA allows for Conditional Fee but does not allow Contingency Fee. Contingency Fee is where the legal team agrees to represent a client based on speculation of the case's success. Contingency Fees are allowed in the USA but not in the UK.

Contractors and sub-contractors can safeguard themselves financially by opting for 'Pre-event' litigation insurance and 'after-the-event' litigation cost insurance. The pre-event litigation insurance is a bolt-on option to the main policy for the prudent contractors. Such policies are tremendously useful in case some unforeseen litigious scenarios arise. Having such a policy aids in the least amount of disruption to the cash flows of the insured contractors and sub-contractors.

After-the-event litigation cost insurance policies are only available to the claimants and not to the defendants. An exception would be where the defendant in the main action is also the claimant in the counterclaim. Such insurance policies take the form of after-the-event litigation costs and respond only in the event of the Claimant losing the case. Such insurance add-ons enable claimants, whether individual or companies, to afford justice. That is, they can seek to enforce their perceived legal rights under a contract and avoid the previous uncertainty of financial risks of losing – specifically, doubling the costs of litigation in case of loss.

7. INDIGENOUS AND TRIBAL METHODS OF DISPUTE RESOLUTION

This section focuses on exploring informal and non-conventional methods of dispute resolutions that are used in rural, indigenous and tribal societies around the world.

ADR is an alternative to formal legal proceedings in court. However, this is partly correct. There are many cultures and communities across the world, even within North American and the Western hemisphere, where litigation is not the norm but is an alternative. These communities prefer to use their own indigenous and tribal methods to resolve their disputes. Consequently, some have advocated that the word 'Alternative' should be replaced with 'Appropriate' ("ADR Options: A Spectrum of Processes," 2018). ADR has been a focus of several critiques, such as its inability to fully protect the rights of the parties involved, and for its failure to understand the culture and context of both the dispute and the parties. Based on 'co-existential justice'(Unknown, 1997), ADR came into public consciousness in the 1970s.

It has also been criticized for attempting to be something new and novel, whereas quasi-ADR forms of dispute resolution have been the norm in indigenous and tribal societies for centuries.

Unlike ADR, which seeks justice, indigenous and tribal dispute resolution focuses on peacemaking. Indigenous or Aboriginal communities follow three forms of dispute resolution: their own processes, Western forms of ADR, adapted forms or Indigenized forms of Western ADR. Such communities seldom resort to court litigation, perhaps because of the associated expense, time, complication, reliance on judge and counsel-dependence, or perhaps because it is not innate for them to do so. Although, some well-organized tribal groups, that have arranged themselves into corporate entities have pursued litigation. It is interesting to note that a critical problem faced by indigenous communities is that of intellectual property rights, stemming from the infringements of their traditional knowledge on medicinal plants, chants, songs, dances, craft, etc.

The United Nations (UN) General Assembly acknowledging the rights of indigenous people, adopted the UN Declaration on the Rights of Indigenous People (UNDRIP) on 13 September (2007). The UNDRIP in its *supra* note 20, article 5 states that 'Indigenous people have the right to maintain and strengthen their distinct political, legal, economic, social and cultural institutions, while retaining their right to participate fully, if they so choose, in the political, economic, social and cultural life of the state'. Indigenous Dispute Resolution (IDR) allows the tribe or its members to resolve their disputes outside of the courtroom within their own cultural and customs confines using 'aboriginal wisdom' (Turner, 2004). IDR based remedies are culturally more appropriate as they are grounded in custom and tradition and include the processes of face-to-face dialogue and calm discussion. IDR, Indigenized Western ADR, and ADR are difficult when applied to Indigenous people, because indigenous community members have different conceptions from mainstream society i.e. they possess a different ontological world view, leaving only a handful of people who understand the indigenous culture; namely, the indigenous themselves and a handful of outsiders. Interestingly, those outsiders that do understand the Indigenous cultures are those working as high-power lawyers, working either to promote the cause of the tribe or fighting against it. Furthermore, government may show reluctance in organizing ADR or upholding IDR. This reluctance stems from, perhaps, them perceiving the issue as unimportant or because it does not need immediate attention or perhaps they wish not to expend energy on dealing with it now.

7.1 The Process of Indigenous Dispute Resolution

The process of IDR is culturally embedded, constrained by customs, and steered by tribal wisdom. Indigenous cultures and customs include: traditional knowledge, respect (for oneself, others, elders, community, animals, environment, etc.), relationships, interconnectedness or a sense of unity, spirituality, prayers, storytelling, 'saving face' (Bauman & Williams, 2004), recounting facts, and emotions. IDR seeks to achieve group consensus, general good relations with other community members, solidarity and reciprocation of obligations (Yazzie, 2004). The IDR process is flexible, cycles through time, gauges success qualitatively, and is people focused. The person made responsible by a tribe for leading its IDR must exemplify their wisdom and knowledge of tradition (Yazzie, 2004). Tribal and Indigenous conflict resolution deploys certain processes while a dispute is being resolved. These are: peacemaking circles, Indian time, shared horizons, feasting, preventing a call to arms, and unforced consensus. These are explained below.

- **Peacemaking Circles:** A way to resolve disputes between family and community members in a face-to-face discussion of an alleged crime between an accused and the victim. The proceedings of a peacemaking circle are guided by tribal elders.
- **Indian Time:** Means sitting together to know one another better.
- **Shared Horizons:** Means sharing oral histories.
- **Feast**: A period of dispute resolution spanning a few days, includes Indian times, singing, protracted recitations of grievances, narrations of stories, sharing horizons*, dancing, sharing food, and gift giving. The feast is an opportunity for the aggrieved party to be heard and terminates when a qualitatively defined measure of success is achieved. The focus of the feast is to make peace.
- **Preventing a Call to Arms:** Something the negotiators strive to achieve. For if negotiations were to breakdown either party may hasten to defend their rights by using aggression. These may escalate into full-blown bloody and deadly armed conflicts. Such tribal wars may end up escalating to groups of ethnic communities e.g. the Tamil conflict in Sri Lanka.
- **Unforced Consensus:** A consensus gained through mutual understanding of an issue through the feast.

It should be noted that IDR is not just used for resolving intra community disputes, but it has been used to solve both inter community disputes and for negotiating with outsiders. Example of where tribal dispute resolution methods have been used and have proved useful include the Maori chiefs in New Zealand (or precolonial Aotearoa) signing a treaty ceding sovereignty to the Crown, whilst retaining (in theory) exclusive and undisturbed possession of their land, estates, etc.

8. FUTURE RESEARCH DIRECTIONS

Future research should focus on qualitative explorations of the role of ADR on the relationships between parties. Additionally, regional and tribal ADR methods may be explored in more detail and compared against more traditional ADR methods. Other issues of interest would include exploring the role of trust and power during ADR proceedings. From a quantitative perspective the effectiveness of ADR may be explored and a case for more effective ADR methods may be built. There is also potential for case studies and longitudinal studies that can aim to explore ADR in action and provide for more thicker and *in situ* descriptions of what goes on when ADR is being practiced.

9. CONCLUDING REMARKS

This chapter has covered a lot of groundwork and provides and quick and through introduction to the concepts and underlying discussions on Alternative Dispute Resolution (ADR). The chapter provided a detailed discussion based on extant literature to differentiate between disputes and conflicts. Then some of the common confusions between terms commonly used in ADR were addressed. Following which various key government acts and reports that shape the state of ADR as we know it were touched upon.

The reader will appreciate that these acts and documents themselves are far too lengthy to be sufficiently described in a single chapter, therefore only those concerns within the documents that directly address ADR or are related to ADR are discussed. It remains a burden on the readers to access these documents themselves to fully appreciate their content.

REFERENCES

ADR Options A Spectrum Of Processes. (2018). Retrieved From Https://Www.Cadreworks.Org/Resources/Cadre-Materials/Adr-Options

Bauman, T., & Williams, R. (2004). *The Business Of Process: Research Issues In Managing Indigenous Decison-Making And Disputes In Land.* AIATSIS Research Disucssion Paper No. 13.

Blake, R. R., & Mouton, J. S. (1964). *The Managerial Grid.* Houston, TX: Gulf Publishing Company.

Blavin, J. H., & Cohen, L. G. (2002). Gore, Gibson, And Goldsmith: The Evolution Of Internet Metaphors In Law And Commentary. *Harvard Journal of Law & Technology*, 16.

Bouygues, U. K. (1999). *Ltd V.* Dahl Jensen UK Ltd.

Bowers, C. P. (1996). Courts, Contracts, And The Appropriate Discount Rate: A Quick Fix For The Legal Lottery. *The University of Chicago Law Review. University of Chicago. Law School, 63*(3), 1099–1137. doi:10.2307/1600250

Bristow, D., & Vasilopoulous, R. (1995). The New CCDC 2: Facilitating Dispute Resolution Of Construction Projects. *Constitutional Law Journal (Newark, N.J.), 11*(2), 95–117.

Bühring-Uhle, C., Kirchhoff, L., & Scherer, G. (2006). Arbitration And Mediation. In *International Business*. New York: Kluwer Law International.

Burton, J. W. (1990). *Conflict Resolution And Prevention*. New York: St. Martin's Press.

Burton, J. W. (1993). Conflict Resolution As Political Philosophy. In H. Van Der Merwe & D. J. Sandole (Eds.), Conflict Resolution Theory And Practice: Integration And Application (pp. 55-64). Manchester, UK: Manchester University Press.

Burton, J. W. (1997). *Violence Explained: The Sources Of Conflict, Violence And Crime And Their Prevention*. Manchester, UK: Manchester University Press.

Burton, J. W. (1998). Conflict Resolution: The Human Dimension. *International Journal of Peace Studies, 3*(1), 4.

Buscaglia, E. (1996). Corruption And Judicial Reform In Latin America. *Policy Studies, 17*(4), 273–285. doi:10.1080/01442879608423713

Buscaglia, E., & Stephan, P. B. (2005). An Empirical Assessment Of The Impact Of Formal Versus Informal Dispute Resolution On Poverty: A Governance-Based Approach. *International Review of Law and Economics, 25*(1), 89–106. doi:10.1016/j.irle.2004.06.004

Carnevale, P. J., & Pruitt, D. G. (1992). Negotiation And Mediation. *Annual Review of Psychology, 43*(1), 531–582. doi:10.1146/annurev.ps.43.020192.002531

Cheung, S. O., Suen, H. C., & Lam, T. I. (2002). Fundamentals Of Alternative Dispute Resolution Processes In Construction. *Journal of Construction Engineering and Management, 128*(5), 409–417. doi:10.1061/(ASCE)0733-9364(2002)128:5(409)

Civil Evidence Act, (1995).

Conlin, J., Langford, D., & Kennedy, P. (1996). *The Relationship Between Construciton Procurement Strategies And Construction Contract Disputes*. Paper Presented At The CIB W92 North Meets South, Durban, South Africa.

Contruction And Regeneration Act, (1996).

Dawnays Ltd v FG Minter Ltd (2 All ER 1389; [1971] 1 WLR 1205 1971).

Diekmann, J., Girard, M., & Abdul-Hadi, N. (1994). *Disputes Potential Index: A Study Into The Predictability Of Contract Disputes*. Academic Press.

Felstiner, W. L., Abel, R. L., & Sarat, A. (1980). The Emergence And Transformation Of Disputes: Naming, Blaming, Claiming.... *Law & Society Review, 15*(3/4), 631. doi:10.2307/3053505

Fenn, P. (2006). Conflict Management And Dispute Resolution. In D. Lowe & R. Leiringer (Eds.), *Commercial Management Of Projects: Defining The Discipline* (pp. 234–269). Blackwell Publishing. doi:10.1002/9780470759509.ch11

Fenn, P., Lowe, D., & Speck, C. (1997). Conflict And Dispute In Construction. *Construction Management and Economics, 15*(6), 513–518. doi:10.1080/014461997372719

Forst, B. (1984). Overburdened Courts And Underutilized Information Technology: A Modern Prescription For A Chronic Disorder. *Judicature, 68*, 30.

Gross, S. R., & Syverud, K. D. (1992). Getting To No: A Study Of Settlement Negotiations And The Selection Of Cases For Trial. *Michigan Law Review, 90*, 323–373. PMID:10115793

Hackett, J. (2000). *Construction Claims: Current Practice And Case Management*. London: LLP Professional Publishing.

Harrisson, T. R. (2003). Victims, Targets, Protectors, And Destroyers: Using Disputant Accounts To Develop A Grounded Taxonomy Of Disputant Orientations. *Conflict Resolution Quarterly, 20*(3), 307–329. doi:10.1002/crq.27

Heath, B., Hills, B., & Berry, M. (1994). *The Origin Of Conflict Within The Construction Process*. Paper Presented At The First Plenary Meeting Of TG15, The Netherlands.

(1992). Hidden Conflict. InKolb, D., & Bartunek, J. M. (Eds.), *Organizations: Uncovering Behind-The-Scenes Disputes*. Newbury Park, CA: Sage.

Hylton, K. N. (1990). The Influence Of Litigation Costs On Deterrence Under Strict Liability And Under Negligence. *International Review of Law and Economics*, *10*(2), 161–171. doi:10.1016/0144-8188(90)90021-K

Jehn, K. A. (1994). Enhancing Effectivenes: An Investigation Of Advantages And Disadvantages Of Value-Based Intragroup Conflict. *International Journal of Conflict Management*, *5*(3), 223–238. doi:10.1108/eb022744

Jehn, K. A., & Mannix, E. A. (2001). The Dynamic Nature Of Conflict: A Longitudinal Study Of Intragroup Conflict And Group Performance. *Academy of Management Journal*, *44*(2), 238–251.

Kahn, R. L. (1964). Introduction. In R. L. Kahn & E. Boulding (Eds.), *Power And Conflict In Organizations* (pp. 1–7). Basic Books.

Kritzer, H. M., Sarat, A., Trubek, D. M., Bumiller, K., & Mcnichol, E. (1984). Understanding The Costs Of Litigation: The Case Of The Hourly-Fee Lawyer. *Law & Social Inquiry*, *9*(3), 559–581. doi:10.1111/j.1747-4469.1984.tb00020.x

Kumaraswamy, M. M. (1997). Conflicts, Claims And Disputes In Construction. *Engineering, Construction, and Architectural Management*, *4*(2), 95–111. doi:10.1108/eb021042

Lax, D., & Sebenius, J. (1986). *The Manager As Negotiator*. New York: Free Press.

Lord Woolf. (1998). *Access To Justice: Interim And Final Reports By Lord Woolf To The Lord Chancellor*. Academic Press.

Mcgovern, F. E. (1996). Beyond Efficiency: A Bevy Of ADR Justifications (An Unfootnoted Summary). *Dispute Resolution Magazine, 3*.

Moffitt, M. L., & Bordone, R. C. (Eds.). (2005). *The Handbook Of Dispute Resolution*. San Francisco, CA: Jossey-Bass.

Moore, C. (1989). *The Mediation Process*. San Francisco: Jossey Bass.

Moore, C. W. (2014). *The Mediation Process: Practical Strategies For Resolving Conflict*. New York, NY: John Wiley & Sons.

Pickavance, K. (2007). *Construction Law And Management*. London: Routledge.

Ponte, L. M. (2001). Broadening Traditional ADR Notions Of Disclosure: Special Considerations For Posting Conflict Resolution Policies And Programs On E-Business Web Sites. *Ohio State Journal Of Dispute Resolution*, *17*, 321.

Price Waterhouse Coopers. (2013). Corporate Choices. In *International Arbitration*. Academic Press.

Priest, G. L., & Klein, B. (1984). The Selection Of Disputes For Litigation. *The Journal of Legal Studies*, *12*(1), 1–55. doi:10.1086/467732

Rahim, M. A. (1986). Managing Conflict. In *Organizations*. New York, NY: Praeger.

Rahim, M. A. (2001). Managing Conflict. In *Organizations* (3rd ed.). Westport, CT: Quorum Books.

Rands, M., Levinger, G., & Mellinger, G. D. (1981). Patterns Of Conflict Resolution And Marital Satisfaction. *Journal of Family Issues, 2*(3), 297–321. doi:10.1177/0192513X8100200303

Rhys Jones, S. (1994). How Constructive Is Construction Law? *Constitutional Law Journal (Newark, N.J.), 10*(1), 28–38.

Robinson, W. (2002). The Effects Of The Human Rights Act 1998 On Arbitration. *Amicus Curiae,* (42).

Schelling, T. C. (1957). Bargaining, Communication, And Limited War. *The Journal of Conflict Resolution, 1*(1), 19–36. doi:10.1177/002200275700100104

Semple, C., Hartman, F., & Jergas, G. (1994). Construction Claims And Disputes: Causes And Cost/Time Overruns. *Journal of Construction Engineering and Management, 120*(4), 785–795. doi:10.1061/(ASCE)0733-9364(1994)120:4(785)

Smith, R. A. (1962). Question Of Arbitrability-The Role Of The Arbitrator, The Court, And The Parties. *Southwestern Law Journal, 16*(1).

Sosa, E. (2010). *The Epistemology Of Disagreement.* His Armchair Philosophy.

Sykes, J. (1996). Claims And Disputes In Construction. *Constitutional Law Journal (Newark, N.J.), 12*(1), 3–13.

The Channel Tunnel Group Ltd v. Balfour Beatty Construction Ltd. (1993).

The Problem. (1997). In J. H. Steyn (Ed.), *Alternative Dispute Resolution, Issue Paper 8 (Project 94).* Pretoria: South African Law Commission.

Turner, D. (2004). Perceiving The World Differently. In C. Bell & D. Kahane (Eds.), *Intercultural Dispute Resolution In Aboriginal Contexts.*

U. (2007). *United Nations Declaration On The Rights Of Indigenous People* (A/RES/61/295). New York, NY: United Nations. Retrieved From Https://Www.Un.Org/Development/Desa/Indigenouspeoples/Declaration-On-The-Rights-Of-Indigenous-Peoples.Html

United Nations Commission On International Trade Law. (2015). *UNCITRAL Model Law On International Commercial Arbitration.* Retrieved from Http://Www.Uncitral.Org/Uncitral/En/Uncitral_Texts/Arbitration/1985Model_Arbitration_Status.Html

Washington State Office Of Administrative Hearings. (2015). *Glossary For Administrative Hearings.* Author.

Wenying, W. (2005). Role Of Conciliation In Resolving Disputes: A PRC Perspective. *The Ohio State Journal On Dispute Resolution, 20*(421).

Winslade, J., & Monk, G. (2000). *Narrative Mediation: A New Approach To Conflict Resolution.* San Francisco: Jossey-Bass Publishers.

Yazzie, R. (2004). Navajo Peacemaking And Intercultural Dispute Resolution. In C. Bell & D. Kahane (Eds.), Intercultural Dispute Resolution In Aboriginal Contexts. Academic Press.

KEY TERMS AND DEFINITIONS

ADR: Alternative dispute resolution.

AJA: Access to Justice Act 1999.

Anticipatory Breach: Also called anticipatory repudiation, is a term in the law of contracts that describes a declaration by the promising party to a contract, that he or she does not intend to live up to his or her obligation under the contract.

CFA: Conditional fee arrangement.

Fiduciary Duty: A relationship between a trustee and beneficiary based on trust.

Hearsay Evidence: The report of another person's words by a witness, usually disallowed as evidence in a court of law.

HGCRA: Housing Grants, Construction, and Regeneration Act.

Jirga: Literally defined as a gathering of elders. It is a term used in the Pashto language of the North Western region of Pakistan and in the Pastho speaking areas of Afghanistan. A jirga is a conflict / dispute resolution process where the disputing parties after agreeing to the jirga process plead their case in front of elders from within their community. The outcome of the jirga is based on either party achieving a two-thirds majority or via a decision recommended by the elders. The higher courts of Pakistan have ruled that jirga's for criminal cases are illegal because their decisions have often proved to be counter to the constitutional rights of the persons in dispute. However, administrative jirga's are allowed within the Federally Administered Tribal Areas of Pakistan and within rural and urban areas to resolve small claims and disputes.

Panchayat: Literally defined as a gathering of five. It is a term used within the rural Punjab provinces of Pakistan and India to define a dispute resolution process similar to the "jirga."

Tort: A wrongful act or an infringement of a right (other than under contract) leading to civil legal liability.

UNCITRAL: United Nations Commission International Trade Law Model Law of International Commercial Arbitration.

Chapter 3
Navigating Moral Reasoning in Mediation

Brian Jarrett
California State University – Dominguez Hills, USA

Kara Dellacioppa
California State University – Dominguez Hills, USA

ABSTRACT

This chapter examines the importance of understanding of moral reasoning processes in individuals involved in mediation. It discusses Lawrence Kohlberg's model of moral reasoning and applies it to a case study of a workplace dispute. The chapter also discusses the care ethic versus justice ethic debate put forth by feminist psychologists challenging mainstream theories of moral reasoning. The chapter concludes by examining the impact of moral reasoning processes on mediation and how it might lead to re-imagining the skill set needed mediate conflict effectively (i.e., skills that involve emotional intelligence).

INTRODUCTION

Mediators and their clients can benefit from understanding the how moral reasoning processes affect decision-making in mediation. Such understanding can provide a schema by which to navigate the kinds of reasoning processes their clients follow during mediation. This is not to suggest that mediators introduce their own moral- reasoning orientation to direct their clients during mediation (Bennett & Hermann, 1999; Moore, 1986). Rather, it is an invitation to mediators to explore moral-reasoning orientations they may observe during mediation (Kohlberg, 1964). Arguably, such analysis is particularly useful when conflicting orientations work to escalate the dispute and, in some instances, prevent any possibility of effective conflict resolution altogether.

Empirical evidence supports the notion that individuals adopt consistent patterns in moral reasoning throughout their lives (Kohlberg, 1964). Disputants' moral reasoning orientations tend to motivate their behavior and steer and their respective legal positions during mediation. Therefore, by becoming aware of the parties' respective moral-reasoning orientations the mediator has an opportunity to discover what is important to them in, what would otherwise be, a turbulent sea of conflicting facts.

DOI: 10.4018/978-1-5225-8516-9.ch003

In situations involving heightened conflict, individuals tend to rely on their dominant moral reasoning orientation to make sense of the world (Kohlberg, 1964). The chosen orientation becomes a framework or reference point through which to navigate conflict. By identifying the disputant(s) dominant moral reasoning orientation, a mediator can assist the parties to communicate more clearly with each other in a non-judgmental manner.

In addition, the mediator can use this awareness to disarm a disputant's attempts to manipulate the co-disputant, the mediator, and/or any aspect of the mediation process. In mediations taking place within organizations or communities, mediators can assist the larger collective to reduce clashes and stand-offs emerging from differences in moral reasoning orientations held by the various competing stakeholders. This can often improve the organizational culture for the betterment of all.

MORAL REASONING AND MORAL DEVELOPMENT

Theories of *moral development* often accompany theories of moral reasoning. Theorists draw links between moral reasoning strategies and antecedent development through childhood into adulthood. The most notable theorist among them is Lawrence Kohlberg.

Kohlberg's Theory of Moral Reasoning Orientations

Lawrence Kohlberg, renowned developmental psychologist, inspired by Piaget's work on cognitive and moral development during childhood, (Piaget, 1932; Piaget 1952); Piaget 1977) was the first to propose a comprehensive theory of moral reasoning orientation. He believed that human beings develop dominant moral reasoning orientations to which they tend to adhere during conflict. To test this hypothesis, Kohlberg presented subjects, both children and adults, with a series of dilemmas in story form, (Boyd, D.R., Bee H.L, & Johnson, P.A. 2011) each of which addressed a specific moral issue, such as the value of human life, i.e., the famous case, in which a man's wife is dying:

[A] woman was near death from a special kind of cancer. There was one drug that the doctors thought might save her. It was a form of radium that the druggist in the same town had recently discovered. The drug was expensive to make, but the druggist was charging ten times what the drug cost him to make. He paid $200 for the radium and charged $2000 for a small dose of the drug. The sick woman's husband, Heinz, went to everyone he knew to borrow the money, but he could only get together about $1000. He told the druggist that his wife was dying, and asked him to sell it cheaper or let him pay later. But the druggist said, "No, I discovered the drug and I'm going to make money from it." So Heinz got desperate and broke into the man's store to steal the drug for his wife (Kohlberg, L. & Elfenbeing D. 1975).

Kohlberg then asked subjects a series of questions, e.g., Should Heinz have stolen the drug? Should Heinz steal the drug if the police told him he should not? Should Heinz steal the drug if the person dying was a stranger, etc? Through the responses to these questions, Kohlberg noticed that subjects appeared to adopt, on a consistent basis, dominant moral reasoning strategies or orientations. Kohlberg concluded that with increasing maturation, the child may or may not pass through three levels of moral development, each containing two sub-stages. See Table 1.

Table 1.

Stages of Moral Development
Level I: Pre-conventional Morality
Stage 1: Punishment and Obedience Orientation. The child decides what is wrong on the basis of what is punished. Obedience is valued for its own sake, but the child obeys because the adults have superior power. Stage 2: Individualism, Instrumental Purpose, and Exchange. The child follows rules when it is in his immediate interest. What is good is what brings pleasant results.
Level II: Conventional Morality
Stage 3: Mutual Interpersonal Expectations, Relationships, and Interpersonal Conformity. Moral actions are those that live up to the expectations of the family or other significant group. "Being good" becomes important for its own sake. Stage 4: Social System and Conscience (Law and Order). Moral actions are those so defined by larger social groups or the society as a whole. One should fulfill duties one has agreed to and uphold laws except in extreme cases.
Level III: Principled or Post-conventional Morality
Stage 5: Contract or Utility and Individual Rights. This stage involves acting so as to achieve the "greatest good for the greatest number." The person is aware that most values are relative and laws are changeable, although rules should be upheld in order to preserve the social order. Still, there are some basic nonrelative values, such as the importance of each person's life and liberty. Stage 6: Universal Ethical Principles. The adult develops and follows self-chosen ethical principles in determining what is right. These ethical principles are part of an articulated, integrated, carefully thought-out, and consistently-followed system of values and principles.

At Stage 1, the individual relies on the physical consequences of his or her actions to determine right from wrong, e.g., if Heinz would go to jail, he should not steal the drug. At Stage 2, the individual believes that one should do those things that bring rewards and avoid punishment, e.g., Heinz should steal the drug so he does not have to pay for the funeral expenses. At Stage 3, the individual believes the "right" choice is what pleases his or her immediate significant social group, e.g., Heinz should steal the drug because it would please his family. At Stage 4, the individual develops a *"law-and-order"* orientation, asserting one should do those things that conform to the rules of the larger society, e.g., Heinz should not steal the drug if it would entail an illegal act. At Stage 5, namely the "*social contract*" orientation, the individual reasons that rules one should uphold the social order, subject to higher values such as the preservation of human life, e.g., Heinz should steal the drug and break the law if it is the only way to save his wife's life. At Stage 6, the highest in Kohlberg's schema, the individual forms a consistent and integrated set of universal ethical principles, accepting responsibility for his or her actions, e.g., Heinz may have to go to jail to do the *right* thing, namely to steal the drug to save his wife.

According to Kohlberg, it is important to recognize that it is not the abstract moral choice that determines the particular stage, but the process of moral reasoning itself (Kohlberg L,1981). In the Heinz dilemma, one could conclude that he should steal the drug and justify this decision from any one of the six stages. In fact, in a number of the above examples, individuals did conclude Heinz should steal the drug, but for different reasons (Kohlberg L. & D. Elfenbein 1975). Thus, it is the reasoning process itself associated with each stage that is the central focus rather than the ultimate choice one might make.

Much empirical research has supported Kohlberg's moral-orientation paradigm. (Boyd, D.R., Bee H.L, & Johnson, P.A. 2011). Longitudinal studies have supported Kohlberg's findings that moral reasoning does, indeed, progress through the six distinct stages in the order he suggests (Snarey, J.R., 1989; Walker 1989). Certain stages correlate with specific ages, from childhood through adulthood, although the adult moral reasoning process may follow any of the six stages (Snarey, J.R., 1989; Walker 1989). Cross-cultural studies have demonstrated that the six stages of moral reasoning tend to hold true in western and non-western cultures, and in industrialized and non-industrialized settings (Snarey, J.R. 1985).

Alternative Conceptions of Moral Reasoning

It is also important to understand how competing conceptions of moral reasoning processes may complement, or even challenge, Kohlberg's analysis of moral development. It is noteworthy that Kohlberg's analysis of moral reasoning has withstood a barrage of criticism. Some critics have argued that Kohlberg is not addressing the development of moral reasoning processes at all, but the development of "reasoning about fairness or justice". In addition, feminist legal scholars have argued that Kohlberg's theory on moral reasoning reflects male bias in its development and application.

Carol Gilligan (1982), a renowned feminist scholar, asserts that there are at least two orientations to moral reasoning, which more accurately conceptualize how individuals make moral choices, namely, a *justice ethic* versus an *ethic of care.* According to Gilligan's theory, men tend to adopt a *justice ethic*, i.e., to treat others fairly. In contrast, she posits that women tend to adopt a *care ethic*, i.e., to notice those in need. The verdict is still out on whether these differences actually exist. Some empirical studies have found gender differences, (Wark & Krebs, 1996) whereas others have not (Walker 1987). This hypothesized difference continues to be the focus of a lively debate (Janoff, 1991).

Carol Gilligan reminds us that it is important to acknowledge alternative conceptions of moral reasoning and is a significant contribution for this reason. In particular, Gilligan asserts that it is misleading to apply moral reasoning processes without regard to the effect of gender. Arguably, an ethic of care itself provides a different orientation to disputes than the *justice ethic*. In mediation, the former emphasizes the welfare of the particular individuals involved in the dispute rather than the disputants as abstract actors with competing justice claims.

Kohlberg was himself cautious in generalizing about moral reasoning. He proffered his stages of moral development and their attendant moral reasoning orientations as evidence of tendencies only and not as categories in any absolute sense. Consequently, it is important to recognize that a stage-model like Kohlberg's cannot provide absolute categorization, but rather simply offer a map of central tendencies in moral reasoning. In addition, his proposed model does not attempt to exclude reference points in moral reasoning that might emerge from an ethic of care.

For mediators, the stages can provide a valuable map by which to navigate and explore dominant moral-reasoning orientations. In doing so, mediator should nevertheless remain cautious in applying Kohlberg's moral orientation schema to reasoning narratives their clients provide during mediation. It is important for mediators to remain mindful to a host of influences, including gender, culture, and other contextual variables that may be contributing to their clients' attitudes, beliefs, and reasoning processes.

The Kohlberg model does not require the mediators to view their clients' respective moral reasoning orientations as irrevocably fixed at any given stage, or to conclude that their clients are inexorably trapped at a certain stage of moral development. This conclusion might pre-dispose the mediators to behave in a dismissive or judgmental fashion toward disputants assessed to be operating through the lens of the lower stages. It is tempting to assign greater value to the higher stages than to their lower counterparts. However, doing so would defeat the very purpose of using the Kohlberg model and potentially breach the mediator's professional duty to act in an unbiased and fair manner toward all parties during mediation.

In addition, Kohlberg warned that while a high degree of correlation exists between moral reasoning and moral behavior, it is not a causative relationship (Kohlberg, 1975). Other factors often account for behavior such as the degree of personal cost associated with a given choice. For example, it may be morally right to sue the potential defendant in a given situation for evident malfeasance, but one may decline to do so because it involves an intolerably high level of risk. Peer group influence and pressures from constituencies can also influence a disputant's decision-making (Mnookin & Susskind 1999). Consider the example of a union advocate in a labor dispute, who feels she must zealously advocate for the general membership of the union, despite the fact that she is more persuaded by the reasoning advanced by management.

Furthermore, the mediator's respective clients may not often reveal their dominant moral-reasoning orientations in an obvious manner. In fact, the mediator will likely have to explore these processes by interpreting the idiosyncrasies of each speaker's language, which will include culturally-embedded language, jargon, code words, techno-speak, and colloquialisms—all potentially familiar to the co-disputant(s), but not necessarily known to the mediator. Therefore the mediator has a particular duty of care to unpack and interpret carefully the narratives each disputant may provide.

In sum, despite the potential risks associated with the application of the Kohlberg moral-reasoning model, it can be an extremely useful tool for mediators. It can provide an important point of reference to assist the mediator in identifying and exploring moral-reasoning orientations that tend to motivate parties to adopt legal positions. In turn, this awareness can enable the mediator to assist the disputants to become cognizant of their respective moral-reasoning orientations in order to facilitate agreements that are more effective and enduring.

ANALYZING MORAL REASONING AS CLUSTERS OF INTERESTS

In order to explore moral-reasoning orientations, the mediator needs to first understand the process of meta-messaging. Narratives that, at first blush, appear to contain only one message, often, on closer examination, contain a variety of messages. (Stone, Patton & Heen 1999).

Meta-Messages and Moral Reasoning

During mediation, parties often disguise or hide more sensitive messages about core values and identity within more mundane factual information (Stone, Patton & Heen, 1999). These oft-embedded 'meta-messages' (Cloke &Goldsmith, 2011) tend to convey information about the particular speaker's moral-reasoning processes (Stone, Patton & Heen). With the passage of time, values tend to shape personal identity (Stone, Patton & Heen, 1999: 5). Parties often have difficulty revealing raw information about their identities, particularly in moments of heightened conflict because they feel vulnerable. If they do express this information at all, they often hide this information within narratives of vilification and blame aimed at the other party (Stone, Patton & Heen, 1999: 15). Disputants tend to find it less embarrassing and less emotionally taxing to blame their co-disputant(s) than to reveal their own core values. They often fear that their co-disputant will attack their sense of self and personal identity. Unfortunately, blaming the other tends to increase hostility, diminish collaborative communication, and thereby reduce opportunities for settlement.

By unraveling the meta-messages contained in the speaker's narrative, the mediator has an opportunity to reframe these messages in the language of the dominant moral-reasoning orientation, which often accompanies the blaming message (Stone, Patton & Heen, 1999: 58). Note, in doing this, it is unnecessary, and potentially distracting, for the mediator to engage in a discussion about the theoretical aspects of Kohberg's model with the parties. Rather the mediator should simply use the model as an internal guide, while teasing out client narratives to help them see the logic of their moral reasoning during the bargaining process. The mediator may strategically wait to reveal insights into her clients' respective level of moral reasoning in the private session (caucus).

Parties tend to be much more concerned about resolving their immediate dispute than engaging in a theoretical discussion on moral reasoning. Therefore, it is important for the mediator to mentally separate the two activities in his or her mind, reframing the disputant's' respective dominant reasoning processes aloud, while silently locating their reference point within the Kohlberg model. This may take several iterations to flesh out an accurate picture of the client's respective moral reasoning orientation. This iterative process complements and can improve *interest* exploration associated with the facilitative approach to mediation, commonly known as the Harvard Method (Fisher and Ury, 1989; Ury, Brett, & Goldberg, 1999).

However, identifying the appropriate stage of moral reasoning goes well beyond an exploration of individual *interests*, as Ury and Fisher have conceived that notion (Fisher, Ury & Patton, 1981). Each stage in Kohlberg's model represents a bundle or constellation of threaded interests and a way to determine personal relevance and priority among a variety of interests, for each party. Consider the following workplace vignette.

Vignette: A Workplace Dispute

Management has invited a mediator to mediate a workplace dispute in a high tech company. A supervisor is seeking to discipline an employee for what he perceives as unjustified absences, erratic work habits, and failure to follow accepted protocols. The employee contests the claim that her absences are unjustified and argues that she is a more productive and creative worker than others who appear to follow the standard protocols. The supervisor values the employee's work but wants the employee to follow the workplace rules, standard protocols, and generally attempt to "fit in" with the organizational culture. The employee enjoys working at the company and she has developed some useful software for the company. Both are interested in improving the workplace relationship. They have therefore asked management to provide an opportunity to mediate the dispute, in a good faith manner. Through interviews, prior to the mediation, the mediator has determined that the supervisor is exhibiting some of the moral reasoning associated with Stage 3 or 4 ('conventional morality') in Kohlberg's Model, while the employee is demonstrating moral reasoning associated with Stage 5('post-conventional morality').

In the above workplace vignette, *Stage 3* expectations of mutual interpersonal conformity represents a constellation of related interests at this stage. In the vignette, these interests would likely include a shared need for recognition of workplace norms, a desire for compliance in the workplace protocols, and a desire for employees to adjust personal behavior based on feedback. *Stage 4* reasoning would add the overlay of the law-and-order orientation so that, in this workplace vignette, the supervisor would be very concerned that the employee follow the company policies and protocols, as a matter of conscience. In this instance, the mediator could anticipate that the supervisor would misattribute the employee's *Stage 5* reasoning to misbehavior when, in fact, the employee might have a genuine interest in producing a successful work-product, i.e., software program, that provide the greatest benefit to the company and its customers.

The mediator might engage the supervisor, exploring the conformity element, in the following questions with regard to employee discipline.

Why are the workplace protocols important for the company? What are the protocols that important to the company? How do you think you might enforce rules in the workplace so that you can provide a fair discipline process and set clear expectations for the employees to follow?

In this way, the mediator affirms the supervisor's conventional moral reasoning while remaining non-judgmental in the process. The questions center on what is important for the supervisor in the dispute, which helps the mediator in this case build genuine rapport and authentic buy-in on the supervisor's part.

The mediator can then turn to the employee and frame her questions in post-conventional language to the employee, without feeling as if she is betraying the moral orientation of the supervisor. For example, the mediator might ask the employee to elicit a response about her interests, using the non-conventional moral frame.

What do you see as the mission of your job? What are your goals in doing this work in the manner that you do it? What is the value that you bring to this job?

The mediator might to do well to allow the employee to explain the values and benefits that she brings to the job, while giving her an opportunity to address her job performance and absences from this post-conventional frame of reference. An employee who is, in fact, productive but unconventional might predictably respond as follows.

Well, as the supervisor knows, I do a good job and produce quality work. I expect to be rewarded for this. I don't just want to sit at my desk or do rote tasks to look *like I am working. It wastes time and does not contribute to our overall mission or work goals. When I finished early I took the time to catch up on some of the projects I had put on the back burner. If I finish faster and produce more results the employer should reward me for that. He should not be standing over me like a policeman or micro-manager. When I have to think about how I look at work, this actually distracts me from doing the work and doing it well. I'm willing to account for my time away from my desk if there is such a rule requires that I do but no one can argue that I have not done a good job. And in the high tech sector productive employees tend to be non-conformists by nature. That is why got involved in this work in the first place.*

The mediator might then turn to the supervisor to see if he is responsive to the employee's framing. The employer may well react with conventional moral logic, as follows.

For our company, obeying the rules is the important thing around here. I have a lot of people in that shop and I need to know that they are following standard protocols to ensure quality of work. We all rely on each other here. A whole chain of employees depend on your work and work product. They need to recognize what you have done and how you have done it. I need to rely on you, as my employee. I am responsible for maintaining order in the chain of work and I just don't want the workplace to devolve into chaos. We are all highly dependent on each other's work. It's only right that people obey the rules. The functioning of the company depends on this. I have to obey the rules myself. Nobody gives me a break on this!

In this response, the supervisor is injecting Stage 4 conventional logic in his attempt to justify adherence to company policies, rules, protocols. The dominant orientation at Stage 4 is *law-and-order*". After some discussion, the mediator may seek agreement between the parties by reframing this Stage 5 moral orientation of the employee with the language that also meets the conventional moral logic of the supervisor, as follows.

Well, a solution here needs to meet your (the employee's) interest in a creative, unfettered work environment where you can be maximally productive in the workplace while meeting your (the supervisor's) need for order in the workplace. We need a solution that meets both sets of concerns. Does that sum it up? Would you agree to that?

In this manner, the mediator sums up the reasoning of both the employee and supervisor in an issue frame that conjoins both sets of concerns, which respects the meta-messages of both and makes their respective moral reasoning processes obvious to each other.

But what happens when a party disagrees with the mediator's assessment. The mediator must be prepared to be flexible and re-assess a party's dominant orientation throughout mediation. For example, in this workplace dispute the supervisor might respond as follows.

No. It isn't just about obeying the rules for their own sake. I want to make sure that I know where my employees are and what they are doing because the lives and safety of my people come first. There are some health risks associated with our product. I don't want any of our employee's health put in jeopardy. That's my ultimate concern. Everyone who goes into the company must have a team member check his or her work, to ensure safety at all times. That is why we have these rules. They ensure safety for everyone and the greater good. .

Here, even though the message might appear to appeal to the '*greater good*' it still frames that "*greater-good*" message within the morally conventional law-and-order logic associated with conventional moral reasoning orientation, albeit at the highest end of that conventional moral framework.. The message does not appear to transition into post-conventional logic, so the mediator can be sure that while the supervisor is navigating principles of goodness and fairness, the person's dominant moral orientation appears to remain conventional.

Throughout the mediation, the mediator would explore the respective of moral framing of the supervisor and the employee. The mediator would identify the interests associated with the dominant logic of both parties. She can do this by posing open questions that reveal the interests and by paraphrasing the party's respective responses. For example, once the mediator feels she has the dominant moral logic of each party, she may then go on to explore associated interests as follows.

Of the supervisor -

So your concern is the safety of your employees and the productivity of the company? Is fair to say you are not as concerned about rules for their own sake, but rather employee productivity and safety? Why must employees work with another team member? What are some of the examples of protocol that might pose a risk to other employees' productivity and safety?

Of the employee -

So your concern is primarily have a workplace in which you can be productive and tap your creativity to do your best work – does that sum it up? What does that look like to you in a given workday? How could the employer maximize these opportunities for you? What do you need to see happen to ensure this optimal level of productivity?

If the parties reach a settlement with reference to inaccurate dominant reasoning orientations, the agreement may lack certain essential elements. In the vignette, an agreement that commits the employee to coworker safety as a mutual aspiration might be far more valuable to the supervisor than one that merely requires the employee to bring his doctor's note to explain his absences. By reframing the employee's comments, in post-conventional language in the Kohlberg model, in conjunction with the supervisor's conventional moral logic, the mediator can now provide a more accurate joint issue restatement as feedback to the disputants.

What we are here to determine is how you (the employee) may have an optimally arranged workspace and set of protocols to maximize your overall work output while meeting your (the supervisor's) paramount concern for worker safety and productivity. Would that be accurate?

This joint-issue restatement is more likely to result in agreement than one that was reflective of the respective moral logic of the parties. Nevertheless, if the joint-issue statement doesn't, then the mediator would simply continue to adjust it, anew, as necessary, to include the dominant moral orientation of each disputant until the parties find agreement on their respective moral framing with regard to the dispute. The discussion following issue restatement tends to focus the disputants, respectively, on what they actually value, as opposed to what they might initially put forth as their espoused concerns. Moreover, this moral reasoning analysis helps the disputants disengage themselves from the need to blame each other for the dispute.

Manipulation and Moral Reasoning

During mediation, one disputant may attempt to draw the other into his or her respective moral framework in a manipulative fashion. In addition, a disputant may attempt to draw the mediator into his moral logic, in order to persuade the mediator of how the party is right and the other party is wrong, in some absolute sense. It is important for the mediator to recognize these attempts and to neutralize their effects (Kritek, 1994). Unchecked, a disputant's successful manipulation of the mediator may serve to validate the disputant's perspective at the expense of her co-disputant and to boost the likelihood of reactive devaluation. Another danger is that the mediator may find him or herself favoring one party over another, not because of the merits of the case, but because she has become fixated in one particularly moral orientation. Even if the mediator can recover, the other party may conclude the mediator has become biased and therefore untrustworthy.

By referring to the Kohlberg's stages, the mediator may deconstruct the argument, to extract those elements that are indicative of authentic moral reasoning from those that are designed to manipulate the co-disputant(s) and/or the mediator. For example, in the workplace vignette, the employee may use the fact that he has not received recognition for her contributions to the organization as a whole and, in particular, her supervisor as a justification for her unexplained absences.

I came here to do a job for you. I've done a great job. You have not recognized me, or the work I've done for you since I started. I don't know why you wouldn't expect me to take time off when I'm not even missed around here. Besides, what's wrong with that if I've done the work and my work is good!

The mediator now has an opportunity to reframe this statement extricating the manipulative element. The mediator could reframe this statement as follows:

You think your boss is not recognizing your contributions. You do a great job and it's very important for you that he and other's in the company recognize you for your good work and contribution to the company as a whole. Is that accurate? You also said the high quality of your work, and the fact that your boss does not recognize your work, justifies your absences. Is that accurate?

Here the mediator highlights the moral reasoning process and, second, exposes the manipulative element, while remaining inoffensive to the speaker. This gives the other party an opportunity to respond to legitimate concerns, i.e., recognition for a job well done, without having to engage in a battle of "rights" and "wrongs" (Ury & Goldberg, 1998; Kritek, 1994). In essence, the mediator validates the moral reasoning but detaches it from the manipulative element.

Manipulation tends to become more evident in circumstances of heightened emotional tension (Garrity & Barris, 1994). Disputants may maintain, more or less, a consistent moral reasoning orientation, but the degree of manipulation may rise or fall with the degree of tension (Goleman, 2001). Also, during mediation, heightened emotional arousal may leave a participant, including the mediator, vulnerable to manipulation (Thompson, 2012). It is particularly important during these moments to have a strategy to neutralize these attempts at manipulation. Adhering to a practice of separating out the moral statement from the other extraneous elements may provide a useful tool for navigating manipulation in the face of heightened emotional intensity. This practice may therefore be useful in breaking impasse or deadlocks where strong emotions, miscommunication, or stereotypical labeling prevent the parties from focusing on the dispute at hand.

CONCLUSION

Kohlberg probably did not foresee the applications of his theory to the contemporary practice of mediation when he first wrote his treatise on the development of moral reasoning. Yet, his moral-reasoning schema can be of significant value to mediators who want help their clients resolve disputes. In fact, an awareness and willingness to explore dominant moral reasoning processes may be essential to effective mediation, by improving self-awareness both on the part of the disputants as well as on the part of the mediator. The mediator can work to explore, in objective terms, disputants' respective moral-reasoning orientations and distinguish them from manipulative and coercive behaviors that these orientations often camouflage. Further, exploring moral reasoning provides the mediator with a framework through which to navigate the oft-chaotic moments during mediation that can lead to impasse. Analyzing moral reasoning goes beyond "interest" exploration, associated with facilitative mediation (the 'Harvard Method'), because it tends to provide an entire bundle or constellation of associated interests and the context for their inter-connection. It provides a useful frame of reference through which to assess the relative weight of various interests in disputants' respective decisions-making processes. Agreements reflecting dominant moral reasoning orientations tend to produce more meaningful, long-term settlements. Therefore, further research concerning moral reasoning in mediation would be of great practical value to mediators and their clients.

FUTURE RESEARCH DIRECTIONS

Recent research indicates a stronger relationship among, emotions, intuition and moral judgement than was previously understood (Gee, 2012). This is especially true in the growing field of positive psychology (Haidt, 2001). In fields such as law enforcement and criminology, research has been advanced that points to emotions as a leading factor in decision-making processes whether focused on buying a car or negotiating with a hostage-taker (Voss, 2016). World renowned security consultant Gavin de Becker goes as far as to argue that people often put themselves at risk by ignoring their own intuition, emotions, and instincts, all of which carry critical information for humans in dangerous situations. De Becker attributes this lack of connection to the "irrational side" of the human mind to modern social conditioning that not only devalues "irrational" in favor the rational but also promotes a societal imperative to "be nice" to everyone in all situations. This makes women, according to de Becker, particularly vulnerable as this "nice" conditioning thwarts their ability to make adequate "threat assessments." Other fields such as the sociology of culture and marketing have long argued that consumer behavior and decision-making is largely irrational (Ewen, 1988).

So how could these insights lead to future research studies in the area of mediation and moral reasoning orientations? First, it might be fruitful to carefully examine the relationship among emotion, intuition, and moral reasoning rather than examining them as discrete, separate entities. In this way, scholarship and practice could move beyond dichotomizing facts vs. values, reason vs. emotions and even the "ethics of justice" vs. the "ethics of care" debate. Taking this approach could lead to a much more robust analysis of gender and moral reasoning orientation in mediation. Second, if this line of research were to uncover a more prominent role for emotion and intuition in moral reasoning, then perhaps the field of mediation might need to reconsider the role of the mediator her/himself and the whole field of mediation might want to reconsider what skill set is needed to play the role of mediator.

REFERENCES

Bennett, M., Hughes, S., & Hermann, M.S.G. (1999). The Art of mediation. Boulder, CO: NITA.

Boyd, D. R., Bee, H. L., & Johnson, P. A. (2011). *Lifespan development.* Toronto: CA Pearson Canada.

Cloke, K., & Goldsmith, J. (2011). *Resolving conflicts at work: Ten strategies for everyone on the job* (3rd ed.). San Francisco: Jossey-Bass.

Debecker, G. (1997). *The gift of fear: Survival signals that protect us from violence.* New York, NY: Dell Books.

Ewen, S. (1988). *All consuming images: The politics of style in contemporary culture*. New York: Basic Books.

Fisher, R., Ury, W., & Patton, B. (1981). *Getting to Yes: Negotiating Agreement Without Giving In*. New York: Penguin Books.

Garrity, C. B., & Baris, M. A. (1994). *Caught in the middle: Protecting the children of high-conflict divorce*. New York: Lexington Books.

Gee, C. (2014). The Role of Emotional Intuitions in Moral Judgments and Decisions. *Journal of Cognition and Neuroethics*, *2*(1), 161–171.

Gilligan, C. (1982). *In a different voice: Psychological theory and women's development*. Cambridge, MA: Harvard University Press.

Goleman, D. (1995). *Emotional intelligence: Why it can matter more than IQ*. New York: Bantam Books.

Haidt, J. (2001). The emotional dog and its rational tail: A social intuitionist approach to moral judgment. *Psychological Review*, *108*(4), 814–834. doi:10.1037/0033-295X.108.4.814 PMID:11699120

Janoff, S. (1991). The influence of legal education on moral reasoning Process. *Minnesota Law Review*, *76*, 193–238.

Kohlberg, L. (1964). *Development of moral character and moral ideology*. New York, NY: Russell Sage Foundation.

Kohlberg, L. (1975). The Cognitive-Developmental Approach to Moral Education. *Phi Delta Kappan*, *56*(10), 670–677.

Kohlberg, L. (1981). *The philosophy of moral development: essays on moral development*. New York, NY: Harper and Row.

Kohlberg, L., & Elfenbein, D. (1975). The development of moral judgement concerning capital punishment. *The American Journal of Orthopsychiatry*, *54*(4), 614–640. doi:10.1111/j.1939-0025.1975.tb01191.x PMID:1180344

Kritek, P. B. (1994). *Negotiating at an uneven table: Developing moral courage in resolving our conflicts*. San Francisco: Jossey-Bass Publishers.

Mnookin, R. H., & Susskind, L. E. (Eds.). (1999). Negotiating on Behalf of Others: Advice to Lawyers, Business Executives, Sports Agents, Diplomats, Politicians, and Everybody Else. Thousand Oaks, CA: Sage Publications.

Moore, C. (1986). *The mediation process*. New York, NY: Jossey Bass.

Piaget, J. (1932). *The moral judgement of the child*. New York, NY: Free Press.

Piaget, J. (1952). *The origins of intelligence in children*. New York, NY: International Universities Press. doi:10.1037/11494-000

Piaget, J. (1977). *Development of thought: equilibration of cognitive structures*. New York, NY: Viking Press.

Snarey, J., Reimer, J., & Kohlberg, L. (1985). The kibbutz as a model for moral education: A longitudinal cross-cultural study. *Journal of Applied Developmental Psychology*, *6*(2-3), 151–172. doi:10.1016/0193-3973(85)90057-7

Snarey, J. R. (1985). A Cross-cultural Universality of Social-moral Development: A Critical Review of Kohlbergian Research. *Psychological Bulletin*, *97*(2), 202–232. doi:10.1037/0033-2909.97.2.202 PMID:3983300

Stone, D., Patton, B., & Heen, S. (1999). *Difficult conversations: How to discuss what matters most*. New York, NY: Viking.

Ury, W., Brett, J. M., & Goldberg, S. B. (1988). *Getting disputes resolved: Designing systems to cut the costs of conflict*. San Francisco: Jossey-Bass.

Voss, C., & Raz, T. (2016). *Never split the difference: Negotiating as if your life depended on it* (1st ed.). New York, NY: Harper Business, an imprint of HarperCollins Publishers.

Walker, L.J. (1989). A Longitudinal Study of Moral Reasoning. *Child Development, 60*, 157-160.

Walker, L.J. (1987). Moral Stages and Moral Orientations in Real-life and Hypothetical Dilemmas. *Developmental Psychology*, *58*, 842–858.

Wark, G. R., & Krebs, D. L. (1996). Gender and Dilemma Differences in Real-Life Moral Judgment 32. *Developmental Psychology*, *32*(2), 220–230. doi:10.1037/0012-1649.32.2.220

ADDITIONAL READING

Haidt, J. (2001). The emotional dog and its rational tail: A social intuitionist approach to moral judgment. *Psychological Review*, *108*(4), 814–834. doi:10.1037/0033-295X.108.4.814 PMID:11699120

Voss, C., & Raz, T. (2016). *Never split the difference: Negotiating as if your life depended on it* (1st ed.). New York, NY: Harper Business, an imprint of HarperCollins Publishers.

KEY TERMS AND DEFINITIONS

Emotional Intelligence: The ability to read people and understand their emotions, and how well you can recognize and respond to feelings and emotions.

Meta-Message: An inner message that could be inferred or implied from a message.

Moral Reasoning: Applies critical analysis to specific events to determine what is right or wrong, and what people ought to do in a particular situation. Both philosophers and psychologists study moral reasoning.

Chapter 4
Collaboration and Conflict in Three Workplace Teams´ Projects

Tom Cockburn
https://orcid.org/0000-0002-4705-0633
The Leadership Alliance Inc., Spain

Peter A. C. Smith
TLA Inc., Canada

Gordon A. Cockburn
GAC ltd, Spain

ABSTRACT

This chapter extends the previous research published in 2016 which looked into the embedding contexts of networks of small firms, in the EU principally, and how collaboration between small to medium enterprises (SMEs) was supported inside national and regional clustering structures and incubators initiated in collaboration with university researchers and governments agencies. The current chapter drills down further to explore the processes at the level of individual firms to see how group and individual conflict and collaboration was generated or sustained within teams in three different case organizations. In other words, the chapter looks at micro level details of conflict and collaboration as well as the observed socioemotional dynamics. The three organizations were involved with executive education programs and the authors were able to access reflective diaries for 2004 to 2012 enabling the authors to triangulate notes taken with interview data and observations used for this chapter.

DOI: 10.4018/978-1-5225-8516-9.ch004

INTRODUCTION

Today competition is global and "world class", mobile and digital technology increasingly the norm in most business transactions with teams, suppliers and customers. The global business environment is recognizably Volatile Uncertain Complex and Ambiguous (VUCA) across all continents (Lawrence, 2013, Smith & Cockburn, 2016, pp. 1-2). National, regional as well as global business environments are in a continuous state of dynamic complexity and evolutionary flux. The emergent cybereconomy is thriving despite global phishing and hacker attacks on both individuals´ and organizations´ computer systems. In this febrile climate the strategic management of corporate positioning, market share enhancement and product innovation are critical objectives for businesses of all kinds. Equally, identity and brand management in the turbulent business world environment requires greater effort at the customer interface, to build trust, perceived reliability and confidence.

Communication underpins all interpersonal relationships in business whether with peers in teams, marketing to clients, negotiating business deals, or when leaders are motivating teams, resolving conflicts and networking, to name only a few. Many of the embedding contexts in and between organization teams, whether face-to-face (f2f) or virtual, supply chain collaboration and customer care require mutuality and reciprocity to varying degrees.

The above entails an overall *commitment* framework that also serves to constitute and reproduce the explicit and tacit rules for emotional engagement within the team and between the team and others in its environment. In order to be trusted, you must first give and then *communicate* trust yourself (Kasper-Fuehrer & Ashkanasy, 2001: 4, Meyerson, Weick & Kramer, 1996). The level of anxiety you have about the *fulfilment* of the obligations entrusted to you, ceteris paribus, gives the measure of your personal integrity and core identity. The extent to which you as an individual, and as a team, *care* about the communication of your 'reputation' for trustworthiness is, as Hogan argues, an 'external' aspect of your personality too (Hogan, 2002:1-2).

The commitment involves an expectation of a personal sense of duty and a concomitant guilt or remorse about failure to meet expectations in the psychological contract terms of reference. The latter terms of reference place a burden of 'fiduciary trust' upon members and teams to enact their trusteeship role on behalf of the 'client', i.e. the employing company. Thus, a) within the commitment framework, trust and anxiety interact as an emotional regime: a part of the context within which the team is embedded. That is b), a *combined* construct of internal and external aspects of personality is reflected in the *intersection* of teams´ enactment of trustworthiness and anxiety levels, which we take as a measure of the *location* of teams *within* the matrix of emotional regimes as seen in table 4. The particular 'touch', c) of that team personality is reflected in the *expression* of specific team conversations and stories within the emotional regimes in which they are embedded.

In a period where rapid organizational co-evolution is also occurring and ´fake news' abounds, there is immense potential for anomie in all areas of human interaction in business whether face-to-face, distributed, networked or virtual enterprises. The sustainable management of staff teams for service delivery and successful project completion includes accessing tacit intellectual and emotional capital of teams as well as recognizing these elements when interacting with suppliers and clients. Such dynamic informational and knowledge development, complexity and fluidity affects all types of organizations. Beyond the technology systems, much of the potential for conflict or for collaboration occurs in how staff are developed and managed as well as how clients interact with the businesses.

All businesses and organizations must inevitably match or exceed their embedding context's rate of change in order to maintain or develop their position whatever the complexity dynamics and speed of change is in that environment. In turbulent times there is a greater likelihood of increased tension, conflict and fractures in professional and personal relationships of all kinds. Conflict is especially likely where debate is stifled by restrictive rules, tacit boundaries, norms and cultural conventions, or it is simply assumed by the dominant leaders that there is no dissent as there is only their 'one best way' to achieve success. However, the processes of collaboration or of conflict are often dynamically complex and 'surprise' is the also often a key feature of global business complexity today (Smith & Cockburn, 2014).

Gibbons et al (1994) indicated that there are two modes of knowledge production and that the 'mode 2' form, whereby the applied elements are the main drivers of change and new knowledge development today. That is practice gets ahead of precept i.e. ahead of explicit theory development. Explicit theory development is typically associated with traditional academic forms of research, wherein explicitly identified theoretical constructs come first and are used to determine the development of new knowledge before any consideration is given to how the theory is to be applied to practice.

However, Gibbons (1994) and others such as Nonaka (1995) recognized the critical importance and the underlying presence of tacit knowledge within organizations, which they identified as a key component of future organizational learning and development, including the development of explicit theories. Gibbons et al (1994) suggested that as we get further into the knowledge era, engaging with global and diverse communities, the major challenge facing most firms will be that of capturing tacit knowledge and thereby linking the internal knowledge management with external opportunities and innovation (Bilandzic,2018). So, how do businesses innovate and differentiate themselves from the rest?

The short answer is by boosting their creativity in capturing and applying tacit knowledge to their business and communities. This is expressed through corporate strategic vision initially and then through the leadership and management of the process of implementation and value creation within the networked business world. So, inclusive leadership is shown via the creative articulation of the processes of symbolic and physical value exchanges within communication and knowledge networks (Simpson et al, 2005, Cockburn, 2006, Smith & Cockburn, 2013, 2014; Cockburn & Smith, 2018; Bilandzic, 2018).

The knowledge industries are especially likely to be subject to VUCA in social and cultural terms as well as differentiated in terms of the innovative business process models, products and service with lead times often less than 1 year for new developments and as global cybersecurity issues emerge. Therefore, these challenges require greater use of "right hemisphere" abilities, listening to voices of diverse others and more systemic analysis and probing the limits as well as the opportunities of VUCA business environments (Cockburn & Smith, 2018).

Not only is the global business environment dynamic but the nature and profile of "consumers" of today extends beyond corporate customers in many directions such as the family and community. Specifically, the term "consumers" in relation to teams and leadership, not only includes subordinates but also a range of other stakeholders both inside and outside of the organisation. In the 24/7, 'always on' world of today's digital natives and consumers, the line between work lives and personal lives continues to fade into the background such that millennials have been (unjustly to a degree) labeled as a demographic that has a consumerist lifestyle and attitude to most matters (Barton, Fromm & Egan, 2012)

BACKGROUND: MARKETS AND REGIONS

Market advantage is increasingly located in 'intangibles' including tacit forms of knowledge often as embodied forms of combined and co-evolving intellectual and emotional resources and capabilities such as know-how, resilience, creativity within the employees or population skill-base, business systems and intellectual property. To address the challenges and opportunities presented, individual firms must be able to combine all their resources in novel ways to develop new products and services, and to dispose of, or reconfigure, resources that are no longer relevant, or seek to acquire untapped resources. The ability to manipulate resources continuously and rapidly - to innovate - becomes an adaptive capability that is not easily imitated by competitors enabling firms to maintain, or improve, their current market positions. As Rousseau (2004) noted, as the organization and team evolve, so, too must the perceived psychological contract terms of staff, whether ´transactional´ or ´relational´ contracts.

Success for a business company within a domestic or international market comes from policies and practices that provide it with the necessary competencies and freedom to permit the maintenance and appropriate development of products for their business environments - this is termed Right to Market (R2M), Koudal & Coleman (2005). For a business organization, R2M means introducing the right products and/or services at the right time in the right contexts with the right supply chains, and then continually updating, optimizing, and retiring them as necessary. Thus, R2M involves the complex, dynamic interplay of dialog and dialectics at various points in the supply chain.

Business organizations must also maintain their economic, social and ecological policies consistent with those of the country in which they operate and with countries where they do business, or have impact. Thus, for a business organization to be classified as operating "sustainably" care must be exercised to make sure that R2M does not negatively impact relevant ecological or social systems – this is termed Right for Market (R4M) (Coakes, Smith & Alwiss, 2011). Such competent company management collaborative dialog in action then provides the fundamentals and stimulus necessary for the business stakeholders and staff to prosper and maintain high social and environmental standards and to reduce dialectical frictions or fissures developing.

Attracting inward investment to an area is presumed to be the result in part, of knowledge spillovers and other synergies emanating from the act of co-locating high tech firms in the vicinity of each other. Belderbos and Somers (2015), however, suggest dominant players in the field are effectively limiting such 'knowledge spillovers' in order to maintain their dominance and so often discourage investors. They refer to research indicating that the larger firms which are dominant in specific fields and which fail to reduce knowledge outflows to neighboring organizations may be 'shooting themselves in the foot' and under-capitalizing on their technology dominance. They further assert that firms seeking to avert potential loss of Intellectual Property will likely thereby have a detrimental effect upon the regional attempts at increasing innovation (Belderbos & Somers, p.21) by discouraging inward investment.

Individual Firm Level

Wilkinson et al (2007) suggests that the dynamics in a small firm promote a familial style and culture akin to the "small is beautiful" end of the continuum with the other end of the continuum suggesting hidden conflict and an authoritarian rule represented by the Dickensian "bleak house" view. The latter view is seen in one of the three case companies as a result of rapid growth. Working toward a common objective, each team strives to (or should strive) reach is positively related to building learning Communities of Practice (COPs). Although some conflict may not always be deemed wholly destructive, e.g. if it leads to positive change within an organizational community of practice (Wenger, 1998, Levi, 2011), sharing knowledge and assisting teammates builds a learning culture is critical. If businesses today are not engaging their people to learn then these businesses and their people will fall behind the 'learning curve' with potential conflict and resistance to change -even where such change may be positive by increasing sustainability-over time. However, Communities of Practice (CoPs) nowadays can be physically co-located, locally networked within a firm´s Intranet), virtual (i.e., networked via the web) or a combination of these. Crucially in firms, CoPs need the support and encouragement of Top Management -often the owner and family in S.M.Es. Hearn & White, 2009 advise us that:

...the key is to foster rather than try to control CoP's. Because they are about learning, not about fulfilling mandated tasks, they will thrive only when members find them valuable and are motivated to participate......

Open and frank dialog incorporating dialectics and challenges is a means to promote greater collaboration and harmony by clarifying potential or actual misunderstandings, anticipating, forestalling or otherwise 'surfacing' and addressing unspoken or latent forms of tension in the teams. We do not use the term dialectics in the strict, deterministic, Hegelian manner indicating a rising tide of contradictions inevitably leading to struggle, contention and ultimate synthesis at a new, higher level of praxis. We refer to dialectics as rational debate, argumentation, conflict or contention between parties that may be overt or may exist latent within the interplay of dialog between them and which may then be surfaced or evolve from emergent conversations concerning the best way forward or the allocation of resources.

However, we also recognize that collaboration may sometimes pose problems for parties to an emergent community of practice as illustrated by Hardy and Phillips (1998). These authors stated: ¨... while collaboration can be highly productive in solving interorganizational problems, conflict also has a clear role in challenging existing frameworks and forcing domain change in directions considered by at least some members to be positive. Both aspects deserve equal attention, since failure to recognize the importance of conflict leads to a preference for the status quo and an implicit adoption of the viewpoint of powerful stakeholders ¨ (Hardy and Phillips, 1998). In fact, innovation usually requires some level of challenge to the pre-existing status quo.

Three cases are used to illustrate key aspects of the need for creative balance of forces and drivers promoting collaboration within and between competition and collaboration in teams and departments of S.M.Es. We provide some broad guidelines for improving policy development and implementation including some relevant Human Resource Management policies and training points.

Three Cases: Context

Innovation as has been pointed out elsewhere, predominantly occurs as a result of interactions between various actors, rather than as a result of an isolated individual's efforts (Håkansson, 1987; von Hippel, 1988; Lundvall, 1992, WEF, 2015). Hargadon (2003) provides numerous examples of collaborative dialogs of the latter sort based on ten years of research. He demonstrates that revolutionary innovations result from the creative combination of ideas, people and objects rather than flashes of brilliance by lone inventors. The World Economic Forum(WEF) suggests a structured approach to ensure innovation is scaffolded equitably across organizations in networks where collaboration occurs with relevant and sufficient preparation of the ground work and systems of collaboration between organizations (WEF,2015). They discuss partnerships between firms of many sizes from SMEs to Multi-National Corporations (MNCs). Today, the socio-digital media alongside trade and tax legislation and subsidies may enable these kinds of horizontal collaborations, mentor-partnering and other integrated interactions between organizations of diverse sizes much more easily across regions (WEF, 2015, pp.22-28, Smith and Cockburn, 2013). This open, collaborative embedding context fits well with Schumpeter (1942) and Tidd's (2001) view of innovation as new combinations of already existing knowledge, ideas, and artifacts *being put into use*.

Leonard-Barton and Sensiper (1998) argued that innovation depends upon the collective expertise of individuals in a community and Wenger (1998) says much the same about learning CoPs. That is, that such innovation and learning is characterized by an iterative process of people working together building on the creative ideas of one another. Stacey (2001) places self-organizing human interaction, with its ability for emergent creativity, at the center of the knowledge creating process, and suggests that organizational knowledge depends on the qualities of the relationships between people. In other words, successful innovation must be based in co-ordination mechanisms that support the problem-solving efforts of the firm's Human Capital, and the dynamic processes of 'sensemaking' within it. Sensemaking is the collaborative dialog involving the workplace community members freely sharing their 'sense' of ideas and concepts about 'how things work' or could work, in an open manner whilst remaining open to consideration of others' views and contributions to that discussion.

The interplay of dialog and dialectics is a multidimensional and multi-spiraling process over time as Kodama (2005, pp. 49-51) suggests when describing the concept of 'dialectical dialog' and specifically, the drive for innovation to meet emergent market or societal demands is also important for the evolving social and action dynamics of the innovating organizations too. Such sensemaking dialogs and dialectics may reside in how individuals, team leaders and experts frame their discussions. In particular, Glynn (1996) points to the existence of "innovation champions" who have the social, political or interpersonal knowledge to influence the acceptance of innovative change (though such people must first be identified).

Research unambiguously shows that young innovative companies tend to grow more than other types. An increase in R&D expenditure by 1% generally stimulates employment in the business sector by about 0.15% (Bogliaccino, Piva, & Vivarelli, 2012). In addition, 3 other aspects strengthen the SME case. These are, 1) smaller firms tend to produce better-quality innovations, 2) R&D subsidy policies based upon size of the firm generally perform better than size- independent policies and 3) supporting small firms' investment in R&D often leads to more growth than subsidizing large firms' (Akcigit, 2009; Coad & Hölzl, 2010; Moncada-Paternò-Castello, 2011). Such fast-growing, innovative SMEs can also play a fundamental role in accelerating economic performance and assist greatly with regeneration and renewal dialog about industrial structure (Moncada- Paternò-Castello, 2011; Cincera & Veugelers, 2012; Czarnitzki & Delanote, 2013; Ciriaci, Moncada-Paternò, & Voigt, 2013).

However, despite the fact that approximately 30% of EU business expenditures on R&D are by firms with less than 500 employees, Europe is still lagging behind in the numbers of such R&D-investing companies compared to places such as the USA. Further, 1 in 3 new European enterprises fail before they reach their second year of trading on average. 50 to 60% never survive beyond the seventh year. Results are not much better elsewhere (Dishman, 2017) with around 50% failing by year 5 in USA. Moreover, the post- Global Financial Crisis (GFC) period makes potential investors wary of engaging in the risky business of establishing new companies (Sauner-Leroy, 2004). Evidence suggests that the average size of R&D intensive firms can explain the overall R&D intensity gap between the EU and the US. These US companies are concentrated in sectors that are intrinsically R&D-intensive, so thereby raising the US's overall R&D performance compared to the EU (Moncada-Paternò-Castello, Ciupagea, Smith, Tübke, & Tubbs, 2010; Ortega-Argilés & Brandsma, 2010).

Scaffolding Innovating Organizations´ Success: Across Communities and Regions

Although less sanguine about future policy success in closing the gap between the EU and the USA or Japan, Moncada-Paternò-Castello and Voigt (2013), point out that two of the five targets of the Europe 2020 strategy are to increase employment and shift towards increased growth of innovative R&D- intensive SMEs to speed up the development of knowledge-based economies in the EU. They see this as fostering innovation and requiring increased R&D investment in the EU to 3% of countries' GDP. Horizon 2020 defines innovation management capacity building as a core element of their support. They define innovation management as systematically covering all the steps in the process of generating innovative concepts, screening them for viability, putting them on the market and making a profit.

Thus, the EU innovation policy makers and planners have aligned the goals with the three core objectives for EU funding or support aiming to improve:

1. European Firms' competitiveness:
2. Begin Structural change in the economy and types of industries:
3. Improve employment rates:

There still remains a number of conflicting areas at distinct levels of analysis such as the contest between community' orientation, collaboration and the business dividend for owners as well as taxpayers; the design and development of partnering and mentoring arrangements between big firms and innovative small firms as well as the benefits accruing to the wider community from such governmental pump-priming funding (Moulaert & Nussbaumer, 2005, pp. 89-90). There are some perceived issues with respect to a lack of owners´ and line managers´ skills in teamworking in the firms since these capabilities also require development; individuals' interest, aptitude, acculturation and personal skills repertoire varies.

In one of the two key competitor countries (Japan) recent case study research has indicated that community engagement is vital to success. Kodama (2005, p.31) states: "Community leaders serve an important function in creating networked strategic communities. The case study shows how community leaders have created networked strategic communities in which the central government, regional governments, universities, hospitals, private businesses and non-profit organizations take part in the advancement of regional electronic networking." Given the intrinsic tendencies of large firms to protect IP and for Big Firm clustering to be a detrimental impact on funds invested, in promoting the innovation cluster policy it might seem that further consideration is needed. There are still ongoing debates however regarding how best to advance the overall regeneration and support growth of fledgling High-tech businesses in national and transnational markets in Europe and elsewhere. Kodama's version of 'dialectical dialog' envisions a network both challenging each member's innovations for robustness as well as engaging in a constructive dialog about collaboration and integration of the innovation into the network's New Product Development (NPD) (Kodama, 2005, pp. 49-51).

Examples of community involvement include cooperatives and ´FabLabs´ (Fabrication Laboratories), which emerged as a result of Digitization, Web 2.0 and other technologies which prompted culture change such as the growing, open source movement and the rising numbers of digital knowledge repositories enabling digitally connected environments to generate complex webs of virtual and physical collaboration, experimentation, and innovation (Smith and Cockburn, 2013). An instance of such innovation and ground-level initiatives is the rise of 'fabrication laboratories (FabLabs). FabLabs are now part of a larger global movement of community-based digital fabrication workshops with roots in an initial outreach initiative of MIT's Centre for Bits and Atoms in 2009. Since then, the Fab Foundation, a US non-profit, has emerged from the MIT Center´s Fab Lab Program.

Any major transformations such as researching and developing new services and products or systems for delivery in an industrial system often has some delay before reaching anticipated or optimum levels of sales, production, market penetration and so on. So, targeting support or allocating extra resources to tackle problems at critical moments in the SME or project lifecycle and orienting them towards scaffolding for success are important to overcome or reduce the dialectical tensions inherent in the R&D capital building and know-how generation processes. In an industrial context, these interactions often follow the value-chain and the supply- chain management. An enterprise facing a particular problem turns to a supplier, a customer, a competitor, or some other related actor such as research centers or financial tools, to get assistance in specifying the problem and defining the terms for the solution. From this follows that the level of analysis for understanding the processes of industrial innovation and change in a country is some notion of an industrial system or network of organizations with their entrepreneurs and innovators, carrying out similar and related economic activity; however, the above discussion confirms that organizations in a country cannot compete as isolated agents.

In today's complex and dynamic environments, national and corporate entrepreneurship and innovation capabilities must also be allied with macro level environmental and social concerns if R4M and long-term sustainability are to be successfully achieved (Cockburn et al 2015). Even though many businesses and governments are now moving towards more sustainable practices, the overall impact of these efforts still seems much less than optimal and are threatened in post-Trump USA. Most methodologies and practices are not holistic enough and display significant problems in implementation due to their individualized or piecemeal implementation, their deficient structures, and their inadequate communication channels.

Therefore, some consideration of systems in use is apposite when reviewing how the team operated and their net performance outcomes. The 4 levels of systems thinking that teams must address as a matter of course according to Senge (1990,1994) and which are individually, and collectively potential sources of conflict are as follows:

1. Events that are isolated, apparently random, occurrences with no visible pattern or discernable trends. An example would be where there appears to be some unfortunate, unforeseen 'accidents' that delay the team in meeting its targets especially in firms with ´blame cultures´ as performance management systems.
2. Patterns of behavior, that indicate (an apparent) general 'drift'/direction. The patterns may highlight a cautious sense of urgency (or of laxity) for instance, but do not necessarily suggest answers or any means to make changes to the perceived trends. For example, the team may notice that time is catching up with them and the project deadline is looming whilst they continue to suffer mishaps or losses of some kind such as absent members, broken tools etc.
3. Systemic structure shows interrelationships between patterns of behavior. For example, one of the case teams below noted that because they were trying to make up for absent colleagues and misunderstood techniques, they had to work extra hours to catch up with work to meet fixed/agreed deadlines. As they worked even harder, taking on more tasks and learning new skills or technologies

not originally assigned them, they were more susceptible to illness and stress and raised project anxiety, causing an amplifying loop and additional cycles of absences or poor work/output and higher workloads, more late nights as time passed and other aspects of the environment get more urgent and so on. They then needed to review how they worked in order to try to 'work smarter' on the current project and in future.

4. Mental Models indicate the basic cultural level norms and assumptions (according to Schein there are three levels) that have a Meta-level applicability. For example, the team referred to above might work smarter, but it would be useful to know what underlying socialized and internalized values encouraged these kinds of team behaviors in the first place? What are the levels of emotional and physical resilience involved and how best to measure these in future.

The conversations that occur in the above relationship web conveys the team narrative and the unfolding action and results obtained. A team story has been described as the ways that people make sense or build coherence from their fragmented experiences in the context or landscape they are embedded within (Cockburn et al, 2005). We use the term here to capture the sense that the team is trying to 'live the brand', to enact their shared, tacit and explicit values in their everyday practice or behavioral routines as well as the transformational and transitional phases of their work processes.

Every organization has a story about its founders, history and values as well as its development, growth and so on. In order to practically encourage the process and awaken team members to the need to critically examine their own and others' 'editorial' conversations around their 'team story' and related sub-texts in teams' actions or project discussions, a systematic approach must be adopted. That is, we must promote reflection-in-action. These reflections must be in real time, upon the ongoing interactive processes of social construction of a team-story as it is unfolding. Such reflection threads through the tapestry of conversations within teams, between teams, and leaders and with the rest of organization or external entities.

Added to the above there is the perceived need to research the physical/technical as well as the cultural means to scaffold and build necessary dialogs to capture and apply organizational innovations and learning in SMEs. Problems of continuity of support are also important as illustrated by one case referred to below.

We have narrowed our focus for the rest of this chapter in order to keep things manageable. Thus, we simply to present 3 case overviews and comparisons or contrasts of the internal team processes involved and the dialectics and dialogs in relationships between them and others in the wider community of actors involved. We will draw upon global indicators and comparisons of best practice where available to support current empirical research with SMEs.

MAIN FOCUS OF CHAPTER

Remarks on Illustrative Cases

As Scheel (2007) asserts, in today's knowledge-based economy, the ability to innovate is more important than cost efficiency in determining the long-term ability of enterprises to flourish. This does not mean that cost considerations are irrelevant, but simply that the combined forces of the globalization of markets and the deepening divisions of labor make it increasingly difficult to base a competitive position on cost-advantages only. The creativity aspects are a continuous thread throughout not just a front-end element as Rickards noted some time ago (Rickards, 2000).

Tacit knowledge is a critical component in innovation generally and particularly in many areas of knowledge work. However, the criticality includes positive as well as a negative impact (Cockburn, 2006, Cockburn and Smith, 2018). Tacit knowledge in the workplace impacts on areas of discretionary behaviour. The tacit component also may be related to the 'emotional labour' aspects in the workplace; what gets attended to or ignored and/or 'emotional intelligence of the leadership. These relate to efficiency and effectiveness in performance and project management and include creativity, workplace 'custom and practice' as well as 'communities of practice', informal peer regulation of the pace of work, workplace climate and learning-in-work.

However, it is often difficult to acquire, define, change and/or preserve if key staff leave the organisation—or if they resist being 'managed' in some ways or reject some or all of their managers' ideas or if these staff members decide to sabotage parts of the organisation or particular projects or people. If such workers have the 'ear' of others who may be Opinion leaders, then they can do much harm or will have to be mollified or in some way encouraged to 'buy into' the project at hand.

Business teams typically have a mix of formal and informal leaders responsible for their team story narrative, execution and results. Formal team leadership - whether transactional or transformational - inhabits a dynamic and complex emotional space in work relationships. There are emotional consequences and influences whether the leader is successful or not. Where there is a high commitment environment in particular, leadership processes generate or amplify both positive and negative loops of emotion (Cockburn 2010). Leaders often try to evoke positive emotions in their staff. ¨Authentic¨ leadership is really leadership with a trusted, human face. What really matters most about authentic leadership is the degree to which the leader comes across to their staff as a genuine, sincere, trustworthy human being.

Like spiders constructing their webs, leaders inhabit the complex emergent structure of team´s emotional meaning-making and meaning-taking that they and their followers are constructing in real time. The latter webs are formed as emotional regimes within which teams operate on their tasks. Rising levels of cognitive dissonance and dysfunctional behaviors generate adverse emotional regimes in teams. Bennis has proposed that communication is central to the four key management competences leaders need. Those are the management of attention, meaning, trust and self. Idealistic or naive accounts of trust in economic life must also to be tempered by reference to the way in which high-trust and low-trust relations have different institutional and cultural reinforcements.

Long-term, high-trust relationships tend to be associated not merely with certain cultural traditions such as forms of kinship relations (pace Granovetter, 1998, for example), but are backed up with institutional, legal and financial circumstances which influence the time-scale over which rates of profit matter and the degree to which firms are exposed to short-term pressures, and the scope for voice relative to exit. Such reinforcements are often lacking in low trust relationships, in virtual organizations (Priest et al, 2006) and also in the growing ´gig economy´ or else one or both parties have a suspicious or untrustworthy identity or history in professional relationships. As Deloitte state in their 2017 trends report ¨The rise of the "gig economy" is making more flexible, project-based arrangements an acceptable alternative to company based employment.¨ So, we suggest a fifth competence, the management of team identity is also necessary to ensure positive emotional regimes within the team underpinned by cognitive consonance, aligned team member behaviors and more consistently positive task and project outcomes. Some teams, for instance have a 'personality', in part related to the collective 'persona' of the team members, their ways of working, implicit values or beliefs, or the culture of their profession or of the organisation (Smith and Cockburn, 2016). Thus, for instance, it is fairly common to distinguish 'professionals' by their adherence to the values of their profession rather than their loyalty to particular business organisations.

Swift Trust, Organizational Evolution, and the Gig Economy

The newer approaches in innovation theory no longer describe innovation as a linear process and recognize the tacit knowledge development is crucial (Carayannis and Campbell, 2009, Wisdom and Chor et al.,2014). It is argued that innovations represent the result of interactions and feedback processes by various different players (firms, knowledge producers, technology transfer institutions) in so-called innovation systems. The development potential of a region (of a country) from this perspective is based on the innovation strength of networks, which are characterized, by self-steered processes, co-operative exchange structures and a greater dynamism and complexity. Inevitably, such dynamic interaction involves emotion and thus contains potential for learning, for conflict and for collaboration.

It is increasingly possible to draw together individuals, groups and teams for temporary transactions and short projects or ´gigs´ using sociodigital technology as UBER taxis and Airbnb has done globally. Thus, those engaged on such projects as managers and team members may not have met their team face-to-face. The team may never have had any unmediated face-to-face contact with clients or customers and may also have been recruited by a third party. In any event, they will only be working together for a short time and may never work together again or not for some time and then under different circumstances, on different projects. Consequently, there will be a number of psychological as well as legal contracts. So, how will they become a team, maximise benefits of the tacit and explicit knowledge and synergy, project a positive image and corporate identity within a short time-frame to the significant others? What motivational calculus can be applied?

An emergent challenge this millennium is the management of corporate identity and socialisation processes in a distributed, networked or virtual company where boundaries between internal and external are increasingly permeable. The nature of company- customer-supplier "constellations" or "value webs" requires and initiates greater levels of collaboration as well as competition. Employees a) may be recruited for specific projects or gigs (short contract periods) b) may never have met superiors or colleagues, c) may also never have had an unmediated face-to-face interaction with clients/customers. Identity, habitus, esprit de corps, corporate image will require different tools and techniques than those currently employed in face-to-face (f2f) environments. Substantial tacit knowledge conversion and capture will thus be necessary in relatively short time periods for new product development, "internal" business relationships, marketing and telephony-based customer service "externally".

Although there are issues concerning the perceived equity of rewards and the new psychological contracts (Rousseau, 1995,2004) amongst employees under the regimes of flexible and agile companies it not a one-sided matter. There is a mix of advantages and disadvantages in this for those involved. They suffer from the lack of the normative structures which foster trust and serve to bind the permanent staff (Meyerson, Weick and Kramer, 1996:167). What psychological and social rewards work for core company members are not necessarily going to work or to be available to those at the periphery on short-term project work.

Those members of disparate professions located around the world who share only the commonality of the specific project or gig are going to work differently from core staff, not least because the habitus of their practice fields vary from one another. Bourdieu defines habitus as the "system of acquired dispositions functioning on the practical level as categories of perception and assessment or classificatory principles as well as being the organizing principles of action."(Bourdieu,1987, 1990) Such a habitus presupposes an identity of interests and institutional frames of reference for action, if not of values and beliefs. It is a kind of cultural prism through which the world, divided into overlapping fields, can be viewed.

The field is the social arena for interaction and contention; where power is claimed and legitimated. The emerging digital economy at the level of the corporation occurs within the field of work principally but could also be seen as intruding into other fields such as leisure, learning, family and domestic activities too.

The team field of interaction within which this habitus is seen to operate in the digital economy will be the network. Within these distributed workplaces, a common currency of symbolic exchanges and power will need to be fashioned from the strands of accepted practice in knowledge work teams. The habitus in the freelancers' professions will not necessarily coincide with that of the employing company nor of the other colleagues engaged for the team. Habitus is clearly not an entirely explicit phenomenon. In fact, insofar as it relates in the main to mental schema and models, it is largely tacit and an unarticulated "given" in individual and corporate thinking.

The learning arena and social field of interaction, for such freelancers, especially in an increasingly digitised environment presupposes that the potential for anomie is counterbalanced by some other means of encouraging collaboration, corporate or brand identification and self-organised learning. Operating via electronically-mediated, geographically-dispersed teams, the cash nexus will not remain a sufficient motivation to generate creative relationships with tasks, customers, colleagues and the company as a whole. Much of the corporate habitus will be embodied as tacit learning, memory and knowledge. Knowledge management for competitive advantage will require collaboration between empowered professional, information workers to profit by organizational learning gains available to such teams.

Emergence, Learning, and Thresholds of Change

However, by definition, teams working at the so ´called ´edge of chaos´, that is ´ Emergence teams´ as outlined by Smith and Cockburn (2016), are usually only formed to tackle serious disruptions. Such teams stand at the threshold of imminent surprise, learning challenges and abrupt, discontinuous change in business landscapes brimming with implicit promise and threat. Their considered actions must always aim to invoke collective learning to survive and thrive within amidst the interweave of people, technology and markets in their web of relationships. As spiders live in the webs they construct, so too do teams inhabit and look outwards at the world beyond from within the webs of relationships they have woven. In organizations, such webs are not merely techno-social structures to enable them to better engage in business but enable their manner of living, acting and thinking about their environment.

The notion of liminal thresholds of change used here includes the idea of learning thresholds. That is a domain of action where double loop learning occurs which challenges pre-existing conceptualisations of how things work, of learning and of former learning paradigms. Threshold concepts, discussed in relation to teaching and learning are characteristically defined as follows:

- **Transformative**: Occasioning a 'significant shift in the perception of a subject'
- **(Probably) Irreversible**: 'The change in perspective occasioned by acquisition of a threshold concept is unlikely to be forgotten'

- **Integrative**: Exposing the 'previously hidden interrelatedness of something'
- **(Possibly Often) Bounded:** 'Any conceptual space will have terminal frontiers, bordering with thresholds into new conceptual areas'
- **(Potentially) Troublesome**: That which appears 'counter-intuitive, alien (emanating from another culture or discourse), or incoherent (discrete aspects are unproblematic but there is no organising principle)' (Meyer & Land, 2006: pp. 7-9)

The team´s perception of a threshold of change may itself be intuitive or tacit and so we need some means of eliciting and extracting such latent learning and knowledge from the ongoing action. We regard tacit knowledge and learning as including and embedding a large measure of emotional content, behaviors and reactions to events which eventuate as a team emotional regime underpinning their ´custom and practice´ and organizational sub-culture whilst they are working on their work projects and tasks. We have reviewed and applied a number of models of these processes as they relate to teams in our research. These are discussed briefly below with reference to collective learning, individual and collective transitions and leadership roles.

Tuckman's (1965,1977) model of team development for instance notes emotions and cognitions as background aspects of team´s or individual´s behaviours. Individual or team emotions are treated in a behaviourist-like fashion as a set of lower order concerns. The model is descriptive rather than analytical in this regard. No expression of the relationship between these processes and the behaviours at each stage of the team development process is provided. Only the progress through each stage is affected i.e. faster or slower depending on the cognitive-affective interactions. The stages are the same irrespective of the emotions. Emotions are however very pertinent to the pace and quality of teambuilding, teamwork and team action as well as outcomes in many instances. Particularly in relation to team bonding, development and the anchoring of collective intellectual and social capital in their routine team project behaviours. Emotional maturation processes in teams are thus underpinned by both tacit and explicit sets of norms.

Although individuals are autonomous agents, this does not preclude interconnections within the team and between the individual and the team as a self-organising learning vehicle. There is no mention of interconnectedness of the emotional development (of the whole team and of the individual members of the team) by Tuckman. Movement per se is not too well represented by this model although it does draw our attention to discernible transitions in explicit behaviours. These transitions are important in terms of complexity and we have now begun to review them in relation to attractors.

Reflecting the multispiral model of tacit knowledge-creation in teams including the transitions in the process of conversion from *individuals' activity* to collective knowledge in a team occurs from inside out (Cockburn,2005). However, this *team-insider* model of knowledge transformation and learning has to be distinguished from the movement of an individual from being a solo-learner to becoming a team-learner (Cockburn, 2006; Wenger 1998). Nonaka's research is not about the outsider becoming an insider as in Wenger's communities of practice model but instead it is about the conversion, transformation and co-creation of knowledge *within* the team. That is, the insider's progress through the body of a collective, which transmits learning and reconstitutes the collective anew in a learning-enriched form (Nonaka, 1994, 1995, Nonaka and Teece, 2001). Unlike Kostopoulus et al´s interpretation of Crossan et al´s (1999) model of team learning and cognition (Kostopoulus,2013, pp1433-1434), we see the tacit components of the emotional learning in teams as embodied in the team action rather than explicitly codified without some form of reflection such as diaries and logs.

A brief outline of history of three projects is given in the rest of the chapter. An overview and outline of each case studyis given in a summary template. The template is used for ease of comparison, contrast and reflection for readers. Tables 1, 2 and 3 give an overview for case 1, case 2 and case 3. Each case outline table is supplemented with two other tables, labelled Table 1b, Table 2b and 2c and Table 3b and 3c. These supplementary tables cover aspects of organizational culture (adapted from Hofstede´s 2001 model), as well as data on team´s emotional regimes (Cockburn, 2006) and systems for evaluating and resolving perceived development and training gaps. All the foregoing tables are used in conjunction with Snowden´s Cynefin diagram and Table 4 model. We recommend that the categories of high trust emotional regimes in teams, i.e. those called ´Trusty Followers´ and ´Responsible professionals´ are the most apt for project work under VUCA conditions. Basically, these two emotional regimes correspond to emergent and best practice approaches though teams still need to upskill best practice to enable teams and leaders need to address complexity.

Complexity theory offers dynamic new insights into living and working within interconnected human systems and organizations. Many of these insights are somewhat paradoxical and move us to reframe our understanding from moment to moment as we co-evolve with our environment. This approach contradicts much of the traditional management theories about generating and maintaining control and compliance in organizations. In addition, complexity theory is part of an evolving family of theories.

Emotional Regimes

We originally used Fineman's (1996) definition of emotional regimes, defined initially as comprising "…the coherent rules governing the complex, emotional 'acts and practices' underpinning the teams' shared values, cognitive schemata and enacted scripts". However, the definition was subsequently amended to 'The dynamic and responsive relationship processes and coherent rules governing the complex, emotional 'acts and practices' underpinning the groups' shared values, schemata and enacted scripts.' A matrix of qualitative factors impacting the development of the regimes in each of the 4 main quadrants was developed.

CASES: NOTE ON CONFIDENTIALITY

The details of each case are derived from observations by one or more of the chapter authors and extracts from semi-structured interviews with staff and owners. As these cases were drawn from consulting projects between 2003 and 2015, those of us involved have signed confidentiality and anonymity agreements with the organizations concerned, we have anonymized the organizations´ names and locations to comply with the agreements we made.

High emotional regime refers to the positivity explicitly expressed by team members verbally e.g. about their engagement and enjoyment of teamwork, tasks and roles for instance and behaviorally confirmed in terms of their observed discretionary behaviors such as working beyond normal hours, doing extra work or being available to work outside their standard role during the expected 6 month transition period, assisting colleagues and building bonds by socializing as a team outside of the workplace at teambuilding events following training initially then as friendships are strengthened in the team. There are 4 main types plus a small number of hybrids as outlined in the figure in Box 1. These form part of

Table 1. Four brothers case

Case Study Field/topic/issue/problem	**4 brothers Case**
Context and situation: Where it took place Organization background Who was involved?	In this New Zealand S.M.E., a medium sized service provider (of IT services and products) previously it has built up a good rep in the industry as a consulting organization. It was regarded as trustworthy and reliable by its customers and a key player in its niche. However, it is now also providing services as well as consulting advice. The four directors are brothers, and each has responsibility for a specific functional aspect of the business. "Each Director is driven by the company's customer service values " (quote from executive director #4, the youngest brother, in charge of HR). However, the CEO, who is the eldest brother, does have the ultimate power in decision making, enabling him to overrule others´ decisions. (*authors´ comment*) There are emotions on all sides. That is, between clients and staff, between staff and managers and between staff and the public-at-large. Some of these disputes have spilled over into the family´s relationships outside of work;.one of the brothers (*director #4*) has distanced himself and his family from the other three brothers and their families as a consequence of their ongoing and increasingly bitter feud about how to run the project team. The firm has sub-contracted some work on system upgrades to a local telecoms provider to overcome a gap in the firm´s staffing capabilities in the interim as they are currently recruiting more network systems engineers.
Change Drivers: What prompted the change? Who sponsored it? Management/owners/ others? Why/ did you choose Action Learning? Who led the change?	"The management has failed to recognize or appreciate the fact that employees and other directors have natural expectations of the organization (an unwritten 'Psychological contract') that are aligned our own perceived personal and professional identities, needs and expectations." The psychological contract is conceptualized against the rational expectations and objectives of both employees and management of the organization, though not all of these are made explicit to managers." (chief *consulting engineer #1*). The brothers have chosen action learning as they see it as 'learning-on-the-job' and the most practical, least intrusive way to make practical business changes. " There are recent instances when the disrupted family

continued on following page

Table 1. Continued

	relationships and business culture of the founders has caused tensions and contradictions in the workplace. Only the CEO has the sign-off on any spend. " (*finance and admin consultant*) These arguments, frictions within the SME ´C suite´ are between siblings and are akin to those in the negative end of the possible relationship spectrum or the "Bleak house" of the Hearn and White (2009) model of S.M.E. organizations (*authors*).
Change Narrative: What did you do? What resources were needed? Policy change/support? Enabling technologies? Other support?	In terms of the '3-dimensional strategy' model of Gratton & Truss (2003), The change strategy was in place, but the systems and action dimensions were not wholly agreed with staff, although staff views were canvassed by email prior to implementation of the transition plan, but trust was a diminishing commodity as the CEO used his casting vote to implement his own favored approach despite concerns expressed by the engineering staff about the system readiness, leading to emergence of a ´suspicious ´ mercenary´ type emotional regime in the teams with cliques acting to ´work-to-rule´ i.e. go-slow, using health and safety legislation as a cover to reduce the pace of system upgrades and testing. The latter strategic weaknesses impacted on the CEO leadership focus in particular, as he saw it as employees sabotaging capability and some other directors as undermining his authority. He then determined to force up the pace of the transition plan with sub-contractors and employees despite some minor system issues. This action caused some tension with two of his brother directors, the youngest director #4 and second youngest director #3, in charge of production.
Key Outcomes: What was achieved? Goals/targets missed or deferred? Advantages? • Disadvantages? Lessons learned?	"It is evident that the transition towards a service company necessitates a change in the compensation and motivation model for this organization. The old incentive model supports more performing individuals rather than a performing team. " (Director #4) Given the extra challenge because of the midway speeding up of the transformation, the renegotiation of the rewards package and contract is challenging. It will likely mean that we need to establish a completely new compensation package as well as a new psychological contract with staff rather than just amend existing ones. Employee involvement is also important part of achieving new psychological contract so that everyone can more clearly

continued on following page

Table 1. Continued

	shape his or her contract and related expectations. Longer-term performance focused goals and cross-functional cooperation are cornerstones for achieving a more relational and balanced psychological contract. For this, there is a need for HR to have broader tools available to support consultants so that they see we have listened and they have trust in the fairness and mutuality of new psychological contract. ¨ (Director #2)
Transformability/Sustainability: Could this case example and learning from it be transferred? To other business/industry contexts? Considering deadlines and resources, is this achievable?	Teams in the two high Trust quadrants in the matrix share high anxiety about doing a good job on projects, so they are already under pressures that others such as those in the suspicious mercenaries or the amorphous pairs and social loafers' categories are not. Connecting autonomy to task and role clarity with peer and management support, are key performance drivers and are an integral part of delivering empowerment and are key motivators by the staff who may be willing to go the extra mile offering higher levels of discretionary behaviors and goodwill as a result.
Where to Next: What is envisaged or planned as a next step? For organization, team, staff member/members etc.	In the longer term, the company will aim to achieve the balanced psychological contract model being capable of balancing the benefits and risks. The company will commit to continuous development of its consultants both with internal and external means. This would mean a tradeoff is required between consultants' willingness to be flexible in their demands and expectations and the pilot version should be implemented immediately, with a follow up in 6 months, making sure the balance and fairness is kept by adapting inputs and outputs to ensure perceived fairness through open and frank discussion and clear, candid communication with all staff. CEO, director #1

each case Table 1. Tables 1c through 3c on emotional regimes for each case study are found in appendix study exercise.

The aim was to survey and then move team emotional regimes in each department into one of the two high trust quadrants as compensation review is implemented and ongoing adjustments made to move from an unstable, dynamic and emergent team context at initial stages of the transition into a complicated context and good practice emotional regime as training, systems and resources are added or augmented and continuously adjusted to compensate or reduce fluctuations over time.

Case 2

Table 2c with emotional regime data for case study organization 2 is shown in the Appendix below.

The following case (AP Ltd case #3, below) draws on the experience of AP Ltd.

Table 1b. Cultural dimensions in the firm

Power distance Perception of this distance increased strongly over time, even though departmentally localized to those teams with issues of missed deadlines, culminating in the resignation of Head of production department after the first quarter results were declared.
Uncertainty avoidance Increased for a time, as some of the family members felt threatened by the CEO changes and distrust increased as they pragmatically held back some innovation until after the completion of the compensation review when tension subsided over the next month.
Individualism Increased for a time as a few of the production department staff members fought to preserve the pre-existing culture from what they saw as the newly-imposed culture and some competition within and between teams increased around speed of completion of their stage.
Masculinity Increased for a while, but naturally declined as other factors such as the changing demographic of staff, increased involvement of female consultants allied to the CEO´s skillful interventions to persuade staff they had a long-term future and HR director´s staff survey and follow-up webpage memo to all about the company´s draft guarantee of gender equality and pay /grade transparency. Pressure also eased by the second quarter as new clients were gained and systems successfully upgraded, reducing some staff fears for their job security.

Adapted from Hofstede et al (2001)

Box 1. Typology of emotional regimes in teams

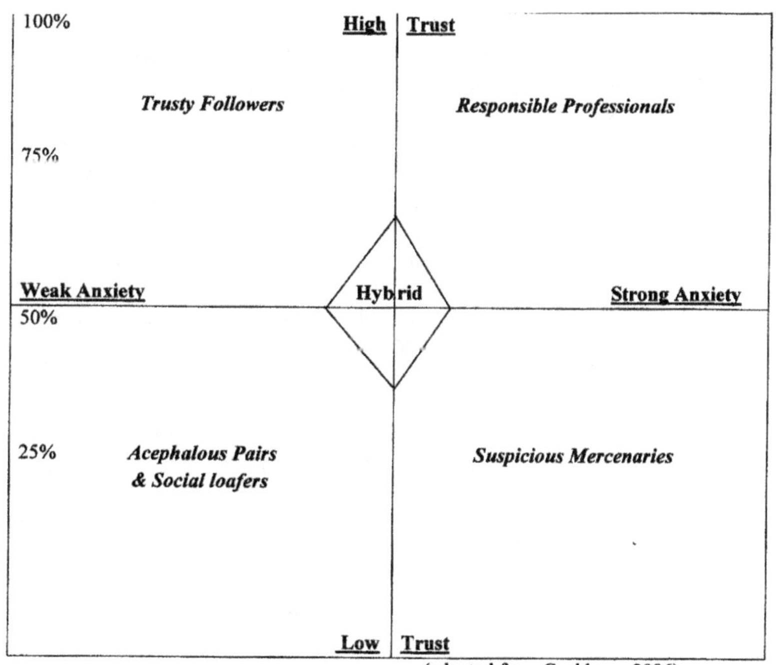

(adapted from Cockburn, 2006)

Source: Snowden (2012)

Table 2. Cardioview franchise case study summary template

Case Study Field/topic/issue/problem	Cardioview franchise Case example
Context: Where it took place Organization background Who was involved?	*Cardioview* case concerns a pilot research project prototype within a local, medical support company in the UK, based upon an adapted Call Center franchise model. *Cardioview* is small with 25 core staff but is expanding. It provides services to physicians. Heart patients are given a monitor which digitises a reading which the patient can then transmit down a freephone line to the company. A Cardiac technician on the other end of the line reads the signal on a computer screen, selects a sample reading to send to the relevant physician treating the patient and will, if it is an emergency situation, alert the appropriate medical services. "We want a highly-committed team to deliver the excellent quality service and reach the company's objectives in the most efficient way" (*CEO*) The CEO, Network engineering manager and chief cardiac technician team were involved along with the 2 of the authors
Change Drivers: What prompted the change? Who sponsored it? Management/owners/ others? Why did you choose Action Learning? Who led the change?	"Action learning seemed to us to be a useful way for the novel aspects of the business situation and our team learning to be harvested, provided we were rigorous in making notes and reflecting and testing the notions and practices. " (*CEO*) "To begin with, it is not face-to-face interaction, the technicians, rather than nurses, are interacting with patients. Secondly, they are not in a hospital environment and they are not dealing with other hospital personnel. Consequently, whilst some of their prior experience and training is relevant and applicable, this is not necessarily true of all of it. They could even be deficient in certain respects. " (*Chief Technician*). "Our aim was to improve the psychology of the interactions between technicians and callers to this virtual business SME. This is, at present, an ephemeral relationship, occurring over a short period when the patient is being monitored (a couple of weeks). The person seeks some reassurance from the technicians and the latter also see this as part of their role. They are already constructing images of callers and negotiating temporary relationships of

continued on following page

Table 2. Continued

	various types. ¨ (*authors*) Currently, these "swift trust" relationships (as Myerson, Weick and Kramer (1996) call them) are reliant on the tacit knowledge and learning of the technicians involved. Most of the technicians have come from a National Health Service background and training and have, thus acquired some ideas and images of "professionalism" derived from that experience. Although some of this is explicit, much is also internalised, tacit and embodied. The specific arena of this private sector company and their current tasks and communications media are significantly different from the technicians´ previous modes of interaction with patients.
Change Narrative: What did you do? What resources were needed? Policy change/support? Enabling technologies? Other support?	The process was in 2 stages. Firstly, we modelled appropriate behaviours. Secondly, initiated a team development sequence leading to corporate visualisation and operationalisation. The latter by actionable steps identified in the "walkback" from the vision. Observations and the application of the proprietary tools and techniques comprising the *beliefs box* and *walkback* methodology will be of value for future employee psychological contract and individual development. This whole process formed the beliefs box which allowed staff to get a handle on their activities. Having opened a door into continuous improvements in work processes, they used an iterative and interactive process to learn, extend, enhance and improve outcomes.
Key Outcomes: What was achieved? Goals/targets missed or deferred? Advantages? Disadvantages? Lessons learned?	The Executive team are currently collaborating privately with a firm of consulting software engineers on the technical set up and people from the local university business school on best practice for commercialisation. ¨The market is growing and developing rapidly so speed is of the essence and although the action learning process has had many advantages for customizing and tailoring the changes to meet our specific company requirements and resource, there is also a drag in terms of the pace for learning to be brought into our practice after we have sifted through what we have gleaned from the project through the learning set´s iterative process for reflective discussions and summing up.¨ (*Sales manager*) ¨ Ambitious standards of business process, technology and patient care are required to continually satisfy external

continued on following page

Table 2. Continued

	stakeholders and internal needs as well as conducive to building a performance-based culture " (*Technician, BG*)
Transformability/Sustainability: Could this case example and learning from it be transferred? To other business/industry contexts? Considering resources and achievements is this achievable?	Some elements can be readily transferred to other contexts. The degree to which they are able to overcome any deficiencies and/or build new mental models of practice and a positive team emotional regime which they can embody and routinise is not yet fully codified. Some staff had a minimalist orientation to the program and to what was required of their development, assuming their NHS training to be sufficient. Some extra effort and resources may be needed to surface some of these aspects and make them an explicit element in staff development programs and actions.
Where to Next: What is envisaged or planned as a next step? For organization, team, staff member/members etc.	"The future plans of *Cardioview* include developing and selling Apps to Health Trusts and building a *Software as a Service* (SaaS) business whilst extending our market into areas where longer-term relationships between callers and technicians are likely to ensue e.g. asthma, diabetes and pregnancy monitoring. " (*CEO*).

Table 2b. Cultural dimensions in the firm

Power distance Perception of this distance reduced strongly over time, even though localized, culminating in the resignation of Head of marketing.
Uncertainty avoidance Increased over time, as one of the founder members felt threatened by changes and distrust increased amongst leadership team
Individualism Increased with time as the department staff members fought to preserve the preferred present culture from what they perceived as the imposed corporate cultural future and perceived anti-trade union bias from US franchise HQ
Masculinity Increased for a while, but naturally declined given the other factors.

Adapted from Hofstede et al (2001)

Table 3c with relevant emotional regime information for this case is seen in the Appendix below.

FUTURE TRENDS

The multispiral models of transformative learning in the emergent, complex responsive systems within teams has potential for future development as a model of the analysis of group tacit learning. The enactive, social construction of meaning and personality entails different modes of learning-in-action as each individual transitions between passive and active learning modes and performative learning states within the team field of action. The fractal learning involved crosses a variety of personal, transactional and

Table 3. AP case study summary template

Case Study Field/topic/issue/problem	AP Ltd Case example 3
Context: Where it took place Organization background Who was involved?	A manufacturer of specialist electronic components based in the south midlands of Britain. The founding partners and executive team are all under 35 years of age and friends from university. The research respondents were CEO and senior executives, in a company-sponsored, Executive Education program run in conjunction with the consortium of universities. Each of these executives were themselves highly-qualified, articulate technical, marketing and production personnel with higher degrees.
Change Drivers: What prompted the change? Who sponsored it? Management/owners/ others? Why did you choose Action Learning? Who led the change?	Our focus groups and interviews made explicit the tensions existing in the professional identities of staff as they began their action research project since it involves a process of learning-by-doing and thus specifying outcomes in advance of the action is problematic especially for some of the engineers. The team opted to select a new leader for each of the distinct phases and for the different technical aspects, based upon expertise and willingness, reflecting their concerns about overstepping professional demarcations -though one executive, MM was seen by others as: "the go-to man for useful advice" (*HR director*).However, the CEO reserved the right to override others if he deemed it necessary or if they failed to reach a consensus. Our role was as observers- a non-voting role- but we might be asked for advice if the CEO felt it necessary.
Change Narrative: What did you do? What resources were needed? Policy change/support? Enabling technologies? Other support?	"The company culture will determine what level of freedom you give your staff to solve problems. If possible, it is better to give the employees the leeway to solve problems at the local level, so they can provide unique solutions to each problem and build a professional, problem-solving culture and brand identity they cherish." (*CEO*)
Key Outcomes: What was achieved? Goals/targets missed or deferred? Advantages? Disadvantages?	The executive team updated and developed their production and marketing systems interface. Goals and targets were all met and mostly within the anticipated deadline. One launch was deferred for a week due to a poor beta test. There were some issues with following the 'walkback' or

Table 3b. Cultural dimensions in the firm

Power distance Perception of this distance is low amongst most of the permanent staff, though the reverse is the case with those on short-term contracts.
Uncertainty avoidance Stable over time, as the owners seen as professional, trustworthy and the business was successful.
Individualism steady as the preferred culture and rewards are not threatened at that time but the sales team retains highest levels
Masculinity low, except for sales teams.

Adapted from Hofstede et al (2001)

interactive thresholds within the teams in their movements towards or between metaphor and metonymy. The team narrative structures capture the embodiment of these stories in the team's performative habitus, and both individual and team levels are linked to the latter in epistemological and ontological terms. Further work and testing within larger communities over longer periods will be required to validate the meaningful processes and patterns within such communities of commitment.

In a networked world,the ability to utilize 'Big data' responsibly comes with the drivers for 'democratization' of leadership and openness in governance and strategizing through forms of collective decision-making using digital social media as the next generation of leaders in business emerges and 'taking the pulse' or 'canvassing opinions' becomes easier (Smith and Cockburn, 2013,2014, Morton and Alireza, 2018, Cockburn, Jahdi and Wilson, 2015). Increasingly emotional aspects of virtual and AI applications for business, particularly avatars which interface with customers, have been researched (Gratch et al, 2007, Sandback et al, 2017). However, there is also some hype and exaggerated fears regarding the rise of machine learning and Artificial Intelligence (AI) displacing people and professions. These concerns encompass legitimate worries about individuals´ privacy and confidentiality in a time of global political turmoil, realignment and terrorism. Other issues around machine learning and AI include the nature of intelligence. Many see AI as ignorant and more artificial than intelligent especially regarding latent, tacit elements underpinning much communication beyond simple commands and statistics gathering. That is, those aspects making the qualitative human differences in levels of understanding and responding to interpersonal communications that result in nuanced, sophisticated grasp of the emotional content of messages and information between people such as empathy, for example.

The gap in understanding is often seen in the amusing ´írony´ deficiency of some AI (and some programmers) failing to see other language tropes such as metaphors, metonymy as well as being oblivious to the diversity and cultural factors of most interpersonal interactions (Ready, 2013, Sandback et al,2017). As Veliz states: ¨It takes a few seconds of interaction with any digital assistant to realize one is not in the presence of a very bright interlocutor¨ (Veliz, 2018). Notwithstanding that mutuality element in interpersonal contexts referred to earlier, such contexts can also stimulate the development of conflict or exacerbate pre-existing tensions, all of which escape the attention of the AI systems in use today (Baciu, 2016). Simply inputting masses of explicit data won´t generate human level comprehension of the layered, culturally-appropriate and tacit levels of meaning that much interpersonal communications are imbued with. That is, unless people adapt by dumbing-down and acting more machine-like or a radically different system is used to make AI learn like people learn.

However, the growth of networked sociodigital media also widely reinforces the rising digital accessibility of 'leaders' and organizations by the wider community including enabling 'whistleblowing' and fact-checking. Cyber security and cyber business opportunities are increasingly critical areas for leaders and managers to address. As a corollary, the R4M aspects must also take on greater significance in leaders' and Boards' agendas for risk management and evaluation of potential for conflict and/or collaboration within and between networks.

CONCLUSION: SUMMARY LESSONS FOR TEAM LEADERS

Overall there is a clear need for better alignment of HR and business strategies via more training for managers in coaching and performance appraisals.

1. Champion and commit to authentic team learning-and 'unlearning'- using a transparent, 'no blame' approach and 'surface´ all of the organizational and team-level undiscussables' to design and implement a more structured and managed career path for staff along with systematic skills building programs aligned to both business goals and individual requirements of staff.
2. Consult, Develop and articulate a shared vision, expressing the high hopes, KPIs and aspirations for all in order to bring energy and a positive focus to the work.
3. Conduct a thorough needs and resources assessment including emotional impact and resilience capability, identifying specific issues to address; build from what's already in place and working well. The Balanced Scorecard is regarded as a standard performance management tool for corporates however, for a SME with no HR department then instead of Balanced Scorecard it is recommended that management implements a Performance Management Cycle with relevant target and meeting dates clearly noted in the work calendar. This will secure ongoing performance evaluation that can be managed by the line manager and used as a constructive tool for dialogue and feed-back.
4. Sometimes innovation may be boosted by more openness in a network or between companies such as when firms deliberately waive some of their intellectual property rights.
5. Sometimes innovation is triggered by customer demand and positive reinforcement through the process of enacting the pilots or beta stage project experiences.
6. Develop an inclusive action plan incorporating the shared goals and objectives as well as a plan for addressing risks and contingencies in the process of attaining, measuring and evaluating their strategic alignment.
7. Select evidence-based programs and strategies and begin to build a shared framework of understanding and vocabulary, to create consistency and coherence for all when reviewing codes of practice and implementation concerns.
8. Conduct initial staff development for inexperienced staff to ensure that each understands and can apply with integrity and consistency the relevant best practices.
9. Launch emotional skills instruction and help staff get familiar with and experienced in these skills. Provide a support infrastructure and network.
10. Revisit activities; adjust for continuous improvement and 'surprising' occurrences in the complex global environment. Check on progress, probe limits in order to resolve problems early.

Network and team interface: things to note

- Networks differ from communities and both differ from small teams. Teams are generally more focused and more tightly knit
- Network and community relationships and emotional bonds are looser than team relationships generally so strengthening and anchoring their social capital including emotional bonds is vital.
- Networks and teams both require leadership styles which motivate and promote focus, capability and the will to complete as well as help in clarify expectations and goals at each stage of a project or Network lifecycle.
- Network and teams both require 'scaffolding' support structures and resources at critical moments.
- Team leaders must encourage and develop action-learning processes including learning from failure.
- The key to a collaborative work environment is that many individuals at *all levels* are responsible for achieving success.

- Voluntarism is important in both network formation and team effectiveness as well as garnering ´buy in´ from team members.
- Team management and systems must ensure dialectical dialog and action learning occurs in parallel in order to capture and strengthen knowledge transfer, creating a positive embedding context for organizational innovation and 'buy in' to decision-making as well as product or services development and thereby also to improved regional knowledge structures as discussed above.
- Lack of equitable incentives and rewards for all collaborators is a barrier to network and team development and restricts knowledge sharing and knowledge building
- Team and network rewards may not always be financial or status symbols, rewards could be a range of more diverse emotional gains derived from inclusion, interesting work, shared workload, sense of civic or professional pride, ¨engaged fellowship¨, for instance.
- No transparency and candor in communication about problems as well as successes will hamper collaboration and dilute trust in teams and networks,
- Insufficient employee input and utilization restricts efficacy of networking actions though too much may also cause ¨paralysis by analysis¨ type of procrastination issues.
- Limitations in effective allocation of resources allied to ineffective technology, legacy systems, bureaucratic processes and procedures also limit agility and responsiveness
- Trust is a valuable element in building collaboration at all levels in networks and in organizations and teams though often much diluted in networks compared to teams, so network managers and sponsors must focus on building trust and 'trustworthiness' in managers and leaders as well as capability and will to complete or follow through without neglecting dialectical dialog.
- Top down corporate direction rather than the informal social, professional or technical linkages autonomously developed between peers may be less effective overall without significant HR input to networks and to teams as above (Bakker, et al., 2006).

REFERENCES

Akcigit, U. (2009). *Firm Size, Innovation Dynamics and Growth. In 2009 Meeting Papers (No. 1267).* Society for Economic Dynamics.

Baciu, A. (2016). *Artificial intelligence is more artificial than intelligent.* Retrieved November 12, 2018 at https://www.wired.com/2016/12/artificial-intelligence-artificial-intelligent/

Bakker, M., Leenders, R. T. A. J., Gabbay, S. M., Kratzer, J., & Van Engelen, J. M. L. (2006). Is trust really social capital? Knowledge sharing in product development projects. *The Learning Organization, 13*(6), 594–605. doi:10.1108/09696470610705479

Barton, C., Fromm, J., & Egan, C. (2012). *The millennial consumer-debunking stereotypes.* BCG.

Belderbos, R., & Somers, D. (2015). Do Technology Leaders Deter Inward R&D Investments? Evidence from regional R & D location Decisions in Europe.2015-02. Regional Studies.

Bilandzic, A. (2018). Social and Spatial Precursors to Innovation: The Diversity Advantage of the Creative Fringe. *The Journal of Community Informatics, 14*(1). Retrieved from http://ci-journal.org/index.php/ciej/article/view/1455

Bogliacino, F., Piva, M., & Vivarelli, M. (2012). R&D and Employment: An application of the LSDVC Estimator using European Microdata. *Economics Letters, 116*(1), 56–59. doi:10.1016/j.econlet.2012.01.010

Bourdieu, P. (1990). *In other Words: Essays Towards a Reflexive Sociology*. Stanford, CA: Stanford University Press.

Bourdieu. (1987). *In Other Words: Essays toward a Reflective Sociology*. Stanford.

Carayannis, E. G., & Campbell, D. F. J. (2009). 'Mode 3' and 'Quadruple Helix': Toward a 21st century fractal innovation ecosystem. *International Journal of Technology Management, 46*(3/4), 201–234. doi:10.1504/IJTM.2009.023374

Cincera, M., & Veugelers, R. (2012). Young leading innovators and the EU's R&D intensity gap. *Economics of Innovation and New Technology*, 1-22.

Ciriaci, D., Moncada-Paternò-Castello, P., & Voigt, P. (2013). *Innovation and Employment: A sustainable relation?* IPTS Working Papers on Corporate R&D and Innovation series - European Commission – No. 01/2013 – EUR 25807 EN.

Coad, A., & Hölzl, W. (2010). *Firm growth: empirical analysis* (No. 1002). Papers on economics and evolution.

Coakes, E., Smith, P. A. C., & Alwiss, D. (2011). Sustainable innovation and right to market. *Information Systems Management, 28*(1), 30–42. doi:10.1080/10580530.2011.536110

Cockburn, T. (2005). Communities of Commitment: Leadership, Learning Spirals, Teamwork and Emotional Regimes on an MBA, 1997-1999. Available from ProQuest and from thc library of the University of Wales, Cardiff, UK.

Cockburn, T. (2006). *A complexity-based typology of emotional regimes in teams*. ITPNZ conference – Research that Counts, Napier, New Zealand.

Cockburn, T. (2010). Employee Commitment and the development of Corruption: A Case Study. In A. Stachowicz-Stanusch (Ed.), *Organizational Immunity to Corruption: Building Theoretical and Research Foundations*. Warsaw: Polish Academy of Sciences.

Cockburn, T., Jahdi, K., & Wilson, E. (Eds.). (2015). *Responsible governance: International perspectives for the new era*. New York, NY: Business Expert Press.

Cockburn, T., Jahdi, K. S., & Wilson, E. (2012). Ethical capital and the culture of integrity: 3 cases in UK and NZ. In W. Amann & A. Stachowicz-Stanusch (Eds.), *Business Integrity in Practice – insights from international case Studies*. New York, NY: Business Expert Press.

Cockburn, T., & Smith, P. A. C. (2018). Vuca and the Power of Emergence Teams. In D. Dalcher (Ed.), *The Evolution of Project Management Practice*. Routledge.

Cockburn, T., Smith, P. A. C., Martins, B., & Valles, R. S. (2016). Conflict of interest or Community of collaboration? Leadership, Dialectics and Dialog issues in community renewal and SME collaboration process. In A. Normore, L. Long, & M. Javidi (Eds.), *Handbook of Effective Communication, Leadership and Conflict Resolution*. IGI Global. doi:10.4018/978-1-4666-9970-0.ch012

Crossan, M. M., Lane, R. E., & White, R. E. (1999). An organizational learning framework: From intuition to institution. *Academy of Management Review*, *24*(3), 522–537. doi:10.5465/amr.1999.2202135

Czarnitzki, D., & Delanote, J. (2013). Young innovative companies: The new high-growth firms? *Industrial and Corporate Change*, *22*(5), 1315–1340. doi:10.1093/icc/dts039

Deloitte plc. (2017). *Technology Industry Outlook 2017 In-depth insight on growth opportunities and challenges in technology*. Retrieved from https://www2.deloitte.com/tr/en/pages/technology-media-and-telecommunications/ articles/ technology-industry-outlook-2017.html

Dishman, L. (2017). *This is the State of Small Business Failure in the US*. Retrieved November 11th,2018 from https://www.fastcompany.com/40435072/this-is-the-state-of-small-business-failure-in-the-u-s

Gibbons, M., Limoges, C., Nowotny, H., Schwartzman, S., Scott, P., & Trow, M. (1994). *The New production of Knowledge-The dynamics of science and research in contemporary societies*. London: Sage.

Glynn, M. A. (1996). Innovative genius: A framework for relating individual and organizational intelligences to innovation. *Academy of Management Review*, *21*(4), 1081–1111. doi:10.5465/amr.1996.9704071864

Granovetter, M., & McGuire, P. (1998). The Making of an Industry: Electricity in the United States. In M. Callon (Ed.), *The Laws of the Markets* (pp. 147–173). Blackwell. doi:10.1111/j.1467-954X.1998.tb03473.x

Gratch, J., Wang, N., Gerten, J., Fast, E., & Duff, R. (2007). Creating Rapport with Virtual Agents. *International Conference on Intelligent Virtual Agents*, Paris, France. 10.1007/978-3-540-74997-4_12

Gratton, L., & Truss, C. (2003). The three-dimensional people strategy: Putting human resources policies into action. *The Academy of Management Executive*, *17*(3), 74–86.

Håkansson, H. (1987). Product development in networks. In H. Håkansson (Ed.), *Technological development: A network approach* (pp. 84–128). New York: Croom Helm.

Hardy, C., & Phillips, N. (1998). Strategies of Engagement: Lessons from the Critical Examination of Collaboration and Conflict in an Interorganizational Domain. *Organization Science*, *9*(2), 217–230. doi:10.1287/orsc.9.2.217

Hargadon, A. (2003). *How Breakthroughs Happen*. Boston, MA: Harvard Business School Press.

Hearn, S., & White, N. (2009). *Communitites of Practice:Linking, knowledge.policy and practice*. London: Overseas Development Institute.

Hofstede, G. (2001). *Culture's Consequences: comparing values, behaviors, institutions, and organizations across nations* (2nd ed.). Thousand Oaks, CA: Sage.

Hogan, R. (2002). What is Personality? *Advantage Hiring Newsletter.* Retrieved on November 2015 at http:// www. Advantagehiring.com/newsletter/1100/n1100_2.htm

Kasper-Fuehrer, E. C., & Ashkanasy, N. M. (2001). Communicating trustworthiness and building trust in interorganisational virtual organization. *Journal of Management*, *27*(3), 235–254. doi:10.1016/S0149-2063(01)00090-3

Kodama, M. (2005). New knowledge creation through dialectical leadership: A case of IT and multimedia business in Japan. *European Journal of Innovation Management*, *8*(1), 31–55. doi:10.1108/14601060510578565

Kostopoulos, K. C., Spanos, Y. E., & Prastacos, G. P. (2013). Structure and Function of Team Learning Emergence: A Multilevel Empirical Validation. *Journal of Management*, *39*(6), 1430–1461. doi:10.1177/0149206311419366

Koudal, P., & Coleman, G. C. (2005). coordinating operations to enhance innovation in the global corporation. *Strategy and Leadership*, *33*(4), 20–32. doi:10.1108/10878570510608013

Lawrence, K. (2013). *Developing Leaders in a VUCA environment*. UNC-Kenan-Flagler Business School whitepaper.

Leonard-Barton, D., & Sensiper, S. (1998). The role of tacit knowledge in group innovation. *California Management Review*, *40*(3), 112–132. doi:10.2307/41165946

Levi, D. (2011). *Group Dynamics for Teams*. Thousand Oaks, CA: Sage.

Lundvall, B.-Å. (1992). *National Systems of Innovation: Towards a Theory of Innovation and Interactive Learning*. London: Pinter.

Meyerson, D., Weick, K. E., & Kramer, R. M. (1996). Swift Trust and Temporary Groups. In Trust in Organizations. Sage.

Moncada-Paternò-Castello, P. (2011). The growth of companies in the EU: the case for a more sophisticated research and innovation policy. IPTS Policy Briefs series – November 2011.

Moncada-Paternò-Castello, P., Ciupagea, C., Smith, K., Tübke, A., & Tubbs, M. (2010, April). Does Europe perform too little corporate R&D? A comparison of EU and non-EU corporate R&D performance. *Research Policy*, *39*(4), 523–536. doi:10.1016/j.respol.2010.02.012

Moncada-Paternò-Castello, P., & Voigt, P. (2013). *The effect of innovative SMEs' growth to the structural renewal of the EU economy-a projection to 2020*. Academic Press.

Morton, J., & Alireza, A. (2018). *Open strategy intermediaries? a framework for understanding the role of facilitators in open strategy-making*. Paper presented at Twenty-Sixth European Conference on Information Systems (ECIS2018), Portsmouth, UK.

Moulaert, F., & Nussbaumer, J. (2005). Beyond the Learning Region: The Dialectics of Innovation and Culture in Territorial Development. In R. A. Boschma & R. C. Kloosterman (Eds.), *Learning from Clusters: A Critical Assessment* (pp. 89–109). Springer. doi:10.1007/1-4020-3679-5_5

Nonaka, I. (1995). *The Knowledge-Creating Company*. Paper delivered at Theseus Institute, Conference on The Emergent Corporation, Sophia Antipolis, France.

Nonaka, I. (1994). A Dynamic Theory of Organizational Knowledge Creation. *Organization Science, 5*(1).

Nonaka, I., & Teece, D. (Eds.). (2001). *Managing Industrial Knowledge*. London: Sage.

Ortega-Argilés, R., & Brandsma, A. (2010). EU-US differences in the size of R&D intensive firms: Do they explain the overall R&D intensity gap? *Science & Public Policy*, *37*(6), 429–441. doi:10.3152/030234210X508633

Priest, H., Stagl, K., Klein, C., & Salas, E. (2006). Virtual teams: Creating context for distributed teamwork. In C. Bowers, E. Salas, & F. Jentsch (Eds.), *Creating high-tech teams* (pp. 185–211). Washington, DC: American Psychological Association. doi:10.1037/11263-009

Ready, K. (2013). *In Search of Japan's Missing Startups*. Retrieved October 2017 at https:// www.forbes.com/sites/kevinready/2013/05/17/in-search-of-japans-missing-startups/#709c868b6f06

Rickards, T. (2000). Creativity and the management of change. *Australian Journal of Communication*, *27*(3), 163–164.

Rousseau, D. (2004). Psychological Contracts in the Workplace: Understanding the Ties That Motivate. *Academy of Management Executive, 18*(1), 120-127.

Rousseau, D. M. (1995). *Psychological Contracts in Organizations: Understanding Written and Unwritten Agreements*. Sage.

Sandbank, T., Schmueli-scheueur, M., Konopnicki, D., Herzig, J., Richards, J., & Piorkowski, D. (2017), *Detecting Egregious Conversations between Customers and Virtual Agents.* ArXiv: 1711:05780v1

Sauner-Leroy, J. B. (2004). Managers and productive investment decisions: The impact of uncertainty and risk aversion. *Journal of Small Business Management*, *42*(1), 1–18. doi:10.1111/j.1540-627X.2004.00094.x

Scheel, C. (2007). Why the Latin American region has not succeeded in building world-class industrial clusters. In *KGCM proceedings*. Winter Garden, FL: International Institute of Informatics and Systems.

Schumpeter, J. A. (1942). Capitalism, Socialism and Democracy. Harper & Brothers.

Senge, P. (1990). *The Fifth Discipline: The Art and practice of the Learning organization*. New York: Doubleday.

Senge, P. (n.d.). Transforming the Practice of Managemen. *HRD Quarterly, 4*(1), 5-32.

Simpson, M., Cockburn-Wootten, C., & Cockburn, T. (2005). Resistance; the unexpected consequences of implementing change. In *International Conference on Case Study teaching and learning*. University of Auckland.

Smith, P., & Cockburn, T. (2013). *Dynamic Leadership Models for Global Business: Enhancing Digitally Connected Environments*. IGI Global. doi:10.4018/978-1-4666-2836-6

Smith, P., & Cockburn, T. (Eds.). (2014). *Impact of Emerging Digital Technologies on Leadership in Global Business*. IGI Global. doi:10.4018/978-1-4666-6134-9

Snowden, D. J. (2012). Retrieved June 6, 2012, from http://en.wikipedia.org/wiki/Dave_Snowden

Stacey, R. D. (2001). *Complex Responsive Processes in Organizations*. London: Routledge.

Tidd, J. (2001). Innovation management in context: Environment, organization and performance. *International Journal of Management Reviews*, *3*(3), 169–183. doi:10.1111/1468-2370.00062

Veliz, C. (2018). *Common Sense for A.I. Is a Great Idea But it's harder than it sounds.* Retrieved on 12th November 2018 at https://slate.com/technology/2018/03/paul-allens-plan-to-teach-artificial-intelligence-common-sense.html

Von Hippel, E. (1988). *The Sources of Innovation.* New York: Oxford University Press.

WEF. (2015). *Collaborative Innovation Transforming Business, Driving Growth.* Geneva: World Economic Forum.

Wenger, E. (1998). *Communities of Practice: Learning, Meaning, and Identity.* Cambridge, UK: Cambridge University Press. doi:10.1017/CBO9780511803932

Wilkinson, A., Dundon, T., & Grugulis, I. (2007). Information but not consultation: Exploring employee involvement in SMEs. *International Journal of Human Resource Management, 18*(7), 1279–1297. doi:10.1080/09585190701393798

Wisdom, J., Chor, K., Hoagwood, K., & Howitz, S. (2014). *Innovation Adoption: A Review of Theories and Constructs, Adm policy Ment Health.* Springer.

KEY TERMS AND DEFINITIONS

Action Learning: A form of learning by using "learning sets" composed of problem-holders who assist each other to work on issues faced by each party.

Dialectical-Dialog: Refers to a concept by Kodama whereby networks seek rational balance between challenge and collaboration enabling constructively-critical evaluation of and "sensemaking" about options with the purpose of getting the best way forward that gets buy in from all parties.

Dialectics: Conflicts between proponents of opposing views which may eventuate in a communication breakdown or in a new synthesis and understanding between parties.

Dialog: A collaborative discussion where parties seek a consensus.

Emotional Regime: Emerge from complex, interweave of trust, anxiety, culture, and behaviors embodied in the team´s achievement of its strategic objectives. Further, they are founded upon and foster tacit knowledge and immanent collective team personas that evolve as they try to enact their project tasks and these.

Sensemaking: Concerns ways that team participants understand and "make sense" of their circumstances and options.

SME: Defined as a small to medium enterprise. Networks or clusters are interconnected, collaborating collectives composed of SMEs, advisors, government or funding body representatives, and relevant others such as researchers.

VUCA: Volatile uncertain complex ambiguous refers to highly turbulent and dynamically complex contexts within teams, organizations and between them and their environment.

APPENDIX: STUDY QUESTIONS

Table 1c. Overall learning performance

OVERALL PERFORMANCE			
	Expected	Current	Gap
OBSERVED EMOTIONAL REGIMES (based on emotional regime typology provided above)	*Responsible Professionals or Trusty Followers*	*Suspicious mercenaries*	-6%
TRAINING & ASSISTANCE	*Graduated but high*	*average*	-10%
RESOURCES & PROCESSES	*Mostly high*	*average*	-9%
Expected and Current ratings			Trust issues
1. Very low (0-20%)			TNA review needed
2. Low (21-40%)		Gap scores	Resource disputes
3. Medium (41-60%)		**Priority area**	Compensation review & Systems upgrade
4. High (61-80%)			Transactional psychological contracts and expected tradeoffs need more focus and detailed attention
5. Very high (81-100%)			

In teams, there are many emotional regimes as discussed above. These emotional regimes impact aspects of teamwork involving issues of trust, commitment and performance anxiety and are evident in the team´s development and in the emergent ´´ team persona¨ (Cockburn, 2005, 2006, 2008). These factors crucially impact upon the ways that projects are carried out and in their success rate, especially within VUCA environments (Smith and Cockburn, 2016). When teams are part of larger systems there is a further complex set of amplifying or dampening feedback and feedforward loops operating across the hierarchy of the organization and the strategic deployment both how that is envisaged by leaders as well as how it is practically implemented. The story that emerges in practice may not be exactly match the one propounded officially unless leaders build a culture of integrity and openness which promotes an empowering, consensus-building process in projects and teams (Smith and Cockburn, 2016, p. 63, pp.152-154). A Triple Impact Evaluation of emotional regimes in teams requires answers to the following set of key questions:

Table 2c. Overall learning performance

OVERALL PERFORMANCE			
	ALL		
	Expected	Current	Gap
OBSERVED EMOTIONAL REGIMES (Based upon emotional regimes typology provided above)	*Responsible Professionals*	*Suspicious mercenaries*	-9.06
TRAINING & ASSISTANCE	*high*	*average*	-1.91
RESOURCES & PROCESSES	*high*	*average*	-16.72
Expected and Current ratings			
1. Very low (0-20%)			Aspects relating to trust and transactional mindsets need work to shift towards relational psychological contracts
2. Low (21-40%)		Gap scores	More resources needed in staff induction to begin transition to new role requirements
3. Medium (41-60%)		**Priority area**	Staff engagement is not as high as it needs to be according to recent staff surveys.
4. High (61-80%)			System tweaks and app development
5. Very high (81-100%)			

1. Is there a latent or manifest emotional expression of positive or negative value within the frames of reference for the current team?
2. Does it elevate or diminish personal or collective power and influence?
3. What is the legitimate team member response in this context?

Overall, in networks there is movement through the life-cycle in bottom-up clusters which seems wave-like: with new projects, coming on line to provide fresh insights informed by, and capitalizing on the achievements (and problems discovered) of previous projects. However, successful progression depends, crucially, upon being able to set the cluster development process in a reflective frame. Failing to achieve that will mean that the wave-like development process will cycle between the initial stages of 'learning the ropes' and ¨projectism´, where project teams continue consuming increasing amounts of resources and undermining the entire teams´ motivation. Trapped in this cycle, a growing series of separate projects (most likely with local success) may be implemented, so long as additional funds can be found, but

Table 3c. Overall learning performance

OVERALL PERFORMANCE			
	ALL		
	Expected	Current	Gap
OBSERVED EMOTIONAL REGIMES(Based upon emotional regimes typology provided above)	*Responsible Professionals*	*Suspicious mercenaries*	-12.06
TRAINING & ASSISTANCE	*high*	*average*	-10.92
RESOURCES & PROCESSES	*high*	*average*	-1.71
Expected and Current ratings			Retraining for virtual interaction with clients and other medical professionals
1. Very low (0-20%)			Telemarketing training for dealing with doctors and patient referrals as well as social services referrals
2. Low (21-40%)		Gap scores	
3. Medium (41-60%)		**Priority area**	
4. High (61-80%)			
5. Very high (81-100%)			

rarely would the cluster emerge, and network management capacity be enhanced, thus there would be no regional impact or only minor impact on the territory. How might that reflexivity scaffolding be applied in a team context? Within a single project or in an ongoing multiple organizational change context? What kinds of emotional regimes would be most useful and how might the other two be turned around to build trust and greater effectiveness? High or low trust and anxiety? What types of psychological contracts may be engendered and how might these impact on the 4 main emotional regimes?

Recent emphasis of EU programs on the creation of emergent industries as a way to reduce Europe's innovation and competitiveness gap with the US and boost growth and employment, has turned the attention to clusters as supportive mechanisms to unlock innovation potential of SMEs on a large scale, promoting the smart use of resources. Under which circumstances clusters would be able to play such role, and how? What should this 'supportive' role be and what it may encompass? Should the cluster incorporate some form of mentoring between S.M.Es and MNCs? If so what sorts of safeguards should be applied, e.g. to protect Intellectual property in the smaller of the two businesses particularly?

Given that assumption,

- What type of methodologies and tools, and roles, are assumed to support the development and leverage teams´ and clusters/networks' generative dynamics towards innovation, growth and/ renewal?

- The aforementioned examples suggest there might be a networking or collaboration readiness level in the individual SME, that pre-exists the bottom-up clustering efforts. Assessing such latent level may draw the line of distinction between both the cluster's failure and success, also both team and cluster life-cycles.
- How is the latent collaborative urge or readiness level defined? What are the elements of the business environment that are most likely to influence it? (Consider the SME, team and the cluster action domains)
- How does the cluster /network organization help other partner companies achieve their business strategies and objectives?
- Given that about two-thirds of European clusters are essentially top-down, how can bottom-up initiatives be integrated into top-down managed clusters to make clusters *and* clustered SMEs more agile and resilient learning communities? Where in the life-cycle would these interventions have the highest impact?

Chapter 5
MAGNUS Leadership:
Using Principled Negotiation to Improve International Negotiation

Alexander Javidi
National Command and Staff College, USA

Larry Long
Illinois State University, USA

Mitch Javidi
National Command and Staff College, USA

Brooks Hill
Trinity University, USA

Anthony Normore
California State University – Dominguez Hills, USA & National Command and Staff College, USA

James Klopovic
Credible Leadership Organization, USA

ABSTRACT

The primary purpose of this chapter is to examine how leadership connects to principled and international negotiation. International negotiation is conceptualized with an in-depth description of the process followed by a description of negotiation styles. A corollary purpose is to extend the discussion of negotiation by introducing and defining MAGNUS leadership and how it can translate into negotiation. The authors offer a few practical tips for beginning the journey of becoming MAGNUS. Recommendation for international MAGNUS negotiators are offered.

DOI: 10.4018/978-1-5225-8516-9.ch005

INTRODUCTION

In 1994, "Principled Negotiation" (Hill, Long, & Javidi, 1994) was proposed as an approach to peaceful international negotiation and conflict management. Two decades ago, the authors noted that:

The increasing interdependence among peoples and nations is a double-edged sword: on the one hand, it compels attention to differences and thus fosters conflict; on the other hand, it provides a wonderful prospect for development of the ability to resolve our differences and conflicts. Despite the promising opportunities presented by this interdependence and an amazing technology the world is a boiling cauldron of conflicts which threaten harmony and the social fabric of many nations and regions of the world. Instead of using the available potential constructively, people are so blinded by self-interest that they engage in destructive actions which sacrifice mutual development. Unfortunately, these episodes are common throughout the world. (Hill, Long, & Javidi, 1994, p. 194)

Although this observation was made in the 1990's, there is evidence that these circumstances still exist and will continue in the foreseeable future. Projections for the years 2010 to 2030 suggest that leading nations, such as G-20 (the 20 major world economies), will not develop and implement appropriate policies to manage international weapons proliferation, deal with increasingly bitter socio-economic divisions, and adjust global environmental constraints (Rogers, 2004). These circumstances underscore the importance of leadership to effectively use negotiation as a key tool for international conflict management now and for the future (Creede, Fisher-Yoshida, & Gallegos, 2012; Hackman & Johnson, 2013; Normore & Erbe, 2013). Recent negotiations (August, 2015) to avoid escalation of military conflict between North and South Korea are a case in point. Furthermore, conflict projections for the future provide justification for revisiting and expanding the concept of "principled negotiation" to include elements of leadership and credibility.

In the latter portion of the Twentieth Century, experts studied the international negotiation process from diverse viewpoints. Much of this was likely motivated by the peace imperative or concern as to whether or not persons with diverse backgrounds (to include gender, age, ethnicity, ideology, geography, religion, language, etc.) can coexist peacefully (Martin & Nakayama, 2008). Clearly, many scholars have been motivated with the hope that people might settle disputes peacefully (Paupp, 2014; Pruitt & Kim, 2004). This body of literature draws heavily upon communication, education, psychology, sociology, political science, management, and other disciplines to discover and create concepts, principles, and best practices that will lead to effective negotiation outcomes (e.g., see Lewicki, Saunders, & Barry, 2006 & 2015; Watkins, 2002; Kolb & Williams, 2003). Regardless of scholarly orientation, no one can contest the centrality of communication in local, national, and international negotiation arenas (Oetzel & Ting-Toomey, 2013).

During the past two decades, scholars and negotiation experts have given more attention to the role of communication, in which credibility plays an important role, as fundamental in the negotiation process. For example, one of the most widely used books about negotiation is Lewicki, Saunders, and Barry's *Negotiation* (2006, 5th Ed. & and 2015, 7th Ed.). For several years and across different editions, the authors have devoted an entire chapter to communication, referring to it as one of the four main negotiation subprocesses (other subprocesses include perception/cognition/emotion, power, and influence). While basically an introductory overview of the communication process, inclusion of the chapter was important recognition of the critical role played by communication during negotiations. In their chapter about influence, Lewicki, et al discuss the impact and importance of source credibility. They provide a three-page discussion of the credibility construct (Lewicki, Saunders, Barry, 2006, pp. 215-218), noting how it directly influences the perception of whether or not a negotiator's messages are believed and the consequence for negotiation outcomes. As a result, communication and credibility have become recognized as essentials of negotiation.

Interestingly, however, negotiation process descriptions rarely recognize the negotiator as a leader. Yet, a review of the published negotiation literature will yield numerous research articles and books elaborating on concepts like leading and managing, power, influence, relationships, teams, interpersonal trust, conflict management, problem solving, managing crises, etc., (Kriesberg, 1998; Pearce & Pearce, 2000). These concepts are also deeply rooted in communication and leadership literature (Bryman, 2013). Leadership and negotiation are often spoken of and written about together, yet infrequently integrated except in a very general way (Hackman & Johnson, 2013). Often, it is assumed that good leaders are good negotiators and are normally effective in "getting their way" and effective at persuasion. This chapter's depiction of international negotiation (see Figure 1) places the negotiator in the prominent role of leader, recognizing the inherent processes of that role, including perceptions of credibility, add significantly to the nature of negotiation outcomes (Watkins, 2002).

While international and intercultural negotiation complexity demands insight from many perspectives, a pragmatic communication and credible leadership perspective guides us more directly to useful negotiation guidelines. Consequently, this chapter will elaborate the sometime neglected dimensions of leadership, credibility, and intercultural communication (see Erbe, 2011; Normore & Erbe, 2013) as applied to the negotiation process. Specifically, the last part of this chapter will offer a communication perspective based upon principled negotiation and credible negotiation leadership.

As was the case when "principled negotiation" was introduced two decades ago, one troublesome use of words needs to be mentioned. The term "international" will be used in such a way as to include "intercultural," even though situation may exist when international negotiation could occur between two or more people of the same culture; nations and cultures typically do not coincide, although instances to the contrary may be found.

The first section of this chapter highlights international negotiation complexities as it defines, provides a model, and analyzes/explains component parts of this process. Notably, this model has been modified with inclusion of the concepts of leadership and credibility. Within this conceptual framework, a general review of negotiation styles lays the groundwork for credible negotiation leadership which is couched in principled negotiation. A final section examines potential application of this position about international negotiation in order to achieve greater intercultural effectiveness.

Definition of International Negotiation

International negotiation is a communication function of international relations that is used for the purpose of mutual adaptation in order to' accomplish specific goals. This definition has several implications: First, international negotiation occurs when two or more persons from different nations (usually possessing different world views, cultures and representing different self-interests) lead (through communication) in order to achieve a particular outcome or goal. Since participants "represent" a position, the presumption of a vested interest supporting the position being represented by the negotiator normally exists. Also, the potential for misinterpretation and misattribution is much greater than in those circumstances where negotiators share a similar culture, experience/s, and psychological frame-of-reference.

Second, this definition emphasizes mutual adjustment through communication between or among negotiators. Mutual adjustment is a two-way process in which all parties participate. When mutual adjustment is absent, negotiation actually does not exist. Rather, the relationship is one-way, based upon taking or winning at the other's expense. When, for example, a country uses its power to impose predetermined outcomes, the negotiation becomes a sham, differences are only temporarily displaced, and they are likely to resurface later.

Third, goal attainment for all participants is the assumed outcome of negotiation. This does not imply that all parties realize complete gains without experiencing concessions. However, the process begins with the assumption that both parties can experience satisfying, productive outcomes that outweigh losses. If not, the negotiation process is compromised and relations between the groups represented may deteriorate.

Contrary to self-serving conceptions of international negotiations, the credible negotiation leadership presumes that effective negotiations, like effective communication, entail mutual achievement and relational development, rather than short-term winning or losing. This approach requires objective focus on the goals of all parties, development of trust, complete collaboration, and emphasis on mutually beneficial outcomes (Austin, 2010).

Components of International Negotiation: World Environment

The twenty-first century provides the international negotiator with new challenges in realizing long-term stability and peace while contributing to the world economy and enhancing the standard of living for all mankind. The past century has contained incomparable wars, devastation of resources, and the consequences of technology; the current century is dealing with that aftermath, particularly those challenges listed earlier by Rogers (2005) and his prognostications for 2010 through 2030. Despite the challenges, when leadership and credibility concepts are combined into the international negotiation model there is additional knowledge to aid the prospects for peace, improving the global environment, and economic growth (Paupp, 2014). Thus, the current model provides a more in-depth analysis and synthesis of negotiating.

No longer can negotiators perceive their actions to be narrowly focused on the issues at hand. Actions taken in one specific instance may directly affect people in many other parts of the world. The fluctuations in the world-wide stock markets during the latter part of August 2015 are testimony supporting that contention. Consider also, the process of trade talks between nations and their indigenous industries. In nearly every instance of negotiation about products and the policies regarding their manufacture and distribution will concern other nations. For example, if China opens its markets to allow a given technology more opportunity, how will this action affect other producers of a similar technology in other parts of the world? If, for example, the USA tightens its restrictions on importation of automobile parts, then how might the Japanese or Koreans' response affect its production facilities in other countries? On an even broader scale, what are the possible ramifications of the policies of other nations, which place tight control on economic relations because of human rights violations and past relations? The world environment contains all acts of negotiations between and among nations, and the environment and negotiation outcomes mutually influence each other.

Components: Contextual Subsystem

The model classifies five dimensions of the immediate context (derived from Hazelton & Long, 1988) which impact on the negotiators and their negotiations. The model includes et cetera which suggests the need to be alert for unforeseen influences. Each of the dimensions is explained and illustrated.

Cultural Dimension

Culture is the behaviors and underlying values, motives, beliefs, knowledge, meanings, ethics, patterns of interaction, etc., that identify a specific "cultural" group and also differentiates it from other cultures. Culture may be related to physical appearance, the way a person dresses, and the manner in which a person communicates. But culture is more than observable characteristics. It contains the underlying values, motives, beliefs, and ethics that stimulate a negotiator's behavior. Culture provides the negotiator with a dominant frame-of-reference that influences the nature and evolution of the negotiator's relationships and communication (Oetzel & Ting-Toomey, 2013). For example, cultures vary in emphasizing the self or the group. When developing a relationship with members of Western societies, it is most effective to stimulate the Westerner's self-interest and encourage participation. In contrast, Eastern cultures emphasize the group and social identity. Thus, it is more effective to develop congenial social relations and focus on relationship, rather than self-interest. Consequently, understanding culture provides the initial template for negotiators to use in developing international relations (Pearce, 2007).

Social Dimension

Growing out of the cultural dimension, social values, norms, rules, and roles are one of the greatest sources of influence on human behavior. Culture and cultural influence as learned phenomena has long assumed a role of importance in understanding human communication. Consequently, an understanding the social environment is a necessary precondition to effective international negotiation because rules of appropriate "social" conduct largely determine communication strategies and tactics that should or should not be used. The social dimension also contains significant individuals and groups, who often serve to lead and influence negotiations more strongly, such as consumers, suppliers, opinion leaders, government, or any group that possesses the potential to influence other dimensions (Pearce, 2007).

Political/Legal Dimension

International treaties and law set limits for negotiation; they constrain behavior and often designate the extent to which concessions can be made. Essentially, the political/legal dimension is comprised of formal rules which govern organizational, governmental, national conduct. It also operationalizes methods for creating rules and methods for rule enforcement. Understanding the political/legal dimension requires consideration of any electoral or position appointment practices, executive or administrative influence, and adjudication processes. Since international agreements are often vague, there is opportunity for self-serving negotiators to insinuate their best interests, skillfully rationalized in terms of the treaties or agreements. Resolution of these conflicts requires consideration of the reason(s) the agreements were originally made, along with the laws and principles of the nations/organizations negotiating.

Technological Dimension

The technological dimension highlights a concern for methods and tools used to accomplish tasks; for purposes of this chapter, this dimension emphasizes transportation and communication/information technologies. A technological innovation spreads quickly as other nations attempt to duplicate or to acquire rights to use it themselves. The transportation and information revolutions have made isolationist doctrines impractical for any nation. Physical proximity to another culture is, at most, 24 hours away. Information transfer across the globe is instantaneous. However, instantaneous information transfer can mean instant communication or miscommunication. Thus, international relations are inevitable and must be effectively managed. The technological development represented by a negotiator sets limits to the amount and type of available resources during negotiation. Likewise, technology may indirectly impact on negotiations through other dimensions. For example, the presence or absence of computer technology and internet access, medical technology, sophisticated robotic systems, etc., will influence social and economic conditions for a nation or culture.

Economic/Competitive Dimension

Social and technological influences have stimulated economic conditions and created international competitive situations. These have, in turn, influenced and have been influenced by political and legal realities. Adoption of North American Free Trade Agreement (NAFTA) by the United States in 1994 is a case in point. NAFTA had both positive and negative effects, with modest positive economic benefit for Mexico, the United States, and Canada; on the other hand, many Canadian companies were taken over by citizens of other countries, corn prices in Mexico fell while internal demand exceeded supply, and in the United States organized labor blamed the agreement for sending 700,000 jobs from the U.S. to Mexico. Clearly, global changes in patterns of competition and economic relations cannot be ignored. The competitive aspects of this dimension consist of all individuals, groups, organizations, nations, or entities who possess goals that may stimulate competition for resources, markets or alliances. Government trade agreements, for example, with respect to electronic technologies were the result of intense competition for international consumer market share and have been invoked to reduce negative aspects of the intense competition. Many international negotiation situations occur among businesses and governments because of economic competition and pressures for market expansion (Ahmad, Francis, & Zairi, 2007; Erbe, 2011). The economic aspects of this dimension influence the availability of resources. In particular, the economic environment directly defines the nature and extent of financial resources which influences the cost of physical, human, and information resources.

Contextual Dimensions Applied

Cultural, social, political/legal, technological, and economic/competitive conditions define, constrain, and guide the use of resources available to negotiators – these contextual elements are inputs that influence negotiators. The negotiators' contextual frames-of-reference are reflected by symbols used to produce messages; messages influence the initiation, maintenance, and termination of negotiation relationships. Consequently, before any negotiation episode begins, application of this model requires that specific questions be answered about the party with which an individual may negotiate. Using the dimensions as a template, and incorporating credible leadership concepts, questions were generated for the Hill, Long, Javidi (1994) model:

- **Culture**
  - What are the dominant values, beliefs, and attitudes expressed by members of the culture?
  - How does language in this culture differ from mine?
  - How easy are translations of language and culture accomplished without loss or distortion of meaning?
  - How is the culture similar or different from mine?
  - How might differences affect the negotiation relationship?
  - How might differences affect perceptions of my credibility; perceptions of my trustworthiness and expertise?
- **Society**
  - What norms, rules, and expectations exist among members of the society?
  - How would members of this society define the negotiation role and what type of outcome would they accept?
  - How is the society similar or different from mine?
  - How might differences in the society affect the negotiation relationship?
  - What primary groups are influencing negotiator choices?
  - What is the society's preferred leadership negotiation style?
- **Political and Legal Processes**
  - What international treaties, laws, and agreements must be observed by members of the nation?
  - What laws and accepted principles for conducting negotiations are followed by members of the nation?
  - How are laws created, interpreted, and enforced among members of the nation?
  - How are political and legal processes in this nation similar or different from mine?
  - How might differences in political and legal processes influence outcomes?
- **Technology**
  - What level of consumer technological sophistication exists for this nation?
  - What level of technological development in transportation and information management exists in this nation?
  - Is technological development similar or different from mine?
  - How might differences in technological development affect the negotiation relationship?
- **Competitive and Economic Conditions**
  - What are the primary contributors to the economy of this nation?
  - How sound is this nation's economy? How volatile are its markets?
  - What competitive pressure does this nation face?
  - Are competitive and economic conditions of all parties compatible or are they incompatible?
  - How might differences in competitive and economic conditions affect the negotiation relationship?

Possessing answers to these and other implied questions allows each person the information necessary to overcome many barriers to successful negotiation outcomes. The next section will focus on MAGNUS leadership, how it relates to principled negotiation and offers a few practical tips for beginning the journey of becoming MAGNUS.

THE MAGNUS LEADER AS THE NEGOTIATOR

Becoming MAGNUS is a process of improving thinking, speaking, action and deeds through the gradual process of improving character. The most provocative part of becoming MAGNUS is by its process, the negotiator, family, work, community and life continually get better and the journey never ends. By becoming MAGNUS, the negotiator helps define and lead the next stage of negotiation evolution, epitomized by the enlightened leader who sets the example by leading with head and heart, with intellect and compassion.

Demands of negotiation require leaders who are not only technically competent, they must continually strive to be virtuous and thus contribute to the best of their ability to family, those around them, career and the community. The greats throughout history practiced and negotiated what they preached. Cicero became one of our greatest orators by life-long study and practice; Mashushi is Japan's greatest Samauri because he lived the Way; and, Benjamin Franklin became one of our most accomplished and revered Founding Fathers by acting on his 13 virtues as a young man and continuously throughout his lifetime. They all had the pursuit of virtue in common. All started humbly, and contributed to making the world a better place. Their enduring message is that everyone has the capacity to be better tomorrow than they are today and consequently improved their world. Essentially, "what matters most is what sort of person you are becoming, what sort of life you are living" (Epictetus, 1995, p. xiv). In terms of negotiation, the following tips are intended to help the negotiator as he/she finds MAGNUS leadership development.

Decide to Be Remarkable: Now

It has been said that a large part of success in life is just showing up. Further, show up ready and able to work and set the example of one guided by a sense of what is right and wrong. What we suggest is that we develop a noble, values-based character which then intuitively guides our every action. This is as simple as always doing the right thing. It is referred to as a moral compass which takes constant practice to get right. This is not a new idea; the ancients prove that it is better to live a life of moderation. This does not mean become a recluse; it means to live within your means and doing simple but meaningful things. Learn to enjoy a dinner with the family. Go to every school event with your children that you possibly can. Participate in making little improvements at work by first doing a lot of listening and moving deliberately to construct an improvement especially with the people who can help you make it happen.

We all have years, if not formative decades, of unproductive habits, counterproductive behaviors, and perhaps a few character flaws to overcome. You cannot change the world without first understanding yourself. Assess your strengths and weaknesses. What matters is that you act; negotiate and correct what can be corrected and polish the positive.

- **Observe**: Perceive what is really going on. Most times what you see is not what is really going on. The face you see on a call for service is but the beginning of what is going on with that person. The first expression of an idea to improve your working situation needs to be understood in the context of the people, processes and procedures required to get it done.
- **Listen**: Carefully listen to what people say; when you are quiet you can hear the nuances of what is being said. Many times, people really do not get to the heart of things unless they are asked the same question posed several different ways which brings them to the gem of information, perspective or bit of wisdom that needs just a little coaxing to reveal. Then you get to the root of a problem to correct.
- **Learn**: Continuously learn. If you are not a reader, pick up a book - right now. Surround yourself with books. A good book especially a classic, is the way to wisdom, better command of language and a lifetime of enjoyment. Never leave home without one. Experience something new, even push your limits a bit. Stretching outside our comfort level increases capability and ads to the quality of life.
- **Act**: In the end you must act. Start small but commit; do something to improve. Then immerse yourself in the process and the journey of becoming MAGNUS. As with all things, the more you practice the better you are at the task at hand.

A successful career is not a matter of a continuous campaign to promote yourself, which is unbelievably stressful. It is a matter of a thousand little things done well and perhaps a little better than you did them the last time. Living and negotiating virtuously is not a big thing; it is awareness of all the little noble things that can be done throughout the day. It is the difference between slogging through the day and feeling accomplished after a workday – It is the practice of simply being useful thus becoming remarkable, becoming MAGNUS. As indicated in Epictetus (1995), "The morally trained, rather than resenting or dodging their current life situation and duties, give thanks for them and fully immerse themselves in their duties to their family, friends, neighbors, and job" (p. 89).

MAGNUS negotiators all have the heart of a guardian. Becoming a MAGNUS negotiator allows us to discover that heart or rediscover it, if it should fade. Becoming MAGNUS opens the doors to opportunities, accomplishment and reward. There is nothing more important than the source of MAGNUS negotiators thoughts, their "Guardian Heart." The Guardian Heart of MAGNUS negotiators regulate the nature of their actions and leadership. In order to manifest The Guardian Heart of MAGNUS negotiators, we have to acknowledge how their virtues and actions impact their relationship with their communities. Thus, The Guardian Heart:

- Produces resilience
- Sources determination
- Incubates (I don't know if incubate is the right word???) courage
- Supports the Cardinal Virtues
- Enables creativity
- Provides passion for clear sense of purpose
- Feeds the pursuit for results

There Is More to the Negotiator Than Negotiating

Because negotiating is evolving it is not enough to just be good at the technicalities of negotiating - what matters is what you permanently build as an individual, *how you* go about it. You can build a good reputation. You can form a cohesive negotiating team. You can devise, negotiate, and lead a permanent solution to a community problem. What matters is that it is done by being guided by a firm sense of MAGNUS virtues. That is, there is more to negotiating than confronting issues and being proactive.

You Are Part of the Next Wave of Negotiation Evolution

This traveling the road of personal discovery and accomplishment which is becoming MAGNUS, helps us realize how great it is *being* MAGNUS. You are living in the age of a new renaissance. History will look back and say that our time is when man began the leap forward to create a better world. In what is little more than a lifetime we have come from the wisest people of the day declaring that it is impossible for man to fly, a waste of time they said, then the bicycle boys happened. We have gone from an expected life span of about 48 years to about 78 years in about the same time; many of you can expect to live to 100 and be vital and vigorous for that age. In that time, we have gone from horses to cars. We have blasted from the agricultural age, through the industrial age, and are sprinting through the information age into the molecular age. This galloping progress demands a new age of negotiation as reinvigorated guardians, keepers of safe, secure communities where families are stable, productive and happy. It is not an easy road, but remarkably rewarding.

Act as If You Will Be Remembered

By committing to the unique honor and privilege to service as negotiators, you are leading the new wave of negotiators in one of the greatest eras of governmental, civil and evolutionary progress. What will you do with this opportunity? How will you grow your Guardian Heart? How will you make a mark with family, art of negotiating, and your community? Will you approach the day with an eye to quitting time, counting the moments to retirement? Or, will you dig into the day and contribute to the wellbeing of all you touch? We are all so fortunate to be alive now in this remarkable, some say moment in history. MAGNUS asks: “Will you act as if you will be remembered?”

Becoming MAGNUS Is Real Work and Real Reward

Make no mistake you are the Vanguard of the next wave of negotiation evolution, the era of the self-aware negotiator who is a fundamental part of our historical experiment in governance and takes his or her part in it with commitment, intention and gusto. Your MAGNUS guide travels the road with you and fully understands that it is a much harder way to negotiate but necessary and remarkably rewarding. The DNA of the Guardian Heart holds the promise of strength, character realized in peace, kindness, goodness, faithfulness, gentleness, selflessness, commitment, harmony, compassion, safety and prosperity for negotiating, community and family. It is the guardian heart of MAGNUS negotiators that obligates them to live a virtuous life and reach an understanding of the various negotiation styles at their fingertips.

NEGOTIATION STYLES

In *Mindsets* (1988) Glenn Fisher defined international negotiation basically as a communication process across cultural boundaries (p. 4). Despite the apparent emphasis on communication, this book emphasized social psychological variables, but did not draw upon communication theory and research sufficiently to reinforce the emphasis reflected in the definition. These omissions by Fisher and other authors prompted development of the earlier international negotiation model, which was needed to integrate intercultural communication theory and research with practical experience. Except for Glenn Fisher's work, few have attempted to relate communication to international negotiation. The expansiveness of the topic, the closed doors of the negotiation process, and the almost proprietary nature of training and preparation in government and industry have, no doubt, contributed to this oversight.

Compared with relevant communication research, the literature about negotiation and conflict resolution is far more extensive (e.g., Kriesberg, 1998), but is narrowly focused in a distinctively western bias and characterized by the readily marketable jargon of trainers and quick-fix artists. Since research and too much of the literature merely "follow the dollar," this overview should come as no surprise. Among these marketable commodities, the substance which underlies the gimmickry sometimes surfaces. Such is the case in *Getting to Yes* by R. Fisher and W. Ury (1988). According to them, a negotiator's style of conflict management and decision-making influences negotiation outcomes. From this perspective, these authors examine outcomes of "soft" and "hard" negotiators. Intent to overcome weaknesses of each, they settle for an alternative style they call "principled negotiation." For Fisher and Ury, this seemed to provide an interesting vehicle capable of carrying far more weight than the authors may have anticipated.

Soft Negotiating Style

To Fisher and Ury a "soft" negotiator is one who emphasizes the importance of relational initiation and maintenance, while not caring too much about accomplishing the negotiation goals and purposes. These negotiators would approach the process by overly accommodating other peoples' goals and objectives. Buckholz, Lashbrook, and Wenburg (1976) described several social styles that emerged during conflict negotiations. One particular style was labeled as "amiable." This social style is indicative of "soft" negotiators. Amiable or "soft" negotiators are low in assertiveness, yet responsive. They are accommodative, seeking to satisfy the other party's concerns while neglecting their own needs and negotiation goals. The "soft" negotiator's philosophy is to avoid conflict use a non-confrontational style, and may even sacrifice productive outcomes in order to avoid confrontation. Consequently, a "soft" negotiator's communication behavior consists of a denial of the existence of differing positions. These negotiators actively deny the existence of conflict and direct conversation, often ambiguously, by shifting topics of discussion away from disagreement. This type of negotiator is most often agreeable and ingratiating. In addition, they may be conforming, unsure, dependable, awkward, supportive, respectful, and willing.

Since keeping other persons happy is an objective of the "soft" negotiator, this person is often characterized as being tentative in their communication behaviors. The "soft" negotiator will infrequently advocate a specific position on controversial issues; this person will tend to equivocate. As a consequence, this negotiator will produce messages that are ambiguous and difficult to understand. Comments are abstract, often containing inconsistent information. In fact, these persons learn to make decisions appear compatible with the person they are talking to at the time. The result is confusion and unclear perceptions among other negotiators. "Soft" negotiators prefer compromise strategies. When possible, these negotiators will allow persons in conflict to work out differences and remain uninvolved. For the "soft" negotiator, differing positions are "bad" and considered as evidence of dissatisfaction. Often, this negotiator will attempt to keep other people happy by distributing grief, or by following a course of avoidance.

"Hard" Negotiating Style

From the "hard negotiator's" perspective other people are viewed as adversaries and "victory" is the primary concern. This style uses what are referred to as "hardball tactics" (Lewicki, Saunders, and Barry, 2006). "Hard" negotiators make threats and apply pressures to get what they want. This style of negotiation is very common among Americans, especially in the corporate environment, since the number of wins provides a culturally-defined index of negotiation effectiveness. Buckholz, Lashbrook, and Wenburg's (1976) "driver" social style is very much like the "hard" negotiator. A "driver" is low in responsiveness to others, but is highly assertive. The driver seeks to win at the expense of the other negotiators. This behavior results from a heightened interest and desire for competition. The driver is pushy, severe, tough, dominating, harsh, strong-willed, independent, practical, decisive, and efficient. The "hard" negotiator will tend to use tactics that include threats, shouting, physical aggression, insults, hostility, and blaming other parties. For the "hard" negotiator, there is minimal concern for establishing trust or maintaining the relationship in the future.

"Hard" and "soft" negotiation styles were considered undesirable by Fisher and Ury. As was evident in the above descriptions, both styles result in short-term accommodations and deny efficient movement toward intermediate and long-term goal attainment. For example, soft negotiators may misrepresent truth and reality in their effort to maintain harmony. This action inevitably leads to future problems, along with lowered perceptions of credibility. In addition, humans naturally tend to resent those who predominantly use a hard, power-driven style. Eventually, these persons may experience a "boomerang" effect when the power differential changes. Cummings, Long, and Lewis (1986) described such a circumstance that occurred at a major American university:

A department chairperson operated as a highly authoritarian manager. Nothing seemed to get done unless the chairperson was there to see that faculty members did as they were told. One particularly unproductive faculty member was threatened with punishment: assignment to undesirable courses, no merit raise, and delays in promotion. This heavy-handed procedure was based upon a continual use of power. The faculty member became a life-long enemy and decided to lie in wait for retaliation. Eventually the opportunity arose. The faculty member became a Dean — that same chairperson's boss. The loser didn't stay a loser; the winner didn't stay a winner.

Determining whether a hard or soft negotiation style is the result of individual preference or the result of environmental influence is often difficult. In reality, it is probably a function of both preference as well as environmental. Since much of the previous work in this area has emphasized social-psychological influence, consideration of socio-cultural elements as sources of influence is warranted. Eastern and western conflict negotiation strategies provide examples of cultural influence on style selection. For example, western organizations often use formal confrontation meetings as a method to help manage conflicts during negotiations (Gibson, Ivancevich, Donnelly, and Konopaske, 2011). The purpose of such meetings is to provide various individuals and groups an opportunity to air their differences. Some Japanese companies have also used this intensive confrontation training to prepare their people to handle conflict situations. In both cases, it is assumed an open, direct avenue of interaction among negotiators will assist in increased understanding, awareness, and resolution of differences. Both presume, however, a limited and stereotypic conception of western negotiation practices.

Eastern organizational members negotiate differences quite differently than their western counterparts. Michael Yoshino (1968) has indicated that Japanese culture encourages the avoidance of open conflict expression. The reason for overt conflict avoidance behavior is to maintain flexibility in making adjustments in positions. Eastern culture tends to view open conflict as "public," and shifts in position cannot occur once a public position is stated. Thus, conflicts are low-key. Members of eastern decision-making groups also tend to be more sensitive than western decision-makers to subtle communication cues. In general, eastern cultures apparently believe that the less public confrontation accompanying conflict negotiation the less polarized and more flexible the parties in conflict tend to be (Long, 2003; Martin & Nakayama, 2008).

Credible Negotiation Leadership and Principled Negotiation Style

Principled negotiation is "designed to produce wise outcomes efficiently and amicably" (Fisher & Ury, 1988, p. 10-11). Essentially, this approach separates people from the problem first by focusing on interests rather than on bargaining positions. Principled negotiation generates a variety of possibilities and insists that the results be based on some objective standards. Thus, principled negotiation focuses on effective problem-solving through an initial understanding of cultural diversity and interpersonal sensitivity. This assumes at least a minimal level of interpersonal communication competence on behalf of all participants. It also presumes that negotiators lead in the process of establishing trust, i.e., credibility, for one another at the onset of negotiation relationship development.

From a human relations development perspective, credible negotiation leaders (CNL) can be characterized as avid users of conflict management tactics as described by Cummings, Long, and Lewis (1986):

- Focus and containment. CNLs determine the location of differences; i.e., are they related to people or positions, individual negotiators or environmental conditions?
- Control threat levels. CNLs avoid "hard" styles and work actively to insure that perceptions of threat by others are reduced.
- Clarify communication rules. CNLs are concerned with reducing uncertainty and adverse emotions that may result; they actively consider cultural influences on the interpretation of messages and inferred motives underlying behavior.
- Early conflict identification. CNLs monitor differences that occur during negotiations and endeavor to insure that these differences do not result in debilitating, personal conflict that damages the relationship.
- Balance dependencies. CNLs endeavor to insure that people perceive one another as relational equals; they are aware that perceived imbalances generate mistrust and suspicion. Development and maintenance of mutual dependence is a preferred strategy.

Credible Negotiation Leaders emphasize satisfying all participants. Parties do not advocate. Negotiators search comprehensively to define and solve problems in the short, intermediate, and long terms. Although these basic strategies are generally accepted methods for managing human relations, Credible Negotiation Leadership, as proposed in this chapter, embraces more than the human relationship; concern for spanning cultural boundaries and developing cultural relations in negotiation is the emphasis.

Using Japanese and American interactions, Hill, Long, and Javidi (1994) illustrated the potential of Credible Negotiation Leadership. Perhaps even more importantly, the approach illustrated how negotiation in other cultures is more informed by an interculturally sensitive perspective than those of the more "short-termed" Americans.

Japanese MAGNUS Negotiators

Harmonious social relations are central to Japanese negotiations. Japanese negotiators tend to relate to one another on a vertical axis. For the Japanese, self-concepts play a relatively insignificant role in a negotiation situation. Enhancement of the group is much more important than satisfaction of personal needs. Loyalty plays an important factor in the way one negotiates, while a formal style of communication is strongly preferred. Japanese also tend to use go-betweens to assure smoothness in social relations and in all kinds of dealing and negotiating. Disagreement in public is distasteful (Pearce, 2007).

American MAGNUS Negotiators

In contrast to the Japanese, Americans view "negotiation sessions as problem-solving exercises" (Fisher, 1988, p. 18). The negotiation process for Americans takes place on a horizontal axis, while in most eastern cultures negotiation occurs on a vertical axis. More specifically, Americans tend to view people as independent, carrying to the negotiation tables a sense of who they are, what they should do, and what they want to accomplish from the negotiation. Americans focus on self-concept primarily in terms of self-awareness, self-image, self-esteem, self-identity, self-reliance, self-assistance, self-actualization, self-expression, and self-determination. Americans accentuate informal communication skills and tend to avoid the use of formal codes of conduct, titles, honorifics, and ritualistic manners. Often, negotiators are equalized in language or symbol selection, regardless of differences in age, sex, status, or rank.

Recommendations for International MAGNUS Negotiators

Restated, international negotiation is a form of communication across cultures in which participants come into contact with each other for the purpose of mutually desirable outcomes. Most individuals, however, usually see only two ways to negotiate: soft or hard. The soft negotiator wants to avoid personal and/or national conflict and so makes concessions readily in order to reach agreement. The hard negotiator, on the other hand, sees every situation as a contest of wills in which the side that has the most extreme positions and holds out longer fares better. Despite the occasional lure of hard negotiations, the authors strongly recommend the long-term results of credible negotiation leadership and principled negotiation which is neither hard nor soft, but rather is both soft and hard. The use of intercultural communication as a primary source of the principles is more strongly recommended.

This approach looks for mutual gains whenever possible, based on common and equitable standards independent of the will of either side. In addition, application of the international negotiation model continually requires that the negotiators monitor variables that influence each other's interactions and corollary information exchanges. This method is hard on merits, but soft on people. It employs the important aspects of intercultural bonding and trust to establish effective, believable communication among participants without any tricks or posturing. This method argues for culturally sensitive negotiation across cultures which is based on improvements of intercultural bonding and relations.

On the world scene many activities illustrate the strengths of this approach to international negotiation. In the trade negotiations between Japan and the USA, the contrast of short-term and long-term strategies regularly complicates relationships. On the one hand, the USA focuses on numerical quotas as a tangible outcome of such importance that the overemphasis threatens long-term relations. For example, US Senator Bradley indicted this behavior – "President Clinton's hardline on Japan trade policy was 'gratuitous brinkmanship' that puts the United States' long-term economic and strategic interests at risk in pursuit of domestic political gains" (quoted by Purdum, 1994). This firm position also threatened the political stability of Prime Minister Hosokawa's government. With similar imprudence, however, the Japanese negotiators did not assess accurately the political circumstances pressing President Clinton. Similar circumstances threatened public support for U.S. Secretary of State John Kerry and President Obama in 2015 as they negotiated in Vienna with other nations and Iran to seal an agreement that would limit Iran's uranium enrichment capabilities; critics argued that Iran would use billions of dollars after sanctions were lifted to beef up its military power. The ultimate significance of this stressful behavior is difficult to predict. Rather than publicly squabble over the particulars, however, the negotiators should recognize the need to strengthen ties through economic relations, especially when the post-Communist world will require innovative, credible leadership from its most powerful nations.

As a final note, the position provided in this chapter complements well other approaches (Erbe, 2011, 2014) to international negotiation and MAGNUS leadership. With the enrichment of intercultural communication and credible leadership some of the following principles assume even greater prominence. Examine them within the perspective of the prior discussion.

- Do not bargain over positions. Instead, try to understand the positions as you come to know the individuals involved. Arguing over positions produces unwise agreements. Arguing over positions is inefficient. Arguing over positions endangers an ongoing relationship. When there are many parties, positional bargaining is even worse. Being nice also is no simple answer.
- Separate people from the task and overcome people problems as an entree to task achievement. Negotiators are people first. Face the problem, not the people. Every negotiator has two kinds of interests, relationship and substance. Balance and proportion the emphasis wisely.
- Avoid presumptions of similarity. Try to learn the other culture as much as possible. Learn about environmental, cultural, socio-cultural, and psychological factors influencing your negotiation.
- Empathize or put yourself within the other negotiator's frame of reference. Do not deduce another's intentions from your fears. Do not blame another negotiator for your problem. Negotiators should discuss each other's' perceptions.
- Recognize and understand emotions through self-analysis and analysis of the other person. Allow negotiators an opportunity to let off steam. Do not react to emotional outbursts. Listen actively and acknowledge what is being said. Speak for a purpose and speak clearly to be understood.

- Remember that Credible Negotiation Leadership, when the above principles are observed, becomes a shared activity, leading to longer term relationships and outcomes that are acceptable to all.

In summary, build a working relationship which is not only effective, but interculturally beneficial as well. For each of the do's and don'ts, many more reasons and pitfalls could be elaborated. But, that is the challenge for credible negotiation and MAGNUS leaders as they work to enhance the world environment.

REFERENCES

Ahmad, A., Francis, A., & Zairi, M. (2007). Business process reengineering: Critical success factors in higher education. *Business Process Management Journal, 13*(3), 451–469. doi:10.1108/14637150710752344

Altaian, I., & Taylor, D. A. (1983). *Social penetration: The development of interpersonal relationships.* New York: Holt, Rhinehart, and Wilson.

Austin, J. (2010). *The collaboration challenge: How nonprofits and businesses succeed through strategic alliances.* San Francisco, CA: Jossey-bass.

Bryman, A. (2013). *Leadership and organizations.* London, UK: Routledge.

Buckholz, S., Lashbrook, W., & Wenburg, J. (1976). *Toward the measurement and processing of social styles.* Paper presented at the International Communication Association, Portland, OR.

Cicero, M. (1971). *Selected works* (M. Grant, Trans.). Middlesex, UK: Penguin Books.

Cicero, M. (2012). *On living and dying well* (T. Habinek, Trans.). London, UK: Penguin Books.

Creede, C., Fisher-Yoshida, B., & Gallegos, P. (Eds.). (2012). *The reflective, facilitative, and interpretive practices of the coordinated management of meaning: making lives, making meanings.* Teaneck, NJ: Fairleigh Dickinson Press.

Cummings, H. W., Long, L., & Lewis, M. (1986). *Managing communication in organizations.* Scottsdale, AZ: Gorsuch-Scarisbrick.

Diddams, M., & Chang, G. C. (2012). Only human: Exploring the nature of weakness in authentic leadership. *The Leadership Quarterly, 23*(3), 593–603. doi:10.1016/j.leaqua.2011.12.010

Epictetus. (1995). *The art of living: The classical manual on virtue, happiness, and effectiveness, (Interpreted by Sharon Lebell).* New York, NY: HarperCollins.

Erbe, N. (2011). *Negotiation alchemy: global skills inspiring and transforming diverging worlds.* Berkeley, CA: Public Policy Press.

Erbe, N. (2014). *Approaches to managing organizational diversity and innovation.* Hershey, PA: IGI Global Press. doi:10.4018/978-1-4666-6006-9

Fisher, G. (1980). *International negotiation: A cross cultural perspective.* Yarmouth, ME: Intercultural Press.

Fisher, G. (1988). *Mindsets*. Yarmouth, ME: Intercultural Press.

Fisher, R., & Ury, W. (1986). *Getting to yes: Negotiating agreement without giving in*. Bergenfield, NJ: Penguin.

Franklin, B. (1950). *The autobiography of Benjamin Franklin and selections from his other writings*. New York, NY: Random House, Inc.

Gibson, J., Ivancevich, J., Donnelly, J., & Konopaske, R. (2011). *Organizations: Behaviors, structures, and processes* (14th ed.). New York, NC: McGraw-Hill Education.

Gudykunst, W. B., & Kim, Y. Y. (1992). *Communicating with strangers: An approach to intercultural communication* (2nd ed.). New York: McGraw-Hill.

Hackman, M., & Johnson, C. (2013). *Leadership: A communication perspective* (6th ed.). Long Grove, IL: Wave Land Press.

Hazelton, V., & Long, L. (1988). Concepts for public relations education, research, and practice: A communication point of view. *Central States Speech Journal, 39*(2), 77–87. doi:10.1080/10510978809363239

Hill, L. B., Long, L. W., & Javidi, M. (1994). Principled Negotiation: Achieving Intercultural Effectiveness. In N. Honna, L. Hill, B. Hoffer, & Y. Tokeshita (Eds.), Organizational behaviors in cross-cultural settings. Vol. II, Intercultural Understanding and Communication. Tokyo: Sanshuusha Publishers.

Hovland, C., Janis, I., & Kelley, H. (1953). *Communication and persuasion*. New Haven, CT: Yale University Press.

Javidi, M., Nash, R., Normore, Hoina, C., Valenti, V., Scott, W., … Javidi, A. (2016). *Magnanimous officers*. The International Academy of Public Safety. Retrieved from, http://leicld.com/magnus/

Kolb, D. M., & Williams, J. (2003). *Everyday negotiation: Navigating the hidden agendas in bargaining*. San Francisco: Jossey-Bass.

Kriesberg, L. (1998). *Constructive conflicts: From escalation to resolution*. Lanham, MD: Rowman and Littlefield.

Lewicki, R. J., Saunders, D. M., & Barry, B. (2006). *Negotiation* (5th ed.). Boston: McGraw-Hill Irwin.

Lewicki, R. J., Saunders, D. M., & Barry, B. (2015). *Negotiation* (7th ed.). Boston: McGraw-Hill Irwin.

Long, L., & Hazelton, V. (1984). Assessing communication behavior: An application within the public relations profession. Journal of Applied Communication.

Long, L. W. (2003). Mapping Organizational Culture: An Integration of Communication and Organizational Design. *Intercultural Communication Studies, 12*(2), 127–142.

Martin, J., & Nakayama, T. (2008). *Experiencing intercultural communication: An introduction* (3rd ed.). Boston: McGraw-Hill.

McCroskey, J. & Young, T. (1981). Ethos and credibility: the construct and its measurement after three decades. *Central States Speech Journal, 32*(981), 24-34.

Mowlana, H. (1986). *Global information and world communication*. White Plains, NY: Longman.

Musashi, M. (1974). *A book of five rings* (V. Harris, Trans.). Woodstock, NY: The Overlook Press.

Normore, A., & Erbe, N. (2013). *Collective efficacy: interdisciplinary perspectives on international leadership*. Bingley, UK: Emerald Group Publishing. doi:10.1108/S1479-3660(2013)20

Northouse, P. (2013). *Leadership: theory and practice* (6th ed.). Thousand Oaks, CA: Sage.

Oetzel & Ting-Toomey, S. (2013). The handbook of communication. Thousand Oaks, CA: Sage.

Paupp, T. (2014). *Redefining human rights in the struggle for peace and development*. New York: Cambridge University Press.

Pearce, B. (2007). *Making social worlds: a communication perspective*. London: Blackwell.

Pearce, B., & Pearce, K. (2000). Extending the theory of the coordinated management of meaning ("CMM") through a community dialogue process. *Communication Theory*, *4*(4), 405–423. doi:10.1111/j.1468-2885.2000.tb00200.x

Pruitt, D., & Kim, S. (2004). *Social conflict: escalation, stalemate and settlement*. New York: McGraw-Hill.

Purdum, T. S. (1994, February 24). Bradley rebukes Clinton on Japan. *The New York Times*, p. C1-C2.

Rogers, P. (2004, June 10-11). *Trends in conflict 2010-2030*. Centre for Humanitarian Dialogue Mediators Retreat, Oslo, Norway.

Tannenbaum, R., Weschler, I. R., & Massarik, F. (1961). *Leadership and organizations*. New York: McGraw-Hill.

Trompenaars, F., & Hampden-Turner, C. (2012). *Riding the waves of culture*. New York: McGraw Hill.

Watkins, M. (2002). *Breakthrough business negotiation*. San Francisco: Jossey-Bass.

Yoshino, M. (1968). *Japan's managerial system: Tradition and innovation*. Cambridge, MA: MIT Press.

KEY TERMS AND DEFINITIONS

Communication Subsystem: The throughput dynamic of the negotiation process that contains the negotiators and messages.

Contextual Subsystem: The input dynamic of the negotiation process that contains cultural, social, political/legal, technological, and economic/competitive dimensions.

Credibility: Perceptions of an individual's trustworthiness and expertise; one's level of believability during communication is influenced by the perceived level of their credibility.

Cultural Dimension: Concern for the behaviors and underlying values, motives, beliefs, knowledge, meanings, ethics, patterns of interaction, etc. that identify a specific "cultural" group and also differentiates it from other cultures.

Economic/Competitive Dimension: Concern for acquisition and management of financial resources; competitive aspects of this dimension consist of individuals, groups, organizations, nations, or entities who possess goals that may stimulate competition for resources, markets or alliances.

Intercultural Communication: Communication (creation and consumption of messages) among individuals from different cultures who often possess differing social norms and rules, as well as different languages, experiences, and world views.

International Negotiation: A communication function of international relations that is used for the purpose of mutual adaptation in order to' accomplish specific goals.

MAGNUS Leadership: The natural pursuit of virtue. The MAGNUS leader continuously seeks ideal character by pursuing virtues and in the process, learns how to serve with distinction and how to live a life worth living.

Outcomes Subsystem: Concern for interaction between people and consequent effects or outcomes; three categories of outcomes are considered tangible, symbolic, and relational results.

Political/Legal Dimension: Concern for formal rules which govern organizational, governmental, national conduct; methods of creating rules/laws/policy and methods for rule enforcement; electoral or position appointment practices, executive or administrative influence, and adjudication processes.

Social Dimension: Concern for the values, norms, rules, and roles; one of the greatest sources of influence on human behavior, emanating from the cultural dimension.

Technological Dimension: Concern for methods and tools used to accomplish tasks; for purposes of this chapter, this dimension emphasizes transportation and communication/information technologies.

Section 2

Leadership and Communication in K-16 Education

Chapter 6
The Use of Online Social Networks and Its Influence on Job-Related Behavior:
The Higher Education Context

Vera Silva Carlos
University of Aveiro, Portugal

Ricardo Gouveia Rodrigues
Universidade da Beira Interior, Portugal

ABSTRACT

Web 2.0 technologies have progressively transformed social interactions among people. In addition, there is plenty of evidence of a positive influence of social relationships on work-related attitudes and behaviors. Within these frameworks, the purpose is to evaluate the effect of using online social networks on the workers' attitudes and behaviors, particularly in the context of higher education. The authors used an online survey to evaluate the attitudes and behavior of 157 faculty members. To assess the use of OSNs, they used a dichotomous variable. The t-student test and the PLS method were used to analyze the data. They conclude that the use of OSNs influences the workers' performance, but not job satisfaction, organizational commitment, or organizational citizenship behaviors (extra-role performance). The relationships they propose in what concerns the workers' attitudes are all empirically supported. Lastly, they describe the study limitations and we suggest some perspectives for future research.

INTRODUCTION

Social networks are a means to conceptualize social groupings and interaction. At a time when technologized sociability is the norm, this blend of everyday human experience with mediated communication is quite significant since social interaction turns out to be a synonym of, and sometimes inseparable from, the technology that allows it. Social networking might, on the whole, be considered a way of describing the design of social interaction practices, which include the ones among family members, friends, neighbors

DOI: 10.4018/978-1-5225-8516-9.ch006

and people from different communities. Thus, we could refer to the social networks of previous school friends, workmates or those that form a hole variety of groups within social institutions, organizations or clubs and that serve our needs and interests. In fact, social institutions and the informal or casual meetings that happen among people give significant background for the keeping and the developing of a wide variety of relationships (Merchant, 2012). The growth and popularity of Online social networks (OSNs) have completely modified cooperation and communication (Cheung, Chiu & Lee, 2011) and social interaction using these sites is abruptly intensifying (Antonci & Sabatini, 2018).

OSNs have affected all Internet users and they are an essential communications tool nowadays (Paul, Baker & Cochran, 2012). All over the world, by being connected, more than a million people cooperate by sharing ideas, work, knowledge and creativity (Cheung, Chiu & Lee, 2011). More than organizations, Higher Education Institutions (HEI) have a better insight of how to make environments easier, where people cooperate by sharing, creating and advancing knowledge (Barnatt. 2008). As well, academic institutions are using social networking sites such as Facebook and LinkedIn more and more to put in contact nowadays students and potential ones and to provide instructional content (Paul, Baker & Cochran, 2012), so HEI would better be ready to harvest value from these new online tools (Barnatt, 2008). This has made the impact of OSN on academic performance and the accuracy of using it as an effective teaching tool an important topic (Paul, Baker & Cochran, 2012). Taking this into consideration, it seems adequate to use the Higher Education (HE) context to assess the influence of using OSNs on the workers' attitudes and behaviors. Specifically, the intention is to evaluate to what extent the use of OSNs to keep contact with co-workers has an influence on Job satisfaction, Organizational commitment, Organizational citizenship behaviors and Individual performance. On the other hand, we intend to check whether there are positive relationships between the workers' attitudes and behaviors – previously supported fully or partially. If the proposed relations are positive, it will be possible to better understand each of the concepts studied and increase their importance in the HE context.

Firstly, the concepts that are being studied are briefly summarized. Then, two research models, based on 10 hypotheses, are proposed. After explaining and stating the hypotheses, the methodology is described and the results are presented and discussed. Finally, we describe the findings, the limitations of the study are explained and some guiding lines for future research are suggested.

THE WEB 2.0

The term Web 2.0 is used to describe applications that distinguish themselves from preceding generations of software by a number of principles (Ullrich et *al.*, 2008). The appearance of Web 2.0 technologies has created new opportunities for producing and sharing content and interacting with others. Also called 'social media', Web 2.0 includes tools that permit individual and collective publishing, sharing of images, audio and video; and the creation and maintenance of OSN (Bennett, Bishop, Dalgarno, Waycott & Kennedy, 2012).

Initially, the World Wide Web was intended to be used to share ideas and encourage discussion within scientific communities. Web 2.0 heralds a return to these original functions and prompts significant changes in the ways the World Wide Web is being used in education. In this context, there is a need to increase awareness of Web 2.0 tools and the opportunities they offer, and an imperative need to carry out quality research to inform better use of Web 2.0 applications (Boulos & Wheeler, 2007).

The growth of social media has altered the ways in which the Internet is experienced by most users. The Internet is no longer a one-way broadcast distribution system where the user downloads data, information and other resources created by a relatively small number of content providers. Instead, it is driven by (and to some level determined through) the activities of users, which has been described as many-to-many rather than one-to-many connectivity. The Web 2.0 is, then, significantly different from the cyberspace-era Internet of the 1990s and 2000s (Selwyn, 2011).

ONLINE SOCIAL NETWORKS (OSNS)

Social media generally refer to the media used to enable social interaction. Social media technology is defined as Web-based and mobile applications that allow individuals and organizations to produce, participate, and share new user-generated or existing content in digital contexts, through multi-way communication. It is important to highlight the difference between user-generated content, which is non-traditional media developed and produced by individual users, and existing content, which usually consists of traditional media (news, magazines, radio, and television) reproduced for the Web. The broad definition of Social media technology includes the totality of digital products and services enabling online, user generated social behavior and interactions around user-generated content. This definition, though, does not include educational learning and content management systems, such as Blackboard, eLearning Suite, WebCT, Desire2Learn (Davis III et *al.*, 2012).

Web 2.0 sociable technologies and social software work as make doers for organizations (Boulos & Wheeler, 2007). They are of important consequence to organizational communication processes as they are able to include behaviors that were difficult or impossible to have combined together before these new technologies entered the workplace (Treem & Leonardi, 2012). These technologies include social networking services, collaborative filtering, social bookmarking, social search engines, file sharing and tagging, instant messaging and online multi-player games. The more popular Web 2.0 applications in Education, namely wikis, blogs and podcasts, are nothing but the tip of the social software iceberg. Web 2.0 technologies stand for, then, a completely different way of managing and repurposing online information and knowledge repositories – including research information –, in comparison to the traditional Web 1.0 model (Boulos & Wheeler, 2007).

OSNs may also function as tools to help individuals in the workforce organize their workload and life. When properly used and integrated into an organization's business plan they allow the organization and its workers to:

1. Increase customer satisfaction;
2. Facilitate communication between customers and experts to share knowledge;
3. Find experts within the organization as well as those outside with similar interests;
4. Provide the whole product to fully meet a customer's needs, since customers can more easily divulge their needs;
5. Understand and visualize real communication paths within the organization the customer; and
6. Extend the shelf life of conferences and organization meetings with an online network of attendees and databases (Asunda, 2010).

OSNs have, then, become an international phenomenon (Sledgianowski & Kulviwat, 2009; Benson, Filippaios & Morgan, 2010; Heidemann, Klier & Probst, 2012), with huge social and economic impact within a few years (Heidemann, Klier & Probst, 2012). They have been shown to facilitate business relationships (Benson, Filippaios & Morgan, 2010), as described above, and to build social capital (Benson, Filippaios & Morgan, 2010; Young, 2011).

Regarding the social perspective, OSNs have a great impact on the way people communicate and interact with each other (Grabner-Kraeuter & Waiguny, 2011, providing an efficient and user-friendly way to maintain social relationships and share information. Mainly, they play a key role in the spread of information at very large scale (Guille, Hacid, Favre & Zighed, 2013).

OSNs allow individuals to simultaneously share information with numerous peers. Measuring the causal effect of these mediums on the diffusion of information encompasses identifying who influences whom, and whether individuals would still spread information in the absence of social signals regarding that information. Though stronger ties are individually more significant, it is the more abundant weak ties which are accountable for the spread of new information, which suggests that weak ties may have a more dominant role in the dissemination of information online than currently believed (Bakshy, Rosenn, Marlow & Adamic, 2012).

Although OSNs may impact an individual's behavior, they reflect the individual's personal activities, interests, and opinions as well. These commonalities make it nearly impossible to determine from observational data whether any specific interaction, method of communication or social environment is responsible for the apparent spread of a behavior through a network. There are three probable mechanisms that may explain diffusion-like phenomena, particularly on Facebook: (1) An individual shares a link, and contact with this information on the news feed leads a friend to re-share that link; (2) Friends visit the same Web page and share a link to that Web page, independently of one another; (3) An individual shares a link within and external to Facebook, and contact with the externally shared information leads a friend to share the link (Bakshy et *al.*, 2012).

The use of Social media interfaces through computer and mobile devices has become widespread and two of the most noticeable interfaces are Facebook and Twitter. Facebook allows users to create profiles, allows those user-operated profiles to interact with each other, allows the expression of interests and the discovery of commonalities among users, and allows users to create and maintain connections and invite other users to join a community. On the contrary, Twitter is a Social media interface that allows users to share a limited amount of user-generated content, rapidly and easily, to an extensive number of users. In this interface, the communication exchange is crucial and the conception and sharing of user profiles is not mandatory. Nevertheless, Twitter can link to profiles that exist on other interfaces (Davis III et al., 2012).

Social networking sites are, therefore, interesting examples of 'maps' of communication paths among users, since they represent rich and popular communication interfaces for hundreds of millions of users (Sledgianowski & Kulviwat, 2009). Likewise, according to Young (2011), OSNs like Facebook fortify existing friendships by complementing traditional forms of communication (like face-to-face or telephone). On the other hand, participation in the Facebook community enables effective and convenient contact to be maintained with a larger and more diverse group of acquaintances, thus, as mentioned, extending potential social capital, that is a sociological concept related to the connections between social networks.

SOCIAL MEDIA ON THE EDUCATION SECTOR

Education likes to explore emerging technologies as new or improved tools to improve instruction and learning (Tess, 2013). However, regardless of the widespread use of Social media technologies, little is known about the benefits of its use in post-secondary contexts and for specific purposes, such as marketing, recruitment, learning, and/or student engagement. Hence, it is essential to begin to examine if and how Higher Education Institutions (HEI) are integrating the use of such technologies (Davis III et *al.*, 2012).

Many HEI and educators find themselves expected to catch up with Social media applications and users (Selwyn, 2011). In a time of change, Higher Education has to adapt to external circumstances created by the prevalent adoption of popular technologies such as Social media, OSNs and mobile devices. Therefore, faculty members need opportunities for concrete practices which are capable of creating a personal belief that a particular technology is worth using and an understanding of the settings in which it is best applied (Kukulska-Hulme, 2012). It is known that Web 2.0 technologies are becoming more prevalent in the daily lives of students (Bennett et al., 2012) and they are progressively evident in HE setting as many instructors resort to technology in order to mediate and enhance their instruction as well as stimulate active learning for students (Tess, 2013).

According to Forkosh-Baruch and Hershkovitz (2012), the use of OSNs in HE promotes knowledge sharing, hence facilitating informal learning within the community and open academic institutes to the community altogether. OSNs can be used as indirect supports for learning as well, providing an emotional outlet for school-related stress, validation of creative work, peer-alumni support for school-life transitions, assistance with school-related tasks and stimulating social and civic benefits, online and offline, which has repercussions for Education (Greenhow, 2011).

One of the main social media platforms is Facebook. Originally, it was privately conceived within and navigated through the social networks of students at Harvard University and, later, at other elite universities. If we consider the birth of this particular OSN at Harvard, we can distinguish it as an example of how mechanisms of a university's social 'community' were quickly transferred onto this online platform. Since its creation, this interface has enlarged across numerous HE communities and, then, quickly covered a wider range of linked networks of individuals and groups all over the world (Davis III et *al.*, 2012).

Although the potential of OSNs as means of sharing academic knowledge in HE has not been actualized, it is now being explored by these organizations as well as by the community (Forkosh-Baruch & Hershkovitz, 2012). Nonetheless, there is a lot of tension between Web 2.0 and educational practices (Bennett, Bishop, Dalgarno, Waycott & Kennedy, 2012). Many scholars debate for the integration of Social media as an instructive tool. However, most of the current research on the usefulness and efficiency of Social media in the HE class is limited to self-reported data and content analyses (Tess, 2013), being, thus, insufficient. It is claimed that there is a technological delay between HE and the rest of society, which can be traced back to the insertion of film and radio throughout the first decades of the 20th century. Unquestionably, as with most of the previous waves of new technology, Social media persist as an area of great expectation and exaggeration. It is vital, then, that the higher educators are able to approach Social media in an objective way (Selwyn, 2011).

Even though the infrastructure to support the presence of Social media exists in most HEI, instructors have been slow in accepting the tool as an educational one. Although Social media has been prevalent on HE, its viability as a learning tool has only been considered recently. On the other hand, OSNs integration in HE is a choice made at the instructor level rather than an institutional determination. Subsequently, the implementation may be more of a test that leads to the need of developing research and, eventually, to more questions (Tess, 2013).

Regarding the awareness and use of OSNs by HE faculty members, they are very familiar with social media (Moran, Seaman & Tinti-Kane, 2011), using these media either for professional purposes (Moran, Seaman & Tinti-Kane, 2011; Veletsianos, 2011) or in their classes - or both (Moran, Seaman & Tinti-Kane, 2011).

A majority of HE researchers are making at least sporadic use of one or more Web 2.0 services for divulging their research activity, for developing and maintaining networks and collaboration or for finding out what others are doing (Jamali, Russell, Nicholas & Watkinson, 2014). Moran, Seaman and Tinti-Kane (2011) concluded that most of faculty members report using at least one social media site in support of their professional career. However, in their research, 19% of faculty members who state they use social media in support of their professional careers do it rarely. Over one-quarter of faculty members report using blogs, LinkedIn and Wikis and just over 10% refer Twitter or Flickr. Professional use of SlideShare and Myspace is under 10%, and daily use of Facebook, at 11%, surpassed that of other social media sites, followed by blogs (5% daily use), YouTube (4%) and Wikis (3%). Also, 70% of faculty members mention privacy concerns as an 'important' or 'very important' barrier to using OSNs. Trust and privacy features of websites have evolved as an important concern for any businesses or interactions, particularly in online networks (Kumar, Kumar & Bhasker, 2018).

Foster, Francescucci and West (2010) stress the importance of privacy in OSNs, as some participants who have privacy concerns may not have developed the confidence to contribute to new communities. Increasingly, people are sharing sensitive personal information via OSNs. While such networks do permit users to control what they share with whom, access to control policies are notoriously difficult to configure correctly, and this raises the question of whether OSN users' privacy settings match their sharing intentions (Madjeski, Johnson & Bellovin, 2011). Within this framework, privacy concerns should be accounted for when analyzing the use of OSNs in every context, even in the context of HE.

WORK-RELATED ATTITUDES AND BEHAVIORS

Considering our goal is to better understand the effect of using OSNs to maintain contact with co-workers on the Lecturing staff attitudes and behaviors, we briefly describe below two work-related attitudes – Job satisfaction and Organizational commitment – and two behaviors – Organizational citizenship behaviors and Individual performance.

Job Satisfaction (JS)

There are few, if any, more central concepts for organizational psychology than for job satisfaction. (Judge et al., 2001, pp. 25)

The concept of Job satisfaction (JS) has been originating some controversy (Staw, 1986), since it is characterized as a "*complex emotional reaction to work*" (Locke, 1968: 9), and also as an attitude (Saari & Judge, 2004). Locke (1990: 1432) defines JS as "the pleasurable emotional state resulting from the perception of one's job as fulfilling or allowing the fulfillment of one's important job values, providing these values are compatible with one's needs".

JS theories may also be divided according to the following classification: (1) situational theories, which support that satisfaction is a result of the nature of work and environmental factors, (2) dispositional theories, according to which satisfaction results from personal and personality factors, (3) interactive theories, which suggest that JS derives from the interaction between personality factors and factors intrinsic to the situation. the most recent are Dispositional theories, but they are also the less developed ones. However, individual differences have been considered since investigation related to JS began (Judge et *al.*, 2001).

The job characteristics pattern was suggested by Hackman and Oldham (1976) to evaluate three classes of variables: work objective characteristics, mediator psychological stages and individual needs of growth. According to this model, the main characteristics of each task – like the range of competencies, the identity and the meaning of the tasks, the autonomy, the feedback given to the worker about his/her performance, that is, the feedback – influence the individual's psychological stage. The function characteristics and satisfaction are also controlled by the worker's need for growth. The model can be used as basic concept to identify the potential of job motivation, the workers' availability to answer positively to work improvement and to reorganize specific characteristics of the jobs that need to be changed. Judge et *al.* (2001) state that, according to this perspective, the jobs that have intrinsically motivating characteristics will lead to higher levels of motivation and even to an increased performance. But, one should keep in mind that the more interested individuals, who want greater challenges and reveal a greater interest for work are, usually, happier and more motivated (Hackman e Oldham, 1976).

Organizational Commitment (OC)

Meyer and Herscovitch (2001) state that the OC definitions, presented in the literature, have two common aspects: (1) commitment consists of a force of connection – a psychological or attitude stage, and (2) commitment determines a direction at the level of the individual's behavior.

Based on previous definitions of OC, Allen and Meyer (1990) created a commitment model, based on the fact that the concept is composed by three dimensions: (1) *affective,* which means a connection, an identification and involvement with the organization; (2) *continuance*, which refers to the commitment based on the expense that the individual connects with leaving the organization and (3) *normative*, related to the feelings of obligation to stay in the organization.

The perspective chosen in this research is the one proposed by Cook and Wall (1980), who support that the OC refers to the affective answers to the characteristics of the employer organization. It is related to the worker's feelings of connection with the goals and values of the organization; to the role that he entails when relating to them and to the connection with the organization with the aim of benefitting it, and not just for its instrumental value. Since this is a positive result of the experience of quality work, the concept can be considered a contributing factor to the well-being at work.

Organizational Citizenship Behaviors (OCB)

The concept of OCB has different origins: (1) in Barnard's (1938) proposal, in which the workers' will to cooperate is essential to the organization, (2) in Katz and Kahn's (1978) differences of behavioural typologies in organizations, and (3) in Organ's (1977) essay, which proposes that people can choose a collaborative behaviour in order to respond to each other, considering the work experiences that provide satisfaction, in opposition to the behaviours inherent to the role, which depend on certain restrictions. Based on Organ's work (1977), Bateman and Organ (1983) measured this new kind of Performance.

From then on, several definitions and dimensions were proposed (e.g.: Graham, 1991; Williams & Anderson, 1991; Organ & Moorman, 1993; Van Dyne, Graham, & Dienesch, 1994; Konovsky & Organ, 1996; Podsakoff, MacKenzie, Paine & Bachrach, 2000).

In González and Garazo's point of view (2006), there are five dimensions of OCB that are more frequently used, which is accordingly to the OCB studies found:

1. **Altruism** (MacKenzie, Podsakoff, & Fetter, 1993; Organ & Lingl, 1995; Konovsky & Organ, 1996; Podsakoff & MacKenzie, 1997; Rego, Ribeiro, & Cunha, 2010): That is defined as 'helping behaviour' (Lo & Ramayah, 2009);
2. **Sportsmanship** (MacKenzie et al., 1993; Organ & Lingl, 1995; Konovsky & Organ, 1996; Podsakoff & MacKenzie, 1997; Rego et al., 2010): Behaviour of warmly tolerating unavoidable irritations (Podsakoff & MacKenzie, 1997);
3. **Civic Virtue** (MacKenzie et al., 1993; Organ & Lingl, 1995; Konovsky & Organ, 1996; Podsakoff & MacKenzie, 1997; Rego et al., 2010): The responsibility of the workers to participate in the life of the organization (Podsakoff et al., 2000);
4. **Conscientiousness** (MacKenzie et al., 1993; Rego et al., 2010): Based on how organized, hard-working and responsible the worker is (Lo & Ramayah, 2009); and
5. **Courtesy** (Organ & Lingl, 1995; Konovsky & Organ, 1996; Rego et al., 2010): Related to the prevention of problems at the workplace (Lo & Ramayah, 2009).

Individual Performance (IP)

In the organizational context, individual performance (JP) is defined as a *multidimensional* (Campbell, McHenry & Lauress, 1990; Motowidlo, Borman & Schmit, 1997; Viswesvaran, 2001; Sonnentag & Frese, 2002; Cheng, Li, & Fox, 2007), *dynamic* (Motowidlo et al. 1997; Sonnentag & Frese, 2002), *behavioural* (Campbell et al., 1990; Motowidlo et al., 1997; Viswesvaran, 2001), *episodic* (Motowidlo et al., 1997) and *evaluative* (Motowidlo et al., 1997; Viswesvaran, 2001) concept.

Viswesvaran (2001) defines IP as behaviors that can be evaluated, but he emphasizes that the difference between behaviors and results is not clear, since IP is made of several behavioral manifestations, that are identifiable only through operational measures and that are different depending on the context in which they are used.

Considering the theory of social capital as a valuable one, according to which the organizational theories that concentrate on costs and on human capital are not adequate to immediately respond to quick changes on the nature of work, on the organizational structures and on the inter-organizational competitiveness (Dess & Shaw, 2001), the workers who are essential for the organization may be recognized for their ability to have a high performance, as well as for their capacity to create value for that same organization. As such, the fundamental workers are those who have an influence on the other workers, who have knowledge and whose performance is characterized by the following aspects: (1) Skills to tackle organizational networks; (2) Skills to transmit organizational memory; (3) Flexible confidence; (4) Skills to actively work with a team; (5) Influence on the performance chain command; (6) Difficulty in being replaced; (7) Innovation characteristics (Xiaowei, 2006).

RESEARCH MODELS AND HYPOTHESES

Literature points out the existence of positive relations among the social relationships established at work and:

1. Job satisfaction (JS) (Castilla, 2005; Hurlbert, 2001);
2. Organizational commitment (OC) (Donaldson, Ensher & Grant-Vallone, 2000);
3. Organizational citizenship behaviors (OCB) (Donaldson, Ensher & Grant-Vallone, 2000);
4. Individual performance (IP) (Castilla, 2000).

Considering that social media have become ubiquitous and have started to influence several organizational phenomena and processes (Leonardi & Vaast, 2017), and that HE faculty members are very familiar with these technologies (Moran, Seaman & Tinti-Kane, 2011), it seems plausible to assume that social relationships developed online, specifically with co-workers, influence the worker's job-related attitudes and behaviors. Thus, we formulate the following research hypotheses:

H_1: The use of OSNs to maintain contact with co-workers (OSN) influences JS.
H_2: OSN influences OC.
H_3: OSN influences OCB.
H_4: OSN influences IP.

The hypotheses can be summarily represented by the research model in Figure 1.

According to some authors (Chang & Chang, 2007; Eker, Eker & Pala, 2008; Malik, Nawab & Naeem, 2010), satisfaction has a positive influence on commitment. In an attempt to assert these studies we propose H_5.

Figure 1. Model 1

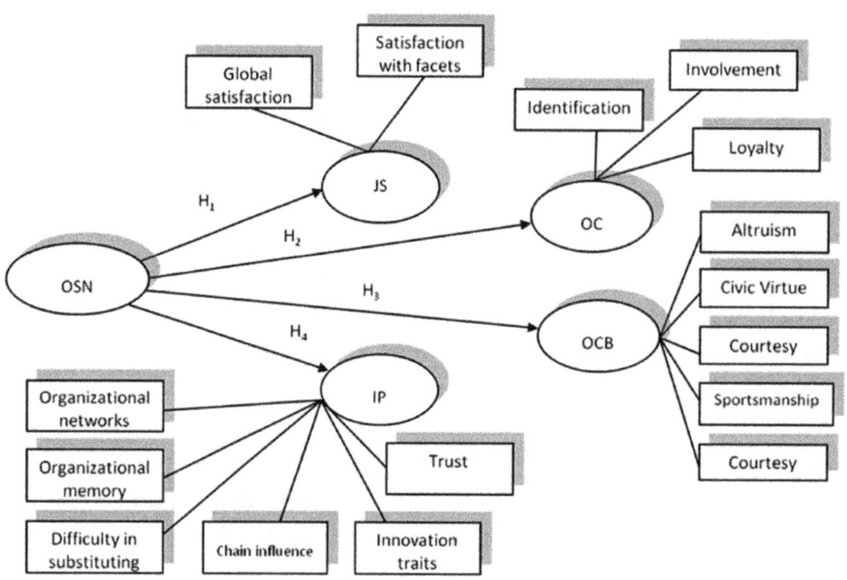

H_5: JS has a positive impact on OC.

Literature also points out that satisfaction is positively related to OCB (Donavan, Brown, & Mowen, 2004; González & Garazo, 2006; Jones, 2006). Thus, we formulate the following hypothesis:

H_6: JS has a positive impact on OCB.

Samad (2005) and Jones (2006) refer that performance is positively influenced by satisfaction. These studies allow the formulation of the following hypothesis:

H_7: JS has a positive impact on IP.

According to Donavan, Brown and Mowen (2004), commitment has a positive impact on the OCB, specifically on the 'altruism' dimension. Lavelle et *al.* (2008) also investigated the relationship between OC and OCB and concluded that the affective commitment has an impact on OCB, characterized by the authors as the participation in meetings or events related to the organization. These studies allow the formulation of the following hypothesis:

H_8: OC has a positive impact on OCB.

Samad (2005) found a positive impact of commitment on performance. The author adopts the perspective of Mowday et *al.* (1982), in which OC is defined as (1) the belief in the organization and the acceptance of its values and goals, (2) the will to make an effort to the well-being of the organization and (3) the will/wish to stay in the organization. Locke, Latham and Erez (1988) argue that the strength of this relationship will depend on the amount of variance in the commitment. According to Meyer et *al.* (2002) commitment has an impact on performance, being this impact positive for to the affective and normative commitment, and negative for the continued commitment. In an attempt to assert these studies we propose H_9.

H_9: OC has a positive impact on IP.

Following Podsakoff and MacKenzie (1997), there is a positive relation between OCB, in the perspective as helping behaviors, and the effectiveness of the organizations. Consequently, a relationship between the OCB and IP is supposed to exist and the following hypothesis is formulated:

H_{10}: OCB has a positive impact on IP.

The six hypotheses can be summarily represented by the research model in Figure 2.

Figure 2. Model 2

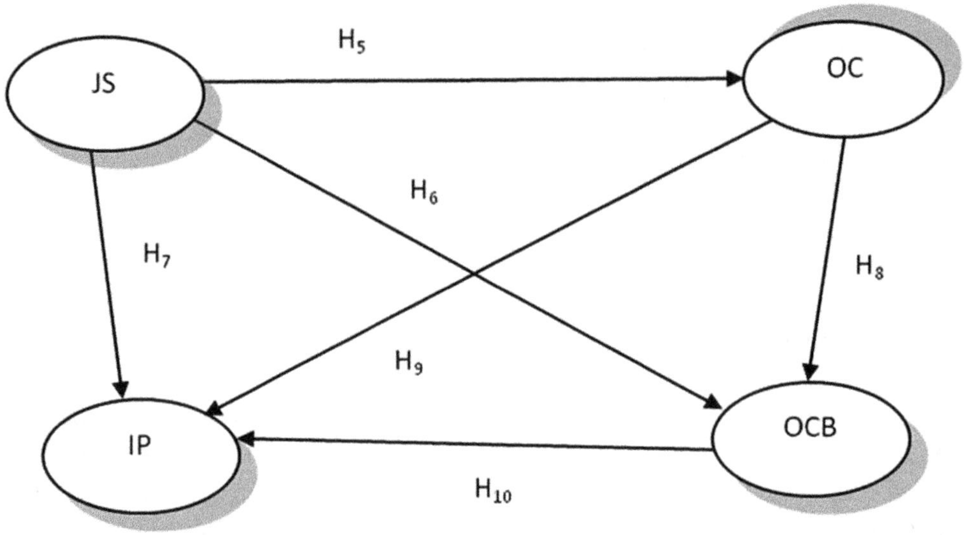

METHODOLOGY

Sample and Data Collection

This research, descriptive in nature and quantitative, is carried out through the deductive method (Ciribelli, 2003) and is based on a model that tries to relate the following variables: the use of OSNs to maintain contact with co-workers (OSN), job satisfaction (JS), organizational commitment (OC), organizational citizenship behaviors (OCB) and individual performance (IP).

Following the information of the National Institute of Statistics[1], updated on the 31st May, 2007, the number of Professors in HE was 37,281, both in the in the public sector (26,098) and in the private sector (11,183). The sample in this study is composed by 157 Professors, of which 137 work in public HEI and 20 in privately-held ones; 101 teach in universities and 56 in polytechnic institutions.

We created a questionnaire in order to assess the use of OSNs. To evaluate work-related attitudes and behaviors, four instruments using 7 points *Likert* type scale, where 1 means 'completely disagree' and 7 means 'completely agree', were used. This scale allows a wide appreciation of the worker's perception about the variables under study. It was necessary to validate the instruments for the Portuguese population by translating them into Portuguese and convert them back into English. The second translations were compared to the original instruments and some mistakes corrected. Because we were dealing with HEI, it was necessary to substitute the expressions 'firm' and 'organization' for the expression 'teaching institution', or just 'institution'. A pre-test was carried out with 6 individuals, which led to the need to make some changes. After these changes were made, the questionnaire was revised. Then, the final questionnaire, divided in five parts, was made available online and all the Portuguese HEI, public and private, were requested, via e-mail, to invite the Professors to participate in this study.

Development of Measures and Scales

Online Social Networks (OSN)

To evaluate the use of OSNs, we built a questionnaire that contained the following questions: (1) Do you use OSNs? (Yes/No), (2) If you answered 'yes', indicate which ones you use, (3) If you answered 'yes', indicate the how often you use OSNs, (4) If you answered 'yes', indicate with who you maintain contact with on OSNs (friends/family/co-workers/unknown people/other), (5) If you answered 'no', indicate why you do not use OSNs (lack of time/lack of interest/high personal exposure/other). OSN is assessed through a 0-1 variable. Since our purpose is to evaluate the influence of OSNs on work-related attitudes, we'll consider the use of OSNs to contact with the co-workers as the independent variable for model 1.

Job Satisfaction (JS)

Job Diagnostic Survey (JDS) was developed to measure three classes of variables: objective characteristics of work, critical psychological states and individual needs for growth. This measurement evaluates the global satisfaction and the satisfaction with job facets. Global satisfaction is measured through three dimensions, which include general satisfaction (5 items), internal work motivation (6 items) and satisfaction with growth (4 items). JDS also measures satisfaction with the following job facets: job security (2 items), pay (2 items), social (3 items) and supervision (3 items). The scores of items 3, 5 and 9 have to be reversed for statistical analysis (Hackman & Oldham, 1975).

Organizational Commitment (OC)

This measure, developed by Cook and Wall (1980), describes, in general, the worker's commitment towards the organization he/she works for. It has nine items, three of them measuring the identification with the organization, other three the involvement with the organization and, the remaining, loyalty. Three of the items are written in the negative form and their score was reversed later for statistical analysis purposes.

Organizational Citizenship Behaviors (OCB)

The scale used to evaluate the OCB was developed by Lo and Ramayah (2009). The instrument is composed of 20 items, which describe five dimensions of the OCB: (1) civic virtue, (2) conscientiousness, (3) altruism, (4) courtesy and (5) sportsmanship. Four of the items were withdrawn from the scale by the authors, since they did not apply to the cultural context in which they used the instrument. However, those items were used in this study. One item is written in the negative form, so the score was reversed for statistical analysis purposes.

Individual Performance (IP)

In this study, the concept of 'individual performance' is measured using the performance traits that characterize the worker. Xiaowei (2006) developed a self-assessment measure of the performance traits, based on the revision of other authors' work. Seven dimensions were considered: the relationship among organizational networks (3 items), the transmission of organizational memory (2 items), trust (4 items), group synergy (2 items), chain influence on performance (2 items), difficulty in substituting (2 items) and innovation traits (3 items). On the whole the measure is made up of 18 items. Seven of the items are written in the negative form, so their score was reversed later for statistical analysis purposes.

Apart from the use of three scales to assess these variables, the respondents were requested to provide further information, such as age, gender and nature of the HEI where they work (public/private and university/polytechnic).

Data Analysis Methods

To analyze the results we used the statistical package *SPSS,* version 18.0.

In this study, among other objectives, we intend to verify whether the means, for each variable, are statistically different depending on the use of OSNs to maintain contact with co-workers. In this case, the method used was the t-student test, for independent samples, which makes it possible to test whether the means of two populations are significantly different (Maroco, 2007).

To test model 2, we used the PLS method. This method has been increasingly used because of its ability to shape latent constructs under conditions of non-normality and small to medium samples. As a technique to create models based in components of structural equations, it is similar to the regression, but it models simultaneously the structural paths, i.e., the theoretical relationships among the latent variables, and it measures the paths, i.e., the relations among a latent variable and its indicators (Chin, Marcolin, e Newsted, 2003). This method was used to study the relationships when the independent variables were not solely 0-1 variables.

FINDINGS AND DISCUSSION

Sample Characterization

The sample is composed mostly by female individuals (62.4%). In what concerns age, the majority of the individuals is 30 to 49 years old (73.8%). A larger number of individuals belong to polytechnic institutions (64.3%) and to a public HEI (87.3%).

Utilization of OSNs

The majority of the sample uses OSNs (72.6%), but out of 157 individuals only 29.9% uses OSNs on a daily basis and only 10.8% uses three or more OSNs. 65,5% use Facebook. Most of the individuals (57.2%) use OSNs to maintain contact with co-workers, although some of them also use it to contact friends, family or unknown people. However, only 29,3% uses OSNs at work.

The reason most often identified by faculty members not to use OSNs is 'high personal exposure', followed by 'lack of interest' (19), 'lack of time' (15) and, finally, 'unawareness' (1).

The concerns shown by faculty members that do not use OSNs suggest that there may be a lack of trust on OSNs, especially with respect to the reason 'high personal exposure'. According to Foster, Francescucci and West (2010), even some individuals that use OSNs have privacy concerns and do not have the confidence to contribute to new communities.

Group Comparisons (Model 1)

In order to evaluate the influence of the use of OSNs to contact with co-workers on work-related attitudes and behaviors, we used, as mentioned before, the t-student test for independent samples.

It is possible to check, regarding the variable 'OCB', that $p = .177 > .05$, so we do not reject H_0, which means that there is no significant statistical difference between the means for the individuals that use OSN to maintain contact with co-workers and the ones that do not, in what concerns OCB.

For the variables JS and OC, $p > .05$, and so H_0 is not rejected, which means there is no significant difference between the means for individuals that use OSN to maintain contact with co-workers and the ones that do not. It is possible to check, regarding the variable 'IP', that $p = .032 < .05$, so we reject H_0, which means that there is a significant statistical difference between the means for the individuals that use OSN to maintain contact with co-workers and the ones that do not.

The results described above lead to and the rejection of H_1, H_2 and H_3. H_4 is supported. The use of OSN to maintain contact with co-workers influences IP, but not JS, OC or OCB. In what concerns commitment, the results found may be due to the fact that the definition of OC is directed towards the employer organization and not to co-workers.

Considering that the results were not significant for JS, OC and OCB, we also evaluated the influence of OSN on the different dimensions that constitute these concepts.

Considering that the results were not significant for JS, OC and OCB, we also evaluated the influence of OSN on the different dimensions that constitute these concepts. The variable OSN has a significant positive influence on satisfaction with job facets (p =.048). This means that the individuals that use OSN are more satisfied in what concerns job facets, such as job security, pay, social and supervision, in comparison to those who do not use OSN. The variable OSN also has a significant positive influence on civic virtue (p =.006), one of the dimensions of OCB, which means that the individuals that use OSN demonstrate more OCB related to the dimension 'civic virtue', that is behaviors that reveal the responsibility to participate in the life of the organization, in comparison to those who do not use OSN.

These results partially corroborate H_1 and H_3.

PLS Method (Model 2)

We used the PLS method to test the relations among the worker's attitudes and behaviors.

The results show that there are positive correlations among all the variables, although the correlations among JS and OCB, JS and IP, OC and OCB, OCB and IP are low. The correlations among the other variables are moderate.

To test the significance of the relations, we utilized the bootstrapping method, which is used to create a high number of samples (in this case, 1000) from the original sample, through systematic eliminations of observations. When $\alpha>.05$ in what concerns a certain relation between variables, that is, when the relation is not supported by the data, we eliminate it from the model. In this study, there was no need to eliminate any of the relations, since they are all significant.

In what concerns the Cross loadings, there were some problems with the correlations among certain indicators, but we did not consider they were important enough to alter the model, also because that could imply the loss of validity of the scale contents.

Figure 3. Final model and direct effects

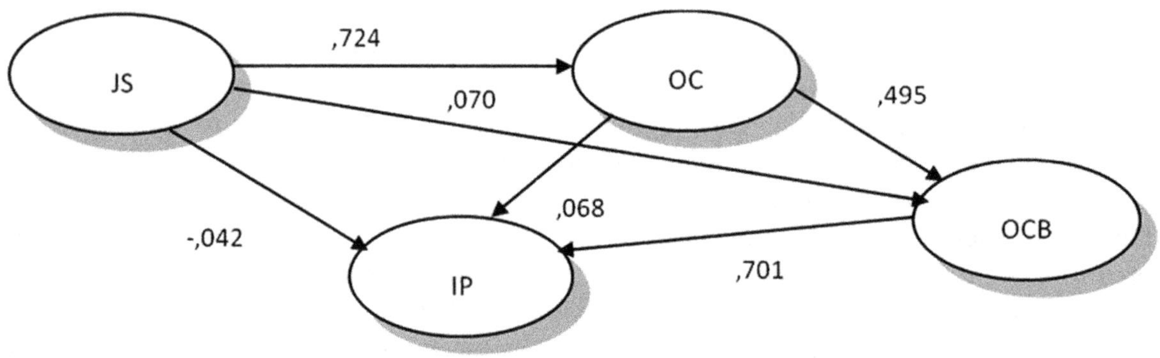

In what concerns the direct effects of the model, JS has a direct positive impact of .724 on OC (H_5), an impact of .070 on OCB (H_6) and it has a negative impact of -.042 on IP. When considering the direct effects between the variables, OC explains 49.5% of OCB (H_8), but only 6.8% of IP (H_9). Finally, OCB explains 70.1% of IP (H_{10}).

There are also indirect positive effects between JS and OCB (.358) – mediated by OC –, between JS and IP (.251) – mediated by OC and OCB –, and between OC and IP (.347) – mediated by OCB.

According to the results shown on Table 4, JS has a positive impact of .724 on OC (H_5), a positive impact of .429 on OCB (H_6) and it explains 30.9% of IP (H_7). OC explains 49.5% of OCB (H_8) and 41.6% of IP (H_9). Finally, OCB explains 70.1% of IP (H_{10}). Using another explanation, when, for example, OCB raises one unit, IP raises .701. These results are in agreement with the studies we identified in the literature review, so all the hypotheses included in model 2 are supported.

Table 1. Indirect effects for model 2

	JS	OC	OCB	IP
JS			.358	.251
OC				.347
OCB				
IP				
JS – Job satisfaction; OC – Organizational commitment; OCB – Organizational citizenship behaviors; IP – Individual performance				

Table 2. Total effects for model 2

	JS	OC	OCB	IP
JS		.724	.429	.309
OC			.495	.416
OCB				.701
IP				
JS – Job satisfaction; OC – Organizational commitment; OCB – Organizational citizenship behaviors; IP – Individual performance				

Explanatory Capacity of the Model and Internal Consistency of the Measures

In order to complete the analysis of the model, it is necessary to verify its explanatory capacity. The R^2 allows verifying what proportion of the variation of Y is explained by the variable X (Manso, 1996). The variable 'OC' explains 52.5% of the model, OCB explains 30.1% and IP explains 52.1% of the variation in the model. The variable 'JS' does not explain any variation in the model because it appears as the predictive variable.

A high composite reliability is a necessary condition to obtain a high validity and it is an important pre-requisite in the application of measures used to evaluate behaviors (Raykov & Grayson, 2003). The value for IP is moderate, while the values for the other variables are high.

Cronbach's alpha allows us to analyze the internal consistency of a measure and provides a sub-estimate of the real credibility of the analyzed instrument (Marôco & Garcia-Marques, 2006). The alpha values of Cronbach for the scale that measures JS (.88), OC (.85) and OCB (.88) are relatively high, suggesting that these theoretical constructs exhibit appropriate psychometric properties (Cronbach, 1951). However, the value for the scale of IP is somewhat low (.61), which means that further improvement of the scale may be needed.

As we can see on Figure 4, the use of OSNs to maintain contact with co-workers only has an effect on IP, if we do not consider the dimensions of the concepts. When considering the dimensions of JS, OC and OCB, we find that OSN influences the dimension 'satisfaction with facets' (JS) and the dimension 'civic virtue' (OCB). The results show that the use of OSNs to maintain contact with co-workers does not influence, at all, commitment.

In what concerns satisfaction with facets (job security, pay, social and supervision) the results make sense, since the variable OSN is related to the use of OSNs to maintain contact with co-workers, and so this may have a positive effect on social relationships at work, including with supervisors.

Figure 4. Combination of model 1 and model 2

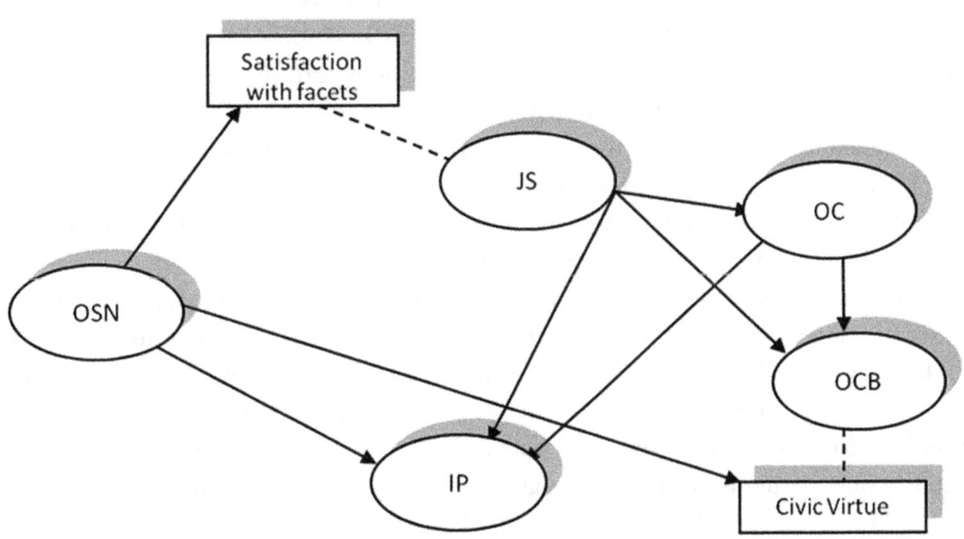

We explain the influence of 'OSN' on 'civic virtue' by the fact that OCB are also related to the worker's performance, and specifically this dimension of OCB could easily be confused with in-role behaviors. On the other hand, the contact that the worker maintains on OSNs with the co-workers could enhance the worker's will to participate actively in the organization's life due to a possible exchange of information regarding the organization on OSNs.

In what concerns the relations among work-related attitudes and behaviors, we verify that IP is also influenced by JS, OC and OCB. OC is positively influenced by JS and OCB is positively influenced by JS and OC.

CONCLUSION

We conclude that the use of OSNs to maintain contact with co-workers, when compared to those that do not use OSNs, influences performance (IP), specifically the individual's performance traits that lead to a higher performance. Interestingly, some of the dimensions that compose the IP measure are directly connected to concepts related to networks, such as 'relationship among organizational networks', 'transmission of organizational memory/knowledge', 'trust' and 'chain influence on performance'.

Although we found that the use of OSNs does not influence commitment (OC), in what concerns job satisfaction (JS) and Organizational citizenship behaviours (OCB), we found that the individuals that maintain contact with co-workers on OSNs show higher satisfaction with job facets – job security, pay, social and supervision –, which may be explained by the fact that the variable OSN is related to the use of OSNs to maintain contact with co-workers, so this may have a positive effect on the worker's social relationships at work, including with supervisors.

The fact that no significant relation between the use of OSNs to contact co-workers and OC was found may be due to the fact that OC is related to the affective reactions to the characteristics of the employer organization, and not to the interpersonal relationships established in the work environment. However, the use of OSNs to maintain contact with co-workers has a positive influence on the participation in the life of the organization (related to OCB), which may seem inconsistent. However, although OCB refer to extra-role performance, 'civic virtue' behaviors could easily be confused with in-role performance. On the other hand, there might be an exchange of information regarding the organization on OSNs that may raise the worker's will to actively participate on the organization's life.

It seems significant to underline that the motive 'high personal exposure', recognized more often by workers as the reason to not use OSNs, reveals a lack of trust on OSNs, a fact that is in agreement with one study we found, that discusses that even the individuals who use OSNs do not contribute as much as they could to online communities due to privacy concerns.

With regard to the worker's attitudes and behaviors, we've empirically supported all the proposed relationships – JS positively influences OC, OCB and IP, that OC has a positive impact on OCB and on IP, and that OCB have a positive effect on IP –, results that had already been found in previous studies. This way, we assure their value for HEI and we reaffirm their importance in the organizational context.

The results found in this study allow us to conclude that, to keep workers that show a high performance in the HE context, the use of OSNs to maintain contact with co-workers should be encouraged. Our conclusion is in agreement with the study carried out by Boulos and Wheeler (2007). The authors mention the need to raise awareness of Web 2.0 tools and the possibilities they offer in the educational context. Moreover, since HEI should be forming environments in which people join forces to create, share and advance knowledge, they should be prepared take the opportunities created by online tools (Barnatt, 2008). Additionally, HEI should assure that their workers are satisfied, thus enhancing commitment and, consequently, in-role and extra-role performance.

FUTURE RESEARCH DIRECTIONS

The use of OSNs to maintain contact with co-workers could have been more deeply assessed. We propose the replication of the study considering the types of exchanges made with co-workers on OSNs.

The relation between the use of OSNs to maintain contact with co-workers and OCB should be studied more accurately, using a different instrument and/or using a different context. We suggest requesting respondents to mention what type of information they exchange with co-workers, in order to enable getting to more precise conclusions in what concerns the influence of 'OSN' on the dimension 'civic virtue'.

We also suggest the evaluation of the quality of interpersonal relationships at work. This way, it could be possible to understand the effect that using OSNs to maintain contact with co-workers has on the relationships that workers keep in the work environment.

In the future, this investigation should be broadened, to include other organizational variables, such as motivation or work-related stress, so the understanding of the concepts used in this study can be highlighted.

A very important aspect which was identified in this study is the need of exploring the understanding about how to use OSNs as an educational tool, and the effects of their integration in this particular context.

Furthermore, considering our results, it would be interesting to probe the effects of using OSNs on the amount and quality of research carried out by academics, as well as on the amount and quality of research developed in cooperation with academics from different HEI, particularly regarding the effects of professional OSNs such as LinkedIn.

We also propose the use of other means to evaluate the variables, particularly performance, as well as the exact reproduction of the study in other contexts, such as service or sales companies, with the aim of comparing and extending the empirical evidence of the proposed relations.

REFERENCES

Allen, N., & Meyer, P. (1990). Organizational socialization tactics: A longitudinal analysis of links to newcomers' commitment and role orientation. *Academy of Management Journal*, *33*(4), 1–18.

Antoci, A., & Sabatini, F. (2018). Online networks, social interaction ans segregation: An evolutionary approach. *Journal of Evolutionary Economics*, *28*(4), 859–883. doi:10.100700191-018-0556-6

Asunda, P. (2010). Productivity, social networks and net communities in the workplace. *Techniques - American Vocational Association*, *85*(5), 38–41.

Bakshy, E., Rosenn, I., Marlow, C., & Adamic, L. (2012). The Role of Social Networks in Information Diffusion. *International World Wide Web Conference*, Lyon, France. 10.1145/2187836.2187907

Barnard, C. (1938). *The functions of the executive* (2nd ed.). Harvard University Press.

Barnatt, C. (2008). Higher Education 2.0. *International Journal of Management Education*, *7*(3), 47–56. doi:10.3794/ijme.73.250

Bateman, T., & Organ, D. (1983). Job satisfaction and the good soldier: The relationship between affect and employee "citizenship". *Academy of Management Journal*, *26*(4), 587–595.

Bennett, S., Bishop, A., Dalgarno, B., Waycott, J., & Kennedy, G. (2012). Implementing Web 2.0 technologies in higher education: A collective case study. *Computers & Education*, *59*(2), 524–534. doi:10.1016/j.compedu.2011.12.022

Benson, V., Filippaios, F., & Morgan, S. (2010). Online social networks: Changing the face of business education and career planning. *International Journal of Business and Management*, *4*(1), 20–33.

Boulos, M. N., & Wheeler, S. (2007). The emerging Web 2.0 social software: An enabling suite of sociable technologies in health and health care education. *Health Information and Libraries Journal*, *24*(1), 2–23. doi:10.1111/j.1471-1842.2007.00701.x PMID:17331140

Campbell, J. P., McHenry, J. J., & Lauress, W. L. (1990). Modeling Job performance in a population of jobs. *Personnel Psychology*, *43*(2), 313–333. doi:10.1111/j.1744-6570.1990.tb01561.x

Castilla, E. J. (2005). Social networks and employee performance in a call center. *American Journal of Sociology*, *110*(5), 1243–1283. doi:10.1086/427319

Chang, C.-S., & Chang, H.-H. (2007). Effects of internal marketing on nurse job satisfaction and organizational commitment: Example of medical centers in southern Taiwan. *The Journal of Nursing Research*, *15*(4), 265–274. doi:10.1097/01.JNR.0000387623.02931.a3 PMID:18080971

Cheng, E. W. L., Li, H., & Fox, P. (2007). Job performance dimensions for improving final project outcomes. *Journal of Construction Engineering and Management*, *133*(8), 592–599. doi:10.1061/(ASCE)0733-9364(2007)133:8(592)

Cheung, M. K. C., Chiu, P.-Y., & Lee, M. K. O. (2011). Online social networks: Why do students use facebook? *Computers in Human Behavior*, *27*(4), 1337–1343. doi:10.1016/j.chb.2010.07.028

Chin, W., Marcolin, B., & Newsted, P. (2003). A partial least squares latent variable modeling approach for measuring interaction effects: Results from a Monte Carlo simulation study and an electronic-mail emotion/adoption study. *Information Systems Research*, *14*(2), 189–217. doi:10.1287/isre.14.2.189.16018

Ciribelli, M. (2003). *Como realizar uma dissertação de mestrado através da pesquisa científica*. Rio de Janeiro: Viveiros de Castro Editora.

Cook, J., & Wall, T. (1980). New work attitude measures of trust, organizational commitment and personal need non-fulfillment. *Journal of Occupational Psychology*, *53*(1), 39–52. doi:10.1111/j.2044-8325.1980.tb00005.x

Davis, C. H. F. III, Deil-Amen, R., Rios-Aguilar, C., & Canche, M. S. G. (2001). Voluntary turnover, social capital and organizational performance. *Academy of Management Review*, *26*(3), 446–456. doi:10.5465/amr.2001.4845830

Donaldson, E., Ensher, E. A., & Grant-Vallone, E. J. (2000). Longitudinal examination of mentoring relationships on organizational commitment and citizenship behavior. *Journal of Career Development*, *26*(4), 233–248. doi:10.1177/089484530002600401

Donavan, D., Brown, T., & Mowen, J. (2004). Internal benefits of service-worker customer orientation: Job satisfaction, commitment and organizational citizenship behaviors. *Journal of Marketing*, *68*(1), 128–146. doi:10.1509/jmkg.68.1.128.24034

Eker, M., Eker, S., & Pala, F. (2008). The effects of job satisfaction on organizational commitment among Turkish health care staff: An empirical study. *Journal of Academic Studies*, *10*(36), 46–68.

Forkosh-Baruch, A., & Hershkovitz, A. (2012). A Case Study of Israeli Higher-Education Institutes Sharing Scholarly Information with the Community via Social Networks. *The Internet and Higher education*, *15*(1), 56–68. doi:10.1016/j.iheduc.2011.08.003

Foster, M. K., Francescucci, A., & West, B. C. (2010). Why users participate in online social networks. *International Journal of Business and Management*, *4*(1), 3–19.

González, J., & Garazo, T. (2006). Structural relationships between organizational service orientation, contact employee job satisfaction and citizenship behavior. *International Journal of Service Industry Management*, *17*(1), 23–50. doi:10.1108/09564230610651561

Grabner-Kraeuter, S. & Waiguny, M. (2011). *Why users stay in online social networks: perceptions of value, trust, subjective norm and the moderating influence of duration of use.* American Marketing Association.

Graham, J. (1991). An essay on organizational citizenship behavior. *Employee Responsibilities and Rights Journal*, *4*(4), 249–270. doi:10.1007/BF01385031

Greenhow, C. (2011). Online social networks and learning. *On the Horizon*, *19*(1), 4–12. doi:10.1108/10748121111107663

Guille, A., Hacid, H., Favre, C., & Zighed, D. A. (2013). Information Difusion in Online Social Networks: A Survey. *Association for Computing Machinery*, *42*(2), 17–28.

Hackman, R., & Oldham, G. (1975). Development of the Job Diagnostic Survey. *The Journal of Applied Psychology*, *60*(2), 150–170. doi:10.1037/h0076546

Hackman, R., & Oldham, G. (1976). Motivation through the design of work: A test of a theory. *Organizational Behavior and Human Performance*, *16*(2), 250–279. doi:10.1016/0030-5073(76)90016-7

Heidemann, J., Klier, M., & Probst, F. (2012). Online social networks: A survey of a global phenomenon. *Computer Networks*, *56*(18), 3866–3878. doi:10.1016/j.comnet.2012.08.009

Hurlbert, J. S. (2001). Social networks, social circles and job satisfaction. *Work and Occupations*, *18*(4), 415–430. doi:10.1177/0730888491018004003

Jamali, H. R., Russell, B., Nicholas, D., & Watkinson, A. (2014). Do online communities support research collaboration? *Journal of International Management*, *66*(6), 603–622.

Jones, M. (2006). Which is a better predictor of job performance: Job satisfaction or life satisfaction? *Journal of Behavioral and Applied Management*, *8*(1), 20–42.

Judge, T., Parker, S., Colbert, A., Heller, D., & Remus, I. (2001). Job satisfaction: a cross-cultural review. In N. Anderson, D. Ones, H. Sinangil, & C. Viswesvaran (Eds.), *Handbook of Industrial, Work and Organizational Psychology* (Vol. 2, pp. 25–52). London: Sage Publications.

Katz, D., & Kahn, R. L. (1978). *The Social Psychology of Organizations* (2nd ed.). New York: Wiley.

Konovsky, M., & Organ, D. (1996). Dispositional and contextual determinants of organizational citizenship behavior. *Journal of Organizational Behavior*, *17*(3), 253–266. doi:10.1002/(SICI)1099-1379(199605)17:3<253::AID-JOB747>3.0.CO;2-Q

Kukulska-Hulme, A. (2012). How should the higher education workforce adapt to advancements in technology for teaching and learning? *The Internet and Higher Education*, *15*(4), 247–254. doi:10.1016/j.iheduc.2011.12.002

Kumar, S., Kumar, P., & Bhasker, B. (2018). Interplay trust, information privacy concerns and behavioural intention of users on online social networks. *Behaviour & Information Technology*, *37*(6), 622–633. doi:10.1080/0144929X.2018.1470671

Lavelle, J., Brockner, J., Konovsky, M., Price, K., Henley, A., Taneja, A., & Vinekar, V. (2008). Commitment, procedural fairness, and organizational citizenship behavior: A multifoci analysis. *Journal of Organizational Behavior*, *30*(3), 337–357. doi:10.1002/job.518

Leonardi, P. M., & Vaast, E. (2017). Social media and ther affordances for organizing: A review and agenda for research. *The Academy of Management Annals*, *11*(1), 150–188. doi:10.5465/annals.2015.0144

Lo, M.-C., & Ramayah, T. (2009). Dimensionality of organizational citizenship behavior (OCB) in a multicultural society: The case of Malaysia. *International Business Research*, *2*(1), 48–55. doi:10.5539/ibr.v2n1p48

Locke, E., Latham, G., & Erez, M. (1988). The determinants of goal commitment. *Academy of Management Review*, *13*(1), 23–39. doi:10.5465/amr.1988.4306771

Locke, E. A. (1968). *What is Job satisfaction?* Washington, DC: American Psychology Association.

Locke, E. A. (1990). The nature and causes of Job satisfaction. In M. D. Dunnette & L. M. Hough (Eds.), Handbook of Industrial and Organizational Psychology (pp. 1297–1349). Palo Alto, CA: Consulting Psychologists Press.

Madjeski, M., Johnson, M., & Bellovin, S. M. (2011). *The Failure of Online Social Network Privacy Settings*. Columbia University Computer Science Technical Reports.

Malik, M., Nawab, S., Naeem, B., & Danish, R. Q. (2010). Job satisfaction and organizational commitment of University teachers in public sector of Pakistan. *International Journal of Business and Management*, *5*(6), 17–26. doi:10.5539/ijbm.v5n6p17

Manso, J. (1996). *Estatística descritiva e previsão* (2nd ed.). Covilhã: Universidade da Beira Interior.

Maroco, J. (2007). *Análise Estatística com utilização do SPSS* (3rd ed.). Lisboa: Edições Sílabo.

Marshall, B., Choi, J., El-Shinnaway, M. M., North, M., Svensson, L., Wang, S., ... Valenzuala, J. P. (2009). Online and offline social ties of social network website users: An exploratory study in eleven societies. *Journal of Computer Information Systems*, *50*(1), 54–64.

Merchant, G. (2012). Unravelling the social network: Theory and research. *Learning, Media and Technology*, *37*(1), 4–19. doi:10.1080/17439884.2011.567992

Meyer, J., & Herscovitch, L. (2001). Commitment in the workplace: Toward a general model. *Human Resource Management Review*, *11*(3), 299–326. doi:10.1016/S1053-4822(00)00053-X

Meyer, P., Stanley, D., Herscovitch, L., & Topolnytsky, L. (2002). Affective, continuance, and normative commitment to theorganization: A meta-analysis of antecedents, correlates, and consequences. *Journal of Vocational Behavior*, *61*(1), 20–52. doi:10.1006/jvbe.2001.1842

Moran, M., Seaman, J., & Tinti-Kane, H. (2011). *Teaching, Learning, and Sharing: How Today's Higher Education*. Boston: Pearson Learning Solutions.

Motowidlo, S. J., Borman, W. C., & Schmit, M. J. (1997). A theory of individual differences in Task and Contextual performance. *Human Performance*, *10*(2), 71–83. doi:10.120715327043hup1002_1

Organ, D. (1977). A reappraisal and reinterpretation of the satisfaction-causes-performance hypothesis. *Academy of Management Review*, *2*(1), 46–53. doi:10.5465/amr.1977.4409162

Organ, D., & Lingl, A. (1995). Personality, satisfaction and organizational citizenship behaviors. *The Journal of Social Psychology*, *135*(3), 339–250. doi:10.1080/00224545.1995.9713963

Organ, D. W., & Moorman, R. (1993). Fairness and Organizational citizenship behavior: What are the connections? *Social Justice Research*, *6*(1), 5–18. doi:10.1007/BF01048730

Paul, J. A., Baker, H. M., & Cochran, J. D. (2012). Effect of online social networking on student academic performance. *Computers in Human Behavior*, *28*(6), 2117–2127. doi:10.1016/j.chb.2012.06.016

Podsakoff, P., & MacKenzie, S. (1993). Citizenship behavior and fairness in organizations: Issues and directions for future research. *Employee Responsibilities and Rights Journal*, *6*(3), 257–269. doi:10.1007/BF01419449

Podsakoff, P., & MacKenzie, S. (1997). Impact of organizational citizenship behavior on organizational performance: A review and suggestions for future research. *Human Performance*, *10*(2), 133–151. doi:10.120715327043hup1002_5

Podsakoff, P., MacKenzie, S., Paine, J., & Bachrach, D. (2000). Organizational citizenship behaviors: A critical review of the theoretical and empirical literature and suggestions for future research. *Journal of Management*, *26*(3), 513–563. doi:10.1177/014920630002600307

Raykov, T., & Grayson, D. (2003). A test for change of composite reliability in scale development. *Multivariate Behavioral Research*, *38*(2), 143–159. doi:10.1207/S15327906MBR3802_1

Rego, A., Ribeiro, N., & Cunha, M. P. (2010). Perceptions of Organizational virtuousness and happiness as predictors of Organizational citizenship behaviors. *Journal of Business Ethics*, *93*(2), 215–235. doi:10.100710551-009-0197-7

Saari, L. M., & Judge, T. A. (2004). Employee Attitudes and Job satisfaction. *Human Resource Management, 43*(4), 395–407. doi:10.1002/hrm.20032

Samad, S. (2005). Unraveling the organizational commitment and job performance relationship: Exploring the moderating effect of job satisfaction. *Business Review (Federal Reserve Bank of Philadelphia), 4*(2), 79–84.

Selwyn, N. (2012). Social Media in Higher Education. In *The Europa World of Learning* (62nd ed.). Routledge.

Sledgianowski, D., & Kulviwat, S. (2009). Using social network sites: The effects of playfulness, critical mass and trust in a hedonic context. *Journal of Computer Information Systems, 49*(4), 74–83.

Sonnentag, S., & Frese, M. (2002). Performance concepts. In S. Sonnentag (Ed.), *Psychological Management of Individual Performance: A Handbook in the Psychology of Management in Organizations* (pp. 3–25). West Sussex, UK: John Wiley & Sons. doi:10.1002/0470013419

Staw, B. (1986). Organizational psychology and the pursuit of the happy/productive worker. *California Management Review, 28*(4), 40–53. doi:10.2307/41165214

Tess, P. A. (2013). The role of social media in higher education classes (real and virtual) – A literature review. *Computers in Human Behavior, 29*(5), A60–A68. doi:10.1016/j.chb.2012.12.032

Treem, J. W., & Leonardi, P. M. (2012). Social Media Use in Organizations: Exploring the Affordances of Visibility, Editability, Persistence, and Association. *Communication Yearbook, 36*(1), 143–189.

Ullrich, C., Tan, X., Borau, K., Shen, L., Luo, H., & Shen, R. (2008). Why Web 2.0 is good for learning and for research: principles and prototypes. *Proceedings of the 17 th International World Wide Web Conference*, 705-714. 10.1145/1367497.1367593

Van Dyne, L., Graham, J., & Dienesch, R. (1994). Organizational citizenship behavior: Construct redefinition, measurement and validation. *Academy of Management Journal, 37*(4), 765–802.

Veletsianos, G. (2011). Higher education scholars' participation and practices on Twitter. *Journal of Computer Assisted Learning, 28*(4), 336–349. doi:10.1111/j.1365-2729.2011.00449.x

Viswesvaran, C. (2001). Assessment of individual job performance: a review of the past century and a look ahead. In N. Anderson, D. Ones, H. Sinangil, & C. Viswesvaran (Eds.), *Handbook of Industrial, Work and Organizational Psychology* (Vol. 1, pp. 110–126). London: SAGE Publications. doi:10.4135/9781848608320.n7

Williams, L., & Anderson, S. (1991). Job satisfaction and organizational commitment as predictors of organizational citizenship and in-role behaviors. *Journal of Management, 17*(3), 601–617. doi:10.1177/014920639101700305

Xiaowei, L. (2006). A test on the systematic fuzzy measures of the key degree for the core employees' performance traits. *Canadian Social Science, 2*(5), 38–43.

Young, K. (2011). Social ties, social networks and the Facebook experience. *International Journal of Emerging Technologies and Society, 9*(1), 20–34.

KEY TERMS AND DEFINITIONS

Attitude: Describes an internal arrangement of the individual in relation to an element of the social world, which guides the conduct they adopt in the presence, real or symbolic, of that element.

Behavior: It is the activity of an organism interacting with its environment.

Higher Education Institutions: Community service providers, specifically of transference and economic value increase of the scientific and technological knowledge, which have as main goals to facilitate environments in which people collaborate to create, share, and advance knowledge.

Individual Performance: Defined as behaviors that can be evaluated, that is, behaviors that are identifiable only through operational measures.

Job Satisfaction: A positive emotional state—feelings and affective responses—or a generalized positive attitude towards work and the experiences that occur in the work environment, that depends on situational factors and/or on personality and personal factors, and that can be measured according to a global approach—based on the attitude towards work in general, not being a result of the sum of different aspects related to work, but depending on them—or to a multidimensional approach—satisfaction that reverses from a number of factors associated with work, being possible to measure satisfaction for each one of them.

Online Social Networks: They function as communication interfaces between millions of users, providing an efficient and user-friendly way to maintain social connections and to easily create and share information.

Organizational Citizenship Behaviors: Characterized as extra-role behaviors, that is, behaviors that arise as a way of acting beyond what is defined by work requirements (in-role behaviors), which means that the workers do non-mandatory tasks without expecting any rewards or recognition.

Organizational Commitment: It is a force of connection—a psychological or attitude stage—with the goals and values of the organization, which determines a direction at the level of the individual's behavior towards the employer organization, with the aim of benefiting it.

Social Networks: They function as communication channels and allow the exchange of resources to several levels, as a form of spreading and sharing ideas. The social relationships established at work are an important tool for the understanding of the workers' outcomes in the organizations.

ENDNOTE

1 Indicators of the teaching staff of HEI in Portugal. Accessed on the 24th May, 2011, on http://www.ine.pt/xportal/xmain?xpid=INE&xpgid=ine_indicadores&indOcorrCod=0000887&contexto=pi&selTab=tab0

Chapter 7
The Case for Effectively Using Existing Business Improvement Models in Australian Schools

Venesser Fernandes
https://orcid.org/0000-0003-3907-7673
Monash University, Australia

ABSTRACT

There is a significant lack of documented research on Australian school improvement that is contextualized within business improvement model settings. This is the case even though Australian schools have been operating within a business environment for a while now. This chapter aims at addressing this gap by discussing what educational quality is within schools. It will present an adapted version for continuous school improvement within school systems in Australia. This adapted version of continuous school improvement provides a theoretical framework on how schools operating as self-managed business systems can ensure that the delivery of educational quality is strategically sustained at the organizational level and that focus remains on the important core business of student learning. This adapted version has been described as strategic TQM and a case is made for its use in Australian schools through five transformations that are brought about through the SCOPE cycle for school improvement.

INTRODUCTION: THE KALEIDOSCOPIC LANDSCAPE OF CONTINUOUS SCHOOL IMPROVEMENT

Making any more mistakes in the "How to" of delivering a quality education will be disastrous to us as a nation, we cannot afford to delay having a world-class education system that builds a stronger future and a fairer Australia that can face the challenges of a globally competitive world. (Commonwealth Of Australia, 2008, p. 34)

DOI: 10.4018/978-1-5225-8516-9.ch007

For decades there has been a concerted effort at the international and national level to improve educational quality as part of both international and national educational reform agendas. However defining and coming to an understanding of what educational quality is, has been an ambiguous and difficult journey. There is in fact no universal agreement on its definition, its processes, its methods for measurement, and the complexity of many simultaneously interacting relevant variables that would need to be analysed. This ambiguity in itself provides credence to the fact that educational quality is not a universally defined phenomenon but something that has to be understood at its point of action albeit having a universally accepted notional framework of understanding that nations strive to achieve. As seen over the years, some of the problems endemic to studies of educational effectiveness have been attributed to a lack of empirical evidence, a lack of longitudinal studies modelling change, the issue of data analysis methods, problems in the choice of measures for the outcomes, the issue of sample size, and statistical adjustments (Hill, Rowe, Holmes-Smith & Russell, 1996).

In a rapidly changing environment of social and economic globalisation, education is identified as a primary centrepiece and a requisite for fulfilling many individual, familial and national aspirations (Adams et al., 2012, p. 6). Hill, Mellon, Laker and Goddard (Hill, Mellon, Laker & Goddard, 2016) suggest that, "The strength of a nation's economy and the vitality of its society depend on the quality of its schools". Hill, Rowe, Holmes-Smith and Russell (1996) go on to describe how, "The provision of schooling is one of the most massive and ubiquitous undertakings of the modern state. Schools account for a substantial proportion of public and private expenditure and are universally regarded as vital instruments of social and economic policy aimed at promoting individual fulfilment, social progress and national prosperity" (p. 1). Taking Australia alone as a case in point, it has been found that Australia's declining performance across maths, reading and science may cost the country approximately $120 billion over the coming decades (Hetherington, 2018). This indicates the substantial role that the quality of education plays in any nation's success. In such an environment, understandings around educational quality have understandably become much more complex and comprehensive.

Schools are open systems where people work together to achieve a common purpose. As open systems, schools are always interacting with their environments and therefore structure themselves to deal with forces within these environments. Betts (1992) suggests that, "The improvement of quality involves the design of an educational system that not only optimises the relationship among the elements but also between the educational system and its environment. In general, this means designing a system that is more open, organic, pluralistic, and complex" (p.40). Adams et al. (2012, p. 2) suggest that there are three major implications that should be considered in improvement efforts across education policy, planning and practice which include: (a) increased centrality of education in national development policy and planning; (b) increased focus and priority on decentralisation and localisation with further empowerment of teachers and administrators; and, (c) the trend towards an emphasis on, and assessment of education quality at all levels. Brooks and Normore (2010) further suggest that "a more glocalised (a meaningful integration of local and global forces) approach to education by the discrete agency of educational leaders is imperative" (p. 52) in being able to develop a deeper understanding of educational quality. As they suggest, "the implications of glocalisation are profound, and the consequences of not understanding the way that the local and global are interconnected will increase over time" (p. 73). Torres and Antikainen (2003) similarly identify that "the presence of globalisation makes the study of education even more complex. Traditional preoccupation with the intersection of classes, race, gender, and the state become magnified with the dialectics of the global and the local" (p. 5). According to Fernandes (Fernandes, 2019a), educational leadership practised within schools that actively demonstrate and practice glocal

Figure 1. A glocalised framework of continuous school improvement

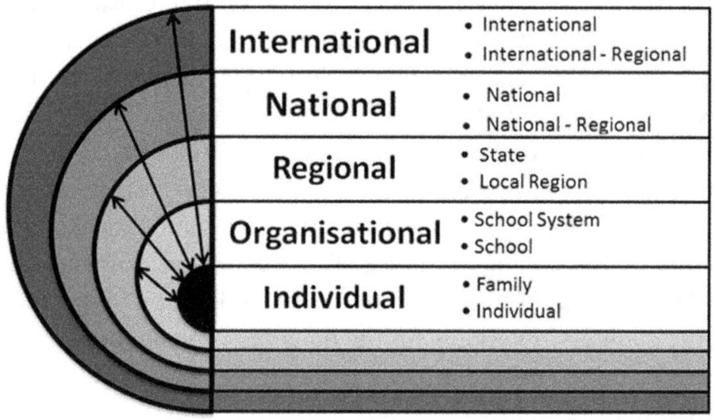

leadership "will provide experientially rich learning to students on how to live, survive and thrive in their future world" (p.27).

Thus, it seems obvious that school improvement initiatives taken to improve educational quality continue to be required at all levels: international, national, state, regional and organisational (see Figure 1). Having a conscious and agentic understanding of the importance of this continuous change for improvement in educational quality is required by stakeholders at every level. Using a strong glocalised approach, educational quality becomes decentralised and localised being situated around continuous and improved educational effectiveness at the individual level as well as at the organisational, regional, national and international levels of educational development. Also, as Figure 1 suggests, it is imperative that whatever the level of improvement, the effect is felt at the individual level – the student learner. The individual learner is central to all educational improvements going on at each of these levels.

Banathy (1991, p.80) describes such an educational system as one that interacts with constantly changing, multiple environments and coordinates with many other systems in the environment. In essence, the question then is how can this dynamic glocalised educational system be understood? Engeström and Glaveanu (2012) use the third generation activity theory as a systems model for theorizing and for empirical studies which expand the unit of analysis from a single activity system to multiple, interacting activity systems. Daniels and Warmington (2007) in discussing Engeström's (2001) third generation activity theory identify the importance of extending beyond a singular activity system such as a school organisation and to examine and work towards the transformation of networks of interacting activity systems such as the school community or other similar schools and multi-organisational fields of activity such as regional departments of education as well as national and international education bodies. Daniels and Warmington (2007) contend that through the interactions of these interacting activity systems and their relative subjects and objects, the transformation of practice, in this case, educational practice, grows and improves itself.

Australian schools have been engaged in school improvement for a number of decades with many theoretical models and frameworks outlining the importance of good practice and good organisation to deliver quality education (Drysdale, Goode & Gurr, 2009; Masters, 2012; Mulford, 2008; Reid, Cranston, Keating & Mulford, 2010; Silins, Zarins & Mulford, 2002). Gammage (2008) suggests that, "since the mid-seventies, the Australian systems of education showed a keen interest towards decentralisations and that evidence of school-based management as a strategy and a major vehicle in introducing education reforms became evident" (p. 665). At the national level, looking at the dominant discourse in Australian education, Reid et al. (2010, p. 27) suggest that there is a public purpose of education that must be maintained in Australian schools over the individual or economic purposes of education and state that, "in a globalising world where the role of the nation state is changing and societies are becoming increasingly culturally diverse, schools are necessary for the public purpose of forming active citizens for democratic publics – people with the will and commitment to shape, and participate in an inclusive and democratic civil society and polity that is responsive to the new environment." Goddard (2010) further suggests that, at the organisational level, "strategies such as democratic governance, a culture of collaboration, a commitment to professional growth, strong leadership, and concern for the equity, success, and well-being of individual students" (p. 47) must be implemented by school administrators and educational leaders. As Gammage (2008) elaborates, "when the private sector embraced a more decentralised, high-involvement management approach, public education systems too started to focus on reforms to provide a more flexible, autonomous and responsive, high-performing schools which are able to meet the complexities of a global knowledge economy" (p. 664). Currently, this is the *modus operandi* within schools, be it in the public, independent or catholic school systems with primary, secondary or K-12 levels, or localised in the urban or regional landscape of Australia (Caldwell, 2005; 2007; Cranston, 2000; 2001; Dellar, 1998; Leithwood & Menzies, 1998; Thomas et al., 2011). De Grauwe's (2005) research into school-based management informs of five common reasons for this being so widely accepted: a democratic system; more relevant with local solutions to local problems; less bureaucratic; allows greater responsibility; and, allows greater mobilisation of resources. Fernandes (Fernandes, 2019b) also discusses how educational business improvement models allow for the unique context of each school and its associated stakeholders to engage in collective and collaborative participation while working through their school improvement agenda making use of both accountability and improvement while working on the many transformative, complex and adaptive problems that schools face today. Interestingly, there is little documented research written at length about Australian school improvement in terms of business improvement (Kovacs, 2009; Robinson, 1996) even though after decentralisation, Australian schools have been operating within a business environment. The objectives of this chapter are as follows:

1. To introduce a new perspective on educational quality that has been framed using a business improvement vernacular geared towards school improvement.
2. To discuss an adapted version of continuous school improvement where schools operate as self-managed business systems and develop themselves as strategically-oriented learning organisations.

BACKGROUND: FRAMING A PROGRESSIVE-REFLECTIVE APPROACH TO EDUCATIONAL QUALITY WITHIN SCHOOLS

The term *Quality* continues to remain hard to define because the concept of quality in itself can mean many things to many people (Cheng & Tam, 1997; Weick, 2000). The understanding of quality has been found to be different for each individual due to the unique existence of a person with their own particular set of life experiences. Hence quality is undefined (Pfeffer & Coote, 1991) and the indicators used to measure quality for one individual may not be the same for another (Fuller, 1986; Hughes, 1988). Uselac (1993) states that "Quality is an attribute of a product or a service. Quality is not [restricted to] products and services but includes processes, environment and people" (p. 20). Sallis (1993) defines quality as both an absolute and relative concept leading to a *consumer definition for quality*. As an absolute, quality relates to rank, demonstrating that it is mainly concerned with performing to the highest standards. Greenwood and Gaunt (1994) define quality as "a product or service delivered to a very high specification at a very high price, only accessible to customers or clients who have high incomes and wealth" (p. 26). Quality as a relative concept is not an end in itself; but the means by which the end product is judged to be up to standard. Thus, quality products must do what they claim to do, and do what their customers expect of them (Sallis, 1993). This definition of quality deals with measuring up to specification by meeting pre-set standards and is known as the producer definition of quality – *fitness for purpose or use* (Murgatroyd & Morgan, 1993). Here a quality assurance system is established to ensure that there is a consistent production of goods or services to a particular standard or specification. Quality Assurance systems such as the ISO 9000 series, the Malcolm Baldrige National Quality Award (MBNQA), the former British Standards (BS5750), European Quality Award (EQA), the Deming Prize (Japanese) or the Australian Quality Award (AQA) which later changed to the Australian Business Excellence Framework (ABEF) are examples of this definition of quality. The last concept of quality integrates the other two, and is commonly known as the customer-driven concept of quality – *quality in perception*. It identifies the *results aspect* (Goetsch & Davis, 2000) of quality. This quality is defined as that which satisfies best and exceeds customer's expectations.

The American National Standards Institute (ANSI) and the American Society for Quality (ASQ) have standardised an official definition for this quality (ANSI/ASQC A3-1978, 1978) which states that "Quality is the totality of features and characteristics of an entity bearing on its ability to satisfy stated and implied needs [of customers or clients]" (p. 3). In short, quality is dynamic – associated with various factors such as: products, services, people, processes and environments that meet or exceed client/customer expectations. For some, this totality perspective has also been defined as Total Quality Management (TQM). When extended to educational systems, a TQM-based educational organisation will work on developing systems and processes that satisfy the expectations of both internal and external stakeholders within that system to ensure that educational quality is maintained. Thus, within the context of education, two central issues for educational quality are: 'Quality of what?' and 'Quality for whom?' The first question, 'Quality of what?' refers to those aspects of educational performance which relate to the overall quality specifications. The second question, 'Quality for whom?' refers to different stakeholders involved within the school. As indicated by Reddy (2007):

[educational] quality is a multifaceted concept viewed from different perspectives by different stakeholders ... though its meaning is not a settled matter, there is consensus on the fact that a high quality of education should facilitate the attainment of knowledge, skills and attitudes that have intrinsic value, for all students, and contributes to economic and social development. (p. 18)

Due to these different concepts, concerns and stakeholders in education, educational quality is assessed using diverse indicators as well as wide-ranging strategies (Cheng & Tam, 1997). In addition, expectations of different stakeholders within education can be different or even contradictory (Hughes, 1988), making the notion of *achieving educational quality* more complex. To unravel this complexity and coming from a business improvement perspective that is grounded in a progressive-reflective approach, the author proposes that two aspects of educational quality need to be considered, i.e. *Quality Assurance* and *Quality Enhancement*.

Defining Quality Assurance Within Educational Quality

Quality Assurance refers to the policies, processes and actions through which the quality of a system is developed and maintained (McKimm, 2003 as cited in Hodgkinson & Kelly, 2007, p. 78). *Quality Assurance* ensures fitness of purpose (Hodgkinson & Kelly, 2007) or use (Murgatroyd & Morgan, 1993). In a *Quality Assurance* educational system two inter-related activities would typically be found (see Figure 2), i.e. one that is concerned with *Management for Quality* (doing the right job) and the other with *Quality Management* (doing the job right) (Hodgkinson & Brown, 2003 as cited in Hodgkinson & Kelly, 2007, p. 78).

The first inter-related activity: *Management for Quality* includes those school improvement processes where the quality of an educational program or service is achieved through certain set goals (Hodgkinson & Kelly, 2007). Looking at the processes involved within the delivery of quality education, Deming's philosophy of profound knowledge and his fourteen principles provide a plausible route for the management of an educational institution to ensure that they are able to deliver good service quality in education (Redmond, Curtis, Noone, & Keenan, 2008). According to Schultz's (2014) discussion of Deming's philosophy, the leader drives this *Management for Quality* where "The system of profound knowledge … requires the leader…to consider all organisational aspects when making decisions. This means recognizing how processes are interconnected and how they function as a whole within the larger environment so that the organisation can reach intended expectations" (p. 6). Hodgkinson and Kelly (2007) suggest *Management for Quality* implies that "there is a tacit understanding of the prescribed quality of the [program] or service that has to be delivered. To be effective, this tacit understanding requires articulation, strategies and actions" (p. 78). Hence, the educational organisation uses a focused and dynamic approach to implement a quality plan and policy. Thus, the activities that come under *Management for Quality* within an educational organisation assist it in staying competitive and having new thinking linked with the challenges of a global economy, new technologies, environmental and social diversity, and customer-oriented management (Lee & Lazarus, 1993).

Figure 2. A schematic diagram of quality assurance mechanisms implemented within school organisations
Source: Adapted from Hodgkinson & Kelly (2007, pp. 78-79)

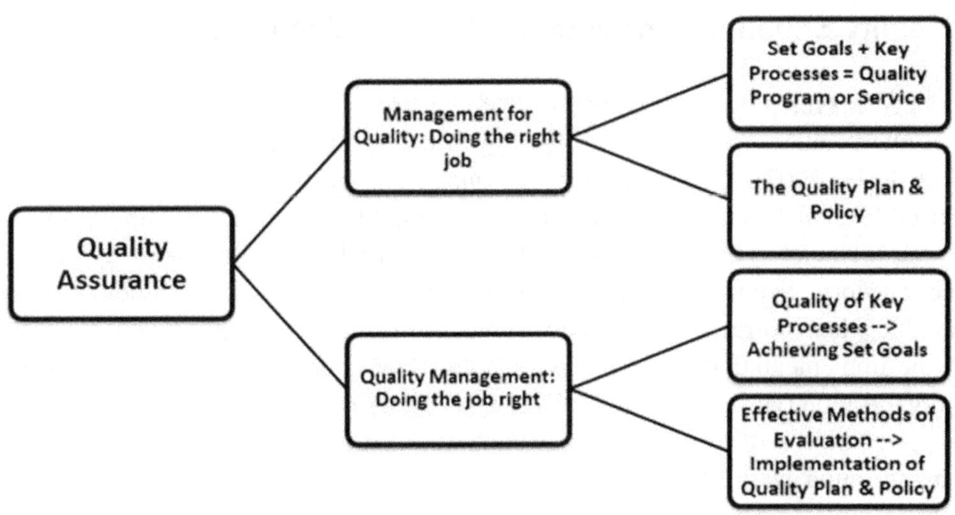

The second inter-related activity: *Quality Management* has been defined as the quality of the processes whereby an educational institution works towards achieving its goals (Hodgkinson & Kelly, 2007). It is that aspect of the overall management function that determines and implements the quality policy which in effect is the collective intentions and directions of the organisation (Van Vught & Westerheijden, 1992). *Quality Management* within an educational organisation is framed within the context of planned cultural change. As Hodgkinson and Kelly (2007, pp.78-79) suggest, "It is dependent upon an understanding of how people learn, how they interact, and how they sustain, develop, or even destroy, a culture… It [involves] well-articulated methods of evaluation of the management processes involved. These methods are often referred to as quality audits or annual monitoring and review" or school accountability frameworks (Montecinos et al, 2014). Furthermore, Montecinos et al (2014) suggest that school leadership plays a significant role in mediating the emotional and motivational effects that arise from these mandated internal and external accountability processes integrated within the school organisational culture (p. 256). Elaborating on this, Emstad (2011) highlights that school leadership plays a central role in building this organisational culture through coordination of problem-solving processes among teachers, organisation of teacher teams and the holding of the entire school accountable for school improvement.

Such a quality culture has been defined by Saraph and Sebastian (1993) as, "the total collective and shared learning of quality-related values as the [educational] organisation develops its capacity to survive in its external environment and to manage its own internal affairs" (p. 73). *Quality Management* is a cultural transformation within an educational organisation. It upholds the organisational goals (*Management for Quality*) as it sustains processes for continuation of a shared organisational vision, a proactive leadership, an effective professional development program, provision of services that satisfy customer needs, and a continuous improvement process of review and evaluation within an educational organisation (Berry, 1997). *Quality Management* provides an organisational culture characterised by increased satisfaction brought about through continuous improvements in educational processes and the proactive participation of all educational stakeholders in these improvement processes (Dahlgaard, Kristensen, & Kanji, 1995; Ngware et al., 2006). These two inter-related activities: *Management for Quality* and *Quality Management* provide schools a comprehensive framework for monitoring *Quality Assurance* mechanisms through a progressive-reflective approach of looking from the inside outwards and looking from the outside inwards.

Defining Quality Enhancement Within Educational Quality

Quality Enhancement refers to the improvement of educational quality brought about through cycles of continuous improvement and innovation that becomes the culture of the educational organisation (Hodgkinson & Kelly, 2007). Through *Quality Enhancement*, services provided are more responsive to stakeholder needs established through processes of continual improvement existing through the understanding and improving of systems (DiPietro, 1993), such as school organisations.

Due to the transformative nature of these continual improvement processes a deliberate change process is put in place that is directly concerned with adding value through improved educational quality and through the implementation of subsequent cycles of on-going transformative change within the educational organisation (Hodgkinson & Kelly, 2007). Under *Quality Assurance* the *'Management for Quality'* and '*Quality Management'* are primary activities for a quality system incorporated within an educational organisation, while *Quality Enhancement* provides the systemic processes required to sustain changes so that long term objectives can be achieved. These systemic processes were first identified

Figure 3. A modified version of Deming's PDSA cycle
Source: Adapted from Brown & Marshall (2008, p. 206)

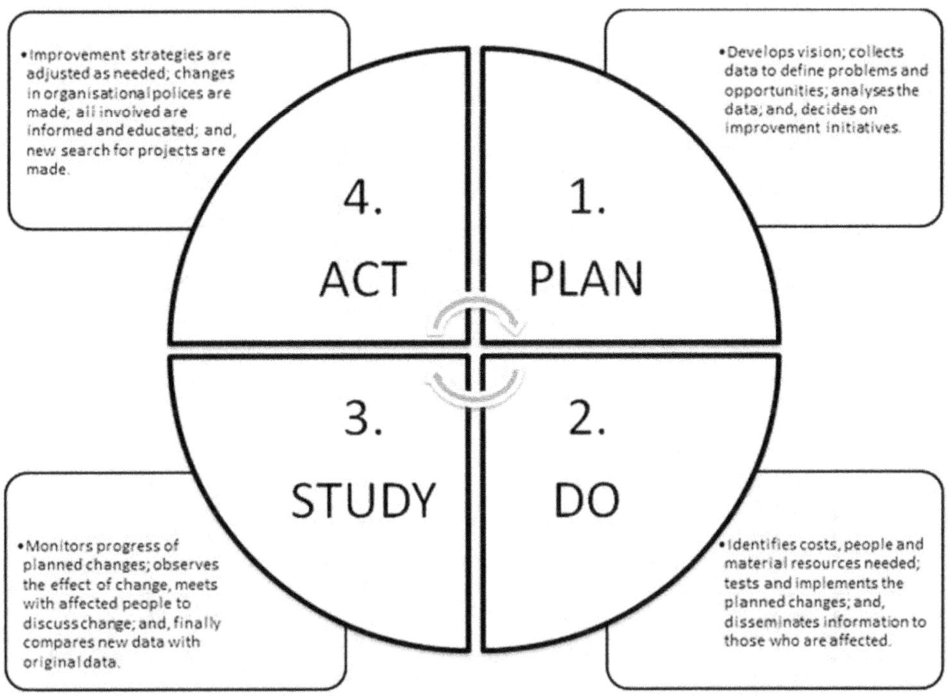

as a '*Continuous Quality Improvement approach*' and were proposed by Walter Shewart (1931). Later, Deming's famous continuous quality improvement cycle of Plan, Do, Study and Act became more widely used and known for this approach (see Figure 3). Svensson and Klefsjö (2006, p. 303) in their TQM-based self-assessment model identify four phases to self-assessment that closely resembled Deming's Continuous Improvement Cycle, which include: Plan, Describe, Analyse and Act.

Svensson and Klefsjö (2006, p. 304) suggest that within an educational organisation self-assessment tasks (PDSA cycles in the Figure 4) and continuous improvement tasks (future projects in the Figure 4) are two interdependent and consecutive cycles. In most instances, the self-assessment task is followed by continuous improvement tasks. Fernandes (2013, p. 59) suggests that the combination of both these tasks: self-assessment tasks and continuous improvement tasks, working interdependently and consecutively in a continuous improvement system leads to a quality-enhanced educational organisation (see Figure 4). In this dynamic continuous improvement system, after the first initial self-assessment task the educational organisation leads itself into a set of continuous improvement tasks (future projects) that are inbuilt with their own self-assessment tasks. These continuous improvement tasks are the first stage of organisational continuous improvement tasks. However, as indicated in Figure 4, each of the stage one continuous improvement tasks as future projects follow their cycles of inbuilt self-assessment tasks (PDSA cycles) which then lead the organisation to a second stage of continuous improvement tasks also having inbuilt self-assessment tasks. These stages then continue to move on in these interdependent and consecutive cycles. The rationale behind this progressive-reflective approach is that system self-assessments are done at each stage to analyse the effect the continuous improvement tasks are having on the whole organisation. This multiple-stage continuous improvement with inbuilt self-assessment tasks

Figure 4. The two interdependent and consecutive cycles of organisational self-assessment and organisational continuous improvement tasks
Source: Adapted from Svensson, M. & Klefsjö, B. (2006, p. 304)

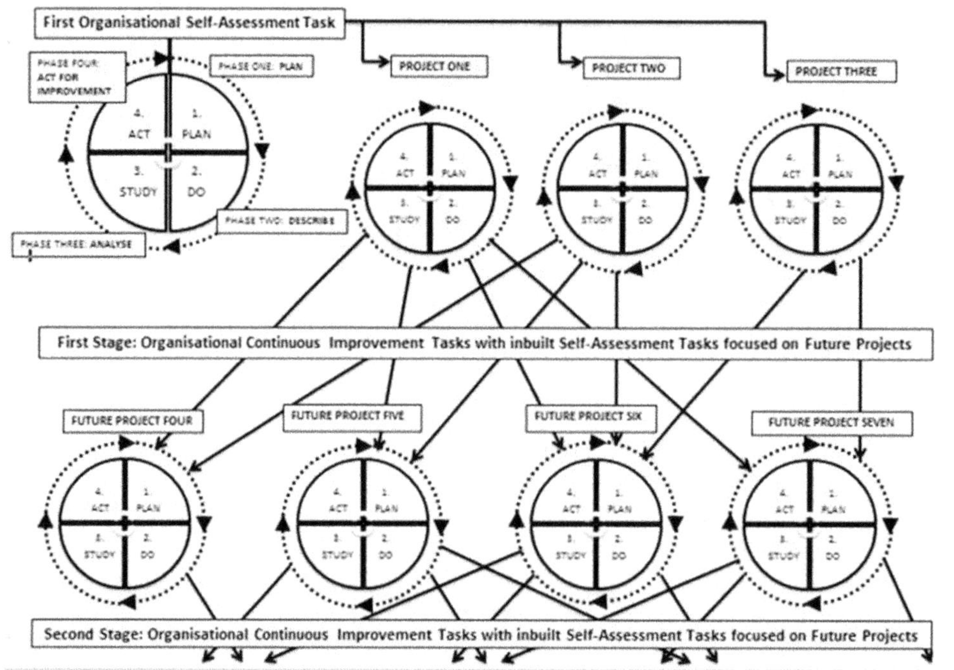

allows the organisation to closely look at the efficiency of the project and to ensure that it is moving to its next desired state of improvement. Thus future projects are in fact but desired states of improvement developed after an organisation has assessed itself on the previous state of improvement.

Svensson and Klefsjö's (2006) study also suggests that for any continuous quality improvement project to succeed it requires the following: 1) a common understanding by all stakeholders on what quality is in their context; 2) a common and shared understanding of what the purpose and core values of the project are; 3) sufficient time and resources spent on planning the self-assessment tasks and continual improvement tasks; and, 4) effective communication within the organisation during the planning, execution and evaluation stages of the project. Brown and Marshall (2008, pp. 206-207) suggest that in using Deming's approach in education, three assumptions must be held: (1) Decisions should be facts-based, evident through the collection and analysis of objective data. (2) People performing the work know it best hence stakeholder involvement at all levels is critical. (3) Teams have more success in problem-solving than individuals. Hence, teams must be trained in the continuous improvement approach. Hodgkinson and Kelly (2007) suggest that, "*Quality Enhancement* is given practical expression through staff appraisal and development, and the fostering of a culture of continuous improvement and innovation" (p. 79). Its successful implementation requires a cultural change and the willingness of stakeholders to participate in a variety of reflective activities or programs (Bone, 1996, p. 44). These organisations have a collegiate management style, allowing the development of school values and providing it with necessary quality enhancement processes that ensure these values are reviewed periodically so that they do not become 'hidden resistors to change'.

In framing educational quality through *Quality Enhancement* approaches, the educational organisation will determine, define and develop its people and its processes based on a system of continuous quality improvements involving a number of self-assessment tasks as well as continuous improvement projects working in consecutive cycles. The educational organisation thus bases its quality policies, processes and actions (*Quality Assurance*) around the approach of systemic continuous improvement (*Quality Enhancement*). Hence there is a symbiotic relationship between *Quality Assurance* and *Quality Enhancement* evident within the educational organisation where they use a progressive-reflective approach with a business improvement perspective that allows them to take a 360 degree view of the continuous improvement path being taken by them at each stage of improvement and ensuring that this path leads them ahead.

MAIN FOCUS OF THIS CHAPTER: REFRAMING EDUCATIONAL QUALITY WITHIN CONTINUOUS SCHOOL IMPROVEMENT

Referring to Reddy's (2007) definition given earlier in this chapter, educational quality is a multi-faceted concept that draws its strength from the consensus that an educational institution delivers a high quality of education which adds value to its students as well as contributes towards the overall economic and social development of the nation. In framing educational quality within school contexts, it is important to consider the school as a social system. Banathy and Jenks (1990) suggest that, "Systems thinking helps us to understand the nature of education as a complex and dynamic system that operates in ever changing environments and interacts with a variety of other societal systems." (p. 7) A system is most commonly defined as a set of elements, principles or procedures that function as a whole in order to meet a common purpose. The system is based on synergy where the parts that make up the system cannot function on their own but instead the whole system is greater than the sum of its parts, i.e. the elements, principles or procedures. This is because the relationship between the parts adds value to the overall system. Betts (1992) suggests, "The improvement of quality involves the design of an educational system that not only optimises the relationship among the elements but also between the educational system and its environment… this means designing a system that is more open, organic, pluralistic, and complex" (p. 40). Similarly, Cheng (2003) suggests that "Educational quality is the set of elements in the input, output and process sections of educational institutions that provide services which completely satisfy internal and external strategic constituencies by meeting their explicit and implicit expectations" (p. 207). Schools are often described as open systems that have a number of complexities and pluralities embedded within their organic nature therefore making the task of leading school improvement processes within schools today more complex than it has been in the past.

Sallis (1996) in focusing upon a systems approach to school improvement processes suggests that Total Quality Management (TQM) provides "a philosophy of continuous improvement, which can provide an educational institution with a set of practical tools for meeting and exceeding present and future customer needs, wants and expectations" (p. 27). This would indicate that business improvement models relying on continuous improvement philosophies and practices could make use of a TQM philosophy to provide the internal and external strategic constituencies with a set of practical tools and processes that help drive the school improvement processes and meet the expectations of stakeholders within that organisation. Betts (1992) advocates a need for using TQM in education as it is 'a total systems approach' and is needed in current times to address the issues surrounding educational quality. As Betts (1992) suggests, "Nearly a century of change has left schools playing catch-up, and it will take a whole-system approach to meet society's evolving needs" (p. 38). There is sufficient evidence to show that schools using TQM approaches have had both positive as well as negative outcomes and while some have managed to sustain the improvement effort put in place, others have not. A closer analysis of this dilemma raises an interesting argument on what type of TQM should be deployed within an educational organisation.

Total Quality Management (TQM) in the educational context of teaching and learning (Chizmar, 2000) has been defined as "a collaborative and holistic implementation of ideas derived from the industrial TQM model" (p. 1). In some ways this definition perpetuates the misconceptions that have been associated with TQM and its application in education. Due to the strong overtones of the industrial model, TQM has found many barriers since the eighties in being implemented within educational institutions such as schools as compared to higher education institutions. Reservations about the use of quality models have been due to their association initially with industry (Hodgkinson & Kelly, 2007) and business (Desjardins & Obara, 1993) where earlier models have strong overtones of industrial language (Kohn, 1993) and business processes (Walpole & Noeth, 2002). Others feel that the application of TQM programs within educational systems can be challenging, costly and time-consuming (Kwan, 1996; Rampa, 2005; Temponi, 2005; Terry, 1996). Successful implementation of quality systems has required a complete commitment from various stakeholders in the organisation, especially the leadership, as well as a large degree of re-engineering and change (Weller, 1998), involving a huge amount of time and resources (Hernandez, 2001; Rampa, 2005). TQM programs can sometimes be met with opposition and reluctance by conservative school teachers (Crawford & Shutler, 1999) and academics in higher education sector who have reservations about students being considered as customers and related processes of customer satisfaction (Eagle & Brennan, 2007; Idrus, 1995; Kwan, 1996).

Also, in education there are many types of "customers" and defining each of them is difficult (Kohn, 1993). While the student is the primary beneficiary of education, other stakeholders ranging from parents, prospective employers and society as a whole, have an interest in what they see as the extent of a successful and appropriate education that meets the needs of the student (Madu & Kuei, 1993). Some researchers define students as customers (Brandt, 1993; Holt, 1993b), while others believe there is a huge difference between students' wants and needs (Chickering & Potter, 1993) to be able to put in satisfactory standards or benchmarks. Some have compared the student to a worker (Schmoker & Wilson, 1993; Siegel, 2000), student knowledge to the product, and education (teaching and learning) to the core operating process (Bonstingl, 1993). However, in education, this "product" is not as tangible as it is in business or industry. The teaching and learning process cannot be mass-produced; instead it is an individual, student-centred process (Kohn, 1993; Sztajn, 1992). TQM critics fear that educators using TQM programs may focus solely on visible and measurable outcomes such as measurable performance indicators, because implementing quality requires data and data-driven decisions. In doing so, they feel that this will inhibit important outcomes of education such as creativity and non-measurable factors such as the love of learning and the enhancement of curiosity (Holt, 1993a). Another concern raised in the use of quality programs is the confusion of many packaged programs being available and the lack of clarity on what would be best-suited for a particular setting. Within educational organisations, there is a wide diversity in what is perceived as quality products or services due to a number of factors such as leadership, teaching staff and their competencies and methods, students enrolled, team building and teamwork, or geographic location of the school (Garbutt, 1996). As such, it becomes difficult to determine which quality program will work best within a particular educational organisation. There are also many misconceptions that seem to be driven by the lack of information about the scope of quality programs and the larger impact of the continuous improvement programs within educational systems (Temponi, 2005). Even when TQM programs have been taken on board and run successfully in schools and school systems, a lack of sufficient research on their impact has left an imbalance in the overall perspective around the effectiveness of TQM in school contexts and has led to a more negative one.

Though all has not been lost and some have suggested that, when managed correctly, TQM is a way of thinking or a philosophy that focuses attention on the management functions that transform learning into 'quality learning' (Rampa, 2005). In success stories, the contribution of quality pioneers such as Edward Deming and the application of his principles through TQM programs within educational organisations have assisted in the provision of a quality service to a diverse group of stakeholders (Redmond et al., 2008). Also, when looking further into this situation, there is sufficient evidence to suggest that TQM has provided a set of guiding principles focused entirely on meeting the needs and expectations of stakeholders within an educational institution with in-built mechanisms of continuous improvement (Steyn, 2000). As Murgatroyd and Morgan (1993) suggest, this is brought through by "the systematic management of an organisation's customer-supplier (or more appropriately stakeholder) relationships" (p. 59) that ensures sustainable, steep-slope improvement in quality performance. The KEYS Initiative developed and run by the National Education Association in USA examined the relationship between organisational characteristics of schools and student learning and found that schools that consistently displayed six key factors of total quality in education directly promoted high student achievement (Hawley & Rollie, 2007). Bernhardt's (2013) work on continuous school improvement underpinned by TQM theory, presents a strong case for educators to understand the impact data can make on educational quality, especially in times of high-stakes accountability, where educators are required to gather, analyse, and use data to improve teaching and learning within schools.

Examples of success in TQM initiatives can be obtained from descriptive reports on cases at Fox Valley Technical College, U.S. (Spanbauer, 1989) and Mt. Edgecumbe High School, Alaska (Hubbard & Menzel, 1995); Oregon State University, U.S. (Coate, 1990); Texas State District, U.S. (Hernandez, 2001); Wolverhampton University, U.K. (Doherty, 1993); Aston University, U.K. (Clayton, 1995); University of Central Queensland, Australia (Idrus, 1995); the Departments of Education in South Australia and Victoria, Australia (Kovacs, 2009; Kovacs & King, 2005); Southwest School, New South Wales, Australia (Robinson, 1996); the Swedish National Agency for School Improvement (Svensson & Klefsjö, 2006); the Kenya Education Master Plan for Education and Training 1997-2010 (Ngware, Wamukuru, & Odebero, 2006); and Otago Polytechnic, New Zealand (Idrus, 1996).

Hence, in effect, TQM has had mixed effects since its inception and integration into educational contexts. As discussed earlier on, it cannot be implemented successfully if an industrial version is used within a school context, although sometimes it has worked to a certain degree in higher education. TQM models need to be adapted to fit into school contexts. Fernandes (2013) provides an adapted version of TQM in school contexts, where the influence of both *Quality Assurance* mechanisms and a *Quality Enhancement* approach provides schools with a more approachable and convenient deployment of TQM within their school improvement processes and a better position for achieving educational quality. This progressive-reflective concept of implementing *Quality Assurance* mechanisms through quality enhancement approaches has been termed in literature as *Strategic TQM* (Combe & Bostchen, 2004; Fernandes, 2016; Mehra, Hoffman, & Sirias, 2001; Sousa, 2003).

In combining *Quality Assurance* and *Quality Enhancement* together, an educational organisation will be using Strategic TQM, not TQM within their continuous improvement systems. This relationship can also be interpreted and called the Strategic TQM equation (see Figure 5).

Figure 5. The strategic TQM equation for educational organisations

Holness (2001) suggests that having a synergistic *Quality Assurance* system as well as a continuous improvement system, i.e. *Quality Enhancement* approach provides an effective and sustainable approach towards educational quality. As Holness (2001) identifies, when a continuous improvement program is used in conjunction with a meaningful *Quality Assurance* program, significant improvements are felt within the organisation. Holness (2001) finds that the results of these are seen over time as a culture for quality is developed. Findings from the study by Hallinger and Heck (2011) also suggest that improvements made within schools lead to changes in the school over a period of time having strong links found between the school context, its collaborative learning-directed leadership, and the academic capacity of school personnel. Ngware et al. (2006) also found that, a successful *Quality Enhancement* approach is found when the school management provides leadership that promotes TQM practices resulting in empowered employees participating in decision-making leading to quality student learning. As Ngware et al. (2006) put it, "school leadership [should] put in place mechanisms to ensure that quality assurance practices are being followed and are being sustained and continuously improved upon" (p. 342). Strategic quality planning becomes increasingly important for the provision of quality services to be sustained over time. Ngware et al. (2006) further discuss that, "*Quality Assurance* is an integral part of TQM in educational organisations. Developing strategic quality plans through continuous improvement systems provides a way of actualizing quality assurance in a systematic and performance-oriented way" (p. 352). Holness (2001) and Ngware et al. (2006) have identified the importance of *Quality Assurance* mechanisms and *Quality Enhancement* programs working together and have identified common elements such as mechanisms for systematic and informed strategic planning, group decision-making, logical and results-oriented performance and on-going evaluation.

Bilich and Neto (Bilich & Neto, 1997, S.88) state that, "An organisation that uses *Strategic TQM* incorporates constant evaluation of its concepts of management and of its administrative practices through the use of innovative strategies applied within a strategic culture." *Strategic TQM* identifies four elements that make a quality management system more integrated: the environment, leadership, method and a systems view (Pruett & Thomas, 1996). *Strategic TQM* is an aspirational model of TQM over its predecessor – the benchmarking deficit model of TQM found in the eighties and nineties. The deficit model of TQM focused on benchmarking and quality control, advocating innovation but firmly fixed in standardisation, encouraging cultural change through open communication and collaborative teamwork but institutionalising managerial control and work place accountability. In *Strategic TQM*, *Quality Assurance* and *Quality Enhancement* work together to develop a thinking framework that aligns with the strategic intent of the school physically embodied through its mission. Various levels of self-assessment and continuous improvement allows school members to ascertain the value of the improvements being made and the strategic direction being taken. It provides a sense of community where an emphasis is placed on a progressive-reflective approach in the drive for continuous improvement. The question however arises as to whether *Strategic TQM* is a suitable frame for continuous quality improvement within schools? Fernandes (2013) suggests that "educational quality cannot be easily assessed by a single indicator…the achievement of satisfactory quality involves considering all stages of the quality loop as a whole within an educational organisation" (p. 40). *Strategic TQM* assists an organisation in addressing this complexity by measuring educational quality through its *Quality Assurance* mechanisms and its *Quality Enhancement* approach. In fact, referring back to the initial discussion in this chapter, the aspect of glocalisation and decentralisation lends itself to the notion that self-managing schools need to develop sustainable improvement processes that allow them to follow the quality loop of Plan, Do, Study and Act in their journey towards educational effectiveness. Schools today are becoming complex organisations of change where all those who participate in the process of schooling are in effect preparing citizens for tomorrow's glocalised world, hence, schools need to be able to intelligently sustain and continuously improve their school systems through a progressive-reflective approach such as *Strategic TQM*.

SOLUTIONS AND RECOMMENDATIONS: THE RELATIVE GAIN OF AUSTRALIAN SELF-MANAGING SCHOOLS TRANSFORMING INTO STRATEGICALLY-ORIENTED LEARNING ORGANISATIONS

Strategic TQM provides schools with a substantial philosophy, tools and processes to meet and sustain change and improve continuously. It offers a transformative framework for school improvement that creates a school culture where the drive for educational quality is critically important. It is best understood as 'a proactive posture' incorporated by school organisations using a quality approach. Grumdahl (2010) states that in effect it is "a valuable [improvement] tool when used in combination with creating a culture in which staff and students experience a sense of belonging, where differences and creativity are valued and celebrated, and where the pursuit of excellence in learning applies to all" (p. 144). In other words, schools work towards improving their quality, and focus on improving their school culture by transforming into learning organisations as this continuously effects the improvements in the quality of their educational offerings. Bilich and Neto (1997, S.88-89) suggest that, "An organisation that administers quality in a strategic way takes advantage of any and every information supplied in order to perfect itself; on the other hand, an organisation that is not preoccupied with quality, considers all and any complaints as more of a nuisance, deriding this important source of information." In further discussing the transformative nature of *Strategic TQM*, Madu, Aheto, Kuei and Winokur (1996) have found that strategically oriented organisations focus upon four critical transformations which include:

1. Structural transformation,
2. Cultural transformation,
3. Organisational transformation, and
4. Process transformation

However, a fifth and equally important transformation being proposed in line with the philosophy of *Strategic TQM* is that of an *Environmental transformation*. These five transformations more appropriately known as 'the SCOPE improvement cycle' provide schools with the tools for ensuring that they have successful, sustained and continuous improvements within their school improvement processes (see Figure 6).

Figure 6. The SCOPE improvement cycle: Five critical transformations in strategically oriented educational organisations

While *Quality Assurance* and *Quality Enhancement* provide an educational organisation with leadership as well as strategic methods, the role of *Strategic TQM* helps to recognise the environmental forces that influence the organisation since it is part of a larger system (Fernandes, 2013). Instead of having its quality improvement strategies limited to quasi-static audited mechanisms, *Strategic TQM* allows organisations to become dynamically responsive to changing trends in society, making them more environmentally proactive (Leonard & McAdam, 2003; McAdam, Leonard, Henderson, & Hazlett, 2006). The *Strategic TQM* approach uses a contingency approach which allows educational organisations to cope with complex and dynamic phenomena associated with rapidly changing internal and external environments (McAdam, Leonard, Henderson, & Hazlett, 2006). It focuses on developing closer ties between all stakeholders inside and outside the educational organisation through its proactive position towards continuous improvement (DiPietro, 1993; Mehra & Ranganathan, 2008). This in turn works towards strengthening the environmental influence and capability of the organisation. Self-managing schools make effective use of both *Quality Assurance* mechanisms and a *Quality Enhancement* approach to assist them in formulating and translating their strategy planning (Mehra et al., 2001; Sousa & Voss, 2002) into effective business and operational plans (Currie, 1999; Sousa, 2003). Herein lies the answer as to why the author supports the notion that while TQM has had mixed results in educational institutions such as schools, *Strategic TQM* is different and works more in sync with the complexity currently faced by school leadership.

As discussed by Bilich and Neto (1997), this transformative nature of Strategic TQM provides an organisation with the advantage of working strategically and becoming a learning organisation in its own right. Peter Senge (1990) suggests that organisations capable of surviving and prospering are indeed learning organisations where people, processes, and systems are all dedicated to continuous learning and improvement. According to Bonstingl (1992), a school that is a *strategically-oriented learning organisation* will have: committed leadership, reflective teaching and learning processes, informed and participative roles of stakeholders and allocation of sufficient human, material, time, and financial resources. Research also indicates that within these schools, the level of organisational learning directly impacts on student participation and engagement with the school, subsequently improving their learning outcomes (Silins & Mulford, 2002). In effect, a *strategically-oriented learning organisation* will be committed to a continuous, progressive-reflective approach of self-evaluation and action.

Fernandes (2013; 2016) suggests that when applied within a school setting, the school is transformed into a *strategically-oriented learning organisation* where each stakeholder in effect becomes a participant in transforming the school and improving its current state. In discussing this further, Fernandes (2013; 2016) identifies four key aspects of a *strategically-oriented learning organisation.* These include: (1) Leadership, (2) Teamwork, (3) Bundling Strategies, and (4) Contextual Influences (see Figure 7). Since *Strategic TQM* involves an educational organisation in transformative and continuous quality improvement, it stands to reason that transformative leadership will be an essential enabler for this to happen. In fact, leadership is a central factor in the transformation of schools into *strategically-oriented learning organisations* (Ah-Teck & Starr, 2013; Leithwood, 1994; Silins, 1994; Silins, Mulford, Zarins, & Bishop, 2000; Montecinos, et al, 2014). Leaders who aspire to transform their schools into learning communities are visionary and life-long learners themselves (Cocklin, 1999; Diggins, 1997; Hale & Whitlam, 1997; Kotter, 1996). Hayes, Christie, Mills and Lingard (2004) found that elements of productive leadership were evident in such schools where a supportive culture works towards collective responsibility. Leadership diffuses throughout the organisation by its transformation from being an individual capacity located in the principal into a group attribute of school improvement teams and finally into an overall organisational property (Hallinger & Heck, 2011). School leaders give away their leadership authority by inducting and coaching others within the school and by actively building up organisational leadership capacity (Johnson, 2000). Through this distribution of leadership, the focus remains on the interactions of leadership practice by those who are both in formal as well as informal leadership roles within the organisation (Harris & Spillane, 2008). Through an integrated leadership model using both transformational as well as instructional leadership in improving school performance the principal elicits a high level of commitment and professionalism from their teacher leaders and works at developing their leadership capacity and as well as working interactively with them (Marks & Printy, 2003; Printy, Marks & Bowers, 2009). The results of this approach are stakeholder improved involvement and satisfaction, improved communication, increased productivity, improved quality and less rework, (Sim & Rogers, 2009).

Redmond et al. (2008) identify that teamwork breaks down organisational and professional barriers allowing the creation of opportunities amongst school stakeholders to generate new insights and ideas for improving the educational quality. Kovacs (2009) suggests that, the team approach builds a critical mass of knowledge where, "embedding the approach throughout the school takes place by 'osmosis' as the experience of the team grows by applying improved practices to their area of responsibility and then supportively informing the efforts of others." (p.260) Robinson (1996) suggests that coupled with a visionary and collaborative leadership style other strategies found in these schools include: a problem-solving approach; collaborative decision-making; trust; empowerment for all stakeholders; delegation of roles and responsibilities; the provision of opportunities of leadership; continuous improvement of processes; effective communication channels; and, training and development programs for staff, parents and members of the community. The shift is from a controlling culture into a learning organisation culture with a nurturing and coaching leadership function.

Figure 7. Four key aspects of a strategically-oriented learning organisation

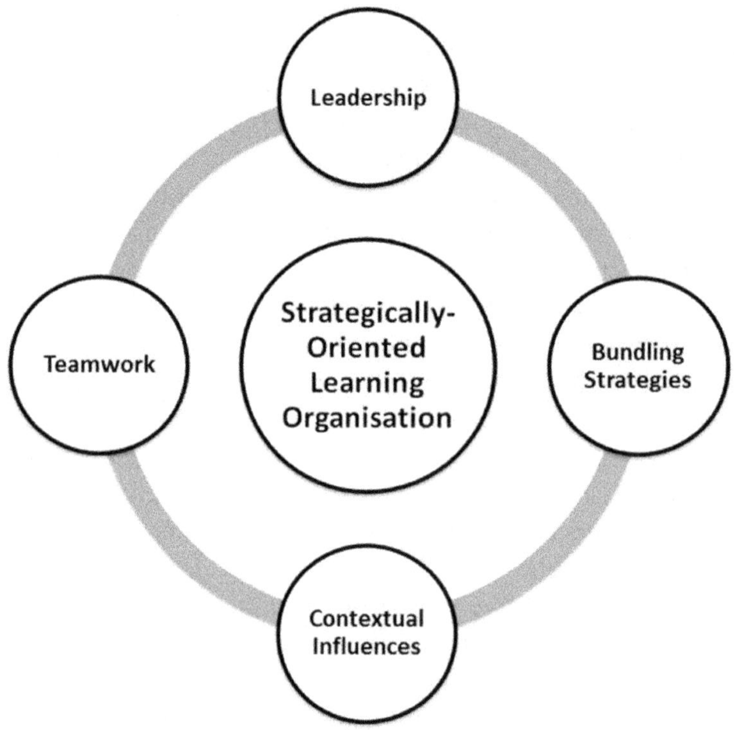

Many quality systems have evolved into comprehensive management systems that have coupled a number of innovations together depending upon the needs and structure of the individual organisation. Modell (2009) has defined this organisational evolution as a 'bundling phenomenon' where organisations go through a diffusing process of innovations, using a reflective-managerial approach, as they map out their own goals and targets over a period of time and make contextually-based adjustments in line with the overall purpose of the organisation. Finally, an important aspect of a *strategically-oriented learning organisation* is that any quality initiative implemented within the organisation is unique to it. Effective implementation of *Strategic TQM* within a learning organisation requires being able to discern what would be the best initiative for a particular organisation (Jones & Seraphim, 2008; Temtime, 2003). While the knowledge and understanding quotient of *Strategic TQM* must be high for successful implementation, each organisation develops its own subset of *Strategic TQM* characteristics and activities that are contextually unique (Jones & Seraphim, 2008). Navaratnam (1997) outlines the metaphor of 'a never-ending journey' of continuous improvement where educational quality can be designed, developed, implemented, achieved, measured and improved incrementally and continuously, through an integrated process view and continuous management practice within the educational organisation. Navaratnam defines this as, 'total quality in education' (1997, p. 19).

FUTURE RESEARCH DIRECTIONS

This chapter has discussed an adapted version of continuous school improvement where schools operate as self-managed business systems and develop themselves as strategically-oriented learning organisations. This concept of *Strategic TQM* (Figure 5) needs to be further investigated within different types of school settings making use of the five critical transformations of the SCOPE Improvement Cycle (Figure 6) and the four key aspects of a strategically-oriented learning organisation (Figure 7).

CONCLUSION: AN ADAPTED FRAME FOR CONTINUOUS SCHOOL IMPROVEMENT IN AUSTRALIAN SCHOOLS

This chapter discussed the importance and need for Australian schools today to understand the complexity and ever-changing landscape of school improvement as they frame educational quality within their own school contexts. Using a progressive-reflective approach, this chapter focused on how schools can use the proposed continuous school improvement frame based on business improvement and consisting of two main aspects: *Quality Assurance* and *Quality Enhancement,* to develop a system of *Strategic TQM*. The relative gain of this adapted version of TQM known as *Strategic TQM* over earlier industrial TQM models indicates that this model will better assist self-managed Australian schools in their achievement of educational quality. In describing the "what" and "how" of Strategic TQM, the author ends the chapter propounding that *Strategic TQM* leads schools through transformative change that results in them becoming *strategically-oriented learning organisations*. Through the actual embodiment of the philosophy and practice of *Strategic TQM*, Australian self-managing schools can work towards transforming into strategically-oriented learning organisations using a system of continuous school improvement that effectively drives all school processes towards the attainment of educational quality and where quality student learning is the core educational service being provided.

REFERENCES

Adams, D., Acedo, C., & Popa, S. (2012). In Search of Quality Education. In C. Acedo, D. Adams, & S. Popa (Eds.), *Quality and Qualities: Tensions in Higher Education* (pp. 1–22). Rotterdam: Sense Publishers.

Ah-Teck, J. C., & Starr, K. (2013). Principals' perceptions of "quality" in Mauritian schools using the Baldrige framework. *Journal of Educational Administration, 51*(5), 680–704. doi:10.1108/JEA-02-2012-0022

American National Standard ANSI/ASQC A3-1978. (1978). *Quality Systems Terminology*. Milwaukee, WI: American Society for Quality Control.

Banathy, B. H. (1991). *Systems Design of Education: A Journey to Create the Future*. Englewood Cliffs, NJ: Educational Technology Publications.

Banathy, B. H., & Jenks, C. L. (1990, April). *The transformation of education: By design.* Paper presented at the Annual Meeting of the American Educational Research Association, Boston, MA. Retrieved from http://files.eric.ed.gov/fulltext/ED323660.pdf

Bernhardt, V. (2013). *Translating data into information to improve teaching and learning*. New York: Routledge. doi:10.4324/9781315853758

Berry, G. (1997). Leadership and the development of quality culture in schools. *International Journal of Educational Management*, *11*(2), 52–65. doi:10.1108/09513549710163943

Betts, F. (1992, November). How Systems Thinking Applies to Education. *Educational Leadership*, *50*(3), 38–41. Retrieved from http://search.proquest.com/docview/224857527?accountid=12528

Bilich, F., & Neto, A. A. (1997). Strategic total quality management. *Total Quality Management*, *8*(2-3), 88–89. doi:10.1080/0954412979767

Bone, D. (1996). Quality management is collegiate management: Improving practice in a special school. In P. Lomax (Ed.), *Quality Management in education: Sustaining the vision through Action Research* (pp. 19–46). London: Routledge and Hyde Publications.

Bonstingl, J. J. (1992). The quality revolution in education. *Educational Leadership*, *50*(3), 4–9.

Bonstingl, J. J. (1993). The quality movement: What's it really about? *Educational Leadership*, *51*(1), 66–70.

Brandt, R. (2003). Is this school a learning organization? 10 ways to tell. *Journal of Staff Development*, *24*(1), 10–16. Retrieved from http://search.proquest.com/docview/211520094?accountid=12528

Brooks, J., & Normore, A. (2010). Educational leadership and globalization: Literacy for a glocal perspective. *Educational Policy*, *24*(1), 52–82. doi:10.1177/0895904809354070

Brown, J. F., & Marshall, B. L. (2008). Continuous quality improvement: An effective strategy for improvement of program outcomes in a higher education setting. *Nursing Education Perspectives*, *29*(4), 205–211. PMID:18770948

Caldwell, B. (2005). *School-based management. Education Policy Series. International Academy of Education and International Institute for Educational Planning*. UNESCO.

Caldwell, B. (2007). *Self managing schools and improved learning outcomes*. Canberra: Department of Employment, Education, Training and Youth Affairs.

Cheng, Y. C. (2003). Quality assurance in education: Internal, interface, and future. *Quality Assurance in Education*, *11*(4), 202–213. doi:10.1108/09684880310501386

Cheng, Y. C., & Tam, W. M. (1997). Multi-models of quality in education. *Quality Assurance in Education*, *5*(1), 22–31. doi:10.1108/09684889710156558

Chickering, A. W., & Potter, D. (1993). TQM and quality education: Fast food or fitness center. *The Educational Record*, *74*(2), 35–36.

Chizmar, J. F. (2000). Total quality management of teaching and learning. *Journal of Economic Education*, *25*(2), 1–8. doi:10.1080/00220485.1994.10844828

Clayton, M. (1995). Encouraging the kaizen approach to quality in a university. *Total Quality Management*, *6*(5/6), 593–601. doi:10.1080/09544129550035242

Coate, L. E. (1990). TQM on campus: Implementing total quality management in a university setting. *Business Officer*, *24*(5), 26–35.

Cocklin, B. (1999). Gumly Gumly Public School as a learning community. In J. Retallick, B. Cocklin, & K. Coombe (Eds.), *Learning Communities in Education* (pp. 265–286). London: Routledge.

Combe, I., & Bostchen, G. (2004). Strategy paradigms for the management of quality: Dealing with complexity. *European Journal of Marketing*, *38*(5), 500–523. doi:10.1108/03090560410529187

Commonwealth of Australia. (2008). *Quality education: The case for an education revolution in our schools*. Retrieved from http://apo.org.au/files/Resource/deewar_quality-education_2008.pdf

Cranston, N. (2000). The impact of school-based management on primary school principals: An Australian Perspective. *Journal of School Leadership*, *10*(3), 214–232.

Cranston, N. C. (2001). Collaborative decision-making and school-based management: Challenges, rhetoric and reality. *Journal of Educational Enquiry*, *2*(2), 1–26.

Crawford, L. E. D., & Shutler, P. (1999). Total quality management in education: Problems and issues for the classroom teacher. *International Journal of Educational Management*, *13*(2), 67–72. doi:10.1108/09513549910261122

Currie, W. (1999). Revisiting management innovation and change programmes: Strategic vision or tunnel vision? *Omega*, *27*(6), 647–660. doi:10.1016/S0305-0483(99)00023-7

Dahlgaard, J. J., Kristensen, K., & Kanji, G. K. (1995). Total quality management and education. *Total Quality Management*, *6*(5), 445–456. doi:10.1080/09544129550035116

Daniels, H., & Warmington, P. (2007). Analyzing third generation activity systems: Labour power, subject, position and personal transformation. *Journal of Workplace Learning*, *19*(6), 377–391. doi:10.1108/13665620710777110

De Grauwe, A. (2005). Improving quality of education through school-based management: Learning from international experiences. *International Review of Education*, *51*(4), 269–287. doi:10.100711159-005-7733-1

Dellar, G. B. (1998). School Climate, School Improvement and Site-based Management. *Learning Environments Research*, *1*(3), 353–367. doi:10.1023/A:1009970210393

Desjardins, C., & Obara, Y. (1993). From Québec to Tokyo: Perspectives on TQM. *Educational Leadership*, *51*(1), 68–69.

Diggins, P. B. (1997). Reflections on leadership characteristics necessary to develop and sustain learning school communities. *School Leadership & Management*, *17*(3), 413–425. doi:10.1080/13632439769953

DiPietro, R. A. (1993). TQM: Evolution, scope and strategic significance for management development. *Journal of Management Development*, *12*(7), 11–18. doi:10.1108/02621719310044910

Doherty, G. D. (1993). Towards total quality management in higher education: A case study of the University of Wolverhampton. *Higher Education*, *25*(3), 321–339. doi:10.1007/BF01383857

Drysdale, L., Goode, H., & Gurr, D. (2009). An Australian model of successful school leadership. *Journal of Educational Administration*, *47*(6), 697–708. doi:10.1108/09578230910993087

Eagle, L., & Brennan, R. (2007). Are students customers? TQM and marketing perspectives. *Quality Assurance in Education*, *15*(1), 44–60. doi:10.1108/09684880710723025

Emstad, A. B. (2011). The principal's role in the post-evaluation process. How does the principal engage in the work carried out after the schools self-evaluation? *Educational Assessment, Evaluation and Accountability*, *23*(4), 271–288. doi:10.100711092-011-9128-0

Engeström, Y. (2001). Expansive learning at work: Toward an activity theoretical reconceptualization. *Journal of Education and Work*, *14*(1), 133–156. doi:10.1080/13639080020028747

Engeström, Y., & Glaveanu, V. (2012). On third generation activity theory: Interview with Yrjö Engeström. *Europe's Journal of Psychology*, *8*(4), 515–518. doi:10.5964/ejop.v8i4.555

Fernandes, V. (2016). Reframing Continuous School Improvement in Australian Schools. In A. Normore, L. Long, & M. Javidi (Eds.), *Handbook of Research on Effective Communication, Leadership, and Conflict Resolution* (pp. 98–124). Hershey, PA: Information Science Reference. doi:10.4018/978-1-4666-9970-0.ch006

Fernandes, V. (2019a). Glocalising Educational Leadership Development in the Asia-Pacific Region. In V. Fernandes & P. W. K. Chan (Eds.), *Asia Pacific Education: Leadership, Governance and Administration*. Hershey, PA: Information Age Publishing.

Fernandes, V. (2019b). Disrupting the Norm? Implementing Educational Business Improvement Models in Pakistani Public-Private School Partnerships. In V. Fernandes & P. W. K. Chan (Eds.), *Asia Pacific Education: Leadership, Governance and Administration*. Hershey, PA: Information Age Publishing.

Fernandes, V. M. (2013) *The Effectiveness of Total Quality Management as a School Improvement Process* (Doctoral dissertation). Monash University, Melbourne, Australia. Retrieved from http://arrow.monash.edu.au/hdl/1959.1/871750

Gammage, D. T. (2008). Three decades of implementation of school-based management in the Australian Capital Territory and Victoria in Australia. *International Journal of Educational Management*, *22*(7), 664–675. doi:10.1108/09513540810908575

Garbutt, S. (1996). The transfer of TQM from industry to education. *Education + Training*, *38*(7), 16–22. doi:10.1108/00400919610130736

Goetsch, D. L., & Davis, S. B. (2000). *Quality management: Introduction to total quality management for production, processing and services* (3rd ed.). Prentice-Hall International Inc.

Goodard, J. T. (2010). Toward Glocality: Facilitating leadership in an age of diversity. *Journal of School Leadership*, *20*, 37–56.

Greenwood, M. S., & Gaunt, H. J. (1994). *Total quality management for schools*. London: Cassell.

Grumdahl, C. R. (2010). *How schools can effectively plan to meet the goal of improving student learning* (Doctoral dissertation). University of Minnesota. Retrieved from:https://conservancy.umn.edu/bitstream/handle/11299/59567/Grumdahl_umn_0130E_10969.pdf?sequence=1

Hale, R., & Whitlam, P. (1997). *Towards the virtual organization*. London: The McGraw-Hill Co.

Hallinger, P., & Heck, R. H. (2011). Exploring the journey of school improvement: Classifying and analyzing patterns of change in school improvement processes and learning outcomes. *School Effectiveness and School Improvement*, *22*(1), 1–27. doi:10.1080/09243453.2010.536322

Harris, A., & Spillane, J. (2008). Distributed leadership through the looking glass. *Management in Education*, *22*(1), 31–34. doi:10.1177/0892020607085623

Hayes, D., Christie, P., Mills, M., & Lingard, B. (2004). Productive leaders and productive leadership: Schools as learning organisations. *Journal of Educational Administration*, *42*(4/5), 520–538. doi:10.1108/09578230410554043

Hernandez, J. R., Jr. (2001). *Total quality management in education: The application of TQM in a Texas school district* (Unpublished doctoral dissertation). University of Texas, Austin, TX. Retrieved November 3, 2008, from Dissertations & Theses: Full Text. (Publication No. AAT 3034546)

Hill, A., Melon, L., Laker, B., & Goddard, J. (2016, October 20). *The one type of leader who can turn around a failing school*. Retrieved on October, 30 2018, from https://hbr.org/2016/10/the-one-type-of-leader-who-can-turn-around-a-failing-school

Hill, P. W., Rowe, K. J., Holmes-Smith, P., & Russell, V. J. (1996). The Victorian Quality Schools Project: A study of school and teacher effectiveness (Report, Volume 1). Centre for Applied Educational Research: University of Melbourne.

Hodgkinson, M., & Brown, G. (2003). Enhancing the quality of education: A case study and some emerging principles. *Higher Education*, *45*(3), 337–352. doi:10.1023/A:1022680504729

Hodgkinson, M., & Kelly, M. (2007). Quality management and enhancement processes in UK business schools: A review. *Quality Assurance in Education*, *15*(1), 77–91. doi:10.1108/09684880710723043

Holness, G. V. R. (2001). Achieving quality using TQM and ISO. *ASHRAE Journal*, *43*(1), 195–199.

Holt, M. (1993a). Dr. Deming and the improvement of schooling: No instant pudding. *Journal of Curriculum and Supervision*, *9*(1), 6–23.

Holt, M. (1993b). The educational consequences of W. Edwards Deming. *Phi Delta Kappan*, *74*(5), 382–388.

Hubbard, S., & Menzel, S. (1995). Mt. Edgecumbe High School case study report. In S. Hubbard & S. Menzel (Eds.), *The Study of School-to-Work Reform Initiatives. Volume II: Case Studies* (pp.5-55). Studies of Education Reform Series. Academy for Educational Development, Washington, DC. National Inst. for Work and Learning. Retrieved from http://files.eric.ed.gov/fulltext/ED397551.pdf

Hughes, P. (Ed.). (1988). *The challenge of identifying and marketing quality in education*. Sydney, Australia: The Australian Association of Senior Educational Administrators.

Idrus, N. (1995). Empowerment as a manifestation of total quality: A study in three countries. *Total Quality Management*, *6*(5 & 6), 603–612. doi:10.1080/09544129550035251

Idrus, N. (1996). Towards total quality management in academia. *Quality Assurance in Education*, *4*(3), 34–40. doi:10.1108/09684889610125850

Jackson, D. S. (2000). The School Improvement Journey: Perspectives on leadership. *School Leadership & Management Development*, *20*(1), 61–78. doi:10.1080/13632430068888

Jones, J. P., & Seraphim, D. (2008). TQM implementation and change management in an unfavourable environment. *Journal of Management Development*, *27*(3), 291–306. doi:10.1108/02621710810858614

Kohn, A. (1993). Turning learning into a business: Concerns about total quality management. *Educational Leadership*, *51*(1), 58–61.

Kovacs, J. (2009). *Facilitating Change in Australian Schools: Applying a Business Quality Improvement Model. Unpublished Doctoral dissertation*. Melbourne, Australia: Swinburne University of Technology. Retrieved from http://researchbank.swinburne.edu.au/vital/access/manager/Repository/swin:14100

Kovacs, J., & King, M. (2005). *Studying the Impact of the Quality in Schools and Quality and Improvement in Schools and Preschools Initiatives: 1997-2003*. Quality Learning and Improvement in Schools and Preschools Summary Report, November 2005 [Electronic Version]. Melbourne: Quality Learning Australia Pty Ltd. Retrieved from http://www.qla.com.au/pathtoitems/QLA_QISP_Report.pdf

Kwan, P. Y. K. (1996). Application of total quality management in education: Retrospect and prospect. *International Journal of Educational Management*, *10*(5), 25–35. doi:10.1108/09513549610146114

Lee, Y. R., & Lazarus, H. (1993). Uses and criticisms of total quality management. *Journal of Management Development*, *12*(7), 5–10. doi:10.1108/02621719310044901

Leithwood, K. (1994). Leadership for school restructuring. *Educational Administration Quarterly*, *30*(4), 498–518. doi:10.1177/0013161X94030004006

Leithwood, K., & Menzies, T. (1998). A review of research concerning the implementation of site-based management. *School Effectiveness and School Improvement*, *9*(3), 233–285. doi:10.1080/0924345980090301

Leonard, D., & McAdam, R. (2003). An evaluative framework for TQM dynamics in organisations. *International Journal of Operations & Production Management*, *23*(5/6), 652–677. doi:10.1108/01443570310476663

Madu, C. N., Aheto, J., Kuei, C., & Winokur, D. (1994). Adoption of strategic total quality management philosophies: Multi-criteria decision analysis model. *International Journal of Quality & Reliability Management*, *13*(3), 57–72. doi:10.1108/02656719610116081

Madu, C. N., & Kuei, C. (1993). Dimensions of quality teaching in higher institutions. *Total Quality Management*, *4*(3), 325–338. doi:10.1080/09544129300000046

Marks, H. M., & Printy, S. M. (2003). Principal leadership and school performance: An Integration of Transformational and Instructional Leadership. *Educational Administration Quarterly*, *39*(3), 370–397. doi:10.1177/0013161X03253412

Masters, G. N. (2010). *Teaching and learning school improvement framework. Melbourne: Australian Council for Educational Research (ACER).* Brisbane: Department of Education and Training.

McAdam, R., Leonard, D., Henderson, J., & Hazlett, S. A. (2006). A grounded theory research approach to building and testing TQM theory in operations management. *International Journal of Management Sciences, 36*, 825–837. doi:10.1016/j.omega.2006.04.005

McKimm, J. (2003). Assuring quality and standards in teaching. In H. Fry, S. M. Ketteridge, & S. Marshall (Eds.), *A Handbook for Teaching and Learning in Higher Education* (2nd ed.; pp. 182–199). London: Kogan Page.

Mehra, S., Hoffman, J., & Sirias, D. (2001). TQM as a management strategy for the next millenia. *International Journal of Operations & Production Management, 21*(6), 855–877. doi:10.1108/01443570110390534

Mehra, S., & Ranganathan, S. (2008). Implementing total quality management with a focus on enhancing customer satisfaction. *International Journal of Quality & Reliability Management, 25*(9), 913-927. doi: 02656710810908070

Modell, S. (2009). Bundling management control innovations: A field study of organisational experimenting with total quality management and the balanced scorecard. *Accounting, Auditing & Accountability Journal, 22*(1), 59-90. doi: 09513570910923015

Montecinos, C., Madrid, R., Fernández, M. B., & Ahumada, L. (2014). A goal orientation analysis of teachers' motivations to participate in the school self-assessment processes of a quality assurance system in Chile. *Educational Assessment, Evaluation and Accountability, 26*(3), 241–261. doi:10.100711092-014-9190-5

Mulford, B. (2008) The leadership challenge improving learning in schools. Australian Education Review. Melbourne: Australian Council for Educational Research (ACER).

Murgatroyd, S., & Morgan, C. (1993). *Total quality management and the school.* Buckingham, UK: Open University Press.

Navaratnam, K. K. (1997). Quality management in education must be a never-ending journey. In K. Watson & S. Modgol (Eds.), *Educational dilemma: Debate and diversity; VI: Quality in education.* London: Cassell.

Ngware, M. W., Wamukuru, D. K., & Odebero, S. O. (2006). Total quality management in secondary schools in Kenya: Extent of practice. *Quality Assurance in Education, 14*(4), 339–362. doi:10.1108/09684880610703947

Pfeffer, N., & Coote, A. (1991). Is Quality Good for You? A Critical Review of Quality Assurance. In *Welfare Services. Social Policy Paper No. 5.* London: Institute for Public Policy Research.

Printy, S. M., Marks, H. M., & Bowers, A. J. (2009). Integrated Leadership: How Principals and Teachers Share Transformational and Instructional Influence. *Journal of School Leadership, 19*(5), 504–532.

Pruett, M., & Thomas, H. (1996). Thinking About Quality and its Links with Strategic Management. *European Management Journal, 14*(1), 37–46. doi:10.1016/0263-2373(95)00045-3

Rampa, S. H. (2005). *The Relationship between Total Quality Management and School Improvement. Unpublished doctoral dissertation*. Pretoria, South Africa: University of Pretoria. Retrieved from http://repository.up.ac.za/bitstream/handle/2263/23595/Complete.pdf?sequence=5

Reddy, S. (2007). *SCHOOL QUALITY: Perspectives from the Developed and Developing Countries*. Azim Premji Foundation. Retrieved from http://www.azimpremjifoundation.org/pdf/Consolidated-SchoolQualityreport.pdf

Redmond, R., Curtis, E., Noone, T., & Keenan, P. (2008). Quality in higher education: The contribution of Edward Deming's principles. *International Journal of Educational Management*, *22*(5), 432–441. doi:10.1108/09513540810883168

Reid, A., Cranston, N., Keating, J., & Mulford, B. (2010). *Exploring the Public Purposes of Education in Australian Primary Schools*. Report on an ARC-Linkage Project conducted in partnership with the Australian Government Primary Principals Association (AGPPA); and the Foundation for Young Australians. Retrieved from: http://www.agppa.asn.au/index.php?option=com_content&view=article&id=28&Itemid=18

Robinson, B. M. (1996). *Total quality management in education: The empowerment of a school community* (Unpublished doctoral dissertation). University of Nebraska, Lincoln, NE.

Sallis, E. (1993). *Total quality management in education*. London: Kogan Page Ltd. doi:10.4324/9780203417010

Sallis, E. (1996). *Total quality management in education* (2nd ed.). London: Kogan Page Ltd.

Saraph, J. V., & Sebastian, R. J. (1993). Developing a quality culture. *Quality Progress*, *26*(9), 73–78.

Schmoker, M., & Wilson, R. B. (1993). Adapting total quality doesn't mean "turning learning into a business". *Educational Leadership*, *51*(1), 62–63.

Schultz, J. R. (2014). *Four-cornered Leadership: A Framework for Making Decisions*. CRC Press, Taylor & Francis Group.

Senge, P. (1990). *The Fifth Discipline: The Art and Practice of the Learning Organisation*. New York: Doubleday.

Shewart, W. A. (1931). *Economic Control of Quality of Manufactured Product*. New York: Van Nostrand.

Siegel, P. (2000). Using Baldridge to improve education: A rationale based on results. *Training & Development*, *54*(2), 66–67.

Silins, H. (1994). Leadership Characteristics and School Improvement. *Australian Journal of Education*, *38*(3), 268–281. doi:10.1177/000494419403800306

Silins, H., & Mulford, B. (2002). Schools as learning organisations: The case for system, teacher and student learning. *Journal of Educational Administration*, *40*(5), 425–446. doi:10.1108/09578230210440285

Silins, H., Mulford, B., Zarins, S., & Bishop, P. (2000). Leadership for Organizational Learning in Australian Secondary Schools. In K. Leithwood (Ed.), *Understanding Schools as Intelligent Systems* (pp. 267–291). Stamford, CT: JAI Press. doi:10.1080/03057640302041

Silins, H., Zarins, S., & Mulford, B. (2002). What characteristics and processes define a school as a learning organisation? Is this a useful concept to apply to schools? *International Education Journal*, *3*(1), 24–32.

Sim, K. L., & Rogers, J. W. (2009). Implementing lean production systems: Barriers to change. *Management Research News*, *32*(1), 37–49. doi:10.1108/01409170910922014

Sousa, R. (2003). Linking Quality Management to Manufacturing Strategy: An Empirical Investigation of Customer Focus Practices. *Journal of Operations Management*, *21*(1), 1–18. doi:10.1016/S0272-6963(02)00055-4

Sousa, R., & Voss, C. (2002). Quality Management Re-visited: A Reflective Review and Agenda for Future Research. *Journal of Operations Management*, *20*(1), 91–109. doi:10.1016/S0272-6963(01)00088-2

Spanbauer, S. J. (1989). *Measuring and Costing Quality in Education*. Appleton, WI: Fox Valley Technical College Foundation.

Steyn, G. M. (2000). Applying Principles of TQM to a learning process: a case study. *SAJHE/SATHO*, *14*(1), 11-14. Retrieved from: http://hdl.handle.net/10500/242

Svensson, M., & Klefsjö, B. (2006). TQM-based self-assessment in the education sector: Experiences from a Swedish Upper Secondary School Project. *Quality Assurance in Education*, *14*(4), 299–323. doi:10.1108/09684880610703929

Sztajn, P. (1992). A matter of metaphors: Education as a handmade process. *Educational Leadership*, *50*(3), 35 37.

Temponi, C. (2005). Continuous improvement framework: Implications for academia. *Quality Assurance in Education*, *13*(1), 17–36. doi:10.1108/09684880510578632

Temtime, Z. T. (2003). The Moderating Impacts of Business Planning and Firm Size on the Total Quality Management Practices. *The TQM Magazine*, *15*(1), 52–60. doi:10.1108/09544780310454457

Terry, P. M. (1996). *Using Total Quality Management Principles to Implement School-Based Management*. Paper presented at the 14th Annual International Conference of the International Association of Management, Toronto, Ontario, Canada. Retrieved from: http://files.eric.ed.gov/fulltext/ED412590.pdf

Thomas, M., Hawkins, A., Christian, F., Merlene, M., & de Meyrick, C. (2011). *Independent Review of the School Based Management Report*. Summary Report (October 2011). Department of Education and Communities, NSW: ARTD Consultants. Retrieved from: https://www.det.nsw.edu.au/media/downloads/about-us/statistics-and-research/key-statistics-and-reports/irsb-management-pilot-sr.pdf

Torres, C. A., & Antikainen, A. (2003). Introduction to a sociology of education: Old dilemmas in a new century? In C. A. Torres & A. Antikainen (Eds.), *The International Handbook on the Sociology of Education: An International Assessment of New Research and Theory* (pp. 1–18). Lanham, MD: Rowman & Littlefield.

Uselac, S. (1993). *Zen Leadership: The Human Side of Total Quality Team Management*. Loudonville, OH: Mohican.

Van Vught, F. A., & Westerheijden, D. F. (1992). *Quality Management and Quality Assurance in European Higher Education: Methods and Mechanics.* Center for Higher Education Policy Studies, University of Twente.

Walpole, M., & Noeth, R. J. (2002). *The Promise of Baldrige for K-12 Education.* ACT Policy Report: ACT Policy Research Inc. Retrieved from https://www.act.org/research/policymakers/pdf/baldrige.pdf

Weick, K. E. (2000). Quality Improvement: A Sensemaking Perspective. In R. E. Cole & W. R. Scott (Eds.), *The Quality Movement & Organization Theory* (pp. 155–172). Thousand Oaks, CA: Sage Publications Inc.

Weller, L. D. (1998). Unlocking the culture for quality schools: Reengineering. *International Journal of Educational Management, 12*(6), 250–259. doi:10.1108/09513549810237959

ADDITIONAL READING

Bass, B. M., & Riggio, R. E. (2006). *Transformational Leadership* (2nd ed.). New Jersey: Lawrence Erlbaum Associates.

Cheng, Y. C., & Mok, M. M. C. (2007). School-based management and paradigm shift in education: An empirical Study. *International Journal of Educational Management, 21*(6), 517–542. doi:10.1108/09513540710780046

Hargreaves, D. (2007). *System re-design – 1: The road to transformation.* London: SSAT.

Harris, A. (2011). Distributed leadership friend or foe? *Educational Management Administration & Leadership, 41*(5), 545–554. doi:10.1177/1741143213497635

Leithwood, K. (2001). School leadership in the context of accountability policies. *International Journal of Leadership in Education, 4*(3), 217–235. doi:10.1080/13603120110057082

Leithwood, K., Mascall, B., Strauss, T., Sacks, R., Memon, N., & Yashkina, A. (2007). Distributing leadership to make schools smarter: Taking the ego out of the system. *Leadership and Policy in Schools, 6*(1), 37–67. doi:10.1080/15700760601091267

Lingard, B., Hayes, D., & Mills, M. (2002). Developments in school-based management: The specific case of Queensland, Australia. *Journal of Educational Administration, 40*(1), 6–30. doi:10.1108/09578230210415625

Senge, P. M. (1990). *The Fifth Discipline: The Art and Practice of the Learning Organization.* New York: Doubleday.

Stoll, L., & Timperley, J. (2009). *OECD: Improving School Leadership – the toolkit.* OECD Publishing.

KEY TERMS AND DEFINITIONS

Continuous Improvement.: Refers to a long-term approach towards improvement that systematically seeks to achieve small, incremental changes in the organizational processes that lead towards improvements in efficiency and quality. It is also known as Kaizen and is the responsibility of every person in the organisation, not just a selected few.

Quality Assurance: Refers to the policies, processes and actions through which the quality of a system is developed and maintained.

Quality Enhancement: Refers to the improvement of educational quality brought about through cycles of continuous improvement and innovation so that it becomes the culture of the educational organisation.

Strategic TQM: It provides schools with a substantial philosophy, tools and processes to organize themselves to meet and sustain change and improve themselves continuously.

Total Quality Management: Refers to a systematic approach to the practice of management within an organization. At the organizational level it requires changes in organizational processes, and strategic priorities; and at the individual level, it requires changes in the beliefs, attitudes, and behaviors of individuals working within that organisation. It is considered both as a philosophy and a set of guiding principles for organizational management.

Chapter 8
The Role of Leadership and Communication:
Challenges Reconceptualizing Graduate Instruction

Heather M. Rintoul
Nipissing University, Canada

ABSTRACT

This chapter explores concerns and challenges associated with the transition to online graduate instruction from the traditional face-to-face format. The author discusses several catalysts for the transition to virtual teaching, the ethics of being present, impediments to learning and communication online, and participant concerns. The chapter also considers online knowledge and meaning-making, online communities, and associated uncertainties. Finally, new financial decisions and considerations leading to hardships for faculty and their families as well as trends for leadership and communication moving forward are addressed.

INTRODUCTION

The pursuant exponential expansion of virtual instruction offers an appropriate opportunity to reflect about the effectiveness of this medium from a leadership and communication perspective as it compares to the traditional face-to-face experience. Conceptual in nature, in this chapter I examine the role of faculty as instructional leaders of graduate online teaching and learning. I first consider two significant pieces of the backstory leading to the implementation of online instruction. Next, I speak to concerns regarding the ethics of 'being present' in the graduate seminar tradition, specifically: instructor presence, interpersonal (social) presence, and cognitive presence while discussing some supplementary perceived impediments to authentic leadership, communication, and learning online. I then consider the (re)-conceptualising of online knowledge acquisition and meaning-making, understandings around the idea of communities and perceptions of relationships online, as well as on-going uncertainties about online instruction and learning. Finally, I envisage possible pathways and new trends for instructional leadership and communication moving forward in the virtual realm.

DOI: 10.4018/978-1-5225-8516-9.ch008

BACKGROUND

The Synergy of Two Catalysts

As economic difficulties related to the recent recession continue to be a challenging global phenomenon, universities in Ontario, Canada have not been exempt from associated financial woes. At the most basic level, financial resources have not kept pace with escalating expenditures, compelling universities to do substantially more with substantially less (Metcalfe, Fisher, Gingras, Jones, Rubenson, & Snee, 2010). The latest victim of diminishing fiscal resources appears to be a heretofore untouchable- the graduate seminar (of Masters and Doctoral programs). In recent years, venues at-a-distance have been on the increase as colleges and universities seek to broaden their student base and their financial bottom line by expanding student access to their programs (Dobbins, 2009). Serving these distant centres with traditional face-to-face graduate seminars, however, has necessarily incurred significant auxiliary expenses for institutions, for example: rental of off-site venues, travel expenses (hotel/meals/gasoline for faculty), and loss of considerable faculty work hours unavoidably spent in travel. As a consequence, in an effort to stem the financial bleeding, many universities initially thought to replace much (and in some cases, all) of their face-to-face graduate teaching with an on-line model (Chau, 2010). Was the purpose and rationale of the new technology-based online model for graduate teaching driven by an ever-strengthening economic component in that graduate education was being viewed as a standardized commodity, with keeping expenses in check emerging as a primary university goal (Power & Vaughan, 2010)? Would such a strategy represent a permanent divergence from the ideological and towards more pragmatic ends- that of servicing a university's bottom line (Braddock, Mahony, & Taylor, 2006)? If so, how could faculty reconcile the experience of on-line teaching and learning as authentic if academic freedom was subjugated to the vagaries of increasingly aggressive fiscal influences? In the short term, this conversion to online appeared to accomplish the desired economic goal in that it reined in faculty expenses (Rich, 2015). There was, however, an equally significant and perhaps unforeseen circumstance that was soon to enter the expenditures fray that would signal an unanticipated consequence.

Lifestyles today have become increasingly demanding and multifaceted. A key component of that complexity appears to rest with the explosion of interest in social media (Facebook, Twitter, and Instagram, for example) and the Internet. No longer tethered by telephone lines, a vast array of revolutionary cordless devices now offers the facility and flexibility to contact anyone from anywhere at any time. Interactive electronic devices and their ever-expanding resources permit instant access to the Internet, not only to keep in touch with others but to search and acquire information on a broad variety of topics: travel mapping, meal options, online purchasing, music, health care, and even the acquisition of a university/college degree. Indeed, almost anything anyone can dream up, can be searched and utilized, all from the comfort of home or, from any place, at any time. The limitless capacity of the electronic world as the leading interactive information highway of people, places, and things now seems as intrinsic to life as breathing, especially so for our younger generation (Dobbins, 2009), our 'digital natives' (Prensky, 2006), who have known only an intensifying cordless world- the one of sophisticated cell phones, progressive electronic devices, and seemingly unlimited data and information exchanges available via the Web, online and the Internet.

With the explosion of the virtual world, computer programs for teaching graduate and other coursework (for e.g. undergraduate massive open online courses, MOOC, Prensky, 2014) began to be widely accessible with students clamoring for a virtual learning experience (VLE) which, from their perspective, adapted more easily to their hectic lifestyles (Johnson, Stewart & Bachman, 2015). Initially, universities saw online learning as a two-pronged positive: a means to satisfy student demand for online instruction as well as an opportunity to reduce expenses associated with travelling faculty. Unfortunately, graduate online programs, for example, 'Elluminate' (synchronous) and 'Blackboard' (asynchronous) themselves come with considerable continuing expenditures. The programs are cost-significant to purchase initially, with on-going annual fees, and of necessity, the availability of specialized teams with technical expertise to upgrade the technology of the program in maintaining its current status, and to help faculty and students when online challenges manifest. While student maximums for face-to-face graduate seminars have risen, in many instances to an academic grouping of 30 or even 35, it has become apparent that online graduate instruction best supports a maximum of 20 individual participants; otherwise, managing the experience becomes unwieldy to the detriment of knowledge-building within the learning community (Rich, 2015). What was initially conceived as a viable option to satisfy much-needed university fiscal re-structuring (Braddock, et al, 2006) has arguably become another significant financial drain on university coffers (Rich, 2015).

THE GRADUATE TEACHING TRADITION: THE ETHICS OF BEING PRESENT

Instructional, Interpersonal, and Cognitive Presence: Do They Matter?

As leaders of learning, many instructional faculty leaders and facilitators of all graduate learning are struggling to make sense and to decipher the intricacies of the new online model. Chief among their concerns is instructional presence. How can faculty instructors, notwithstanding, effectively communicate ethical purpose and simultaneously model an ethical environment for their online participants when they are not actually physically present with their students (Garrison, Anderson, & Archer, 2000; author, 2011)? Assuming that the main aspiration of graduate teaching continues to be the nurturing and support of graduate students in an authentic way, how can we construe this new online standard to achieve the stated goal? Where and who are our faculty models for conceptualizing and/or contextualizing content and for facilitating authentic interactive communication in the new online convention? Where are the faculty role models who set high standards and enforce the discipline needed to achieve these benchmarks when students are associating only with their online peers? Should online learners themselves be re-conceptualized within this new environment? Specifically, what criteria should be considered in this re-conceptualization and who should make this determination? Current faculty, mostly digital immigrants (Prensky, 2006), who struggle to navigate the new medium may themselves become the leader models for a new generation of graduate instructors. If so, the necessity and burden for faculty to 'get it right' for current students, as well as for present and future instructors alike, seems even more acute.

Those who teach graduate education have honed their craft by experiencing graduate education first as students, learning from and being guided by professor mentors as they, in turn, hypothesized and made meaning of their own graduate teaching. Customarily, it has been the task of faculty, as instructional leaders and facilitators, to model an ethical purpose, to develop new scholars to their full potential, and to authentically support each individual's connection to learning (Leonard & Rintoul, 2010; Metcalfe et al., 2010). This graduate model has historically been defined largely as face-to-face academic nurturing, with faculty and students interacting, often on a daily basis, as learners master the content and methods necessary to become the new trailblazers and intellectuals in their field. The graduate class itself, a significant cornerstone of this connection piece, has traditionally been conceptualized as a small aesthetic seminar of about 15 to 20 individuals engaged in the immediacy of intelligent, face-to-face conversational exchanges, scholarly discussions, lively debates and workshops, all in an ethical learning environment (Leonard & Rintoul, 2010). The face-to-face interaction model of both faculty and students has generally been considered largely successful within the stated aims and goals of graduate education, and as such has been a fundamental characteristic of graduate seminar instruction for decades, perhaps even centuries. This practice has been refined over time with considerable dedication and skill by each instructor to become the authentic learning experience each believes her/his present standard to be. With the transition to on-line graduate teaching and learning, however, some might speculate how and whether we can replicate genuine student/instructor rapport if we are sublimating what we currently understand as authentic pedagogy to the purpose and goal of (as yet unproven) financial viability.

With virtual instruction (VLE), there continues to be much talk about the new 'global village/community' with unlimited access to resources and individuals using the latest technological advancements and engaging in the social construction of information to enhance scholarly achievements (Hibbert & Rich, 2006; Li, 2009). But, what does this new community look like? We have always understood that the one constant of the traditional graduate model has included faculty and students physically together in a seminar room. Perversely, the current online model appears to be that of a solitary individual in front of a computer, often counties, countries, and even continents apart engaging in *some form* of self-directed learning. The phrase '*some form*' is significant because, as faculty, we have no way of truly understanding what *form* that self-direction takes. Tech-savvy graduate students are communicating and networking constantly it seems, skipping along the surface of one website to another, but valuable intellectual pursuits of an in-depth nature may not necessarily be part of that agenda. Darting impulsively from one website after another like hummingbirds sampling flowers may ultimately be counter-productive to the graduate experience by promoting a type of intellectual superficiality, an inability and unwillingness to concentrate (Flaherty, 2010). A virtual world rife with numerous jolts of astounding information bytes available in seconds does not appear to bode well for instructors attempting to engage participants in higher-level thinking, nor perhaps does it augur well for the patience and dedication required for reading academic tomes and thinking intensely about complex scholarly content. Even so, there are strong advocates of virtual instruction for 'digital natives' suggesting the banning of paper books at university altogether in favour of online technology (Prensky, 2011).

Many individuals may comfortably embrace self-directed learning and autonomy while others may seem adrift, anxious, and unable to experience quality education without the nurturing presence of the instructor. Neither is self-directed learning without its challenges. Although the instructor-centric model has changed, at least online, to a learner-centric view (Rosenberg, 2003), even those individuals who are comfortable with autonomous learning may require, from time to time, some degree of support, affirmation, and even re-direction. When the instructor is not physically present to guide and mentor, students who ostensibly appear to be contributing online, may be treating course content cursorily much like skimming websites or just responding to the online discussion without even bothering to read the preparatory documents. Faculty have long been aware that students enter graduate school with differing levels of expertise, ability and motivations. Without the presence of strong instructional leadership these discrepancies may be widening such that the triangle of instructor, learner, and course content may not be as intellectually vigorous with the current online paradigm as it is with the traditional face-to-face format wherein skilled instructors are available to assess, scaffold and re-direct as necessary. Further, how can we as graduate learner leaders and course facilitators be assured and trust that students are actually acquiring, reading, and engaging with the content of the prescribed course pack or text? Even more troubling, from an ethical perspective, how is it possible to guide online behaviour and guarantee the authenticity of online responses when we really do not know our graduate students or have a personal relationship with them?

To further compound the complexity of the problem, students are subscribing to online courses in record numbers (DeCosta, Berquist, & Holbeck, 2015) but their reasons for doing so, in many instances, may not necessarily be pedagogically sound. Even key courses described as 'degree required,' which initially were reserved for the traditional face-to-face format, are now commonly available online to allow access for the maximum number of students, culturally diverse, from a wide variety of locations, both nearby and at a distance. Although the reasons for enrolling might not be always pedagogically pure, the burgeoning number of students embracing the online format has perhaps served to strengthen the case that online is the desired learning format of students (DeCosta, et al., 2015). What is not clear is whether the perceived demands of students regarding course format should supercede the beliefs and considerations of experienced faculty, arguably a form of professional de-skilling. Nonetheless, online offerings are on the increase. Required courses available online typically have long waiting lists, sometimes necessitating a parallel course offering. Is there some way forward to manage the authenticity of the face-to-face teaching/learning traditional paradigm attendant with the new online learning model, a model which appeared, at least initially, to be so financially expedient and the preferred choice of students? To confound thinking even further, studies have revealed that face-to-face graduate modes of instruction scored significantly better on 2 of 3 measures of evaluation (see Ferguson & Tryjankowski, 2009) as well as on preference, performance and pass rates for White and minority Master's students (Richardson, 2012).

Learning and training are not the same. Learning involves a process of translating information into knowledge, a very intimate and human activity, whereas training is a means to facilitate this pursuit (Rosenberg, 2003). The processes around managing and presenting course content has traditionally been the purview of faculty, but with no tutoring other than that associated with program practicalities, the urgency to make meaning of this new format and to render the experience a quality one for graduate learners have also become matters of on-going concern. Content itself is rather one-dimensional and flat but comes alive with on-going exchanges of discovery, questioning, interaction and debate. To merely offer content online as flat information (Malamed, 2009) seems antithetical to the graduate experience which historically has created dimension by challenging theory, urging us to examine our own beliefs and practices and thereby, through interactive discussion, put substance to that which is flat. Is it possible for faculty to nurture meta-cognitive thinking and put flesh on flat content from a distance? If so, how is this actuality to be accomplished? Are faculty presently satisfied that they are able to adequately provide an achievable interpersonal dimension to these 'flat' conversational threads online (Garrison, et al., 2000; Hauser, Paul, Bradley, & Jeffrey, 2012)? More importantly, how can faculty adjudicate such viability in a medium when we are not there in person to investigate and make a coherent and ultimately crucial determination?

Most learning builds on that which is known and slowly incorporates that which is unknown and unfamiliar (Malamed, 2009). It seems reasonable then that faculty, in preparing online graduate courses, quite naturally would begin with what they believe constitutes quality graduate education, an experience probably both comfortable and familiar, and '*somehow*' translate it to the new and relatively unknown online milieu. But some may question the wisdom of such a plan. To assume that the simplified understanding of one mode (face-to-face) may be transferable and even applicable to another (online) seems ingenuous and myopic at best, yet, what else is currently available, tested and successful? Although graduate investigation in particular, has tended to endorse and encourage self-directed inquiry, faculty were always present as buttressing assistance to facilitate and re-direct. There may be specific literacies, certain competencies, and abilities essential to comfortable online learning which would enable students to make the most of their electronic environment. Are graduate faculty confident that they have facility with these essential literacies and competencies for competent online learning and able to intercede effectively when appropriate and imperative? Without the scaffolding physical presence of the instructor, are isolated participants feeling able to safely negotiate the dynamics of the asynchronous platform in terms of meaning-making and knowledge-building (Kop, 2011)? If struggling students are not communicating their difficulties, how are we, as instructors-at-a-distance, able to know, intervene and mediate?

Online learning (and this includes graduate learning) is socially-constructed through the practicality of the social community or, as Hibbert and Rich (2006) identify –communities of practice, but the traditional supportive 'in-the-flesh' *relationship* component is absent online. Information shared online, by definition, lacks authentic interpersonal depth because participants are not physically present with each other. Many online contributors use the same 'personal paragraph' to share from one graduate course to the next, much like a desultory form letter summarizing their likes, dislikes, and current activities, with this superficial introductory paragraph somehow posturing as the initial stage of an 'authentic' interpersonal connection. When we are physically together, 'in-the-flesh' so to speak, interpersonal activities abound: visual cue exchanges, eye contact, perhaps dining/shopping together, chatting about the trivialities of daily life, sharing and exchanging beliefs, ideas, and innermost thoughts. It is this intensely intimate interactive interchange that begins to weave our personal 'fabric' with that of another, shaping and crafting a kind of 'interpersonal quilt' we can describe as a *relationship*. When an interpersonal relationship develops and becomes established, meaning-making becomes authentic, caring, and more in-depth, rather than casual and perfunctory (Noddings, 2012).

Similarly, there is the possibility too, that online graduate discussions can become mere assemblages of existing information, a rather cursory activity, rather than processes of knowledge-building in a thought-filled meta-cognitive way that being physically present with others seems to actively inspire. Similarly, there is on-going concern about the perceived tone of online conversations. Considerable skill is required in crafting online commentary that stimulates cutting edge thinking and dynamic conversational dialogue but does not read to others as abrasive, abrupt and even rude. In face-to-face conversation, tone of voice is a powerful motivator, but is absent with online. Electronic words are inanimate with no apparent soul until a meaning, rightly or wrongly, is placed upon them by another. Rather than risk being accused of online rudeness or even bullying and harassment, participants may 'play it safe' and not push the conversational boundaries, thus eliminating the possibility of engaging in higher level reasoning and learning. Faculty can pose questions that encourage meta-cognitive thinking and debate but the impersonal nature of online coupled with inherent time delays and fears of being labelled a bully (Clark, Werth & Ahten, 2012) may relegate the potential for profound discussion to languish among the myriad of other unremarkable posting dialogues. On the other hand, when the potential interaction has at its foundation a personal affiliation and vested interest, such as is commonly found in face-to-face communication, the presence of strong interpersonal relationship capital is perhaps much more likely to inspire authentic high level conversational engagement (Major, 2014).

Student-centred learning is not new, but in an online paradigm students are different regionally, demographically, ethnically, as well as in motivation and expectations. In face-to-face learning graduate participants have to make a significant commitment: driving to the venue, setting aside time to attend, preparing academically by pre-reading, perhaps engaging individuals to care for their children, and a myriad of other obligations. Online graduate learning can be 'attended' at a level of marginal preparation and contribution- a participant may be simply fulfilling minimal program requirements with course credit as the primary goal. As a consequence, there is a legitimate concern that online courses may be increasingly limited to cognitive learning, just the acquisition of knowledge/credentials- a form of reductionism. Other learner participants who really want authentic meta-cognitive interaction may be anxious (Hauser, et al, 2012), feeling that their course is being 'watered down' by the lack of dynamic and stimulating online graduate-level discussions. If graduate online learning is conceived as an interactive process, a convergence of inquiry, debate and discovery with 'present' individuals forming a learning community, what, then, ensues if one or more individuals fail to attend online in a timely manner? Starratt (2005) proposes an expectation of interdependence on each other, such that if one partner is not fully engaged "the mutuality of presence is diminished" (p.403). This interdependence underscores that online courses are *not* usually conceived as an isolationist experience, but rather as an interactive community of learning and knowledge-building (Hibbert & Rich, 2006; Nicol, Minty, & Sinclair, 2003). The participant may be sitting alone but any contribution, like a strand of a double helix, is inextricably generated as part of the knowledge-building collective (Garrison, Anderson, & Archer, 2010). Graduate online group work though does not necessarily appear to be a satisfactory answer for increasing communication as participants may feel there are fewer channels for communication than available with face-to-face (Smith, Sorensen, Gump, Caris, Heindel & Martinez, 2011).

Online (graduate) exchanges are typically featured as non-spontaneous dialogue and interactive responses with individuals able to carefully contemplate and edit their involvement before posting online as they attempt to move the conversation forward. Once a posting is available online, it is ready to be interpreted, perhaps differently by each individual reader, with the originating author having little occasion for elucidation unless queried directly. Likewise, the graduate instructor has no immediate opportunity to pose clarifying questions until some misdirection becomes obvious. All posting, reading, and questioning by participants takes considerable time, with responses and any remediation, especially in the instance of perceived online harassment, delaying the consolidation of learning and knowledge-building within the online graduate community even further. Additionally, are individual participants able, and perhaps more importantly, *should* they be willing to place their trust with unknown members of their online learning cohort? Whether we care to embrace the digital world of communication, it is certainly the wave of current and future interaction, especially among the younger generation, who are, perhaps, the most comfortable with this medium. Ease of communication, however, should not necessarily mean that such relationships are what they appear to be as all our sensory filters are not really engaged. Individuals can easily disguise their true selves and hide behind the words written online. We can scarcely perceive whether the words on the computer screen have actually originated from and by the designated sender. With every new digital advancement and discovery, there seems to be an equal number of charlatans', scam artists, and those who mean to do us harm using the advancement.

Conceptualizing Knowledge-Acquisition and Meaning-Making

Traditionally, universities and their libraries were repositories of scholarly collections, contributed by learned men and women. Tangible works were gathered over decades and centuries since the beginning of the written and printed word: books, periodicals, newsprint, film, documents, microfiche and the like, were accessed by students, researchers and scholars physically on site browsing, searching and gathering information from material available in the library stacks. Most of this early information along with the most recent is now readily available online as university libraries have also embraced the virtual world by acquiring their current (and even past) collections making them available for learner acquisition online as virtual electronic 'paper'. As a natural consequence of electronic media and internet advances in the virtual world, access to the electronic 'information highway' requires only a few taps of an electronic device that heretofore required hours, days, weeks and sometimes months to search, procure, and print information from paper-based libraries. In the current academic environment, seminar participants no longer need to be physically present on campus to 'browse' the library stacks. They can do their browsing virtually with an electronic device and an Internet connection from places as far-flung as world travel and connectivity will allow.

Online Environment Apprehension: Potential Impediments to Authentic Communication and Learning

Were faculty leaders commonly consulted when computer-supported online programs were in the design phase? If so, who were they? There appears to be no discussion around these technically generic inventions regarding any consideration for pedagogical soundness and instructional individuation, nor is there necessarily any alignment with current academic programming and practices. These feats of technical origination are simply created by those with specialised electronic expertise to be adapted as, arguably, a means of educational convenience, purchased at considerable expense, and made available to faculty as 'fait accompli' programs ready-for-use. Universities can then claim they are up-to-date and in line with current educational experiences as they proudly showcase these costly virtual accommodations. Any personalization of the online template must be undertaken by faculty instructors, who perhaps have little or no facility with the practicalities of the online paradigm. With any new instructional instrument, especially those that are computer-based, there is considerable new up-front and in-progress learning necessary to acquire the technical competency for navigating and trouble-shooting the online program and its latest revisions, as well as the online medium itself. Skill acquisition and a high level of comfort are essential for faculty whom students immediately consult as their 'technical' expert and leader when electronic issues manifest. Any failure by faculty to resolve electronic difficulties promptly has immediate negative implications for the smooth progression of learning within the practising learning community. Regrettably, when on-going electronic issues become the focus, all leadership, communication, and learning are negatively affected and in-course knowledge-building quickly falls into disarray or is truncated completely until the issue is resolved. Faculty and students are no longer physically in the same room to attempt a temporary solution together, nor is technical staff always immediately available. This frustrating and interruptive gap in the pragmatic aspects of the virtual learning instrument further complicates the resolution of any but the most elementary of electronic glitches.

As a tentative step into these uncharted online waters, faculty, at first, often utilized a combination of synchronous and asynchronous learning strategies. Synchronous learning (for example, using Skype or Elluminate) more closely models the traditional face-to-face experience, in that, students are required to log on and participate at the same time as their cohort members. One difficulty quickly became apparent. Although online connectivity reduced geographical barriers, location actually *does* matter in synchronous learning. Time differences among remote locations around the world meant that some students had to log on in the middle of the night or, as is common for adult student income earners, during an inopportune time of their workday, just to be in the 'virtual class' with their cohort. In an attempt to alleviate this challenge, synchronous attendance with the instructor was allowed at different times, but regrettably, the goal of all participants attending together was rarely achievable. As a consequence, synchronous learning was/is not always the best option. Enter the asynchronous learning environment whereby students logged in at times that were most convenient for them.

Leaping Into the Abyss: Troubling Practicalities and Possibilities

With the asynchronous on-line experience, it seems reasonable to speculate too, about who is teaching and what is being taught/learned online when graduate faculty are not a constant presence to guide and mentor. The context for ethical communication and authenticity appears to have changed with the on-line environment perhaps, because unlike much of face-to-face teaching and learning interaction, online communication is time-delayed with deliberately-planned 'written' dialogue and non-spontaneous interaction. As a corollary, faculty may speculate about who is actually doing the learning? Are graduate students actually who they say they are and how can faculty verify that course work is being completed by the registered student? This latter concern seems especially troubling.

When first introduced, the use of online instruction was left to individual faculty choice, many feeling apprehensive about purpose and content, as well as the teaching and learning processes of this relatively untested electronic medium. Adjunct graduate instructors were the most frequent consumers of the online paradigm, while many site-based university faculty resisted online instruction, mentioning course quality as a major concern. The university, initially placing their faith in online as a means to address both financial strife and student interest; and students, enrolling in significant numbers (Johnson, et al., 2015), seemed to be conspiring against the traditional norm (and excellence perhaps?) of graduate education. Face-to-face graduate seminars began to be cancelled for want of sufficient enrolment, signalling a necessary shift in thinking by apprehensive mainstream faculty who reluctantly began to sample the online prototype (Rintoul, 2011). For their part, graduate students whole-heartedly embraced the ability to learn from the comfort of their home, or indeed, from anywhere in the world, at any time (Parry, 2010). Rejoicing in the freedom and flexibility this mode of learning afforded, student online enrolment ballooned exponentially (DeCosta, et al., 2015).

There remain, however, many reservations and uncertainties to contemplate, consider and confront. As efficiency is gained (and this has by no means been confirmed), have interpersonal connections and instructional practices as we know them been subjugated by online standardization? Graduate students continue to endorse the virtual learning environment, ranking it enthusiastically as their favourite mode of learning (Johnson, et al., 2015), but numerous questions remain. A significant number of students clamoring enthusiastically for online graduate courses have themselves never experienced instruction via a face-to-face model (Rintoul, 2011). One might query whether those who have only been exposed to one delivery mode, that of online, are even qualified to make such arbitration? Should faculty concerns about the authenticity of online instruction be trumped by student demands for ease of access to virtual course instruction? Do these changes to satisfy format demands from students with scant regard for the quality of courses represent a trend toward de-skilling of university instructors (Flaherty, 2010)? Further, is this change, although seemingly significant, merely an essential re-tooling to keep abreast of current trends and practices or could there be something much more fundamental happening to contemporary instructional practices?

The pragmatics of the new technology, perhaps of necessity, has been put in place first, but little else, as we leap blindly into the abyss of the virtual world. While many have embraced the virtual teaching/learning milieu (Prensky, 2014), others may cautiously argue that there has not been enough time to appreciate, comprehend and assess the nuances of the on-line graduate experience. Is this new milieu redefining interactive behaviour in seminars- and if so, in what way(s)? Does the explanation lie with the re-design of graduate courses or is it our understandings that must change- or both? How then should online courses to be crafted, led and assessed? Should the parameters for interaction and appraisal of participants' work be somehow parachuted from the face-to-face experience (Topper, 2007) or is it now appropriate and necessary to initiate new philosophies and practices styled specifically for the new literacy of electronic instruction and online interaction? What are these new philosophies and new practices and who should undertake these significant decisions?

Attempting to manage the technology of online, while simultaneously fostering a fulfilling and appropriate learning experience for individuals of unknown personas, has generated significant trepidation and a litany of concerns for faculty (Rintoul, 2011). Some might question whether the allure of innovative technology mechanisms itself might interfere and obfuscate the true reason for schooling- learning to think. In the transition to technology-based online graduate seminars, faculty have strong resources available for university-sponsored programs such as 'Blackboard,' but that assistance, although necessary and helpful, is more of a pragmatic and practical nature dealing with the functioning and navigating of the online milieu. Resources do not offer, nor are they intended as, assistance regarding (re)conceptualizing and (re)contextualizing content, re-considering online leadership/communication, and perhaps most significantly, appraisal practices appropriate for the new literacy of online learning. Preliminary discussions comparing face-to-face and online graduate course evaluations have begun (e.g. see Berk, 2013; Topper 2007) but certainly more qualitative study would be helpful. Many faculty remain unclear and unconvinced about the viability of virtual learning and may not feel predisposed to undertake these momentous decisions, however, there appears to be no one else with the scholarly acumen to do so.

RECOMMENDATIONS

Trending Uncertainties: Re-Conceptualizing and Re-Designing- Some Considerations for Moving Forward

The new digital literacy for our learning society has emerged as an essential and energizing aspect of our social phenomenology- both practical and intellectual (Florica, Mozelius, Shabalina, Balan, Malliarakis, Miller & Jones, 2013; Pendlebury & Enslin, 2000). The virtual door has been opened wide and wholly embraced universally as we move forward at lightning speed (with)in the virtual realm. Perhaps it is now expedient to embrace this new paradigm as an innovative stimulating adventure with the capacity to support a quality, yet discrete, experience that can be as meaningful and satisfying for both leaders and learners as the more traditional modes of discovery and interaction, **if** prepared thoughtfully and administered well (Hauser et al., 2012). Instructing graduate faculty must find a way to comfortably navigate the new medium and uncover imaginative techniques to offer students the stimulating and scholarly graduate course experience they have come to expect, all while continuing to maintain high standards. As lifelong learner leaders, the path for graduate instructors to accomplish this task will, of necessity, be fraught with uncertainty, trepidation, trials, successes, and even disheartening setbacks. The successful instructional learner leader must now not only understand course content and the nuances of the ever-changing technology, but also comprehend the synergy of these two aspects working together to support authentic learning opportunities (Karchmer-Klein & Shinas, 2012; Moten, Fitterer, Brazier, Leonard, & Brown, 2013) for a vast array of participants with disparate experiences and motivation, from diverse cultures, beliefs, and locales.

The online dynamic is dissimilar from face-to-face in many key aspects as I have noted throughout this chapter yet faculty goals to achieve an authentic learning experience within a quality learning environment must continue (Armstrong & Thornton, 2012). Displaying ethical sensitivity and moral erudition together with care-filled reasoning, graduate instructors, in my view, must navigate a path that facilitates a re-conceptualization of online as a contemporary and provocative scholarly and social community in a medium for progressive communication and learning, not instead of face-to-face learning, but as another viable mode of graduate knowledge-building and interaction. I suggest that this path must of necessity include online conversation with lively discussion as a significant component facilitating discovery, learning and erudition. The key to robust student engagement and spirited participation online may well lie in the structure (Prensky, 2005/2006) and precision of the details: the thoroughness and clarity of course design outlining the purpose(s) and outcomes of learning and collaborative conversational interaction, together with timely, detailed, and thoughtful instructor feedback. Such strategies are not new as these particulars were, and continue to be, the benchmark of a quality face-to-face graduate experience. Unlike undergraduate teaching, most graduate seminars have long ago moved from lecturing to a conversation-driven experience, therefore, the transition to online, arguably, may be more seamlessly achieved. Another favorable aspect moving forward is that graduate students, for the most part, seem wholly engaged with virtual learning and the online environment as a key component of daily learning and communication.

A new dimension with innovative abbreviated language has permeated casual online communication, for example, the blurring of words, numerals, letters and symbols to convey meaning and emotions (the latter pictorials are termed 'emoticons') and this language has seeped into graduate online participation. There are many of these letter/symbol mixes but even their connotations are not universally consistent, probably because this new language is still in its infancy- for example 'lol' at last count (August, 2015) has 111 suggested meanings on Google. Although some may consider this online 'street' language the wave of the future, as even now it occasionally finds its way into scholarly papers submitted for grading, graduate instructors may be concerned that students' competence with traditional writing and grammatical structure to convey meaning clearly and eloquently is on the wane. There is a plethora of troubling examples: the use of the pronoun 'this' without a discernable antecedent, the use of 'then' for 'than,' to offer but two. While these grammatical errors of structure and syntax may, from a cursory view, seem relatively minor, complexity and complication occurs when intended meaning becomes obscured through lack of precision in writing. Sentence comprehension, at the graduate level certainly, should not be reduced to a guessing game of 'what's the intended meaning'? As a consequence, it may be that graduate faculty will feel it necessary to re-imagine online seminar conversation as an exercise in promoting and strengthening writing skills through a variety of purposive and purposeful writing experiences.

In traditional graduate instruction/learning, the rhythm of a dynamic and vibrant energy among cohort members sitting across from one another in seminar passionately and spontaneously debating an issue verbally has been the standard of excellence by which all graduate teaching has been compared. Such free-wheeling, real time interactive conversation suddenly seems to have gone the way of the dinosaur, leaving in its wake an online literacy model of physical isolation and potential ambiguity as participants sit solitarily struggling to make meaning of the written word, both their own and that of others. This new literacy appears to be socially constructed and conceptualized as an on-going written dialogue of ideas and knowledge-building that may not always read or flow well, subject to the vagaries of posting times as well as the whims and commitment of seminar participants, if they even seize the online conversational mantle at all!

Alternatively, when participants take the time to contemplate and craft their responses carefully, online collaboration can lead to complex knowledge-building by these virtual communities (Hibbert & Rich, 2006). In consideration of this new online reality, it seems even more imperative that students acquire and demonstrate effective writing and thinking skills to convey their viewpoints, philosophies, and responses both concisely and clearly. Taking extra care with the composition of written posts may help alleviate the necessity for endless queries regarding intended meaning as well as accusations of bullying (Clark, at al., 2012; Park, Na, & Kim, 2014). The latter is a very real concern as individuals read and place their own interpretation on written posts, with those opaquely constructed being especially vulnerable to misunderstanding. Interpersonal skills have taken on a new meaning as online participants struggle to write their conversational postings intelligently and scholarly yet in a sensitive interpersonally-mindful way. Consistent and helpful instructor feedback on writing mechanics, both scholarly and ethically sensitive, as well as suggestions of books offering advice on grammatical structure and syntax may be initial steps to assist individuals in their quest to become better online writers. The challenge for instructors may lie in our ability, or lack thereof, to inspire participants to take extra care with their writing *before* posting, especially when we are not physically present to assist, support, and re-direct.

Online structure seems to be of critical importance (Hauser, et al, 2012). To promote care-filled writing and as a catalyst to robust engagement, instructors may deem it necessary to be more prescriptive and to apply certain parameters to regulate the frequency and length of online responses. The goal of such strategies is not only for participants to show they are attempting to move the dialogue and debate forward by posting at least a minimum number of times within a sessional time frame, but also to prevent never-ending quantities of 'empty' text within each post. The latter tends rather quickly to disengage reader-participants. Posting individuals will be required to *'say what they need to say'* succinctly and unambiguously within the given parameters, with the course syllabus clearly and succinctly outlining the requirements. Of necessity, participants will have to learn to edit their work carefully to improve their 'conversational' writing competencies in order to avoid negative feedback (clarity and intended meaning issues) from their cohort members and, of consequence, a lower participation grade from the instructor. Control over posting, in some respects, may seem antithetical to the free-flowing process of typical face-to-face graduate student interactive involvement, but for online participation, doing so may assist in prompting the highly-valued reciprocity that is associated with, and is intensely valued in, spontaneous oral conversation. After all, online postings are part of a continuing social dialogue, not meant to simply remain inert and nebulous but rather to actively supplement meaning and to engage the learner in the facilitation of thinking and discovery; and to shape understandings as individuals react and counter, join and riposte, expanding theory and the knowledge base of the practicing learning community. To facilitate this atmosphere of continuing dialogue, it may be appropriate that sessions will close at the end of a prescribed time frame such that participation cannot be 'made up.' Participants have been known to forget about posting sessions and then email the instructor their posts in a non-contextualized electronic lump (Rintoul, 2011). Clearly, the interaction aspect of postings should be considered a significant part of the participation grade and directly stated as such in the course outline. Even though participants are not actually together in the same physical space, online dialogue is an inherent part of the social learning and knowledge-building experience of the online graduate community.

In an effort to offer a more (w)holistic experience and to supplement what appears to be a rather solitary graduate experience, it seems appropriate to consider team-prepared activities and presentations online such as interactive workshops, critiques of individual short writing assignments online (instructor graded), as well as the availability of an ungraded online Lounge or Bistro where individuals can 'chat' about topics not necessarily related to course materials or to expand on a theme that particularly resonated with them in the graded and posting dialogue of the course. The ungraded portions are always available for all to utilize as little or as often as time and inclination permit. These team-prescribed assignments, both arbitrary (graded) and the ungraded Lounge or Bistro may encourage more interpersonal familiarity, thus helping to promote stronger interactive connections which generally may serve to enhance the comfort of the online milieu while easing some misgivings and trust among cohort members. It is worth noting, though, that there is often less satisfaction associated with online group work and its fewer channels of communication to resolve logistical difficulties than group work done in a face-to-face setting (Smith, et al., 2011).

More Tribulations Ahead

Extreme Measures

In Ontario, just as faculty were becoming more familiar and comfortable with the vagaries of online teaching and learning, the winds (or is it 'whims'?) of change once again would thrust some faculty and their personal lives into considerable turmoil. Following several years of much consternation and consequent re-consideration of their financial circumstances, many universities continue to find they are contending with ever-diminishing budgets and increased bureaucratic oversight. Many are now trending toward increased utility of their existing physical centres, that is, their main campuses ('Not enough students to fill university campuses, expert says,' 2016; 'University of Guelph closing 2 satellite campuses,' 2015; 'University of Windsor closing its centre,' 2013). With universities shutting all or most of their satellite campuses and terminating any attendant face-to-face seminars, both students and faculty are left confused and distressed, with their personal and professional life in turmoil. The face-to-face seminars from recently-closed satellites are now being harvested as either additional online courses or as new face-to-face instruction in the existing core physical structures of the main university campuses only (see for e.g. University of Guelph, Nipissing University, Wilfrid Laurier University, and Laurentian University). In the short term, fiscal relief following the closure of outpost campuses should, at least temporarily, alleviate the financial hardships associated with the practicalities of satellite campus service and maintenance. Intriguingly, forcing these closures may be somewhat the right decision but perhaps for the wrong reason. Face-to-face learning has generally been accepted by most university instructors as the atmosphere for the best knowledge-building and student learning (reasons discussed elsewhere in the chapter). Unfortunately, there is no sense at all that universities are making these decisions for pedagogical concerns but rather for the improved fiscal stability of their financial bottom line. Students who thrived in the face-to-face environment at satellite campuses are suddenly left with just online instruction or, alternatively, distance-driving to attend the 'new' face-to-face teaching available only at the central or main campuses.

Challenges for Faculty

With this trend towards the core, universities also appear to be placing their academic faculty at risk with this new reality. The province of Ontario has always been known as having a climate subject to extreme weather variables, but as a further consequence of global warming, these seasonal hazards are on the rise (*The Weather Network*, 2018). Navigating precarious and unpredictable weather patterns, especially in late fall, winter, and early spring can be an additional source of stress and danger for drivers on roads that are prone to black ice, snow drifts, flash flooding and temperature extremes.

In Ontario, distances between a university's main campus and their satellite campuses can be significant, often 2 or 3 hours distant or more in heavy traffic, especially when considering the busy 401 and 400 corridor series highways. Tenured faculty, many of whom moved their family circumstances years ago to better access and service these satellite campuses, are facing personal hardships and challenges associated with driving long distances back and forth at their own expense to teach at universities' main campuses (Milia, Rogers, & Akerstedt, 2012). Travelling long distances before and after work can be hazardous have a deleterious effect on mental and physical well-being over time (Milia et al., 2012). I doubt that when Parker Palmer wrote in 1998 about having 'the courage to teach,' his words did not refer to the new dangers of driving long distances in harrowing conditions to our place of work to do that teaching. Some individuals have reluctantly taken early retirement rather than face the prospect of these overly-long and perilous drives (Shields, 2018).

In the wake of these retirements some universities may potentially be facing a 'brain drain', losing some of their most experienced, dedicated, and valued faculty. Some, for whom retirement is not an option, may decide to rent a small apartment by themselves or with a colleague enabling them to live near the main campus where they are teaching. Doing so has the potential to be personally disruptive, causing increased financial strife trying to maintain 2 residences and ultimately perhaps the bifurcation of the family unit. In some instances the pressure on one spouse to take on the parenting duties usually managed by two parents, may be overwhelming, resulting in emotional and mental breakdowns and even marriage collapse. In the extreme, in an effort to keep their families together, some faculty may find it a necessity to sell their homes and uproot their families once again to secure lodging nearer the main campus where they now are working, resulting in more financial and emotional discord for all family stakeholders. This ultimate sacrifice may not even be viable because in many families both parents are necessarily employed and such extreme measures such as re-location may just not be reasonable or feasible for one of the working parents, not to mention displacing children from their friends, extended families, and a familiar academic milieu.

Mental and Emotional Stress

Verbal promises, and even written contractual ones, are often fractured or severed when university circumstances change. The concept of university teaching being considered a craft (Lindsay, 2018) becomes little more than "well, everyone has to teach/do something they're not comfortable doing' when someone in administration decides to make a change. The result is an eroding of faculty confidence while increasing feelings of disenfranchisement and insecurity in professional abilities (Rintoul, 2018). Couple these negative feelings with being a single parent and disaster cannot be far behind. Single parent households resulting from bifurcated families often have less inter-familial support available to assist them in an on-going daily basis, let alone when emergencies arise. Single parent faculty and their children can be especially vulnerable when placed in these situations of unwanted, oppressive and substantial professional and life changes. Remarks such as, "Oh this will be good for you" just underscores how uncaring and devoid of empathy some administrators can be. Faculty are commonly required to assist their students to achieve their best, but if faculty themselves are under severe personal, emotional, and psychological duress, how can they advise their students and do their best teaching when they are themselves tired, worn out, over-worked, and anxiety-ridden? Academic planning that, in the university Board room and on paper, may seem a great idea for financial viability, should not be taken lightly as the lives of faculty who are, after all, the university's front-line, may be increasingly and dangerously at risk.

Faculty members are not nor should they be considered inanimate pieces on a chess board to be moved capriciously. Communication is commonly a two-way process of listening and speaking and should not, at the university level, be uni-directional. What has happened to the ability of faculty to offer meaningful input and to have a voice in changes that have the potential for significant changes with far-reaching effects to our personal lives? That choice should not be a 'jump on board, do what you are told, or lose your job" type of selection but rather a willingness to work collegially in an equitable manner, enabling everyone to decide what is best for their family circumstances and themselves, professionally and personally in order to excel and lead productive lives.

FUTURE RESEARCH DIRECTIONS

It may be that graduate instruction has moved from the philosophical and scholarly and toward the more practical and pragmatic with acquisition of graduate degrees for individuals and financial viability for institutions as the main goals. Alternatively, it may be that virtual learning is at the threshold of a revolution in the phenomenology of knowledge-building. Certainly, online graduate education is 'of the moment' and perhaps the wave of the future. Opportunities for future research and consideration of this dynamic and innovative paradigm might include more in-depth study of the evaluation and content viability of online graduate programs as contextualized by both instructional faculty and our graduate participants.

CONCLUSION

Graduate faculty, especially digital immigrants, may be struggling to keep abreast of the exploding advances of the virtual universe and this whole process may at times feel a bit messy, clumsy and laborious but, in many respects, a slower pace allows for careful re-thinking, re-tooling and refinement of strategies moving forward- what works, what doesn't and especially, what needs to be re-conceptualized, re-contextualized and how stated goals might be achieved. I would argue that ultimately, it remains the role of faculty, the learner leaders, as the final guardians of scholarly instruction, communication and course facilitation to ensure that online graduate teaching still inspires meta-cognitive thinking in an intellectually stimulating environment that enriches and strengthens graduate learning and knowledge-building of our burgeoning future scholars in their various fields of study.

The scholarly academy generally has always been considered highly collegial and interactive, appreciative of the individual, encompassing an atmosphere of support, understanding, and equity. As active members of the tertiary learning environment of the university academy, we have long known that personal happiness is foundational for professional realization so why then are so many of our members feeling diminished and disenfranchised? We know that when faculty members are happy and feel valued it becomes much easier for them to be successful and valuable assets to their institution. As a consequence, every instructor and every student together with the institution of which they are a part, benefits greatly from their achievements. The new urgency for universities may be to re-consider and re-visit, in a meaningful way, how substantial changes are adjudicated, authorized and administered, especially those that have the potential of impacting in critical and on-going ways the professional and personal lives of faculty and students.

REFERENCES

Armstrong, A., & Thornton, N. (2012). Incorporating Brookfield's discussion techniques synchronously into asynchronous online courses. *The Quarterly Review of Distance Education*, *13*(1), 1–9.

Berk, R. (2013). Face-to-face versus online course evaluations: A 'consumer's guide' to seven strategies. *Journal of Online Teaching and Learning*, *9*(1), 140–148.

Braddock, R., Mahony, P., & Taylor, P. (2006). Globalisation, commercialism, managerialism and internationalisation. *International Journal of Learning*, *13*(8), 61–67.

Chau, P. (2010). Online higher education commodity. *Journal of Computing in Higher Education*, *22*(3), 177–191. doi:10.100712528-010-9039-y

Clark, C., Werth, L., & Ahten, S. (2012). Cyberbullying and incivility in the online learning environment, Part I: Addressing faculty and student perceptions. *Nurse Educator*, *37*(4), 150–156. doi:10.1097/NNE.0b013e31825a87e5 PMID:22688872

DeCosta, M., Berquist, E., & Holbeck, R. (2015). A desire for growth: Online full-time faculty's perception of evaluation processes. *The Journal of Educators Online*, *13*(2), 73–102.

Dobbins, K. (2009). Feeding innovation with learning lunches: Contextualising academic innovation in higher education. *Journal of Further and Higher Education*, *33*(4), 411–422. doi:10.1080/03098770903272495

Ferguson, J., & Tryjankowski, A. (2009). Online versus face to face learning: Looking at modes of instruction in Master's level courses. *Journal of Further and Higher Education*, *33*(3), 219–228. doi:10.1080/03098770903026149

Flaherty, J. (2010 October/November). Bridging the digital divide: A non-technical approach to the use of new technology in post-secondary teaching and learning. *Academic Matters Journal of Higher Education*, 21-26.

Florica, T., Mozelius, P., Shabalina, O., Balan, O., Malliarakis, C., Miller, C., & Jones, P. (2013). An international approach to creative pedagogy and students' preferences of interactive media. *Proceedings of the International Conference on E-Learning*, 479-487.

Garrison, D., Anderson, T., & Archer, W. (2000). Critical inquiry in a text-based environment: Computer conferencing in higher education. *The Internet and Higher Education, 2*(2-3), 87–105. doi:10.1016/S1096-7516(00)00016-6

Garrison, D., Anderson, T., & Archer, W. (2010). The first decade of the community of inquiry framework: A retrospective. *Internet and Higher Education, 13*(1/2), 5–9. doi:10.1016/j.iheduc.2009.10.003

Hauser, R., Paul, R., Bradley, J., & Jeffrey, L. (2012). Computer self-efficacy, anxiety and learning in online versus face to face medium. *Journal of Information Technology Education, 11*, 141–154. doi:10.28945/1633

Hibbert, K., & Rich, S. (2006). Virtual communities of practice. In J. Weiss, J. Hunsinger, & J. Trifonas (Eds.), *The international handbook of virtual learning environments* (pp. 563–579). Springer. doi:10.1007/978-1-4020-3803-7_22

Johnson, R., Stewart, C., & Bachman, C. (2015). What drives students to complete online courses? What drives faculty to teach online? Validating a measure of motivation orientation in university students and faculty. *Interactive Learning Environments, 23*(4), 528–543. doi:10.1080/10494820.2013.788037

Kop, R. (2011). The challenges to connectivist learning on open online networks: Learning experiences during a massive open online course. *International Review of Research in Open and Distance Learning, 12*(3), 19–37. doi:10.19173/irrodl.v12i3.882

Leonard, P., & Rintoul, H. (2010). An international collaboration: Examining graduate educational leadership in Louisiana and Ontario. In A. Normore (Ed.), *Advances in educational administration, 11. Global perspectives on educational leadership reform: The development and preparation of leaders of learning and learners of leadership* (pp. 301–321). Emerald Group Publishing Limited. doi:10.1108/S1479-3660(2010)0000011018

Li, Q. (2009). Knowledge building in an online environment: A design-based research study. *Journal of Educational Technology Systems, 37*(2), 195–216. doi:10.2190/ET.37.2.f

Lindsay, P. (2018). *The craft of university teaching*. Toronto: University of Toronto Press.

Major, W. (2014). Contagion in the classroom: The need for physical and emotional connectedness for deep learning classrooms offering social experience. *Liberal Education, 100*(4), 66–69.

Malamed, C. (2009). *10 ways to organize instructional content.* E-Learning podcast 2.0.

Metcalfe, A., Fisher, D., Gingras, Y., Jones, G., Rubenson, K., & Snee, I. (2010, October/November). How influential are faculty today? Responses from the Canadian Professorate. *Academic Matters Journal of Higher Education*, 16-20.

Milia, L., Rogers, N., &Akerstedt, T. (2012). *Sleepiness, long distance commuting and night work as predictors of driving performance.* /journal.pone.0045856 doi:10.137/1

Moten, J., Fitterer, A., Brazier, E., Leonard, J., & Brown, A. (2013). Examining online college cyber cheating methods and preventative measures. *The Electronic Journal of E-Learning, 11*(2), 139–146.

Nicol, D., Minty, I., & Sinclair, C. (2003). The social dimensions of online learning. *Innovations in Education and Teaching International, 40*(3), 270–280. doi:10.1080/1470329032000103807

Noddings, N. (2012). *Philosophy of education* (3rd ed.). Boulder, CO: Westview Press.

Not enough students to fill university campuses, expert says. (2016). Retrieved from https:// www.cbc.ca/news/canada/sudbury/laurentian-university-barrie-campus

Palmer, P. (1998). *The courage to teach*. San Francisco, CA: Jossey-Bass.

Park, S., Na, E., & Kim, E. (2014). The relationship between online activities, netiquette and cyberbullying. *Children and Youth Services Review, 42*, 74–81. doi:10.1016/j.childyouth.2014.04.002

Parry, M. (2010). Tomorrow's college. *Chronicle of Higher Learning, 57*(11), 84–86.

Pendlebury, S., & Enslin, P. (2000). Lifelong learning for a new society. In J. Field & M. Leicester (Eds.), *Lifelong learning: Education across the lifespan* (pp. 149–157). New York: Routledge Falmer.

Power, M., & Vaughan, N. (2010). Redesigning online learning for international graduate seminar delivery. *Journal of Distance Education, 24*(2), 19–38.

Prensky, M. (2006). Listen to the natives. *Educational Leadership, 63*(4), 8–13.

Prensky, M. (2011). In the 21st century university, let's ban (paper) books. *The Chronicle of Higher Education, 58*(13), 309.

Prensky, M. (2014). Innovation experimentation and courage in the education of students for the future. *Educational Technology, 54*(1), 64.

Richardson, J. (2012). Face to face versus online tuition: Preference, performance and pass rates in White and ethnic minority students. *British Journal of Educational Technology, 43*(1), 17–27. doi:10.1111/j.1467-8535.2010.01147.x

Rintoul, H. (2011). *Transforming educational practices. The online graduate experience: Concerns, challenges and dilemmas*. Paper presented at the annual meeting of the Center for the Study of Leadership and Ethics in Education, Victoria, Canada.

Rosenberg, M. (2003). Redefining e-learning. *Performance Improvement, 42*(3), 38–41. doi:10.1002/pfi.4930420307

Smith, G., Sorensen, C., Gump, A., Heindel, A., Caris, M., & Martinez, C. (2011, March). Over-coming student resistance to group work: Online versus face to face. *Internet and Higher Education, 14*(2), 121–128. doi:10.1016/j.iheduc.2010.09.005

Starratt, R. (2005). Cultivating the moral character of learning and teaching: A neglected dimensions of educational leadership. *School Leadership & Management, 25*(4), 399–411. doi:10.1080/13634230500197272

The Weather Network. (2018). Retrieved from www.theweathernetwork.com

Topper, A. (2007). Are they the same? Comparing the instructional quality of online and face-to-face graduate education courses. *Assessment & Evaluation in Higher Education, 32*(6), 681–691. doi:10.1080/02602930601117233

University of Guelph closing 2 satellite campuses. (2015). Retrieved from www.thestar.com/news/queenspark/2015

University of Windsor closing its centre for studies in social justice. (2013). Retrieved from Nationalpost.com/…to-join-ghostly…haunting-university-campuses

ADDITIONAL READING

Benton, S., & Cashin, W. (2012). *Student ratings of teaching: A summary of research and literature.* Manhattan, KS: The IDEA Center.

Berk, R. (2010). The secret to the 'best' ratings from any evaluation scale. *Journal of Faculty Development*, *24*(1), 37–39.

Del Barrio-Garcia, S., Arquero, J., & Romero-Frias, E. (2015, July). Personal learning environments acceptance model: The role of need for recognition, e-learning satisfactions and students' perceptions. *Journal of Educational Technology & Society*, *18*(3), 129–141.

Rothman, T., Romeo, L., Brennan, M., &Mitchell, D. (2011). Criteria for assessing student satisfaction with online courses. *International Journal for e-Learning Security, 1*(1-2), 27-32.

Taylor, P., Parker, K., Lenhart, A., & Moore, K. (2011). *The digital revolution and higher education.* Washington, DC: Pew Internet & American Life Project.

KEY TERMS AND DEFINITIONS

Asynchronous Program: A program whereby participants attend online at different times (e.g., Blackboard).

Digital Immigrant: A person who became familiar with computers as a young adult or later in life.

Digital Native: A person who has been familiar with computers, the Internet, and other digital technology from a very young age.

E-Learning: Learning conducted via electronic media, typically on the internet.

Graduate Programs: These programs include both Masters and Doctoral seminars.

MOOC: Massive open online courses.

Self-Directed Learning: Each individual takes responsibility and accountability for his/her own learning.

Synchronous Program: A program facilitating all participants attending face-to-face together online at the same time (e.g., Elluminate, Skype).

Virtual Learning Environment: Web-based platform for the digital aspects of course study.

Chapter 9
Leading Teacher Professional Learning:
Shared Language for Shared Goals

Doron Zinger
University of California – Irvine, USA

Jenell Krishnan
University of California – Irvine, USA

Nicole Gilbertson
University of California – Irvine, USA

Kate Harris
Pittsburgh CAPA, USA

ABSTRACT

Teacher professional development is a critical component of teacher learning and improving classroom instruction. Effective communication is key in facilitating professional development. In this chapter, the authors present one aspect of communication in teacher professional development, building shared understanding of key terminology and ideas. they present three case studies of professional development program from across English, history, and science. These cases highlight professional development design and implementation approaches that produced varying degrees of success. The potential pitfalls and effective approaches to facilitating the development of shared language about key ideas are presented. Lessons learned and implications for those who work with diverse groups and conduct professional development are discussed.

DOI: 10.4018/978-1-5225-8516-9.ch009

INTRODUCTION

Every year, educational leaders and educators come together and spend countless hours, and billions of dollars working to improve instruction in schools (Darling-Hammond & Berry, 2006; Wilson, 2013). They face a challenge found in almost any field, developing a shared understanding of concepts, ideas, and discipline-specific terms as they work collectively in groups (Innes & Booher, 1999). A lack of shared understanding can create confusion, lead to miscommunication and misunderstandings, and undermine collective goals (Dickson, 1999). But how often do we consider these concepts and ideas when beginning to work in collaborative groups? And how do we address different conceptualizations to build shared meaning? In this chapter we examine these questions through the lens of teacher professional development for improved classroom instruction. Professional development often brings diverse groups together. They include school district leaders, researchers, instructional coaches, teacher leaders, and teachers. We present three illustrative cases from English language arts, history, and science to highlight the challenges of developing shared understandings around key concepts and ideas between participating teachers and leaders of professional development. In the three cases, we explain how a lack of shared meaning was identified or avoided and how each group approached the building of shared meaning to facilitate collective work. Our goal through these cases is to show how others may avoid or overcome some of the challenges we encountered.

BACKGROUND

Improving Instruction in K-12 Schools

Improving instruction in the public education system has been an ongoing priority in the United States (Duschl, Schweingruber, & Shouse, 2007). Central to these efforts has been a focus on improving teaching as a critical lever to improving student learning (Darling-Hammond, 2010). A primary approach used to improve teacher instruction has been the implementation of various forms of professional development (Scott & Mouza, 2007). Professional development can take many shapes, but typically involves teachers coming together and working with experts or facilitators that can include teacher leaders, instructional coaches, researchers, and school district staff in a particular learning context (Borko, 2004). Nonetheless, and despite significant financial and human investment, the outcomes of professional development have been mixed (Wilson, 2013). That is, the impact of what teachers learn from professional development, and the impact of professional development on student learning remains negligible at times (Buczynski & Hansen, 2010).

Whereas numerous studies have examined the structures and design of professional development, fewer studies examine more nuanced aspects of professional development and how these teaching learning experiences can adapt and change to better meet teacher needs (Zinger et al., 2017; Guskey & Yoon, 2009). Furthermore, although developing shared understanding has been raised as an important consideration for professional development, there are few examples of how negotiation of language to build common understanding works through this collaborative design (Little, 1988).

A Promising Approach to Improving Professional Development

In recent years, new approaches have been adopted to improve professional development (PD). These approaches are designed to better serve teachers with the goal of creating professional learning opportunities that will improve instruction and student learning (Russell, Jackson, Frank, 2013; Penuel, Fishman, Cheng, & Sabelli, 2011). These includes research-practitioner partnerships (Penuel, Coburn, & Gallagher, 2013), and various design-based implementation research (DBIR) strategies or methods (Fishman, et al., 2013). These approaches have shown promise in the way they support teacher learning (Zinger et al., 2017; Wang, Hsu, Reeves, Coster, 2014) At their heart, DBIR focuses on identifying problems of practice and addressing them in collaboration with teachers. DBIR allows for the renegotiation of more traditional relationships between teachers and those leading the professional learning. The hierarchical relationship is replaced with an open interaction between researchers and teachers who have shared goals to support teaching and learning. The teacher feedback and experiences directly informs the design of the professional development as it evolves to better meet the needs of teachers. By viewing research as central to teacher professional development, by making design and program choices in consideration of where teachers' problems of practice and professional needs, and by considering that the context in which teacher PD programs evolve as a potential source of change in the nature of the program itself, we change deep-rooted perspectives on how research can best contribute to the development of effective teacher PD programs for educational improvement (Supovitz, 2013).

Thus we present detailed cases of how professional developers and researchers worked with teachers to create shared language for shared goals across different types of professional development. We pay particular attention to contexts as these vary and are likely to impact professional learning (Zinger et al., 2017). We offer examples of how professional development can involve participating teachers in building a shared language and moving towards building coherent, collective visions for teaching practices.

THREE ILLUSTRATIVE CASES

The three cases presented below illustrate how common understandings of discipline-specific concepts underlying professional development were created and the impact this shared language had on teacher learning. In the first case, we describe how building shared meaning prior to the development of a program has meaningful effects on teacher professional development. In the second case, we highlight what may happen when explicit questions about shared understanding are raised as a program begins and how it informs program design. In the third case, we highlight what may happen when professional development is enacted without explicit examination of, and consideration for, what teacher may or may not know prior to engaging in a program. We use pseudonyms for the participants in all cases.

Case 1: Close Reading (What Is Close Reading?)

Setting: Southern California, diverse schools
Actors: Mrs. Nguyen
Goal(s): Develop instructional materials that align with ELA teachers' goals for close reading.

Defining Close Reading: The Case of Mrs. Nguyen

Thanh, a 13-year-old English language learner, enters Mrs. Nguyen's English language arts (ELA) classroom where small, mixed ability groups will be asked to engage in close reading. Mrs. Nguyen invites her students, a culturally and linguistically diverse group, to read today's learning objective aloud. This class of 32 8th graders reads, *Scholars will be able to analyze the effects of using sentence fragments by engaging in close reading of a memoir.* This specific objective is intended to support students' larger learning goal to identify features of a memoir and to analyze the author's style. But what exactly is close reading, and how does it support the language learning needs of Thanh and her peers?

Contemporary Education Initiatives and Close Reading

The Common Core State Standards for English Language Arts (CCSS, 2010) ask teachers to engage students in close reading: "to determine what the text says explicitly and to make logical inferences from it" and to "cite specific textual evidence when writing or speaking to support conclusions drawn from the text" (p. 1).

Similarly, the Partnership for Assessment of Readiness for College and Careers (PARCC, 2011) explains that by focusing on textual meaning and structure, students may "reflect on the meanings of individual words and sentences; the order in which sentences unfold; and the development of ideas over the course of the text, which ultimately leads students to arrive at an understanding of the text as a whole" (p. 7).

Brown and Kappes (2012) describe the activity of close reading in this way:

Through text-based questions and discussion, students are guided to deeply analyze and appreciate various aspects of the text, such as key vocabulary and how its meaning is shaped by context; attention to form, tone, imagery and/or rhetorical devices; the significance of word choice and syntax; and the discovery of different levels of meaning as passages are read multiple times (p. 2).

Brown and Kappes (2012) refer to "focus on discrete elements of the text," and suggest that in close reading, it is "the author's word choices and repetition, specific sentences, literary devices, academic vocabulary, or particular passages containing information that is key to the curricular objective" (p. 3). They stress, however, that close reading needs to be situated within a comprehensive literacy framework where it serves disciplinary goals. The challenge for teachers is to develop questions that focus students on text in ways that make the close reading serve those larger goals. Given these education initiatives, it is unsurprising that Mrs. Nguyen and her colleagues place particular emphasis on close reading during their ELA instruction. However, to support ELA teachers in their instructional goals, education leaders and researchers who are responsible for designing teacher professional development opportunities must understand how close reading is being defined and how it is being enacted in the classroom.

Understanding the Context

Mrs. Nguyen took part in a district-wide literacy intervention during 2016-2017 academic year that tested the effects of a digital scaffolding tool on students' reading and writing outcomes. Other participants included 50 7th and 8th grade teachers from ten middle schools in their large, urban public school district, teaching 170 ELA classes with 3,472 students (2,097 8th graders; 1,375 7th graders; 73% eligible for free or reduced price lunch). Twenty-seven percent of these students were English language learners, 44% were redesignated as English Language Proficient, and 27% were native speakers of English. As part of the intervention, ELA teachers taught reading for 50 minutes each week (i.e. treatment classes were exposed to digitally reformatted texts and control classes were exposed to traditionally formatted texts). The results of the broader study indicate that students who read with visual-syntactic text formatting (VSTF) earned significantly higher overall scores on California state assessments for ELA compared to students who read traditionally formatted texts (Tate et al., 2019).

To maximize teachers' use of the reformatted texts, and to support their implementation of these materials through intervention-related PD, the research team needed to understand the nature of reading instruction and the nature of teacher PD in the district. The following table highlights the ways that researchers and district education leaders worked toward a shared language for PD and reading instruction, broadly, and the design of close reading materials, specifically, prior to and throughout the intervention year.

Designing Close Reading Materials

This multi-tiered approach to developing a shared understanding of how close reading is defined and enacted throughout this district's ELA team allowed for the development of close reading materials that 96% of teacher reported using throughout the intervention year. Because these materials were designed using teacher-reported instructional goals, they fit seamlessly into their grade-level curricular pacing guides and supported teachers, like Mrs. Nguyen, in engaging students in close reading of informational and literary texts. Below, we provide an example of one close reading document. It features a text-dependent question, theoretically-informed close reading tip, and an excerpt from the informational text.

Enhancing Close Reading Materials

A shared understanding of what these teachers' goals were for supporting teaching and learning in the classroom supported the design and implementation of the close reading materials during the intervention

Table 1. Information seeking activity and corresponding insight gained

Information Seeking Activity	New Insight for Shared Language
Researchers were invited to participate in a six-hour, district-level PD facilitated by curricular experts on reading for language and meaning	District PD sessions used specific strategies for same-site and cross-site collaboration; these strategies were incorporated into intervention-related PD.
Researchers were invited to attend ten 90-minute, school-site PD sessions facilitated by TOSAs on Google Apps for Education and one-to-one mobile technologies	Teachers' experience and comfort with instructional technology varied within and across school sites; focal areas were identified for intervention-related PD; teacher leaders were identified and invited to share best practices during intervention-related PD.
Researchers were invited to observe 250 hours of classroom instruction across 10 schools and participated in research-practice work groups with the district's curricular experts and teacher leaders	Through the Gradual Release of Responsibility Instructional Framework, teachers first asked students to read for gist understanding. Next, they engaged in close reading using specific, visually organized documents that featured analytical text-dependent questions, corresponding excerpts, and space for text annotation; 124 close reading analysis tasks (62 in VSTF and 62 in traditional format), including theoretically-informed close reading tips were developed for teachers' use during instruction.

Figure 1. Sample close reading document featuring theoretically-informed reading tip

1. Read As you read lines 1—31, begin to collect and cite evidence. Circle the question at the beginning of the essay. In the margin, explain what Vernikos says about the human spirit in lines 5—7. Then, underline the main idea in each of the next two paragraphs.

Close Reading Tip: Locate the words "human spirit". Notice that the sentence with those words has two parts, highlighted by the two verbs in red. What does the human spirit 'seek'? What does the process of 'seeking' help the human spirit to 'explore'? What is 'human endurance'? How can 'endurance' be both physical and psychological? Answer these questions to restate what lines 5-7 are telling us about the human spirit.

Annotate	Explain
Why explore? Asked why he kept trying to climb Everest, English mountaineer George Mallory reputedly replied, "Because it was there." Exploration is intrinsic to our nature. It is the contest between man and nature mixed with the primal desire to conquer. It fuels curiosity, inspiration and creativity. The human spirit seeks to discover the unknown, and in the process explore the physical and psychological potential of human endurance.	

year. This understanding, too, helped researchers identify ways that they could enhance the materials for greater teaching and learning outcomes. This took place from the development of theoretically-informed close reading tips that were featured on select text-dependent questions.

At the end of the intervention year, teachers were surveyed about their experiences participating in the study. Specifically, teachers were asked "*Have the close reading tips helped you learn anything new about supporting close reading? If so, what?*, and "*Did the close reading tips help students succeed who would have struggled with the analytical tasks? How do you know?*" Teachers reported that they learned that close reading should focus on specific, short segments of a text and that students need to be given specific steps for engaging in this activity. Teachers also reported that the close reading materials designed to be used during the intervention were structured and stimulated classroom discussion, the tips drew attention to pivotal passages, and provided students with ways to tackle complex texts. These teaching and learning outcomes related to close reading were made possible through a shared understanding of what it means to engage in close reading in service of larger learning goals.

Results of Shared Language for Shared Goals

Successful close reading requires attention to the language an author uses, in service of coming to deeper understand of meaning of the text being read (Moore & Schleppegrell, 2014). By focusing on a shared language and through shared goals, close reading tips were developed and used to enhance the established curricular materials and activities. This offered teachers new ways of thinking about support for close reading by drawing attention to the ways language works to present meanings of different kinds.

By using the close reading materials, Mrs. Nguyen and her colleagues supported their students' English language development by engaging them in interaction that drew their attention to the relationship between language and meaning in text. Teachers reported that the close reading tips were typically used in activities where students interacted with each other to answer the questions, or participated in whole class discussion about their thinking as they read closely. Most importantly, by drawing students' attention to particular aspects of the language authors use, the close reading tips helped students consider larger questions relevant to English language arts: how characters develop, how conflicts are introduced and resolved in a narrative, how arguments are structured and what counts as evidence, and how authors' craft creates meaning in language choices. This is the overarching goal of close reading: to support students' disciplinary learning in ELA as they engage in literary analysis and exploration of informational and argumentative texts. Ultimately, by investing in a solid understanding of the nature of this district's teacher professional development and how ELA teachers conceived of close reading, the education leaders and researcher team created meaningful instructional materials and learning experiences intended to meet these groups' shared goals.

Case 2: Historical Thinking (What Is Historical Thinking?)

Setting: East Coast of the United States, diverse schools
Actor: Jamie Collins
Goal(s): Teachers learned disciplinary skills to implement a digital archive in their history courses

What Is Historical Thinking, an Overview?

Ask most adults about their history classes and they will either complain that they were required to memorize too many dates or will rave about a teacher who told the best stories. Through both of these responses, it is clear that history class once consisted mainly of teachers sharing narratives that required students to remember what happened in the past. We assumed that current history teachers have a deeper understanding of history and historical methods than most adults, but as we started our professional development program with teachers, we thought we would ask them what they thought historical thinking was. Our purpose was to better plan professional development that would focus on the skills of historical thinking, rather than memorization. In order to create meaningful workshops, we acknowledged it was important to know what teachers already knew about historical thinking.

We hoped that participant definitions would connect or overlap with a definition of historical thinking that we had previously developed. Our definition of historical thinking is based on literature in the field and emphasized primary sources like the kind teachers would have access to while in this professional development program. While there is no one definition of historical thinking shared by experts in the field, the methods employed by historians include: inquiry and developing questions, primary and secondary source analysis, and the use of conceptual frameworks such as point of view and change over time (Seixas, 2013, Wineburg 2001, Duquette, 2015, Lesh, 2011). In working with this group of teachers, we shared a definition of historical thinking on the first day and provided specific models of this concept, hoping to expand upon the teachers' own understandings of historical thinking and to preview the types of activities we hoped to share later on. We defined historical thinking as an interpretation that responds to an inquiry question and uses evidence (primary and secondary sources) to make meaning grounded in a deep understanding of a particular time and place. To construct an interpretation, we rely on certain conceptual lenses and practices involving discipline-specific skills. Conceptual lenses are the ways that historians organize their interpretation to provide an explanation for what happened in the past. These lenses include: cause and effect, change over time, historical significance, and perspective/point of view.

Figure 2. Historical thinking graphic

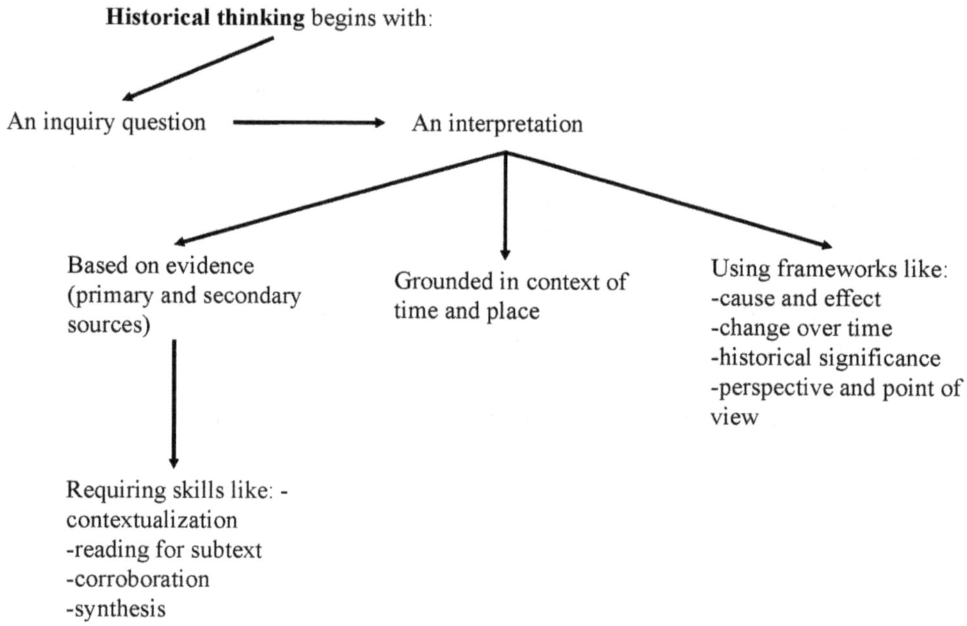

The skills that historians (and students of history) engage in that allow them to make meaning from primary and secondary source material include the skills of contextualization, reading for subtext, corroboration, and synthesis. This definition of historical thinking has been informed by the work of scholars engaged in history education and cognition (Seixas 2013, Wineburg, 2001, Duquette, 2015, Lesh, 2011).

The Context of Teaching Historical Thinking

Our study is situated in the context of a professional development program aimed at high school history teachers who were taught in the use and implementation of a digital archive of primary sources. This digital archive was a searchable platform that allowed users (teachers, students, or the general public) to search for artifacts and sources, collect them into groups for instructional purposes, and annotate the sources for future use. Primary sources are documents from the past and are the foundation for the work that historians do; they are the "stuff" of history. The teachers in this program were all high school history teachers from or near a large city in the Eastern United States. Most of the participants were experienced teachers, with 27 of the 29 teachers having taught more than four years, and the majority of those having taught for over eleven years. Eight had degrees in history, eight others had degrees in humanities or social sciences; so most of the group had training in history at the post-secondary level.

At the outset, we wanted to know what these teachers thought about historical thinking, in order to help build a shared language and develop stronger plans for future professional development sessions. At the beginning of the first meeting with teachers, we asked them to individually define historical thinking in a written response (see figure 3). This would help us establish a baseline of the teachers' knowledge. Most definitions contained ideas, lists, and a description; these included full sentence descriptions, whereas others drew images. Some answers include: "Understanding moments in history," "What is the story the narrative," and "Knowing dates." Other responses focused on the skills of history, such as:

discussing, questioning, analyzing, and interpreting. We synthesized all of the responses and created a word cloud (see figure 4). The word cloud represents the words that were used to define "historical thinking." Words that were repeated more frequently are larger in the cloud. The largest word, thus the word used most frequently, is "past," and "event" is the second most frequently used word. Both of these may reflect the notions that history is a study of past events, which may or may not require students to engage in the work of historians of doing primary source analysis to develop an interpretation. Based on these initial definitions of historical thinking, we realized that we needed to clearly define the term (as outlined in the previous section), provide teachers with models of historical inquiry, and allow teachers to engage in historical thinking themselves using the resources in the digital archive.

Figure 3. Sample historical thinking definition

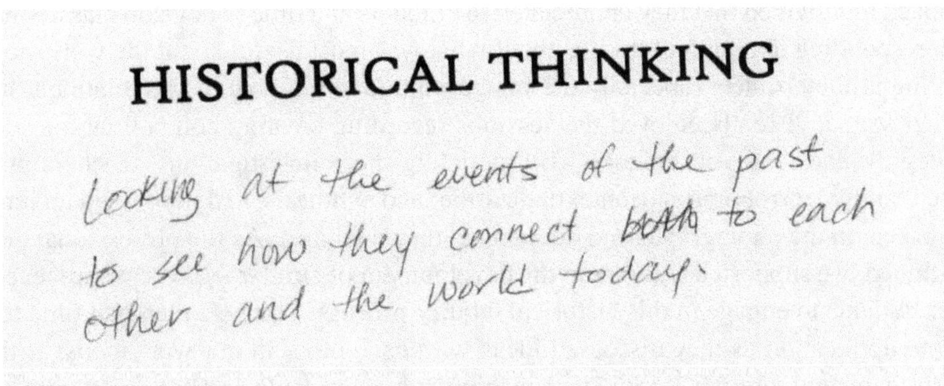

Figure 4. World cloud synthesizing the initial (pre) definitions of historical thinking

Teaching About Historical Thinking

To offer examples of historical thinking at each session, we shared strategies, modeled inquiry and analysis, and allowed teachers to develop lessons around collections of primary sources. We wanted teachers to understand how to incorporate primary source materials in a way that emphasized inquiry and so built lessons around collections of source material that teachers would use to construct a narrative. For example, in the digital archive, we created a collection of primary sources relating to East Coast immigration in the early 20th century and allowed teachers to experience instruction as students, and consider how they might develop a narrative based on these sources. We also provided teachers with model questions, such as "How did ordinary people respond to the Depression?" that they could use as a basis for developing their own set of primary sources. These sources would then be used in the classroom and students would analyze them and use them as evidence to develop a historical interpretation. Teacher feedback highlighted that they appreciated the models and time to develop classroom activities. For example, responding to a prompt asking about what was most useful about the workshop a teacher wrote, "Looking at the artifacts especially the images and learning how to formulate questions about them." Another stated, "I really enjoyed the sessions regarding creating compelling questions, visual thinking strategies, and search techniques." By modeling these investigations, teachers practiced the skills of close reading, corroboration, contextualization, and synthesis, and developed an interpretation of their own based on the photographs and documents they analyzed. As the professional development program continued, we supported teachers in the development of similar lessons, where teachers would ask their own students to engage in this historical inquiry process. Teachers then had time to reflect on their classroom application as they discussed ideas with each other in our workshops, at their school sites with their team, and through school-site coaching, where each teacher partnered with an expert to develop and discuss implementation.

Teachers deepened their understanding of historical thinking through practical application. As we developed the workshop program, we used teacher feedback to inform our planning for subsequent workshops. Teachers requested time to collaborate and learn from colleagues to research and analyze primary sources and to then translate these experiences into lessons for students. Another teacher comment reflects this approach, as they appreciated, "Sharing new ideas for techniques on how to use [the digital archive], and then actually using those techniques to create an assignment!"

At our last session with the teachers, we asked each teacher to again provide their definition of "historical thinking," reflecting any new understandings based on the professional development program. After reviewing the data, we developed a word cloud synthesizing their new definitions (see figure 5). While the teacher responses continued to include "event" and "history," they also highlighted specific historical thinking skills and concepts. The post-professional development response highlights that teachers emphasized specific skills associated with historical thinking, the same skills that we engaged in through the program. These include: analyze, context, and primary sources. Their responses were much more detailed and nuanced as can be seen from the word cloud that includes a variety of specific understandings of how historians construct narratives, such as "cause and effect," "continuity and change," and "make." This highlights that history can be a narrative of the past, but is also subject to interpretation based on specific shared practices and methods that constitute historical thinking.

Figure 5. Word cloud synthesizing the post definitions of historical thinking

Lessons Learned

When comparing the pre- and post- definitions, it became clear that a greater number of teachers were using more words and phrases about the interpretative nature of history--including: students developing arguments, creating new understandings, or making meaning based on primary and secondary source evidence. In the first round of definitions, there were only two clear statements regarding this: one teachers defined historical thinking as "interpreting and synthesizing various accounts to achieve a deeper understanding of the past" and another wrote, "analyzing data, images, video to make sense of past events." However, by the last workshop, there were 18 different phrases that alluded to history as interpretation.

This change was echoed in many of the definitions written by individual teachers. For example, Jamie Collins' (pseudonym) first definition of historical thinking was "time, place, documents, pictures, relevant to history…". By the end of the program, Jamie wrote "using primary sources to evaluate" and "cause-->effect." Her change in phrasing reflects an understanding that history instruction requires students to take an active role in developing their own learning. An emphasis on students engaging in primary source analysis and using these as a way to deepen their understanding of historical concepts and events was echoed by the way her instruction shifted as well. At her first observation, Collin's lesson was content-focused and teacher-led: she reviewed immigrants' experience at Ellis Island through video, discussion, notes, and a vocabulary worksheet. Subsequent observations of her instruction highlighted that she increasingly engaged students in primary source analysis skills, using sources related to content they were currently studying. For example, during the final observation of her class, Collin's students were working independently on computers to analyze photographs and artifacts related to the labor union movement in the United States, responding to guiding inquiry questions that she created.

A post-observation debrief after the lesson also revealed Collin's new confidence with implementing teaching strategies that engaged students actively in making meaning for themselves through the study of primary sources. For example, she identified possible modifications like reducing the number of images in order to allow students more time to focus on each one. Through the professional development program, Collins learned strategies for developing historical thinking skills and implemented these with her students. The opportunity for reflection and feedback on this process offered her an opportunity to further refine these practices to emphasize instruction where students critically engaged with primary sources as a way to develop their understanding of historical content and develop analytical skills at the heart of the discipline.

Collins' definitions and instruction highlight the ways that historical thinking can be reflected in the classroom to support student learning. The professional development program centered on the concept of historical thinking and grounded teachers' learning and practice so that they could engage in the process of historical thinking together. At each session, teachers worked together to develop lessons that reflected these disciplinary methods and then discussed the implementation in the classroom with their colleagues. By beginning our work with a pre-assessment where we collected teacher data on their individual understanding of historical thinking, we could center our work together to discuss what this concept meant for each of us, while moving toward a shared definition of this concept. By modeling specific strategies and instructional practices where teachers did the work of historians, they developed the understanding of how to analyze, synthesize, and interpret primary sources, which they in turn could implement with their students. Creating opportunities for teachers to discuss lesson ideas with each other and during coaching visits at their school-site gave them additional opportunities to develop their definitions of historical thinking and further shape the experiences of the students in their classrooms.

Case 3: Developing Inquiry Science Instruction With Elementary School Teachers (What Is Inquiry in Science?).

Setting: Southern California, school serving historically underrepresented students.
Actors: Expert teachers, professional developers, researchers, classroom teachers.
Goal(s): Improve science instruction and student learning.

Discussion as Part of Scientific Inquiry

As part of a large intervention to improve elementary student science learning, over 80 third through fifth grade teachers participated in a week-long professional development. A significant component of the program focused on preparing participating teachers to teach three inquiry-based Earth science lessons. During the professional development participating teachers engaged in inquiry activities as well as experienced and had opportunities to ask question about the lessons they would be teaching. They were given the curriculum and materials to then teach the lesson in their own classroom.

Once teachers began teaching the lesson, we visited some classrooms to see what instruction looked like. The following unfolded in a veteran teachers' classroom. As the lesson was coming to a close, Alice, the teacher, engaged students in a task where they described each of the steps of weathering, erosion, deposition, and sedimentation. As she walked around the classroom, she reminded students, "so you are *discussing* it, what is the first step?" as she checked on individual groups she praised her students, "My goodness, this is amazing, people are getting all the steps...I hear a lot of good *discussion* there."

Through the lesson and through the *discussion*, Alice engaged her students in inquiry, or inquiry as she understood and perceived it.

When presented with this scenario, the organizers, instructional coaches, and researchers that developed the professional development that Alice participated in were confronted with a larger problem and question. Although Alice used words such as discussion, her enactment of inquiry and discussion did not align with the vision and goals of instruction of inquiry desired by the program. Specifically, discussion being part of a critical analysis of a scientific inquiry. Alice's perceptions of inquiry were not an isolated case, and reflected the perceptions of inquiry and discussion of nearly all participation teachers. So why was there such a disconnect between the intended goal and understanding of inquiry and the way they were enacted? Before we attempt to answer these questions, we should examine what we know about inquiry instruction and the context of teaching science in elementary grades, which are the backdrop of our inquiry.

The Goals of Scientific Inquiry and Instruction

Efforts to improve science teaching and learning emphasize an inquiry approach where students generate questions, present ideas, and defend their hypotheses while teachers facilitate rather than direct (National Science Education Standards [NSES], Next Generation Science Standards [NGSS]). Indeed, the NGSS represent a shift in what and how students are expected to learn and show mastery of learning. Whereas prior standards focused on students knowing facts, the NGSS calls for students to engage in scientific practices such as discussing, arguing, and defending conclusions they reach (NGSS lead states, 2013). Nonetheless, although inquiry approaches to teaching science date back to Dewey and have evolved over the last century (Barrow, 2006), a precise definition of inquiry which guides some of the NGSS principle is still lacking (Anderson, 2002; Windschitl, Thompson, Braaten, & Stroupe, 2012).

Conceptions of inquiry include specific practices such as planning and designing ways to answer questions, conducting experiments, analyzing data, sharing ideas and receiving feedback (Krajcik, Blumenfeld, Marx, & Soloway, 1994), and examining "why" explanations of the natural world, language and disciplinary thinking, and connecting to student real lives (Windschitl et al., 2012). Additionally, more general concepts such as communicating, problem solving and developing thinking skills have been used to frame inquiry (van Zee, 2000). The lack of precise definition juxtaposed with the ubiquity of the word inquiry may be at the root of the challenge of having a shared definition. That is, inquiry is frequently used to describe a type or set of activities in science classroom. Individuals may have deeply ingrained understandings of what the word means, and assume others share this understanding. Yet even within the community of science education, there are widely varying definitions. Nonetheless, despite the lack of consensus, both reform and inquiry pedagogies point to student-centered and student-generated thinking and processing of information and ideas as cornerstones of inquiry (Anderson, 2002).

Discourse and discussion are critical to engaging student in meaningful scientific sense making. As highlighted by the NRC (2000), in inquiry learning "teachers orchestrate discourse among students about science ideas" (p. 22). Additionally, the NGSS standards call for students to ask questions, and engage in argumentation around evidence (NRC, 2011). Discourse moves can engage students in constructing their own explanations which are central to inquiry teaching (Braaten & Windschitl, 2011). In an inquiry-based classroom, students would be expected to generate questions and demonstrate knowledge building. Indeed, some have used classroom discourse as a way to determine if a class is engaged in inquiry (Marshall, Smart, & Horton, 2010). By these definitions, what we observed in Alice's classroom, the *discussion* students engaged in would not constitute meaningful discourse or a discussion as it was framed. Students were simply stating steps in a process and were not generating any new meaning. But why do so many teachers perceive this to be inquiry in action?

The Context of Science Instruction in Elementary Grades

Researchers and professional developers of science instruction, and even more specifically of inquiry-based instruction, are often experts in inquiry-based approaches as well as their specific subject area. Nonetheless, the lived experience of elementary teachers is quite different than that of researchers and instructional experts. Elementary school teachers are charged with teaching multiple subjects, including math, English, social studies, physical education, and more in addition to science (Davis & Smithey, 2009). Within science, they are expected to cover a broad range of areas including, life, physical, and Earth sciences (Davis & Smithey, 2009). Furthermore, the vast majority of elementary school teachers have little background beyond their own experiences in the K-12 system in learning or teaching science (Epstein & Miller, 2011). The lack of content area expertise may contribute to the fact that elementary school teachers also tend to feel least comfortable teaching science as compared to other subjects (Banilower et al., 2013).

In elementary grades, the importance of science instruction is nonetheless emphasized through policies and standards focusing on developing children's ideas and concepts of science (NRC, 2007). However, science standards and policies exist in a broader policy context, where English and math may be prioritized over science. Indeed, elementary school teachers report that the time they can allocate to teaching science can be restricted by prioritization of other subjects, as well as limited access to the materials and resources needed to teach science. On the whole, despite efforts from well-intentioned elementary school teachers and their willingness and desire to participate in professional development opportunities, many engage with professional development with limited content knowledge of science and limited instructional experience with science.

Finding the Incongruence

In this case, our work with elementary science teachers was undermined by a lack of shared meaning about key terms and ideas that were central to the learning goal of the professional development. Specifically, the intended definition of *inquiry* and *discussion* that were central to what teachers were being asked to do and their understanding of these ideas were misaligned. Classroom observations, teacher interviews, and teacher surveys were necessary to identify this misalignment. As teachers completed the initial professional development, there were no clear indicators about the misalignment, with teachers largely satisfied with the program. Nonetheless, the leaders and instructors of the professional development had been talking about inquiry as were participating teachers, but were unaware of how they perceived inquiry differently.

Central to the lack of a shared definition was that professional developers understood inquiry and discussion to be closely aligned with the instructional standards and students analyzing, interpreting, questioning, and justifying experimental findings. The teachers, on the other hand saw inquiry as engaging student in some sort of activity. Teachers saw discussion, as exemplified by Alice's talk with students, as potentially rote, such as reciting the steps of the rock cycle. We conjecture that the difference in expertise about the nature of inquiry and their typical work environment between the teachers who led the professional development and participated in the program were central to the misalignment. Specifically, the professional development leader included teachers of the year, and science subject area specialists, who were not teaching all subjects as a typical elementary teacher would, or were teaching in school setting very different than those the participating teachers came from.

Beginning to Address the Incongruence

The discovery of the incongruence occurred after the initial round of professional development. Thus, the first step to address the incongruence was to provide the professional development leadership team with a clear picture of the classroom interaction and instruction of the participating teachers. This provided an important perspective of the lived experience of the classroom teachers, the challenges they faced, and why it was that they held the definitions of inquiry and discourse that they did. This helped the leadership team understand the starting point or place where they should meet teachers at. The second step was to critically consider how to meet teachers where they were. Specifically, the team reflected on the complexities of inquiry and considered their own level of expertise and how they built it. Ultimately, the team decided to focus on one component of inquiry, questioning and the formulation of questions as a realistic entry point for the subsequent professional development. The team realized that trying to unpack the entirety of inquiry was unrealistic, and the use of questioning would be a good starting point. Specifically, the goal for the subsequent professional development became to facilitate the participant's understanding of the type of learning and engagement students would experience given different types of questions. Different types of questions were ultimately tied to the inquiry that they afforded.

CONCLUSION

In the three cases presented in this chapter we saw improvement minded instructional leaders and classroom teachers working together to improve instruction. We saw some common themes emerge across the cases, including (a) attending to the teachers' lived experiences and meeting them where they are instructionally; (b) using multiple types of data to identify incongruences and misunderstandings; and (c) the importance of developing a shared or common understanding of key ideas and terms. We also saw some differences in the cases in terms of the impact of identifying the incongruences or misunderstandings at different points of the professional development process. Specifically, we saw how identifying incongruences prior to a large scale rollout, or early in a large scale rollout provided teachers better learning opportunities. We detail each of these emergent themes.

Understanding where teachers were coming from was fundamental to developing shared understanding with the participating teachers in all three cases. Indeed, in all three cases, the leaders of the professional development were experts in the areas they were addressing—close reading, historical thinking, and scientific inquiry. These leaders, however, were not experts, at least not initially, in what the daily lives of the teachers were like and how their classrooms operated. Indeed, the more specialized knowledge that was the strength of the professional developers provided them with little insight into where to meet the participating teachers as learners. Once the leaders became aware of the teachers' lived experiences and existing understanding of key ideas, they were better able to design and implement professional development for teacher learning.

Central to understanding where teachers were coming from were a number of different data sources and types. We see across the cases that classroom observations, surveys, focus groups, interviews, and instructional materials all played key roles in understanding how and why teachers held particular definitions or made sense of key ideas and terms. We note the importance and challenges to using multiple data sources. We see, for example, that surveys, in the cases of historical thinking and scientific inquiry, were useful in providing a broad overview— the *what*—but classroom observations and interviews helped better understand the *how* and *why*. We are mindful of the challenges and commitments required for more in-depth data collection such as classroom observations. Nonetheless, we note that even small scale observations of just two or three classrooms can provide useful insight and inform a localized professional development program, when used with other forms of data such as surveys.

Ultimately, we saw the importance of developing shared language for shared goals. We saw two examples, close reading, and historical thinking, where negotiating the shared understanding early in a professional development program helped shape the program and produce desired outcomes. Additionally, offering space for teachers to engage in discussions about these shared understandings and disciplinary practices reinforced their learning. In the case of scientific inquiry, we saw how addressing shared understanding helped the subsequent iteration of the professional development, but not the current. This was primarily due to the focus on shared language arising after the professional development, rather than before or early on in the process. Nonetheless, in all cases, we saw that in all programs that the instructional leaders were able to take the information about their participating teachers and put it into action for systematic improvement.

IMPLICATIONS

Although our focus here is on teaching, implications may be useful to other groups and individuals who lead professional learning or training. Our three cases highlight the importance of using multiple sources of data to understand learners, especially as it related to the key ideas and concepts that are central to the professional development. Additionally, the cases point to the value of investing time and efforts early on in projects to design meaningful learning experiences. Developing and implementing professional development with little regard for what the participating teachers know, or do not know, is likely to be an ineffective endeavor. It may be equally ineffective to make claims about participating teachers without understanding their lived experience.

Our three cases illustrate that learning outcomes of participating teachers are likely to improve when in addition to the substance or content of what is intended to be taught, the participant's background knowledge is considered. We suggest that investing time in classroom visits, surveying participating teachers, and talking to individual or groups of participating teachers is a critical step in obtaining important information that can productively shape a professional development. Taking this approach will provide professional developers with information that allows them to meet their learners where they are rather than providing generic instructional opportunities that only benefit a few participating teachers.

FUTURE RESEARCH DIRECTIONS

Looking forward, we see opportunities to extend on the work presented here by examining approaches to professional development that more deliberately and systematically establish shared language early in the process to facilitate understanding between facilitators and participants of professional development. We also see opportunities to extend on this approach and focus on shared meeting around key ideas in other aspects of schooling, such as in the classroom, where terminology can often have multiple and complex meanings. Beyond the field of education, there are opportunities to examine how shared meaning or lack thereof around key ideas or terms supports or constrains the work of groups towards a common goal.

REFERENCES

Anderson, R. (2002). Reforming science teaching: What research says about inquiry. *Journal of Science Teacher Education*, *13*(1), 1–12. doi:10.1023/A:1015171124982

Banilower, E. R., Smith, P. S., Weiss, I. R., Malzahn, K. A., Campbell, K. M., & Weis, A. M. (2013). *Report of the 2012 national survey of science and mathematics education*. Chapel Hill, NC: Horizon Research, Inc.

Barrow, L. H. (2006). A brief history of inquiry: From dewey to standards. *Journal of Science Teacher Education*, *17*(3), 265–278. doi:10.100710972-006-9008-5

Borko, H. (2004). Professional development and teacher learning: Mapping the terrain. *Educational Researcher*, *33*(8), 3–15. doi:10.3102/0013189X033008003

Braaten, M., & Windschitl, M. (2011). Working toward a stronger conceptualization of scientific explanation for science education. *Science Education*, *95*(4), 639–669. doi:10.1002ce.20449

Brown, S., & Kappes, L. (2012). *Implementing the Common Core State Standards: A Primer on "Close Reading of Text"*. Washington, DC: Kaplan Institute.

Buczynski, S., & Hansen, C. B. (2010). Impact of professional development on teacher practice: Uncovering connections. *Teaching and Teacher Education*, *26*(3), 599–607. doi:10.1016/j.tate.2009.09.006

Darling-Hammond, L. (2010). Teacher education and the American future. *Journal of Teacher Education*, *61*(1-2), 35–47. doi:10.1177/0022487109348024

Darling-Hammond, L., & Berry, B. (2006). Highly qualified teachers for all. *Educational Leadership*, *64*(3), 14.

Davis, E. A., & Smithey, J. (2009). Beginning teachers moving toward effective elementary science teaching. *Science Education*, *93*(4), 745–770. doi:10.1002ce.20311

Dickson, D. (1999). Barriers to communication. In *Interaction for practice in community nursing* (pp. 84–132). London: Palgrave. doi:10.1007/978-1-349-14757-1_5

Duquette, C. (2015). Relating Historical Consciousness to Historical Thinking Through Assessment. In *New Directions in Assessing Historical Thinking*. New York: Routledge.

Duschl, R. A., Schweingruber, H. A., & Shouse, A. W. (2007). *Taking science to school. Learning and teaching science in grades K-8*. Washington, DC: National Academies Press.

Epstein, D., & Miller, R. T. (2011). Slow off the mark: Elementary school teachers and the crisis in science, technology, engineering, and math education. *Science Progress*. Retrieved from www.americanpress.org

Fishman, B. J., Penuel, W. R., Allen, A. R., Cheng, B. H., & Sabelli, N. O. R. A. (2013). Design-based implementation research: An emerging model for transforming the relationship of research and practice. *National Society for the Study of Education, 112*(2), 136-156.

Guskey, T., & Yoon, K. (2009). What works in professional development. *Phi Delta Kappan, 90*(7), 495–500. doi:10.1177/003172170909000709

Innes, J. E., & Booher, D. E. (1999). Consensus building and complex adaptive systems: A framework for evaluating collaborative planning. *Journal of the American Planning Association, 65*(4), 412–423. doi:10.1080/01944369908976071

Krajcik, J. S., Blumenfeld, P. C., Marx, R. W., & Soloway, E. (1994). A collaborative model for helping middle grade science teachers learn project-based instruction. *The Elementary School Journal, 94*(5), 483–497. doi:10.1086/461779

Lesh, B. (2011). "Why won't you just tell us the Answer?" Teaching historical thinking in grades 7-12, Portland, OR: Stenhouse Publishers.

Little, J. W. (1988). Seductive images and organizational realities in professional development. In A. Lieberman (Ed.), *Rethinking school improvement*. New York, NY: Teachers College Press.

Marshall, J. C., Smart, J., & Horton, R. M. (2010). The design and validation of equip: An instrument to assess inquiry-based instruction. *International Journal of Science and Mathematics Education, 8*(2), 299–321. doi:10.100710763-009-9174-y

Moore, J., & Schleppegrell, M. (2014). Using a functional linguistics metalanguage to support academic language development in the English Language Arts. *Linguistics and Education, 26*, 92–105. doi:10.1016/j.linged.2014.01.002

National Governors Association Center for Best Practices and Council of Chief State School Officers. (2010). *Common core state standards for English language arts and Literacy in history/social studies, science, and technical subjects*. Washington, DC: Authors.

National Research Council. (2000). *Inquiry and the National Science Education Standards*. Washington, DC: National Academy Press.

National Research Council. (2007). *Taking science to school: Learning and teaching science kindergarten to eighth grade*. Washington, DC: National Academy Press.

National Research Council. Committee on Conceptual Framework for the New K-12 Science Education Standards. (2011). A framework for K-12 science education: Practices, crosscutting concepts, and core ideas. Washington, DC: National Academy Press.

NGSS Lead States. (2013). *Next Generation Science Standards: For States, by States*. Washington, DC: The National Academies Press.

Partnership for assessment of readiness for college and careers (PARCC). (2011). *PARCC model content frameworks for ELA-literacy*. Author.

Penuel, W. R., Fishman, B. J., Haugan Cheng, B., & Sabelli, N. (2011). Organizing research and development at the intersection of learning, implementation, and design. *Educational Researcher*, *40*(7), 331–337. doi:10.3102/0013189X11421826

Russell, J. L., Jackson, K., Krumm, A. E., & Frank, K. A. (2013). Theories and research methodologies for design-based implementation research: Examples from four cases. *Yearbook of the National Society for the Study of Education*, *112*(2), 157–191.

Scott, P., & Mouza, C. (2007). The impact of professional development on teacher learning, practice and leadership skills: A study on the integration of technology in the teaching of writing. *Journal of Educational Computing Research*, *37*(3), 229–266. doi:10.2190/EC.37.3.b

Seixas, P., & Morton, T. (2013). *The Big six: Historical thinking concepts*. Boston: Cengage Learning.

Supovitz, J. (2013). Situated research design and methodological choices in formative program evaluation. *National Society for the Study of Education Yearbook*, *112*(2), 372–399.

Tate, T. P., Collins, P., Xu, Y., Yau, J. C., Krishnan, J., Prado, Y., & Warschauer, M. (2019). Visual-Syntactic Text Format: Improving Adolescent Literacy. *Scientific Studies of Reading*, 1–18.

van Zee, E. (2000). Analysis of a student-generated inquiry discussion. *International Journal of Science Education*, *22*, 115–142.

Wang, S. K., Hsu, H. Y., Reeves, T. C., & Coster, D. C. (2014). Professional development to enhance teachers' practices in using information and communication technologies (ICTs) as cognitive tools: Lessons learned from a design-based research study. *Computers & Education*, *79*, 101–115. doi:10.1016/j.compedu.2014.07.006

Wilson, S. M. (2013). Professional development for science teachers. *Science*, *340*(6130), 310–313. doi:10.1126cience.1230725 PMID:23599481

Windschitl, M., Thompson, J., Braaten, M., & Stroupe, D. (2012). Proposing a core set of instructional practices and tools for teachers of science. *Science Education*, *96*(5), 878–903. doi:10.1002ce.21027

Wineburg, S. (2001). *Historical thinking and other unnatural Acts: Charting the future of teaching the past*. Philadelphia: Temple University Press.

Zinger, D., Naranjo, A., Gilbertson, N., Amador, I., & Warschauer, M. (2017). A design-based research approach to improving professional development of the Smithsonian Learning Lab. *Contemporary Issues in Technology & Teacher Education*, *17*(3).

ADDITIONAL READING

Avalos, B. (2011). Teacher professional development in teaching and teacher education over ten years. *Teaching and Teacher Education*, *27*(1), 10–20. doi:10.1016/j.tate.2010.08.007

Brown, A. L. (1992). Design experiments: Theoretical and methodological challenges in creating complex interventions in classroom settings. *Journal of the Learning Sciences*, *2*.

Dede, C., Jass Ketelhut, D., Whitehouse, P., Breit, L., & McCloskey, E. (2008). A research agenda for online teacher professional development. *Journal of Teacher Education*, *60*(1), 8–19. doi:10.1177/0022487108327554

Loucks-Horsley, S., Stiles, K. E., Mundry, S., Love, N., & Hewson, P. W. (2009). *Designing professional development for teachers of science and mathematics*. Thousand Oaks, CA: Corwin Press.

Oliveira, A. W. (2009). From professional development to classroom instruction: Addressing issues related to science inquiry discourse. *Cultural Studies of Science Education*, *4*(4), 865–873. doi:10.100711422-009-9195-4

Penuel, W., Fishman, B., Yamaguchi, R., & Gallagher, L. (2007). What makes professional development effective? Strategies that foster curriculum implementation. *American Educational Research Journal*, *44*(4), 921–958. doi:10.3102/0002831207308221

van Driel, J. H., Meirink, J. A., van Veen, K., & Zwart, R. C. (2012). Current trends and missing links in studies on teacher professional development in science education: A review of design features and quality of research. *Studies in Science Education*, *48*(2), 129–160. doi:10.1080/03057267.2012.738020

Zinger, D. (2016). Developing instructional leadership and communication skills through online professional development: Focusing on rural and urban principals. In A. H. Normore, L. W. Long, & M. Javidi (Eds.), *Handbook of Research on Effective Communication*. Hershey, PA: IGI Global. doi:10.4018/978-1-4666-9970-0.ch019

KEY TERMS AND DEFINITIONS

Close Reading: A multi-step process of reading that moves beyond a cursory understanding of a text and attend to the fine details of a text.

Design-Based Research: Research that focuses on problems of practice identified collaboratively with practitioners and researchers. The goal of design-based approaches is to address problems of practice as well as develop theory that can be applied more broadly for systematic improvement.

Discussion, Scientific: A form of talk in which scientific sense-making and analysis is central. Discourse between individuals where participants contribute more than simple canonical knowledge or regurgitate scientific facts.

Historical Thinking: Interpretation that responds to an inquiry question and uses evidence to make meaning grounded in a deep understanding of a particular time and place.

Professional Development: A formal structure or program within schools where teachers gather with facilitators or experts to work on improving some aspect of instruction. Professional development may be ongoing, occurring multiple times, or in a single event.

Shared Understanding: Having a common interpretation of a concept of idea which may have multiple and varied meaning even within a specific context.

Visual-Syntactic Text Formatting (VSTF): A format designed to display text in a cascading pattern rather than a block approach. The format is intended to facilitate identification of grammatical structures in text.

Section 3

Identifying Challenges and Opportunities in Public Safety Leadership and Management

Chapter 10
Identifying Blind Spots in Leadership Development

Timothy W. Turner
https://orcid.org/0000-0002-3606-7237
Independent Researcher, USA

Richard J. Conroy
Dallas Baptist University, USA

ABSTRACT

A plethora of market available 360-degree assessment tools add value to the work of organizational leadership and management professionals. This chapter examines 360-degree assessments in terms of leadership development, training, and coaching. Multi-rater assessment use is reviewed in the context of emotional intelligence competencies. Leadership development is enhanced when benchmarks are established for leaders in the area of emotional intelligence. Organizations can identify keys to leader development by recognizing specific competencies in "star performers" (high performers). Self-report assessment instruments are generally useful in identifying key leadership competencies, but are limited by an individual's self-awareness. 360-degree multi-rater assessments enhance and support the recognition of these specific competencies but more so serve to identify blind spots or gaps in competency areas. Any divergence is often between a leader's self-reporting and observations gleaned from a 360-degree perspective by peers, subordinates, managers, family members, friends, and others.

INTRODUCTION

The leadership literature in diverse fields as business, history, higher education, political science, and others abounds with various tools, questionnaires, and assessment instruments designed to allow individuals to understand their own personal traits, characteristics, skills, behaviors, competencies, talents, and styles when it comes to leadership. This abundance of assessment tools is no different from a similar abundance of leadership definitions that have filled the social science literature for years. A foundational challenge for any student of leadership includes how to define leadership. Further, how does one come to an understanding through assessment, of the cognitive as well as conceptual skills and traits

DOI: 10.4018/978-1-5225-8516-9.ch010

related to self-development of leadership? This chapter examines the underlying foundational theories of transactional and transformational leadership, leading to a specific focus on the role of competencies in leadership as well as emotional intelligence development. Successful leadership development can be enhanced when behavioral benchmarks are established for leaders using competency based 360-degree assessments related to emotional intelligence (EI). Acceptance of this premise will lead to a review of an assessment method of evaluating proficiencies, attributes, and competencies related to leadership.

The examination will suggest self-report psychometric assessment instruments are generally useful in helping identify leadership competencies related to emotional intelligence. Further, the examination will identify that 360-degree multi-rater assessments enhance and support the recognition of specific EI competencies and behaviors, but more so, serve to help identify blind spots or gaps in competency areas that are valuable to a leader's development. Despite a number of different models of emotional and social intelligence that have emerged in the literature since the early 1980s, three primary models (Bar-On, 1997, Goleman, 1995, and Salovey and Mayer, 1990) will be discussed. More specifically, the examination will address the advantages gained in the identification of leadership competencies as well as blind spots using the Bar-On EQ-i (1997) instrument when paired with the EQ-360 instrument—Bar-On's multi-rater version of the EQ-i).

FOUNDATIONAL LEADERSHIP THEORIES: BACKGROUND

Interest in and fascination with leadership and all that it entails is not a new development. Social scientists, academicians, and intellectuals have been intrigued by the study of leadership since the times of Plato, Freud, Einstein, Gandhi, Churchill, Roosevelt, Kennedy, King, and others (Burns, 1978). The study of leadership is often viewed as a broad and generic discipline with applicability across multiple fields, including academia, politics, military, and business. This popularity seems to have transcended more than academia and the corporate world and has become of general interest socially as well. Despite its popularity, the leadership field can also be complex to understand. Where does one begin focused and worthwhile research in the leadership arena? Are people simply born with natural leadership traits? If not, can leadership traits, competencies, and skills be learned through training and education? Because leadership means different things to different people, it is understandable that myriad definitions have been coined following the evolution of leadership studies over a long period of time. In an early 1970's work, Stogdill (1974) posited that a review of leadership literature indicated there are as many definitions for the term, as there are people who have attempted to define it.

In its evolution, the leadership field has also developed its own nomenclature with various sub-fields, styles, terms, and traits. Burns (1978) suggested society in general has both a "desire and hunger for leaders who are both compelling and creative," (p.1). As a part of this hunger, leadership definitions have primarily focused on the characteristics and dynamics that make one person perceived as a more effective leader than someone else. Burns' book *Leadership* remains the classic benchmark text that introduced *transformational* leadership, which takes place when one or more persons "engage" with others in such a way that leaders and followers raise one another to higher levels of "motivation and morality." (p.19). This concept of transformation is contrasted to transactional leadership, a more traditional view holding that followers are led by managers who supervise by offering rewards and punishments in order to accomplish group goals (Northouse, 2013, Wren, 2006).

Burns (1978) theorized the relationship between leaders and followers is framed around either a transactional or transformational format. He described transactional leadership as a leader's ability to motivate a follower based upon rewards of an economic, political, or psychological nature. In this framework, both leaders and followers are cognizant of the other's role as well as what is at stake. However, the transactional bargaining process did not form a true relationship between the parties. In contrast, Burns also suggested transformational leadership involved leaders and followers engaging in developing a purposeful relationship in order to achieve a higher level of motivation and ethical aspiration. Burns posited power alone was not responsible for making a person transactional or transformational, whereas leadership does.

Transactional Leadership

Burns (1978) made the specific distinction leaders are either transactional or transformational. In general, transactional leadership refers to the vast and overwhelming majority of leadership models and focuses on the interpersonal exchanges that occur between leaders and followers (Northouse, 2013). This approach emphasizes the importance of the relationship between leaders and followers. Significant here are the mutual benefits that come by way of a quid-pro-quo "contract" through which the leaders deliver things such as rewards or recognition in return for commitments as well as loyalty from followers.

Grounded in exchange theory, transactional leadership posits leaders use contingent rewards, management-by-exception (active or passive), or laissez-faire styles when exchanging punishment and rewards for follower compliance and effort in order to achieve organizational performance (Bass, 1985). The focus of transactional leadership is centered solely on a leader's ability to set up agreements or contracts with followers to accomplish specific goals based upon rewards and punishments rather than establishing relationships (Ardichvili and Manderscheid, 2008; Avolio & Bass, 2002; Bass & Avolio, 1994).

In Texas, Sarver (2007) examined the leadership styles of Texas polices chiefs and the correlates of the most effective leaders. With negligible differences, this data demonstrated more Texas police chiefs were identified as transactional leaders. The data also suggested the transformational leadership style is the more effective leadership style. If one agrees with Sarver's assessment that the personality attributes of transformational leaders can be characterized as optimistic, positive, open-minded, non-judgmental, and considerate of feelings, then the hypothesis could be that transformational leaders are indeed more likely to be emotionally and socially intelligent leaders.

Transformational Leadership

Leadership is also viewed as a process that has the potential to positively influence organizations, teams, and individuals alike. In contrast to transactional leadership, Burns suggested transformational leaders induce followers to act in order to achieve certain goals. These goals represent values and motivations, but additionally the wants, needs, aspirations and expectations of leaders and followers alike. Northouse (2013) suggested these goals are long-term and often concerned with ethics, standards, and more importantly—with emotions.

Bryman (1992) offered transformational leadership is not only the latest, but also the most-effective leadership paradigm when it comes to facilitating change in both organizations as well as individuals. Transformational leadership also draws upon and uses the motivation of followers to effectively accomplish goals that are mutually held (Avolio, 1999). Northouse (2013) further observed transformational leadership includes: 1) inspirational motivation, 2) idealized influence, 3) concern for individuals, and 4) intellectual stimulation.

Bass (1985) extended the work of Burns (1978) by developing a formal theory, model, and measure of transformational leadership in order to understand further, specific factors related to leadership behavior (Bass & Avolio, 1994). Bass and Avolio (2004) expanded that model by identifying what they called full range leadership (FRL). This was a combination of styles per se—including transformational and transactional as well as a variety of laissez-faire frameworks.

Transformational leadership is thought to be the most effective managerial behavior, wherein a leader builds positive relationships with followers to move lower level objectives to higher levels of performance (Ardichvili and Manderscheid, 2008; Avolio & Bass, 2002; Bass and Avolio, 1994, 2004). Bass and Avolio's (1994) transformational leadership model was designed not to replace transactional leadership, but to expand the leadership style from simple leader–follower exchange agreements to inspiring and motivating followers to achieve goals beyond their own personal expectations.

Avolio and Bass (2002) contended that to some extent, all leaders have a certain level or combination of transactional, transformational, and possibly other styles of behavior in their leadership toolkit and there are likely certain situations wherein each style may be relevant and needed. Among the end results of transformational leadership are 1) social change, 2) getting followers to do more than is or was expected, 3) improving follower performance, 4) developing followers to their fullest potential, and 5) the satisfaction of authentic needs of followers—their wants, values, and morals.

Transformational Leadership and Behavioral Competencies

Any discussion of transformational leadership and its non-cognitive traits should also include a close look at the concept of behavioral competencies. Organizations not only want, but expect their leaders to have critical skills and competencies to help make organizations more effective. Emotional intelligence has been identified as an essential skill likely necessary for effective leaders (Goleman, Boyatzis & McKee, 2002). Although research on the topic continues to expand, some believe that there is a relationship gap that exists between an individual's perception of their leadership (self-awareness) and their actual leadership capabilities. Empirical evidence supports a strong positive correlation between self-awareness and the leadership styles of managers experiencing change in their organizations (Bar-On, 2006a, 2006b; Bolden, 2007; Goleman, 1995; Parker & Sorensen, 2008). While the literature may be divided on the beneficial relationship between transformational leadership and behavioral competencies, for the purpose of the current examination, there is support that such a relationship exists (Barbuto & Burbach, 2006; Clarke, 2010; Parker & Sorensen, 2008; Sayeed & Shanker, 2009).

As early as 1872, in Darwin's third book, "*The Expression of the Emotions in Man and Animals*" he discussed behavioral genetics. In 1920, Edward L. Thorndike developed his "social intelligence theory" but was never able to create a way to measure it—despite a significant awareness of its importance[1]. Thorndike's son, R. L. Thorndike (1937) also tried to measure social intelligence but was unable. Although social intelligence was difficult to measure, Carnegie (1936) recognized its importance in contributing to an individual's success. With that understanding, he developed ways to improve social intelligence and enumerated those in his book and seminars called "How to Win Friends & Influence People". The modern study of behavioral competencies is relatively new in the social science literature, primarily since the early 1990's.

Despite psychologists such as Abraham Maslow believing as early as the 1950's that people can grow emotionally and socially (Coy, 2005), the first real emergence in the literature was the dissertation work of Payne (1985), followed in the late 1980's by the seminal work of Yale University and University of New Hampshire psychologists Salovey and Mayer (1988) which reviewed the adaptive and maladaptive qualities of emotion related to social intelligence and explored the role of emotion in traditional intelligence conceptions. Their work, along with a colleague David Caruso, has served as the benchmark in developing scientific research against which the theory of EI can pass scrutiny. The contrast to the scientific research side of the EI discussion is of EI can pass scrutiny. The contrast to the scientific research side of the EI discussion is sometimes referred to as the "commercial aspect" (Landy, 2005).

Landy (2005) contrasted the scientific research work of Salovey and Mayer in the 1990s with the "commercial" work of Goleman (1995), author of "*Emotional Intelligence*", a best-selling book on the subject. Despite the popularity of Goleman's work, including his own statements "that the most effective leaders are alike in one crucial way—they all have a high degree of what has become known as emotional intelligence," and research suggesting that "emotional intelligence is the sine qua non of leadership," (Goleman, 1998, p. 94), his work has critics. Some claim his research and data is proprietary and has not been shared due to his affiliation with the Hay Group, a private research consortium.

Others claim Goleman has strayed far from his educational background as an organizational psychologist in order to continue the promotion and publication of best-selling books, hence the "commercial aspect" label. In defense of Goleman, Landy (2005) reported that compelling behavioral research in more than 500 organizations by the Hay Group and Goleman showed: 1) EI is twice as important as any other factor in predicting outstanding employee performance, 2) EI accounts for more than 85 per-cent of star performance in top leaders, 3) EI—not IQ, advanced degrees, or technical experience—is the single most important factor in the ability to build and sustain relationships, and 4) EI can be learned and enhanced—relatively quickly—through specialized assessments, training and coaching (p. 412).

When it comes to effective leadership and management, Ashkanasy (2004) cautioned not to downplay or otherwise discount the concept of emotions, saying to do so would not be a wise choice on the part of any manager and the emotional dimension is critical when trying to understand how people are managed successfully. He opined that if a leader cannot manage their own emotions or those of subordinates, the leader simply would not be effective.

EMOTIONAL INTELLIGENCE MODELS

Generally speaking, the EI literature includes a number of different models or constructs. For purposes of this review related to identifying leadership development blind spots, three models including an ability model (Salovey & Mayer, 1990), and mixed models (Goleman, 1995 and Bar-On, 1997) combining aspects of the ability and trait models are presented, although Bar-On rejects classifying his EI model as a "trait" model and provides empirical findings that justify this rejection (Bar-On, 2006a).

Mayer and Salovey (MSCEIT)

Mayer and Salovey (1988, 1990) suggested EI can be measured in four areas including: 1) identification and perception of emotions in oneself and others, 2) facilitation of thought; ability to generate an emotion and deal with it, 3) understanding emotional meanings, including complex emotional chains of transition from one emotion to another, and 4) regulation and management of emotions in oneself and others. The scale yields six scores. An overall emotional intelligence score expressed as an emotional intelligence quotient or EIQ; two area scores Experiential Emotional Intelligence (EEIQ) and Strategic Emotional Intelligence (SEIQ); and four branch scores corresponding to the four branches of emotional intelligence. Each score is expressed in terms of a standard score with a mean score of 100.

Goleman (ESCI) Emotional Social Competency Inventory

Goleman's ESCI (1998) instrument is based on the measurement of 20 emotional competencies organized into four constructs including: self-awareness, social awareness, self- management, and social skills. This is a multi-rater instrument providing for self, direct report, and peer ratings for behavioral indicators of emotional intelligence. Table 1 summarizes both the self (personal) and other (social) competencies measured by Goleman's ESCI instrument.

Bar-On (EQ-i and EQ-i 2.0)

Bar-On's (1997) work originated with the belief that emotional intelligence is a sub-set of social intelligence, and he conceptualized the term "emotional and social intelligence" or "emotional-social intelligence" (ESI). Key components include: a) the ability to recognize, understand and express both emotions and feelings; b) the ability to understand how others feel and relate with them; c) the ability to manage and control emotions; d) the ability to solve problems and manage change associated with personal and interpersonal issues; and e) the ability to generate positive emotions and be self-motivated. Table 2 represents the components and sub-components of Bar-On's original EQ-i model of emotional intelligence.

Table 1. Goleman's (2001) emotional competency inventory

	SELF	OTHER
	Personal Competence	**Social Competence**
	Self-Awareness	**Social Awareness**
RECOGNITION	Emotional Self-Awareness	Empathy
	Accurate Self-Assessment	Service Orientation
	Self-Confidence	Organizational Awareness
	Self-Management	**Relationship Management**
	Self-Control	Developing Others
	Trustworthiness	Influence
REGULATION	Conscientiousness	Communication
	Adaptability	Conflict Management
	Achievement Drive	Leadership
	Initiative	Change Catalyst
		Building Bonds
		Teamwork & Collaboration

Table 2. Components of Bar-On's original model of emotional intelligence

Components	Sub-Components
	Self-Regard
	Emotional Self-Awareness
Intrapersonal	Assertiveness
	Independence
	Self-Actualization
	Empathy
Interpersonal	Social Responsibility
	Interpersonal Relationship
	Reality Testing
Adaptability	Flexibility
	Problem Solving
Stress Management	Stress Tolerance
	Impulse Control
General Mood Components	Optimism
	Happiness

Bar-On's Emotional Quotient Inventory (EQ-i) was empirically developed to measure his conceptual model of EI (1997). Useful in personal and professional development, the instrument identified and assessed competencies and behaviors that allow a person to be successful as well as those that stand in the way of progress. The Bar-On EQ-i was the first scientifically validated self-report measure of emotional intelligence that was made commercially available, and it is still one of the most widely used instruments for assessing emotional intelligence (Stein, 2010). The EQ-i was mildly revised in 2011, which created the current EQ-i 2.0 version comprising five composite scales with each including three scales the measure different aspects of social and emotional intelligence. As such, the revised EQ-i 2.0 includes 15 subscales. Table 3 represents the composite scales and subscales of the EQ-i 2.0 instrument.

To reiterate, Bar-On's original 1997 version of the EQ-i was revised in 2011; and the resultant EQ-i 2.0 was released in 2012. As is the case with other assessment tools, the revision was conducted in an effort to avoid the language from becoming dated. According to the publisher's technical manual, the EQ-i 2.0 is described as a "revised psychometric instrument" based on the original Bar-On model. Moreover, the manual reveals that the overall correlation between the EQ-i 2.0 and the original EQ-i is .90 and that the correlations between the scales of the two versions range from .49 to .90; and based on a series of factor analyses that were conducted, the findings support, for the most part, the original 15-factor structure of the Bar-On conceptual model. These findings mean that the EQ-i 2.0 assesses what the original EQ-i assessed for the most part.

Table 3. Components of Bar-On's EQ-i 2.0 model of emotional intelligence

Composite Scale	Sub-Scales
	Self-Regard
Self-Perception	Self-Actualization
	Emotional Self-Awareness
	Emotional Expression
Self-Expression	Assertiveness
	Independence
	Interpersonal Relationships
Interpersonal	Empathy
	Social Responsibility
	Problem Solving
Decision Making	Reality Resting
	Impulse Control
	Flexibility
Stress Management	Stress Tolerance
	Optimism

ASSESSMENT OF LEADERSHIP

Historically, leadership has been assessed in a variety of ways including structured interviews, experience-based interviews, biographical information (past accomplishments), cognitive ability measures, and personality measures (Miller, Watkins, & Webb, 2009). Psychometric assessment instruments, primarily consisting of self-report models have become the norm among human resource practitioners, executive coaches, and leadership and organization development professionals. A number of published performance tests measure distinct components that are often similar to emotional intelligence (Brackett, Rivers, & Salovey, 2011). Dussault, Frenette, and Fernet (2013) developed a 21-item leadership self-report scale consisting of "a third-order dimension (leadership), two second-order dimensions (transactional and transformational leadership), and one first-order factor (laissez-faire leadership)" (p.432).

Myriad other self-report measures are available with varying degrees of reliability and validity among the different models and constructs of emotional intelligence. Workplace self-report instruments have been heavily marketed and remain a popular choice among corporate and employment studies Muyia, 2009). Most experienced leaders are acutely aware that emotional and social competencies are critical to managerial success. The EQ-i 2.0 self-report and the EQ-i 360 multi-rater assessment have been beneficial in assisting organizations formulate clear profiles and development plans for up-and-coming leaders (Stein & Book, 2010).

Hogan and Hogan (2001) suggested the variety of methods used in empirical literature to evaluate leadership is mostly unsatisfactory. Their view of leadership includes the ability to build and maintain effective teams that are capable of out-performing competitors. As such, they opine that the single best way to evaluate a manager or leader's performance is using subordinate ratings. Shipper and Wilson (1991) also documented that subordinates' ratings of a manager's performance are reliably correlated with team performance. The problem though, is that many subordinates don't really know what their managers' responsibilities, duties or job descriptions are, nor are they with them all day, so how can they effectively rate their performance?

Key to multi-rater assessment effectiveness is using them as a developmental tool rather than tying them to performance (Dalton, 1996; Maylette & Riboldi, 2007) and London & Turnow (1998) indicated leadership competencies can be improved through the use of multi-rater assessments. Donnithorne (1994) believed that character leadership is a way of life and is an evolving lifelong process striving for excellence and establishing a lasting legacy through feedback. The difference between good leaders and exceptional leaders is that the latter have the self-discipline to postpone gratification in pursuit of long-term goals. Donnithorne stated that "leaders-in-training need to know the extent of their own limitations before they can begin to grow further as leaders" (Donnithorne, 1994, p. 21).

Senge (1994) believed "the discipline of working with mental models starts with turning the mirror inward; learning to unearth our internal pictures of the world, to bring them to the surface and hold them rigorously to scrutiny" p.9). Carnegie (1993) believed self-awareness is the key to relationships and to be effective one must "keep your mind open to change all the time. Welcome it. Court it. It is only by examining and re-examining your opinions and ideas that you can progress" (p.1)

360-Degree Feedback Assessments

"If followership is the beginning of leadership, the beginning of followership is getting to zero; realizing all that you don't know, and then opening yourself to the possibility of being remade into something more. This is important because one is not born a leader; one is made by self-awareness and the feedback of others" (Donnithorne, 1994, p. 20). Multi-rater feedback is a process designed to assess job and leadership performance. A broad holistic view of strengths and areas for improvement can be identified using data gleaned from peers, supervisors, direct reports when balanced against self-report information. Staub (1996) illustrated that multi-rater instruments were critical in order to validate what success looked like as well as evaluating, benchmarking, and comparing so as to set standards for leadership performance. Significantly important to multi-rater assessment effectiveness, is using them as a developmental tool rather than linking the information gleaned to an individual's performance appraisal (Dalton & Hollenback, 1996). London (1998) argued that leadership competencies could be improved through the use of 360-degree assessment instruments.

The concept of 360-degree feedback acknowledges the increasing complexity of modern organizations by looking for feedback from those groups of people with whom an individual works. This allows a complete picture to be developed of how a person's work is perceived (Dewing, et al, 2004). The 360-degree assessment tool allows individuals at all levels in an organization to share feedback in a constructive manner with each other. The goal here is to improve an organization's process of developing leaders. Feedback is gleaned not only among subordinates, but also among peers as well as managers and supervisors of the individual being assessed (Sones, 2009). There are also clear and specific benefits (Westerman & Rosse, 1997) supporting use of 360-degree assessment instruments. These benefits impact not only the person being rated but the organization as well. The benefits suggest 360-degree feedback helps a person develop a broader awareness of what, and how, they do well and also ways the individual might improve. This format also encourages development of an organizational culture where employees actually solicit feedback from each other. Thus, the specific feedback serves as the foundation for developing work teams that value openness and trust in their overall discussions related to group performance.

After analyzing research regarding U. S. police chiefs, Porter et al (2000) indicated, "the ideal process for achieving self-awareness and learning what competencies need improvement is using 360-degree feedback surveys coupled with individualized leadership coaching" (p. 183). The key to success at the executive level, at least in law enforcement, is "know themselves" and executives should do this through choosing the correct competencies for incorporating into leadership development, seeking new perceptions on oneself, implementing a leadership development plan into their and their department's schedule.

According to Caruso (1999) emotional intelligence has four specific applications at work: career development, management development, team effectiveness, and selection. Caruso argued many selection-measuring instruments have little to do with the job (face validity), whereas emotional intelligence measures those skills needed and used by managers. Research by Taylor (2001) provided support for the belief that emotions affect the processes of reasoning and rationality. Brain research has shown that implicit memory, which is inaccessible to conscious recollection, ascertains who we are and influences present behavior by establishing control of habits, attitudes and preferences. Richmond et al (2004) determined though their research, that leaders considered emotional intelligence competencies of more importance than traditional business and financial acumen. Leaders ranked vision, strategic thinking, relationship building, and people development as critical leadership competencies.

Indeed, "feedback" is the breakfast of champions. 360-degree multi-rater assessments enhance and support the recognition of star performance in leadership as well as organizational effectiveness. More importantly, use of 360's can identify change in leadership behavior and whether an individual is different at home, at work, or in other organizations that they participant in, such as church or social organizations. As a development tool, these instruments serve to help identify blind spots or gaps in competency areas. Any blind spot divergence is often between a leader's self-reporting of competencies and those observed from a 360-degree perspective by peers, subordinates, managers, family, or friends.

Inflation and Reality

An EI study using the Emotional and Social Competence Inventory 360 was given to over 1200 participants and provided information not revealed in previous research (Church, 1997). The study indicated a "self-inflation" by higher-level participants compared to lower level individuals indicating that higher-level participants over-rated themselves, while lower-level participants were more accurate (Sala, 2001). Sala posited that higher positions generate self-aggrandizement or suffered from a lack of effective feedback. According to Krug (1994) current culture and super egos of many executives' supports a self-deception and a fear of hearing what others think and feel about their leadership. By allowing fear to become endemic in many organizations, including law enforcement, it also creates a blind spot for leadership development. In discussing self-image and personal performance, Krug (1994) stated, "to the degree that people have a poor self-image or low self-esteem, the predominance of their attention, at least subconsciously, is focused on what's wrong with themselves and how to keep others from seeing their weaknesses" (p.69). Additionally, many leaders suffer from what Jackman and Strober (2003) called 'fear of feedback'—characterized by fear, procrastination, denial, brooding, jealousy, and self-sabotage.

LEADERSHIP DEVELOPMENT

Indispensable to leadership development is feedback from all available sources (Blank, 2001). From within and outside of organizations, leaders should look and listen for ways to establish patterns of improvement and to uncover "blind spots" in development. In doing so, excellence becomes the leadership standard and feedback from others becomes the measurement tool. The key to effective growth is the depth, guidance, and heart of feedback, which must be connected to the values, vision and mission of the organization (Staub, 1996). Pragmatically, Staub suggested a relevant key to understanding feedback is acceptance that it is simply information—it is neither good, nor bad, and the single biggest barrier to accepting feedback is ego. Acceptance and understanding of feedback is also about interpretation, perception, and willingness to create a feedback loop that clarifies and creates personal meaning by enhancing correction and effectiveness (Staub, 1996).

According to Cooper and Sawaf (1997), emotional feedback consists of paying attention to every emotion and feeling, while recognizing the value of being realistic and truthful to oneself. The research is clear that technical skills are of importance to leadership improvement and development but it is equally critical for organizations to identify, select, promote, and develop leadership based on behavioral competencies (Cherniss & Goleman, 2001; Howell & Costley, 2006). "When it comes to promotions and succession planning, emotional intelligence should be a major criterion, particularly to the extent that a position requires leadership," (Cherniss & Goleman, 2001, p. 43). Successful leadership development is enhanced when behavioral benchmarks are established for leaders in the area of emotional intelligence (Stein & Book, 2010; Turner, 2006).

Johari's Window

In the mid 1950's Luft and Ingham (1955) developed a communication model that has become widely used to improve understanding between individuals within teams and in-group settings. Based on disclosure, self-disclosure, and feedback, the Johari Window is founded on two assumptions. First, that individuals can build trust between themselves by disclosing information about themselves second, individuals can learn about themselves and come to terms with personal issues with the help of feedback from others. The Johari Window addresses the degree to which individuals both receive and disseminate information. "The underlying concept of the Johari Window is that open, two-way communication enhances interpersonal effectiveness and that when information is mutually held and freely exchanged, organizational productivity will increase, (Little, 2005, p. 4). Figure 1 is an illustration of the concept of identification of "blind spots" in learning about oneself through feedback and the Johari Window.

The two information sources in the Johari scheme, *Self* and *Others*, contain information that is pertinent to the overall relationship between parties. At the same time, each party is missing information that is equally germane. Thus, there is relevant and necessary information, which is *Known by the Self, Unknown by Self, Known by Others*, and *Unknown by Others*. The *Self/Other* combinations of known and unknown information make up the four regions within the interpersonal space and characterize the various types and qualities of relationships possible within the Johari framework.

Figure 1. Using Johari's window for feedback on blind spots
(Source: adapted from Jay Hall, 1973. Communication revisited. California Management Review, 15(3), p. 177).

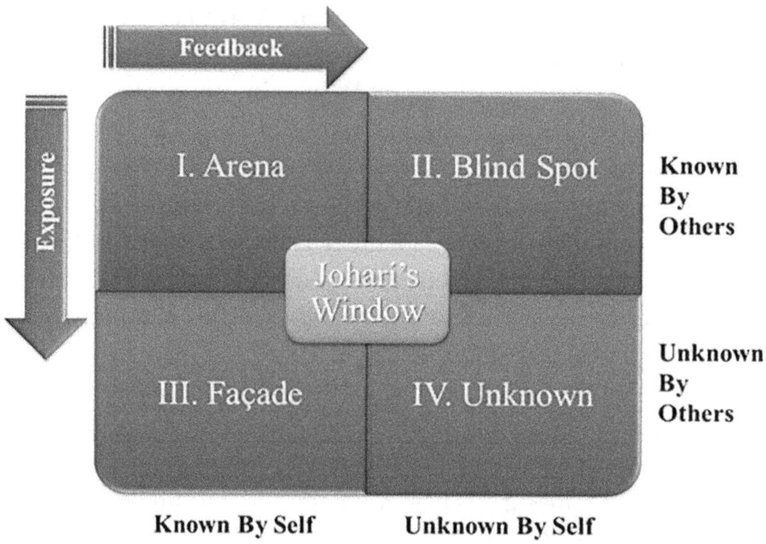

The Johari Window graphic represents the various kinds of data available for use in establishing interpersonal relationships, including emotional and social intelligence. The "blind spot" area constitutes that portion of the total interpersonal space in which information is *Known by Others* but *Unknown to Self*. This constitutes an interpersonal handicap for the *Self*, since one can hardly understand the behaviors, decisions, or potentials of others if one does not have the data upon which these are based. *Others* have the advantage of knowing their own reactions, feelings, perceptions, and the like while the *Self* is unaware of these. The blind spot can be described as an inhibitor to interpersonal or emotional and social intelligence effectiveness. Reducing a leader's blind spot should serve to improve both interpersonal and emotional intelligence effectiveness. Jules (2009) conceptualized that transformational leadership effectively must include a strategy that uses leadership assessments that measure personality attributes and provide truthful multi-rater input to the leader. This view is necessary as a support and development system for transformation to occur.

Relying solely on self-report instruments for accurate collection of leadership development information in the area of emotional intelligence can have drawbacks. A few emotional intelligence models are classified as ability models—that recognize specific abilities related to perception of emotion, use of emotion, understanding of emotion, and managing emotion. Significant limitations can occur when pairing an ability conceptualization together with a self-report instrument. Borges, Kirkham, Deardoff, and Moore (2012) correctly identify that this combination can be inherently problematic. The potential exists for data objectivity to be reduced by social desirability and ego protection with the use of self-report instruments paired with ability identifying assessments.

EQ-i 2.0 and EQ-360 Assessment: Best Practice Example

Turner (2006) suggested the key to successful leadership development is establishing benchmarks of successful behaviors by labeling the emotional and social intelligence competencies that are responsible for those same behaviors. After identifying the cluster of emotional and social intelligence competencies defining exceptional or star performance, organizations should immediately implement training and coaching initiatives. In addition to coaching, these efforts should incorporate mentoring programs that help in efforts toward continuous growth as well as on-going critical reflection. Knowledge of the star performance clusters associated with emotional and social intelligence will help in hiring, retention, and leadership development, which in turn will benefit organizational succession programs. Utilizing the EQ-i 2.0 self-report together with the Bar-On's EQ-360 instrument represents a logical solution and best practice approach in establishing a leader's emotional and social intelligence benchmarks as well as determining where the competency gaps or blind spots may exist in an assessment profile.

Reliability and Validity

Reliability indicates the extent to which individual differences in test scores are attributable to "true" differences in the characteristics under consideration (Ary, Jacobs, & Razavieh, 2002). Reliability studies, including internal consistency and test-retest, carried out on the EQ-i 2.0 demonstrated more than adequate reliability (MHS, 2011). In terms of internal consistence, the EQ-i 2.0 total scale alpha coefficient was .97. The alpha coefficients for the five composite scales ranged from .88 to .93 and all subscales showed a minimum Cronbach alpha of .77. These alpha coefficients held also for the age and gender normative groups (MHS, 2011). In terms of test-retest, the EQ-i 2.0 had a correlation of .92 over a 2-4 week time interval. The test-retest scores ranged from .86 to .91 for the five composite scales, and .78 to .89 for the subscales. Eight-week test-retest correlations for 104 individuals were .81 for the total score, .76 to .83 for the composite scores, and .70 to .84 for the subscales.

Construct validity is the degree to which a test measures the construct it sets out to measure. In terms of convergent/concurrent construct validity, the EQ-i 2.0 scores correlated .90 (MHS, 2011). Correlations in the expected directions with other psychological measures add further support to the convergent validity of the EQ-i 2.0. Total EI was positively and significantly correlated with both the Social Skills Inventory (Riggio & Carney, 2003) total score ($r = .54$), as well as the majority of the SSI subscales. The EQ-i 2.0 total score also positively and significantly correlated with Extraversion ($r = .57$), Agreeableness ($r = .36$), and Conscientiousness ($r = .61$) measured by the NEO-FFI (Costa and McCrae, 1992). In summary, users of the EQ-i 2.0 can be confident that the scores generated by this assessment are consistent and reliable, and that the results accurately measure emotional intelligence.

A total EQ score provides a general indication of the respondent's emotional and social competencies, and how they influence the way the respondent perceives and expresses himself, maintains social relationships, copes with challenges, and uses emotional information in a meaningful way. The five composite areas of the EQ-i 2.0 assess a broad array of competencies that are important in dealing with workplace, social, and leadership demands.

In the broader context of understanding blind spots in leadership development, the self-perception subscales in the assessment address the 'inner-self' and assess feelings of inner strength, confidence, pursuit of meaningful goals as well as understanding of what, when, why, and how different emotions impact thoughts and actions. The self-expression subscales in the assessment are an extension of self-perception as they assess the outward expression or the action part of an individual's internal perception. Such skills as openly expressing thoughts and feelings in a constructive way and remaining self-directed are included in this composite section. The interpersonal composite includes sub-scales which measure an individual's ability to develop and maintain relationships based on trust and compassion, articulate an understanding of another's perspective, and act responsibly, showing concern for others, team members or the greater community/organization. The decision making sub-scales in the assessment composite address the way in which one uses emotional information by understanding the impact emotions have on decision making. This includes the ability to resist or delay impulses and remain objective so to avoid rash behaviors and ineffective problem solving. Finally, the stress management area in the assessment contains subscales which address how well one can cope with the emotions associated with change and unpredictable circumstances, while remaining hopeful about the future and resilient in the face of setbacks and obstacles.

Table 4 presents a sample scoring profile including self-reporting and 16 360-degree peer raters among four group categories. The normative data raw scores are converted to scaled scores and normed on a 100-point mean, with a standard deviation of 10. Any score falling within the 90 to 110 range is considered to be in the average or mid-range. Any score greater than 110 is considered to be in the high range; any score less than 90 is considered to be in the low range. Both the self-report and the 360 instruments include 133 questions designed to be answered by those age 17 and older and take approximately 30-45 minutes to complete. Questions are presented in the form of a self-statement, rated on a five-point Likert scale.

Table 4. Self vs raters response summary

	Self	Managers	Peers	Fam/Friends	Others	Mean others	SD
Total Overall EQ-i 2.0	108	121	110	115	111	114.25	4.99
Self- Perception Composite	109	**122***	112	**119***	115	117.00	4.39
Self-regard	111						
Self-Actualization	107						
Emotional self -awareness	104						
Self-Expression Composite	106	**116***	107	113	105	110.25	5.12
Emotional Expression	110						
Assertiveness	102						
Independence	101						
Interpersonal Composite	101	**115***	110	**111***	**113***	112.25	2.20
Interpersonal relationships	92						
Empathy	105						
Social responsibility	108						
Decision Making Composite	111	120	111	115	112	114.50	4.04
Problem Solving	105						
Reality Testing	117						
Impulse Control	105						
Stress Management Composite	108	**120***	106	109	103	109.50	7.40
Flexibility	102						
Stress Tolerance	112						
Optimism	105						
**** indicates that there is a significant difference between the 360 raters group score and the SELF score***							

When viewed in the context of the Johari Window framework, Table 4 demonstrates there are blind spots when comparing the self-report information to the 360-rater information. In this case, managers rated the individual higher, often by 1.0-1.5 standard deviations above the self-report scores in four of the five composite areas. It is also helpful to review scores in the context of different rater groups as an additional leadership development tool. As presented, there was almost a two standard deviation difference in the individual's stress management composite as viewed by managers and other raters. A key to the depth of this information is not only alignment or lack of alignment between rater groups, but also by the number of raters per group and how long and how well the raters have known the respondent.

Profile Gap Analysis

Figure 2 provides an overview of the level of agreement between self-report and the 360 degree information from others and identifies "blind spots" in agreement. The horizontal axis shows how much agreement there is between the self-score and the scores received from rater groups, across the various subscales.

Subscales appearing to the far right indicate consensus between self-reporting of those behaviors much in the same way as others raters view the respondent. The vertical axis shows the person's self-rating. Higher scoring subscales will appear towards the top of the graph and lower scoring subscales at the bottom. Subscales that overlap with each other indicate a consistent experience of those particular emotional intelligence behaviors. The terms gap and agreement are used throughout the assessment

Figure 2. Level of agreement between self-report and 360 information

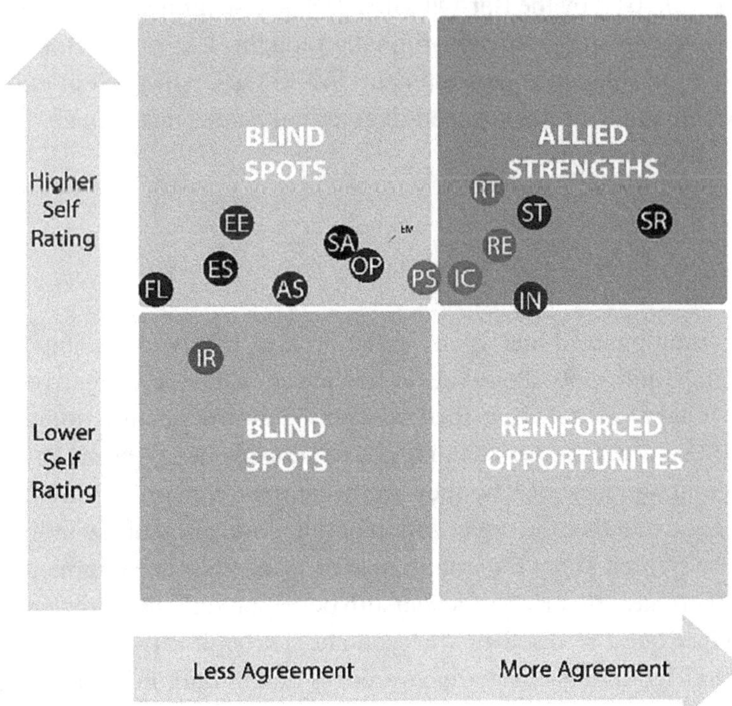

report in order to address differences or similarities that exist between rater groups. A gap exists when one group sees the individual significantly different than does another rater group. Gaps of 10 points or more are considered significant. In contrast, agreement exists when there is less than a 10 point difference between rater group scores.

BEYOND EMOTIONAL INTELLIGENCE: A MULTIFACTOR MEASURE OF PERFORMANCE (MMP)

The construct measured by the EQ-i 2.0 and the EQ-360 have effectively served to help understand the role of emotional and social intelligence in leadership development. More recently, Bar-On (2016, 2018) has developed a new model of performance measurement conceptualized as comprehensive in examining, understanding, and enhancing significant critical contributors to performance as well as leadership — that go beyond emotional intelligence. The Bar-On Multifactor Measure of Performance (MMP3) "is an operational framework designed 1) to help understand why some people perform better than others and 2) to determine which contributing factors need to be strengthened in order to enhance performance in individuals who are underperforming" (Bar-On, 2016, p. 104).

Recently completed research (Conroy, 2017) demonstrated that the factors assessed by the Bar-On MMP3 adequately predict effective leadership. More succinctly, this instrument was shown to be a robust predictor of the sub-scales of transformational leadership in a sample of 454 agency executive law enforcement officers (sheriffs). The predictive model that emerged, from multiple regression analysis in this study, indicated that most of the variance of this type of leadership can be significantly accounted for [$R = 0.76$ ($F = 35.00, p < 0.001$)] by the Bar-On MMP3™. A re-examination of the dataset suggests that its predictive ability is even greater than was originally thought. Use of the Bar-On MMP3 instrument (Bar-On, 2016, 2018), alongside an in-development 360-MMP3 will present expanded opportunities to more accurately examine and strengthen 360-degree multi-rater instruments in terms of leadership development, training, and coaching.

CONCLUSION

Identification of self-development blind spots in the area of behavioral competencies is critical for leadership improvement. Blind spots should never be viewed solely in a negative connotation. Leaders can also be positively blind to areas where they may not be aware they are doing something well. The key is to 'know thyself', so that followers can in turn be transformed. Absent knowledge of their blind spots, leaders have a limited picture of who they are, what their capabilities are, and how best to move others forward for the good of either the organization or the moral good of the individual follower. Many leadership scholars have written about the importance of leadership development as self-development. Kouzes and Posner (2008) have theorized, "leadership development is self-development. The quest for leadership is first an inner quest to discover who you are. Through self-development comes the confidence needed to lead. Self-confidence is really awareness of and faith in your own powers. Learning to lead is about discovering what you care about and value" (p. 343).

Results of the research indicate that blind spots can result in leadership derailment and could be due to intrapersonal flaws such as being authoritarian, too ambitious, poor work relations and conflict with upper management and not due to technical competencies. After behavioral competency training, organizations have reported significant improvements in individual performance and have documented financial increases representing tens of millions in additional revenues (Stein & Book, 2001).

REFERENCES

Ardichvili, A., & Manderscheid, S. V. (2008). Emerging practices in leadership development. *Advances in Developing Human Resources*, *10*(5), 619–631. doi:10.1177/1523422308321718

Ary, D., Jacobs, L. C., & Razavieh, A. (2002). *Introduction to research in education*. Wadsworth, Thomson Learning.

Ashkanasy, N., & Rush, S. (2004). Emotional rescue: A conversation with Neal M. Ashkanasy. *Leadership in Action*, *24*(4), 15–18. doi:10.1002/lia.1078

Avolio, B. J. (1999). *Full leadership development: Building the vital forces in organizations*. Thousand Oaks, CA: Sage Publications.

Avolio, B. J., & Bass, B. M. (2002). *Developing potential across a full range of leadership*. Mahwah, NJ: Erlbaum.

Bar-On, R. (1997). *Bar-On Emotional Quotient Inventory: Technical manual*. Toronto, Canada: Multi-Health Systems.

Bar-On, R. (2006a). *EQ-i leadership user's guide*. Toronto, Canada: Multi-Health Systems.

Bar-On, R. (2006b). The Bar-On model of emotional-social intelligence. *Psicothema, 18,* 13-25.

Bar-On, R. (2016). *Beyond IQ and EI: The Bar-On Multifactor Model of Performance*. In U. Kumar (Ed.), *Personality Assessment: The Way Forward*. London: Wiley.

Bar-On, R. (2018). The Multifactor Measure of Performance: Its development, norming, and validation. *Frontiers in Psychology*, *9*(140), 1–16. PMID:29515479

Barbuto, J., & Burbach, M. E. (2006). The emotional intelligence of transformational leaders: A field study of elected officials. *The Journal of Social Psychology*, *146*(1), 51–64. doi:10.3200/SOCP.146.1.51-64 PMID:16480121

Bass, B. M. (1985). *Leadership and performance beyond expectations*. New York: Free Press.

Bass, B. M., & Avolio, B. J. (1994). *Improving organizational effectiveness through transformational leadership*. Thousand Oaks, CA: Sage Publications.

Bass, B. M., & Avolio, B. J. (2004). *Multifactor leadership questionnaire: Manual and sample set* (3rd ed.). Redwood City, CA: Mind Garden, Inc.

Blank, W. (2001). *The 108 skills of natural born leaders*. New York, NY: American Management Association.

Bolden, R. (2007). Trends and perspectives in management and leadership development. *Business Leadership Review, 4*, 1-13. Retrieved from http://www.mbaworld.com/bss/blr

Borges, N. J., Kirkham, K., Deardorff, A. S., & Moore, J. A. (2012). Development of emotional intelligence in a team-based learning internal medicine clerkship. *Medical Teacher, 34*(10), 802–806. doi:10.3109/0142159X.2012.687121 PMID:23009257

Brackett, M. A., Rivers, S. E., & Salovey, P. (2011). Emotional Intelligence: Implications for Personal, Social, Academic, and Workplace Success. *Social and Personality Psychology Compass, 5*(1), 88–103. doi:10.1111/j.1751-9004.2010.00334.x

Bryman, A. (1992). *Charisma and leadership in organizations*. London: Sage Publications.

Burns, J. (1978). *Leadership*. New York: Open Road Integrated Media.

Carnegie, D. (1936). *How to win friends and influence people*. New York, NY: Simon and Schuster.

Carnegie, D. A. Inc. (1993). The leader in you. New York, NY: Pocket Books.

Caruso, D. R. (1999). *Applying the ability model of emotional intelligence to the world of work*. Retrieved from cjwolfe.com/article.doc

Cherniss, C., & Goleman, D. (2001). *The emotionally intelligent workplace*. San Francisco, CA: Jossey-Bass.

Church, A. H. (1997). Managerial self-awareness in high-performing individuals in organizations. *The Journal of Applied Psychology, 82*(2), 281–292. doi:10.1037/0021-9010.82.2.281 PMID:9109286

Clarke, N. (2010). Emotional intelligence and its relationship to transformational leadership and key project manager competences. *Project Management Journal, 41*(2), 5–20. doi:10.1002/pmj.20162

Conroy, R. J. (2017). *Beyond emotional intelligence: A correlational study of multifactor measures of performance and law enforcement leadership styles (Order No. 10643144)*. ProQuest Dissertations & Theses Global.

Cooper, R. K., & Sawaf, A. (1997). *Executive EI: Emotional intelligence in leadership & organizations*. New York, NY: Grosset/Putnam Inc.

Costa, P. T. Jr, & McCrae, R. R. (1992). *Revised NEO Personality Inventory (NEO–PI–R) and NEO Five-Factor Inventory (NEO–FFI) professional manual*. Odessa, FL: Psychological Assessment Resources.

Coy, D., & Kovacs-Long, J. (2005). Maslow and Miller: An exploration of gender and affiliation in the journey to competence. *Journal of Counseling and Development, 83*(2), 138–145. doi:10.1002/j.1556-6678.2005.tb00590.x

Dalton, M., & Hollenbeck, G. P. (1996). *How to design an effective system for developing managers and executives*. Greensboro, NC: Center for Creative Leadership.

Dewing, J., Hancock, S., Brooks, J., Pedder, L., Adams, L., Riddaway, L., & O'Connor, P. (2004). An account of 360° review as part of a practice development strategy. *Practice Development in Health Care, 3*(4), 193–209. doi:10.1002/pdh.156

Donnithorne, L. R. (1994). *The west point way of leadership: From learning principled leadership to practicing it*. New York, NY: Doubleday.

Dussault, M., Frenette, E., & Fernet, C. (2013). Leadership: Validation of a self-report scale. *Psychological Reports, 112*(2), 419–436. doi:10.2466/01.08.PR0.112.2.419-436 PMID:23833872

Goleman, D. (1995). *Emotional intelligence: Why it can matter more than IQ*. New York, NY: Bantam Books.

Goleman, D. (1998, November). What makes a leader? *Harvard Business Review*, 92-102.

Goleman, D. (2000). Leadership that gets results. *Harvard Business Review, 78*(2), 78–90.

Goleman, D., Boyatzis, R., & McKee, A. (2002). *Primal leadership: Realizing the power of emotional intelligence*. Boston: Harvard Business School Press.

Hall, J. (1973). Communication revisited. *California Management Review, 15*(3), 177. doi:10.2307/41164439

Hogan, R., & Hogan, J. (2001). Assessing Leadership: A View from the Dark Side. *International Journal of Selection and Assessment, 9*(1/2), 40–51. doi:10.1111/1468-2389.00162

Howell, J. P., & Costley, D. L. (2006). *Understanding behaviors for effective leadership* (2nd ed.). Upper Saddle River, NJ: Prentice Hall.

Jackman, J. & Stober, M. (2003, April). Fear of feedback. *Harvard Business Review*.

Jules, C. (2009). Feedback as a unit of work: A data-driven approach to organizational coaching. *OD Practitioner, 41*(3), 8–12.

Kouzes, J. M., & Posner, B. Z. (2008). *A Leader's Legacy*. San Francisco, CA: Jossey-Bass.

Krug, D., & Oakley, E. (1994). *Enlightened leadership: Getting to the heart of change*. New York, NY: Simon & Schuster.

Landy, F. J. (2005). Some historical and scientific issues related to research on emotional intelligence. *Journal of Organizational Behavior, 26*(4), 412. doi:10.1002/job.317

Little, L. (2005). Leadership Communication and the Johari Window. *Administrator, 24*(3), 4.

London, M., & Tornow, W. (1998). 360-degree feedback - more than a tool. In W. Tornow, M. London, & C. Associates (Eds.), *Maximizing the value of 360-degree feedback* (pp. 1–8). San Francisco, CA: Jossey Bass.

Luft, J., & Ingham, H. (1955). The Johari window, a graphic model of interpersonal awareness. In *Proceedings of the western training laboratory in group development*. Los Angeles, CA: UCLA.

Maylett, T. M., & Riboldi, J. (2007). Using 360° Feedback to Predict Performance. *Training & Development*, (September): 48–52.

Miller, H., Watkins, R., & Webb, D. (2009). The use of psychological testing to evaluate law enforcement leadership competencies and development. *Police Practice and Research, 10*(1), 49–60. doi:10.1080/15614260802128575

Multi-Health Systems. (2011). MHS: 2011 catalog. Ontario, Canada: Academic Press.

Muyia, H. (2009). Approaches to and instruments for measuring emotional intelligence: A review of selected literature. *Advances in Developing Human Resources, 11*(6), 690–702. doi:10.1177/1523422309360843

Northouse, P. (2013). *Leadership: Theory and practice* (6th ed.). Thousand Oaks, CA: Sage Publishing.

Parker, P. A., & Sorensen, J. (2008). Emotional intelligence and leadership skills among NHS managers: An empirical investigation. *International Journal of Clinical Leadership, 16*(3), 137–142. Retrieved from http://www.radcliffe-oxford.com /journals/J24_The_International_Journal_of_Clinical_Leadership/default.htm

Payne, W. (1985). *A Study of Emotion: Developing Emotional Intelligence; Self-Integration; Relating to Fear, Pain and Desire (Theory, Structure of Reality, Problem-Solving, Contraction/Expansion, Tuning In/Coming Out/Letting Go)* (Doctoral dissertation). Available from Worldcat Dissertations. (437626710)

Porter, C., Neal, S., & Medina, A. (2000, October). Leadership development at the executive level. *The Police Chief,* 179 - 187.

Richmond, S. L., Rollin, P. F., & Brown, J. M. (2004). *What makes a successful leader*. Retrieved from http://ideashape.com/leadership-research.htm

Riggio, R. E., & Carney, D. (2003). *Manual for the Social Skills Inventory* (2nd ed.). Redwood City, CA: Mind Garden.

Sala, F. (2001). *It's lonely at the top: Executives' emotional intelligence self (mis) perceptions*. Retrieved from http://www.eiconsortium.org

Salovey, P., & Mayer, J. D. (1988). Emotional Intelligence. *Imagination, Cognition and Personality, 9*(3), 185–211. doi:10.2190/DUGG-P24E-52WK-6CDG

Sarver, M. B. (2008). *Leadership and effectiveness: An examination of the leadership styles of Texas police chiefs and the correlates of the most effective leaders* (Doctoral dissertation). Available from ProQuest Dissertations and Theses database. (UMI No. 3311989)

Sayeed, O. B., & Shanker, M. (2009). Emotionally intelligent managers & transformational leadership styles. *Indian Journal of Industrial Relations, 44*, 593–610. Retrieved from http://www.srcirhr.com/ijir.php

Senge, P. M. (1994). *The fifth discipline: The art & practice of the learning organization*. New York, NY: Doubleday.

Shipper, F., & Wilson, C. (1991). *The impact of managerial behaviors on group performance, stress, and commitment.* Paper presented at The Impact of Leadership Conference, Center for Creative Leadership, Colorado Springs, CO.

Sones, E. (2009, October). 360 assessment, an easier pill to swallow: Implementation of peer assessment for captain's career course students and staff. *U.S. Army Medical Department Journal,* 59-63.

Staub, R. E. I. (1996). *The heart of leadership: 12 practices of courageous leaders*. Provo, UT: Publishers Press.

Stein, S. J., & Book, H. (2010). *The EQ edge: Emotional intelligence and your success*. Ontario, Canada: John Wiley & Sons.

Stogdill, R. (1974). Handbook of leadership. New York: The Free Press: A Division of McMillan Publishing.

Taylor, E. W. (2001). Transformative learning theory: A neurobiological perspective of the role of emotions and unconscious ways of knowing. *International Journal of Lifelong Education*, *20*(3), 218–236. doi:10.1080/02601370110036064

Thorndike, E. L. (1920). Intelligence and its use. *Harper's Magazine, 140,* 227-235.

Thorndike, R. L., & Stein, S. (1937). An eval- uation of the attempts to measure social intelligence. *Psychological Bulletin*, *34*(5), 275–285. doi:10.1037/h0053850

Turner, T. W. (2006). *Identifying emotional intelligence competencies differentiating FBI national academy graduates from other law enforcement leaders*. ProQuest Dissertations & Theses Global. (304965891)

Westerman, J. W., & Rosse, J. G. (1997). Reducing the threat of rater nonparticipation in 360-degree feedback systems: An exploratory examination of antecedents to participation in upward ratings. *Group & Organization Management*, *22*(2), 288–309. doi:10.1177/1059601197222008

Wren, J. (2006). A quest for a grand theory of leadership. In G. Goethals & G. Sorenson (Eds.), *The quest for a general theory of leadership* (pp. 1–38). Cheltenham, UK: Edward Elgar Publishing. doi:10.4337/9781847202932.00008

ADDITIONAL READING

Annis, B., & Gray, J. (2014). *Work with me: The 8 blind spots between men and women in business*. New York, NY: St. Martine's Press.

Banaji, M., & Greenwald, A. (2016). *Blindspot: Hidden biases of good people*. New York, NY: Bantam Books.

Baumeister, R., Dale, K., & Sommer, K. (1998). Freudian defense mechanisms and empirical findings in modern Social Psychology: Reaction formation, projection, displacement, undoing, isolation, sublimation, and denial. *Journal of Personality*, *66*(6), 1081–1124.

Bazerman, M., & Tenbrunsel, A. (2013). *Blind spots: Why we fail to do what's right and what to do about it*. Princeton, NJ: Princeton University Press.

Canaday, S. (2012). *You—According to them: Uncovering the blind spots that impact your reputation and your career*. Austin, TX: T&C Press.

Doepker, D. (2015). *Break through your bs: Uncover your brain's blind spots and unleash your inner greatness*. ExcuseProof.com

Glaser, J. (2017). *Blind spots: Shedding light on old habits*. Retrieved from https://www.psychologytoday.com/us/blog/conversational-intelligence/201705/blind-spots

Haudan, J., & Berens, R. (2018). *What are your blind spots? Conquering the 5 misconceptions that hold leaders back*. New York, NY: McGraw Hill.

Razzetti, G. (2018). *How to conquer your blind spots: The elephant in your life*. Retrieved from https://blog.liberationist.org/the-elephant-in-your-life-how-to-conquer-your-blind-spots-dc5982372576

Vazire, S. (2010). Who knows what about a person? The self-other knowledge asymmetry (SOKA) model. *Journal of Personality and Social Psychology*, *98*(2), 281–300.

KEY TERMS AND DEFINITIONS

Assessments: Assessments include profiles, tools, instruments, and questionnaires designed to assist individuals in evaluating, predicting, measuring, or developing their potential for leadership success.

ENDNOTE

1 Generally referred to as people skills or the ability to get along cooperatively with others. Includes those things that govern situational awareness and interaction strategies that help individuals meet their objectives when dealing with others. Often governed by one's own self-awareness, insights and perspectives.

Chapter 11
Finding Star Performer Leaders: The Secret to Running Successful Organizations

Reuven Bar-On
National Command and Staff College, USA

ABSTRACT

This chapter describes an innovative and valuable method for creating predictive models designed to assist in hiring high performing leaders—"star performers"—as well as to continue to enhance their ability to perform on an even higher level. This approach—"Star Performance Modelling"—is described in detail including the process involved and how best to apply the star performer models that are created. The author also demonstrates that the application of these models has a significant impact on organizational effectiveness and profitability. Moreover, it will be explained how star performance modelling is based on analyzing and applying results generated by multifactor assessment instruments such as version 3.0 of the "Bar-On Multifactor Measure of Performance" (MMP3). The author additionally presents a number of examples showing how star performance models have been applied to help organizations save and/or earn hundreds of millions of dollars.

INTRODUCTION

Every organization wants and *needs* to be successful. But, how is this best achieved? It is achieved by hiring and promoting the right people for the job – the star performers – who are the ones who drive organizational effectiveness. And, how do organizations find and more efficiently develop star performer employees and leaders? This is based on Star Performance Modelling (SPM), which is what this chapter is about. The author also discusses the reasons for developing MMP3™ and SPM (version 3.0 of the Bar-On Multifactor Measure of Performance™).

DOI: 10.4018/978-1-5225-8516-9.ch011

BACKGROUND

This section explains the author's reasons for developing Star Performance Modelling (SPM) as well as a comprehensive assessment instrument – the Bar-On Multifactor Measure of Performance™ (MMP3™) – which plays an integral part in this type of model-building. Creating such a multifactor assessment instrument naturally prompts a discussion on how best to apply it. As such, the author describes the reasons for developing the MMP3™ as well as a more detailed discussion on how to apply it (SPM).

One of the basic reasons for beginning the extensive research that led to developing the Bar-On MMP3™ (version 3.0 of the Multifactor Measure of Performance™) emerged from reviewing a wide variety instruments that have been designed to assess various aspects of human behavior and performance (Bar-On, 2016, 2018). This review indicated a need to create multifactor assessment instruments capable of concomitantly evaluating a *combination* of key predictors of performance, in order to hopefully reduce the need for time-consuming and costly *batteries of tests* in psychological assessment. Additionally, this need to develop multifactor assessment instruments, designed to measure human performance, emerged from the desire to, metaphorically, "go beyond IQ and EQ" (Bar-On, 2016, p. 104) as well as other concepts that focus on only a few and questionably robust predictors, by including a wider array of physical, cognitive, intra-personal, inter-personal and motivational contributors to performance. Furthermore, the author's overall approach to this endeavor was purposely a-theoretical in nature from the outset, in order to avoid being restrained by rigid conceptual frameworks that run the risk of restricting rather than facilitating the ability to examine and potentially include a wider range of contributors to human performance. Essentially, the author envisioned the development of a multifactor assessment instrument that attempts to include as many significant contributors to performance as possible and to combine them in order to enhance overall predictive ability. It was thought that such an instrument could eventually be used in career counseling, human resources as well as leadership assessment and development, to help make better decisions in the workplace.

The above-mentioned need for creating *a better assessment instrument* was confirmed, moreover, by a survey that the author conducted of existing pre-employment tests (Bar-On, 2018). Based on a random sample of 120 of the 359 pre-employment tests listed in the 20th edition of the *Mental Measurement Yearbook* (MMY), there appears to be eight major categories describing the vast majority of currently available tests (Carlson, Geisinger & Jonson, 2017). A review of these categories indicated the percentage of pre-employment tests that are designed to obtain the following information from individuals exploring careers and job applicants: 1) 9% identify vocational and career interests; 2) 20% evaluate employability as well as general and specific employment skills; 3) 37% examine cognitive or academic potential; 4) 14% assess intra-personal competencies and personality traits; 5) 5% estimate inter-personal compatibility and communication skills; 6) 3% tap managerial and leadership skills; 7) 8% focus on job commitment, social responsibility, work ethics, honesty and dependability; and 8) 3% attempt to screen for possible disruptive psychological problems and potential criminal behavior. It was also interesting to note that almost none of the pre-employment tests reviewed evaluate motivational drive, which is thought to be an important predictor of performance in the workplace and elsewhere (e.g., Halbesleben & Wheeler, 2008; Markos & Sridevi, 2010; Rich, Lepine & Crawford, 2010). While the Bar-On MMP3™ was not designed to identify vocational interests or specific occupational skills, it is capable of assessing most of the factors that many of the pre-employment tests are designed to evaluate as well as additional factors that they do not assess. The author's examination of the pre-employment tests reviewed by MMY also suggests that they focus on an average of only five potential predictors of performance, while the

MMP3™ focuses on 23 contributors to performance in the workplace and elsewhere. This assessment instrument also *combines* multifactor contributors to performance in one instrument including 1) physical, 2) cognitive, 3) intra-personal, 4) inter-personal and 5) motivational factors. It therefore has the potential of significantly reducing the need to create a *battery* of tests to obtain a more comprehensive evaluation of job applicants, provided by only *one* assessment instrument, completed in *one* sitting and in approximately half an hour. Last, the predictive validity of many pre-employment tests listed is not always available in the MMY nor is it frequently convincing when findings are available.

The main reason for developing the Bar-On MMP3™ can be briefly summarized as *the need to develop a better assessment instrument than previously existed*. Moreover, the ultimate aim of creating such an instrument was to substantially contribute to the study, assessment and enhancement of human performance including leadership.

MAIN FOCUS OF THE CHAPTER

Even if it is hypothetically possible to create *the best assessment instrument* that has ever been created, the author – as an organizational psychologist – was also well aware that a better approach to applying test results needed to be applied in order to make wiser decisions in hiring and promoting the best people for the job (i.e., "star performers") as well as in employee, team and leadership development. In an attempt to address this challenge, the focus of the present chapter therefore deals primarily with Star Performance Modelling.

SOLUTIONS AND RECOMMENDATIONS: *STAR PERFORMANCE MODELLING*

This section explains what Star Performance Modelling (SPM) is, how it works and why it is so effective. This discussion requires a description of the 3rd version of the Bar-On Multifactor Measure of Performance™ (MMP3™) that is applied to collect data used to create this model. When SPM and the MMP3™ are combined, one has a very sophisticated, accurate and robust tool for selecting, developing and promoting the right people for the job as will be shown below.

What Star Performance Modelling Is: A Brief Description

Star Performance Modelling (SPM) is a process designed to improve an organization's ability to find and develop high performers as well as to increase organizational effectiveness. It is important a to emphasize that it is a *process*, based on the way it works. It is also important to stress that because SPM is organization-specific (i.e., specifically describes performance in the organization in which it is developed), it minimizes potential cross-cultural problems that are often encountered when various assessment and development models are used in organizations. More succinctly, these models are based on the specific corporate culture of the organization in which it was developed.

The SPM process generates a statistical or mathematical *snapshot* of high performance, which is then used as a valid and reliable *roadmap* in selection and development. In that this snapshot of high performance is based on the culture of the organization in which it is developed, it accurately describes what is high occupational performance and successful leadership in that particular organization and in that specific unit within the organization.

While SPM was originally based on data generated by Bar-On's 15-scale Emotional Quotient Inventory™ (the Bar-On EQ-i™), it is presently based on his 23-scale Multifactor Measure of Performance™ (MMP3™) that assesses more than 50% of additional competencies, skills and behaviors than the Bar-On EQ-i™ did. This means it will provide a more comprehensive and in-depth picture thus significantly enhancing data interpretation.

After applying this approach and seeing the results since 1996, the author is convinced that SPM is one of the most efficient and cost-effective methods of applying important multifactor concepts such as the one measured by the Bar-On MMP3™.

How Star Performance Models Are Created: The Process

Star performance models are created by the process of Star Performance Modelling, which is described here in detail.

First, a group of individuals performing a specific task in a particular organization are requested to complete a valid multifactor measure such as the MMP3™. Next, their current performance is rated by co-workers. Multiple Regression Analysis is then applied to examine the ability of the questionnaire to predict the employees' occupational performance. This process generates a statistical model – referred to as a "star performance model" – of high performance by pinpointing those scales that predict performance the most.

In addition to completing the MMP™ and having their current performance rated by a minimum of three co-workers, it is recommended that clients rate their satisfaction with the product and/or service they are receiving. It is also recommended that an indication of the overall organizational effectiveness is assessed, for example, by looking at the difference in annual profit growth from the past 12 months to the present. These additional parameters will serve to enhance the sensitivity, accuracy and strength of the star performance model that is created.

The number of participants required in SPM, when using the Bar-On MMP3™ is applied, is a minimum of 160 individuals.

Performance ratings can be very simple such as 1) *performing below expectations*, 2) *performing according to expectations* and 3) *performing above expectations*, or it can be based on annual or biannual reports that many organizations use. Job satisfaction and customer satisfaction can also be rated in a very simple manner, such as 1) *not satisfied*, 2) *satisfied* and 3) *very satisfied.*

What Is Needed to Create Star Performance Models: Valid Multifactor and Comprehensive Measures of Performance Such as the Bar-On MMP3™

The 15-scale Bar-On EQ-i™ was previously used when Star Performance Modelling (SPM) was originally developed and applied (e.g., Handley, 1997; Langhorn, 2004a, 2004b; Lennick & Kiel, 2005; Turner, 2006). The 23-scale Bar-On MMP3™ is currently being used. Assessing a larger number of variables capable of predicting performance will normally increase the overall predictive validity of the assessment instrument used (Anastasi, 1988; Tabachnick & Fidell, 2001). This more comprehensive assessment instrument is briefly described below, with a more detailed description found elsewhere (Bar-On, 2016, 2018).

A Description of the Bar-On MMP3™

The Bar-On MMP3™ (Multifactor Measure of Performance / version 3.0™) is a self-report measure of key factors that predict performance. This assessment instrument comprises 142 brief items and uses a response format that ranges from 0% to 100%, designed to capture the degree to which the individuals' responses accurately describe the way they behave and perform most of the time. The degree of correlation found between the MMP3™'s validity scale – "Self-Image Accuracy" – and the questionnaire's other scores suggests that social bias and the desire to present an overly positive image could artificially increase scores to some degree (Bar-On, 2018). As such, the author has recognized the need to adjust raw scores as he has done with other assessment instruments (Bar-On, 1997). This is done by multiplying raw scores by non-standardized beta weights obtained from applying Multiple Regression Analysis to examine the degree of correlation between the questionnaire's validity scale and its other scales. Software is presently being developed to proportionally reduce significantly high raw scores, by converting them to adjusted scores.

It normally takes no more than half an hour to respond to all of the items that are presented online (Conroy, 2017). Scores are computer-generated and automatically summarized in an individual report together with a number of suggestions designed to strengthen the relatively weaker predictors of performance that are identified. The individual report is emailed to the respondent immediately upon completing the questionnaire and exiting the testing site. Test results can also be made available to create star performance models for organizations upon request. In addition to a total performance score, scores are provided for the following 23 scales that evaluate physical, cognitive, intra-personal, inter-personal and motivational predictors of performance:

- Physical Predictors
    - Physical Fitness & Well-Being
    - Discomfort Tolerance & Stamina
- Cognitive Predictors
    - General Cognitive Competence
    - Situational Awareness
    - Applying Experience
    - Flexibility & Adaptability
    - Resourcefulness & Resilience
    - Decision-Making
    - Preparedness & Readiness
    - Coping & Endurance
- Intra-Personal Predictors
    - Self-Awareness
    - Self-Control
    - Self-Reliance
    - Decisiveness
    - Courage
- Inter-Personal Predictors
    - Social-Awareness
    - Connectedness

    - Responsibility
- Motivational Predictors
    - Finding Meaning
    - Engagement
    - Self-Motivation
    - Determination
    - Perseverance

A description of what is measured by each of the above scales appears in the Definitions of Key Terms section at the end of this chapter. In addition to providing more detailed information about the Bar-On MMP3™ and what it assesses, this will provide a deeper understanding of the importance of Star Performance Modelling and its potential as described in this chapter.

Why the Bar-On MMP3™ Was Developed

The author's fundamental reason for creating this instrument was to address the need for developing more reliable and valid multifactor measures of performance, as was previously mentioned, by concomitantly assessing the following five groups of factors that contribute to performance: 1) physical factors; 2) cognitive factors; 3) intra-personal factors; 4) interpersonal factors; and 5) motivational factors. Moreover, this was an attempt to comprehensively capture and evaluate *the whole person* when studying, assessing and enhancing performance – i.e., "body, mind and soul" as well as *everything in between and more*. Additionally, this was an attempt to assess the above-mentioned groups of contributors to performance by employing only *one* psychometric instrument, in *one* sitting and in a relatively short period of time as was previously mentioned. To reiterate, it was hoped that this would significantly reduce the need to combine results obtained from applying a number of different instruments in order to evaluate all of the key factors described above and, in turn, substantially reduce the time and cost involved in testing. To briefly summarize the primary reasons for creating the MMP3™, the author wanted to create a comprehensive operational framework designed to help understand why some people perform better than others and to determine which contributing factors need to be strengthened in order to enhance performance in individuals who are underperforming. In addition to flagging those factors that need to be strengthened, identified by the low scores, the summary report that is automatically emailed to respondents contains a number of straightforward suggestions for enhancing performance. In addition to individually exploring the application of these suggestions for self-improvement, they can be shared with a coach to continue enhancing performance with a professional. Additionally, star performance models can be created based on group scores to develop cost-effective training and coaching programs in order to strengthen those areas that need to be collectively addressed to enhance overall organizational performance.

How the Bar-On MMP3™ Was Developed

The author began developing the idea of a multifactor model of human performance in the late 1970s, before creating his model of emotional intelligence (Bar-On, 1988, 1997, 2006). The process of developing these two models was very similar. While he chose to submit a *limited* doctoral proposal that focused on a separate sub-set of factors that impact "optimal emotional and social functioning" (Bar-On, 1988), the more comprehensive explanation of human behavior, performance and well-being was essentially temporarily paused. The author then returned to his earlier idea of creating a more comprehensive conceptual and psychometric model of human performance which eventually led to the Bar-On MMP3™. The basic approach adopted in creating this assessment instrument involved the following steps (Bar-On, 2018): 1) systematically identifying factors in the literature thought to predict human behavior and performance; 2) receiving input from expert consultants who have worked in performance assessment and/or development; 3) initially selecting and defining nearly 30 potential predictors of performance; 4) creating a large item pool for the beta version of the instrument based on the way the author defined these factors; 5) selecting and further editing these items; and 6) applying multivariate statistics to examine the results obtained from the beta version of the instrument, in order to both reduce the number of items and psychometrically strengthen the assessment instrument while progressing from the first to the third version of this questionnaire. The author is continuing to norm and validate the current version of the questionnaire across cultures.

The key findings, to date, indicate that the MMP3™ is a reliable and valid measure of performance including leadership (Bar-On, 2018; Conroy, 2017; Murphy, 2018) as is explained below.

The Factorial Structure of the MMP3™

Exploratory Factor Analysis (EFA) was used to estimate the factorial structure of this questionnaire (Bar-On, 2018), which examined the responses generated by 2,380 individuals in North America. Nine consecutive EFAs were carried out, in which factor output was limited by progressing from 18 to 26 factors. The simplest and most logical factorial structure of the MMP3™ appeared to emerge from limiting factor output to 22 factors, confirming 22 clearly structured factors to be assessed by 22 MMP3™ scales verifying most of the items in the original scales (Bar-On, 2018). In addition to estimating that the factorial structure of the MMP3™ accounts for nearly 82% of the total variance that it was designed to capture, approximately 85% of the original scales were retained. The average factor loading of the third version of this questionnaire was .55 (Bar-On, 2018), which suggests the potential for significant factorial validity; but, this will need to be confirmed by Confirmatory Factor Analysis in future studies that need to be conducted on larger and more diverse independent samples. When considering which scales and items should be retained from beta versions of assessment instruments, typically those with highest reliability and validity are retained. Additionally, the original conceptual model – the *theory* – is also taken into consideration when making final decision regarding the nature of the final version. As such, one of the biggest challenges for the author was that the original Self-Awareness scale, included in the two previous versions of the questionnaire, did not survive the EFA stage described above. The original items of this scale loaded more heavily on a few other factors that emerged. In spite of this, the author was well aware that self-awareness is an important contributor to performance and represents the foundation for other important contributors to performance such as social awareness and impulse control (Bar-On, 1988, 1997) as well as represents the basis for self-development and self-improvement. As such, the author wanted *to give it another chance* by the continued norming and validation of the MMP3™ and re-examine its factorial structure further on. The Self-Awareness scale was thus retained in the questionnaire as its 23rd scale.

MMP3™'s Basic Psychometric Properties

Based on the normative sample (n=2,380), the skewness and kurtosis of all of the scales fall within the acceptable ±2.0 range (Trochim & Donnelly, 2014); and the mean scores of the scales appear to be normally distributed (Bar-On, 2018).

MMP3™'s Reliability

The approach used to estimate the MMP3™'s reliability was to evaluate the internal consistency of its scales with Cronbach alphas. The results indicate that all of the scales possess more than adequate reliability (Bar-On, 2018), based on the assumption that reliability coefficients equal to or greater than .70 indicate adequate reliability for scales (Anastasi, 1988; Tabachnick & Fidell, 2001). Other researchers have also obtained similar results regarding MMP3™'s reliability (Conroy, 2017; Murphy, 2018). In that the MMP3™'s test-retest reliability has not yet been examined, the consistency of test scores over relatively short periods of time is not presently known. However, research findings do indicate that the questionnaire's scores increase with age (Bar-On, 2018) suggesting that scores change over time as a result of *experience*, in general, and are also expected to increase as a result of participating in focused courses, training and coaching designed to enhance performance. This also means that the MMP3™ could be used to reliably evaluate intervention progress and effectiveness made by comparing pre- and post-intervention assessments.

MMP3™'s Validity

The author's findings indicate that nearly all of the MMP3™ scales are capable of significantly discriminating between high and low performers except for Self-Reliance (Bar-On, 2018). However, all of the scales, including Self-Reliance, are capable of predicting performance (Bar-On, 2018). More precisely, the overall multivariate correlation between the MMP3™ and performance is .56 ($F = 7.39$, $p <.001$) suggesting that it possesses relatively high predictive validity. It is also important to note that a 2017 doctoral study (Conroy, 2017) demonstrated that the MMP3™ appears to be a very robust predictor of leadership ($R = .76$ ($F = 35.00$, $p<.001$)). In an additional doctoral study that was recently conducted, the researcher also demonstrated that the MMP3™ possesses significant predictive ability based on a Multiple Regression coefficient of.52 (Murphy, 2018). When these findings are compared with other approaches to predicting performance, including most pre-employment testing involving cognitive factors and personality traits moreover, the MMP3™ outperforms other assessment instruments in this regard. More specifically, Morgeson and his colleagues reported findings from 13 meta-analyses (n=40,230) indicating that the average predictive coefficient of cognitive testing is .25 accounting for only 6% of the variance of occupational performance (Morgeson, Campion, Dipboye, et al., 2007, p. 700); and based on 12 meta-analyses (n=23,413), the average predictive coefficient of personality traits is only .15 accounting for a mere 2% of the variance (Morgeson, Campion, Dipboye, et al., 2007, p. 700, p. 705). This comparison highlights a major accomplishment in test-construction and especially for those psychometric instruments frequently used in pre-employment assessment of potential performance in the workplace.

How Star Performance Models are Used and Where: Applications and End-Users

To date, there are two basic ways of applying Star Performance Modelling (SPM): In hiring and development. A third application of SPM is in promoting employees, which is used less often but could be used more often. SPM could also be used in downsizing when needed, in order to help make difficult decisions especially during times of economic downturn in order to help create smaller, stronger and more productive organizations (i.e., by (a) hiring and (b) retaining the star performers and downsizing those who are underperforming). End-users of SPM have included the following industries and occupational sectors to date: 1) healthcare; 2) education and career counseling; 3) human resources in organizations; 4) employee, team and leadership development; 5) financial services and banking; 6) public safety including law enforcement and emergency management; 7) security and defense; and 8) hospitality.

Why Star Performance Modelling is a Valuable Cost-Effective Tool: Empirical Evidence

This section discusses the primary benefits from using simple group profiles and especially from applying the more sophisticated star performance models, based on its significant impact on occupational performance and profitability.[1] The seven examples below are presented to empirically demonstrate the importance and value of Star Performance Modelling (SPM). In the first four examples, it will be shown that star performance models normally have a substantial impact on the organization's "bottom line" by saving and/or making millions of dollars for the organization. Before presenting the examples below, it is important to explain why SPM is cost-effectiveness in general. When comparing the cost of SPM with that of Assessment Center (AC) assessments for example, it is important to note that the initial cost per individual model – based on the minimum of 160 participants required for developing MMP3™-based models – includes the cost of initially creating a star performance model. However, the cost of the continued use of SPM-based assessments, after building the initial predictive model, fairly quickly decreases the more the model is used; and even the cost per individual in the initial stage of building the model is a fraction of AC assessment per person—(which was an average of $1,200 the last time the author examined the cost involved). Additionally, the average correlation between SPM-assessed employees and occupational performance is .55 based on findings to date. By comparison, the correlation between AC-assessed employees and their performance is .28 (Hermelin, Lievens & Robertson, 2007) based on a meta-analysis of 26 studies (n= 5,850). Here it is important to note that Assessment Centers have been considered *the gold standard* in occupational assessment for years. Last, the time it takes to conduct an SPM-based assessment and receive the results – less than an hour on the average – is much less than the time it typically takes to conduct an average AC-based assessment (often more than seven hours per assessee). Additionally, more individuals are involved in AC-based assessments, which often include at least one psychologist and at least one professional from the organizational unit for which the candidate is being considered. Therefore, AC assessments take more man-power hours which partly explains the greater cost of this type of assessment when compared with SPM assessments. In the end moreover, AC assessments are less effective (the correlation is .28 between results and occupational performance as was previously mentioned).

The first-known application of SPM was conducted in 1996 in the US Air Force (USAF) by Handley together with the author (Bar-On, 2006; Bar-On, Handley & Funds, 2006; Handley, 1998). A sample of 1,171 military recruiters completed the Bar-On EQ-i™, and Multiple Regression Analysis was used to examine the ability of the resultant star performer model to predict the ability of the recruiters to recruit individuals to the USAF. A predictive coefficient of .53 confirmed the predictive validity of the model that emerged. This model was then used in selecting potentially high performing recruiters. After one year of its application in selection, it proved to increase the USAF's ability to accurately select star performers by nearly threefold and decreased mismatches by 92% saving the military approximately $3,000,000 the first year alone. The GAO (US Government Accountability Office) submitted a Congressional Report to the Senate Committee on Armed Services, in January 1998, praising the USAF's application of this approach and recommended its use throughout the military (GAO, 1998).

After the success of the USAF's initial application of SPM, the military was interested in seeing if this approach could be used to reduce costly mismatches in selecting individuals for a special ops course. The cost per mismatch in this two-year course cost the government approximately $250,000. A sample of 200 individuals participated in this study, in which they examined the differences between those who completed the course and those who did not. A number of factors thought to predict performance in the course were examined with Discriminant Function Analysis. The predictive coefficient was found to be .45, and the accuracy level of the star performance model was calculated to be 75%, meaning that this model could be used to spot nearly 8 out of 10 who would complete the course. This, in turn, was thought to significantly reduce costly mismatches. The military's conservative estimate was that the use of this star performance model in selection would save the government $190,000,000 over a five-year period. The application of this approach was praised by RAND Corporation (Manacapilli, Matthies, Miller, et al., 2012). Such an approach should be examined in selection for other military special ops courses as well as in law enforcement units like SWAT.

An additional example based on an early SPM approach used in leadership development was carried out at American Express by Lennick (Lennick & Kiel, 2005), who was a former VP in charge of the organization's 12,000 financial investors at the time. They examined the difference in creating revenue between those who participated in this project and those who did not. It was found that those who participated out-performed those who did not by 18% in generating revenue amounting to $200,000,000 in the first year. In addition to being initially described by Goleman (1998) and later by Lennick (2005), this project was also discussed on the Oprah Winfrey Show when the project was first described.

The HR Director at Whitbread Corporation described an additional example of SPM in his doctoral dissertation (Langhorn, 2004a, 2004b). He examined the ability of 161 restaurant managers' emotional and social adeptness to impact the profitability of the restaurants they managed as well as their leadership performance as managers, team satisfaction and customer satisfaction. Multiple Regression Analysis was applied to the data to develop a star performance model. The model that emerged showed that the managers' emotional and social adeptness had a significant impact on the annual profit growth of the restaurants they managed (.51) as well as on their leadership performance (.54), the employees' satisfaction (.43) and on guest satisfaction as well (.40). This study also found that the combined effect of managerial emotional and social adeptness, leadership performance, employee satisfaction and guest satisfaction had a very significant impact on annual profit growth which increased exponentially (.71). Moreover, the restaurants run by the star performers in this study showed an annual profit growth of 22% when compared with other managers. This amounted to an estimated increase in £110,000,000 for Whitbread Corporation.

Turner's doctoral research (2006) examined the difference in emotional and social competencies between a group of candidates who were not admitted to the FBI National Academy and those who graduated. He found that there were significant differences in the competencies studied between the two groups ($F = 4.22$, $p = .041$), which clearly defined the star performers in his research.

Conroy's research demonstrated that the Bar-On MMP3™ can predict effective leadership (2017). More succinctly, this psychometric instrument was shown to be a robust predictor of "transformational leadership" in a sample of 454 senior law enforcement officers. The predictive model that emerged clearly indicated that most of the variance accounting for effective leadership (nearly 60%) can be accounted for by this model when the MMP3™ is applied ($R = 0.76$ ($F = 35.00$, $p < 0.001$)).

A doctoral study recently completed by Murphy (2108) created a star performance model with mildly high predictive validity based on the MMP3™. In addition to finding significant differences between 396 emergency managers and a random sample of 1,614 individuals from the normative population, his star performance model was able to significantly predict performance for certified emergency managers (Multiple $R = .52$, $F = 3.94$, $p <.001$).

FUTURE RESEARCH DIRECTIONS

The findings presented in this chapter will hopefully encourage other researchers and practitioners to use the Bar-On MMP3™ in Star Performance Modelling (SPM), in order to significantly enhance leadership assessment and development. The author is in the process of analyzing SPM results created by individuals from a number of different public safety occupations who have completed this questionnaire. The author together with Drs. Richard Conroy, Timothy Turner, Howard Murphy and Mitch Javidi will shortly begin to summarize findings from a sample of over 1,000 individuals, which will include star performance models for law enforcement officers, first responders, emergency managers and others working in closely associated fields. Additionally, Bar-On Test Developers is partnering with Prof. Isaac Ashkenazi and a software company to develop a VR simulator to assess and develop emergency management.

In addition to the above-mentioned projects, there is a need to reach out to other researchers and practitioners to help develop additional star performance models for a wide range of industries and occupational sectors. Star performance models will need to be created, applied and examined in hiring and training "the right people for the job" as well as to study their impact on a number of different organizations. Moreover, it will be important to examine the ability of the Bar-On MMP3™ to predict occupational performance rated by co-workers, direct reports and supervisors. Additionally, it will important to evaluate differences between pre- and post-intervention assessments before and after leadership development programs as well as to evaluate their ability to increase occupational performance and to examine the MMP3™'s incremental validity compared with other performance assessment instruments. Those who are interested in studying these and other aspects of SPM can contact the author.

CONCLUSION

In light of the fact that this chapter has presented a cost-effective and powerful approach to hiring and developing star performers who have a significantly valuable impact on organizations, it is the author's hope that a greater number of organizations will apply Star Performance Modelling.

REFERENCES

Anastasi, A. (1988). *Psychological testing* (6th ed.). New York, NY: Macmillan Publishing.

Bar-On, R. (1988). *The development of a concept of psychological well-being* (Doctoral dissertation). Grahamstown, South Africa: Rhodes University.

Bar-On, R. (1997). *The Bar-On Emotional Quotient Inventory (EQ-i): Technical manual.* Toronto, Canada: Multi-Health Systems.

Bar-On, R. (2006). The Bar-On model of emotional-social intelligence (ESI). *Psicothema, 18*, 13–25. PMID:17295953

Bar-On, R. (2016). Beyond IQ & EQ: The Bar-On Multifactor Model of Performance. In U. Kumar (Ed.), *The Wiley handbook of personality assessment* (pp. 104–118). London, UK: John Wiley & Sons. doi:10.1002/9781119173489.ch8

Bar-On, R. (2018). The Multifactor Measure of Performance: Its development, norming, and validation. *Frontiers in Psychology, 9*(140), 1–16. PMID:29515479

Bar-On, R., Handley, R., & Fund., S. (2006). The impact of emotional intelligence on performance. In V.U. Druskat, F. Sala, & G. Mont (Eds.), *Linking emotional intelligence and performance at work.* Mahwah, NJ: Lawrence Erlbaum Associates.

Carlson, J. F., Geisinger, K. F., & Jonson, J. L. (2017). *The Twentieth Mental Measurements Yearbook.* Lincoln, NE: Buros Center for Testing.

Conroy, R. J. (2017). *Beyond emotional intelligence: A correlational study of multifactor measures of performance and law enforcement leadership styles* (Doctoral dissertation). Dallas Baptist University.

GAO / US Government Accountability Office. (1998). *Military Recruiting: The Department of Defense Could Improve Its Recruiter Selection and Incentive Systems.* A United States Congressional Report Submitted to the Committee on Armed Services in the United States Senate on the 30th of January, 1988 (GAO/NSIAD – 98 – 58).

Goleman, D. (1998). *Working with emotional intelligence.* New York, NY: Bantam Books.

Halbesleben, J. R. B., & Wheeler, A. R. (2008). The relative roles of engagement and embeddedness in predicting job performance and intention to leave. *Work and Stress, 22*(3), 242–256. doi:10.1080/02678370802383962

Handley, R. (1997, April). AFRS rates emotional intelligence. *Air Force Recruiter News.*

Hermelin, E., Lievens, F., & Robertson, I. T. (2007). The validity of assessment centres for predicting supervisory performance ratings: A meta-analysis. *International Journal of Selection and Assessment, 15*(4), 405–411. doi:10.1111/j.1468-2389.2007.00399.x

Langhorn, S. (2004a). *The role of emotions in service encounters* (Doctoral dissertation). University of Luton.

Langhorn, S. (2004b). How emotional intelligence can improve management performance. *International Journal of Hospitality Management, 16*(4), 220–230. doi:10.1108/09596110410537379

Lennick, D., & Kiel, F. (2005). *Moral intelligence: Enhancing business performance & leadership success.* Upper Saddle River, NJ: Wharton School Publishing.

Manacapilli, T., Matthies, C. F., Miller, L. W., Howe, P., Perez, P. J., Hardison, C. M., & Sims, C. S. (2012). *Reducing attrition in selected Air Force training pipelines.* Santa Monica, CA: RAND Corporation.

Markos, S., & Sridevi, M. S. (2010). Employee engagement: The key to improving performance. *International Journal of Business and Management, 5*(12), 89–96.

Morgeson, F. P., Campion, M. A., Dipboye, R. L., Hollenbeck, J. R., Murphy, K., & Schmitt, N. (2007). Reconsidering the use of personality tests in personnel selection contexts. *Personnel Psychology, 60*(3), 683–729. doi:10.1111/j.1744-6570.2007.00089.x

Murphy, J. H. (2018). *A quantitative study of key indicators of effective management leadership* (Doctoral dissertation). Piedmont International University.

Rich, B. L., Lepine, J. A., & Crawford, E. R. (2010). Job engagement: Antecedents and effects on job performance. *Academy of Management Journal, 53*(3), 617–635. doi:10.5465/amj.2010.51468988

Tabachnick, B. G., & Fidell, L. S. (2001). *Using multivariate statistics* (4th ed.). Needham Heights, MA: Allyn & Bacon.

Trochim, W. M., & Donnelly, J. P. (2014). *Estimates of statistics for the behavioral sciences* (8th ed.). Belmont, CA: Wadsworth.

Turner, T. W. (2006). *Identifying emotional intelligence competencies differentiating FBI national academy graduates from other law enforcement leaders* (Doctoral dissertation). University of Virginia.

ADDITIONAL READING

Conroy, R. J., Turner, T. W., Murphy, J. H., Javidi, M., & Bar-On, R. (2018). Applying key predictors of star performance in law enforcement. *Law Enforcement Today*, 1-10.

KEY TERMS AND DEFINITIONS

Applying Experience: In addition to appropriately and effectively applying past experience in order to facilitate current problem-analysis, problem-solving and decision-making, this is the ability to apply experience in understanding and dealing with current challenges and problematic situations. This requires the capacity to effectively combine past experience with new information and approaches, which is an important contributor to effective cognitive functioning.

Connectedness: In addition to being able to connect with other people and to establish and maintain mutually satisfying interpersonal relationships, this is the capacity to establish and maintain good relationships with others, get along with friends and colleagues as well as to enjoy social interactions in general.

Coping and Endurance: In addition to managing one's feelings in stressful situations, this is essentially how well people typically cope and function under pressure. This includes how effective they are in dealing with anxiety-provoking situations.

Courage: In addition to being able to overcome one's apprehensions and fears to act courageously, this is the capability of individuals to protect, stand up for and support others even when there might be negative consequences for doing so. Additionally, it is the extent to which people are even prepared to risk their life to save another person's life.

Decision Making: In addition to generating potentially effective solutions to problems, weighing the pros and cons of each possibility and deciding on the best solution, this is the ability to make good decisions in general. Moreover, it is the ability to come up with a potentially effective plan that requires coping with ambiguity and exercising sound judgement even when working under pressure and dealing with potential risks.

Decisiveness: In addition to expressing oneself openly, clearly and boldly as well as being able to confidently convey feelings, beliefs and ideas, this is the ability of people to be assertive and decisive as well as to set firm limits with others when necessary but without being aggressive or hostile.

Determination: In addition to being committed to decisions that are made and goals that are set as well as being determined to follow through with them, this is essentially how resolute people are in the choices and decisions they make. This requires the resolve to begin what they decide to do and to move into "action mode" after decisions are made.

Discomfort Tolerance and Stamina: In addition to the ability to temporarily suspend everyday physical needs and comforts in order to complete a task, this is the willingness to eat at irregular times, work longer hours with less sleep as well as to work on weekends in order to meet deadlines and finish the work on time.

Engagement: In addition to being committed to one's work which builds on feeling passionate about what one enjoys doing that enhances overall motivational drive, this is the degree to which people feel positive about what they do or have done and understand the positive impact it has or might have on others.

Finding Meaning: In addition to finding meaning in what one does as well as being passionately involved in meaningful pursuits that benefit others in addition to oneself, this is the ability to live a meaningful and rewarding life as well as to follow one's calling.

Flexibility and Adaptability: In addition to coping with and adapting to change as well as dealing with unexpected, unpredictable and confusing situations, this is the ability to flexibly "think on one's feet" and deal with the unexpected, finding ways to improvise and adapt when the unpredictable occurs, and to make the necessary adjustments to overcome. This often requires one to re-reframe setbacks and not to see them as personal or permanent.

General Cognitive Competence: In addition to one's ability to learn new information and apply learned knowledge, logic and reasoning for the purpose of understanding and solving problems, this is the capacity to learn more about the challenges one is faced with, to first understand them and then think about a reasonable course of action, to apply potentially effective solutions and weigh conflicting evidence, as well as to take into account the short-term and long-term consequences of potential solutions being considered.

Perseverance: In addition to persevering and following through with a task until it is completed, this is the drive to pursue goals in general.

Physical Fitness and Well-Being: In addition to striving to obtain and maintain good physical fitness, which contributes to overall well-being, this factor is a combination of physical (primarily) and emotional well-being. It is how people feel in general about their physical fitness, eating and sleeping habits as well as how energetic they typically are in what they do.

Preparedness and Readiness: This is the ability of individuals to be prepared and ready to cope with immediate situations that arise and/or to execute some form of goal-oriented action based on what they have learned. This includes immediately sizing up what is presently happening in the here-and-now, deciding on the best course of action and rapidly implementing it, which appears to be what is cognitively needed in dealing with emergency situations.

Resourcefulness and Resilience: In addition to the ability to be innovative and consider different ways of coping with situations, this is the capacity of individuals to generate different approaches to dealing with challenges and setbacks as well as to resiliently recover from them. If previous approaches are ineffective, resourceful individuals typically come up with alternative approaches that work for them; and this often depends on formulating an effective course of action aimed at going from the current situation to a better one for them.

Responsibility: In addition to living according to a set of principles, values and beliefs which guide one's decisions and ability to do the right thing, this is also the consistency of one's moral integrity when one is with family members, friends and/or colleagues. Fundamentally, this is based on the ability to understand the difference between *right* and *wrong* and to act accordingly.

Self-Awareness: This is the ability to accurately look inward at oneself in order to better understand and accept oneself, including one's weaknesses as well as one's strengths.

Self-Control: In addition to controlling emotions and maintaining self-composure, this is essentially "the ability of people to control their emotions so they work for them and not against them." Moreover, it is the ability to effectively deal with challenges while maintaining outward composure.

Self-Motivation: In addition to being positive, optimistic and energized in doing what one does, this is the degree to which people are capable of motivating themselves. This enhances their drive to get as much as they can out of what they enjoy doing and energizes them to perform on an even higher level.

Self-Reliance: In addition to being independent from others and being able to think things out alone, make decisions and act independently when needed, this is essentially the capacity to think and act independently rather than depending on others. Moreover, it is the ability of people to act alone when need be, even though they might be open to receive input and suggestions from others.

Situational Awareness: In addition to being attentive to the immediate situation, paying attention to detail and understanding, clarifying and closing gaps between the perception of subjective reality and objective reality, this has to do with how attentive people are to their surroundings and how well they size up the situation. This appears to be based on an ability to update their assessment of situations in response to changes in the immediate environment as well as to filter out irrelevant information, in order not to get distracted.

Social Awareness: In addition to being aware of others, their feelings and concerns which helps one interact with people and become a more cooperative, constructive and contributing team player, this is the ability to understand nonverbal communication, to know how others feel and to be attentive to their needs.

ENDNOTE

1 The difference between "group profiling" and "star performer modelling" is that the former is created by simply averaging the test scores of individuals in the same occupation, organization or organizational unit; and the latter is created by applying sophisticated multivariate statistics to generate powerful regression models that very accurately predict performance based on the most robust predictors examined.

Chapter 12
First-Line Police Supervisory Leadership:
A Pivotal Role in Effective Communication and Engagement

Brian Ellis
Sacramento Police Department, USA

Anthony Normore
California State University – Dominguez Hills, USA

ABSTRACT

In this chapter, the authors highlight the extant literature on organizational leadership and its pivotal role in effective communication and engagement processes. The authors focus on first-line supervisors and the impact of communication and engagement on officers under their supervision. Employee trait, state, and behavioral constructs coupled with the culture of emotional connection between police officers and the police organization are explored. Further, in this chapter, the authors examine the principles of effective empowerment including meaningfulness, competence, mastery, choice, and impact and its applicability to effective police leadership. The outcome of the relationship between effective leadership and employee engagement is directly linked to innovation, participation, teamwork, accountability, and the ability to face challenges. Conclusions and recommendations for future research are discussed.

INTRODUCTION

While there are many organizations studying the implications of employee engagement, minimal information exists in the study of employee engagement within police organizations. In western policing, the profession has seen many standards of performance, with regards to the training and readiness of their police forces in the field. Unfortunately, little is required to supervise this new workforce. In California for instance, while a police academy offers approximately 664 hours of instruction, only 80 hours of training is mandated to become a supervisor (www.post.ca.gov). To complicate the issue of training,

DOI: 10.4018/978-1-5225-8516-9.ch012

the higher an officer promotes in a police organization, the less education is required. In a hierarchical setting such as police organizations, it remains essential that leaders within those organizations have the competency necessary to enhance performance and make police organizations vibrant places where officers remain highly engaged to deliver great customer service. This occurs through the ability of leaders to understand what drives employees to do excellent work, and how to better attach employees to organization values.

Like any other professional, police officers have signature strengths. Those strengths are seen as traits or interests that allow officers to flourish in some environments and become frustrated in others (Buckingham & Coffman, 1999; Seligman & Csikszentmihalyi, 2000). It becomes central for leaders to identify the needs of each individual, which may include their individual traits, behaviors, and work setting to maximize their abilities (Macey & Schneider, 2008). Furthermore, police leaders must be effective at utilizing empowerment. Empowerment stems from understanding and proper application of the numerous sources of empowerment: *meaningfulness*, where employees attach themselves to the work itself by understanding how the work makes a difference; *competence,* the ability to become proficient at a job, where one feels they have mastery of a role or task; *choice,* or the ability for one to do work in a fashion that compliments them; and *impact,* which is knowing that the work they complete is making a difference (Yukl & Becker, 2006). Finally, for police leaders to deliver the next generation of best practices, they need an understanding of all who are positively impacted by an engaged employee. Within this context, the authors argue that there are positive impacts for the police employee, the organization, and the public they serve and protect. We further argue that engagement and communication lead police employees to improved teamwork, creativity and innovation, accountability, and the ability to more effectively deal with any potential organizational adversity (Lakshmi, 2012).

This chapter will expand on the above-mentioned concepts (i.e., engagement, communication, leadership) and its applicability within police agencies. In understanding the process of effectively engaging employees (e.g. police officers), the leaders (e.g., first-line police supervisors) must first focus on social processes (e.g. cultural, personal, professional, and organizational). Northouse (2010) asserts that leadership is the act of influencing others where most power comes from things such as referent and reward bases and "have an ethical responsibility to attend to the needs and concerns of followers" (Northouse, 2010, p. 4). Towards this end, we will highlight the extant literature on organizational leadership and its pivotal role in effective communication and engagement processes. First, we provide examples of employee trait, state, and behavioral constructs (e.g., Mark & Schneider, 2008; Seligman & Csikszentmihalyi, 2000) as seen in police organizations. Then, we discuss the culture of emotional connection between police officers and the police organization (Tomlinson, 2010). Next, we highlight the synergistic effect of the four principles of effective empowerment including *meaningfulness, competence, choice, and impact* (Yukl & Becker, 2006) and its applicability to effective police leadership. We articulate the outcomes of effective leadership (Gladwell, 2008) and employee engagement (Chughtai, Buckley & Finian, 2008; Harter, Schmidt, & Hayes, 2002) and how employee engagement has direct links to innovation, participation, teamwork, accountability, and the ability to face challenges (e.g., Lakshmi, 2012). Conclusions and future research directions are articulated.

LEADERSHIP AND THE FIRST-LINE POLICE SUPERVISOR

Leadership has a critical role within any police agency and is often considered the key element in determining a division or department's success or failure. The leadership of the chief of police and the command staff down through the ranks (e.g., middle management of captains and lieutenants) to first-line supervisors (sergeants) to the patrol officer often acts as a catalyst for promoting or devaluing the goals and objectives of a police department (Waters, 2004). Although "every position within a police agency presents leadership challenges - the role of the first-line supervisor is often the most crucial" (Waters, para.1).

According to research on police supervisors (e.g., Baker, 2000; Tully, 2002; Waters, 2004) the first-line supervisor is considered the backbone of any police agency. The leadership - or lack of leadership - shown by a sergeant "can have a dramatic effect on how the agency is perceived by the community… upper management can have the most well thought-out strategic planning initiatives, but without the first-line supervisor's leadership ability to move his or her subordinates toward the implementation of those goals, they will remain just ideas" (para.15). According to Baker (2000), "Sergeants must be able to organize, plan and evaluate their officers to reach department objects. Frustrated police personnel can lead to negative productivity." (p. 89). The first-line supervisor has to be able to "quickly identify potential problems and seek remedies that will promote growth for the department and the affected employee" (para. 15). Of equal importance, they are expected to provide opportunities for officer engagement, motivate subordinates, and communicate effectively (Baker, 2000). While engagement might be challenging for a first-line supervisor to measure, they can look for 'work energy,' which can be seen in subordinate's behavior and overall attitude at work. High energy levels lead to the development of high-performance settings (Ellis, Normore & Javidi, 2018; Rafi, 2017).

COMMUNICATION AND ENGAGEMENT IN POLICING CONTEXT

A police organization benefits from communication and engagement as people become more connected to an agency's strategies that lead to positive outcomes (Harter, Schmidt, & Hayes). Engaged police officers leads to better service, thereby positively impacting customer satisfaction (Crabb, 2011). Further, the engagement-oriented police leader looks for ways to impact people that not only make a social impact for the groups they belong to, organizations, and communities, but show the moral responsibility to their followers (Northouse, 2010). The way a supervisor interacts and models certain behaviors with their subordinates impacts the way in which employees will interact with the public. From an extant review of literature one can find numerous reasons to pay attention to employee engagement. Based on the work by Mone and London (2009), engaged employees produce more for their organizations. They feel more involved, committed, and empowered in their workplace. It is important to understand the desired outcomes, but to also understand that influential positive behavior of first-line police supervisors, managers, and anyone in a police leader role is a path to more engagement. When the aforementioned groups fail to communicate with their employees, fail to provide them with learning and development opportunities, and fail to recognize good work, subsequent positive engagement is thwarted (Mone & London 2009). Additionally, counterproductive leadership deters engagement opportunities for police forces. Counterproductive leadership is best described by the US Army and can be defined as:

Counterproductive leadership can take different forms, from incompetence to abusiveness, all of which have detrimental impacts on individuals, the unit, and the accomplishment of the mission. Counterproductive leadership behaviors can span a range of behaviors to include bullying, distorting information, refusing to listen to subordinates, abusing authority, retaliating, blaming others, poor self-control (loses temper), withholding encouragement, dishonesty, unfairness, unjustness, showing little or no respect, talking down to others, behaving erratically, and taking credit for others' work (US Army, 2017, p.8)

This should help send a message to leaders that on-going positive commitments to employees as well as communication are essential to maximize the workplace.

There are layers of the communication process which can impede the flow of information depending on the number of layers (Buckingham & Coffman, 1999). Based on these authors research there is a universal understanding of the technical process of communication. For example, many people have experienced the different messaging that takes place at work setting where multiple people come out of the same meeting and heard different things being said. This is because people import their unique and different personal histories into the way they experience things, leading to the different ways in which communications are encoded, transmitted, received, and understood (Pfeiffer, 1994). That is why leaders must ensure that the message carries the same force within each layer of our organization. Otherwise, it becomes diluted. Leaders can do this by over-communicating simple messages and using various mediums to communicate. Examples of this are to use a wide array of tactics such as email, team and organizational meetings (informational, strategy, training, and feedback settings), and one-on-one interactions to properly communicate key issues. Leaders can also rely on groups and personal relationships to carry messages effectively, thus ensuring the right message is understood. Finally, Buckingham and Coffman (1999) indicated that far too often supervisors and managers look at employees' weaknesses and not their strengths. This is significant for police organizations, as officers are trained early on to look for deception in an investigative setting. Unfortunately, this negativity biases finds its way into police supervision and management situations frequently, and the adept police leader must look beyond negativity biases to get the most out of employees (Enter, 2006).

If organizations want the best out of employees, they should identify their strengths and bring the best out of them while simultaneously managing their weaknesses. In turn, leaders create opportunities to reduce resistance, reflect on the presence of irritants, and build motivation and commitment in a manner consistent with being credible, authentic, deliberate, and intentional (Keis & Javidi, 2014). In police work, there are myriad assignments to choose from including but not limited to: Investigations, Special Weapons and Tactics (SWAT), or school resource officer. Officers gravitate towards assignments that are aligned with their current or emerging identity, while the organization sends the message that in order to promote, officers need to be well rounded. While the authors agree that people who seek promotional opportunities should be well rounded, they also understand there are many organizational opportunities present to fulfill such requirements without causing unnecessary engagement challenges. One author has witnessed people taking field and/ or investigative assignments merely to fulfill what they believed to be a requirement for advancement; when they had no desire to work in the job itself. This creates issues for the others that work in these environments and sends the message (particularly if they are a supervisor or manager) that they do not want to be there nor care about the work being done.

Keis and Javidi assert that employee well-being and job satisfaction are the desires of the individual, while commitment and performance are that of the organization. Consequently, it is paramount that leaders understand how to balance individual and organizational needs for maximum performance.

Communication is expected to be simple, yet there are times where it is the pitfall that stands in the way of organizational effectiveness. Many times when supervisors communicate the message, it is derailed by the negative message that is delivered, whether intended or not. The "don't do that", "not on my watch", or "look what you have done this time" are negative messages that impede the essential communication that rallies effective engagement, happiness and optimism (Ellis, Javidi, & Normore, 2018; Keis & Javidi, 2014).

Seligman and Csikszentmihalyi (2000) explored the enablers of happiness and traits (e.g., optimism) in the relation to how these enablers affect health. Through their personal discoveries and life lessons, these authors found that people often ignore the needs of others out of selfishness, a behavior that leads to chaos and despair. The authors argued that people cannot be excluded from organizational culture because of their poor attitudes but rather a need exists to develop and reinforce positive attitudes. Positive attitudes such as optimism lead to a great deal of preventative measures while increasing strengths and capacities for interpersonal skills, honesty, and hope. They further articulated that people with high optimism levels tend to have better moods, to be more preserving and successful, and to experience better physical health. Developing positive attitudes in police agencies not only develops the relationship between supervisor and subordinate, but also between the police officer and community member.

Seligman and Csikszentmihalyi (2000) also noted that peak performance is a product of people using their signature strength. This is a process where one knows and understands their work and feels they have excellent skills in completing the task at hand. As a result, leaders create opportunities for employees to recommit to their work and become re-motivated in the work place while the organization enjoys the benefits of maximizing resources. To do otherwise, leaders can create an atmosphere of resentment, hostility, and excuses. We argue that police leadership must strive to have a talent pool greater than the number of specialty jobs available. Tomlinson (2010) asserts that the hopes of employee engagement is to create a culture of emotional connection between the employees and the organization. This in turn leads to perpetual commitment and attachment to the company.

To return to the key findings from the Gallup organization (2010) pertaining to employee engagement, it is clear that engagement is critical for any organization's success. In their meta-analysis of over 199 research studies across over 152 organizations, and reaching over 950,000 employees, Gallup concluded that organizational leadership is desperately in need of a more engaging atmosphere. Key findings revealed that only 11% of the workforce is engaged; 62% is unengaged; and 27% are actively disengaged.

Similar studies (e.g., Kahn, 1990; Macey & Schneider, 2008) have been completed by both larger and smaller companies where the engagement numbers are similar. Even police departments and cities have completed similar studies, both pointing for a need of more employee recognition and a need to better understand the metrics that assist in creating engagement.

ELEMENTS OF ENGAGEMENT: TRAIT, STATE, AND BEHAVIORAL

Kahn described engagement as,

The simultaneous employment and expression of a person's "preferred self" in task behaviors that promote connectedness to work and to others, personal presence (physical, cognitive, and emotional), and active, full role performances. To employ such dimensions is to drive personal energies into physical, cognitive, and emotional labors. People who are personally engaged keep their selves within a role, without sacrificing one for the other. People become physically involved in tasks, whether alone or with others, cognitively vigilant, and empathically connected to others in the service of the work they are doing in ways that display what they think and feel, their creativity, their beliefs and values, and their personal connections to others (p. 700).

Researchers (e.g., Macey & Schneider, 2008; Yukl & Becker, 2006) suggest that employee engagement is a complex system, which has *trait*, *state*, and *behavioral* constructs under an umbrella of work conditions that may facilitate behavioral and state engagement. We now explain these three elements and include our own professional examples of how these are recognized in police agencies.

Trait

Trait engagement deals with personality attributes of the individual such as being positive and energetic about work (Macey & Schneider, 2008). These attributes are considered the inner personal process of being a proactive person. In policing, discovering past work products in an employee's background might tell supervisors a great deal about the trait aspects of a person. Police leaders have many opportunities to understand their workforce. From checking employee's personnel files and/or to talking to past supervisors. In addition, leadership must set unambiguous goals and strategies that are reinforced and checked on frequently. Police organizations are filled with many people who show high trait value, as seen in the many alpha personalities who strive to be better. As great of a quality that is, it can also hinder success of these people who do not have the humility, as they can potentially resist leadership movement. Humility allows people to see the best in others and in the plans they bring forward. While a 'can-do' attitude is a great quality in employees; it should not be at the expense of creating an environment of hubris. Humility also translates into sharing opportunities beyond the top performers. We contend that leadership is about making all people in the organization as successful as possible, not just the highest performers. As important as leveraging the entre workforce is for leadership to not over depend on those who achieve frequently. There is a natural tendency to reward hard work with more work; thus, sending a message that the reward for working hard is more work. This creates stagnation in the development of others and reduces engagement. We further assert that when leaders play favorites or make excuses such as not having enough time in rank or needing more experience while concurrently giving opportunities to others who have limited qualifications, is a potential failure of leadership.

Great trait qualities can be seen in police over-achievers. Unfortunately, all over- achievers do not always have good organizational reputations. From our own experience, perceptions of other sergeants and managers can be that these people have an air of arrogance or insecurity about who they are as people and/or as officers and as a result are threatened by the stellar performance of some. Additionally, cultural riffs between supervision style creates ambiguous environments where it becomes difficult to gage what great performance actually looks like, as the same activity appreciated or demanded by one sergeant is treated indifferently by another (Engel, 2003; Van Maanen, 1973). This can and has led to some over-achievers being blind-sided in their careers, which subsequently leads to unengagement and underperformance. For example, we have experienced situations where patrol officers want to spend their shift apprehending criminals. As a rule, this could be considered an admirable quality and directly aligned with the protection of community members. There is, however, much more to being an effective problem solver in the community being served. Examples include working through every call not to only effectively problem solve, but to build relationships that aid officers in the ability to have a greater opportunity to know what is going on in the neighborhoods they patrol. When officers favor efficiency over effectiveness in these moments, they lose out on the opportunity to build the trust that opens the gates of communication; leading them to more opportunities to do the kind of work they are interested in. Our best employees often create much extra work for supervisors. Great employees are involved in a lot of police work; therefore supervisors have additional paperwork through the checks and balances (e.g., use of force reports, pursuit reports, injured on duty forms, etc.). The last thing first-line police leaders want is for employees to apologize for doing great work because it makes work for them. Police leadership ought not to worry about the additional work that's created at the expense of great work being done for the community. To curb these behaviors, leaders should make it a priority to provide opportunities for each team member to show signature strengths in the workplace and appreciate them often.

Unfortunately, some sergeants and managers get caught up in the "numbers game" and rely on those who are well known throughout the agency to produce. Sadly, the reward for doing a good job is usually recognized in the form of more work assigned. Supervisors and managers get bogged down in work that they simply want to give it to people who will get it done, while shying away from developing others along the way. Essentially, this type of leadership buries top performers and creates a lack of development opportunities within the organization. Police supervision can be very mission-focused and lose sight of all the processes that garner better leverage for the organization. When management continues to throw large loads onto an employee, sooner or later, they take on too much and are burdened by an overwhelming amount of work, and might not accomplish anything at all, or simply burn out.

State

State engagement is associated with work setting where a person can have feelings of energy, dedication, enthusiasm, and pride (Yukl & Becker, 2008). This happens through an attitude created by factors, which happen at work such as being valued by your supervisor, or-organizational value programs. Leaders can learn more about this from their people with well-crafted employee surveys that question organizational pride, advocacy, overall satisfaction, and commitment. This connects largely with the intrinsic rewards to which leaders align their people (Ellis & Normore, 2015).

One of the more effective ways to create new energy within a team is to create small wins for team members early and frequently (Macey & Schneider, 2008). Police leaders should first look at the work setting and seek feedback about processes or workplace settings that irritate or complicate work conditions for employees prior to engaging a team towards a new mission. For example, officers may be frustrated with working conditions or processes that can be easily fixed or eliminated. If officers do not have a clear understanding of purpose that drives these practices, they may feel buried with endless work expectations with no real concrete outcome. First-line police leaders cannot expect people to be effective in their daily workspace if leaders are not making workspaces that are full of energy and user friendly.

Creating "wins" for employees assists efforts of change (Macey & Schneider, 2008). Changes to policies and procedures that are either not relevant anymore or complicate the process create easy victories for leaders. As long as they are not detrimental to customer service or impact criminal investigations, in the long run, they are worth exploring. Research indicates that the best way to start this process is to reach out to trusted sources and ask for feedback about these irritants existence in the workplace (Yukl & Becker, 2006). Some of the frustration employees have comes from the very way policies are created and updated. Often members of police management are tasked with writing and/or updating policies and often rely on the way they "use to do it" and/or collaborating with other managers to rewrite the policy rather than asking for line-level opinions. We contend that in order to be a good police agency leader it means having the ability to reach out to line-level troops and frequently ask, "What do you think?" By doing so, employees are not simply learning the tasks required to do their job, but become active participants in the business of the business and begin to understand the impact of their work for the community and the organization (Hams, 2012).

Behavioral

The behavioral component of employee engagement is an adaptive process that can describe a range of behaviors such as doing more and/or something different (Macey & Schneider, 2008). In police work, officers have to be comfortable with change. It is an essential part of the criminal justice system. This is where an employee's willingness to work towards the organization's values appears. For example, for a police department, its values are demonstrated by the way an officer acts in an effort to enhance customer service. Police leaders must frequently align the work of employees with organizational values (Ellis & Normore, 2015). It's our experience that when police leaders weave individual officer's values into organizational values it allows officers to see how their work directly reflects on their personal values while simultaneously empowering the officer to achieve satisfaction on both personal and professional levels. This type of engagement between police officer and police leader is then representative of the organizational conditions that enhance relationships, or introduces additional behavioral engagement (Ellis & Normore, 2014; Macey & Schneider, 2008) through the effective use of empowerment within the police agency

EMPOWERMENT PRINCIPLES: MEANINGFULNESS, COMPETENCE, CHOICE, AND IMPACT

In their work, *Effective Empowerment in Organizations*, Yukl and Becker (2006) suggest that engagement is directly related to empowerment. These researchers assert that when employees believe they can adjust their work roles to accomplish assignments, engagement naturally happens. Further, they theorize that empowerment comes from four independent principles that have a synergistic effect when used in combination: *meaningfulness, competence, choice, and impact*. The following section provides an overview of the principles of empowerment with professional examples added for purposes of understanding how these translate into practice.

Meaningfulness

Meaningfulness is the attachment an employee makes with the work itself. This is described by Yukl and Becker (2006) as the "engine" of empowerment. In police work, officers are very attached to their identity as police officers. This is reinforced through various mechanisms - namely being a police officer 24-7, personal values, and shift work which tends to isolate officers to only socialize with other officers. When work is in line with an individual's values, there is a greater attachment to the work being completed (Yukl & Becker, 2006). While one might think the policing profession does this well, there are still several issues to be considered. An officer's work can be very meaningful. However, when all of the moving parts of the criminal justice system are not collaborating, the balance becomes chaotic (Bone, Normore, & Javidi, 2015).

There are many instances where police agencies, District Attorney's offices, probation/ parole Departments, and the courts find themselves in conflict with the same cases they have been assigned. For example, an officer makes what he/she believes to be a great arrest on a chronic offender. Upon filing the criminal charges at the DA's office, the case is referred to parole due to the status of the individual. With parole being inundated with the large percentage of recidivism of offenders, sentences are often shortened. The officer sees the same career criminal on the street just a short time later reoffending. Upset, the officer looks to see that there were never any charges filed on the last case. After a while, this officer begins to ask himself/herself why he/she should work as hard as he/she does to keep criminals off the street. Subsequently, he/she finds himself/herself in an ethical dilemma related to his/her discretion such as reducing their number of self-initiated stops. That same officer now begins to heavily monitor all future cases and can become very cynical about the system to the point where he/she does not put forth the same effort as before. The officer feels like it is a personal attack on him/her, when in fact it is a system simply trying to survive on its individual set of rules.

The saturation of the criminal justice system puts all of the cogs in positions in order to be selective of the work they do. It begs the question if society should gage a DA's office, the court system, or police investigators on conviction/clearance rates, or rather how much the entire system disrupts crime in a region? Perhaps this is where regionalization can finally make its mark on the criminal justice system? What does this mean for law enforcement leaders? What are the fixes to the problem? Does this lie with providing officers with more training so that their cases are better suited to get filed? Or is it an issue related to unrealistic dispositions for criminal cases? The answer is complicated and maybe the best answer is "it depends." The real nexus to leadership in these moments is to identify when these actions happen and attempt to stay abreast of them. Simply asking the right questions and illuminating roadblocks of confusion allows employees to see impacts and how they can help rather than to take something that happens personally. It allows for officers to problem-solve for solutions to the problems they inevitably face daily. Policing in today's world is the act of problem solving (Ellis, Normore, & Javidi, 2018c). Problem solving has internal (workplace) and external (community) components. We assert that when the synergistic effects of the criminal justice system fall out of balance it has consequences for the overall organization in that the organizations will inevitably lose a great deal of employee engagement. It is up to first-line supervisors to properly monitor and identify events to ensure they are raised up on the correct flagpole for executives to fine-tune the system.

A second area where police leadership can better attach meaningfulness is to be more mindful of expressing gratitude and appreciation to officers for a job well done. By publically acknowledging and celebrating the good work of officers, leaders create a culture of recognition therefore enhancing meaningfulness. This could be done by simply reading a citizen's thank you letter in a police roll call. At the same time, leaders create responsibility and accountability. Recognition however should not be cut short. Far too often, supervisors expedite and privatize recognition such as sending an employee an email for a job well done. While it seems appropriate, such recognition can be seen as insensitive and does not allow a supervisor to model behavior for the other employees he or she supervises. Recognition which is energetic produces energy in employees. Accountability comes from officers knowing that leaders are paying attention to their work (Ellis & Normore, 2015).

Competence

The **competence** component from Yukl and Becker's work is derived from the notion that people like to complete skills of which they have a personal mastery. This is the self-belief of employees of successfully completing tasks (Ellis & Normore, 2015). To illustrate with an example, prior to graduation night from the police academy one of the academy staff expressed to the class, "Congratulations, you are now all police officers. It will take you five years on the job to become cops." In retrospect, the academy staff was right in many ways. There is a real difference between the two. Police officers are the people who wear a badge, whereas cops are the intellectual property of people who are passionate about their purpose and provide value each and every minute for their organizations and the citizens they serve. The hopes of any leader are to have an organization of cops. People like to play their strengths and leaders are responsible in assuring the organization has the ability to maximize the potential of every employee. Personal mastery is a link to those strengths that police leaders should use to get officers excited about their work by linking them to the things for which they have a passion (Bone & Normore, 2015; Keis & Javidi, 2014).

Mastery

Mastery is about the personal experiences and life lessons on the job. Personal mastery allows for what Peter Senge (1990) calls the difference between what's important, what we want, and where we are now, which produces "creative tension." Creative tension is generated and maintained through the forces of personal mastery (Anderson, Gisborne, & Holliday, 2012, 2017). When reflecting about mastery and an appropriate example to share with the reader, we chose to look at a particular job skill over the course of one author's career to see how it has changed. We decided to look at the "name game," a staple of deception within policing. It is universally agreed that most cops are familiar with the "name game" but for those who are unfamiliar with it, it is arguably one of the more thought-provoking experiences in police work – especially for a detective or a patrol officer. This is a game of wits where an officer intellectually jousts with some of society's "slipperiest" people. In the early stages of his career, Brian found himself dealing with a seasoned criminal. In retrospect, he wonders how many criminals were so successful in playing this deception game. Add a significant amount of experience playing this game and the name game has now become easy due to experience. Yet, Brian is not always certain as to why that is. He understands there are some telltale signs in the interaction, but there is also that certain feeling an officer confronts when he has played the game repeatedly. To understand the nuances of the "name game" we offer a sample scenario below between a cop and a criminal subject eluding capture:

An officer makes a contact, either via an enforcement stop or via a consensual contact someone in public. The officer drums up some conversation with the subject and then asks for some identification during a casual conversation, using humor and a relaxed spirit to keep the conversation going. Yet, most criminals do not carry their identification with them for fear of being identified. While all of the content is not here, the essence of it situation is paraphrased in the following:

COP: Do you mind if I ask your name since we've been talking?
BAD GUY: Why are you asking for my name? I haven't done anything wrong? (Or some other kind of stall tactic like "what?", "huh", "what did you say?")

COP: I never accused you of anything; I just like to know who I'm talking to. Geesh, talk about having a guilty conscious.
BAD GUY: My name is John, John Doe.
COP: How old are you John, we look like we are the same age?
BAD GUY: I'm 39.
COP: May I ask your date of birth?
BAD GUY: (Quietly and anxiously provides a birth date, usually a few numbers off, or a birthdate other than his own that he easily remember, such as a sibling.)
COP: The date of birth you gave me would make you 42, why did you tell me you were 39? You wouldn't lie to me would you? (Now it becomes a game of math. Trying to play deception math on the fly is difficult and this is where the game can fall apart, or another early sign of deception appears.)
BAD GUY: Uh, 42 I meant to say 39, sorry boss, I am just nervous and have problems with numbers (or a number of other excuses for not getting it right. Now if the numbers do not add up, the cop has him. Note however, the cop probably had him prior to that - based upon body language, eye movement such as looking for potential escape routes, and overall nervousness).

This process continues from one lie to another. Some cops will extend this game even when they already know they have caught the subject in a lie. As officers engage in this "name game" over a period of time their skills become more and more refined. An officer will gain much confidence that upon the first set of deception, he puts a criminal on notice and because the officer carries so much conviction about it, the offender comes clean. This is mastery. In retrospect, the scenario draws parallels to Malcolm Gladwell's (2008) 10,000 Rule. Gladwell suggests it takes 10,000 hours to become great at anything. The leadership lesson here is for leaders to empower employees with opportunities that will enhance their skills at tasks they find meaningful and to subsequently provide them with the tools to master those skills.

Choice

The third empowerment principle introduced by Yukl and Becker is choice whereby the employee chooses to complete a task in a manner of his/her choice. This is the individual's sense of having a choice of initiating the work that he/she is planning to do. Police work is filled with choice. Officers often ask themselves, should I stop this violator or that one? Should I give this person a ticket? How do I best mediate this neighborhood dispute so I do not have to return? Then there is the choice of assignments: Patrol, detectives, SWAT, and other various specialized units.

One would think that police work is filled with so much choice that this is an easy win for policing. However, supervisors and managers have their work to do here as well. First, officers will often emulate those who they want to be more like; such as a senior officer who has credibility amongst their peers. Police leaders should attempt to have conversations with newer employees to ensure they understand that individuality is a benefit for problem-solving and learning. Second, while officers might desire to work in certain roles, sometimes their career goals fall short. When this happens, police leaders have an obligation to pivot employees or come to their aid, so that organizational energy is not lost. Finally, delegation is an important skill needed early in leadership. Delegation is a critical piece of being a leader. Learning to let go becomes a critical piece of this process, and one that most leaders find challenging. It requires people to be a little vulnerable and to give up control. According to Enter (2006), everyone faces burnout if leadership tries to shoulder the load. Leaders also miss valuable educational opportunities for themselves and their staff (Enter, 2006). Being "in charge" is not about having all of the answers but rather being as resourceful as possible for those under one's leadership. For choice to be meaningful, leaders have to identify problems with employees and ask for their input, then facilitate teaching and learning opportunities to the same employees so they can solve problems on their own, or as a collective (Enter, 2006).

Impact

The final principle of empowerment is the role of impact. Impact is the sphere of "making a difference." (Yukl & Becker, 2006, p. 229). Police work is replete with opportunities to make a difference such as the search for the criminal element that victimizes society and subsequently bring justice to the incident that unfolded within a community. Furthermore, there are the personal opportunities such as the ability to make a difference in someone's life. There are, however, instances where police work is not about impactful work. An illustration of this is the false alarm call or a non-injury vehicle accident where there is no opportunity to impact events in others lives. Yet, as first responders, police officers have a duty to do this work. They are law enforcers, guardians, counselors, and numerous other trades weaved within their roles. While all of these forces create impactful work, police leaders must recognize those instances where impact is affected and/or non-existent. In those instances, the challenge is to find ways to create impactful work from those reactive forces. It is also an opportunity to challenge the forces that stand in the way of great work such as the disequilibrium in the criminal justice system mentioned earlier. One way of doing this is to realign officers to the statements they made upon entering the profession. Most applicants when asked during the hiring process as to why they choose to do this kind of work will respond with "to help people." Along the way, they get to chase "bad guys". They are assigned other types of autonomous duties, which create conflicting desires about what the officer feels needs to be done.

One author is aware of these types of conflicts because he was once considered his effectiveness by the sheer number of trips he took to jail (e.g., arrests). Many other parts of the job created obstacles that he needed to quickly "jump" through in order to create another opportunity to jail another criminal or make another arrest. In that time, people can short-cut calls and undermine an officer's other duties. Opportunities for organizational problem solving creates healthy officers and a healthy agency. Metaphorically stating, these problem-solving instances fills the belly, the heart, and the mind all the while being filled with action-oriented processes. Still, problem solving can be challenging for officers because they are action-oriented individuals.

Police leaders need to reinforce why the work officers do has an impact and makes a difference. Policing is filled with all kinds of styles and communities would benefit from officers assigned to specific work they do best. For example, it stands to reason that a police leader would not want to assign an officer who he/she depends on to arrest criminals to work instead a traffic complaint, or in parking enforcement. There is a school of thought that every officer is a leader (see Anderson et al., 2012, 2017) and needs to be well rounded. While we mostly agree with this statement we also argue that the health of any police agency (or any organization in general) would benefit more from leaders who take the initiative and care to ensure assignments are delegated to those who have special knowledge and training in specific areas. When the leader assigns a task to someone on the team for the sake of well-roundedness and is unsuited for the task, we question the level of communication and positive engagement the employees are in fact receiving.

OUTCOMES OF ENGAGEMENT: FUTURE RESEARCH DIRECTIONS

There are quite a number of outcomes of employee engagement that range from direct benefits to the employee, to the organization and customer benefits. Studies point to a relationship between trust and work engagement, which ultimately leads to additional performance (Chughtai, Buckley & Finian, 2008). In a research project, the Gallup organization teamed up with the University of Iowa and the U.S. Department of Immigration and Naturalization (Harter, Schmidt, & Hayes, 2002) to examine the relationship between satisfaction, employee engagement, and business outcomes. In their meta-analysis of over 7,900 business units in 36 companies, Gallup findings revealed a substantial relation between individual job satisfaction and individual performance. Researchers concluded that employee satisfaction and engagement are related to meaningful outcomes at such a magnitude that organizations should take a closer examination (Ellis, Normore, & Javidi, 2018a). Other research (e.g., Lakshmi, 2012) concluded that employee engagement has been linked to innovation, participation, teamwork, accountability, and the ability to face challenges. Furthermore, Crabb (2011), a senior consultant with A&DC, a leading talent management consultancy company in the UK linked engagement to elevated levels of customer satisfaction.

We now propose several research directions concerning the significance of potential positive influence of leadership, engagement, communication, and empowerment on an organization's health and well-being. For our purpose, we reflect on these processes as they pertain to police agencies, first-line police supervisors, and police officers. Future research directions made as a result of the findings suggest that police agencies need to conduct further research on the impact of supervisor and officer engagement as a key component for improving an agency's performance. With such positive attributes as those listed in earlier research (see above), it is undoubtedly a force-multiplier for police agencies, and therefore every attempt should be taken to understand and develop engagement opportunities tailored to supervisor and officer workspace as well as for the entire agency.

From Kahn's studies in the early 90's to present time (2015), academics and organizational personnel have continued to research employee engagement in search of the link between communication, engagement and organizational performance. A large amount of useful information has resulted from the studies while organizations still find the same problem of a mostly disengaged workforce. It stands to reason that more qualitative research is warranted in this area to determine why police agencies and their police supervisory leaders continue to miss the mark in leading their agencies forward to a healthy space in time.

In understanding the process of engaging employees, Northouse (2010) asserts that organizational leaders must first focus on social processes. Northouse reiterates that leadership is the act of influencing others where most power springs from organizational culture such as referent and reward bases. Consequently, leaders "have an ethical responsibility to attend to the needs and concerns of followers" (Northouse, 2010, p. 4). To this end, we suggest longitudinal study is necessary on the professional and organizational leadership socialization processes of police supervisors, and the self-efficacy of officers while in the training academy, and subsequently during the promotional processes. Such a study could help determine what factors play a role in the understanding of leadership versus management, the reasons for entering the police force, job satisfaction, employee engagement, communication forms (e.g., lateral, top-down, bottom-up), and the dynamics of creating an agency's institutional culture.

There appears to be no viable system which police agencies could put into action whereby the success of every officer is guaranteed (Normore, 2017). Still, police leaders should strive to connect with as many officers as possible. The organizational and individual values ought to be aligned for any process to succeed. At the very least, the organizational goals of formal and informal leaders within the organization need to be aligned with the organizational direction. Unfortunately, this is not the usual way in police agencies. If the circle of power, or the sphere of influence, excludes organizational input from all its members, there is a likelihood that some members will not be valued despite their high productivity level. We argue for the maximizing of "wins" in order to understand that every department has those people who have "street credibility" with their peers. These people are at times distractions for organizational movement because they can be seen as cynical (Anderson et al., 2012, 2017). Leadership is often about reducing resistance and removing irritants. If leaders can at the very least remove irritants in order to build credibility, they could most likely leverage the trust of new allies to reduce resistance to future programs and productivity levels. If leaders ignore or attempt to forcefully move these key allies within departments, it will be futile. Police leaders need energy and drive that officers possess in order to create an impact. The old formula of "strength plus speed equals power" helps to illustrate how a leader's power cannot live up to that leader's potential without rallying layers of informal leaders throughout the agency. Informal leaders could likely provide speed to the cause. We propose further research in the area of organizational health so police leaders and officers are provided opportunities to share real-time input concerning the respect of the agency's values, philosophy, and long-term vision. Such a study could reveal the factors that lead to organizational cynicism.

It is common in community-oriented policing events for police officers to push the community to engage with their neighbors (Ellis & Normore, 2014) where officers preach the old adage of "strength in numbers". Leaders, however, sometimes forget how compelling such an external relationship is for building internal organizational health and work satisfaction. As noted earlier, employee well-being and job satisfaction are the desires of the individual, while commitment and performance are that of the organization (Keis & Javidi, 2014). It is paramount that leaders understand how to balance individual and organizational needs for maximum performance.

CONCLUSION

Leadership holds the key to the ability to create force multipliers and it is the action that is necessary to move this momentous stone. Think about it in terms of physical fitness. When you have been hitting the gym hard, you reap the rewards of feeling and looking great. Then life gets in the way with one thing or another and you find yourself a little out of shape. It is really the same with the engagement process? If we are not developing relationships at all times and doing authentic actions that make people feel they are a part of the team, we will find those relationships will atrophy. When you get back into any routine, the hardest part is the beginning. After awhile you adapt to the new workload and actually crave more. This is the very process we are chasing. We must take action towards the sometimes unquantifiable processes that build trust. It is here that we will find employee engagement.

REFERENCES

Anderson, T. K., Geisborne, K., & Halliday, P. (2017). *Every officer is a leader: Coaching leadership, learning and performance in justice, public safety and security organizations*. Holly Spring, NC: International Academy of Public Safety.

Anderson, T., Gisborne, K. D., & Holliday, P. N. (2012). Every officer is a leader: Coaching leadership, learning, and performance in justice, public safety, and security organizations. Trafford Publishing. Retrieved from www.trafford.com

Baker, T. (2000). *Effective police leadership*. New York, NY: Looseleaf Law Publications, INC.

Bone, D., Normore, A. H., & Javidi, M. (2015). *Human factors: police leaders improving safety while developing meaningful public trust. FBI Law Enforcement Journal.*

Bone, D., & Normore, A. H. (2014). Progressive law enforcement leaders effectively manage departmental risk. *Law Enforcement Today (LET): The Law Enforcement Community.* Retrieved from http://www.lawenforcementtoday.com/2014/07/13/striving-for-educational-excellence-in-law-enforcement-leadership-the-case-of-jefferson-parish-sheriffs-office/

Buckingham, M., & Coffman, C. (1999). *First, break all the rules: What the world's greatest managers do differently*. New York, NY: Simon & Schuster.

Chughtai, Buckley, & Finian. (2008). *Work engagement and its relationship with state and trait trust: A conceptual analysis*. Retrieved from, http://findarticles.com/p/articles/mi_qa5335/is_200809/ai_n29493978/?tag=content;col1

Ellis, B., Normore, A. H., & Javidi, M. (2018a). Getting left of boom: Troubleshooting poor outcomes. *Law Enforcement Today.* Retrieved from, https://www.lawenforcementtoday.com/getting-left-boom-troubleshooting-poor-outcomes/

Ellis, B., Normore, A. H., & Javidi, M. (2018b). Auftragstaktik': Building organizational leadership through mission control. *The Tactical Edge (National Tactical Officers Association), 2018*, 82-86. Retrieved from, http://public.ntoa.org/default.asp?action=issue&year=2018&season=3%20-%20Summer&pub=Tactical%20Edge

Ellis, B., Normore, A. H., & Javidi, M. (2018c). How leadership training is an effective tool against civil liability. *Police Chief Magazine.* Retrieved from, http://www.policechiefmagazine.org/police-leadership-training-effective-tool-against-civil-liability/

Ellis, B., Javidi, M., & Normore, A. H. (2018). The toxicity of the spiteful leader. *Law Enforcement Today.* Retrieved from, https://www.lawenforcementtoday.com/toxicity-spiteful-leader/

Ellis, B., & Normore, A. H. (2016). Effective engagement and communication between first-line police supervisors and police officers. In *The handbook of effective communication, leadership, and conflict resolution (pp. 479 – 493)*. Hershey, PA: IGI Global Publishers. doi:10.4018/978-1-4666-9970-0.ch025

Ellis, G., & Normore, A. H. (2015). Performance management strategies for effective leadership in law enforcement: An accountability process. *FBI Law Enforcement Bulletin*. Retrieved from http://leb.fbi.gov/2015/february/performance-management-strategies-for-effective-leadership-an-accountability-process

Ellis, B., & Normore, A. H. (2014). Police leadership: Connecting with communities through a partnership initiative. *Peace Officers Research Association of California Law Enforcement.* Retrieved from http://porac.org/

Engel, R. (2003). *How police supervisory styles influence patrol officer behavior*. Washington, DC: US Department of Justice. Retrieved from https://www.ncjrs.gov/pdffiles1/nij/194078.pdf

Enter, J. (2006). *Challenging the law enforcement organization: The road to effective leadership*. Dacula, GA: Narrow Road Press.

Gallup, Inc. (2010). *The state of the global workplace: A worldwide study of employee engagement and wellbeing*. Retrieved from http://www.gallup.com

Gladwell, M. (2008). *Outliers: The story of success*. New York, NY: Little, Brown & Company.

Hams, B. (2012). *Ownership thinking: How to end entitlement and create a culture of accountability, purpose, and profit*. New York, NY: McGraw Hill.

Harter, J., Schmidt, F., & Hayes, T. (2002). Business-united-level relationship between employees satisfaction. *The Journal of Applied Psychology*, *87*(2), 268–279. doi:10.1037/0021-9010.87.2.268 PMID:12002955

Kahn, W. A. (1990). Psychological conditions of personal engagement and disengagement at work. *Academy of Management Journal*, *33*(4), 692–724.

Keis, K., & Javidi, M. (2014). *Deliberate leadership: Creating success through personal style*. Vancouver: CRG Publishing.

Lakshmi, K. (2012). Employee engagement- A corporate boon. 10 ways for effective engagement. *Advances in Management Journal*, *5*(2), 64–65.

Pfeiffer, W. (1994). *Basic communication model*. Pfeiffer & Company library of theories and models: management. Retrieved from, http://home.snu.edu/~jsmith/library/body/v25.pdf

Macey, W., & Schneider, B. (2008). The meaning of employee engagement. *Industrial and Organizational Psychology: Perspectives on Science and Practice*, *1*(01), 3–30. doi:10.1111/j.1754-9434.2007.0002.x

Mone, E., & London, M. (2009). *Employee engagement: Through effective performance management*. New York, NY: Taylor-Francis Group.

Normore, A. H. (2017). Prologue: Police leadership from a futurist viewpoint. In T. Anderson, K. Geisborne, & P. Halliday (Eds.), *Every officer is a leader: Coaching leadership, learning and performance in justice, public safety and security organizations* (pp. 459–464). Holly Spring, NC: International Academy of Public Safety.

Northhouse, P. (2010). *Leadership: Theory and practice* (5th ed.). Thousand Oaks, CA: Sage.

Rafi, Y. (2017). *Productivity secrets of high-performance employees at Google & Apple*. Retrieved from https://blog.taskque.com/productivity-secrets-high-performance-employees-google-apple/

Seligman, M., & Csikszentmihalyi, M. (2000). Positive psychology: An introduction. *The American Psychologist*, *55*(1), 5–14. doi:10.1037/0003-066X.55.1.5 PMID:11392865

Senge, P. (1990). *The fifth discipline: The art & practice of the learning organization*. New York, NY: Doubleday.

Tomlinson, G. (2010). Building a culture of high employee engagement. *Strategic HR Review*, *9*(3), 25–31. doi:10.1108/14754391011040046

Tully, E. (2002, May). The slippery slope. *National Executive Institute Associates, Major Cities Chiefs Association and Major County Sheriff's Association Leadership Bulletin,* 1-11.

United States Army. (2017). *Army profession and leadership policy*. Regulation 600-10. Department of the Army. Retrieved from, http://data.cape.army.mil/web/repository/doctrine/ar600-100.pdf

Van Maanen, J. (1973). *Working the street: A developmental view of police behavior*. Retrieved from https://dspace.mit.edu/bitstream/handle/1721.1/1873/SWP-0681-14451100.pdf

Waters, M. (2004). The leadership role of the first-line supervisor in police operations. *Florida Police Chief Magazine*. Retrieved from, http://www.clearwaterpolice.org/articles/waters.asp

Yulk, G., & Becker, W. (2006). Effective empowerment in organizations. *Organizational Management Journal*, *3*(3), 210–231. doi:10.1057/omj.2006.20

ADDITIONAL READING

Ellis, B., & Normore, A. H. (2015). Has the term law enforcement run its course in police agencies? *Law Enforcement Today (LET): The Law Enforcement Community.* Available [Online]: http://www.lawenforcementtoday.com

Harari, O. (2002). *The leadership secrets of Colin Powell.* New York, NY: McGraw –Hill.

Kruse, K.E. (2012). *Employee engagement 2.0: How to motivate your team for high performance (A real-world guide for busy managers).* An Amazon.com Company: CreateSpace Independent Publishing Platform

Marciano, P. T. (2010). *Carrots and sticks don't work: Build a culture of employee engagement with the principles of RESPECT*. McGraw-Hill.

Murrell, K., & Meredith, M. (2000). *Empowering employees*. New York, NY: McGraw-Hill.

Normore, A. H., Javidi, M., & Anderson, T. (2015). Developing future police leaders. *Blue Line: Canada;s National Law Enforcement Magazine*. Available [Online]: http://blueline.ca/

Normore, A. H., Javidi, M., Anderson, T., Normand, N., Scott, W., & Hoina, C. (2014). *Moral compass for law enforcement professionals*. Holly Springs, NC: International Academy of Public Safety.

Primicerio, J., & Normore, A. H. (2018). Historical context of policing and community relations: An American perspective. *Police Chief Magazine*. Retrieved from, http://www.policechiefmagazine.org/transformation-of-community-police-relations-through-history/

Starhawk (2011). *The empowerment manual: A guide for collaborative groups*. Gabriola Island, BC, Canada: New Society Publishers.

Tully, E. (1997, December). Misconduct, corruption, abuse of power-what can the chief do? *National Executive Institute Associates, Major Cities Chief's Association and Major County Sheriff's Association Leadership Bulletin,* 1-8.

Watt, R., Javidi, M., & Normore, A. H. (2015). Identifying and combatting organizational leadership toxicity. *California Peace Officer. Journal of California Law Enforcement*, *49*(2).

Werder, E. (1996, January). The great sergeant! *National Executive Institute Associates, Major Cities Chief's Association and Major County Sheriff's Association Leadership Bulletin*, 1-9.

KEY TERMS AND DEFINITIONS

Communication: The process of exchanging information, both verbal and non-verbal, within an organization. An organization may consist of employees from different parts of the society. In order to unite the activities of all employees, communication is crucial. Communicating necessary information to the entire workforce becomes necessary.

Empowerment: Sharing information, rewards, and power with employees so that they can take initiative and make decisions to solve problems and improve service and performance. Empowerment is based on the idea that giving employees skills, resources, authority, opportunity, motivation, as well holding them responsible and accountable for outcomes of their actions, will contribute to their competence and satisfaction.

Engagement: Emotional connection an employee feels toward his or her employment organization, which tends to influence his or her behaviors and level of effort in work related activities. The more engagement an employee has with his or her company, the more effort they put forth.

First-Line Police Supervisor: Produces the police departmental product/service to the citizens of the community. Usually a sergeant who accomplishes this task by having direct contact with the officers he or she supervises to ensure accountability and performance objectives. Because of the first-line supervisor's close interaction with the patrol officers, they are the key element in identifying and reducing potential misconduct incidents within police organizations.

Chapter 13
Dynamic Presence Rather Than Command Presence:
How Communicative Intelligence Influences Police/Citizen Interactions

Renée J. Mitchell
University of Cambridge, UK

Kendall Zoller
Sierra Training Associates, USA

ABSTRACT

Human beings are social animals inhabiting a world where unspoken, nonverbal body language dominates the perception of the listener. It has been shown that nonverbal behaviors effect perception more intently than verbal communication. Police-citizen interactions are a complex process where verbal and nonverbal interactions are occurring simultaneously and interpreted immediately, leading to multiple chances for misunderstanding or misinterpretation of the officer's intent. With little research on the actual techniques to create the perception of police legitimacy, the authors intend to link communicative intelligence to the verbal and physical behaviors officers should engage in to enhance procedural justice and improve police legitimacy. They posit that the citizen's perceived level of police fairness is derived from the officer's treatment of the citizen which is significantly influenced by how the officer communicates with the citizen.

INTRODUCTION

Human beings are social animals inhabiting a world where unspoken, nonverbal body language dominates the perception of the listener. It has been shown that nonverbal behaviors effect perception more intently than verbal communication (Matsumodo, Keltner, Shiota, & O'Sullivan, 2008) and increasingly so if the listener feels as though they are being misunderstood (Chan & Frey, 1992). Police-citizen interactions are a complex process where verbal and nonverbal interactions are occurring simultaneously and

DOI: 10.4018/978-1-5225-8516-9.ch013

interpreted immediately, leading to multiple chances for misunderstanding or misinterpretation of the officer's intent. Misperception of an officer's intent during a conversation can affect a civilian's view of the legitimacy of that officer or authority. Civilian perception of police behavior is an important aspect of police legitimacy, which makes the interpretation of police nonverbal behavior an important component of procedural justice and police legitimacy.

As a society, there are social norms that prescribe process and outcome in the criminal justice system, and when these are violated, we object (Tyler, 1990). Citizens encounter these processes when interacting with police officers. Officers have constitutional laws, city and state laws, and standard operating procedures of their departments that they must follow during an encounter with the public. The process that underlies a police-citizen encounter is nuanced and varied. But it is this encounter and how the officer treats the citizen that defines a citizen's sense of procedural justice. Tyler (1990) asserts that "the justice of the procedures through which outcomes are distributed and decisions made" is procedural justice. Outcomes are the result of the contact, i.e. arrest, citation, removal from the area, etc. and the decisions are the multiple determinations an officer makes throughout the contact to resolve the issue at hand. The outcomes and decisions the officer makes influence the public's perception of police legitimacy (Mazerolle, Sargeant, Cherney, Bennett, Murphy, Antrobus, & Martin, 2014) Police legitimacy is defined as the belief that police are a legitimate authority that the public will defer to and obey (Sunshine & Tyler, 2003b). Police legitimacy allows society to function smoothly. The authors assert that during this encounter, the citizen's experience with the officer defines the level of procedural justice, which in turn, creates the degree of police legitimacy.

America was founded on a citizen's right to procedural due process in regards to "life, liberty, or property". This belief was well founded in common law even before the constitution codified it in the Fifth and Fourteenth Amendments (Orth, 2003). These Amendments ensure fair treatment of an offender when charged with a legal violation. There are three essential features of due process: adequate notice, a fair hearing, and judgment based on evidence (Fogler, Konovsky, & Cropanzano, 1992). Citizens contacted by police officers over a potential violation are at the mercy of the police that they have a fair hearing and a judgment based on unbiased evidence. Officers collect evidence at the scene of the crime, take eyewitness testimony, and often provide testimony themselves. If citizens view the officer as incapable or unwilling to conduct the investigation in fair and equitable manner the citizen will view the encounter as a violation of their procedural due process or procedural justice. By definition, policing is procedural justice. The police make the initial decisions about which procedures and outcomes are distributed to the public (Tyler, 1990). All police/citizen contacts involve procedure and outcomes; thus, every police contact will involve a modicum of procedural justice.

Enforcing the law is one of the fundamental duties of a police officer. To do this an officer must make contact with a citizen and communicate the observed violation. And although they have discretion in their enforcement, they are often required to make arrests or administer citations due to policy or legal concerns. There are four aspects of a police contact that affects a citizen's perception of the police: the citizen is allowed active participation in the decision-making, the officer's decision-making is neutral and objective, the officer's motives are trustworthy, and the citizen is treated with dignity and respect (Tyler, 2004). "Quality of treatment" and the "quality of decision-making process" are the two overarching themes by which the public judges the officer's interaction (Reisig, Bratton, & Gertiz, 2007, p.1006). Whether the outcome for the citizen was positive or negative, it is the treatment by the officer that influenced the citizen's satisfaction with the police (Tyler, 1990). Restated, the outcome of the contact is less important to the citizen as the officer's decision making and the regard given to the citizen. The treatment received by the citizen shapes the citizen's perception of police legitimacy. Legitimacy, according to Tyler (1990), is "a quality possessed by an authority, a law, or an institution that leads others to feel obligated to obey its decision and directives". Legitimacy drives a citizen's willingness to obey the law.

We posit that the citizen's perceived level of police fairness is derived from the officer's treatment of the citizen which is significantly influenced by *how* the officer communicates with the citizen. Therefore, officers who enhance their communication and build rapport through the development of their communicative intelligence (CI) can have more positive perceptions of procedural justice by the citizen. CI is the integration of cognitive and emotional resources with behavioral abilities that creates experiences and develops relationships to solve problems, catalyze change, and create new meaning (Zoller, 2008). According to Zoller (2015):

CI focuses on the cognitive and emotional elements of communication. It is behaviorally demonstrated through verbal and nonverbal channels. At its foundation, CI can be used to initiate and maintain rapport. Rapport is a foundation with which to build relationships (p. 305).

Officers may not have total control over the outcome of a police/citizen contact, but they do have control over the type of treatment the citizen receives from them. A DDynamic Presence approach, which is a behavioral ability of CI, achieves this by the officer adjusting to a citizen's shifting emotional needs during a contact. Dynamic Presence rather than command presence is a skill that can be developed. Dynamic Presence supports citizen's active participation, conveys an air of neutrality, and enhances dignity and respect. Research is limited as to what actions officers should take to convey those principles, but we know the foundation of policing and procedural justice is communication (Tankebe & Liebling, 2014). One way an officer can transmit his intentions are through his verbal skills and body language. The author's assert that officers adept in Dynamic Presence have higher levels of procedural justice and police legitimacy than officers who do not possess adept communication skills. As communication skills are foundational to procedural justice and police legitimacy, the authors offer communicative intelligence as a framework to support positive police-citizen interactions. When mastered, CI supports the ability of officers to communicate with greater consciousness and strategic purpose affording them the insight to be proactive with their communicative strategies while at the same time evaluating their communicative interactions.

Communicative intelligence is a communication theory based on five capabilities: interdependence, consciousness, craftsmanship, efficacy, and flexibility (Zoller, 2015). The five capabilities were first defined by Costa and Garmston as a tool for educators using Cognitive Coaching (2002, 2015). Communication requires two people, which means we rely on other human beings when we want to communicate an idea, thereby creating interdependence. Consciousness occurs when a person is aware of their ability to influence another person with words and actions. Craftsmanship is the idea that we can master communication skills. Efficacy is the feeling that one is competent in their ability to communicate effectively. Flexibility is closely aligned to Dynamic Presence as being flexible is a key skill in adapting to another's communication style and emotional state. Zoller (2015) adapted these concepts into a communication framework - CI. The theory of CI integrates both emotional capabilities with behavioral actions to give officers skills to nimbly adjust their approach to any citizen contact. These minor adjustments within communication can influence a citizen's perception so a citizen feels as though they were treated in a neutral manner, while keeping their dignity intact and being respectfully listened to which leads to improved perceptions of police legitimacy.

Adapting the CI framework to the police officers can be summarized as: A skill that improves the relationship between the police and the community (*interdependence*) that requires the officer to have the ability to recognize the influence they wield; interactions between others' and how those interactions influence both sides (*consciousness*), having the knowledge that they can succeed (*efficacy*) by deploying an array of skills (*craftsmanship*) in an unpredictable and ever changing environment (*flexibility*) which will result in better office safety and improve the quality of the relationship with the community. CI consists of over fifty-five patterns of verbal and physical behaviors officers can use to enhance procedural justice and improve police legitimacy. The framework linking CI to police legitimacy and procedural justice is supported in the following discussion on motivation theory and communicative intelligence.

BACKGROUND

Why Is Procedural Justice Important to the Police?

There are two types of motivation - instrumental and social. Instrumental motivation comes from the outside – it is the incentives, sanctions or punishment we might receive from performing or refraining from an act (Sunshine & Tyler, 2003a). Citations and jail are two forms of instrumental motivation. People are motivated by self-interest, but when citizens are engaged in a group or community, they will begin to view the interest of the group as being aligned with their own interests (DeCremer & Tyler, 2005). Instrumental motivation will have a stronger effect if people are more motivated by self-interest. Instrumental motivation requires the sanctioning body (police) to be present, requiring the increased use of resources. Of the two types of motivation, social motivation lasts when the sanctioning authority isn't around while instrumental motivation does not (Mcluskey, 2003). If people are only instrumentally motivated, they will resume illegal activity when authorities are not around. This is true for employees and employers, civilians, and with those who enforce the law. Social motivation comes from within, it is internally centered while instrumental motivation is externally centered (Tyler, 1990). Social motivation is comprised of attitudes, values, identity, motive-based trust and procedural justice. A sense of procedural justice enlists a person's sense of community and increases the likelihood they will comply with the law.

There are three things that influence people's willingness to cooperate or obey the law: procedural fairness, legitimacy, and instrumental concerns (Tyler, 2003). When people obey the law out of concern for instrumental motivation, they weigh the risk of getting caught for a crime, the ability of the police to combat crime, and how the law is enforced in the community (Tyler, 2003). Instrumental motivation supports the theory of deterrence, that citizens are rational beings and will weigh the costs and benefits of committing crime (Nagin, 1998). Laws are an external motivator intended to deter crime. General deterrence can occur through police contact, police visibility and word of mouth about police activity on the street (Sherman, 1990). For policing to influence crime and disorder, an offender must have the perception that there is a high risk of swift and severe reaction by the police and then refrain from committing the act (Erickson, Gibbs, & Jensen, 1977). The challenge to this approach in policing is that the amount of resources necessary to create greater police visibility is expensive (Bayley, 1996). When motivation is external people tend to hide their behavior, thus resources are consumed to continuously monitor people (Tyler, 2010). The deterrent effects of increasing police resources to an area can be short lived. Often reduction in crime and social disorder is temporary and may not last longer than two hours after the appearance (Koper, 1995). The ability for a police department to allocate this high level of resources might be impossible.

Alternatives to allocating these expensive resources must be identified and social motivation may be one alternative. Because social motivation is internal it is a cheaper motivator than external. Social motivation originates from attitudes, values and beliefs about the world and our institutions (Tyler, 2010) and of the two types of motivations, social motivation lasts when the sanctioning authority is not around (McCluskey, 2003). Treating a citizen in a procedurally just manner taps into their social motivation and will have longer lasting effects on behavior than instrumental motivation. It is the internal motivation, driven by police action, that contributes to procedural justice.

Police tactical and communicative actions contribute to and define procedural justice. If the definition of procedural justice is "the justice of the procedures through which outcomes are distributed and decisions made" then by definition policing is procedural justice (Tyler, 2010, p. 42). The police officer distributes outcomes and makes decisions that affect the public. Officers can control their actions and can have influence on a citizen's perception of procedural justice. Officers can influence the public's perception of the police even when the outcome is not in favor of the citizen (Tyler, 1990). Tyler further asserts a citizen's treatment during a police contact carries slightly greater weight in their perception of an authority than the outcome of their contact. Their treatment (the process they are subjected to) matters more than the outcome that is being enforced (Tyler, 1990). This occurs because there is an unwritten social contract that an authority figure will "act in the interests of those for whom she exercises authority," that citizens can trust officers (Tyler, 1990). People will trust that even when the outcome is negative, the officer made the decision for the good of the people. Tom Tyler (2010) described it this way:

If people are allowed to present their concerns to a neutral authority, they are more likely to trust it. Further, when people feel treated with dignity and respect they are more trusting. Authorities can facilitate these beliefs by justifying their decisions in ways that make clear that they have considered the arguments raised and either can or cannot accept those arguments. It is also important for authorities to make clear that they are sincerely interested in the well-being of the parties involved – for example, through acknowledging the needs of those involved the difficulties they may be operating under, and/or their efforts to act in good faith (p. 106).

Public cooperation is imperative to an officer's ability to enforce laws. Although the public does not always cooperate most of them do. The police often need cooperation from the very people least likely to give it; those whose freedoms are about to be taken away by the authority of the officer. Cooperation from a suspect or violator is one facet to procedural justice. Another facet to cooperation is that a suspect or violator may also be a witness. This duality of identity adds complexity to the paradigm of cooperation.

People involved in crime can also be witnesses to crime. And all civilians (even suspects) are more likely to comply with a legal authority when they view the authority as legitimate. Legitimacy, according to Tyler & Huo (2002), is "a quality possessed by an authority, a law, or an institution that leads others to feel obligated to obey its decision and directives" (p. 201). When the public views the police as "legitimate", they are more willing to cooperate because they view law enforcement values as congruent with or the same as their values (Sunshine & Tyler, 2003a). When viewed as legitimate people do not renege on their agreements and still heed an officer's advice, even when the officers leave the area (Mastrofski, Snipes, & Supina 1996, p. 283). Legitimacy leads to cooperation, cooperation leads to following the law even when sanctions are not imminent, and cooperation makes the police more effective in fighting crime (National Research Council, 2004). Social motivation is the foundation of cooperation. Summarizing Sunshine & Tyler, Mastrofski et al., and National Research Council, treating citizens with dignity and respect, allowing citizens to have active participation in the decision-making process, making decisions that are neutral and objective, and ensuring the officer's motives are trustworthy are all necessary components of a procedurally just police contact. And although it is unknown which of these components is the strongest conveyor of procedural justice, communication underlies each of the four elements of procedural justice (Mazerolle et al., 2014). Thus, we suggest the mastery of CI and understanding how to engage in Dynamic Presence will strengthen all four components of procedural justice no matter which of the four is the greater predictor of police legitimacy.

THE FOUR COMPONENTS OF PROCEDURAL JUSTICE: VOICE, RESPECT AND DIGNITY, FAIR AND IMPARTIAL TREATMENT, AND NEUTRALITY

The components of procedural justice were previously mentioned, yet in this section we examine each of the elements more thoroughly. Tyler asserts Procedural Justice has four components and when these four components are fully expressed, fairness emerges (Tyler, 2004). Procedural Justice emerges from perception and communication influences perception. We assert CI can be used to influence the perceptions of PJ - the judgment one makes in reference to fairness. Fairness is an important trait to human beings. In a policing context, procedural justice is the perception of fairness when a citizen has legal contact with an authority (Tyler, 1988). Procedural justice is the "fairness of the process through which the police make decisions and exercise authority" (Sunshine & Tyler, 2003, p.514). The determination of fairness is made by the communication surrounding the legal decisions the officer makes about the individual (Tyler, 1988). There are two procedural elements citizens consider when determining fairness the quality of the decision making and the quality of the treatment in the interaction (Tyler, 2003). In game theory if a player is being treated unfairly, they will respond with vindictiveness and if treated fairly will respond in kind (Rabin, 1993). When people are shown kindness they respond in kind, when receiving hostility people will often respond with increased hostility surpassing the originator, becoming brutal at times (Fehr & Gaechter, 2000). The two procedural elements, the quality of decision making and the quality of treatment, are made up of four underlying foundational pieces; being treated with dignity and respect, having a voice in the decision-making process, being treated in a neutral manner and outcomes are fair and impartial (Mazerolle et al., 2014). When officers demonstrate behavior that support these processes, citizens view them as a legitimate authority and follow their direction. It is still unknown which of the four processes is the strongest predictor of the perception of police legitimacy (Mazerolle et al., 2014). However, there is some support that voice plays a strong role in reducing citizen noncompliance (Dai, Frank, & Sun, 2011). Additionally, whether subjects are given a voice before or after a decision is still viewed as fairer than a decision where the subject was afforded no input (Lind, Kanfer, Earley, 1990). The strongest tactic for gaining citizen cooperation was allowing a citizen to have input in the decision-making (Dai et al., 2011). The citizen also needs to believe they have been listened to and understood. Communicative Intelligence offers the Dynamic Presence skills officers can employ to increase the probability a citizen will feel listened to and understood.

HOW DOES COMMUNICATIVE INTELLIGENCE AND DYNAMIC PRESENCE RELATE TO PROCEDURAL JUSTICE?

Communicative Intelligence (Zoller, 2015) is a theory merging cognition and action when communicating. It is presented here as a way of influencing procedural justice. We call the cognitive elements of Communicative Intelligence the *5 Capabilities of CI* (modified from Costa & Garmston, 2002). They are capabilities in that they are future directed, can be developed, and contribute to the ability to think and problem solve. How do these *five capabilities* accomplish all that? To begin to make sense of these *five capabilities*, consider each a mental discipline representing a unique perspective of mental focus. Refining mental capabilities require focus on the mental processes you follow before you speak, gesture, or pause. A mental focus that has clarity increases energy and confidence when thinking and problem solving. The five capabilities of CI can be thought of as how you think about communication. If one of the capabilities is weak or missing you cannot master communication. The goal is to master communication and use it as an intelligence when making decisions and thinking critically. The five Capabilities are interdependence, consciousness, efficacy, craftsmanship, and flexibility.

The five Capabilities appear a little daunting at first glance as a way to think about communication, but when broken apart it, emerges as a strategic and attainable approach to communicating with deliberate intention. Interdependence is the ability to recognize that your verbal and non-verbal communication has a symbiotic effect on those around you. When you speak or move, people around you respond to the inflection of your voice, the movement of your hand, the direction of your gaze, and the pattern of your breathing. We are in tune with each other when we are communicating and sometimes, we are not in tune and miscommunication occurs. Being in tune is considered rapport. Rapport is part of the foundation of trust in relationships and a significant component of social intelligence (Goleman, 2006), whether the relationships are professional, interpersonal, or in this case, initiated by an officer.

Consciousness is the ability to step outside of yourself as you are speaking to see the interaction as though from a balcony. According to Costa and Garmston (2015), "the function of consciousness in humans is to represent information about what is happening outside and inside the body in such a way that it can be evaluated and acted upon by the body" (p. 117). Consciousness includes being cognizant of how your speech tones, inflections, and pauses influence those you are speaking to. Consciousness is about knowing what you know and being able to process what you see. Consciousness is not only about understanding what a person sees and hears, it is also about what to do when they see and hear what is perceived.

Efficacy is the ability to have confidence in your communication skills, to know what speech patterns to engage in to achieve the response you are looking for (Costa & Garmston, 2002, 2015). Efficacy is a belief and it "is grounded in the confidence that a person can effectively and appropriately respond and react to people when communicating" (p. 308). Efficacy is an internal drive emerging from the belief a person has about their ability to influence and positively impact a situation (Zoller, 2015). A collateral outcome of efficacy is confidence. High efficacy is a characteristic needed to be mindful and resourceful when communicating. People with "robust efficacy are likely to expend more energy in their work, persevere longer, set more challenging goals, and continue in the face of barriers or failure" (Costa & Garmston, 2002, p. 127). According to Garmston and Wellman (2015) "the main purpose of the brain is survival" (p. 110) and "efficacy is a determining factor in the resolution of complex problems" (p. 110). Survival and resolution to complex problems are foundational to policing.

Craftsmanship is the process of mastering a practice. Craftsmanship of communication is knowing what technique or speech pattern you are going to use and then having the ability to execute it. "Excellence is the soul of craftsmanship" (Costa & Garmston, 2015, p. 121). Craftsmanship in CI is the *what* of communication skills. It is driven by the desire to seek precision, refinement, and specificity when communicating (Costa & Garmston, 2015). Craftsmanship is the foundation essential to support flexibility. Craftsmanship is the driver of continuous learning, refinement, and excellence leading to mastery (Costa & Garmston, 2002). By having a variety of skills at your disposal you can execute from multiple pathways. Craftsmanship includes several elements of communication; voice tone, speech pace, voice volume, gestures, breathing, eye contact duration, points of reference, and proxemics. We trust officers high in craftsmanship because we believe they will lead us in the right direction, show us the correct way, or effectively demonstrate how something can be accomplished. Craftsmanship leads to trustworthiness. Within the framework of CI are more than 50 verbal and nonverbal patterns found in a variety of languages and cultures (Poyatos, 2002a; Zoller, 2008; Zoller & Landry, 2010).

Interdependence is the sense and awareness of community. As Costa and Garmston assert (2015), "interdependence means knowing that we will benefit from participating in and contributing to work (p. 125). Zoller (2015) posits that Interdependence is a willingness to influence and be influenced by others and it includes a desire to contribute (p. 310). The link between interdependence and procedural justice and police legitimacy is cooperation. Relationships with high levels of interdependence have high levels of cooperation (Costa & Garmston, 2015). Interdependence creates trust and people are more likely to cooperate when they trust the other person (Tyler, 2010) Established at the beginning of the chapter, social motivation is stronger than instrumental motivation (Tyler, 1990). Interdependence is deeply human; it is our drive to be connected to others and to know we are part of a larger whole. Our personal relationships bring deep levels of purpose and meaning. Our professional interdependence increases our safety, social purpose, and courage. As social beings in need of reciprocity and community, we grow and nurture relationships with others. Besides communication, the other aspect of policing officers are involved with one hundred percent of the time is the community whether it is a neighborhood, a district, a street, a precinct or a whole agency. These social facets are inter-connected through complex relationships. The healthy community is one where interdependence thrives. People are dependent on each other at various levels at different times of the day and different days of the week. To become exceptional, police officers have to understand interdependence. Citizens cooperate with law enforcement when they are socially interdependent. This cooperation is a socially motivated attribute that will continue even when a supervising entity is removed. An officer who understands interdependence will have influence on the public to obey the law (Tyler, 2010). A

Communicating using CI allows officers to actively engage in conversations with the public that support procedural justice and improve police legitimacy. Mastering the *five capabilities* allows a police officer to consciously and proactively evaluate their interactions with the community, which includes suspects. Small adjustments to an officer's behavior can improve community relations. An officer's nonverbal and verbal behavior has a direct and observable effect on another's behavior and with practice can be adjusted in milliseconds to gain a citizen's cooperation and increase the safety of a situation. This ability to consciously and deliberately make small adjustments in behavior in an instant is why mastering EVERY component of the five states capabilities is so important. Mastering the five capabilities has a direct effect on an officer's ability to interact with their community in a fair and respectful manner.

THE TRIAD: WHAT IS PROCEDURAL JUSTICE, POLICE LEGITIMACY AND COMMUNICATIVE INTELLIGENCE

To recognise always that the power of the police to fulfil their functions and duties is dependent on public approval of their existence, actions and behaviour, and on their ability to secure and maintain public respect – Robert Peel

Without legitimacy, the police could not exist. If the public does not give the police permission to monitor their behavior we would return to a feudal system. Before there were organized police departments, local constables settled matters. And even in remote tribes, the chief resolved disputes between members (Williams & McShane, 1998). Today, the United Kingdom actively promotes policing by consent. It has become part of their national agenda in line with Peelian views that unless the public approves of the police force, they will not be able to carry out their function as law enforcers. Just like beauty, police legitimacy lies in the eye of the beholder. The citizen's perception of the police officer is what determines a citizen's approval (Tyler, 1990). And the citizen's view is based on the four components of procedural justice. Figure 1 listed below visually demonstrates how the relationship between the two ideas flow.

An officer conveys due process by acting in a procedurally just manner. The elements of procedural justice are: dignity and respect, voice, fairness/impartiality and trustworthiness. We believe improving CI skills leads to officers mastering a Dynamic Presence. Dynamic Presence can provide officers with greater flexibility when communicating that increases the probability of a positive police/citizen contact. If a citizen believes that they did not receive a fair and impartial outcome from the officer/citizen contact, they will leave the interaction with a lowered perception of police legitimacy. For the citizen to perceive their interaction as procedurally just, they must feel they were an active participant in the decision-making, the decision-making was neutral and objective, the officer's motives were trustworthy, and they were treated with dignity and respect (Tyler, 2004). The only way to convey these four components of PJ is through communication or a dialogue (Tankebe & Liebling, 2013).

Figure 1.

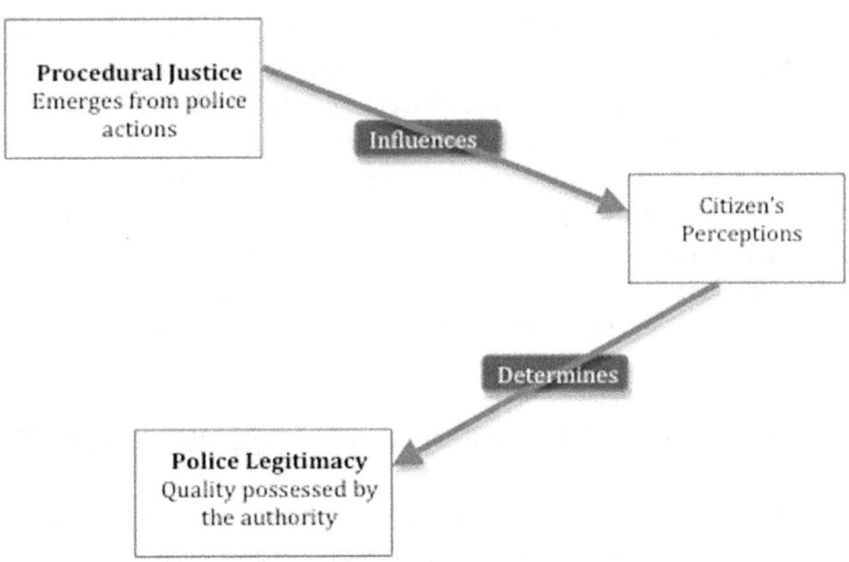

CI aims to break communication down into behaviors and patterns that can be learned and practiced to communicate exactly what is intended and to positively influence the citizen. In this case, it is important for officers to become skilled in CI as the public's perception of an individual officer's communication skills affect the public's view of the police department as a whole (Mazerolle, Antrobus, & Bennett, 2012b). Officers who are conscious of their influence on others can become a powerful force for improving police legitimacy. Officers skilled in Dynamic Presence will influence how citizens perceive a whole profession. Increased skill comes with increased responsibility and officers will have to learn *Duco pro bono publico*, Latin for Influence for the benefit of the public, or Influence for the greater good. The intent of improving Dynamic Presence skills is not to manipulate for self-serving reasons, it is to influence for the greater good to settle someone down so an officer can get information or to get someone to understand another's point of view, to calm someone who is frightened, to successfully conduct a death investigation interview with awareness of cultural and religious beliefs. Dynamic Presence is a powerful tool that when used with integrity can improve a citizen's perception of police legitimacy.

HOW PROCEDURAL JUSTICE INFLUENCES A PERSON'S WILLINGNESS TO COOPERATE?

Tyler (2004) asserts that citizens who have a positive sense of being treating fairly (high procedural justice) will cooperate. Sir Robert Peel maintained the following when establishing the first police force in 1829; "The ability of the police to perform their duties is dependent upon *public approval* of police existence, actions, behavior and the ability of the police to secure and maintain *public respect*" (Sir Robert Peel's Principles of Law Enforcement, 2015, p.1). Citizen cooperation is the goal of any police/citizen contact so encouraging and creating processes for officers that allow increased citizen cooperation should be a priority for every police department (Tyler & Huo, 2002). Research has demonstrated that people cooperate when they are treated in a procedurally just manner in both their work place and when interacting with a public official (Tyler, 2010). The perceptions of fairness citizens have of a police officer influence the citizen's reaction to the officer (Dai, et al. 2011). Citizen/police interaction begins with unequal status, an imbalance of power (Sykes & Clark, 1975). The imbalance of power requires the officer to set the tone and context for the contact to put the citizen at ease. When citizens are in a position of disadvantage, as they are during a police contact, they view procedures that favor them as more fairly than a procedure that advantages the officer (Thibaut, Walker, LaTour, & Houlden, 1973). Because the officer is in a role where he is being paid to represent the city or state, it is incumbent on him to adjust his approach to the citizen and not the other way around. The officer has control over their own behavior, not that of the citizen. If citizens perceive the officer is treating them with disrespect this affects their social identity and they will respond with treatment in kind (Dai et al., 2011). But if officers engage in respectful policing and allow the citizen to participate in decision-making the citizen will be more compliant and be more likely to follow the law even when officers are not around (Tyler, 1990).

COMMUNICATION IS THE FOUNDATION OF PROCEDURAL JUSTICE

Thus far, we have argued procedural justice is grounded in CI. Procedural legitimacy is a perception that influences cooperation (Tyler, 2010). And the common theme across these sociological frameworks is communication. Developing an officer's ability to communicate is grounded in understanding a framework of communication. CI offers the framework in both intellectual and actionable fields. Establishing an environment where the citizen feels listened to and understood requires communication strategies that engage the citizen at an emotional level. If this can be accomplished, it will result in higher levels of respect for the police and improved perceptions of police legitimacy.

Communication is not just about the words that fall from a person's mouth. It's about which words you choose, the speed at which you say them, the way you hold your head, purse your lips, and breathe. Communication ultimately is about the micro-level processes that symphonize to create meaning. If the goal of procedural justice is to make a citizen feel as though they were treated with dignity and respect and as though they had a voice in the process, then officers must understand the micro-processes that create those feelings (Tyler, 1990). The five capabilities of communicative intelligence offer a path to understanding.

Communicative intelligence and the five foundational capabilities are the foundation for procedural justice. The five capabilities provide an officer with the ability to perceive and respond to situations with greater effectiveness. The five capabilities are the tools we use to make choices and act. Unlike thinking styles, the *five capabilities* are at once innate to human processing and at the same time developmental meaning they can be learned and refined. Through the lens of police legitimacy, craftsmanship is the drive to hone a skill to perfection to ensure the citizen's and officer's safety and the citizen's perception of procedural justice. Efficacy is the knowledge and belief that the officer can overcome any obstacle. Or in the case of communication, the officer will be comfortable communicating no matter the direction the citizen takes during the conversation. Flexibility is the officer's ability to shift their approach with a citizen based on the citizen's response or participation. Consciousness is the officer's ability to understand how their emotions influence thinking and decision making when communicating – to recognize their triggers. Consciousness is also the officer's ability to recognize, name and assess what is being said by the citizen while simultaneously being able to choose the best communication technique available. Interdependence is when the officer knows how their actions contribute to the greater whole of an organization, a community, or to the public. The five capabilities create an atmosphere of procedural justice through officers understanding that effective communication requires all five capabilities to seamlessly move a citizen from a reactive emotional state to an accepting emotional state.

THE FOUR ABILITIES: THE BEHAVIORAL ELEMENTS OF COMMUNICATIVE INTELLIGENCE

The *Four Abilities* comprise the behavioral elements of the CI model. Drawing from the fields of behavioral psychology, linguistics, and biology (Kendon, 1997; McNeill, 1992; Poyatos, 2002b) the four abilities of CI define specific patterns of communication that can be used to influence communication, emotion, and perception. During active communication, the patterns of communication identified in the four abilities are not distinct and isolated. The patterns are intertwined and complex, nuanced by subtle changes in breathing, eye gaze, and speed of deployment. Communication is dynamic and complex and looks and sounds differently in each culture.

Although the deployment of a communication pattern may be culturally unique, the patterns are universal in their appearance, which makes the patterns important to learn. Some common nonverbal skills than span cultures include gesture, voice tone, and pausing (Poyatos, 2002a, 2002b; Kendon, 1997,

2004). Nonverbal communication provides context to the words we speak. What is relevant about CI in police legitimacy is that nonverbal skills provide meaning beyond the words; CI teaches officers to be aware of their communication beyond their words (Beattie & Shovelton, 1999; Bevalas, Chovil & Row, 1995; Burgoon, Byuller, Hale & deTurck, 1984; Goldin-Meadow, 1997, 1999, 2002). CI is a model that officers can use to increase their deliberate and conscious use of verbal and nonverbal skills. The four abilities of CI are comprised of verbal and nonverbal patterns of communication.

RECEPTIVITY

The important skills of receptivity are voice tone, stance, mirroring, and paraphrasing. These skills have influence on the emotional and cognitive receptivity of the listener. Furthermore, the skills of receptivity can be influential even when the message challenges a person's knowledge, abilities, values and beliefs. Receptivity is recognized by the presence of abdominal levels of breathing (Grinder, 2008). An officer can use the patterns of receptivity to attempt to increase the citizen's state of receptivity to a message.

Receptivity is enhanced by rapport. According to Zoller and Landry (2010), rapport is "a short-term psychological state in which the lines of communication are wide open" (p. xxiv). Forming relationships is dependent on the ability to develop rapport (Milgram, Dunn, & Price, 1993) and mirroring the gestures of a speaker when listening contributes to rapport (Valdesolo & DeSteno, 2011). Officers can quickly get into rapport by knowing these skills and knowing when best to use them to achieve the desired outcomes. When citizens are in rapport they are more likely to be receptive and more likely to leave the conversation with the officer with a more positive attitude. This positive attitude is a direct measure of procedural justice.

The authors taught a course on Communicative Intelligence and Procedural Justice at a large Northwestern Police Department. The officers were taught specific skills on voice, stance, gestures and how to use these behaviors to get into rapport with citizens. One of the students described a contact with an overwrought teenager and how he used the skills taught in the course to build rapport with a female student:

One of the students at the high school had brought her iPhone to school and it was stolen. She was hysterical. She was crying uncontrollably, taking in large gulps of air, and was unable to calm herself down enough to explain to the officer what had happened. The school counselor kept telling the student that she broke the rules by bringing the IPhone to school and if she would have made better decisions she wouldn't have this problem. The counselor said, "I'm sorry you lost your phone but there is nothing we can do about it now." The officer had been listening to the student talk about how her deceased grandmother's photos were on the phone. There were multiple pictures of the two of them together. The officer matched her stance and gestures stating, "So what you are really upset about is losing the photos of your grandmother." The student took a breath, wiped her eyes, and nodded her head. She continued to breathe deeply taking deep breaths to settle herself down and began telling the officer exactly what happened.

The preceding story illustrates an example of a clarifying paraphrase (Garmston & Wellman, 2013). In this story the paraphrase was used to acknowledge the specificity of the girl's emotional focus. Once she felt understood, she shifted her breathing and got into rapport with the officer.

A third component to receptivity is credibility. Credibility is the listener's perception that the speaker is worth listening to. This is important to police legitimacy because to have high levels of legitimacy, the citizen needs to believe the officer is capable of doing the job. The perception of credibility is enhanced through the use of voice tone, pausing, and stance (Poyatos, 2002; Zoller, 2008; Zoller & Landry, 2010). A narrow voice tone is perceived as more credible than a rhythmic voice tone. The pause is a naturally occurring pattern in communication. Pausing to influence credibility is best accomplished by standing still at the same time while simultaneously breathing abdominally (Zoller, 2008).

Receptivity is influenced by the patterns of rapport. People engaged in conversation are in rapport when they can be observed mirroring each other. Valdesolo & DeSteno (2011) found higher levels of receptivity when mirroring was present than when these behaviors were not evidenced. In addition to rapport, empathy contributes to procedural justice by making the citizen feel they have been heard and understood from their perspective.

EMPATHY

Empathy is a state of awareness in others where they feel they are understood contextually and emotionally. When there is empathy, trust emerges. With trust, a sense of procedural justice emerges. Empathy is dependent on effectively establishing rapport. According to Goleman (2006), what makes empathy unique from rapport is that the person being spoken to feels understood beyond their words. Goleman (1996, 2006) further asserted that empathy and rapport form the foundations of social intelligence and emotional intelligence.

When a person feels understood, they display a shift in their breathing and take more abdominal breaths and often the blood pressure and tensions lower (Grinder, 2008). An officer can create that moment by effectively paraphrasing the citizen. When the paraphrase is delivered in a way that matches the energy and meaning of what the other person initially said, empathy emerges. Tyler (2010) suggested officers need to "make clear" they are "sincerely interested" to improve legitimacy outcomes, when empathy emerges citizens will feel heard. Garmston and Wellman (1998, 2013) assert that paraphrasing is a listening skill as opposed to a language skill. The paraphrase is used to convey to the citizen they are understood by their works and also understood at an emotional level. Understanding a citizen is important when conveying that the officer has considered the citizen's argument (Tyler, 2010). When empathy is conveyed, the potential for defensiveness is reduced. With reduced defensiveness comes increasing receptivity and increased cooperation (Dai et al., 2011).

AGILITY

Agility is the ability to move quickly and easily with nimbleness. Human interactions are complex and unpredictable (Zoller, 2015). Officers with high levels of agility have flexibility and can react quickly. Consciousness and flexibility are the energy sources for agility. To be agile is to simultaneously recognize culturally specific patterns among individual's unique patterns and the influences. In policing this means an officer engaging a citizen must be able to read the nonverbal patterns of the citizen, assess the situation, and choreograph a response congruent with their intended goal. Agility requires the ability to see from the citizen's perspective. This is called the allocentric perspective (Garmston & Wellman,

2013). Being allocentric is evidenced by expressing empathy. Agility is the ability to see or respond to the unique patterns and behaviors during a citizen contact. Dynamic Presence is the ability to respond in ways that maintain receptivity and empathy with a citizen in the hopes of establishing a positive sense of procedural justice. A citizen who feels listened to and understood as well as empathized should hold high levels of police legitimacy.

DYNAMIC PRESENCE

Doyle and Strauss (1976) equate human interactions as an "impromptu, syncopated dance with unpredictable humans" (p. 89). This view is consistent with the situations officers face during citizen contacts. To navigate this state of unpredictability with Dynamic Presence an officer relies on sensory acuity and the CI patterns that support receptivity and empathy. The energy states supporting Dynamic Presence include consciousness, because consciousness is necessary to acknowledge and process incoming data, as well as craftsmanship and flexibility. To process the incoming data accurately and thoroughly the officer must go beyond the words and respond also to emotions. Dynamic Presence as opposed to command presence allows an officer to shift with a citizen's emotions rather than staying in a static with the individual. Command presence is taught in the academy, yet no approved definition of it exists in the literature. Command presence is a muddy ideology that expects an officer to control a situation through a dominate presence, using a stern voice and telling people what to do. Dynamic Presence still attempts to control volatile situations, but through matching a person's emotional energy and attempting to guide them to a successful resolution. The officer shifts into a state that is necessary for the moment.

WHY IS COMMUNICATIVE INTELLIGENCE IMPORTANT TO PROCEDURAL JUSTICE?

At the heart of procedural justice is the citizen's perception of fair treatment. We hear our young children cry out, "That's not fair" when they feel someone else is getting something better, bigger, or more valuable than they are. Fairness is a value that runs deep within all societies. Officers trained in Communicative Intelligence gain skills that allow them to be more responsive to the public's need for fairness. When treated in a procedurally just way citizens are more likely to cooperate and have improved opinions of the police officers in general (Mazerolle, Bennett, Antrobus, & Eggins, 2012a; Tyler, 2010). Suspects recidivate less in domestic violence situations when treated in a procedurally just manner (Paternoster, Brame, Bachman, & Sherman, 1997). These two areas alone, cooperation and reduction of spousal assault are reasons enough for officers to be trained in specific behaviors that improve a citizen's perception of the police.

HOW DOES COMMUNICATIVE INTELLIGENCE INFLUENCE PROCEDURAL JUSTICE?

The skills of CI are the undercurrent of human communication. Just as a river can look smooth and slow moving on the surface but have fast moving eddies of water that can pull you to your death, so too with communication. It looks smooth on the surface unless you are trained to observe the undercurrent of communication. CI skills give officers this tool. Citizens want to be treated in a procedurally just way by any person or institution that has power over them (Tyler, 2010). When they are not treated in this manner they become angry and/or frustrated and may lash out (Dai et al., 2011). CI teaches skills that when used properly can assist a citizen in becoming more receptive to a negative outcome (Engel, 2005). Officers generally are called when something is not going well. Through CI officers can influence how the citizen views the outcome. By using receptivity, empathy, and Dynamic Presence in an agile manner the officer can create an atmosphere of procedural justice.

HOW CAN POLICE OFFICERS USE COMMUNICATIVE INTELLIGENCE?

Officers respond to a variety of situations that can change in a moment's notice. Officers need skills that allow them to shift rapidly from one approach to another, from one weapon to another, from one verbal tactic to another. The nature of policing requires an officer to have the agility and Dynamic Presence to shift in the moment to a new approach. Officers develop these skills anecdotally by their fifth year on the street. They pick up cues from other officers or citizens and create micro-adjustments to their communication techniques over time. Often officers that are good with the citizens cannot articulate what it is they do that puts a citizen at ease, they just know that it comes naturally and easily to them. CI training develops the vocabulary of the officer, so they can teach others how to get a citizen to relax and become receptive. Additionally, CI training can decrease the amount of time a new officer takes to become adept at speaking to people during tense situations. CI skills allow officers the awareness of what it is about their body language that is either increasing a citizen's receptivity to direction or decreasing it. By being aware of which skills they are engaging and the reaction of the citizen the officer will be more adept at consciously choosing which techniques to engage in with different types of citizens.

PROCEDURAL JUSTICE + COMMUNICATIVE INTELLIGENCE = POLICE LEGITIMACY

Police legitimacy is in the eye of the beholder. Legitimacy is a quality held by an authority that determines whether a citizen will obey its decisions and directions (Tyler, 2006). The citizen's perception of legitimacy is influenced by their sense of procedural justice. When citizens feel as though they have been treated impartially, respectfully, fairly, and were listened to, they will acquiesce to the decisions and directions of the police (Tyler, 2010). CI allows officers to choose which skills they will employ when trying to build rapport with a citizen, when trying to show empathy, and when breaking rapport in a gentle manner. Understanding the components of procedural justice and the skills of CI allow officers to determine what level of legitimacy a citizen walks away with. Without both sets of skills, officers will continue to use trial and error to learn communication skills that work on the street.

HOW DOES COMMUNICATIVE INTELLIGENCE IMPACT THE PUBLIC?

Police decisions impact people's lives on a daily basis. Police officers have been imbued with the power to seize property, seize people, and take lives. The communication that is exchanged before any of these measures are taken are imperative to the outcome of those situations. Giving officers tangible skills that can be practiced and measured is a significant step towards creating a more procedurally just approach to police/citizen contacts. Improving perceptions of police legitimacy can lead to lower incidents in use of force (Dai et al, 2011). Officers often escalate situations when citizen's first communication is one of disrespect and vice versa, citizens will escalate if an officer's first communication is one of disrespect (Dai et al., 2011). When someone feels disrespected it diminishes their social identity and they react to feeling "less than" by showing they cannot be coerced (Dai et al., 2011). When officers are aware of CI, they can make conscientious decisions about how their first communication will be made. They can consciously decide to be approachable or credible, whether to build or break rapport. CI allows officers to influence a situation to maintain officer safety. Additionally, CI allows officers to reduce the stress of the police/citizen interactions for both the officer and the citizen. By maintaining a Dynamic Presence officers can consciously keep both themselves and the citizen in a receptive state. Remaining in a receptive state allows citizens to feel understood and heard, to remain calm in the face of adversity and to walk away from a situation feeling as though they received the best outcome possible.

SOME OF THE CURRENT BARRIERS TO INTRODUCING POLICE TO COMMUNICATIVE INTELLIGENCE: COMMAND PRESENCE VERSUS DYNAMIC PRESENCE

Command presence is a concept without a universal definition. The term is discussed in the academy from the first day as a recruit and as a trainee out in the field, but the definition is a vague combination of body language, voice projection, and professionalism. Chief Ron Richards described command presence in *Command presence: Feeding your own self confidence* as, "essentially presenting yourself as someone in authority, trusted and respected" (Richards, August, 2015). He goes on to say that you need to walk with intent and your head up, project an air of "I am in charge of the situation", speak clearly, groom yourself neatly and behave professionally to project command presence. Command presence is challenging to measure because it is subjective. How do you walk with intent? What projects an air of being in charge? It is a concept without a concrete set of behaviors that can be taught and then measured.

Dynamic Presence on the other hand is based on patterns of CI. These patterns can be taught and measured in the field when officers are in training. They can be reinforced. Dynamic Presence teaches that an officer can control a situation by influencing the officer/citizen interaction through rapport and empathy rather than coercive means. Dynamic Presence feels more like respectful negotiation between an authority and a citizen rather than a forceful directive. CI is tangible whereas command presence is ambiguous. Officers, when dealing with divergent situations multiple times a day, need skills they can practice and then artfully master to deal with the ever-changing society around them. These skills include pausing, gaining rapport, matching and mirroring the nonverbal and verbal signals of the citizen they are talking to. Perhaps the most important skill is paraphrasing.

Paraphrasing is a listening skill as Costa and Garmston assert. The challenge for officers is that they are proficient at summarizing what a citizen says and in many cases the officer feels this is evidence of listening. Summarizing is evidence of the literal message. Summarizing is not evidence of listening beyond the words. The paraphrase is the communication skill that when done effectively acknowledges the meaning of communication beyond the words.

The structure of effective paraphrases contains the language, "you" and not "I". Then a person responds by saying, "If I understand you correctly…" it is about the listener. When a person responds by saying, "For you…" it is about the speaker. When a person feels they have been listened to and understood the listener gains a level of permission that was not previously present. By permission, we mean the speaker is in a psychological state where they are more likely to provide additional information and feel a greater sense of trust (Costa & Garmston, 2002).

The following story describes the interactions between a citizen and two officers. The story provides an example of the influence of paraphrasing on the perception of being understood.

During a class given by Mitchell and Zoller a police student described an attempt to build rapport with a distressed women. He was assisting another officer, as a cover officer, on a disturbance call. The contact officer was speaking with an angry woman when the cover officer arrived on scene. The woman was breathing high, pacing, and yelling at the officers. She told the officer she allowed friends of hers to move into her house. She described how they were now taking advantage of her kindness, not paying rent, staying up late, and eating all of her food. She spoke loudly and quickly. Her breathing is high in the chest. She told the officer, "I want them out of my house!"

The contact officer told the woman, I understand you are upset but there is nothing we can do. We cannot throw the tenants out of your house. You have to give them a thirty-day notice." She then began screaming and yelling profanities at the officer ending the rant with "You are worthless!"

The contact officer kept saying, "Calm down ma'am, just calm down" to no avail. Each time the officer said to calm down, she became more agitated and loud. A second officer decided to try and build rapport with her, based on the training from the class he was experiencing. His goal was to get her to shift her emotion to a lower energy state so she was more receptive to police direction. He thought about her fear, frustration, and disappointment and in a voice volume that matched hers as well as gestures that mirrored her, he said, "You are so frustrated right now. Your friends have taken advantage of you and when you call the very people who are supposed to help you, the police, you find out that we can't even help you." She stopped pacing, turned to the officer, taking a deep breath, she snarled with a significant decrease in volume, "That's right mutha fucka!"

The officer mirrored and paced her to get her to become open to police direction. And although this was not a conventional reaction she did shift emotionally for the officer and began to listen.

FUTURE RESEARCH

The current literature articulates what procedural justice is and how engaging in procedural justice practices improve the public's perception of police legitimacy. Researchers are still uncertain on which components of procedural justice are the strongest indicators of police legitimacy (Mazerolle et al., 2014). We do not have a clear understanding of whether respect and dignity influences police legitimacy more strongly than having a voice. We also do not understand what components of an officer's actions influence the public's perception. Dai & Sun (2011) demonstrated that "disrespect" by an officer leads to disrespectful behavior by a citizen. It still needs to be determined what conveys "disrespect" to a citizen; is it the tone an officer takes, a look of contempt, the words the officer uses, or does social status create a skewed lens from which the citizen views the officer.

Communicative Intelligence and specifically Dynamic Presence accord the officer's skill sets to learn, practice, and master. Training in communicative intelligence allows an officer to become agile in the reciprocal exchange that occurs between officers and citizens. Having specific skills to measure allows for definitive research to take place on whether the patterns have influence on a citizen's perception. Engel (2005) demonstrated that citizen's perceptions change based on whether they receive a traffic citation or not. Studies like this make evident the possibility that research can be designed to test the effectiveness of CI patterns on the public's perception.

CONCLUSION

Police attitudes and behaviors are at the forefront of a negative national conversation about policing. Police are given relatively little training on communication when compared to shooting, arresting, and driving techniques. Communication training when taught is often explained within a control framework. It teaches officer how to use command presence to control people and to use communication techniques that benefit the officer over the citizen. Communicative Intelligence afford officers the opportunity to learn specific patterns of behavior to influence a citizen's attitude and behavior in a subtle way that supports police legitimacy. Training officers in Dynamic Presence to create rapport within the framework of procedural justice offers a flexibility that tactical communication techniques do not. Communicative Intelligence as a police practice is an approach that needs greater development and study.

REFERENCES

Bavelas, J. B., Chovil, N., & Roe, L. (1995). Gestures specialized for dialogue. *Personality and Social Psychology, 21*(4), 394–405. doi:. doi:10.1177/0146167295214010

Bayley, D. H. (1996). *Police for the Future*. Oxford, UK: Oxford University Press.

Beattie, G., & Shovelton, H. (1999). Iconic hand gestures that accompany spontaneous speech. *Journal of Language and Social Psychology, 18*(4), 438–463. doi:10.1177/0261927X99018004005

Burgoon, J. K., Byuller, D. B., Hale, J. L., & deTurck, M. A. (1984). Relational message associated with nonverbal behaviors. *Human Communication Research, 10*(3), 351–378. doi:10.1111/j.1468-2958.1984.tb00023.x

Costa, A. L., & Garmston, R. J. (2002). *Cognitive coaching: A foundation for renaissance schools.* Norwood, MA: Christopher-Gordon.

Costa, A. L., & Garmston, R. J. (2015). *Cognitive coaching: Developing self-directed learners and leaders.* Lanham, MD: The Rowan & Littlefield Publishing Group, Inc.

Dai, D., Frank, J., & Sun, I. (2011). Procedural justice during police-citizen encounters: The effects of process-based policing on citizen compliance and demeanor. *Journal of Criminal Justice, 39*(2), 159–168. doi:10.1016/j.jcrimjus.2011.01.004

De Cremer, D., & Tyler, T. R. (2005). Managing group behavior: The interplay between procedural justice, sense of self, and cooperation. *Advances in Experimental Social Psychology, 37*, 151–218. doi:10.1016/S0065-2601(05)37003-1

Doyle, M., & Straus, D. (1976). *How to make meetings work.* New York, NY: Berkeley Publishing Group.

Engel, R. S. (2005). Citizens' perceptions of distributive and procedural injustice during traffic stops with police. *Journal of Research in Crime and Delinquency, 42*(4), 445–481. doi:10.1177/0022427804272725

Erickson, M. L., Gibbs, J. P., & Jensen, G. F. (1977). The deterrence doctrine and the perceived certainty of legal punishments. *American Sociological Review, 42*(2), 305–317. doi:10.2307/2094607 PMID:860865

Fehr, E. & Gaechter, S. (2000). *Fairness and Retaliation: The economics of reciprocity.* Academic Press.

Folger, R., Konovsky, M. A., & Cropanzano, R. (1992). A due process metaphor for performance appraisal. *Research in Organizational Behavior, 14*, 129–129.

Garmston, R., & Wellman, B. (1998). *The adaptive schools sourcebook.* Norwood, MA: Christopher-Gordon.

Garmston, R., & Wellman, B. (2013). *The adaptive schools sourcebook.* Lanham, MD: Rowman & Litchfield Publishers, Inc.

Goldin-Meadow, S. (1997). When gestures and words speak differently. *Current Directions in Psychological Science, 6*(5), 138–143. doi:10.1111/1467-8721.ep10772905

Goldin-Meadow, S. (2002). *Hearing gestures: How our hands help us think.* Cambridge, MA: Belknap Press.

Goldin-Meadow, S., Kim, S., & Singer, M. (1999). What the teacher's hands tell the student's mind about math. *Journal of Educational Psychology, 91*(4), 720–730. doi:10.1037/0022-0663.91.4.720

Goleman, D. (1996). *Emotional intelligence.* New York, NY: Bantam Books.

Goleman, D. (2006). *Social intelligence.* New York, NY: Bantam Books.

Grinder, M. (2008). *The elusive obvious.* Battle Ground, WA: Michael Grinder and Associates.

Kendon, A. (1997). Gesture. *American Review of Anthropology*, *26*, 109–128.

Kendon, A. (2004). *Gesture: Visible action as utterance*. Cambridge, UK: Cambridge University Press; doi:10.1017/CBO9780511807572

Koper, C. S. (1995). Just enough police presence: Reducing crime and disorderly behavior by optimizing patrol time in crime hot spots. *Justice Quarterly*, *12*(4), 649–672. doi:10.1080/07418829500096231

Lind, E. A., Kanfer, R., & Earley, P. C. (1990). Voice, control, and procedural justice: Instrumental and noninstrumental concerns in fairness judgments. *Journal of Personality and Social Psychology*, *59*(5), 952–959. doi:10.1037/0022-3514.59.5.952

Mastrofski, S. D., Snipes, J. B., & Supina, A. E. (1996). Compliance on demand: The public's response to specific police requests. *Journal of Research in Crime and Delinquency*, *33*(3), 269–305. doi:10.1177/0022427896033003001

Matsumoto, D., Keltner, D., Shiota, M. N., & O'Sullivan, F. M. (2008). Facial expressions of emotion. Handbook of emotions, 211-234.

Mazerolle, L., Antrobus, E., Bennett, S., & Tyler, T. R. (2012b). Shaping citizens perceptions of police legitimacy: A randomized field trial of procedural justice. *Criminology*, *51*(1), 33–64. doi:10.1111/j.1745-9125.2012.00289.x

Mazerolle, L., Bennett, S., Antrobus, E., & Eggins, E. (2012a). Procedural Justice, routine encounters, and citizen perceptions of police: Main findings from the Queensland Community Engagement Trial (QCET). *Journal of Experimental Criminology*, *8*(4), 343–367. doi:10.100711292-012-9160-1

Mazerolle, L., Sargeant, E., Cherney, A., Bennett, S., & Murphy, K. (2014). Procedural Justice and Police Legitimacy in Policing. Academic Press.

McCluskey, J. D. (2003). *Police requests for compliance: Coercive and procedurally just tactics*. LFB Scholarly Pub.

McNeill, D. (1992). Hand and mind: What gestures reveal about thought (1st ed.). Chicago, IL: Chicago University Press.

Milgram, R. M., Dunn, R., & Price, G. E. (Eds.). (1993). *Teaching and counseling gifted and talented adolescents: An international learning style perspective*. Westport, CT: Praeger.

Nagin, D. S. (1998). Criminal deterrence research at the outset of the twenty-first century. *Crime and Justice*, *23*, 1–42. doi:10.1086/449268

Orth, J. V. (2003). *Due process of law: A brief history*. University Press of Kansas.

Paternoster, R., Brame, R., Bachman, R., & Sherman, L. W. (1997). Do fair procedures matter? The effect of procedural justice on spouse assault. *Law & Society Review*, *31*(1), 163–204. doi:10.2307/3054098

Poyatos, F. (2002a). *Nonverbal communication across disciplines* (Vol. 1). Philadelphia, PA: John Benjamins.

Poyatos, F. (2002b). *Nonverbal communication across disciplines. Paralanguage, kinesics, si- lence, personal and environmental interaction* (Vol. 2). Philadelphia, PA: John Benjamins. doi:10.1075/z.ncad2

Rabin, M. (1993). Incorporating fairness into game theory and economics. *The American Economic Review*, 1281–1302.

Reisig, M. D., Bratton, J., & Gertiz, M. G. (2007). The construct validity and refinement of process-based policing measures. *Criminal Justice and Behavior, 34*(8), 1005–1028. doi:10.1177/0093854807301275

Richards, R. (n.d.). *Command presence: Feeding your own self confidence.* Retrieved from the internet August 30, 2015, http://www.withthecommand.com/2004-May/PA-Richards-commandpresence.html

Sherman, L. W. (1990). Police crackdowns: Initial and residual deterrence. *Crime and Justice, 12*, 1–48. doi:10.1086/449163

Sir Robert Peel's Principles of Law Enforcement. (n.d.). Retrieved on October 12, 2015 from https://www.durham.police.uk/AboutUs/Documents/Peels_Principles_Of_Law_Enforcement.pdf

Sunshine, J., & Tyler, T. (2003a). Moral solidarity, identification with the community, and the importance of procedural justice: The police as prototypical representatives of a group's moral values. *Social Psychology Quarterly, 66*(2), 153–165. doi:10.2307/1519845

Sunshine, J., & Tyler, T. R. (2003b). The role of procedural justice and legitimacy in shaping public support in policing. *Law & Society Review, 37*(3), 513–548. doi:10.1111/1540-5893.3703002

Sykes, R. E., & Clark, J. P. (1975). A theory of deference exchange in police-civilian encounters. *American Journal of Sociology, 81*(3), 584–600. doi:10.1086/226109

Tankebe, J., & Liebling, A. (2013). *Legitimacy and criminal justice: An international exploration*. OUP Oxford. doi:10.1093/acprof:oso/9780198701996.001.0001

Thibaut, J., Walker, L., LaTour, S., & Houlden, P. (1973). Procedural justice as fairness. *Stanford Law Review, 26*(6), 1271. doi:10.2307/1227990

Tyler, T. R. (1988). What is procedural justice?: Criteria used by citizens to assess the fairness of legal procedures. *Law & Society Review, 22*(1), 103–135. doi:10.2307/3053563

Tyler, T. R. (1990). *Why people obey the law*. Princeton University Press.

Tyler, T. R. (2003). Procedural justice, legitimacy, and the effective rule of law. In M. Tonry (Ed.), *Crime and justice: A review of research* (Vol. 30, pp. 431–505). Chicago: University of Chicago Press.

Tyler, T. R. (2004). Enhancing police legitimacy. *The Annals of the American Academy of Political and Social Science, 593*(1), 84–99. doi:10.1177/0002716203262627

Tyler, T. R. (2010). *Why people cooperate: The role of social motivations*. Princeton University Press. doi:10.1515/9781400836666

Tyler, T. R., & Huo, Y. (2002). *Trust in the law: encouraging public cooperation with the police and courts through*. Russell Sage Foundation.

Valdesolo, P., & DeSteno, D. (2011). Synchrony and the social tuning of compassion. *Emotion (Washington, D.C.)*, *11*(2), 262–266. doi:10.1037/a0021302 PMID:21500895

Williams, F. P., & McShane, M. D. (1998). Criminology Theory: Selected Classic Readings (2nd ed.). Cincinnati, OH: Anderson Publishing Co.

Zoller, K. (2008). Nonverbal patterns of teachers from 5 countries: Results from the TIMSS-R video study. *Dissertation Abstracts International. A, The Humanities and Social Sciences*, *68*(9-A), 154.

Zoller, K. (2015). The Philosophy of Communicative Intelligence. In Cross-Cultural Collaboration and Leadership in Modern Organizations. IGI Global.

Zoller, K., & Landry, C. (2010). *The choreography of presenting: the 7 essential abilities of effective presenters*. Thousand Oaks, CA: Corwin Press.

KEY TERMS AND DEFINITIONS

Command Presence: Essentially presenting yourself as someone in authority, trusted and respected.

Communicative Intelligence: The integration of cognitive and emotional resources with behavioral abilities that creates experiences and develops relationships to solve problems, catalyze change, and create new meaning.

Consciousness: The ability to step outside of yourself as you are speaking to see the interaction as though from a balcony.

Craftsmanship: Is the repertoire of skills of communication, knowing what technique or speech pattern you are going to use and then having the ability to execute it.

Efficacy: The ability to have confidence in your communication skills, to know what speech patterns to engage in to achieve the response you are looking for.

Police Legitimacy: A psychological property of an authority, institution, or social arrangement that leads those connected to it to believe that it is appropriate, proper, and just.

Procedural Justice: The justice of the procedures through which outcomes are distributed and decisions made.

Section 4

Strategies for Improved Communication

Chapter 14
Mobile Communication in Hospitals:
Problems, Possibilities, and Solutions

Terje Solvoll
University Hospital of North Norway, Norway

ABSTRACT

Mobile communication for healthcare workers is a critical part of hospitals infrastructure. Many of these systems do not work well together, leading to difficulties regarding multiple communication devices with different usage area, unavailable or missing equipment, and alarm fatigue. Physicians and nurses often need information fast, and any delay between the decision and the action taken could cause medical errors. One suggested solution for this problem is to implement wireless phone systems. However, psychological theory and empirical evidence, both suggest that wireless phones have the potential of creating additional problems related to interruptions. The fact that hospital workers prefer interruptive communication methods before non-interruptive methods, amplifies the risk of overloading staff. The key is how to handle the balance between increased availability and increased interruptions. In this chapter, the authors present solutions and possibilities based on context aware communication systems that aim to reduce interruptions and thereby also alarm fatigue.

INTRODUCTION

Mobile communication for health care workers are a critical part of today's hospital infrastructure. Unfortunately, many of these systems do not work well together, leading to difficulties regarding, multiple electronic communication devices with different usage area, which they have to carry around during their shift, unavailable or missing equipment at the hospital, and alarm fatigue. The work setting in hospitals is communication intensive and can lead to significant difficulties also related to interruptions from co-workers and alarm fatigue. Physicians and nurses often need information fast, and any delay between the decision made and the action taken could cause medical errors. Nurses in, at least Norwegian hospitals, are handling patients' alarms (bed and toilet alarms) through pagers, which is a one-to-many relationship

DOI: 10.4018/978-1-5225-8516-9.ch014

network where pagers are subscribing to alarm information, and alarm signals are broadcasted to every pager associated with a department (Solvoll, T., et al., 2017). As a consequence of unnecessary interruptions, this solution is a known source for alarm fatigue. We also know from earlier studies within health care that physicians in hospitals are interrupted unnecessary by mobile devices in situations where such interruptions should be avoided (Scholl, Hasvold, Henriksen, & Ellingsen, 2007; T. Solvoll & Scholl, 2008; Terje Solvoll, Scholl, & Hartvigsen, 2010, 2013). Unnecessary interruptions can cause concentration difficulties and disturb the activity performed (Hersh et al., 2002). Unwanted interruptions should be minimized in order to avoid distraction that can lead to intolerable action or decisions, especially during surgery, patient examinations and medication. This is a problem in today's hospital settings, and a solution to reduce such unnecessary interruptions from mobile devices is needed and wanted (T. Botsis, T. Solvoll, J. Scholl, P. Hasvold, & G. Hartvigsen, 2007; Scholl, et al., 2007; T. Solvoll & Scholl, 2008; Terje Solvoll, et al., 2013). A lot of research has been done within this area, and solutions has been suggested, which include possibilities to solve other problems in hospital settings. Some of this work will be presented in the next sections, but we cannot see that the situation has changed too much lately. In this chapter, which is an update of the earlier chapter (Solvoll, T., 2013) and (Solvoll, T., 2016), we will present some earlier work on context sensitive systems for mobile communication in hospitals (internal communication systems, not including public networks (GSM/2G/3G/4G/5G)) that aims to improve the communication situation, reduce interruptions, but at the same time include smartphone functionality and 3 party applications.

BACKGROUND

Physicians' and health care workers in general working conditions rely on mobility. They move frequently between in-patient ward, out-patient ward, emergency ward, operating theatres, etc., and often do not stay more than a few minutes in the same location. High mobility requires mobile communication systems, which enables physicians' and nurses to communicate with colleges at any time and place, to avoid any delay between the decision made and action taken. Such delays could result in medical errors (Hersh, et al., 2002), and mobile communication systems have been suggested as a solution to improve communication in hospitals (Coiera & Tombs, 1998). The challenge when deploying mobile communication systems is to handle the balance between the increased availability and possible interruptions (Scholl, et al., 2007; T. Solvoll & Scholl, 2008; Terje Solvoll, et al., 2010, 2013). Most hospitals still rely on a mobile communication infrastructure with dedicated devices for each role, where pagers still are the most dominant mobile communication device.

Pagers provide a cheap and reliable way for contacting staff. They are ubiquitous and several physicians carry numerous pagers simultaneously to cover the various work roles they have been assigned. Pagers suffer from a number of problems due to their simplicity. The most obvious limitation is that it requires the staff to locate a telephone (landline or wireless) in order to respond to a page. This might cause unnecessary delays and communication overhead, since the person placing the page is not always near the phone when the page is returned (Spurck, Mohr, Seroka, & Stoner, 1995). Pagers also create a large amount of unnecessary interruptions (Blum & Lieu, 1992; Katz & Schroeder, 1988), which is unpleasant and can cause medical errors (Hersh, et al., 2002).

Currently, a common way to handle bed and toilet alarms, at least in Norwegian hospitals, is a one-to-many relationship network where pagers are subscribing to alarm information, and alarm signals are broadcasted to every pager associated with a department. The nurses at the department have to pick up their pager, look at the room and bed information and remember if the care of this patient is their responsibility. Finally, to turn off the alarm, the nurse have to push a button inside the room of the patient. In a small hospital department, more precisely the Oncology department at the University hospital of North Norway the alarm bells ring up to as much as 2800 times during a one week period (Solvoll, T., et al., 2017). Most of these alarms are related to patients asking for small favors, like opening a window, saying that they are ready to take their medicine, ask for a glass of water and similar. Even though many of these messages are meant for a specific nurse, and also quite frequently not are time sensitive, signals are sent to everyone using a pager within the department, making pagers ring quite frequently. Moreover, alarms are interruptive by nature, and they are designed to catch the attention of the receiver. Furthermore, several patients explained that they get stressed of continuous alarm rings, because they feel like the nurse that visits them is needed somewhere else. It is clear that desensitization to alarm signals is a serious concern in hospital environments (Mitka, M., 2013), and multiple nurses have told us that after being at work for a while, they no longer hear their pager. Sound produced by pagers are considered background noise, and their way to check for running alarms is to make it a habit to often check the pager display. Another nurse continued and said that blocking and ignoring the sounds, quote: "is the only way to get something done, and not constantly lose focus" (Solvoll, T., et al., 2017).

Alarm fatigue appears when someone has been surrounded by a high frequency of alarms throughout a substantial period of time. These alarms are very interruptive in their behavior, and as such our human body desensitize our perception of these particular sounds and light signals, making us less aware of them. Studies like (Weigl, M., et. al., 2012) try to prevent alarm fatigue by reducing false positives. They accomplish this by customizing some settings to levels that are less likely to trigger an alarm, while they are still ensuring safety for the patient.

While the Advanced Safety in Medical Technology (ANSI/AAMI/IEC 60601-1-8 standard) suggests three severity levels for alarms:

- **High**: Requires immediate response from hospital staff, and where it is assumed that delayed reaction will result in injury or death in the interval from seconds to a couple of minutes,
- **Medium**: Requires prompt response from hospital staff, where it is assumed that delayed reaction will result in injury or death if not attended within "several to many" minutes, and
- **Low**: Requires awareness of clinicians, no acute danger.

It is argued by (Block, F. E., 3rd, & Block, F. E., Jr., 2016) that some committees do not recognize that not all alarms generated from equipment should have the maximum priority level. They continue with the claim that clinicians control their own workflow and that there are no human or electronic system that sets priority levels to different work tasks. Hence, health care personnel are responsible to undertake additional work and weave it into their already tight schedule. They conclude with a clarification of the already stated severity levels for alarm:

- **High**: Requires an interruption in the caregiver's current workflow
- **Medium**: Requires replanning of the caregiver's current workflow
- **Low**: Requires planning of the caregiver's current workflow

According to Lipschultz, A. (2014), a forthcoming book by Frank Block, one of the authors of (Block, F. E., 3rd, & Block, F. E., Jr., 2016), claims that broadcasting of alarms will be replaced by systems that designate alarms to individual caregivers, resulting in a drastic decrease in interruptions caused by alarms. Today however, most middleware platforms available provides these types of functionality:

- Only create sound when it is high priority
- That are distinct, vocal and explanatory
- Notify the caregiver in a reasonable time
- Notify the caregiver on urgency

However, the most intuitive solution to improve the communication situation in hospitals is to provide physicians with wireless phones. However, phones can be even more interruptive than pagers (Scholl, et al., 2007; T. Solvoll & Scholl, 2008; Terje Solvoll, et al., 2010, 2013). In (Scholl, et al., 2007) a physician states that; "with a pager you just have to glance down at your coat pocket to see who is paging, while with a phone, you have to pick it up from your pocket to see who is calling. Having done that, it is easier just answering and explaining that you are busy" (T. Solvoll & Scholl, 2008). However, today the trend is that healthcare workers also bring their own private mobile phone to work. The device is sometimes used for contacting other health care workers, or to answer a page, but at the same time also for medical applications, i.e. Medical references and so on.

Preliminary studies points at a diversity of potential benefits from wireless phones in hospital settings, using both mobile text and voice services (Acuff, Fagan, Rindfleisch, Levitt, & Ford, 1997; Eisenstadt et al., 1998; Minnick, Pischke-Winn, & Sterk, 1994 ; Spurck, et al., 1995). Even though these studies are quite old, they reveal potential technological limitations that is still relevant today and can explain some of the challenges of gaining acceptance. Text-chat is a less obtrusive medium than other forms of workplace communication (Bradner, Kellogg, & Erickson, 1999). It is therefore unlikely that mobile text-messaging creates the same amount of interruptions as mobile voice services. Improved asynchronous communication systems have in fact been recommended for improving hospital communication practices as early as 1998 (Coiera & Tombs, 1998). In addition to mobile synchronous communication systems, mobile text-messaging systems are therefore an interesting medium to explore in hospitals settings.

However, the current generation of mobile-text messaging systems (secure systems) seems ill suited for hospital environments. Early studies of mobile text-messaging usage in hospitals have revealed difficulties related to small screen size (Eisenstadt, et al., 1998), and problems related to forcing doctors to carrying an additional device (Acuff, et al., 1997). It has to be taken into account that these studies are some years old. Today displays and keyboards are significantly improved, which might have changed the situation. A continual problem with mobile text messaging is that senders often need an acknowledgement that an asynchronous message has been read by the receiver (Coiera & Tombs, 1998). This is still not the case for secure systems used in hospitals. The acknowledgement challenge could be solved by a forced feedback when the message has been opened. Actually, there are several commercial messaging systems available for private use today that offers feedback if a message has been delivered and opened. The question is if these systems are suitable for hospital use? Another solution that may ease the difficulties with text messaging, is automatic suggestions for replies. It has been reported that predefined messages can meet up to 90% of the mobile text-messaging needs for some hospital workers (Jakob E. Bardram & Hansen, 2004).

Mobile communication systems for hospitals, is still an important research area since hospitals are noted to suffer from poor communication practices. The combination of wireless phones and fact that hospital workers prefer interruptive communication methods before non-interruptive methods (Blum & Lieu, 1992; Coiera & Tombs, 1998; Katz & Schroeder, 1988) and often exhibit "selfish" interruptive communication practices, may result in unnecessary interruptions for conversations that otherwise would' not occur (Parker & Coiera, 2000). This amplifies the risk of overloading limited resources with special knowledge, experience, and the power of taking medical decisions. The balance between getting immediate access to resources and causing interruptions in moments where it is not appropriate, has similarities with the classical problems regarding collaboration and sharing of resources, such as of disparity in work and benefit, "prisoner's dilemma" and "the tragedy of the commons" (Grudin, 1994). A critical issue for voice services is the potential of make people "fatally available" (Spurck, et al., 1995), which cannot be overlooked, since health care is a knowledge intensive activity where consulting colleagues or senior staff members is a necessity in many situations (Coiera, 2000). One way of attacking this problem is to provide the caller with context information from the receiver's situation. Context information could be any kind of information which helps to decide if the receiver is available or not, such as; location, activity, surrounding noise, role, etc. In a study by (Avrahami, Gergle, Hudson, & Kiesler, 2007) they revealed that if the caller is provided with context information about the receiver's situation, it reduces the mismatch between the caller's decision and the receiver's desires.

To address the conflict between physicians' and nurses' needs for mobile communication, the interruptions from mobile devices in hospitals and alarm fatigue, we have been looking at context sensitive (also called context aware) systems for mobile communication first in general and then in hospital settings. A number of studies have focused on context-sensitive systems for hospitals; however, a lot of this work has focused on scopes not covered by this chapter, including issues related to mobile learning and privacy, accessing clinical data, or on multimedia communication at terminals with fixed locations (Mitchell, Spiteri, Bates, & Coulouris, 2000).

CONTEXT SENSITIVE COMMUNICATION SYSTEMS

There have been many suggestions on how to reduce interruptions from mobile devices during the years. In this chapter we will focus on context sensitive/aware communication systems that aims to reduce interruptions, first in general, and then within hospital settings. But first of all we need to define context sensitive/aware systems. We will use the terms context aware and context sensitive as equal terms during this chapter.

Identifying Context Sensitive Systems

A system is a set of interacting or interdependent components forming an integrated whole. The behaviour of this whole has observable Inter-Process Communications. Further, to define what we mean by context, we had to look into some of the definitions defined during the years by the research community

(Bisgaard, Heise, & Steffensen, 2004; Lieberman & Selker, 2000; Schilit, Adams, & Want, 1994), and came up with (Abowd et al., 1999) as the most suitable definition for this chapter:

Context is any information that can be used to characterize the situation of an entity. An entity is a person, place, or object that is considered relevant for the interaction between a user and an application, including the user and applications themselves.

This definition highlights the importance of which information that is relevant or not in a context sensitive system. A Context sensitive system could therefore be defined as a system allowing interactions between multiple entities using relevant information. Abowd, et al., (1999) states; "a system is context-aware if it uses context to provide relevant information and/or services to the user, where relevancy depends on the user's task". This definition shows that a context-aware system can change its behaviour and send some relevant information according to the context, which reflects our view. So, what is relevant information? What are the most common types of contextual information used by context aware applications? (Mizzaro, Nazzi, & Vassena, 2008) identified some common types of information:

- Spatial
- Temporal
- Social situation
- Resources that are nearby
- Physiological measurements
- Schedules and agendas
- Activities
- Identity

Only a small number of these crucial information types are applied in existing applications. Only the information that satisfies the requirements of the targeted application, technology available, and environmental constraints, is used. The trend has been to offer the user as much information as possible in order to provide more sophisticated and useful services, and at the same time making the users more available. A preliminary study on the Aware Media system by Jakob E. Bardram, Hansen, & Soegaard (2006), presented in this book, they suggest a classification that splits the above listed information along three main axes:

- **Social Awareness**: `Where a person is', `activity in which a person is engaged on', `self-reported status'.
- **Spatial Awareness**: 'What kind of operation is taking place in a ward', 'level of activity', 'status of operation and people present in the room'.
- **Temporal Awareness**: 'Past activities', 'present and future activities' that is significant for a person.

This classification describes social aspects regarding knowledge about a person, spatial aspects regarding information about a specific place, and temporal aspects describing information about history and future plans of a subject.

The adoption of context-aware services based on these definitions is growing in a variety of domains, as mention in (Hristova, 2008):

- **Smart Homes:** Context aware applications provide useful services to the residents in order to increase their quality of life and help disabled or elderly people to be more independent, such as; supervising health care functions to monitor the person's biomedical functions: glucose levels, blood pressure, heartbeats or provide reminders about daily medication.
- **Airports:** Context-aware solutions are used to identify possible threats or emergency conditions providing automatic mechanisms aimed at delivering immediate security notification to the appropriate department such as maintenance, fire department or police. Services linked to passenger's behaviour have been developed as well. Most of them are able to send information to passengers' mobile devices about shopping zones, exits, gates, arrivals and departures delay according to their location.
- **Travel/Entertainment/Shopping:** Information provided, typically on mobile phone, is about nearby restaurants, theatres, festivals, events, shops, sales and other data related to the area where the user is located.
- **Museum:** Context aware applications are often used to detect user's position within a building, in order to guide visitors through a predefined path. Typically, these applications are developed on suitable portable devices able to sense the location and capable to provide video/audio information relating paintings, statues and other objects within a museum.
- **Offices:** Context-aware systems are usually aimed at monitoring the status of equipment and providing better allocation of human resources by changing the shift schedules considering location and activity performed by the workers.

Spatial information is perhaps the most frequently used type of contextual information, pertaining to user location. It can be as simple as knowing whether a user is at home or at work or more precise, by specifying which office floor for their current location. The benefits of using this kind of information is obvious. Trying to find someone is a lot easier when you know which building. In addition, if a user uses a context aware system in order to find someone, the system can inform the user that the person they are looking for is currently in a meeting, and thereby not available.

Temporal information can be of high value when collecting contextual data, and several different ways of presenting the information has been proposed (Omar, A., et al., 2007; Steve B Cousins and Michael G Kahn, 1991; Robert Wu et al., 2011). An example of how to use temporal information is to use it to check for colliding or overlapping events in calendars and schedulers. Other example uses involve combining temporal data with, as an example, sales data, and looking for connections between time of day and sales of certain items. Horvitz et al., (2002) presents a system allowing for setting of thresholds regarding alerts on desktop and mobile, depending on urgency, availability, and other factors, including temporal data.

Knowing which resources are available nearby can be used in order to help the users in a variety of situations. This could be as simple as; informing the user that a meeting room is now available, or where the closest available projector is located. However, taking this to the next level, then the system might recognise that a user currently located in a meeting room is about to make a presentation due to an event in the user's schedule, and as a result it automatically connects the users laptop to the projector and speaker system located in the room.

Having access to the users schedule can include a lot of information. Knowing when people are attending meetings, seeing their doctor, or taking vacation, can be very useful for providing relevant information without the user having update this themselves. An example of using this kind of information: The interaction between Google's services, Gmail offers functionality that automatically import event data to your calendar. Many applications also exist in which automatically puts your phone in silent mode during meetings and other events, by checking your calendar. Similarly, a phone system can note that a callee is in a meeting, and thereby inform the caller when it is appropriate to call back, or it can present the caller with a set options as to what to do depending on the context of the callee, as presented in Chihani et al. (2011).

The identity of the user, as well as those attempting to contact them or contacted by them, is also useful to know in terms of context. We mentioned earlier that a context aware system could be used in order to reduce the availability of the user if they were in a meeting, but what if the one calling is someone with an urgent need to contact the user, an acute situation? The fact is that people are often willing to be interrupted if the responsible party has a valid reason for it (Daniel Massaguer et al. 2009). Identity can also be used in order to tailor the users' surroundings. A user might have his office set up as the lighting is adjusted based on the time of day, or having the temperature turned down and the lights turned off when they aren't there. Chen et al. (2000) features more examples of how various contextual information can be utilized.

While the term context aware was first used to describe a system in 1994 (Bill N Schilit, David M Hilbert, and Jonathan Trevor, 2002), the concept had already been in use for years. Bill N Schilit and Marvin M Theimer (1994) and Albrecht Schmidt et al. (1999) gives a good overview of some earlier systems, the usage of context-aware systems, and design objectives that they believe should be considered.

One of the first system developed was the Active Badge System first deployed at Cambridge early 1990 (Roy Want et al., 1995; Andy Harter and Andy Hopper, (1994). The system used lightweight badges, carried by the users. These badges used infrared (IR) communication in order to send a short signal that could be picked up by network sensors, which were placed around the building. The information gathered by these sensors could be presented on a standard PC display showing users' name, location, and the probability of the given location. The probability of a user being in their last location were based on whether the system noticed that the user have been moving around recently. The system was primarily used by receptionists who used the presented information in order to forward phone calls. Though some were sceptical towards the system at first, it quickly became a useful tool, and many praised the system for making their lives easier in regards to responding to people trying to reaching them, though they wanted more control over when calls were forwarded (Roy Want et al., 1995).

Another early system that used similar techniques was the PARCTAB system develop at Xerox PARC in the early nineties (Norman Adams et al., 1993; Mark Weiser, 1991). PARCTAB was a Personal Digital Assistant (PDA) whose applications mostly ran on remote machines and was primarily meant for use in buildings. Like the Active Badge System (Roy Want et al., 1995) it uses IR communication in order to communicate with these applications. While the Active Badge System had network sensors, which only picked up signals from the badges, the PARCTAB system used a series of transceivers.

More recently, some businesses and retail stores have started to take advantage of the possibilities offered by context-aware systems. As an example, Estimote (www.estimote.com), a company that produces lightweight Blue Tooth (BT) beacons, which can be used for location tracking. They promotes the idea of combining BT beacons with an application on the consumer's phone, which can notify the user of sales and other deals going on when the application detects that the consumer is in close range to the store. In addition, the application can also show the consumer where in the store the desired product is located. These kinds of systems can be categorised as continuation of guidance systems like Cyberguide as (Sue Long et al., 1996) introduces. Similarly the aptly named recommendation systems, systems that try to predict the users interest in an area, product, or event, have also begun using contextual information in order to offer better information to their users (Roy Want et al., 1992; Julie Parker and Enrico Coiera, 2000; Gediminas Adomavicius and Alexander Tuzhilin, 2011).

Context aware system's also share similarities with another concept known as ubiquitous computing, a term initially introduced in the late eighties at Xerox PARC (Johanna I Westbrook et al., 2011; Mark Weiser, Rich Gold, and John Seely Brown, 1999). The general concept is the idea of computers being everywhere and adapting to our presence and surroundings, without the users necessarily realising or having to think about it. An example of how ubiquitous computing is becoming more widespread is that more and more devices and items are connected to Internet. This collection of devices is often referred to as the Internet of Things (IoT), and is often used when presenting ubiquitous devices. IoT consists of billions of devices, and increases every day. Cisco features a device counter on their site, which keeps track of the number of devices connected to the Internet, and estimates that the IoT will count more than 50 billion units by 2020, if the growth continues at its current rate.

While the use of context aware system's can potentially offer a lot of functionality, some people are still sceptical. Some context aware systems often gather large amounts of personal data used to offer additional utilities, which for many users do not outweigh the loss of privacy that the system generates. As a result, privacy is often referred to as the biggest concern when talking about context aware systems (Jason I Hong and James A Landay, 2004). We will not focus on privacy issues. Privacy is a large field and needs more investigation than we will be able cover in this chapter.

Context Sensitive Communication Systems to Control Interruptions

One approach for generalizing context aware communication systems that aims to reduce interruptions, is to divide them into two categories (Ashraf Khalil & Connelly, 2006). The first category includes systems where the phone automatically changes configuration (Ashraf Khalil & Connelly, 2005; Nelson, Bly, & Sokoler, 2001; Schmidt, Takaluoma, & Mäntyjärvi, 2000; Siewiorek et al., 2003). This includes quiet calls where the receiver could negotiate with the caller through text or pre-recorded audio messages (Nelson, et al., 2001), which will not reduce personal interruptions due to the user is supposed to act upon the received call. SenSay (Siewiorek, et al., 2003) is an interesting context-aware mobile phone that adapts to dynamically changing environmental and physiological states. It combines information from several different sensors to catch the user's context, and adapt the ringer volume, the vibration and the feedback to the caller based on the phones context. It also makes call suggestion to users when they are idle. Contextual information is gathered by using 3-Axis accelerometers, Bluetooth, ambient microphones, and light sensors, mounted on different part of the user's body. A central hub mounted on the waist is the central component that receives and distributes data coming from the sensors to the decision logic module. The decision logic module analyzes the collected data and changes the state of the phone. The system provides four states: Uninterruptible, Idle, Active and Normal state. A number of settings on the phone are automatically changed within the different states. The uninterruptible state turns off the ringer and turn on the vibration only if the light level is below a certain threshold. This state is entered when the user is involved in a conversation (recognized by the environmental microphone) or is involved in a meeting recognized from the phones calendar. In this state, all incoming calls are blocked and with feedback messages sent to the caller. The caller does have an option to force the call in case of emergency. When high physical activity or high ambient noise level are detected by the accelerometer or microphones, the active state is entered. This means that the ringer is set to high and the vibration is turned on. When there activity level is low and the detected sounds of the surroundings are very low, the idle state is entered. In this state the phone reminds the user of pending calls. As the name indicates, the normal state will configure the ringer and vibration to default values. Figure 1 shows the overall architecture of the SenSay system, from sensor box to platform, to mobile phone. In another system presented in (Schmidt, et al., 2000), they use wireless application protocols (WAP) to automatically change the phones setting based on the recognized context, and in (Ashraf Khalil & Connelly, 2005) they use calendar information with the users scheduled activity stored, to automatically configure the phone.

The second category (Ashraf Khalil & Connelly, 2006) deals with systems that gives the caller information about the receivers context and thereby helps the caller to make decisions when it is appropriate to make the call (Milewski & Smith, 2000; Pedersen, 2001; Tang et al., 2001). In one study by (Avrahami, et al., 2007), they revealed that if they provided the caller with context information about the receiver's situation, it reduces the mismatch between the caller's decision and the receivers desires. In (Milewski & Smith, 2000) they provide information about the receiver's presence using the phone book and location, like the "buddy list" in instant messenger services. An interaction web-page that gives caller information about the receivers' situation and the available communication channels is used in (Pedersen, 2001), and in (Marmasse, Schmandt, & Spectre, 2004) they formed some kind of member-list combined with a prototype of a wristwatch that captures the user's context and share it to the members of the list, which use the information to check the availability before calling.

Context Sensitive Communication Systems for Hospitals

Context aware systems for hospitals are a promising application domain. Hospitals are dependent of a wide and reliable communication infrastructure for exchanging different kinds of data, such as patient

Figure 1. SenSay; from sensor box, to platform, to mobile phone. This is a simplified version of the overall system architecture presented in (Siewiorek, et al., 2003).

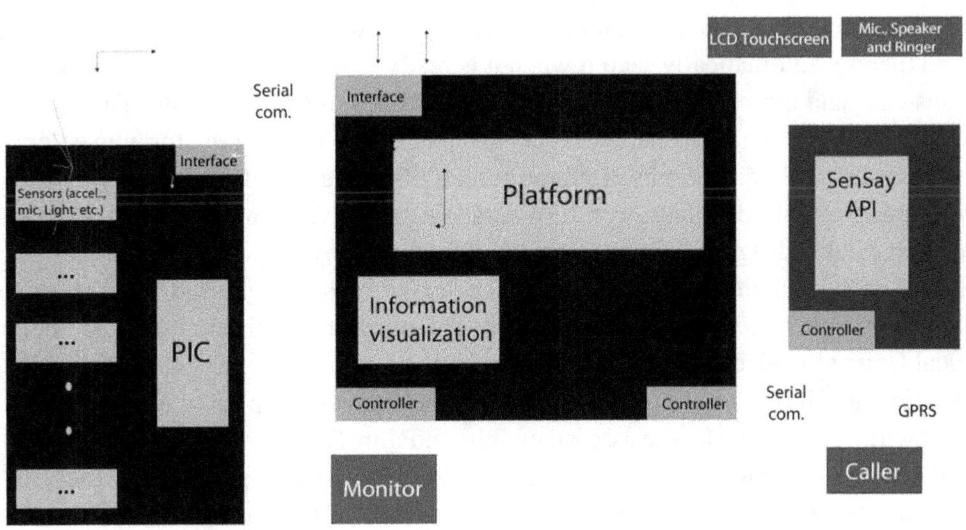

reports, lab tests and working shifts, together with text, voice and alarm services. This means that the security needs to be on a certain level. The management of this information is difficult and requires considering a wide variety of problems that should be avoided in order to properly meet the needs of hospital professionals. Context-aware applications for mobile communication seem to be a valid solution, which also can be used to move parts of the workers activities over to computers. While the society outside of hospitals have embraced mobile phones (GSM/2G/3G/4G and the forthcoming 5G), have health care only shown limited use of the technology. This is mainly due to an older prediction of possible interference with medical equipment. However, some earlier studies showed that the benefits from this technology could outweigh the risk of interference (Kidd, Sharratt, & Coleman, 2004; Myerson & Mitchell, 2003). This has been challenged by Van Lieshout et al., (2007), which in 2007 classified incidents of electromagnetic interference (EMI) by mobile phones (GSM/2G/3G) on critical care medical equipment. Latest years, the introduction of smartphones and medical applications available, has also made smartphones interesting for hospital communication, despite the fair for interference and the fatal available issues.

Several other studies have been carried out within hospital settings, with improved communication and interruption reduction in mind (Acuff, et al., 1997; Coiera & Tombs, 1998; Eisenstadt, et al., 1998; Minnick, et al., 1994 ; Sammon, Karmin, Peebles, & Seligmann, 2006; Spurck, et al., 1995). In (Coiera & Tombs, 1998) they recommend a variety of approaches to improve communication, including support and asynchronous communication with acknowledgement. Different kind of text messaging systems for hospitals has also been revealed as positive (Acuff, et al., 1997; Eisenstadt, et al., 1998), but also showed concerns for character limits, small displays, and yet another device to carry. Of course, a lot have been improved within text messaging systems and mobile devices, regarding small displays and keyboards, since these studies were carried out, which may obliterate these concerns. The introduction of Smartphones has probably changed this. Other studies have shown positive results when providing nursing teams with wireless phones (Spurck, et al., 1995), wearable radio transmitters (Minnick, et al., 1994), and wireless hands-free headsets which interfaces the phone system (Sammon, et al., 2006). The feedback was; quicker updates to patient information, easier to locate nursing staffs, and reduced noise levels, but also concerns about being too available.

PDA have been used by (Munoz, Rodriguez, Favela, Martinez-Garcia, & Gonzalez, 2003) in a contextual message exchange system. This solution, developed at IMSS General Hospital in Ensenada Mexico, uses handheld devices that allow users to specify when and where they want to send messages and/or data to other colleagues. Physicians' can, for example; specify who will be the recipient of a patient's lab test result, and thereby automatically send it when it is ready. Moreover, within this system it is enabled that physicians can send messages without knowing the names of the recipients. This is done by sending the lab tests to any physician in charge for the next shift, or to the first doctor who enters a specified room the next day. In another system by Holleran et al. (2003), they used PDAs for simple text services.

PDA's with built in mobile phones, web-browsers, electronic versions of commonly used UK medical reference text books, drug interactions compendium, anatomy atlases, International Classification of Diseases – 10 (ICD-10), guidelines, and medical calculators, has been used by (Aziz et al., 2005) to enrich communication between health care workers. The purpose of this study, carried out at the Academic Surgical Unit at St. Mary's Hospital (London), was to verify whether PDAs with built-in phones, could be an efficient solution to improve communication between hospital workers. This solution was also compared with pagers. During the assessment phase, Palm Tungsten PDAs were given to a surgical team. The information used to evaluate the communication efficiency gained with these devices, was the time clinicians needed to respond to a call. After 6 weeks of tests and questionnaires filled out by the involved participants, the results were encouraging. It showed a general benefit in replacing pagers with the new advanced PDA devices. In a study described in (Mendonca et al., 2004) they used PDA's with access to patent data and with virtual white boards, which allows health care workers assigned to the same patient know about each other's work progress.

In (Skov & Høegh, 2006) they evaluated a context-aware solution based on mobile phones capable to give nurses patient information. The provided information included the nurse's daily tasks, timing constraints and positions. Moreover, the mobile devices could also be used to insert collected data during the daily work, and to view previously stored patient's information in order to monitor changes. After the development, an assessment phase was conducted. The identified problems mainly concerned the complexity of the automatic update mechanism of the devices: Some subjects did not understand how to navigate between the different interfaces and they felt forced to undergo the information displayed on the phone. Others felt confused when the system suddenly changed the interface while they were reading the information displayed. Some of the nurses also expressed uncertainties about the validity of the data previously entered into the system, and they were not sure if the information was saved properly when using the device.

Intelligent Hospital, QoS Dream Platform, is an application proposed by (Mitchell, et al., 2000). It is based on wired touch-sensitive terminals ubiquitously scattered throughout the hospital. These terminals makes is possible for clinicians, after an authentication process, to request a video call with a colleague without knowing the location of the person they want to contact. The call is routed to the nearest terminal of the recipient, who can choose to accept the call, or refuse it. The user's location is tracked by an active badge system worn by the clinicians. The application is used for: Remote consultation between doctors (e.g. discussions regarding patients and their treatments), and consultation of patient's data enabled by an event notification infrastructure that allows pushing clinical data directly into the terminal's display. The Intelligent Hospital application was built to demonstrate a real application within the QoS Dream middleware platform. This platform supports context aware, event driven applications, and solutions based on multimedia contents where user mobility is a predominant factor. It is based on four main conceptual components: Operating system with resource management and overall control functionality, a dynamic multimedia streaming component based on the DJINN platform used to re-route video streaming contents according to the movement of the participants, an event-based infrastructure based on the HERALD architecture, and a set of APIs for building applications using the technologies within the system.

Other systems like the AwareMedia and the AwarePhone systems to Bardram et al. (Jakob E. Bardram & Hansen, 2004; Jakob E. Bardram, et al., 2006), supports context aware communication. Figure 2 shows the AWARE system architecture divided into four layers: the Client layer, the Awareness layer, the Context layer, and the Monitor and Actuator layer (Jakob E. Bardram & Hansen, 2010). It was developed in centre for Pervasive Health care at the University of Aarhus in Denmark. These systems in combination, forms a complete communication system for clinicians in a surgical ward. The tracking system is tracking clinicians in selected areas, using Bluetooth tags/devices worn by the clinicians. The AwareMedia shows information on a number of large interactive touch screen displays scattered throughout the hospital. The information includes; location from the tracking system along with the clinician's schedule, what kind of operation is currently performed at a specific ward, status of the operation, which physicians present in the room, actual stage of the operation through dynamic colored bars, and status of the work schedule (e.g. delays or cancellations) provided by displaying visual signs and text messages. Further, in a dedicated area of the display, the application shows the status on other physicians' activities, their location, status, and future schedules. The AwarePhone system is an application running on a mobile phone (GSM/3G), which allows clinicians to call or send a message to a person in an operating theatre. Messages sent directly to the room, is shown to all people presented in that room through the Aware-Media Screen. The feedback from the use of these systems focusing on privacy issues as one of the big drawbacks deploying a system like this.

To solve some of the challenges within hospital communication, an intelligent, efficient and context sensitive communication system called CallMeSmart has been developed by T. Solvoll at the Norwegian Centre for E-Health research. This phone system is described later in this chapter (see figure 3)and is fully described in Solvolls PhD dissertation (Solvoll, T., 2013-1). CallMeSmart is a context sensitive mobile communication system designed for use in hospitals. The system aims to improve communication and information flow and to reduce unnecessary interruptions in clinical settings. A first version of the system has been tested by physicians and nurses in a lab setting. The feedback was primarily positive and has been used as input for the further development and improvement of the system, moving from prototype to production.

The system supports voice, text-messaging, paging and alarm services in an efficient and non-interruptive manner. It intends to avoid interruptions when health personnel is busy; for example, when nurses are involved in important conversations with patients or relatives. This kind of context information, which affects the workers' availability, is normally extracted automatically from different sensors, calendar information, work schedule and so on. With this device, individual users can change their availability manually or automatic according to the context information. If a user is busy, the call will be forwarded to another professional at the same level and with the same role, and the caller will be given feedback about the health care workers' availability.

Using these phones, health care workers needs to carry only one device in total, instead of one device for personal use and one for each professional role they have. The role-based communication also enables other users to contact someone assigned on an 'on-call' duty at a specific department, even if they do not know the name of that person. The system enables acute calls and alarms to be forced through, balancing between availability and interruptions.

Figure 2. The AWARE system. This is a simplified version of the AWARE overall system architecture presented in (Jakob E. Bardram & Hansen, 2010).

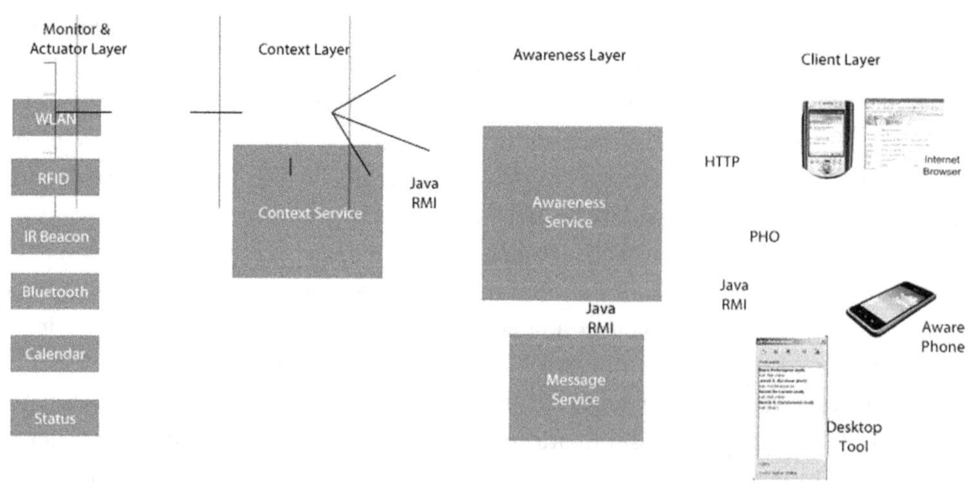

(Johnsen, E., et al., 2016) and (Bergmo, T. S., et al. 2016) investigates if and how the intelligent communication system CallMeSmart affects and improves the communication and information flow among nurses. They collected the empirical material through a multi-method research approach using both quantitative and qualitative data. The data were from phone logs, six individual face-to-face interviews, a focus group interview and informal discussions. They categorised the empirical data into two main groups. One group was for the benefits the nurses experienced. The nurses liked the dedicated phone system, and they gave many examples of how the system could facilitate communication and information flow in their work practice. The second group was for the negative experiences, and it included problems the nurses experienced while using the technology. The phone log material showed the usage of the system. Their conclusion is that this dedicated phone system has great potential in facilitating hospital communication. However, the condition to realise this potential is that the problems that were registered should be resolved.

FUTURE RESEARCH DIRECTIONS

A number of studies have focused on context-sensitive systems for hospitals. Much of this work has focused on scopes not covered by this chapter, including issues related to mobile learning and privacy, accessing clinical data, or on multimedia communication at terminals with fixed locations (Mitchell, et al., 2000). The work done on context-sensitive mobile communication within hospital settings has identified some important elements of context, including location tracking, work role, delivery timing and artifact location, and user state (Munoz, et al., 2003). As presented in the previous sections, this model has been applied to an instant messaging system based on PDAs enabling contact based on these contextual elements. This approach, however, requires workers to carry additional mobile devices in order to support voice and paging services, since it is not compatible with existing hospital communication infrastructure. Another issue, by our knowledge not covered in previous work on role-based contact, is how to design interaction forms that allow users to easily switch work roles.

A variety of models for detecting interruptability have been created for stationary (Fogarty et al., 2005; Eric Horvitz & Apacible, 2003; E. Horvitz, Koch, Kadie, & Jacobs, 2002) and mobile settings (Bernstein, Vorburger, & Egger, 2005; Sawhney & Schmandt, 2000; Siewiorek, et al., 2003). In general, these models focused on office workers and social settings, and used information such as a user's calendar, interactions with computing devices, switches to determine if doors are open, accelerometers, microphones and motion sensors. Accuracy rates of approximately 80% to 90% have been reported for directly predicting interruptability and user state, such as "standing" or "walking", and social context, such as "lecture", "conversation" etc. None of these models, by our knowledge, has been explored in health care settings, and there are several factors that suggest the development of new health care relevant models is needed. First; studies on context aware communication for hospitals suggest information not included in these interruptability models, such as work role, are critical for detecting proper context in health care settings (Munoz, et al., 2003). Second; another issue is elements such as location and social relationships are inherently different within health care, and needs to be accounted for in health care appropriate models. For example, scenarios such as "visiting patients", "in surgery" etc. needs to be considered in combination with the work roles of the person initializing the contact and the contacted person.

In addition, appropriate forms for user-interaction with these interruptability models also needs to be investigated. It has been reported that users tend to use the information provided about a person's availability for communication, as a presence indicator instead of using it to control interruptions. This suggests that automatic configuration of devices may be the most appropriate approach (Fogarty, Lai, & Christensen, 2004). As previous presented in this chapter, the "SenSay" context-aware mobile phone (Siewiorek, et al., 2003) uses a hybrid approach that automatically blocks calls, and also generates text messages notifying the caller that their call have been blocked. Then they are allowed to override the blocking by calling back within a predetermined number of minutes from the same phone number. This problem needs to be reinvestigated in health care settings, since there are some situations where certain calls should not be blocked (such as those for a specific role) whereas other calls may need to be restricted. Thus, the context of both the caller and person being called will need to be considered.

The use of semi-structured messages has shown to be particularly useful for work coordination (Malone, Grant, Lai, Rao, & Rosenblitt, 1987). Preliminary studies have estimated that up to 90% of mobile text-messages used by hospital workers could be met by the use of such messages (Jakob E. Bardram & Hansen, 2004). However, we have not been able to find any published work on the style and function of such messages, nor any studies that demonstrate if they would actually be adopted, or if they would have any effect during real work practice. The possibility to create automatic replies, and suggestions for replies, is also an advantage when using predefined messages, but the appropriate replies have not been studied in the context of mobile-text messaging. This could be particularly useful within health care settings, since such replies actually offers acknowledgement when a message has been read (Coiera & Tombs, 1998).

During the latest years, the industry has started to develop and launch systems for health care that in different levels controls the communication, and introduces smartphones for internal hospital communication. These systems are not presented in this chapter since we have not been able to find any research on the effectiveness or usage of the systems. Vocera (www.vocera.com), Ascom (www.ascom.com), Cisco (www.cisco.com) are examples of such companies/systems.

CONCLUSION

We know from earlier studies within health care, but also from our own studies (Scholl, et al., 2007; T. Solvoll & Scholl, 2008; Terje Solvoll, et al., 2010, 2013) that physicians in hospitals are interrupted unnecessary by mobile devices in situations where such interruptions should be avoided. This is a problem in today's hospital settings, and a solution to reduce such unnecessary interruptions from mobile devices is needed and wanted. A lot of work, as presented in the previous sections, has been done within the area during the years, but we cannot see that the situation has changed. The introduction of systems like Vocera, could have changed this, but we have not been able to find any research on this. We believe that one of the problems that is applicable to most of the earlier systems developed, is that they requires both new devices and infrastructure, and/or is based on public networks like GSM/2G/3G/4G, which in both cases requires considerable investments. A system based on existing infrastructure and devices used in hospitals, would be much cheaper, and will probably require less training and maybe less resistance from health care workers when introduced. This is important since early studies shows that over half of medical informatics systems fail because of user and staff resistance (Anderson, 1993). However, this is an old study, but the situation does not seems to have changed a lot. We believe that; by knowing and understanding health care workers work situation, the nature of unnecessary interruptions, and also by involving the participants in the design process, it is possible to build a system suited for their communication patterns and work situations, on top of an existing communication infrastructure, using devices already in use at hospitals. Our studies (Taxiarchis Botsis, Terje Solvoll, Jeremiah Scholl, Per Hasvold, & Gunnar Hartvigsen, 2007; Scholl, et al., 2007; T. Solvoll & Scholl, 2008; Terje Solvoll, et al., 2010) contributes to such knowledge, and were used as input in when we designed and developed a context sensitive system for mobile communication in hospitals, CallMeSmart. Figure 3 presents the overall system architecture of the system developed. The system aims to reduce unnecessary interruptions from mobile devices in situations where interruptions should be avoided, like; when involved in a surgery (dressed in sterile clothing), doing patient examination at the outpatient clinic, having serious conversations with patients/relatives in conversation rooms, etc.

The system focuses on context sensitive interfaces, middleware, and new interaction forms for mobile devices that support multi-modal communication in hospitals. These devices supports media such as voice services, text-messaging and paging services, in an efficient and non-interruptive manner, as well as enable support for individual and role-based contact on a single device. That is, the user only need to carry one device for both personal and role based communication, which enables other users to, for example, contact someone assigned as "on-call" duties at a specific department, even if they do not know who that person is. At the same time, it aims to balance between availability and interruptions, while it enables acute calls and alarms forced through. Currently, by our knowledge, similar devices are not generally available for internal communication systems in hospitals.

CallMeSmart senses the context automatically from different sensors, calendar information, work schedule, etc., to change the physicians'/health care workers availability and the phones profile, according to the collected context information. At the same time, the caller is given feedback about the physicians'/ health care workers availability, and thereby it is possible for the caller to force through an emergency call, or forward the call to another physician/health care worker at the same level, that is available. The system is based on the ideas from earlier studies on interruptions in combination with the ideas from (T. Botsis, et al., 2007; Terje Solvoll, Fasani, Ravuri, Tiemersma, & Hartvigsen, 2010; T. Solvoll & Scholl, 2008; Terje Solvoll et al., 2011, 2013; Talaei-Khoei, Solvoll, Ray, & Parameshwaran, 2011, 2012). A first version of the system is ready, and has been tested in lab-settings with physicians/nurses as test users. The tests were performed as scenarios observed from real situations. The feedback was mostly positive and has been used as input for improvement and further development of the system moving from prototype to production (Solvoll, T., Gironi, L., & Hartvigsen, G., 2013; Solvoll, T., Gironi, L., Giordanengo, A., & Hartvigsen, G., 2013). The overall system architecture is presented in figure 3, and the system has been tested in clinical settings. (Johnsen, E., et al., 2016) and (Bergmo, T. S., et al. 2016) investigated if and how CallMeSmart affects and improves the communication and information flow among nurses, with positive feedback. This was done during a small pilot at the University Hospital of North Norway. The pilot was running between May 2014 – May 2016.

CallMeSmart supports several forms of communication between users in the form of calling, messaging, and the ability to send out and answer alarms. Differing from many other alarm systems, which will alert all users when sending out an alarm, CallMeSmart uses contextual information in order to only send alarms to relevant users. Calls are performed using Session Initiation Protocol (SIP). The differences from a ordinary phone system comes from the context aware services of the system that decides what action to take, depending on the availability setting of the user receiving the call. Messaging works similar to regular Short Messages Services (SMS), but in CallMeSmart the user is also getting feedback when a message has been delivered to a phone, and when the user has opened the message. This helps the user to know if an important message has been received and read.

Figure 3. CallMeSmart overall system architecture (www.callmesmart.no)

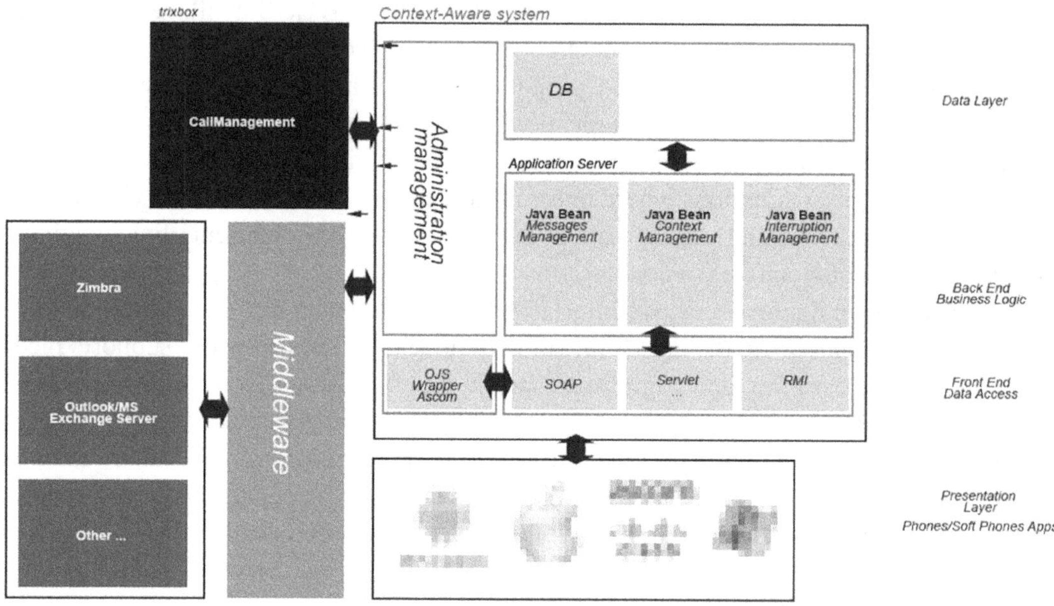

Within CallMeSmart it is developed a system for tracking users, which is redeveloped using a series of Bluetooth Low Energy (BLE) beacons that sends signals to the users' smartphones in order to track the devices location (Solvoll, T., Hanssen, Baard, Giordanengo, A., & Hartvigsen, G., 2015). This system is under development and planned to include tracking of hospital equipment. As resent research has shown, a lot of hospitals equipment like wheel chairs, is "lost" or misplaced, and when needed, hospital personnel uses a lot of time just searching for needed equipment. This could in its worst consequence be life treating. By tagging this kind of equipment, like medicine pumps, wheel chairs and so on, it will in our mind be more efficient and easier to find vacant equipment when needed, and thereby save time and money, which in last stage will benefit patient care. The results of this development and research will be published internationally.

REFERENCES

Abowd, G. D., Dey, A. K., Brown, P. J., Davies, N., Smith, M., & Steggles, P. (1999). Towards a Better Understanding of Context and Context-Awareness. *Proceedings of the 1st international symposium on Handheld and Ubiquitous Computing*. 10.1007/3-540-48157-5_29

Acuff, R. D., Fagan, L. M., Rindfleisch, T. C., Levitt, B. J., & Ford, P. M. (1997). *Lightweight, Mobile E-Mail for Intra-Clinic Communication.* Paper presented at the 1997 AMIA Annual Fall Symposium, Nashville, TN.

Adams, G., & Schilit, T., & Want. (1993). An infrared network for mobile computers. *Proceedings USENIX Symposium on Mobile & Location-Independent Computing,* 10.

Adomavicius & Tuzhilin. (2011). Context-aware recommender systems. In *Recommender systems handbook* (pp. 217–253). Springer. doi:10.1007/978-0-387-85820-3_7

Alonso, O., Gertz, M., & Baeza-Yates, R. (2007). On the value of temporal information in information retrieval. *SIGIR Forum, 41*(2), 35-41. 10.1145/1328964.1328968

Anderson, J. G. (1993). *Evaluating Health Care Information Systems: Methods and Applications*. Sage Publications, Inc.

Avrahami, D., Gergle, D., Hudson, S. E., & Kiesler, S. (2007). Improving the match between callers and receivers: A study on the effect of contextual information on cell phone interruptions. *Behaviour & Information Technology, 26*(3), 247–259. doi:10.1080/01449290500402338

Aziz, O., Panesar, S., Netuveli, G., Paraskeva, P., Sheikh, A., & Darzi, A. (2005). Handheld computers and the 21st century surgical team: A pilot study. *BMC Medical Informatics and Decision Making, 5*(1), 28. doi:10.1186/1472-6947-5-28 PMID:16109177

Bardram, J. E., & Hansen, T. R. (2004). The AWARE architecture: supporting context-mediated social awareness in mobile cooperation. *Proceedings of the 2004 ACM conference on Computer supported cooperative work*. 10.1145/1031607.1031639

Bardram, J. E., & Hansen, T. R. (2010). Context-Based Workplace Awareness. *Computer Supported Cooperative Work, 19*(2), 105–138. doi:10.100710606-010-9110-2

Bardram, J. E., Hansen, T. R., & Soegaard, M. (2006). AwareMedia: A shared interactive display supporting social, temporal, and spatial awareness in surgery. *Proceedings of the 2006 20th anniversary conference on Computer supported cooperative work*. 10.1145/1180875.1180892

Bergmo, T. S., Johnsen, E., Johansen, M. A., & Solvoll, T. (2016). Evaluation of a context spesific communcation system based on smartphone. In *eTELEMED 2016, The Eight International Conference on eHealth, Telemedicine, and Social Medicine*. International Academy, Research and Industry Association (IARIA).

Bernstein, A., Vorburger, P., & Egger, P. (2005). *Direct Interruptablity Prediction and Scenario-based Evaluation of Wearable Devices: Towards Reliable Interruptability Predictions*. Paper presented at the First International Workshop on Managing Context Information in Mobile and Pervasive Environments MCMP-05.

Bisgaard, J. J., Heise, M., & Steffensen, C. (2004). *How is Context and Context-awareness Defined and Applied? A Survey of Context-awareness*. Department of Computer Science, Aalborg University.

Block, F. E. III, & Block, F. E. Jr. (2016). Understanding Caregiver Workflows: A Proposal for Alarm Condition Priorities. *Biomedical Instrumentation & Technology, 50*(2), 114–116. doi:10.2345/0899-8205-50.2.114 PMID:27046686

Blum, N. J., & Lieu, T. A. (1992). Interrupted care. The effects of paging on pediatric resident activities. *American Journal of Diseases of Children, 146*(7), 806–808. doi:10.1001/archpedi.1992.02160190038016 PMID:1496947

Botsis, T., Solvoll, T., Scholl, J., Hasvold, P., & Hartvigsen, G. (2007). Context-aware systems for mobile communication in healthcare - A user oriented approach. *Proceedings of the 7th Wseas International Conference on Applied Informatics and Communications*, 69-74.

Bradner, E., Kellogg, W. A., & Erickson, T. (1999). The adoption and use of \“BABBLE\” a field study of chat in the workplace. *Proceedings of the Sixth European conference on Computer supported cooperative work.*

Chen & Kotz. (2000). *A survey of context-aware mobile computing research.* Technical report, Technical Report TR2000-381, Dept. of Computer Science, Dartmouth College.

Chihani, B., Bertin, E., Jeanne, F., & Crespi, N. (2011). Context-aware systems: a case study. In Digital Information and Communication Technology and Its Applications (pp. 718-732). Springer. doi:10.1007/978-3-642-22027-2_60

Coiera, E. (2000). When Conversation Is Better Than Computation. *Journal of the American Medical Informatics Association*, *7*(3), 277–286. doi:10.1136/jamia.2000.0070277 PMID:10833164

Coiera, E., & Tombs, V. (1998). Communication behaviours in a hospital setting: An observational study. *BMJ (Clinical Research Ed.)*, *316*(7132), 673–676. doi:10.1136/bmj.316.7132.673 PMID:9522794

Cousins, S. B., & Kahn, M. G. (1991). The visual display of temporal information. *Artificial Intelligence in Medicine*, *3*(6), 341–357. doi:10.1016/0933-3657(91)90005-V

Eisenstadt, S. A., Wagner, M. M., Hogan, W. R., Pankaskie, M. C., Tsui, F. C., & Wilbright, W. (1998). Mobile workers in healthcare and their information needs: Are 2-way pagers the answer? *Proc AMIA Symp.*, *1998*, 135–139. PMID:9929197

Fogarty, J., Hudson, S. E., Atkeson, C. G., Avrahami, D., Forlizzi, J., Kiesler, S., ... Yang, J. (2005). Predicting human interruptibility with sensors. *ACM Transactions on Computer-Human Interaction*, *12*(1), 119–146. doi:10.1145/1057237.1057243

Fogarty, J., Lai, J., & Christensen, J. (2004). Presence versus availability: The design and evaluation of a context-aware communication client. *International Journal of Human-Computer Studies*, *61*(3), 299–317. doi:10.1016/j.ijhcs.2003.12.016

Grudin, J. (1994). Groupware and social dynamics: Eight challenges for developers. *Communications of the ACM*, *37*(1), 92–105. doi:10.1145/175222.175230

Harter, A., & Hopper, A. (1994). A distributed location system for the active office. *IEEE Network*, *8*(1), 62–70. doi:10.1109/65.260080

Hersh, W., Helfand, M., Wallace, J., Kraemer, D., Patterson, P., Shapiro, S., & Greenlick, M. (2002). A systematic review of the efficacy of telemedicine for making diagnostic and management decisions. *Journal of Telemedicine and Telecare*, *8*(4), 197–209. doi:10.1258/135763302320272167 PMID:12217102

Holleran, K., Pappas, J., Lou, H., Rubalcaba, P., Lee, R., & Clay, S. (2003). Mobile Technology in a Clinical Setting. *AMIA ... Annual Symposium Proceedings - AMIA Symposium. AMIA Symposium*, 2003. PMID:14728368

Hong & Landay. (2004). An architecture for privacy-sensitive ubiquitous computing. *Proceedings of the 2nd international conference on Mobile systems, applications, and services*, 177-189.

Horvitz, E., & Apacible, J. (2003). Learning and reasoning about interruption. *Proceedings of the 5th international conference on Multimodal interfaces.*

Horvitz, E., Koch, P., Kadie, C. M., & Jacobs, A. (2002). Coordinate: Probabilistic forecasting of presence and availability. *Proceedings of the 18th Conference in Uncertainty in Artificial Intelligence (UAI'02)*, 224-233.

Hristova, A. (2008). *Conceptualization and Design of a Context-aware platform for user centric Applications. Master of Science in Communication Technology Master.* Trondheim: Norwegian University of Science and Technology.

Johnsen, E., Bergmo, T., Johansen, M., & Solvoll, T. (2016). Evaluation of a Context Specific Communcation System Based on Smartphone. Nurses Use and Experiences. *Proceedings from The 14th Scandinavian Conference on Health Informatics 2016.*

Katz, M. H., & Schroeder, S. A. (1988). The sounds of the hospital. Paging patterns in three teaching hospitals. *The New England Journal of Medicine*, *319*(24), 1585–1589. doi:10.1056/NEJM198812153192406 PMID:3200267

Khalil, A., & Connelly, K. (2005). Improving Cell Phone Awareness by Using Calendar Information. Human-Computer Interaction - INTERACT 2005, 588-600.

Khalil, A., & Connelly, K. (2006). *Context-aware Telephony: Privacy Preferences and Sharing Patterns.* Paper presented at the CSCW'06, Banff, Alberta, Canada. 10.1145/1180875.1180947

Kidd, A. G., Sharratt, C., & Coleman, J. (2004). Mobile communication regulations updated: how safely are doctors' telephones used? *Qual Saf Health Care, 13*(6), 478. doi:10.1136/qhc.13.6.478

Lieberman, H., & Selker, T. (2000). Out of context: Computer systems that adapt to, and learn from, context. *IBM Systems Journal*, *39*(3-4), 617 - 632. doi:10.1147j.393.0617

Lipschultz, A. (2014). The complexity of clinical alarm systems. *Biomedical Instrumentation & Technology*, *48*(3), 204–210. doi:10.2345/0899-8205-48.3.204 PMID:24847931

Long, S., Aust, D., Abowd, G., & Atkeson, C. (1996). Cyberguide: Prototyping context-aware mobile applications. In *Conference Companion on Human Factors in Computing Systems, CHI '96* (pp. 293–294). New York: ACM.

Malone, T. W., Grant, K. R., Lai, K.-Y., Rao, R., & Rosenblitt, D. (1987). Semistructured messages are surprisingly useful for computer-supported coordination. *ACM Transactions on Information Systems*, *5*(2), 115–131. doi:10.1145/27636.27637

Marmasse, N., Schmandt, C., & Spectre, D. (2004). WatchMe: Communication and Awareness Between Members of a Closely-Knit Group. UbiComp 2004: Ubiquitous Computing, 214-231.

Massaguer, D., Hore, B., Diallo, M. H., Mehrotra, S., & Venkatasubramanian, N. (2009) Middleware for pervasive spaces: Balancing privacy and utility. In *Proceedings of the 10th ACM/I- FIP/USENIX International Conference on Middleware, Middleware '09* (pp. 13:1-13:20). New York, NY: Springer-Verlag. 10.1007/978-3-642-10445-9_13

Mendonca, E. A., Chen, E. S., Stetson, P. D., McKnight, L. K., Lei, J., & Cimino, J. J. (2004). Approach to mobile information and communication for health care. *International Journal of Medical Informatics, 73*(7), 631–638. doi:10.1016/j.ijmedinf.2004.04.013 PMID:15246044

Milewski, A., & Smith, T. (2000). Providing presence cues to telephone users. *CSCW '00: Proceedings of the 2000 ACM conference on Computer supported cooperative work.* 10.1145/358916.358978

Minnick, A., Pischke-Winn, K., & Sterk, M. B. (1994). Introducing a two-way wireless communication system. *Nursing Management, 25*(7), 42–47. doi:10.1097/00006247-199407000-00011 PMID:8044475

Mitchell, S., Spiteri, M. D., Bates, J., & Coulouris, G. (2000). Context-aware multimedia computing in the intelligent hospital. *Proceedings of the 9th workshop on ACM SIGOPS European workshop: beyond the PC: new challenges for the operating system.* 10.1145/566726.566730

Mitka, M. (2013). Joint commission warns of alarm fatigue: Multitude of alarms from monitoring devices problematic. *Journal of the American Medical Association, 309*(22), 2315–2316. doi:10.1001/jama.2013.6032 PMID:23757063

Mizzaro, S., Nazzi, E., & Vassena, L. (2008). Retrieval of context-aware applications on mobile devices: how to evaluate? *Proceedings of the second international symposium on Information interaction in context.* 10.1145/1414694.1414710

Munoz, M. A., Rodriguez, M., Favela, J., Martinez-Garcia, A. I., & Gonzalez, V. M. (2003). Context-aware mobile communication in hospitals. *Computer, 36*(9), 38–46. doi:10.1109/MC.2003.1231193

Myerson, S. G., & Mitchell, A. R. J. (2003). Mobile phones in hospitals. *BMJ (Clinical Research Ed.), 326*(7387), 460–461. doi:10.1136/bmj.326.7387.460 PMID:12609917

Nelson, L., Bly, S., & Sokoler, T. (2001). Quiet calls: talking silently on mobile phones. *CHI '01: Proceedings of the SIGCHI conference on Human factors in computing systems.* 10.1145/365024.365094

Parker, J., & Coiera, E. (2000). Improving Clinical Communication: A View from Psychology. *Journal of the American Medical Informatics Association, 7*(5), 453–461. doi:10.1136/jamia.2000.0070453 PMID:10984464

Pedersen, E. R. (2001). Calls.calm: enabling caller and callee to collaborate. *CHI '01 extended abstracts on Human factors in computing systems.* 10.1145/634067.634207

Sammon, M. J., Karmin, L. S. B., Peebles, E., & Seligmann, D. D. (2006). *MACCS: Enabling communications for mobile workers within healthcare environments.* Paper presented at the MobileHCI'06.

Sawhney, N., & Schmandt, C. (2000). Nomadic radio: Speech and audio interaction for contextual messaging in nomadic environments. *ACM Transactions on Computer-Human Interaction, 7*(3), 353–383. doi:10.1145/355324.355327

Schilit, B., Adams, N., & Want, R. (1994). *Context-aware computing applications.* Paper presented at the Mobile Computing Systems and Applications. 10.1109/WMCSA.1994.16

Schilit & Theimer. (1994). Disseminating active map information to mobile hosts. *Network, IEEE, 8*(5), 22-32.

Schilit, Hilbert, & Trevor. (2002) Context-aware communication. *Wireless Communications, IEEE, 9*(5), 46–54.

Schmidt, A., Aidoo, K. A., Takaluoma, A., Tuomela, U., Van Laerhoven, K., & Van de Velde, W. (1999). Advanced interaction in context. In *Handheld and ubiquitous computing* (pp. 89–101). Springer. doi:10.1007/3-540-48157-5_10

Schmidt, A., Takaluoma, A., & Mäntyjärvi, J. (2000). Context-Aware telephony over WAP. *Personal and Ubiquitous Computing*, *4*(4), 225–229.

Scholl, J., Hasvold, P., Henriksen, E., & Ellingsen, G. (2007). *Managing Communication Availability and Interruptions: A Study of Mobile Communication in an Oncology Department*. Pervasive Computing.

Siewiorek, D., Smailagic, A., Furukawa, J., Krause, A., Moraveji, N., & Reiger, K. (2003). SenSay: a context-aware mobile phone. *Wearable Computers, 2003. Proceedings. Seventh IEEE International Symposium on*. 10.1109/ISWC.2003.1241422

Skov, B., & Høegh, T. (2006). Supporting information access in a hospital ward by a context-aware mobile electronic patient record. *Personal and Ubiquitous Computing*, *10*(4), 205–214. doi:10.100700779-005-0049-0

Solvoll, T. (2013a). Mobile Communication in Hospitals: What is the Problem? In C. Rückemann (Ed.), *Integrated Information and Computing Systems for Natural, Spatial, and Social Sciences* (pp. 287–301). Hershey, PA: Information Science Reference. doi:10.4018/978-1-4666-2190-9.ch014

Solvoll, T. (2016). *Mobile Communication in Hospitals: Is It Still a Problem? In Handbook of Research on Effective Communication, Leadership, and Conflict Resolution* (pp. 545–564). Hershey, PA: IGI Global. doi:10.4018/978-1-4666-9970-0.ch029

Solvoll, T. (2013b). *From being interrupted by mobile devices to CallMeSmart - a context-sensitive communication system for mobile communication in hospitals*. UiT The Arctic University of Norway.

Solvoll, T., Arntsen, H., & Hartvigsen, G. (2017). Alarm Fatigue vs User Expectations Regarding Context-Aware Alarm Handling in Hospital Environments Using CallMeSmart. *Stud Health Technol Inform, 241*, 159-164.

Solvoll, T., Fasani, S., Ravuri, A. B., Tiemersma, A., & Hartvigsen, G. (2010). *Evaluation of an Ascom/trixbox system for context sensitive communication in hospitals.* Paper presented at the 8th Scandinavian Conference on Health Informatics, Copenhagen, Denmark.

Solvoll, T., Gironi, L., Giordanengo, A., & Hartvigsen, G. (2013). CallMeSmart: A VoIP Softphone on Android Based Mobile Devices Using SIP. In *eTELEMED 2013, The Fifth International Conference on eHealth, Telemedicine, and Social Medicine* (Vol. 15, pp. 198-203). International Academy, Research and Industry Association (IARIA).

Solvoll, T., Gironi, L., & Hartvigsen, G. (2013). *CallMeSmart: An Ascom/Trixbox Based Prototype for Context Controlled Mobile Communication in Hospitals.* Paper presented at the Information Science and Applications (ICISA), 2013 International Conference on Information Science and Applications. 10.1109/ICISA.2013.6579344

Solvoll, T., Hanssen, B., Aring, R.D., Giordanengo, A., & Hartvigsen, G. (2015). CallMeSmart: Location Tracking Using BLE Beacons. *Proceedings from The 13th Scandinavien Conference on Health Informatics.*

Solvoll, T., & Scholl, J. (2008). Strategies to reduce interruptions from mobile communication systems in surgical wards. *Journal of Telemedicine and Telecare, 14*(7), 389–392. doi:10.1258/jtt.2008.007015 PMID:18852324

Solvoll, T., Scholl, J., & Hartvigsen, G. (2010). Physicians interrupted by mobile devices – relations between devices, roles and duties. *Studies in Health Technology and Informatics, 160*, 1365.

Solvoll, T., Scholl, J., & Hartvigsen, G. (2013). Physicians Interrupted by Mobile Devices in Hospitals: Understanding the Interaction Between Devices, Roles, and Duties. *Journal of Medical Internet Research, 15*(3), e56. doi:10.2196/jmir.2473 PMID:23470528

Solvoll, T., Tiemersma, A., Kerbage, E., Fasani, S., Ravuri, A. B., & Hartvigsen, G. (2011). Context-sensitive Communication in Hospitals: A User Interface Evaluation and Redesign of Ascom Wireless IP-DECT Phones. *eTELEMED 2011, The Third International Conference on eHealth, Telemedicine, and Social Medicine*, 37 – 46.

Spurck, P. A., Mohr, M. L., Seroka, A. M., & Stoner, M. (1995). The impact of a wireless telecommunication system on time efficiency. *The Journal of Nursing Administration, 25*(6), 21–26. doi:10.1097/00005110-199506000-00007 PMID:7776003

Talaei-Khoei, A., Solvoll, T., Ray, P., & Parameshwaran, N. (2011). Policy-based Awareness Management (PAM): Case study of a wireless communication system at a hospital. *Journal of Systems and Software, 84*(10), 1791–1805. doi:10.1016/j.jss.2011.05.024

Talaei-Khoei, A., Solvoll, T., Ray, P., & Parameshwaran, N. (2012). Maintaining awareness using policies; Enabling agents to identify relevance of information. *Journal of Computer and System Sciences, 78*(1), 370–391. doi:10.1016/j.jcss.2011.05.013

Tang, J. C., Yankelovich, N., Begole, J., Kleek, M. V., Li, F., & Bhalodia, J. (2001). ConNexus to awarenex: extending awareness to mobile users. *Proceedings of the SIGCHI conference on Human factors in computing systems.* 10.1145/365024.365105

van Lieshout, E., van der Veer, S., Hensbroek, R., Korevaar, J., Vroom, M., & Schultz, M. (2007). Interference by new-generation mobile phones on critical care medical equipment. *Critical Care (London, England), 11*(5), R98. doi:10.1186/cc6115 PMID:17822524

Want, Schilit, Adams, Gold, Petersen, Goldberg, … Weiser. (1995) An overview of the parctab ubiquitous computing experiment. Personal Communications, IEEE, 2(6), 28 43.

Want, R., Hopper, A., Falcao, V., & Gibbons, J. (1992). The active badge location system. *ACM Transactions on Information Systems, 10*(1), 91–102. doi:10.1145/128756.128759

Weiser, M. (1991). The computer for the 21st century. *Scientific American, 265*(3), 94–104. doi:10.1038cientificamerican0991-94 PMID:1675486

Weiser, M., Gold, R., & Brown, J. S. (1999). The origins of ubiquitous computing research at parc in the late 1980s. *IBM Systems Journal, 38*(4), 693–696. doi:10.1147j.384.0693

Westbrook, Woods, Rob, Dunsmuir, & Day. (2011). Association of interruptions with an increased risk and severity of medication administration errors. *Archives of Internal Medicine, 170*(8), 683-690.

Wu, R., Rossos, P., Quan, S., Reeves, S., Lo, V., Wong, B., ... Morra, D. (2011). An evaluation of the use of smartphones to communicate between clinicians: A mixed-methods study. *Journal of Medical Internet Research, 13*(3), e59. doi:10.2196/jmir.1655 PMID:21875849

Chapter 15
Complex Action Methodology for Enterprise Systems (CAMES): A System to Contextualize the Behavioral Management Issue as Quantum Mechanical Variable

Olaf Cames
University of Liverpool, UK

Meghann Drury-Grogan
Fordham University, USA

ABSTRACT

This completed action research utilizes the conceptual framework of quantum mechanics in action science field studies for bias-free behavioral data collection and quantification. The research question tied to experimental verification if action research field studies can practically utilize the theory of communicative action and the theory of quantum mechanics to contextualize the quantification with pathological and distorted behavioral pattern. The result is a quantum-like formalism that provides intermediary conceptuality for organizational intervening initiatives. This process of contextualization behavior in projects via quantum probability experimentally evidenced. The chapter concludes by reviewing the results of two experiments that the hypotheses that the theory of quantum mechanics and the theory of communicative action qualifies as a building block for a planned methodological approach to intervene and steer problematic social structures in the desired direction.

DOI: 10.4018/978-1-5225-8516-9.ch015

INTRODUCTION

For more than two decades, practitioner studies have shown most Information Technology (IT) projects are not prosper- ous and state behavioural patterns as decisive factors for success or non-success. The IT practice lacks procedures to determine and predict project and organisational member behaviour with certainty.

Current action research methodologies bias observations se- verely and render quantification models of subjective data uncertain. Thus, this research thesis aims to design a scien- tifically rigorous action-science methodology process that is operational for action researchers and practitioners to lower the rate of non-successful IT projects where failure is at- tributable to human behaviour in organisational contexts. This investigation aims to apply scientific rigour to this issue and to verify the general applicability of mathematical formalism of quantum mechanics to address organisational venture that includes a wicked problem of how to communicate and collaborate appropriately. The subjective data collection and quantification models of this thesis build on the quantitative formalism of quantum mechanics and qualitative formalism of the theory of com- municative action. Mathematical and ontological formalism combine into a novel research strategy with planned instru- mentation for action research field studies summarised under the term 'Complex Action Methodology for Enterprise Systems' (CAMES). The outcome is a process to understand the behavioural action of project participants better. The process requires that participants act under a new identity, a virtual identity. Data collection occurs in one block with an average duration time of 10 minutes in a virtual location. The practice can, therefore, use these procedures for bias- free quantification of subjective data and prediction of an individual's future behaviour with certainty. Prediction of an individual's future behaviour with certainty provides to the IT practice what IT practice lacks but urgently requires. The certainty that claimed findings of behaviour in projects and organisational context requires to intervene and steer. Certainty and justification for planned intervening and steering initiatives secure funding.

Lack of Bias-Free Collection and Quantification of Subjective Data in Data Sciences

Conventional social sciences research methodologies bias observations and render quantification models of subjective data uncertain. Researcher bias on observations is severe and reason to dismiss classical quantification models. Influ- ences by the researcher and interaction of measuring research instrumentation on the observed result in methodo- logical flaws, false measures and incomplete interpretation of data. Biased research renders observations unreliable and invalidates data gathered from such biased observations. Collecting and quantifying the interaction occurring by and through biased individuals is considered unsolvable. Behavioural inner dynamics of biased individuals for steering and intervening purposes is not measured. Prediction failures deepen the gap between theory and practice (Kieser & Leiner, 2009). Management science mainstream, traditional understanding to explain behaviour lead to severe deficien- cies for its claimed findings. Direct influences from scien- tists on the observed or researcher contamination of envi- ronmental factors in research setup result in biased measure- ments and render the observed useless for bias-free quanti- fication of subjective data and prediction of an individual's future behaviour. To bias-free collect subjective data, the principles of quantification of subjective data and the re- searcher's analytical procedures require a research strategy with upfront planned instrumentation.

Quantum Mechanical and Ontological Formalism for Bias-Free Collection and Quantification of Subjective Data in Social and Data Sciences

CAMES subjective data collection and quantification models build on the quantitative formalism of quantum mechanics and qualitative formalism of the theory of communica- tive action. Mathematical and ontological formalism com- bine into a novel research strategy with planned instrumen- tation for action research field studies summarised under the term 'Complex Action Methodology for Enterprise Systems' (CAMES).

General Principles for Bias-Free Research Strategies

A practical research design combining bias-free quantitative instrumentation with qualitative reviews is practical. Researcher utilising validated instruments on observations produce meaningful findings (Miles, Huberman & Saldana, 2014). Instrumentation that either measure or reduce or avoid biasing effects are validated instruments. Qualifying research instrumentation as bias-free research instrumentation requires validation procedures for the quantitative instrumentation deployed.

General Principles for Quantification of Subjective Data

The unifying interdisciplinary schema for quantification of subjective data is the interference pattern. The interference pattern proved successful to explain data in research aimed to understand behavioural paradoxes. Novel analytical routines and corresponding formal logic had been successfully applied to explain observed human behavioural reasoning phenomena not entirely explainable with traditional concepts (Busemeyer et al. 2009; Wang et al., 2018a). The interference effect is defined in quantum theory as measurable and predictable and is expected to be there, naturally occurring. The presence of interference indicates quantum behaviour. Measured interference represents a healthy, standard, natural emerging and measurable condition (Von Neumann, 1933). The disappearance of interference indicates loss of fully exposed quantum behaviour (Aerts, Broekaert & Smets, 1999).

Interference defines as noise and disturbance in conventional theories. Interference violates conventional theories basic assumptions and renders methodologies based on such conventional theories useless for further investigation of interferences (Conte et al., 2007).

Explanations for data resulting in better understanding of human behaviour by utilising interference pattern render other methods treating the interference phenomena as noise and annoying factor less appropriate for further consideration. A satisfactory explanation by using the conceptual framework of the theory of quantum mechanics is direct evidence for the flaws in the theory of total probability. Con- servative, mainstream methodologies for an explanation of human behaviour base on the flawing theory of the law of total probability and apply methodologies based on the flawing assumption, e.g. all Markov property-based methodologies (Wang & Busemeyer, 2013; Wang et al., 2018a).

Measures and predictive analytics applying the conventional framework of quantum mechanics explain complete human behavioural phenomena (Aerts & de Bianchi, 2015). Clinical, experimental research inform about comparison studies applying both theories that resulted in better understanding for human behavioural phenomena like conceptual combination (Aerts, 2009), perception (Atmanspacher, et al., 2004; Conte et al., 2009), judgments (Khrennikov, 1999), disjunction effect (Busemeyer & Bruza, 2012), conjunction fallacy (Yukalov & Sornette, 2011; Busemeyer, Matthew & Wang, 2006; Franco, 2007;

Figure 1. Avoidance of researcher contamination with his research subject and research environment

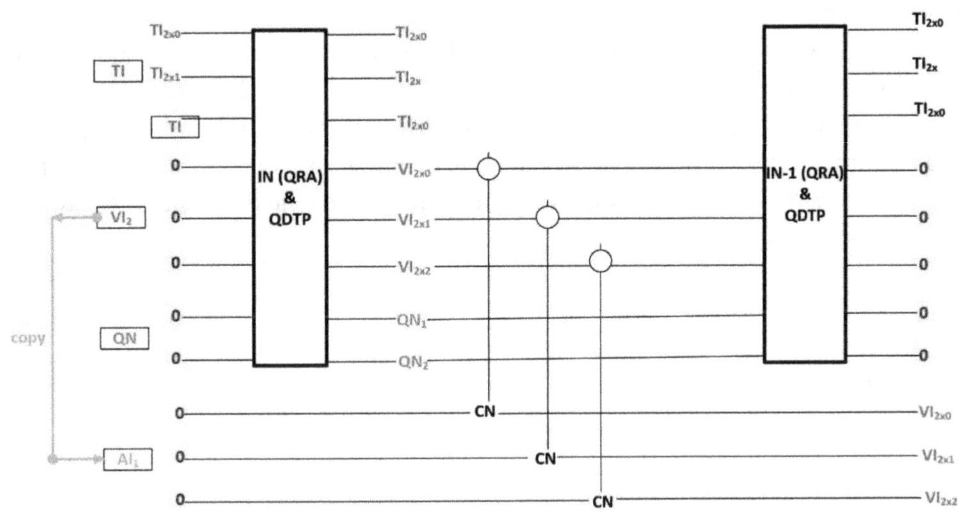

Khrennikov, 2008), liar paradox (Aerts, Broekaert & Smets, 1999) and con- texts and meanings (Yukalov & Sornette, 2011). Those ex- perimental studies expose failing, traditional, classic methodologies, their incomplete explanation of data and their classifications of phenomena as researcher induced methodological flaws. Flawing methodologies apply conventional, standard Markov observation techniques. Such introduced interference instead of measuring and explaining them. It is the conventional mainstream research design that prevents complete interpretation of subjective data and introduces researcher induced interference in measuring and analysis that renders the claimed findings useless (Yukalov & Sornette, 2011; Busemeyer, Wang & Lambert-Mogiliansky, 2009; Aerts, 2009b).

Across non-physics disciplines like social sciences, finances, game theory, decision sciences, cognitive science, psychology, genetics, medicine and economy, empirical validity and evidence for claimed findings emerge naturally by application of quantum structured interference pattern. The conceptual framework of quantum mechanics provides logical steps and proof with certainty for claimed contextual influences (Denolf, 2017), emerging behavioural dynamics (Aerts & de Bianchi, 2014), the presence of interference (Yukalov & Sornette, 2011), and the degree of entanglement with biasing environmental factors (Masuch, 1985; Bruza, et al. 2009).

METHODOLOGY

This methodology defines a planned, constructed research instrumentation (Miles, Huberman & Saldana, 2014). The research instrumentation strategy, definitions of the targets of the investigation, specifications for the action on targets, and performance indicators for evaluation outlines.

Preservation of Uncontaminated Research Environment

This methodology preserves an uncontaminated research environment. The researcher does not influence the data itself during scientific rigour application of subjective data collection and quantification.

The procedure is designed to permit interaction and evolution between the target of evaluation and its environment as ongoing.

Ongoing observation of project and organisational member communicative actions focus on state changes. Evolution operators compare previous and actual user communicative actions. Measurement occurs on models of mirrored superposition of data collected rather than on superposition and data collected itself. Mathematical procedures target logical operations on the mirrored superposition of superposition (Marsh & Briggs, 2009). Operating on mirror avoids the direct interaction of a measuring apparatus with the observed (Figure 1).

Table 1. CAMES notation

CAMES Notation (Non-Linear Orthography Logograms (CNLOL))		
1	TI	Targeted Identity
2	VI	Virtual Identity
3	^{T}ix	Observed components
4	^{T}iy	Observed components
5	^{V}ix	Superposition components
6	$^{T}ix2$	Additional environmental in-put
7	$^{V}ix2$	"AND" of TI observables
8	$^{TI}2x0$	Targeted Identity copied, ob-served component
9	$^{TI}2x2$	Targeted Identity additional copied, observed component
10	TI_R	Repository of environmental observed
11	$^{VI}2x0$	Copy of TI_{2x0}
12	$^{VI}2x1$	Copy of TI_{2x1}
13	VI_2	$^{TI}2x0$, $^{TI}2x1$, $^{TI}2x2$ repository Copy of TI
14	$^{AI}1 \leftarrow {}^{VI}2$	Augmented Identity
15	IN	Instances of Quantum Algo-rithms
16	QN	Nullifiable results of quantum operations
17	CN	CNOT gate. The data repre- sentation of VI cognitive dissonance.
		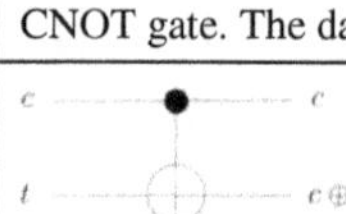 Logogram visualisation of cognitive dissonance in mathematical formalism of the theory of quantum mechanics.
18	IN-1	Reversible gate
19	QBIRAn	Quantum reversible algorithm
20	QBIDTP	Quantum data transformation injection point

continued on following page

Table 1. Continued

CAMES Notation (Non-Linear Orthography Logograms (CNLOL))		
21	adnTI	Attitudes, desires, needs (behavioural action preferences)
22	TIspace	Shared variable. Hosts all observed mental vectors and mental states
23	TIV	Mental vector
24	VIV	Mental vector
25	TIST	Mental state
26	qbiXY	qubit (pure state)
27	QRA1	Coding of companion TI, or VI or TIX/TIY influence on TI
28	QRA2	Additional Virtual Identity in- fluence freeze/defreeze procedures - preservation of time reversibility – anytime ad hoc previous TI state calculations from current VI state prediction analytics
29	QRA3	Acquire the original experimental environment observables from practitioner usage scenario participant (TI, TIx, TIy) again at any given time from VI2 predictive analytics operations
30	AI	Augmented Intelligence / Artificial Intelligence
31	FMn	Formation of "vicious circles of mediocrity" Masuch, 1985, p. 28)
32	IAn	Initial amplitudes Preferences for actions.
33	TIEO	Time-indexed evolution opera tor
34	FPT	Focused predictive task
35	DM	Dynamic momentum. Cogni- tive dissonance.
36	GIF	General Interference Detection
37	DS	Dominating mindset
38	CV	2-argument research question
39	CV	Context variable
39	KPI	Meaningful measure. Key performance indicator. Magnitude baseline.
39	Prb	Predicted behaviour

Organisational and Project Interaction Data Encoding/Decoding

Work context interaction, organisational, and real-world project communication and typical, critical usage scenarios are subject of researcher's notation encoding and decoding the observables. A defined listing of characters, numbers, symbols, punctuation, and letters sequence into a specific format ensures efficient co-negotiation between academics and practitioner (Table 1). Establishing a common language between academic driven further theoretical development and practice usability verification is vital to the translate the complexity and subtlety of ideas into evidence-based management in a particular work context (Rousseau, 2006). Encoding ensures project and organisational member interaction data persists. Decoding ensures project and organisational member interaction data retrieval between co-negotiation transmissions between an academic researcher and project practitioner. Those agreed notations obfuscate the complexity of the mathematical-logical procedures and eliminate the necessity for the project and organisational management to communicate in mathematical terminology (Table 1).

Transform Mathematical Complexity Into Ontological Simplicity

CAMES notation transforms the complexity of 4- dimensional Hilbert space state expressions into ontological state simplifications. Interventionists receive shorthand notation to apply quantum-like formalism into intermediary conceptuality (Aerts, Broekaert & Smets, 1999).

CAMES formal notation is a diagnostic framework in which communicative pathologies identify, localise, diagnose, and therapize. Formal normative notation reveal techniques to empirically evidence distorted communication patterns. Such human behavioural phenomena are subject of already existing and scientifically proven quantum-like quantitative procedures like behavioural anomaly detection in conceptual combination (Aerts, 2009), illusionary effects in human perception (Atmanspacher, et al., 2004), disjunction effect (Busemeyer & Bruza, 2012), affinities to fall for conjunction fallacies (Yukalov & Sornette, 2011; Busemeyer, Matthew & Wang, 2006; Franco, 2007; Khrennikov, 2008), biasing judgments (Khrennikov, 1999), and truth irritations by liar paradoxes (Aerts, Broekaert & Smets, 1999).

Empirical data for behavioural anomaly detection apply as values to non-local variables by observing interactions in context. As CAMES notations are universally applicable across different action contexts, non-local validity for its findings is the logical consequence. In this sense, CAMES notations are universal (Habermas, 2002). Applying formalities of CAMES notation leads therefore to the identification of universal conditions. Those conditions are communicative pathological explanations.

Universal applicability is claimed by quantum mechanics as well. Quantum cognitive sciences claim universal applicability because of mathematical procedures capable of projecting all possibilities with certainty into and out of naturally occurring Hilbert space and interference phenomena (Aerts & de Bianchi, 2014; Aerts & de Bianchi, 2015).

Applying CAMES notations in conjunction with quantitative measures, therefore, results in new behavioural pathologies and re-interpretation of behavioural pathologies that had previously identified, localised, diagnosed and therapized (Lawless & Schwartz, 2002; Rich & Craig, 2012). Those results can only materialise if universal explanations and re-interpretation apply to a context.

Prediction of an Individual's Future Behaviour With Certainty

Equations and Procedure

For simplicity of illustration, the figures are limited to illustrate equations using the Dirac notation because of its notational minimalism (Miller, Resnick & Zeckhauser, 2005). Dirac notation is a useful, effective alternative to conventional mathematical notation. It is the standard notation in quantum mechanics. Every organisational member participant receives a new identity. This new identity is virtual identity. The virtual identity establishes anonymity and confidentiality. Virtual participation provides contextualised disruption of the status quo (Gioia & Chittipeddi, 1991). Anonymity, confidentiality and contextualised disruption of the status quo is therefore at the disposition of the action researcher's experimental setup.

The sample equation depicts a participant who received virtual identity Surrogate252@action-science2.org and his observed mental vectors and mental states variables (Figure 2; Figure 3).

Figure 2. Observed mental vectors and mental state variables

$$TI_{space1}TI_{st}(TI(VI_v(Surrogate252@action\text{-}science2.org)) \doteq \{|G,D>, |G,F>, |B,D>, |B,F>\}$$

Figure 3. Amplitude reset to zero at the initial start of an experimental observation

$$(ia_{GD}(0), ia_{GF}(0), ia_{BD}(0), ia_{BF}(0) \doteq (|IA_I|^2 = 1)$$

$$(ia_{GD}(0), ia_{GF}(0), ia_{BD}(0), ia_{BF}(0) \doteq (|IA_I|^2 = 1)$$

$$(ia_{GD}(0), ia_{GF}(0), ia_{BD}(0), ia_{BF}(0) \doteq (|IA_I|^2 = 1)$$

$$(ia_{GD}(0), ia_{GF}(0), ia_{BD}(0), ia_{BF}(0) \doteq (|IA_I|^2 = 1)$$

Virtual identity resets prior internalised roles and influences to the level of influenced external elements set by the by the uncontaminated research setup (Figure 1).

Attitudes, perceptions, inner thoughts, perspectives and emotion formulate according to implications and directions set by the researcher (Koles & Nagy, 2012; Paniaras, 1997). Each row of IAI (Figure 1; Figure 3) provides the reset of measures to zero for one of the states in TIspace1TIst(TI(VIv(Surrogate252@action-science2.org)) (Figure 2).

Context Variables

A questionnaire asks the same question in a different context. Three questions obtain a particular individual's preferences and intentions to behave and act. The first question obtains values for two mental vectors. The second question obtains additional values for two other mental vectors. The third question obtains additional values to predict future behaviour by spin theory (Pauli, 1940).

Judgement 1

Every participant is forced into conflict. The conflict forces the participant to decide on one of two possible arguments.

This decision is a judgement on how to act and behave. Question 1 enforces judgement 1.

This judgement (Figure 4) delivers observable truth values for the research question into a vector (VIv) of Hilbert spaces (TIspace1) (Figure 1) for good (G), bad (B), defensive (D) and friendly (F) (Townsend et al., 2000; Busemeyer, Wang & Lambert-Mogiliansky, 2009). In case the 0- hypothesis confirms, ranked values are obsolete. Truth logic of research questions enter as shared variables and transform into projectors (Figure 5 and Figure 6).

Figure 4. Judgment 1: Truth values for the research question (sample instance)

$$\text{TIspace}_1\text{TI}_{st}(\text{TI}(\text{VI}_v(\text{Surrogate252@action-science2.org})) \doteq \{|\mathbf{G},D>, |\mathbf{G},F>, |\mathbf{B},D>, |\mathbf{B},F>\}$$

Figure 5. Judgment 1: Initial amplitude distribution for the research question hypothesis IAI = IAG

$$(ia_{GD}(1), ia_{GF}(1), ia_{BD}(0), ia_{BF}(0) \doteq (|IA_I|^2 = 1) \doteq ia_{GD}|^2 + |ia_{GF}|^2 = 1$$

Figure 6. Judgment 1: Initial amplitude distribution for the research question 0-hypothesis IAI = IAB

$$(ia_{GD}(0), ia_{GF}(0), ia_{BD}(1), ia_{BF}(1) \doteq (|IA_I|^2 = 1) \doteq ia_{BD}|^2 + |ia_{BF}|^2 = 1$$

Figure 7. Judgment 2: Truth values for the research questions (typified)

$$\text{TIspace}_1\text{TI}_{st}(\text{TI}(\text{VI}_v(\text{Surrogate252@action-science2.org})) \doteq \{|G,\mathbf{D}>, |G,\mathbf{F}>, |B,\mathbf{D}>, |B,\mathbf{F}>\}$$

Judgement 2

Every participant is forced into a new conflict. The conflict forces the participant to decide on one of two possible arguments. This decision is a judgement on how to act and behave. Question 2 enforces judgement 2.

This judgement delivers additional observable truth values for another, different research question into another vector (VIv) of modified state (TIst) in augmented Hilbert space (TIspace1) (Figure 7). In case the 0-hypothesis confirms, ranked values are obsolete.

Judgement 3

Every participant is forced into a new conflict. The conflict forces the participant to decide on five possible arguments. This decision is a judgement on how to act and behave. Question 3 enforces judgement 3. Truth logic of research questions enter as shared variables and transform into projectors (Figure 8). Judgement 3 superposes between states in judgement 1 (Figure 9).

Figure 8. Judgment 3: Initial amplitude distribution for intentions to act and behave

$$IA_I = (ia_G \cdot IA_G + ia_B \cdot IA_B)$$

Figure 9. Judgment 1 states

$$|ia_G|^2 + |ia_B|^2 = 1$$

Result: General Interference Detection (GIF)

In judgement 3 the context variable is superposed between states in judgement 1 (Figure 9). The context variable represents an individual that is superposed between possibilities to act and behave (Busemeyer & Bruza, 2012). This decision conflict is measurable as interference (Wang et al., 2018a; 2018b). The Interference pattern applies (Aerts & de Bianchi, (2015).

The theory of quantum mechanics measures interference as a naturally occurring mathematical and physical phenomena. This methodology applies measures to test for the presence or absence of interference phenomena in observed behaviours in projects and organisational context (Aerts, Broekaert & Smets, 1999; Wang et al., 2018a).

The presence of interference at the time participants responded to research questions obtains two verifications. First, the certainty that fully quantum behaviour is observed (Sasaki & Carlini, 2002; Aerts, Broekaert & Smets, 1999; Busemeyer & Bruza, 2012). Second, the certainty that research instrumentation did not interact leading to biasing interferences on the naturally occurring phenomena (Wang et al., 2018). Both measures provide certainty that applying quantum models predicting the probability of behaviour lead to practical outcomes.

This methodology transforms an empirical case of field study observed behaviours in projects into multiple-valued two-argument logical observables in TIspace1 (Figure 1) (Tarlacı & Pregnolato, 2016; Vaas, 2001a; Bruza, Widdows & Woods, 2006; Chadha et al., 2009; Cattaneo et al., 2009; Cignoli, d'Ottaviano & Mundici, 2013; Dubois & Toffano, 2016). Predictions derived from the quantum model generate intentions to act and behave for this individual, and the group made up of such individuals (Yukalov & Sornette, 2011; Ashtiani & Azgomi, 2016; Fuller, 2018; Wendt, 2015).

Judgement 2

Judging discrepancy measures per experiment participant per judgement. If variances are high, then context variables are of known truth, validity and utility. The larger the variance for judgement 2, the more significant the discrepancy between judgement 1 and judgement 2.

Judgement 3

Weighting expresses the degree of variance between decision making in question 1 and decision making in question 3. Weights are 0, 1, 3, 4, and 5. The smallest weight is 0, and 4 is the most substantial weight. A variance weighted as 0 represents no variance. A variance weighted as 4 represents the most substantial variance. The larger the variance for judgement 3, the more significant the discrepancy between judgement 1 and judgement 3.

Applying Interference Pattern

In case of GIF measure confirms the observation of fully quantum behaviour, literature researched pattern of interference effects in human behaviour apply (Sasaki & Carlini, 2002; Behrman et al., 2006). In the case of GIF, measure disconfirm observation of a fully quantum behaviour pattern of interference effects in human behaviour do not apply.

DISCUSSION

Project management applies false assumption that human behaviour is predictable by applying standard common sense and standard probability logic in conjunction with the lack of action research bias-free subjective data collection and quantification methodologies (Jaafari, 2004; Williams, 2002). Human affinity to disregard standard probability logic requires to switch to another probability logic.

Figure 10. Quantum model prediction of post-questionnaire behavior (sample instance)

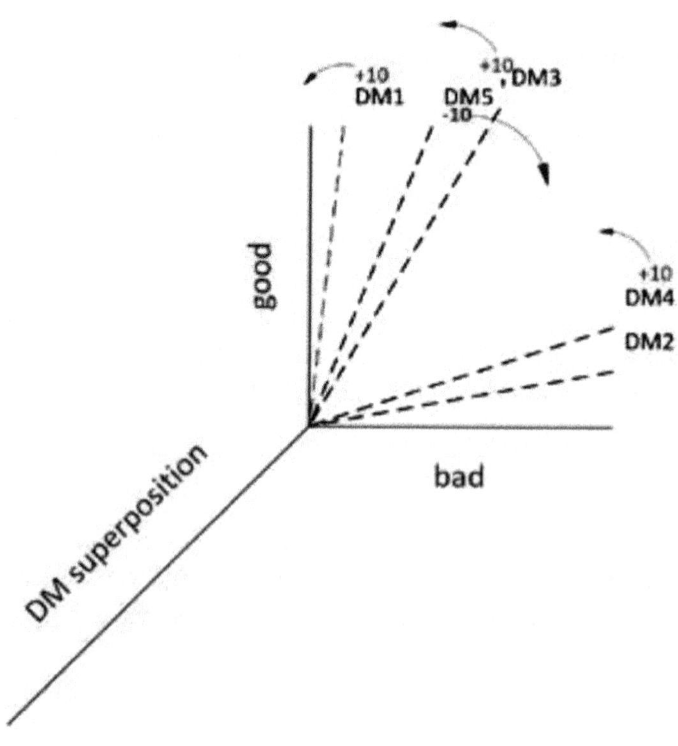

CONCLUSION AND FUTURE WORK

Future research must substitute simple patterns for desired or undesired behaviour in projects with complex behavioural patterns, a.k.a. As organisational sciences power law (Wang & von Tunzelmann, 2000). Future research explores augmented intelligence tools to substitute failing humans as project manager. The next step is to move on from the mathematical-analytical singletons of action science and action research into practical, mass scale execution on quantum computer.

REFERENCES

Aerts, D. (2009). Quantum structure in cognition. *Journal of Mathematical Psychology*, *53*(5), 314–348. doi:10.1016/j.jmp.2009.04.005

Aerts, D., Broekaert, J., & Smets, S. (1999). The Liar-paradox in a Quantum Mechanical Perspective. *Foundations of Science*, *4*(2), 115–132. doi:10.1023/A:1009610326206

Aerts, D., & de Bianchi, M. (2014). The extended Bloch repre- sentation of quantum mechanics and the hidden-measurement so- lution to the measurement problem. *Annals of Physics*, *351*, 975–1025. doi:10.1016/j.aop.2014.09.020

Atmanspacher, H., Filk, T., & Römer, H. (2004). Quantum Zeno features of bistable perception. *Biological Cybernetics*, *90*(1), 33–40. doi:10.100700422-003-0436-4 PMID:14762722

Bruza, P., Kitto, K., Nelson, D., & McEvoy, C. (2009). Is there some- thing quantum-like about the human mental lexicon? *Journal of Mathematical Psychology*, *53*, 362-377. doi:10.1016/j.jmp.2009.04.00

Busemeyer, J., & Bruza, P. (2012). *Quantum Models of Cognition and Decision*. Cambridge University Press. doi:10.1017/CBO9780511997716

Busemeyer, J., Matthew, M., & Wang, Z. (2006). A quantum in- formation processing theory explanation of disjunction effects. In R. Sun & N. Miyake (Eds.), Proceedings of 28th annual confer- ence of the cognitive science society & the 5th international conference of cognitive science (pp. 131–135). Academic Press.

Busemeyer, J., Wang, Z., & Lambert-Mogiliansky, A. (2009). Empirical comparison of markov and quantum models of decision making. *Journal of Mathematical Psychology, 53*(5), 423 – 433. doi: .2009.03.002 doi:10.1016/ j.jmp

Conte, E., Todarello, O., Federici, A., Vitiello, F., Lopane, M., Khrennikov, A., & Zbilut, J. P. (2007). Some remarks on an experiment suggesting quantum-like behavior of cognitive entities and formulation of an abstract quantum mechanical formalism to describe cognitive entity and its dynamics. *Chaos, Solitons, and Fractals*, *31*(5), 1076–1088. doi:10.1016/j.chaos.2005.09.061

Franco, R. (2007). *Quantum mechanics, Bayes' theorem and the conjunction fallacy.* arXiv preprint quant-ph/0703222

Khrennikov, A. (1999). Classical and quantum mechanics on in- formation spaces with applications to cognitive, psychological, social, and anomalous phenomena. *Foundations of Physics*, *29*(7), 1065–1098. doi:10.1023/A:1018885632116

Khrennikov, A. (2008). Bell-Boole inequality: Nonlocality or probabilistic incompatibility of random variables? *Entropy (Basel, Switzerland)*, *10*(2).

Marsh, S., & Briggs, P. (2009). Examining trust, forgiveness and regret as computational concepts. In *Computing with social trust* (pp. 9–43). London: Springer.

Masuch, M. (1985). Vicious Circles in Organizations. *Administrative Science Quarterly*, *30*(1), 14-33.

Von Neumann, J. (1933). Mathematische Grundlagen der Quantenmechanik. *Monatshefte Für Mathematik*, *40*(1), A31.

Wang, B., Song, D., Wang, B., Zhang, P., Li, J., Song, D., & Shang, Z. (2018a). Exploration of Quantum Interference in Doc- ument Relevance Judgement Discrepancy. *Entropy (Basel, Switzerland)*, *18*(4), 144. doi:10.3390/e18040144

Wang, Z., & Busemeyer, J. (2013). A Quantum Question Order Model Supported by Empirical Tests of an A Priori and Precise Prediction. *Topics in Cognitive Science*, *5*(4), 689–710. doi:10.1111/tops.12040 PMID:24027203

Yukalov, V., & Sornette, D. (2011). Decision Theory with Prospect Interference and Entanglement. *Theory And Decision: An International Journal For Methods And Models In The Social And Decision. The Sciences*, *70*(3), 283–328.

Chapter 16
Strategic Communication in Crisis:
Winning May (Not) Be Everything

Lauren J. Keil
Optum, USA

Angela M. Jerome
Western Kentucky University, USA

ABSTRACT

When faced with crises, organizational leaders must identify, prioritize, and communicate with organizational stakeholders. Increasingly, organizational leaders find themselves responding to crises made by persons that represent or are associated with the organization in some way. However, most case studies of image repair campaigns focus on the individual that has transgressed rather than on the often-simultaneous campaigns undertaken by the organizations with which they are associated. To study these issues more closely, this chapter uses The Ohio State University's (OSU's) tattoos for memorabilia scandal as exemplar and offers meaningful insight and pragmatic considerations for practitioners dealing with similar situational constraints.

INTRODUCTION

Image repair[1] undeniably operates at the intersection of strategic communication, leadership, and conflict management in modern organizations. In times of crisis, organizational leaders must identify, prioritize, and communicate with stakeholders. Stakeholder prioritization, regardless of public relations task, is most often based on audiences' legitimacy, power, and urgency (Rawlins, 2006). Research indicates that post-crisis audience prioritization can be particularly troubling for organizational leaders for a number of reasons. Perhaps nowhere is this prioritization more problematic than in the world of sports.

Kruse's (1981) work on apologia in team sport explicates how these issues are problematized in the world of sports. She argues sports is a "sphere of social reality separate from the sociopolitical world" (p. 271). Building on the work of Edwards (1973), Novak (1976), and others, she asserts that because

DOI: 10.4018/978-1-5225-8516-9.ch016

athletic teams, players, fans, and all others associated with the organization form a "family," members may temporarily set aside ethical norms if the option to win is present because winning "controls all of the sport world's ethical precepts" (p. 283). Thus, an act that may be considered unethical or be disapproved of in the regular world may be viewed as acceptable in the sports world because the end goal is to win, regardless of the means to achieve it (Kruse, 1981). She notes, however, that there are cases in which an unethical act is seen as morally reprehensible enough to surpass the need to win, such as when a player places his/her own selfish needs above those of the team, when a vital team member leaves the team or does not play to the best of their ability, or when individual members display "behaviors that indicate an overly casual or frivolous attitude toward the team or the game" (Kruse, 1981, p. 276). In such cases, family members will allow for a punishment that fits the crime.

Though a great deal of work has been done in the area of image repair and sports, most case studies focus on the image repair campaigns of individuals who have transgressed rather than on the, often simultaneous, campaigns undertaken by the organizations that the transgressors represent or with which he/she/they is/are associated. However, when athletes/coaches violate the rules, laws, and/or ethical mores of their governing body (e.g., the NCAA, NFL, NBA), the organizations to which they are members often have to mount their own image repair campaigns. In doing so, the organizations often face complex stakeholder dichotomies. When this occurs, the organization has to decide whether it should fine/suspend/terminate the, often beloved, coach or athlete(s) accused. Further, the organization must evaluate how its decisions may help/harm the institution's image in the eyes of its fans and governing body that often have differing opinions on the issue.

A few studies (e.g., Fortunato, 2008; Len-Rios, 2008; Sisler, 2015) illuminate the value of inquiry that places primacy on the image repair campaigns of organizational leaders who are forced to mount image repair campaigns resulting from actions perpetrated by the athletes representing their organizations. However, additional studies are warranted. The current study examines the image repair campaign undertaken by the leadership of The Ohio State University (OSU) following its tattoos for memorabilia scandal in an effort to offer pragmatic considerations and recommendations for organizational leaders dealing with similar situational constraints. The solutions and recommendations offered herein are discussed in a manner that will benefit practitioners operating both inside and outside of the sports arena.

BACKGROUND

Before delving into the case analysis, it is necessary to provide background in three different areas. First, this crisis has an intricate backstory that warrants telling. Second, an outline of the relevant scholarship on which the arguments herein are based is needed. Third, the methodology undertaken by the authors is discussed.

Case Background

On April 2, 2010, former OSU football player, Chris Cicero, and head football coach, Jim Tressel, exchanged emails about tattoo parlor owner, Ed Rife, who was under investigation for drug trafficking by the U.S. Department of Justice. Cicero informed Tressel that Rife had purchased autographed memorabilia from OSU football players; Tressel thanked him for the information (Associated Press, 2011a; Farrey,

2011). This was a problem because NCAA policy does not allow student-athletes to sell "institutionally issued athletic awards, apparel, and/or equipment" for personal gain (as cited in Farrey, 2011, n.p.), and Tressel did not relay this information to anyone on OSU's leadership team (Associated Press, 2011a). Two weeks later, Cicero again initiated an email exchange with Tressel, providing specific details about what types of memorabilia had been traded and sold to Rife; again, no member of OSU's leadership team was informed (Associated Press, 2011a; Farrey, 2011). On September 13, 2010, Tressel signed the NCAA's annual certificate of compliance signifying he knew of no violations and/or had reported all possible violations to school officials (Associated Press, 2011a).

The OSU crisis came to a boiling point on December 7, 2010, when OSU officials were informed by the Office of the U.S. Attorney that government raids on the home and business of Rife unearthed OSU memorabilia traded for tattoos and/or cash by six OSU football players, a list that included OSU's star quarterback, Terrelle Pryor; the raid turned up 36 items of Buckeye memorabilia, including a $7,000 Bowl Championship Series ring from 2002 (Associated Press, 2011a; Dohrmann & Epstein, 2011; Farrey, 2011).

Interestingly, OSU leaders knew before they hired Tressel that he had a questionable performance history. He was accused of providing the Youngstown State University (YSU) quarterback with $10,000 in cash and cars in 1998 during his tenure as YSU's head football coach; Tressel denied any knowledge of the activity and received no punishment for it (Farrey, 2011). Such accusations were not a one-time occurrence. After leaving OSU in 2002, star running back, Maurice Clarett, alleged Tressel assisted him in acquiring the use of vehicles from a Columbus car dealership while an OSU student-athlete (Farrey, 2011; Friend, 2011). In 2008, Pryor received a ticket while driving a car owned by a Columbus, OH car salesman, Aaron Kniffin; two similar instances subsequently occurred (Farrey, 2011). In July 2010, OSU looked into the relationship between its athletes and Kniffin after receiving an anonymous letter accusing student-athletes of trading autographed memorabilia for the use of cars with employees of the new car dealership at which Kniffin was employed. Doug Archie, OSU's NCAA Compliance Officer, found no violation of NCAA rules (Farrey, 2011). Through all this Tressel, remained one of the most respected coaches in college football (See Dohrmann & Epstein, 2011). Beyond his admirable reputation, Tressel had the most successful 10-year career in OSU history and an overall winning record in the Big Ten, including his 9-1 record against rival and fellow football powerhouse the University of Michigan ("Ohio State players," 2011).

Literature Review

To analyze the image repair strategies used by OSU's leadership team in this case, the current study uses Benoit's (1995, 2015) typology because the plethora of case studies done using this typology as a methodological base offer an aggregate of findings from which to offer practical recommendations. Benoit's typology outlines five categories for image restoration: denial, evading responsibility, reducing offensiveness, corrective action, and mortification. The first strategy identified is *denial*, which includes *simple denial* and *shifting the blame*. When utilizing simple denial, an actor simply denies that the act occurred, that he/she performed it, or, as suggested by Brinson and Benoit (1999), that the act was not harmful to others or the public. In using shifting the blame, the accused actor points to another actor as the transgressor. *Separation*, developed from shifting the blame, involves not just blaming another actor but also trying to distance oneself from the other (Brinson & Benoit, 1999).

The second overarching strategy, *evasion of responsibility*, may be selected by actors who were involved in the performance of the act in question, but hope to reduce the perceived responsibility. In using the first sub-strategy of evasion of responsibility, *provocation*, an actor acknowledges commission of the offensive act but attempts to justify the act by claiming another actor provoked the act. The second subcategory, *defeasibility*, is used when the accused claims a "lack of information about or control over important factors in the situation" (Benoit, 2015, p. 23). The third subcategory is *accident*, in which the accused blames the situation on forces beyond his/her/its control. The last subcategory, *good intentions*, as the name implies, is utilized when the accused wants to show the public that the act was committed with good intentions.

The third category, *reducing offensiveness,* is comprised of six subcategories. The first of these subcategories, *bolstering*, "may be used to mitigate the negative effects of the act on the actor by strengthening the audience's positive affect for the rhetor" (Benoit, 2015, p. 24). This is a common strategy used when actors know they cannot deny the accusations but still attempt to alter the audience's opinion about the situation, person, or organization by highlighting positive traits. *Minimization* focuses on decreasing "the amount of negative affect associated with the offensive act" (Benoit, 2014, p. 24). 5*Differentiation* is used by an accused to compare the act to other more offensive or harmful acts in an effort reduce the public's negative perception of the accused's act. The difference between the two is further explained by Benoit (2014) with exemplars. Minimization is represented by the statement "I broke 5your vase, but it was not an expensive one," while differentiation is represented by the statement "I borrowed your laptop without asking; I didn't steal it" (p. 28).

The fourth subcategory is *transcendence*. This strategy is best explained in the context of the current study by Brinson and Benoit (1999) who describe it as placing "the act in a broad, positive context to help improve the offender's image and includes appeals to other persons, values, or group loyalties" (p. 488). The fifth subcategory, *attacking the accuser*, is used when an actor calls into question the credibility of the person or persons behind negative accusations, such as general publics, media outlets, or competitors (Brinson & Benoit, 1999). Finally, *compensation* is used to reimburse those who have experienced physical, emotional, or material harm because of the event/act in question.

The fourth major category is *corrective action.* In using this strategy, the accused vows to repair any harm done by his/her act and ensure the act will not occur again. The last major image restoration strategy identified by Benoit is *mortification*, which requires the accused to apologize to those harmed and ask for forgiveness.

Space does not allow for a comprehensive overview of case studies done using Benoit's typology. What follows is a sampling of findings from case studies that employed Benoit's typology to analyze image repair campaigns in the sports arena that provide valuable insight for the current study.

Using Benoit's typology as a guide, Fortunato (2008) and Len-Rios (2008) examined Duke University's response to three of its lacrosse players being indicted for physically and sexually abusing an exotic dancer hired for a team party. In examining this crisis response largely led by Duke's President, Richard Brodhead, Fortunato (2008) focused on the framing that was used in the response while Len-Rios (2008) focused on local news portrayals during various stages of the crisis. Together, these works identify points of congruity between Duke's chosen strategies and image repair theory.

Len-Rios (2008) points out that Duke did not respond to the incident for almost 10 days and that, coupled with charges that it did not take the incident seriously enough in the beginning, left Duke at a serious disadvantage. Of Brodhead's initial response Fortunato (2008) notes, he did not try to deny the acts had occurred, and "consistently described the behavior as inappropriate for Duke students" (p.

120). The university also cancelled the lacrosse team's season and vowed stricter oversight in subsequent years. Further, it took responsibility for creating an environment where such an incident could occur, but bolstered its value as an organization and its commitment to corrective action where it could. To indicate his commitment to creating such an environment, Brodhead announced the university's establishment of five different committees to examine the history of the lacrosse team's behavior, analyze Duke's response to the scandal, audit the student judicial process at Duke, investigate the campus culture, and guide university administrators (Fortunato, 2008). Brodhead also noted that Duke should be a national leader in dealing with such issues. In statements specifically aimed at alumni and parents of undergraduate students, he reiterated his position by noting that Duke should use this incident as an opportunity to become a better institution (Fortunato, 2008).

Len-Rios' study adds more nuance to the understanding of Duke's response as her study highlights a few other strategies of note and went beyond a framing analysis to assess the effectiveness of the response as indicated by local news coverage. She observes that the university's initial response contained simple denial, repeating statements made by players and the athletic director that denied sexual assault had taken place, and reiterated the student-athlete's mortification for engaging in the embarrassing party. She also notes that in the early days of the crisis, the university also used a host of other strategies such as bolstering efforts to improve the university's relations with the black community and attacking "the news media for alleged sensational and inaccurate coverage" (Len-Rios, 2008, p. 278). However, she notes that Duke's statements focused most on the corrective action/separation efforts such as terminating the team's coach in addition to the other actions noted above.

It is the function of a new strategy Len-Rios deems "expression of disappointment" (p. 278) that is most important to the current study. Len-Rios argues expressions of disappointment, are related to, but different from separation because instead of "placing responsibility on a group member and disassociating the organization from the member, expression of disappointment acknowledges bad judgment or behavior, but does not definitively sever the member from the group" (p. 279). The significance of this strategy is that it "serves as an intermediate "safe" response and could be interpreted as a step in the process of "corrective action" (i.e., replacing the lacrosse coach, punishing players)" (p. 279). However, she goes on to argue, "The difficulty with expression of disappointment is that it may be interpreted as a middle ground response and as too cautious and indeterminate, thereby not satisfying parties who were hoping the university would take a strong position either way" (p. 279).

Regardless of Brodhead's efforts, Len-Rios found that in the early stages of the crisis, few news stories portrayed Duke athletics positively. Months later, district attorney, Michael B. Nifong, resigned from the case amid ethical questions. As a result, Duke shifted its attacks onto him (Len-Rios, 2008). Eventually, all charges against all three lacrosse players who were indicted were dropped. Two of the accused students were allowed to return to Duke; the third had graduated before he was charged (Fortunato, 2008). Therefore, Duke's need for image repair was significantly diminished as the dropped charges indicated judicial officials' belief that the players were innocent.

In light of this outcome, Len-Rios argues that Duke's refusal to comment on the criminal allegations in the early stages of the crisis was a beneficial decision. However, the outcome of this case also highlights the problematic nature of expressions of disappointment. The university expressed its disappointment in the players numerous times, indicating it "did not condone the behavior or alleged behavior of the students" (p. 279). Thus, some argued those expressions of disappointment, coupled with its corrective action efforts, insinuated the university believed the players were guilty. In fact, the players waged a lawsuit against Duke predicated on that argument. Regardless, news stories about Duke athletics produced in the late stages of the crisis were "overwhelmingly positive" (Len-Rios, 2008, p. 283).

Building on the work of Benoit and Kruse, Brazeal (2008) examines the image repair campaign of NFL player, Terrell Owens, following a failed contract negotiation with the Philadelphia Eagles. She notes that while Owens "boorish behavior" (p. 145) was often disregarded during his career because of his prowess on the field, his belligerent interactions with coaches and public criticism of the team's quarterback, Donovan McNabb, after the Eagles refused to renegotiate, which lead to his deactivation, left him in need of image repair. His image repair campaign failed, according to Brazeal, for several reasons. First, his agent erroneously sought to paint Owens as a victim. In line with Kruse's findings, Brazeal notes that this was poor choice because it went against the team sport ethic, which calls for athletes to place the team and the game above self. Second, though Owens and his representative tried to recover from their early, failed attempts by "giving lip service" to the audience's values and downplaying the events in question, they ultimately failed in their image repair attempt because "they failed to argue that Owens would conform to the culture in the future" (Brazeal, 2008, p. 149).

Though not directly predicated on Benoit's work, several other case studies of image repair add insight into the current case study. The following paragraphs overview these works.

Like that of Kruse and Brazeal, the work of Jerome (2008) highlights the effect winning may have on an image repair campaign in the sports arena when assessing the image repair campaign of NASCAR driver Tony Stewart following a 2002 incident in which he punched a photojournalist. Jerome (2008) found that Stewart used a well-received rhetoric of atonement in his image repair campaign, but drawing on Kruse's assertions, remarked that Stewart's status as one of the winningest competitors in the sport also may have offered him leeway that would not have been afforded a weaker competitor. Though she does not make the claim, there is reason to believe such situational factors may also aid other entities in their image repair campaigns. For example, Coombs (1995) noted the effect performance history has on organizations responding to crises. Winning, whether on the field, politically, or in the stock market, shapes stakeholders' perceptions.

Jerome's (2008) study also demonstrates the nuanced care that must be taken by organizational leaders in the sports arena to respond successfully to diverse audiences following a crisis. She observes that Home Depot's decision to fine NASCAR driver Tony Stewart (of whose car it was the primary sponsor) after the incident rather than suspend/fire him, before stakeholder reactions to the crisis could be accurately gauged, functioned to signal Home Depot's derision with Stewart for stakeholders who felt some punishment was warranted, but also allowed Home Depot to avoid backlash from stakeholders who felt suspension/termination was not warranted.

Bruce and Tini's (2008) work, which focuses on the function of the diversion strategy in the area of sports image repair, echoes the importance of selecting strategies that can aid sports organizations in navigating complex audience dichotomies in the world of sport. In examining the image repair campaign employed by an Australian rugby team that broke the salary cap rules set by its governing body, the authors found that the team successfully "diverted attention away from management by focusing on the players, and later the fans, as innocent victims" (p. 112), allowing for successful organizational rebuilding. Though Bruce and Tini acknowledge a diversion strategy may not have much use outside of the sports and entertainment industries, as may also be the case with some of the above findings, the work of Koerber and Zabara (2017) demonstrates that lessons learned from the study of image repair in the sports arena may well be beneficial to an overall enhanced understanding of organizational image repair.

Building on the work of Coombs (2007, 2015), Koerber and Zabara argue that scholars of image repair should pay a great deal more attention to preexisting situational "buffers" that may well alter an organization's crisis response strategy selection. While Coombs' work focuses primarily on the buffers of crisis history and favorable reputation, Koerber and Zabara argue that in the sports arena, and perhaps in other organizational contexts, other buffers clearly exist. For example, they outline two newly conceptualized buffers, the bonds of community and political economy. Of import to the current study is their discussion of the bonds of community. They argue that the bonds built between a team and its fans and between fans affords organizations a great deal more leeway in crisis response than is often afforded other types of organizations. In building their case, they refer to Kruse's conceptualization of a team and its fans a family and contend,

In this conceptualization, crises cannot damage images and disconnect fans from their teams quite as easily as in other industries because fans have much more to lose than just a product. Giving up on a team in crisis means giving up on the entire community, long-created and nurtured with friends and family in public and private spaces. (p. 197)

However, Koerber and Zabara (2017) assert, "The strength of these communal bonds in relations to sports teams is explained by the psychology of identification" (p. 196) Therefore, it seems this buffer may be established by any type of organization because the presence of communal bonds is likely predicated not on industry, but on the ability of an organization to build identification with its audience members. Not surprisingly, they conclude their piece by stating,

While the world of organized sports seems inherently predestined for the development of buffers based on the unique relationships it creates, buffers should not be disregarded by crisis communicators in other fields, such as business and politics. In fact, crisis communicators working in those fields would do well to emulate some of the conditions for creating buffers described in this article, which may very well help them weather their own unique crises. (p. 199)

Ulmer, Sellnow, and Seeger's (2015) offer the last conceptualization of import to the current study, the discourse of renewal. They argue that crises provide organizations an opportunity for positive post-crisis discourse. According to Ulmer et al. (2015), a discourse of renewal requires four elements: organizational learning, ethical communication, prospective vs. retrospective vision, and effective organizational rhetoric. In an earlier work, Ulmer, Seeger, and Sellnow (2007) noted that a discourse of renewal should focus on the provisional rather than the strategic, be rooted in the values of the organizational leader, and focus on corrective action and change. Further, they noted that organizational leaders should be the model for renewal and that renewal strategies will work best with stakeholder groups with which the organization has a positive relationship pre-crisis. As clear from the above studies, winning and communal bonds establish a positive pre-crisis relationship for many sports organizations facing crisis. Therefore, a discourse of renewal should be considered for a post-crisis response campaign.

Method

The study that serves as the exemplar for the central arguments in this chapter was conducted via case study analysis. While case studies do not produce generalizable results, Seeger (2006) argues that one may generate a list of best practices by generalizing "from other forms of communication" and extrapolating "from the now considerable body of largely case-based research in crisis communication" (p. 233-234). For example, he asserts that multiple case studies illustrate the value of communicating with honesty, candor, and openness in post-crisis messages. Likewise, Benoit (2015) concludes that lying is never an effective image repair strategy because, "if the truth emerges and the original accusations are shown to be true, the accused now has an additional problem" (p. 124). Benoit (2015) illustrated the lessons that may be learned from case studies of image repair in five areas: sports/entertainment, corporate, political, international, and third party. The studies appearing in Blaney, Lippert, and Smith's (2013) collection, *Repairing the Athlete's Image,* also focus on the lessons that can be learned from image repair campaigns conducted in a sports context. Thus, case study analysis is an appropriate methodology for the current study.

To complete this analysis, a variety of articles and websites relating to OSU, Tressel, and the tattoos-for-memorabilia scandal were analyzed. These included articles and videos from websites such as Sports Illustrated, ESPN, Fox Sports, the Columbus Dispatch, the OSU newsroom, and YouTube. While it was impossible to gather all existing information on the scandal from all possible sources, artifacts collected from these sources were representative of the overall campaign. News websites such as ESPN.com and Sportsillustrated.com were the first websites accessed for potential information because these sports news outlets contained detailed information about the scandal. Other articles and videos were also found, as needed for clarification/detail, by typing key words from the scandal into the Google search engine. The first round of data for this study was retrieved and analyzed between June and August 2011.

A critical analysis was the chosen procedure to analyze the collected data for this study. Once the initial data was collected, the first author began the process of analysis by organizing the information chronologically to understand the rhetorical trajectory of the image repair strategies used by both Tressel and OSU's leaders. After these artifacts were organized, Benoit's (1995/2015) image restoration typology was used as the primary framework for initial message analysis. Linkages were drawn between strategy use and function to compose a first draft of this text.

Then, the second author took the first draft and necessary texts and reexamined the rhetoric to expand/clarify the arguments made herein and to better situate these arguments within the broader scholarly context, focusing specifically on the rhetoric of OSU Athletic Director, Gene Smith, and President, Gordon Gee, as they were the organizational leaders most prominent in the organization's image repair campaign. Further, she collected texts and literature between July and October 2015 that allowed for a more nuanced discussion of the rhetorical success of OSU's leadership post-scandal and the pragmatic considerations for practitioners dealing with similar situational constraints as those faced by OSU in this crisis. Further, the second author ensured the analysis was in line with Benoit's (2015) updated typology and that the state of OSU football and image repair theory in 2018 were adequately reflected in the analysis and discussion.

ANALYSIS

This analysis is laid out in five sections. These are: Initial Responses, Emails Discovered, Separation, Attempting Renewal, and Returning to the Top.

Initial Responses

On December 7, 2010, the U.S. Attorney's office notified OSU leadership that a raid of Rife's home and office uncovered the OSU memorabilia described above (Farrey, 2011). On December 16, OSU officials spoke with the six players cited in the Rife scandal. Three days later, OSU self-reported to the NCAA and declared all student- athletes involved ineligible (Associated Press, 2011a; "OSU athletic director," 2010). On December 23, Smith and Tressel held a press conference about the incidents. In his statement, Tressel combine *denial, corrective action,* and *bolstering* strategies. In essence, he denied prior knowledge of the incidents, but accepted responsibility for their occurrence (See Farrey, 2011; "OSU Coach," 2010). Smith provided a timeline of events from December 7 forward and explained the NCAA's initial decision on student-athlete suspensions (their suspensions would be served during the following season, allowing them eligibility for the quickly approaching Sugar Bowl) (Associated Press, 2011a; "OSU athletic director," 2010). Further, he *bolstered* the character of the student-athletes involved when asserting that they were "honest," "forthright," and "remorseful" in their interviews "which allowed us to move expeditiously" ("OSU athletic director," 2010, n.p.).

The substantive part of Smith's statement focused on *denial and minimization;* he stated,

There are no other NCAA violations around this case. We're very fortunate we do not have a systemic problem in our program. This is isolated to these young men, isolated to this particular incident. There are no other violations that exist. (as cited in Staples, 2011, para. 16)

Around this same time, Smith also stated that OSU hoped the players involved would receive reduced penalties through the NCAA appeals process because some of the cash received in the transactions went to help the student-athletes' family members who were struggling financially ("Ohio State football," 2010). In another statement Smith demonstrated OSU's continued commitment to *corrective action* noting that though student-athlete education on the issue of impermissible benefits was lacking between 2007 and 2009, the university "began to significantly improve" its education on these issues in November of 2009 and would continue to do so moving forward (NCAA, 2010, para. 12).

These strategies allowed OSU to navigate the dichotomy noted above smoothly at this point in the crisis largely because college sports fans and media commentators are notoriously critical of the NCAA. A great deal of that criticism arises from the double standard inherent in the NCAA's impermissible benefits policy (See Jenkins, 2013; Solomon, 2013). The NCAA and its member institutions make millions of dollars each year (Berkowitz, 2013) while student-athletes may not benefit from their athletic prowess beyond scholarships. The NCAA's choice to allow the student-athletes in question to play in the 2010 Sugar Bowl and serve their suspensions during the 2011 season demonstrates this double standard. The NCAA said its decision was based on the fact that the student-athletes had not received proper education concerning NCAA rules on such issues (Walker, 2010). However many, like Dave Walker, a correspondent for *The Bleacher Report,* felt it was based on the NCAA's potential loss in television revenue if the student-athletes in question were ruled ineligible for the game. He wrote, "So what will the penalty against them be? All are suspended for five games next year. Not this year. Not in a big money BCS game…" (Walker, 2010, para. 5-6). Though Walker felt the suspensions should start immediately, he argues the violations were "tacky at best" (para. 19) and the sentiment of his piece suggests he believed the punishment far harsher than the crime (Walker, 2010).

Given the above, the work of Kruse (1981) and Koerber and Zabara (2017) indicates that most fans likely would not even see the violations problematic. Though the team might lose the games for which the players would be suspended, the team had a whole year to plan for that, and the NCAA and its oft-criticized rules were an easy scapegoat. While OSU leaders needed to reassure fans, the situation afforded Smith the opportunity to prioritize the NCAA as the primary audience for his rhetoric. To avoid lack of institutional control penalties from the NCAA which come with harsh punishments, OSU leaders needed to convince the NCAA that these were isolated incidents, that they had no prior knowledge of them, that they were telling the truth, and that there was committed to correcting the problem. The strategies chosen served that purpose, but the crisis was far from over.

Emails Discovered

A little less than a month later, OSU's legal affairs office uncovered the Tressel/Cicero emails (Associated Press, 2011a; Farrey, 2011; "Tressel resignation," 2011) and what could have been a blip on the NCAA violations radar became a full blown NCAA compliance and image repair nightmare for OSU. OSU officials questioned Tressel in mid-January 2011, and he admitted to committing a major NCAA violation on February 8, 2011 (Associated Press, 2011a; Farrey, 2011; "Tressel resignation," 2011). The dichotomy would now get more treacherous for OSU leaders to navigate.

In his response, Tressel used *bolstering, good intentions, minimization, differentiation, defeasibility,* and *corrective action* strategies. For example, his statements indicated the student-athletes were his first priority and implied he felt compliance with NCAA rules was less important than potential disruption of a confidential federal investigation. Further, he noted that none of the student-athletes was named in the drug trafficking allegations and that he should have asked OSU legal counsel how to handle the situation. Last, he remarked on the personal growth that would come from the scandal (See Tressel, 2011).

While OSU knew people continued to defend Tressel as "an otherwise perfect coach who made one little mistake" (Staples, 2011, para. 5), it also knew that Tressel broke at least one of the two unforgiveable NCAA violations: allowing players impermissible benefits and lying to the NCAA (Staples, 2011). For these reasons, appeasing both the NCAA and fans would be virtually impossible.

It is not surprising that OSU leaders mirrored Home Depot's strategy at this stage; they handed Tressel a two-game suspension and fined him $250,000, which would be used to pay for OSU's defense of itself to the NCAA (Farrey, 2011; Marshall, 2011). However, OSU officials continued to support Tressel. A March 11, 2011, statement sent to the NCAA and signed by Smith, Gee, and faculty athletics representative, John Bruno, stated that Tressel's "behavior in this situation is out of character for him and is contrary to his proven history of promoting an atmosphere of NCAA compliance within the football program" and noted, "Since his hiring as the head football coach in 2001, he and his staff have attended NCAA rules education sessions on a consistent basis, regularly sought interpretations and self-reported secondary violations" (as cited in Boren, 2011, para. 5). In its public response to Tressel's admission OSU expressed its disappointment in Tressel stating, "The institution is very surprised and disappointed in Coach Tressel's lack of action in this matter" (as cited in Associated Press, 2011a, para. 22). However, Smith reiterated OSU had self-reported Tressel's violation to the NCAA in the hopes that "the governing body of college sports will agree with the sanctions handed out by the Buckeyes officials" (as cited in Marshall, 2011, para. 4). Smith went as far as to say, "Wherever we end up at the end of the day, Jim Tressel is our football coach. He is our coach and we trust him implicitly. There is no question in my mind that his decision was from the heart" (as cited in Marshall, 2011, para. 5).

Further, when Gee was asked whether he had considered terminating Tressel, he replied "No, are you kidding?" (as cited in Marshall, 2011, para. 7). Gee then quipped the now infamous statement: "I hope he doesn't fire me" (as cited in Forde, 2011, para. 6). Gee's reluctance to terminate Tressel indicates his keen awareness of the ethic of team sport outlined by Kruse. However, he failed to realize the perception his joke created. Clearly, OSU was looking for the soft response provided by expressions of disappointment as described by Len-Rios (2008); however, what it experienced was the shortcomings that can accompany this strategy that she also describes.

For example. Shaw (2011) jested, "It was hard to tell if Tressel were being disciplined or enshrined in The Hall of Fame at The Ohio State University" (para. 9). Because of this, Shaw argued that Gee's statements significantly harmed OSU's case with the NCAA because they insinuated that he believed Tressel was "invulnerable" (para. 3). In a retrospective of the case, Lesmerises (2014a) stated, "Gee's involvement with Ohio State's NCAA issues always will be remembered with eight words: "I'm just hopeful the coach doesn't dismiss me." (para. 1). In hindsight, Gee also noted the negative affect this statement had on the case (Lesmerises, 20014a).

OSU Separation

On April 19, OSU announced that Tressel's fine may not cover its investigative costs, and it released the compliance form on which Tressel lied (Associated Press, 2011a). On April 21, the NCAA's Notice of Allegations was released and alleged that Tressel "knew or should have known that at least two football student-athletes received preferential treatment from and sold institutionally issued athletic awards, apparel, and/or equipment to Rife, but he failed to report" the violations to school authorities (as cited in Farrey, 2011, n.p.). In early May, OSU and the Ohio Bureau of Motor Vehicles (OBMV) announced its second investigation into questionable used-car purchases made by student-athletes (Boren, 2011; Farrey, 2011). The investigation by the OBMV found the car dealer's paperwork to be in order, but examining NCAA violations was not part of its job. Yet, OSU "dropped its plan to hire experts to conduct an independent investigation of vehicle purchases by players and their family members" (as cited in Boren, 2011, para. 12).

In late May 2011, OSU's campaign fell apart for two reasons. First, former OSU wide receiver, Ray Small, publicly admitted that he sold two of his Big Ten Championship rings (around 2008) for approximately $2,000 to pay rent and a car payment on a car he had purchased from Kniffin; however, he claimed no one in OSU's program was aware of his actions (Farrey, 2011; Meisel & Oldham, 2011). Second, *Sports Illustrated* informed OSU officials that its problems were far worse than first thought. *Sports Illustrated* learned that similar incidents had occurred as far back as 2002 and involved at least 28 current and former players (Dohrmann & Epstein, 2011). OSU's problems were not isolated; they were systemic.

In response, Gee wrote in a letter to OSU's Board of Trustees that stated,

As you all know I appointed a special committee to analyze and provide advice to me regarding issues attendant to our football program. In consultation with the senior leadership of the university and the senior leadership of the board, I have been actively reviewing the matter and have accepted coach Tressel's resignation (as cited in Associated Press, 2011b, para. 12).

For his part, Smith delivered a video statement to "Buckeye Nation" (as cited in "Smith: Tressel's," 2011, para. 2) in which laid out the steps in the resignation process, including information regarding Tressel and Luke Fickell's (the interim head coach) speeches to the team. He then moved into *bolstering* and a form of *transcendence* with this statement about Fickell's meeting with the team, "This happens to be finals week; they obviously need to focus on finishing their classes, which is really what we're all about—making sure they get their education and their degree" (as cited in "Smith: Tressel's," 2011, para 5). Further, he went on to argue that Fickell had his priorities straight and would keep the team and the university on the right track, noting the highest academic performance of the team's student- athletes in program history (*"Smith: Tressel's," 2011)*. Smith also noted that the university would not be discussion anything to do with the NCAA's investigation, only stating, "We will do what we always do. We respond to them, we collaborate with the NCAA and try and find the truth" (as cited in *"Smith: Tressel's," 2011,* para. 6). In another statement Smith avowed,

We look forward to refocusing the football program on doing what we do best-representing this extraordinary university and its values on the field, in the classroom, and in life. We look forward to supporting Luke Fickell in his role as our football coach. We have full confidence in his ability to lead our football program. (as cited in "Tressel resignation," 2011, n.p.)

Though Smith could not use transcendence as it was conceptualized by Benoit (1995, 2015) or his predecessors (Ware & Linkugel, 1973; Scott & Lyman, 1968), who argued transcendence places the scandal in a broader context such that it may viewed as less egregious or justified, he did argue that the scandal was secondary to the central mission of the university, educating students and preparing them for life beyond the university.

While OSU had previously supported the coach through the allegations, it is not surprising it moved from using expressions of disappointment to a separation strategy. Staples (2011) explains this best. Before his admitted transgression,

Tressel was packaged and sole as a paragon of virtue in a college football universe teaming with schemers and bloodsuckers. As long as he beat Michigan and won the Big Ten, most people seemed more than happy to swallow that narrative. (Staples, 2011, para. 9)

However,

They want you to think this is all a Jim Tressel problem and not an Ohio State problem. A Jim Tressel problem means Ohio State needs a new coach. An Ohio State problem means brutal NCAA sanctions that could cripple the program for years (Staples, 2011, para. 8).

Though OSU players and alumni continued to support Tressel (see "Ohio State players," 2011), that buffer was superseded by the looming NCAA investigation. It left administrators little choice but to separate from Tressel if it hoped to escape lack of institutional control charges from the NCAA (Staples, 2011). Staples notes,

What infuriates Ohio State fans most is that other head coaches have sailed along with no personal punishment or a mere wrist slap. Those fans fail to understand that those coaches wore the armor of

plausible deniability…The moment Tressel responded to a Cicero e-mail—thereby acknowledging its receipt—he stripped himself of his armor. (para. 13)

He goes on,

If it ever emerged that Smith or anyone in that athletic administration knew of the e-mails and didn't report them, they could be charged with the same unethical conduct violation as Tressel, and the Committee on Infractions almost certainly would blast the program for a lack of institutional control. (para. 19)

Eight days later, Gee responded to allegations that Tressel's resignation was forced (Lesmerises, 2011). He noted that early decisions were based on the facts as OSU leaders knew them at the time and on Tressel's "incredible body of work as the football coach and as a university citizen," but continued,

We have a process at the university in which we do not immediately make decisions. We try to be deliberate and that was the process. Two months later, I think there were a lot of additional facts, and I think there was also the reality that were are facing serious issues. And the coach realized that and made what I think is the best decision on behalf of the university, which was to resign. (as cited in Lesmerises, 2011, para. 3-4).

He argued that OSU had allowed Tressel to stay so long after admitting his participation in the emails with Cicero in order to give him a chance to "make his case" and "engage in appropriate conversation about the mistakes he had made" (as cited in Lesmerises, 2011, para. 11). Even though Gee claimed OSU had acted correctly in immediately reporting and investigating the allegations, he remarked, "We as an institution have to be appropriately humble and contrite about the mistakes we've made, and then move on from there" (as cited in Lesmerises, 2011, para. 9). Interestingly, he never enumerated to what mistakes he was referring, but noted that the scandal had not affected fundraising or student applications (Lesmerises, 2011).

Though no one ever proved OSU leadership knew about the e-mails or any of the other incidences in this case, a July 2011 article in the *Columbus Dispatch* publicly called the integrity and practices of both Tressel and OSU leadership into question (Pyle & Ludlow, 2011). Through an open records request, Pyle and Ludlow (2011) found that prior to Smith's hiring in 2005, Tressel's performance evaluations indicated a problem. The previous Athletic Director, Andy Geiger, had warned Tressel six times that there was a need to "improve his compliance with NCAA regulations;" these warnings were documented in writing (Pyle & Ludlow, 2011, n.p.). Further, for 2005-2006, the compliance office noted that the speed with which Tressel reported violations was "unacceptable" (Pyle & Ludlow, 2011, n.p.). One review, written in 2003, specifically asked him to pay attention the vehicles his players were driving and to report any "unusual circumstances" to the compliance office (as cited in Boren, 2011, para. 3). Mysteriously, once Smith was hired, no written documents about compliance were placed in Tressel's personnel file even though OSU football had 10 violations from 2008-2010. This was not the evaluation process for any other high-profile employee at OSU, including its President or its men's basketball coach (Pyle & Ludlow, 2011).

Given Tressel's admission, what OSU leaders knew of his compliance record, and the fact that there was no written record of his compliance evaluations under Smith, OSU no longer had hope of satisfying both its fans and the NCAA with Tressel at the helm. While OSU officials might have wanted to spare Tressel to appease fans, concern about NCAA sanctions left them with little choice but to focus on image repair with the NCAA at this juncture because of the legitimate power it had over the future of OSU football. Essentially, the university found it easier to replace one person, Tressel, than rebuild an entire football program from the ground up.

Attempting Renewal

While the NCAA had to take primacy, OSU could not ignore its fans. It needed fan support to thrive if it was to remain a strong program long-term. Not surprisingly, it would make a move to do that in notable style.

Following Fickell's year as Interim Head Coach, OSU hired former Florida Head Football Coach, Urban Meyer, a proven championship-caliber coach. This hire went a long way to repairing OSU's image with disgruntled fans. Though the NCAA handed down a one-year bowl ban for OSU based on its violations and banned OSU from Big Ten Championship eligibility for one year, placed it on three years of probation, and forced it to forfeit nine scholarships over a three-year period (Smith, 2011; The Ohio State University, 2011), OSU was not charged with lack of institutional control, a violation which would have all but killed the OSU football program. In response, Smith shared the university's disappointment with the decision, but noted that the decision would not be appealed in the interest of moving on. He also contended that he knew the student-athletes would find a way to turn the situation "into something positive" and noted that the "embraces its leadership responsibilities and affirms its long-standing commitment to excellence in education and integrity in all it does" (as cited in "The Ohio State University," 2011, para. 2). Further, he thanked the university community for its support, and closed by touting the academic and athletic accolades won by OSU student-athletes ("The Ohio State University," 2011). This statement depicts a discourse focused on renewal. Spoken by an organizational leader at the center of the crisis, it privileges a prospective vision for the future, a future in which OSU would be a leader. Though some may have questioned the ethical communication of OSU's leadership to this point, Smith demonstrated organizational learning in his words by focusing on corrective action and reaffirming OSU's core values.

Both Gee and Smith survived the crisis unscathed. Gee remained the President of OSU for two years after the crisis, leaving in 2013 after "jokingly referring to 'those damn Catholics' at Notre Dame and poking fun at the academic quality of other schools" (Welsh-Huggins, 2013, para. 1). However, he was granted President Emeritus status at OSU (Lesmerises, 2014a). Smith remains at OSU and has been promoted to Senior Vice President and Wolfe Foundation Endowed Athletics Director (Lesmerises, 2014c; "The Ohio State," 2018a).

Returning to the Top

As for OSU football, Meyer led the team to an undefeated season his first year, (Lesmerises, 2014b). In his six years at OSU, Meyer has accumulated a 73-8 record, led the Buckeyes to the 2014 College Football Playoff National Championship by defeating the University of Oregon 42-20 with a third-string quarterback, and took the team to the playoff again in 2017 ("Ohio State Buckeyes," 2014; "The Ohio State," 2018b). As Kruse's work indicates, such success likely healed old wounds with fans who did not agree with the statements and actions of OSU leaders during the tattoos-for-memorabilia scandal.

SOLUTIONS AND RECOMMENDATIONS

This essay adds meaningful insight into the study of image repair campaigns and addresses pragmatic considerations central to the issues at the heart of this text. It clearly illustrates the unique rhetorical intricacies faced by colleges/universities when their coaches/student-athletes violate NCAA rules. However, the lessons learned herein may benefit practitioners in a variety of industries.

First, while numerous works, from Kruse (1981) to the current case study, focus on how the ethic of winning creates a unique crisis situation for sports organizations, crisis scholars at least as far back as Coombs (1995) have noted the effect performance history has on organizations responding to crises. Winning, which is indelibly linked to the concept of performance history, is not a uniquely athletic endeavor. For example. winning also happens in the political and economic arenas. Thus, the same ethic may be afforded organizations in those industries as well. The same may be argued about the bond of community buffer outlined by Koerber and Zabara (2017).

Second, this case calls into question the decision to hire someone whose performance history is questionable. Sports organizations are notorious for such hires. However, the potential for such hires crosses organizational contexts. Third, if such a hire is made, this case highlights the value of written performance evaluations. In an interview, Paul McConnell, President and CEO of Orlando-based McConnell & Co., who works in higher education, contended, "It's highly unusual not to require a written evaluation, especially for someone so prominent" (Pyle & Ludlow, 2011, n.p.). The authors could find no evidence that OSU officials ever explained the reason for the switch to oral evaluations for Tressel. One has to wonder if it was done to offer OSU leaders the protection of *defeasibility* should another set of violations arise. After all, documentation demonstrates Tressel and/or his players were connected to shady dealings on at least three occasions prior to 2010. However, it left them with no way to prove their own innocence. During Lesmerises' (2014a) retrospective interview, Gee revealed,

As a university president…I always felt I spent relatively minute amounts of time on athletics…You have great athletic directors, you let them run it, you keep yourself informed, but I'm not the athletic director, I'm the president of the university. But all of the sudden this whole thing overwhelmed us…" (para. 26-27)

Had Gee put the checks and balances in place to make sure rigorous, documented reviews of Tressel continued under Smith, as they had under Geiger, this crisis may have been avoided altogether.

Fourth, given what organizational leaders knew of Tressel's performance history, the use of denial and minimization strategies in the initial stages of the campaign was a mistake. Even though Tressel initially denied prior knowledge of this particular set of violations, taking the word of Tressel and the players was tenuous given Tressel's troubled past. Further, the raid uncovered memorabilia from as far back at 2002, but the university insisted this was a contained incident. While the 2002 players had long-since left OSU, it still indicated a systemic problem. The authors cannot know why OSU administrators chose to use these strategies. Did they do so because they put too much trust in Tressel and his players or did they do so because they knew they had a systemic problem and chose to lie to the NCAA in the hopes warding off harsher penalties?

Regardless of the answer, this case adds support for existing research, such as that of Benoit (2015), which indicates OSU officials may have been better served by telling the truth if they knew it or that of Rowland and Jerome (2004) that notes the value of seeking the root cause of the issue through an exhaustive investigation and providing an extensive corrective plan once the investigation is complete.

Smith did mention corrective action in his early statements, but they lacked detail. Further, though Gee mentioned a thorough review in the latter stages of the case, OSU leaders claimed these were isolated events a mere eight days after the Office of the U.S. Attorney apprised them of the situation. Gee's own statements (See Lesmerises, 2011) indicated they made an error in making definitive statements before all facts were gathered. Drawing harried, definitive conclusions early in a crisis or lying likely will not be beneficial to any type of organization.

This case also teaches practitioners a great deal about managing stakeholders during crises of this nature. At the outset, OSU's leadership was able to focus almost solely on repairing its image with the NCAA because, as Kruse (1981) notes, highly dedicated fans and other organizational members that consider the team a family are willing to forgive a variety of transgressions. However, it also reveals that organizational/leader survival may call forth the need to go beyond expressions of disappointment and separate from a beloved organizational member. Though fan support was important to OSU, the ability to continue its football program had to take primacy. This is in line with the work of Rawlins (2006) who noted, "the enabling and functional linkages have the greatest priority as stakeholders because their power/dependency/influence relationship is frequent and critical to the regular operations of the organizations" (p. 8). Further, he argued that prioritization will change based on situation and other stakeholder characteristics such as likelihood they will be outspoken about an issue and whether that activism will be supportive or adversarial. Key publics, he contended, are those "whose participation and cooperation are required to accomplish organizational goals" (p. 12) and should be those that receive the highest priority. Benoit's (2015) final chapter echoes these assertions.

However, because fan support would be important to the long-term future of OSU, its leaders needed to renew their faith. While Smith did move to a discourse of renewal toward the end of the crisis, OSU's hiring of Meyer and the team's continued winning performances likely did more to repair OSU's image with fans than any focus on academics or corrective action campaign could have done. Smith echoed this sentiment in his retrospective interview when saying of Meyer, "He's perfect for the situation we had. He's perfect for The Ohio State University, being from Ohio, being here before, his wife being from Ohio. It was a little bit of a Camelot from that perspective." (as cited in Lesmerises, 2014c, para. 28). Once more, this strategy is not unique to NCAA violations crises. Winning transcends sports. Just as sports organizations want to win games, organizations of all other varieties seek wins (e.g., in sales numbers, membership).

Some may wonder why OSU did not attack its accuser, the NCAA. After all, media commentators and fans continually note their distaste for the NCAA's regulatory decisions on a number of fronts. Nevertheless, the authors argue that such a strategy would rarely be beneficial for OSU or any other college/university given the NCAA's position as ultimate arbiter of all things college sports. Again, this factor is not unique to colleges and universities. All organizations have to contend with regulatory agencies daily (e.g., the SEC, the EPA). While there have been occasions where decisions made by governing bodies have been met with so much public ire as to goad the body into overturning its original decision, such occasions are rare. Thus, it is not surprising, given Kruse's (1981) assertions, that as the actions taken by Tressel caused excessive strife for the university, OSU administrators' dedication to Tressel dwindled.

FUTURE RESEARCH DIRECTIONS

As with any study, limitations exist. These include the obvious limitation that this study was based on only one case. Further, this study is completely dependent on press statements and media reports. Thus, the authors had no ability to assess the closed-door decision making processes of OSU administrators that would have undoubtedly added insight to strategy choice. In addition, it is impossible to know what would have happened if OSU had made different rhetorical choices. Along with these limitations, some areas of future research deserve mention. First, OSU found itself facing a new crisis in the summer of 2018 when it was revealed that Urban Meyer, perhaps knowingly, employed a domestic abuser, Zach Smith, on his staff. Because it felt "their actions relating to Zach Smith were insufficient" (Gatto, 2018, n.p.), The Ohio State Board of Trustees suspended both Meyer and AD Gene Smith. Both were later reinstated. A study that examines how that crisis was handled by Smith and new university leadership has the potential to extend the findings of the current study. Second, in the interest of contributing to the broader context off strategic communication, leadership, and conflict management in modern organizations, the claims made herein should be tested on other types of organizational image repair campaigns.

CONCLUSION

This study extends the study of sports rhetoric in important ways. However, it also clearly contributes to the ever-growing body of knowledge about image repair, organizational leadership, and conflict management. Last, it offers insights beneficial to all organizations dealing with dichotomous situational constraints.

REFERENCES

Associated Press. (2011a, April 19). A timeline of Tressel's NCAA troubles. *USA Today*. Retrieved August 28, 2015 from http://usatoday30.usatoday.com/sports/college/football/2011-04-19-2215755358_x.htm

Associated Press. (2011b, May 30). Jim Tressel resigns as Ohio State's coach. *CBS News*. Retrieved August 28, 2015 from http://www.cbsnews.com/news/jim-tressel-resigns-as-ohio-states-coach/

Benoit, W. (1995). *Accounts, excuses, and apologies: A theory of image restoration*. State University of New York Press.

Benoit, W. (2015). *Accounts, excuses, and apologies: Image repair theory and research*. State University of New York Press.

Berkowitz, S. (2013, May 2). NCAA had record $71 million surplus in fiscal 2012. *USA Today*. Retrieved March 17, 2014 from http://www.usatoday.com/story/sports/college/2013/05/02/ncaa-financial-statement-surplus/2128431/

Blaney, J. R., Lippert, L. R., & Smith, J. S. (2013). Repairing the athlete's image. Lanham, MD: Lexington Books (Rowman & Littlefield).

Boren, C. (2011, July 15). Report: Ohio State's Jim Tressel had history of compliance violations. *The Washington Post.* Retrieved October 18, 2015 from https://www.washingtonpost.com/blogs/early-lead/post/report-ohio-states-jim-tressel-had-history-of-compliance-violations/2011/07/15/gIQAJjbFGI_blog.html

Brazeal, L. M. (2008). The image repair strategies of Terrell Owens. *Public Relations Review, 34*(2), 145–150. doi:10.1016/j.pubrev.2008.03.021

Brinson, S. L., & Benoit, W. L. (1999). The tarnished star: Restoring Texaco's damaged public image. *Management Communication Quarterly, 12*(4), 483–519. doi:10.1177/0893318999124001

Bruce, T., & Tini, T. (2008). Unique crisis response strategies in sports public relations: Rugby league and the case for *diversion. Public Relations Review, 34*(2), 108–115. doi:10.1016/j.pubrev.2008.03.015

Coombs, W. T. (1995). Choosing the right words: The development of guidelines for the selection of "appropriate" crisis response strategies. *Management Communication Quarterly, 8*(4), 447–476. doi:10.1177/0893318995008004003

Coombs, W. T. (2015). *Ongoing crisis communication: Planning, managing, and responding.* Los Angeles, CA: Sage.

Dohrmann, G., & Epstein, D. (2011, May 30). SI investigation reveals eight-year pattern of violations under Tressel. *Sportsillustrated.com.* Retrieved June 14, 2011 from http://www.si.com/more-sports/2011/05/30/jim-tressel

Farrey, T. (2011, May 30). Timeline: Jim Tressel's fall. *ESPN.com.* Retrieved July 19, 2011 from http://sports.espn.go.com/ncf/news/story?id=6607982

Forde, P. (2011, May 30). Tressel's end fits with saga's pattern. *ESPN.com.* Retrieved June 14, 2011 from http://espn.go.com/espn/print?id=6607408&type=story

Fortunato, J. A. (2008). Restoring a reputation: The Duke University lacrosse scandal. *Public Relations Review, 34*(2), 116–123. doi:10.1016/j.pubrev.2008.03.006

Friend, T. (2011, May). Maurice Clarett tells his side. *ESPN.com.* Retrieved October 24, 2015 from http://sports.espn.go.com/ncf/news/story?id=1919246

Gatto, T. (2018, August 24). Urban Meyer and Zach Smith: A timeline of key events in abuse scandal. *The Sporting News.* Retrieved from http://www.sportingnews.com/us/ncaa-football/news/zach-smith-urban-meyer-timeline-domestic-violence-allegations-ohio-state-florida-courtney-smith-ex-wife/qdg-wf1d3j9n41skbguxgqsql0

Jenkins, S. (2013, January 20). NCAA touts amateurism rules over open market, but which is more corrupt. *The Washington Post.* Retrieved January 22, 2014 from http://www.washingtonpost.com/sports/colleges/ncaa-touts-amateurism-rules-over-open-market-but-which-is-more-corrupt/2013/09/20/511e18ea-2204-11e3-a358-1144dee636dd_story.html

Jerome, A. M. (2008). Toward prescription: Testing the rhetoric of atonement's applicability in the athletic arena. *Public Relations Review, 34*(2), 124–134. doi:10.1016/j.pubrev.2008.03.007

Koerber, D., & Zabara, N. (2017). Preventing damage: The psychology of crisis communication buffers in organized sports. *Public Relations Review*, *43*(1), 193–200. doi:10.1016/j.pubrev.2016.12.002

Kruse, N. W. (1981). Apologia in team sport. *The Quarterly Journal of Speech*, *67*(3), 270–283. doi:10.1080/00335638109383572

Len-Rios, M. E. (2010). Image repair strategies, local news portrayals and crisis stage: A case study of Duke University's lacrosse team crisis. *International Journal of Strategic Communication*, *4*(4), 267–287. doi:10.1080/1553118X.2010.515534

Lesmerises, D. (2011, June 7). Ohio State President Gordon Gee: "Flurry of activity" led to Jim Tressel resignation. *Cleveland.com.* Retrieved October 27 from http://www.cleveland.com/osu/index.ssf/2011/06/ohio_state_president_gordon_ge.html

Lesmerises, D. (2014a, June 3). Gordon Gee: 'I think everyone won'-closing the book on the Ohio State tattoo scandal. *Cleveland.com.* Retrieved October 27 from http://www.cleveland.com/osu/index.ssf/2014/06/gordon_gee_i_think_everyone_wo.html

Lesmerises, D. (2014b, June 5). Urban Meyer: 'I can tell you there is nothing behind door no. 2'-Closing the book on the Ohio State football scandal. *Cleveland.com.* Retrieved October 28, 2015, 2015 http://www.cleveland.com/osu/index.ssf/2014/06/urban_meyer_i_can_tell_you_the.html

Lesmerises, D. (2014c, June 11). Gene Smith: 'We moved forward a long time ago"- Closing the book on the Ohio State football scandal. *Cleveland.com.* Retrieved October 27 from http://www.cleveland.com/osu/index.ssf/2014/06/gene_smith_our_kids_are_much_f.html

Marshall, A. (2011, March 8). Ohio State football coach Jim Tressel suspended 2 games, fined $250,000 in aftermath of Yahoo report. *Cleveland.com.* Retrieved June 14, 2011 from http://www.cleveland.com/osu/index.ssf/2011/03/post_36.html

Meisel, Z., & Oldham, J. (2011, May 24). Ray Small tells all: Ex-Buckeye says he sold memorabilia, some players don't 'think about' rules. *The Lantern.* Retrieved October 14, 2015 from http://thelantern.com/2011/05/ray-small-tells-all-ex-buckeye-says-he-sold-memorabilia-some-players-dont-think-about-rules/

NCAA. (2010, December 23). *NCAA Requires Loss of Contests for Six Ohio State Football Student-Athletes.* Retrieved August 29, 2015 from http://www.dispatch.com/content/stories/sports/2010/12/23/text-of-ncaa-press-release.html?sid=101

Ohio State Buckeyes-2014 NCAA Football Champions. (2014). Retrieved July 29, 2015 from http://www.ohiostatebuckeyes.com/sports/m-footbl/2014-championship.html

Ohio State football players sanctioned. (2010, December 26). *ESPN.com News Service.* Retrieved August 29, 2015 from http://sports.espn.go.com/ncf/news/story?id=5950873

Ohio State players, alums stand behind Tressel. (2011, May 31). *Sportsillustrated.com.* Retrieved June 1, 2011 http://sportsillustrated.cnn.com/2011/football/ncaa/05/30/tressel-reaction.ap/index.html

OSU athletic director Gene Smith on timeline of events. (2010, December 23). *WEWSNewsChannel5.* Retrieved August 29, 2015 from https://www.youtube.com/watch?v=aJ3z7_oM5W0

OSU coach Jim Tressel on Suspensions. (2010, December 23). *WEWSNewsChannel5.* Retrieved August 29, 2015 from https://www.youtube.com/watch?v=OuqH3PVQJAg

Pyle, E., & Ludlow, R. (2011, July 16). *Ohio State football: Tressel had early history of warnings.* Retrieved October 14, 2015 from http://www.dispatch.com/content/stories/local/2011/07/16/tressel-had-early-history-of-warnings.html

Rawlins, B. (2006). Prioritizing stakeholders for public relations. *Institute for Public Relations.* Retrieved October 18, 2015 from http://pdfcast.org/pdf/prioritizing-stakeholders-for-public-relations

Rowland, R. C., & Jerome, A. M. (2004). On organizational apologia: A reconceptualization. *Communication Theory, 14*(3), 191–211. doi:10.1111/j.1468-2885.2004.tb00311.x

Seeger, M. W. (2006). Best practices in crisis communication: An expert panel process. *Journal of Applied Communication Research, 34*(3), 232–244. doi:10.1080/00909880600769944

Shaw, B. (2001, March 9). What, Gee worry? OSU president's lack of concern over the Tressel scandal will likely raise some with the NCAA: Bud Shaw's sports spin. *Cleveland.com.* Retrieved October 27, 2015 from http://www.cleveland.com/budshaw/index.ssf/2011/03/what_gee_worry_osu_presidents.html

Sisler, H. E. (2015). Crisis of man to crisis of men: Ray Rice and the NFL's transition from crisis of image to crisis of ethics. *TopSCHOLAR.* Retrieved October 18, 2015 from http://digitalcommons.wku.edu/theses/1520/

Smith, E. (2011, December 20). Ohio State hit with bowl ban, Tressel gets show-cause penalty. *USA Today.*

Smith: Tressel's speech to team "eloquent." (2011, May 30). *USA Today.* Retrieved August 28, 2015 from http://usatoday30.usatoday.com/sports/college/football/2011-05-30-4107396395_x.htm

Solomon, J. (2013, August 6). Jay Bilas uses NCAA store to highlight Johnny Manziel scandal. *AL.com.* Retrieved September 16, 2014 from www.al.com

Staples, A. (2011, May 30). Tressel tries to take brunt of NCAA wrath with Ohio State resignation. *Sportsillustrated.com.* Retrieved June 1, 2011 from http://sportsillustrated.cnn.com/2011/writers/andy_staples/05/30/Jim.Tressel.OSU/index.html

The Ohio State University. (2011, December 20). *Statement on NCAA sanctions.* Retrieved August 28, 2015 from http://www.ohiostatebuckeyes.com/genrel/122011aab.html

The Ohio State University. (2018a). *Gene Smith.* Retrieved from http://ohiostatebuckeyes.com/staff/gene-smith/

The Ohio State University. (2018b). *Urban Meyer.* Retrieved from http://ohiostatebuckeyes.com/coach/urban-meyer/

Tressel, J. (2011, March 8). Jim Tressel press conference 3/8/11. *Eleven Warriors.* Retrieved from http://www.youtube.com/watch?v=_wyQwtXvCC4

Tressel resignation: A timeline of quotes (2011, May 30). *The Columbus Dispatch.* Retrieved August 28, 2015 from http://www.dispatch.com/content/stories/sports/2011/05/30/timeline-in-quotes.html

Ulmer, R. R., Seeger, M. W., & Sellnow, T. L. (2007). Post-crisis communication and renewal: Expanding the parameters of post-crisis discourse. *Public Relations Review*, *33*(2), 130–134. doi:10.1016/j.pubrev.2006.11.015

Ulmer, R. R., Sellnow, T. L., & Seeger, M. W. (2015). *Effective crisis communication: Moving from crisis to opportunity*. Thousand Oaks, CA: Sage.

Walker, D. (2010, December 23). Ohio State Buckeyes: Why Terrelle Pryor and others should sit out the Sugar Bowl. *The Bleacher Report.* Retrieved October 27, 2015 from http://bleacherreport.com/articles/551973-bad-buckeyes-why-terrell-pryor-and-others-should-sit-out-the-sugar-bowl

Welsh-Huggins, A. (2013, June 5). Ohio State President Gordon Gee resigns. *The Boston Globe.* Retrieved October 25, 2015 from https://www.bostonglobe.com/sports/2013/06/05/ohio-president-gee-resigns/ifaooLYgKU6YAiqkjzOaSK/story.html

ADDITIONAL READING

Benoit, W. L., & Hanczor, R. S. (1994). The Tonya Harding controversy: An analysis of image restoration strategies. *Communication Quarterly*, *42*(4), 416–433. doi:10.1080/01463379409369947

Brown, K. A. (2016). Is apology the best policy? An experimental examination of the effectiveness of image repair strategies during criminal and noncriminal athlete transgressions. *Communication & Sport*, *4*(1), 23–42. doi:10.1177/2167479514544950

Brown, K. A., Dickhaus, J., & Long, M. C. (2012). LeBron James and the decision: An empirical examination of image repair in sports. *Journal of Sports Media*, *7*(1), 149–175. doi:10.1353/jsm.2012.0010

Compton, J., & Compton, J. (2014). College sports, losing seasons, and image repair through open letters to fans. *Communication & Sport*, *2*(4), 345–362. doi:10.1177/2167479513503542

Coombs, W. T. (2007). Protecting organization reputations during crisis: The development and application of situational crisis communication theory. *Corporate Reputation Review*, *10*(3), 163–176. doi:10.1057/palgrave.crr.1550049

Coombs, W. T. (2014). *Ongoing crisis communication: Planning, managing, and responding*. Thousand Oaks, CA: Sage.

Edwards, H. (1973) Sociology of sport (rpt. Homewood, III.: The Dorsey Press, 1977).

Hearit, K. M. (2006). *Crisis management by apology: Corporate responses to allegations of wrongdoing*. Mahwah, NJ: Lawrence Erlbaum.

Hopwood, M. (2007a). The sport integrated marketing communication mix. In S. Chadwick, & J. Beech (Eds.), *The marketing of sport*. Financial Times Management.

Hopwood, M. (2007b). Sports public relations. In S. Chadwick, & J. Beech (Eds.), *The marketing of sport*. Financial Timcs Management.

Jerome, A. M., & Russell, M. (2018). The rhetoric of sorrow: A subgenre of organizational apologia. *Western Journal of Communication*, *82*(5), 537–553. doi:10.1080/10570314.2018.1440000

L'Etang, J. (2013). *Sports public relations*. London: Sage Publications. doi:10.4135/9781526435910

Millar, D. P., & Heath, R. L. (2004). *Responding to crisis: A rhetorical approach to crisis communication*. Mahwah, NJ: Lawrence Erlbaum.

Nelson, J. (1984). The defense of Billie Jean King. *Western Journal of Speech Communication*, *48*(1), 92–102. doi:10.1080/10570318409374144

Novak, M. (1976). *The joy of sports: end zones, bases, baskets, balls, and the consecration of the American spirit*. New York: Basic Books.

Pfahl, M. E., & Bates, B. R. (2008). This is not a race, this is a farce: Formula One and the Indianapolis Motor Speedway tire crisis. *Public Relations Review*, *34*(2), 135–144. doi:10.1016/j.pubrev.2008.03.019

Reirson, J. L., Sellnow, T. L., & Ulmer, R. R. (2009). Complexities of crisis renewal over time: Learning from the tainted Odwalla Apple Juice case. *Communication Studies*, *60*(2), 114–129. doi:10.1080/10510970902834841

Scott, M. B., & Lyman, S. M. (1968). Accounts. *American Sociological Review*, *33*(1), 46–62. doi:10.2307/2092239 PMID:5644339

Smart, B. (2005). *The sport star: Modern sport and the cultural economy of sporting celebrity*. London: Sage.

Stoldt, G. C., Dittmore, S. W., & Branvold, S. E. (2012). *Sport public relations: Managing stakeholder communication*. Champaign, IL: Human Kinetics.

Utsler, M., & Epp, S. (2013). Image repair through TV: The strategies of McGwire, Rodriguez and Bonds. *Journal of Sports Media*, *8*(1), 139–161. doi:10.1353/jsm.2013.0002

Varma, T. M. (2011). Crisis communication in higher education: The use of "negotiation" as a strategy to manage crisis. *Public Relations Review*, *37*(4), 373–375. doi:10.1016/j.pubrev.2011.08.006

Walsh, J., & McAllister-Spooner, S. M. (2011). Analysis of the image repair discourse in the Michael Phelps controversy. *Public Relations Review*, *37*(2), 157–162. doi:10.1016/j.pubrev.2011.01.001

Ware, B. L., & Linkugel, W. A. (1973). They spoke on defense of themselves: On the generic criticism of apologia. *The Quarterly Journal of Speech*, *59*(3), 273–283. doi:10.1080/00335637309383176

KEY TERMS AND DEFINITIONS

Apologia: The act of rhetorical defense undertaken following an event that threatens one's image.

Bolstering: Listing the positive actions of actors in a crisis.

Corrective Action: Taking steps to ensure similar events/acts will not take place in the future.

Crisis: An event that threatens the legitimacy of an actor with key stakeholders.

Defeasibility: An argument made by an actor that focuses on his/her ignorance of the event/act pre-crisis.

Differentiation: A statement showing the difference between the current crisis and one that could have been much worse.

Good Intentions: An attempt to decrease the egregiousness of an act by arguing that it was undertaken with goodwill.

Expression of Disappointment: An acknowledgement that the organization does not condone the act in question.

Image Repair: An attempt to restore or transform one's image following a crisis.

Minimization: A strategy used by those in crisis that attempts to decrease the perceived harm done.

NCAA: The National Collegiate Athletic Association, governing body of Division 1-3 collegiate athletics programs.

Renewal: A rhetorical strategy undertaken to capitalized on the lessons learned from a crisis.

Separation: Rhetorical action taken to place blame onto another.

Transcendence: An attempt to move past a crisis by appealing to higher values.

ENDNOTE

1. Image repair studies were born out of earlier studies on apologia. For this reason, the terms are used interchangeably in this essay.

Chapter 17
Help Me Understand: Effectively Communicating Across Generations

Carolyn N. Stevenson
Purdue University Global, USA

ABSTRACT

Higher education leaders need to identify differences among generations of employees and students and develop a strategic plan for managing and motivating across the generations. This case study addresses the following question: "How do higher education leaders lead and motivate multigenerational employees and online students?" An understanding of the common characteristics of each generational group is the first step for developing a strategy for motivating all employees and students in higher education. Communication, mentoring programs, training, respect, and opportunities for career advancement are components valued by all. It is important for higher education leaders to understand the values, work ethic, and communication style of the different generations. The implications for higher education leaders lie in establishing an organizational culture that promotes satisfaction for all individuals in the higher education setting.

BACKGROUND

The number of adult learners have increased as individuals are re-inventing themselves and working longer to meet the extension of the retirement age. As such, higher education leaders need to be mindful about the different generations working in various capacities in the higher education setting. College leaders, such as department chairs or other leaders responsible for training and hiring faculty members, also need to be aware of the differences across the generations. This is especially true for online instructors who do not meet face-to-face with students.

According to DeMarco (2018), "Now that four generations, and in many cases five, are working together in offices across the country, how will workplace customs change when it comes to communication?" (p.1). As such, the topic of engaging and managing the multigenerational workforce calls for further research. Educational leaders at all levels are challenged with leading various generations. This

DOI: 10.4018/978-1-5225-8516-9.ch017

has had a major impact on higher education leadership in terms of retention, recruitment, motivation, and productivity. Faculty members also need to be aware of the differences between multigenerational students, especially in the online classroom, and establish communication models where all students are motivated to perform at the highest level.

INTRODUCTION

At the present time, there are five generational groupings of employees in the workplace and in the higher education classroom. Grensing-Pophal (2018) describes the generational groupings as:

- **Traditionalists**: Born before 1946
- **Baby Boomers**: Born between 1946 and 1964
- **Generation X**: Born between 1965 and 1976
- **Generation Y, or Millennials**: Born between 1977 and 1997
- **Generation Z**: Born after 1997

As individuals are working well into their late 60's or early 70's, higher education leaders need to adapt their leadership styles to effectively manage, motivate, and retain employees from various generations. As Grensing-Pophal (2018) states, "By 2024, about 25% of the workforce is projected to be over the age of 55. That compares to only about 12 percent of the workforce in 1994. In fact, in some workplaces, 55 doesn't even begin to signify time to retire. Those in their 60s, 70s, and even 80s also are deciding to stay in place either full time or part time. This trend has resulted in a new phenomenon: more generations in the workplace," (p.1). Additionally, the flexibility of online learning promotes many adults to return to college. Students across generations have different communication styles and study habits. Online instructors need to be mindful of these generational differences and adapt a teaching style that promotes success for all students in the online classroom.

The diversity of generational workers and students impacts motivation and retention of employees. Additionally, higher education leaders, such as department chairs, need to train instructors on communicating with multigenerational students. This is especially imperative in the online classroom where nonverbal cues are absent. As such, college leaders and instructors need to be knowledgeable of the differences across generations and leverage the strengths of each group. "When communicating across generations most likely it isn't just one. Most of us are trying to reach a mix of individuals, but how does each generation like to be reached and how do we combine them," (Aalgaard, 2015, p.1).

While higher education leaders and instructors may be aware of the various generations in their institutions and classrooms, implications for motivating and managing across the generations may not have been considered. "Research indicates that people communicate based on their generational backgrounds. Each generation has distinct attitudes, behaviors, expectations, habits and motivational buttons. Learning how to communicate with the different generations can eliminate many major confrontations and misunderstandings in the workplace and the world of business," (Hammill, 2015).

While the core values are similar, college leaders need to take a different approach when attempting to meet the needs of multigenerational employees. According to Moss (2017) the challenges of blending a mutigenerational workforce include:

- Doing more with less, which means teamwork is necessary.
- Showing employees and managers how to communicate with each other.
- Keeping up with new workplace trends and regulations.
- Supporting work/life balance to create a happier workforce.
- Understanding what motivates each generation (p.1).

Online instructors also need to be mindful of these differences in the classroom and adjust communication styles to meet the needs of the diverse generational groupings of the students.

This chapter discusses the differences in communication, motivation, and work styles of multigenerational workers and students. Having an understanding of the different characteristics of multigenerational employees in the higher education setting will assist in motivating all employees. Regardless of the generational group, employees value a positive work environment, fun environment, respect, and appropriate benefits. Higher education leaders need to acknowledge the differences among the generations, keep communication lines open, and develop an environment where all employees are motivated to perform their best. College leaders also need to train instructors on communicating with multigenerational students in the online classroom. While students may have the desire to succeed, learning styles are also different across the generations.

Following is a case study discussing the issues related to leading across generations. It is important to note that the differences discussed are generalizations. While each individual is unique, there are commonalities that exist among members of all the generational groupings.

CASE DESCRIPTION

The Organization

The organization selected for this case study was a two-year college in a suburb near a large metropolitan city in the United States. Students may take classes in the traditional classroom format, online, or through a hybrid option. All courses are taught via the learning management system BlackBoard.

For this case study, four full-time faculty members were selected. Each faculty member teaches in both the online and face-to-face format. The four faculty members are of different academic rank and represent each of the four generational groupings. All of the participating faculty members agreed to discuss their experience working with leaders and other faculty members from different generational groupings. Each participant, as well as the official name of the college was changed to ensure confidentiality of the institution and the faculty members. Due to space limitations, highlights of the interviews are represented in the vignettes that follow. Participants did go into greater detail and responded to eight interview questions. The passages were selected based on the relevance to the topic.

Statement of the Problem

Literature and observation reveal that there are workplace differences in work ethic, leadership styles, communication styles, and preferred method for communication among the four generations in the workplace. Additionally, differences exist in factors which motivate individuals from the various groups to perform responsibilities to their best abilities. Some researchers argue that there really is no difference between the four generations. It is simply the time in their lives in which the groups exist. Others are concerned that educational and organizational need to recognize these differences to promote an organizational culture that fosters success and job satisfaction among all employees. This is especially important for college leaders whose employees have a direct impact on student success. The findings of the research illustrate there is a need for both college leaders and faculty to understand differences among generations in their institution and develop a plan for enhanced communication and job satisfaction at the institution.

It is reasonable to suggest there is a need for higher education leaders to identify differences among the generations of workers and develop a strategic plan for managing and motivating across the generations. This is a topic of interest for many higher education leaders as well as faculty members. College leaders are faced with a number of factors concerning creating a positive institutional culture among multigenerational workers.

Firstly, deans, faculty members, and other college leaders must employ strong leadership skills as well as knowledge of the generational differences of the individual. Communicating effectively across the generations is challenging and college leaders must be able to motivate others to see the value each generation brings to the institution. College leaders must be open to suggestions from others regarding changes within the institution. A basic knowledge of generational differences is also needed to guide deans, faculty members, and other college leaders in understanding the workplace values of the different generations and establishing an organizational culture that promotes motivation for all employees.

Secondly, college leaders and faculty members must re-think teaching methods and curriculum design for online courses. Four generations of learners are in the online classroom. Assignments, projects, and discussion board questions should foster critical thinking, collaboration, and creativity for all students. Market demands often influence the decision as well. Oftentimes institutions attempt to keep abreast with the competition without reflecting on the needs of the individual institution and the student population specific to the organization. In addition, teaching methods must also be considered. Online learning allows for flexible approaches for students to actively gain knowledge, but also requires instructors to guide students in learning course material through individual learning styles. Inclusion of experiential learning opportunities also allow for a holistic approach to teaching and learning.

Lastly, identifying differences among the generations of workers and developing a strategic plan for managing and motivating across the generations involves attention to a future vision and establishment of specific policies and procedures. Training for all employees at the institution needs to be designed and implemented. The institution must be committed to investing in designing online curriculum that will motivate students from all generations. College leaders must also be committed to continual training as new generations of employees and students enter the institution. While the diversity of generations continues to increase, college leaders need to cautiously develop appropriate policies, but must quickly devise new guidelines regarding motivating and retaining employees and students across generations.

Based on these facts, it is reasonable to assume that college leaders, faculty members, and other employees at the institution have a different perspective on leading and motivating across generations. Additionally, college leaders are challenged with addressing a number of issues associated with retaining quality employees and students. The problem presented in this study is to investigate and determine the perspectives of faculty members on communicating and leading students and other faculty members across the generations. Findings from this case study will assist higher education leaders in leading and motivating multigenerational employees.

Purpose of the Study

The purpose of this study was to describe and explain selected faculty member perspectives on working with multigenerational leaders, students, and faculty. The results may assist higher education leaders in three areas.

The findings of the study will inform higher education leaders, faculty members, and other college leaders of the generation differences of individuals and students at the institution. The findings will also inform current and future college leaders and faculty members of the ways to motivate and retain employees, faculty, and students in the institution. The study will provide the basis for greater understanding of the leadership needed in educational settings that both want and have an interest in communicating, motivating, and training multigenerational employees, faculty, and students.

Research Question

The purpose of this study was to describe and explain selected faculty member perspectives on working with multigenerational leaders, students, and faculty. The exploratory questions that guided the study were:

1. What elements constitute this perspective in for working with multigenerational colleagues?
2. What variables influence this perspective working with multigenerational colleagues?
3. What beliefs do these faculty members hold which support or negate this perspective?

Methodology

The decision to conduct a qualitative study was influenced by the characteristics of qualitative design discussed by Janesick (2011). She describes research as being alive and active. It is a way of looking at the world and interpreting the world. This study focused on qualitative methods as means to understand the multiple complexities existing in the social world (Janesick, 2011).

Qualitative research involves passion for the work. The qualitative researcher is interactive in the sense used by John Dewey (1934) when writing about artists:

An "expression of the self in and through a medium, constituting the work of art, is itself a prolonged interaction issuing from self with objective conditions, a process in which both of them acquire form and order they did not first possess." (p. 65)

This immersion into the research process actively involves the qualitative researcher in the quest for gaining a deeper understanding of the social phenomena. A case study was selected for this study. Case studies involve an in-depth study of this bounded system and rely on a number of data collection materials. The cases used in this study were four faculty members teaching in an online format from four generation. The study sought to gain understanding of the perspectives of faculty members on working with multigenerational employees and students.

Presentation of the individual cases provides the reader the opportunity to gain understanding of the views, observations, and opinions of the individual participant perspectives on working with multigenerational leaders, students, and faculty. Direct quotes from the participants were used in the case studies as an attempt to portray the participant as an individual entity.

Data Collection

Interviews, researcher reflective journal, observations, researcher field notes, documents, artifacts, and transcripts were collected. At least two in-depth interviews were conducted with the participants. In an attempt to gather the rich, descriptive information required for qualitative research, semi-structured interviews with open-ended questions were used. The first step in the data collection process was conducting interviews with the study participants. The information qualitative researchers seek to gain is rich, thick descriptions of the participants in their social setting. Thus, open-ended questions were used to elicit the most complete and thorough responses from the participants.

The nature of qualitative research is flexible, as participants are being studied in their social setting. While variables in the social world cannot be controlled, the researcher can follow a format to help ensure items such as equipment are functioning.

In addition to interviews, participant observation was used to supplement the data collected in the interviews. Janesick (2011) alludes to observation as the immersion into the social setting which allows the researcher to begin to experience the experiences of the participants. The researcher observed each participant at least one time. Settings for potential observations included faculty in their offices, department meetings, and faculty interaction with others at the institution.

Observations also provided a check as to the credibility of the other data collected. Observations do require a series of planned steps. There are limitations as to the amount of information individuals reveal in the interview. Observations served as a means for verifying that the participants' actions match their words.

Document and artifact analysis, researcher field notes, and a researcher reflective journal also served as other sources of data for this case. The researcher gathered documents and artifacts from all participants as an attempt to further understand selected faculty member perspectives on working with multigenerational leaders, students, and faculty. Field notes consisted of supporting interview and observation notes. Format for the field notes collected during interviews and observations followed suggestions provided by Janesick (2011). A researcher's reflective journal was also kept as another means of data collection. The reflective journal served as means for the researcher to express emotions, ideas, and reactions to the study. During the data analysis stage, the reflective journal provided another resource for identifying emerging themes and sub themes.

Participant Selection

Four faculty members from a two-year college in a large suburb in the U.S. were interviewed individually regarding their perspective on working with multigenerational leaders, students, and faculty. The four faculty members taught in an online format only. Each faculty member represented a member of the four generations in the workplace and online classroom: one Traditionalist, one Baby Boomer, one Generation Xer, and one Millennial. Following the recommendations of Janesick (2011), the researcher relied on collection and analysis of various forms of data. Each online faculty member was interviewed at least two times for a total of eight formal and informal interviews. The online faculty members were audiotaped for the formal interviews. Data were also collected from three observations, thirteen documents and artifacts, and nineteen researcher reflective journal entries.

The online faculty members were selected because of the representation of the four generational groupings, their willingness to talk about their experiences, and their ability to provide different perspectives. Each participant had been at the institution for at least three years, had first-hand experience working with higher education leaders, other faculty members, and other leaders at the institution.

Mike was the only male involved in this study. This was not intentional but due to the fact that the other online faculty members willing to participate in the study were female. Jane was selected because of her dual role of faculty member and her extensive administrative responsibilities at the institution. Kayla and Kendra were selected because of their willingness to participate in the study, their role as faculty member for the college for at least three years, and their interaction with other college leaders. Each participant, as well as the official name of the college was changed to ensure confidentiality of the institution and the faculty members. Table 1 shows the basic profile of each participant.

Each participant discussed his or her perspective on working with colleagues from different generational groupings. A summary of the responses follows.

Mike: The Traditionalist

Mike was the oldest member of the participants and has also been at the college the longest. He is nearing retirement, but remains in his position because he enjoys working in higher education. In addition to his administrative role, he also teaches one online class. When asked why is does not wish to retire he responded, "I love what I do." Prior to working in higher education he worked as a Certified Public Accountant for several years. He began teaching part-time and decided he enjoyed teaches so much, he made it his career. Additionally, he stated, "It is a great way to share my experience with others."

When asked about working with different generational groupings, he described his experience as the following:

I enjoy working with all people. One of the benefits of being the oldest kid on the block is that I hold a wealth of experience—both in the classroom and in the boardroom. However, it is difficult at times working with younger individuals who try and rush through decisions without following procedure. I also wish younger faculty would seek out my experience more often.

When asked about the preferred method of communication, Mike responded:

Table 1. Case ordered matrix, participant characteristics

Faculty Member	Gender	Position	Years at College	Time in Position
Mike	Male	Dean, General Studies	18 years	13 years
Jane	Female	Professor, Philosophy	11 years	8 years
Kayla	Female	Associate Professor of Communications	7 years	6 years
Kendra	Female	Assistant Faculty, Composition	3 years	3 years

I prefer a phone call for a complex issue or a face-to-face meeting. There are bi-monthly meetings with my full-time faculty members and semester meetings with my part-time faculty members. It is important to sit around the table and discuss student issues, university issues, changes in policy, and other topics.

When asked about what motivates him at work, Mike responded:

The students motivate me. I enjoy when they have an 'ah-ha' moment. You know, when the light goes on in their head and they really understand the concept. Also, in my administrative role as department chair, I enjoy being part of the decision-making process. In this role, I have the opportunity to meet with a number of leaders across the College. The sharing of ideas is what makes my department and the College run smoothly.

Jane: The Baby Boomer

Jane is a full-time faculty member that teaches both in the traditional classroom setting and in an online. She enjoys teaching in both formats but prefers the face-to-face classroom because of "the connection she can make with the students." Jane started her career working as a librarian. She enjoyed the work but wanted to challenge herself professionally. She went back to college to earn her Ph.D. in Philosophy later in life and completed her degree when she was 47 years old. She began teaching for the College part-time and then accepted a full-time position. She also is a member of the College Assessment Committee and interacts with individuals various departments at the College.

When asked about working with different generational groupings, she described her experience as the following:

The diversity of individuals promotes fresh ideas. When you work with a variety of age groups, people bring experience and creativity to the table. One of the challenges I have is when new faculty complain about the amount of work involved in teaching. It is not just teaching but service to the College, service to academic community, and research. At times, younger faculty complain that there is no mentorship program to help them with their research. I never had a mentor. You have to work hard in academia—both in the classroom as well as in fostering professional development. It is part of your job, but you need to be self-motivated.

When asked about the preferred method of communication, Jane responded:

I prefer a phone call or a meeting when working with faculty members or leaders. Email is essential for the online instructor, but I also encourage students to call during my office hours. It can be easier to explain things with a phone rather than going back and forth on email. Face-to-face meetings are also important when discussing important issues as well as for keeping in touch with your colleagues.

When asked about what motivates her at work, Jane responded:

I love my job and I love to work with both students and leaders. Research is also something I value and effort is made to stay on top of changes in my field. Conference attendance and participation are very important and I am motivated by new ideas presented by scholars in the field. Going into higher educa-

tion was a choice because I enjoy helping students understand the historical and practical applications of philosophy. There is nothing better than reviewing student evaluations and seeing how much they enjoyed the Introduction to Philosophy class and how much they learned.

Kayla: The Generation Xer

Higher education was a second career choice for Kayla. After graduating college, she began her career in publishing. She worked for a major college textbook publisher for three years and then two years for a medical publisher. She began her master's program immediately after undergraduate school and completed her master's degree in communication within two years. Like many of her friends, she changed companies frequently the first ten years. There was a saying that they were part of the "job of the year club." She also worked in the insurance industry and as a technical consultant. After moving to the city, she began working part-time nights for a junior college and discovered a passion for teaching. After getting married and thinking about a family, she realized that a 9-5 job would not be conducive to raising a family. She found a full-time job in teaching and was able to balance raising children and working full-time.

When asked about working with different generational groupings, she described her experience as the following:

I never really thought about the age differences of my colleagues. Reflecting on that point, there are obvious differences, especially when it comes to communication. My department chair is older and likes to hold face-to-face meetings. Meetings are appropriate when there is a critical issue to discuss. However, meeting just to meet is frustrating for me. I would rather do my work during office hours then talk, talk, talk without an agenda or an action item. It also seems like some younger co-workers need a lot of hand-holding on projects. My work style is just to give me a project and let me go. I'll ask questions when needed. However, some of the younger workers need constant reassurance.

When asked about the preferred method of communication, Kayla responded:

Email is the communication method I prefer. It is a quick and easy way to send and receive information. For my online students, it is the only form of communication. Also, with my iPhone I can check email anytime anywhere. However, phone calls or meetings are appropriate to ensure communication of complex issues occurs. On a person level, I would rather text for short, simple messages rather than make a phone call.

When asked about what motivates her at work, Kayla responded:

I love my job and am self-motivated. Being an instructor, especially teaching online, provides a great deal of flexibility. This creates a more balanced life, especially spending time with my family. Also, I enjoy working with my colleagues on research projects. When you work with a talented, experienced group of individuals, it creates a sense of motivation for the project as well as a feeling of being engaged with other members of the College. But most of all, my students motivate me. Working with a large percentage of adult learners, especially online, really has opened my eyes to their dedication. The way the students balance work, family, school, and social issues is amazing. They inspire me every day. Yes---I do cry at graduation when I see how proud they are of themselves and how proud their family is for their ac-

complishments. It is such a wonderful feeling to know that I played a role in helping them achieve their dream of graduating college.

Kendra: The Millennial

Kendra always knew she wanted to be a college professor. Both of her parents were college professors and she loves the higher education setting. Upon completing her Ph.D., she was fortunate to land a full-time job and the College. She did have an opportunity to teach one part-time class prior to obtaining the full-time position. She enjoys working at the College and the fact the College in the suburb where her friends and family also live.

When asked about working with different generational groupings, she described her experience as the following:

Since I am the youngest faculty member in my department, it can be frustrating at times. Although I don't have the experience like many other faculty, I have creative ideas. At times it feels like my voice is not heard. Also, I thought that I would be able to get more direction and mentorship when being at the College. I am new to teaching and really wished someone could have had mentored me my first year. On the positive side, the different age groups does allow to learn from the information shared at meetings. There are also a number of younger workers at the College that work in other departments and we do go to lunch every day which is enjoyable.

When asked about the preferred method of communication, Kendra responded:

I prefer social networking tools like Facebook or Twitter. Email is used for almost all communication with my students. However, I like working in groups on special projects and prefer to meet face-to-face with my team members on these special projects. Group work for me is enjoyable, especially when talented and creative people can share ideas openly. When we can support each other, it can be a positive experience.

When asked about what motivates her at work, Kendra responded:

It is motivating to teach others. I have always wanted to be a college professor and I enjoyed working with the students. I am also motivated by projects that allow me to express by ideas. Last spring I was able to re-design a course which made it much more current to today's students. I do wish there was more recognition for great teacher evaluation or work done on a project.

Major Themes

The themes of engagement, motivation, and mentorship were major themes from the interviews. While the participants varied in age group, all faculty members were motivated by their students. There was a major difference in the preferred form of communication. The Traditionalist and Baby Boomer preferred phone calls or face-to-face meetings, while the Generation Xer and Millennial preferred electronic forms of communication. The preferred communication style was also consistent with the literature. Another important theme was that of mentorship. The Traditionalist spoke about enjoying his work, and wanting to share his experience. The Millennial has a strong desire for a mentor.

SOLUTIONS AND RECOMMENDATIONS

Since the four generations of workers (and very soon five) have very different viewpoints about job satisfaction in the workplace, college leaders need to find ways to meet these needs. The older generations of workers, specifically the Traditionalists and Baby Boomers, need to feel valued in the workplace. Online students share the same need in the classroom. Since these two groups have the most workplace experience, there is an expectation that their experience is valued by other employees. While Traditionalists only make up a small percentage of the workplace, their communication style must be considered. "This is the generation who firmly believes in an "Honest day's pay for an honest day's work." They're extremely loyal and enjoy being respected for that. Since they're conformists, they value most job titles and money," (Rampton, 2017, p.1).

Baby Boomers are one of the largest generational groups and due to delayed retirement, still constitute a large percentage of the workforce. "Boomers are often ambitious, loyal, work-centric, and cynical. They prefer monetary rewards, but also enjoy nonmonetary rewards like flexible retirement planning and peer recognition. They also don't require constant feedback and have all is well unless you say something mindset" (Rampton, 2017, p.1).

Generation Xer's can be motivated by assigning workplace projects that allow for their sense of independence and problem solving to utilized to their fullest potential. "Gen Xers prefer to work independently with minimal supervision. They also value opportunities to grow and make choices, as well as having relationships with mentors. They also believe that promotions should be based on competence and not by rank, age, or seniority," (Rampton, 2017, p.1). In the online classroom, students enjoy projects where creativity can be applied. Online students also enjoyed being challenged to go deeper into discussion board posts.

Millennials hold the title of the largest generation of employees in the workplace. As more Baby Boomers retire, there will be more leadership opportunities within organizations for this group. The smaller number of Generation Xer's will not be sufficient to fulfill these vacant leadership roles. As such, managers need to mentor and channels the talents of the Millennial group. "Millennials also thrive when there's structure, stability, continued learning opportunities, and immediate feedback," (Rampton, 2017, p.1). In the online classroom, this group enjoys collaboration and creative projects. By encouraging creativity in assignments and discussion posts, students of this group will perform their best. Students new to online learning would also benefit by have a peer mentor during their first term of classes.

Soon a fifth generation will have a strong presence in the workforce, known as Generation Z. This is a large group with many in college. They make-up one-quarter of America's population, making this generation larger than baby boomers or Millennials (Rampton, 2007). Faculty and educational leaders need to have an understanding of their motivational and communication styles and foster growth in these future leaders.

It is important that educational leaders and faculty recognize the importance of understanding the motivational styles of this large group. "This generation is motivated by social rewards, mentorship, and constant feedback. They also want to be do meaningful and be given responsibility. Like their predecessors, they also demand flexible schedules. What's most intriguing about Gen Zers is that 53 percent prefer face-to-face communication, (Rampton, 2017, p.1).

It is essential that open, honest communication occurs among the generations. As described in an article by *New Zealand Management* (2012), "The future of our society is dependent upon a respectful and constructive interaction between the generations. We need many more such conversations to grow in focus and diversity; this was just a beginning," (p.23). According to the American Management Association (2015), "A leader's primary responsibility is to ensure that everyone in the organization understands that "working together" is not negotiable. Create a respectful, open and inclusive environment where workers of all ages and cultural backgrounds can share who they are without fear of being judged, "fixed," or changed," (p.1). As such, leaders in higher education need to actively pursue ways to encourage communication among generational groups.

The differences between the generations are often easy to see in the workplace. However, it's important to recognize their similarities as well. Successful organizations are ensuring that company leaders not only understand these similarities, but create work environments that support them. According to recent research conducted by Randstad and the Center for Creative Leadership, employees across the generations agree that:

- Work is a vehicle for personal fulfillment and satisfaction, not just for a paycheck.
- Workplace culture is important.
- Being trusted to get the job done is the number one factor that defines job satisfaction.
- They need to feel valued by their employer to be happy in the job.
- They want flexibility in the workplace.
- Success is finding a company they can stay with for a long time.
- Career development is the most valued form of recognition, even more so than pay raises and enhanced titles (Raines, 2015, p.1).

College leaders, such as Department Chairs, should offer training for online faculty working with multigenerational groups. Additionally, Student Services should provide resources promoting academic success and career development. The following suggestions are suggestions for motivating and retaining online students from all generations:

- Offer peer mentoring opportunities for all first-term students. The mentoring program would allow leadership skills to be exercised by all generations.
- Provide a strong Career Services department. Students from all generations need resources for current and future career searches.
- Offer new student orientation webinars to prepare students for the world of online learning.
- Provide set policies and clear expectations in course syllabi.
- Require instructors to keep virtual office hours at a set time.
- Encourage all students to share personal and professional experience in discussion board responses.

Employee recognition is important for all generations. *The Wall Street Journal* (2011), "Even simple gestures like a pat on the back or positive email congratulations can help boost productivity with Gen Xers. Boomers may seek status so may respond best to an office-wide memo that announces that they are meeting or exceeding their goals. Millennials may seek validation and approval so will appreciate increased responsibility and additional training opportunities. To this end, Millennials may also prefer more frequent employee reviews," (2011).

IMPLICATIONS FOR LEADERS

While placing categories of workers or students into categories based on a set of characteristics can be seen as stereotyping, it is important for college leaders and online instructors to be aware of some of the common traits. As Fox (2011) states, "A stereotype is an oversimplified characterization and therefore doesn't apply to every person of a group at all times in all situations. However, people fall back on stereotypes related to age, physical appearance or gender when interacting. So, real or imagined, stereotypes play a role in how people are judged and how their actions and words are perceived," (Fox, 2011, p.1).

There are personal and lifestyle characteristics common among the generations. A summary of these personal and lifestyle characteristics by generations described by Hammill (2015) are summarized as follows:

- Traditionalists have core values characterized by respect for authority, conforming, and discipline. The preferred communication media are landline phones, one-on-one meetings, and written memos.
- Baby Boomers have core values characterized by optimism and involvement. The preferred communication medium is phone with a "call me anytime" attitude.
- Generation Xers have core values characterized by skepticism, fun, and informality. The preferred communication media is cell phone (call me only at work) or email.
- Millennials have core values characterized by realism, confidence, extreme fun, and highly social. The preferred communication media is social media (such as Facebook and Twitter), Smartphones, and email.

According to the research, there are also workplace characteristics that are common among the generations. A summary of these workplace characteristics by generations described by Hammill (2005) are summarized as follows:

- Traditionalists have work ethics characterized by hard work, respect for authority, sacrifice, duty before fun, and adherence to rules. Work is considered an obligation. The leadership style is directive and command and control. The feedback and reward system is "no news is good news" and "satisfaction in a job well done." The message that motivates is that your experience is valued.
- Baby Boomers have work ethics characterized by being workaholics, working efficiently, crusading causes, desiring quality, and questioning authority. Work is considered an exciting adventure. The leadership style is consensual and collegial. The feedback and reward system is "don't appreciate it." The message that motivates is time and money.
- Generation Xers have work ethics characterized by being direct, being self-reliant, demanding structure, and being skeptical. Work is considered a challenge and a contract. The leadership style is everyone is the same, challenge others, and ask why. The feedback and reward system is "sorry to interrupt, but how am I doing?" and "freedom is the best reward." The message that motivates is forget the rules and do it your way.
- Millennials have work ethics characterized by multitasking, tenacity, tolerant, and goal-oriented. The leadership style is collaborative. The feedback and reward system is "whatever I want, at the push of a button" and meaningful work. The message that motivates is you working with other bright, creative people.

The different generations bring about various communication challenges in the workplace. "The communication challenge arises in that each of the four different generations has been raised in different times, political influences, education, technology, social and economic influences. All of this 'nurturing' delivers different beliefs, expectations and most importantly, different ways of seeing the world around us," (Murray, 2017, p.1).

To best illustrate the key differences, the following table lays out three of the four generations in the workplace today (Generation Z are just entering the workplace now and not a lot is known about what they want):

Working with multigenerational employees is not a new phenomenon. Traditionalists, Baby Boomers, and Generation Xer's have all worked side by side for several years. The same is true for online students. Due to the flexible nature of online learning, adult learners of all ages have been drawn to the virtual classroom for many years. However, this is the first time four generations will be in the workforce and online classroom at the same time. Each generation has brought a set of core values, beliefs, and technological aptitude in the workplace. However, these qualities do change over time as work/life priorities shift and change. According to INITIATIVEONE (2018), "Stereotypes in the wrong hands can be dangerous. That's why it helps when thinking about the characteristics of generations we interact with to remember that it's all just information. Strictly speaking, generations are nothing but a marker of time and facts of history," (p.1). Since the generations work in various positions, creating a collaborative work environment is needed to ensure both the success of the individual as well as the institution.

In an effort to develop a strategic plan for managing, recruiting, retaining, and motivating employees across generations, an understanding of the common characteristics is needed. Several factors impact the common traits of the various generations. Societal issues, economics, and technology all impact the values and ethics of the workers. "Members of the Silent Generation, or Traditionalists, grew up during the devastation of the Great Depression and came of age under the sacrifices of World War II. They witnessed the growth of the federal government as Social Security programs created jobs and safety nets for the poor and the elderly. Therefore, Traditionalists' values in the workplace tend to be frugality, adherence to rules, loyalty to employers, and a deep sense of responsibility and sacrifice for the good of the organization," (Fox, 2011). Although Traditionalists make up a smaller percentage of the workforce, their work ethics and values are very much aligned with traditional corporate structure. "The culture they created is fiscally conservative, rewards tenure and loyalty, is rules-focused, and measures performance based on the number of hours worked," (Fox, 2011).

Table 2. Communication styles

	Baby Boomers	Generation X	Millennials
Communication	Face-to-face	Email or IM	'Just text me'
Attitude to Work	Loyal to my job	I work to live	Play then work
Information	Print me a copy	Send me a copy	I'll Google it
What they want at work	Respect my title	Respect my ideas	Respect my skills
Areas of Focus	Focus on process	Focus on results	Focus on involvement
Priorities	Work comes first	Family comes first	Friends come first

Source: Murray, R. (2017).

The Baby Boomers represent the largest number of workers in the workforce. "Independence and social consciousness are Baby Boomers' bedrock values. They marched against 'the establishment' to bring about equal rights and an end to the Vietnam War. Competitive and independent, Baby Boomers are workaholics, with identities closely aligned to their professions," (Fox, 2011).

Generation X is often considered the "lost generation," since this is the smallest group in the workforce. Growing up, members of this group were often latchkey children, with both parents working outside the home or divorced. "This generation saw the invention of the personal computer, a deregulated airline industry, and multiple recessions. They became technologically astute, more mobile and highly educated, as they went back to school when they couldn't find jobs. Self-management, pragmatism, and cynicism are traits associated with Generation X," (Fox, 2011).

The impact of the economic, social, and technical advancement had an impact on the way this group views corporate loyalty. "Their value set is focused on gaining transferable skills so that they can be ready when the rug is pulled out from under them—as it has throughout their lives. All the major institutions fell apart around them—marriage, family, corporations and the economy. Their attitude is, 'You've never done anything for me. Why should I do something for you?' "(Fox, 2011).

Millennials have been raised around technology. This group also is a heavy user of social media such as Twitter and Facebook. This sense of creating a collaborative network also translates into the Millennials' work preference for working in teams. As children of Baby Boomers, they were raised with the "Everyone Gets a Trophy Mentality." This group had been characterized in the research as needing constant praise and views career advancement based on work performance rather than seniority, (John & Johnson, 2010). "Raised by Baby Boomers who desired peer-like relationships with their children, Millennials have been constantly coached, praised and encouraged for participation—rather than for accomplishments," (Fox, 2011).

While Generation Xer's seek to find a work/life balance, "Millennials view work as a key part of life, not a separate activity that needs to be 'balanced' by it. For that reason, they place a strong emphasis on finding work that is personally fulfilling. They want work to afford them the opportunity to make new friends, learn new skills, and connect to a larger purpose," (Meister & Willyerd, 2010). This characteristic is important to job satisfaction of this group. Employers need to be aware of the high standards that Millennials set for themselves and their employers and seek out ways to motivate and retain this group.

College leaders should also acknowledge the challenges faced by employees when younger members of the institution serve as a supervisor for an older worker. In a 2010 survey conducted by Career Builder, more than half (53 percent) of workers ages 45 and up said they have a boss younger than them, followed by 69 percent of workers ages 55 and up. According the survey Career Builder (2010), workers reported that there are a variety of reasons why working for someone younger than them can be a challenge, including:

- They act like they know more than me when they don't
- They act like they're entitled and didn't earn their position
- They micromanage
- They play favorites with younger workers
- They don't give me enough direction (CareerBuilder, 2010, p.1).

CareerBuilder (2010) offers the following suggestions for older generations with younger supervisors:

- **Understand Others' Point of View**: Different generations tend to have differing opinions on a variety of topics, from management style to pop culture. Put yourself in others' shoes to better understand where they're coming from.
- **Adapt Your Communication**: Younger workers tend to favor communicating frequently using technology, such as e-mail and instant messenger. Older workers may prefer more face-to-face contact. Both parties should take this and other communication differences into consideration when interacting.
- **Keep an Open Mind**: Try not to make assumptions about those who are of a different age group than you. All workers have different skill sets and strengths, so see what you can learn from others rather than making judgments based on their age (CareerBuilder, 2010, p.1).

The suggestions offered by CareerBuilder (2015) are useful for both college leaders as well as online faculty members. Leaders can use the suggestions for training faculty to be aware of the ways older students may communicate with younger students and younger instructors. Being aware of generational differences, without stereotyping individuals, can assist in creating more satisfying work and classroom environments.

FUTURE RESEARCH DIRECTIONS

The study findings and review of the literature raise interest related to the diversity of multigenerational workers in higher education settings. This is a trend that will continue to increase both on a national and international level as more of the Millennials enter the workplace and take on leadership roles in higher education. The research also shows that members of the Millennial group require mentoring and are looking for growth in their career in an environment that fosters collaboration and creativity.

The field of higher education is competitive on a global scale. With the number of online for-profit institutions and traditional on-ground institutions all competing for the same students, it is imperative that higher education leaders recruit and retain the best employees in an environment that fosters growth. This covers individuals across the institution: financial aid, student services, faculty, advising, and admissions.

Once hired at the institution, it is important that higher education leaders keep these employees. With four generations of workers in the institution, each group needs to feel valued and respected in their individual role. College leaders can leverage this diversity by channeling into the factors that motivate the different groups. For example, the Millennial group often seeks mentorships. Mentors can be provided from older workers to coach new employees or faculty.

Online faculty members need to be aware of the multigenerational groups of students in the classroom. This may be difficult because unless students self-disclose this information on a discussion board or in a webinar, there is no way to track the age of the student. Since the majority of online students are adult learners, faculty need to be trained on communication styles for all the generations. While Millennials may send numerous emails and ask for sample projects, a Baby Boomer may ask for a phone call to ask questions about a project. Setting clear expectations in the course syllabus is important for students of all generations. Well-defined rubrics are also important in outlining the expectations for the students.

Higher education leaders may consider reviewing other case studies established by corporations that address multigenerational concerns. Businesses can provide a viable model for implementing a strategy for creating a collaborative spirit in the educational environment. At times, there may be a tendency to view higher education as an entity separate from business. However, the mission to provide a service to individuals is the same. As such, there is a common need to create an environment in which people want to work, be it a corporate or educational setting.

Many businesses have done extensive studies on ways to create a cohesive multigenerational workplace. Higher education leaders can use the experience from these corporations to also address multigenerational concerns and remain competitive in a global economy. For example, Cisco is one company that can be used as a model for higher education leaders charged with enhancing motivation, leadership, and communicating across multigenerational workers and faculty.

The American Management Association (2018) offers the following suggestions for cross-generational leadership:

Expand Your Communication Strategies

Most companies rely too heavily on one strategy for corporate communication. By making the same message available in multiple formats (thus increasing the number of times you communicate a message), you'll ensure that you reach all workers. Silents and Baby Boomers may appreciate verbal communication about changes in policy or procedures, while Generation Xers and Millennials may prefer the use of e-mail, instant messages, or corporate broadcasts.

Conduct generational information awareness/sharing sessions. A great way to get people to work together across the generations is to provide them with an opportunity to educate each other about each generation's own history, characteristics, milestone events, culture, language, and norms. Rather than talking at your people, have representatives from each age-based generation put together programming to educate people and facilitate dialogue.

Make Mentoring a Constant

As more established and experienced workers head toward retirement, develop strategies to ensure knowledge transfer and capture organizational memory.

The more structure you can lend to your mentoring program to create knowledge transfer the better. First determine younger employees' goals and developmental needs, and then pair them with older, more experienced employees to create cross-organizational dialogue among generations.

Train yourself and your managers to develop strong interpersonal skills to foster relationships with employees and each other. A leader's primary responsibility is to ensure that everyone in the organization understands that "working together" is not negotiable. Create a respectful, open and inclusive environment where workers of all ages and cultural backgrounds can share who they are without fear of being judged, "fixed," or changed.

Leaders must remain open to new ideas and provide constant feedback, working with managers and staff to shape the company's strategic vision. They must avoid projecting their own expectations about work and remain open to different perspectives based on generational attitudes.

With the variety of multigenerational employees in today's workplace, companies can no longer abide by traditional rules of leadership and management. Organizations can achieve real strategic advantage by embracing the diversity among generations to create a flexible work environment that values all people and keeps them productive, regardless of age (American Management Association, 2018, p.1).

Organizations succeed when they create a work culture that encourages people from all generations to contribute to their fullest potential. According to Raines, 2015), these organizations:

- Know their company demographics—internally and externally. They gather data about their current customers and target where they want to increase market share. They gather data and learn about their employees and consider how well their staff mirrors current and projected customers.
- Are intentional about creating and responding to generational diversity. They identify needed skill sets within the company and recruit new staff from across the generations. They seek out individuals from under-represented generations for work teams, boards and advisory groups.
- Build on strengths. The most effective mixed-generation work teams recognize the unique strengths of each individual. Successful companies find ways to bring out those strengths and help each individual develop his or her talents so they can reach their own potential and contribute in their own ways.
- Offer options. They recognize that people from a mix of generations have differing needs and preferences and design their human resources strategies to meet varied employee needs. They offer a variety of benefits, flexible schedules, and an array of opportunities for professional growth and advancement.
- Develop an understanding of and appreciation for generational differences and strengths. They find ways to learn about their employees' needs, perspectives and interests and share that learning across the organization. They structure opportunities for less experienced employees from each generation to learn from their more experienced and knowledgeable colleagues.
- Train people to communicate effectively across generations. Communication styles and levels of comfort with varied technologies differ from one generation to the next. Successful companies recognize those differences, employ an array of communication methods and teach employees how to reach out effectively to their colleagues and insure that their communication approaches are inclusive and welcoming (p.1).

There are several opportunities for further research based on themes that emerged from the research and review of the literature. Higher education leaders may wish to conduct studies from the students' perspective. Understanding how multigenerational students learn in the online classroom would benefit the institution and promote student success. Additional research on the perspectives of higher education leaders would also call for further study. Specially, researching the ways multigenerational leaders promote engagement from all employees across the institution. Additional information from the faculty perspective calls for further research. The faculty members who participated from this study were from one institution. Drawing opinion from online, traditional settings, for-profit, and not-for-profit institutions would offer a more diverse perspective. Finally, the research should be done on a global scale. This study was limited to the U.S. higher education leaders would benefit from the global perspective.

CONCLUSION

In summary, the findings of this study and review of the literature conclude that higher education leaders must assess the challenges and benefits associated with working with multigenerational employees. The Millennial group is the largest generational grouping since the Baby Boomer era and will soon hold more leadership roles at institutions of higher learning. More junior-level faculty will also be from this generational grouping and higher education leaders need to develop a plan to motivate and retain this group of individuals.

There have been numerous studies outlining ways to communicate, motivate, engage, and retain multigenerational employees and higher education faculty. Yet there have been few studies that describe and explain from the students' perspective ways to engage and motivate multigenerational peers in the online classroom. Gaining a better understanding of the faculty members' perspective on working with multigenerational peers had led to the identification of major themes and sub-themes related to mentorship, engagement, leadership, and motivation. These findings may be useful to future researchers who investigate educational leadership, communication, and diversity issues. Additionally, higher education leaders who are responsible for making hiring decisions may also utilize the findings in this study to enhance their understanding of the need to train and mentor new employees and faculty members on ways to work in a multigenerational college setting.

The findings of the research questions presented here, if conducted, may help to further understand the questions about working with multigenerational employees and faculty in higher education on an international level, faculty resistance and administrative pressure related to change, and the impact of student demographics and socioeconomic status on student success in online learning courses. As the student population of higher education is becoming more diverse in terms of gender, race, demographics, and sexual orientation, gaining an understanding of the ways to motivate and retain students because a critical issue. In an era of a rapidly changing landscape in higher education, higher education leaders need to look at the value the multigenerational groupings bring to the institution and assess ways to motivate and retain quality faculty members, leaders, other institutional employees, and students.

REFERENCES

Aalgaard, J. (2015). *Communicating Across the Generations*. Retrieved from http://gettingsmart.com/2015/01/communicating-across-generations/

American Management Association. (2015). *Leading the Four Generations at Work*. Retrieved from http://www.amanet.org/training/articles/Leading-the-Four-Generations-at-Work.aspx

CareerBuilder. (2010). *More than four-in-ten workers over the age of 35 currently work for a younger boss, finds new CareerBuilder survey*. Retrieved from http://www.careerbuilder.com/share/aboutus/pressreleasesdetail.aspx?id=pr554&sd=2/17/2010&ed=12/31/2010&siteid=cbpr&sc_cmp1=cb_pr554

Dewey, J. (1934). *Art as experience*. New York: Minton, Malach, and Co.

Fox, A. (2011). Mixing it up. *Society of Human Resource Management, 56*(5). Retrieved from http://www.shrm.org/Publications/hrmagazine/EditorialContent/2011/0511/Pages/0511fox.aspx

Grensing-Pophal, L. (2018). *How to handle 5 generations in the workplace*. Academic Press.

Hammill, G. (2015). Mixing and matching four generations of generations of employees. *FDU Magazine Online*. Retrieved from: http://www.fdu.edu/newspubs/magazine/05ws/generations.htm

INITIATIVEONE. (2018). *Are generational differences that important to workplace culture?* Retrieved from: https://www.initiative-one.com/insights/blog/generational-differences-in-the-workplace/

Janesick, V. J. (2011). *Stretching exercises for qualitative researchers* (3rd ed.). Thousand Oaks, CA: Sage. doi:10.1177/136078041101600402

John, L., & Johnson, M. (2010). *Getting the most from an age-diverse workforce*. Retrieved from http://www.generationsincbook.com

Management, N. Z. (2012). A conversation across the generations. *New Zealand Management, 59*(6), 21.

Meister, J. C., & Willyerd, K. (2010). Mentoring millennials. *Harvard Business Review*, (May): 1–5. PMID:20429252

MeMarco, M. (2018). *The multigenerational workforce: How communication styles impact office culture*. Retrieved from: https://www.staffmanagement.com/blog- multigenerational-workforce-communication-styles/

Moss, D. (2017). *5 generations + 7 values = endless opportunities*. Retrieved from: https://www.shrm.org/hr-today/news/hr-news/conference-today/pages/2017/5-generations-7-values-endless-opportunities.aspx

Murray, R. (2017). *Communication among different generations*. Retrieved from: http://robert-murray.com/communication-among-different-generations/

Raines, C. (2015). *4GenR8tns: Succeeding with colleagues, cohorts & customers*. Retrieved from http://www.generationsatwork.com/articles_succeeding.php

Rampton, J. (2017). Different motivations for different generations of workers: Boomers, *Gen X, Millennials, and Gen Z*. Retrieved from: https://www.inc.com/john-rampton/different-motivations-for-different-generations-of-workers-boomers-gen-x-millennials-gen-z.html

ADDITIONAL READING

Chang, C., & Tung, M. (2016). Intergenerational appeal in advertising: Impacts of brand–gender extension and brand history. *International Journal of Advertising, 35*(2), 345–361. doi:10.1080/02650487.2015.1030282

Friemel, T. N. (2016). The digital divide has grown old: Determinants of a digital divide among seniors. *New Media & Society, 18*(2), 313–331. doi:10.1177/1461444814538648

GunrajD. N.Drumm-HewittA. M.DashowE. M.UpadhyayS. S. N.KlinC.

Knoll, J., Matthes, J., Münch, A., & Ostermann, M. (2017). How long does celebrity meaning transfer last? Delayed effects and the moderating roles of brand experience, celebrity liking, and age. *International Journal of Advertising*, *36*(4), 588–612. doi:10.1080/02650487.2016.1213062

Kreuz, R., & Roberts, R. (2017). *Getting through: The pleasures and perils of cross-cultural communication*. Cambridge, MA: MIT Press. doi:10.7551/mitpress/10845.001.0001

M. (2016). Texting insincerely: The role of the period in text messaging. *Computers in Human Behavior, 55,* 1067–1075. . doi:10.1016/j.chb.2015.11.003

Metrix, A. (2014), 3 television advertising techniques to grab millennials' attention. *Ace Metrix.com*. Retrieved from: http://www.acemetrix.com/insights/blog/3-television-advertising-techniques-to-grab-millennials-attention/

Nielsen, T. (2017). Millennials on Millennials: A look at viewing behavior, distraction, and social media stars. Retrieved from: http://www.nielsen.com/us/en/insights/news/2017/millennials-on-millennials-a-look-at-viewing-behavior-distraction-social-media-stars.html

Pankoke, M. (2016). Three stereotypes to avoid when marketing to millennials. *Advertising Age*, Retrieved from: http://adage.com/article/digitalnext/stereotypes-avoid-marketing-millennials/305872/

Riordan, M. A. (2016). *Appear happier: Text with emojis*. Presentation at the *57th annual meeting of the Psychonomic Society*, Boston, MA.

Riordan, M. A. (2017). The communicative role of non-face emojis: Affect and disambiguation. *Computers in Human Behavior, 76*, 75–86. doi:10.1016/j.chb.2017.07.009

Taipale, S. (2016). Synchronicity matters: Defining the characteristics of digital generations. *Information Communication and Society*, *19*(1), 80–94. doi:10.1080/1369118X.2015.1093528

KEY TERMS AND DEFINITIONS

Baby Boomers: Individuals born between 1946 and 1964. Work ethic and values for this group include being a workaholic and a high level of personal fulfillment.

Collaborative Learning: This term is used to refer to students working on a computer-based learning program that requires them to collaborate by, for example, taking different roles, operating different controls, etc.

Experiential Knowledge/Learning: This term describes knowledge gained through experience/learning through experience. Contrasts, and moreover conflicts, with academic knowledge and learning through instruction.

Generation Xers: Individuals born between 1965 and 1980. Work ethic and value for individuals in this group include wanting structure and direction. This group was the first focus on work/life balance.

Holistic: This term is used to describe an integrated knowledge structure or an approach to learning that recognizes that knowledge needs to be integrated.

Mentoring Programs: Formal or informal programs in which more experienced individuals assist individual with limited experience. Mentor programs can occur in the workplace as well as the classroom.

Millennials: Individuals born between 1965 and 1980. Work ethic and value for individuals in this group include questioning what is next and multitasking. This group also has a high interest in creating work/life balance.

Multigenerational Work Groups: The representative of four generations in the workplace. This includes Traditionalists, Baby Boomers, Gen Xers, and Millennials.

Traditionalists: Individuals born pre-1945. Work ethic and values for individuals in this group include sacrifice and completion of tasks before personal enjoyment.

Virtual Teams: Groups of individuals working in a professional or academic setting set out to achieve comma goals or completion of a project. Communicating is not face-to-face but occurs via electronic format.

Work/Life Balance: Creating a balance between achievement and enjoyment. Work can also refer to tasks that need to be completed in the household in addition to a formal place of employment.

Chapter 18
Strategic Managerial Communication in the Digital Era:
Implications for Ethical-Unethical Behavior

Isabell Carolina Camillo
Niagara University, USA

Angelo A. Camillo
Sonoma State University, USA

ABSTRACT

Managerial communication is considered integral to business related disciplines such as strategic management, leadership, strategic marketing, and business ethics. However, within the context of global strategic management, managerial communication follows under the broad umbrella of "business communication," Communication with internal and external stakeholders demands careful-ethical considerations, regardless of the industry. Having an inclusive-ethical strategic managerial communication policy in place, allows for strategic information dissemination as well as the protection of transmission of confidential data. This chapter discusses the topic of communication with emphasis on ethical managerial communication within the global context. The result of the study confirm that effective-ethical communication strategies and appropriate communications policy implementation is conducive to the firm's success. Within the framework of management, ethical managerial communication refers to communication within the context of business management and not media communication.

DOI: 10.4018/978-1-5225-8516-9.ch018

INTRODUCTION

Within the framework of strategic managerial communication, we define business ethics as "a set of moral rules and principles to protect the interest of all stakeholders including but not limited to, employers, employees, customers, society, business associates, and the industry as a whole, while communicating with others."

Within the context of communication, trying to persuade what is ethical and what is not may influence the management's ability to communicate ethically and effectively.

The "inability" communicative with full transparency within the company and with stakeholders outside the company may lead to complex problems. Consequently, managerial decisions must be taken which could lead to unintended consequences. For example, an expatriate managing a family owned enterprise may discover that a relative working in management is embezzling company money. Should the expatriate manager communicate the problem to the ownership? If so, how? Will they believe him/her? Will they understand and support the expatriate, or will the owners retaliate again him/her? If there is no clear communication policy in place, the expatriate will have to make a tough decision: a) say nothing; b) communicate the discovery in an ethical manner to the ownership; c) contact the embezzler first and explain and inform him/her about the responsibility to inform the owners; or d) consult a legal counsel first. Obviously, there are no easy answers unless an inclusive - strategic communication plan has been implemented for all stakeholders, regardless of the role or responsibility.

The current global business environment is characterized by an explosion in information technology, globalization of the economies, localized - acute ecopolitical crisis, and increased pressure from consumers, organized labor, and government regulations/ deregulations. It is clear that communicating freely and ethically becomes challenging. As a result, managers often chose "silence" over communication, in the hope that bad things will just go away, instead problems only escalate the majority of times. Ethical managers can create a certain image (positive or negative) of the organization, both within the company, and in the community and society. Therefore, considering that global corporations are becoming bigger and more powerful, there is a need for managers to communicate in an ethical and socially responsible manner. Over the last decade, there has been an overwhelming interest by scholars on the importance of socially responsible communication. Social scientists are dynamically engaging in the much-discussed topic of "micro aggression in managerial communication" and ethics in communication (Makau, 2009; Sue, 2010).

In a broad sense, Managerial Communication today is an integral component of many business-related disciplines (strategic management, leadership, strategic marketing, international negotiation, business ethics, etc.). Cross-cultural communication, however, encompasses every area of communication including interpersonal communication (Lustig & Koester, 2010). This topic is usually integrated in courses under the discipline of Media Communication, which does not fall within the scope of this research.

A global search on the topic of cross-cultural communication within the global business context reveals that the discipline is under-researched. In fact, since 2010, UNESCO (United Nations Education Scientific and Cultural Organization) has been running a multilingual program called Transcultural Communication in the Digital Age (UNESCO, 2010). Its scope is to strengthen research in the field of multilingual and transcultural communication, including multilingual computing methods, e-learning, multilingual web content management, and related methods; to promote the development of a multilingual social web, harnessing semantic web technologies and strengthening transcultural communication patterns using a wide range of language resources and technologies; and multilingual computing methods, multilingual e-learning and cultural diversity management procedures (UNESCO).

However, within the global business management context and to a certain extent, Managerial Communication falls under the broad umbrella of "Business Communication", which is at the core of this chapter. In fact, when researching global competitive advantage, a major research question comes to mind: Why are some competitors more successful than others? Further, why do some executives consistently make the right decisions while others invariably fail? This paper provides an explanation by asserting that one of the most significant attributes to global managerial success is *effective and ethical managerial communication*. In an attempt to exploit the true meaning of managerial communication, we theorize that when humans interact they create relationships. We base our approach to theories and applications on a polycentric point of view by thinking of *communication* as being more universal in nature than ethnocentric based. And, because we are different in nature, different people act and react differently. Since we are actively interacting, we adapt and learn the rules of the surroundings which condition the interaction, whether it is at the work place, at school, or on the golf course. By interacting, we acquire each other's culture and integrate our exchanged behavior, knowledge, experience, etc., thus becoming multicultural. Consequently, we adapt to the way we interact and communicate, and according to each given situation. Hence, when adaptation is not possible, we fail.

Indeed, failure due to lack of effective communication with all stakeholders leads to lower productivity, lower profitability, and short-term survivorship. Increased managerial communication effectiveness, however, enables practitioners at all management levels to realize the benefits of proper communication. In order to achieve effective communication, a firm must have well defined communication policies and plans in place. Communication policies are designed to enable a member of an organization to understand the finer points of internal communication with employees and external communication with business associates (Stevens, 2005). Through appropriate training and effective policy implementation, companies aim to develop communication skills, which can be applied to all levels of the organization, especially at middle to upper management levels. This process is conducive to the development and best practice of ethical communication and communicative behaviour.

However, policies and plans can only be developed and implemented with effective and continuous training, by using new and more efficient supporting tools such as developing communication technologies, and by having effective and ethical communication leadership.

To support this objective, certain fundamental elements are necessary. The management must have the ability to manage and deliver what it promises, and must possess a high level of communication competence - including but not limited to - ethical communication skills, language proficiency, cross-cultural awareness, intelligence, expertise, adaptability, and understanding (Hammer, 1989 pp. 247-261; Cushner & Brislin, 1996; Earley & Ang, 2003; Arasaratnam & Doerfel, 2005; Abbe, Gulick, & Herman, 2007).

Within this framework, Strategic Managerial Communication can be described as "an integrative theory-practice methodology that enables the management to sensibly apply the knowledge acquired to any situations, within the perspective of business communication, based on the long-term view of the firm." In other words, it is the process that interconnects knowledge with competent practice not only tactical but strategic (Ting-Toomey, 1999). Furthermore, Managerial Communication can be interpreted as "the skill to efficiently communicate activities/messages to stimulate an anticipated reaction in a specific situation and without offending anyone in the process." Specifically, competent management needs to master the art of interaction and apply it efficiently with the people and the environment, and at the same time fulfil its own communication goals using this capability (Chen & Starosta, 1998: pp. 241–2). Hence, all of the above must be practiced in an ethical-effective way.

BACKGROUND

Meaning and Application of Strategic and Ethical Managerial Communication

Scholastically, managerial communication, within the framework of applied business communication, is considered a discipline (Gross, 2011) and a research topic in the field of social sciences (Calhoun, 2011), which has reached the classroom of many business schools around the globe. In fact, many graduate business programs now include managerial communication and also strategic managerial communication in their curriculum. Strategic communication is instructed as a foundational management competence instrumental in amplifying general performance at personal, company, financial, and strategic strata. It is applied to key managerial fields of study, which include crisis management, multicultural leadership, ethical communication, informational vs. persuational leadership, and team building, amongst others. Practitioners have long seen the necessity of effective communication.

In early 1980s, the topic of managerial communication engaged scholars in finding its clear definition. In 1986, Henderson proposed “A Conceptual Explication and Model for Guiding Future Research” (Henderson, 1986). Since then many definitions have emerged. To a certain extent, managerial communication today can be defined as *the communication between manager and subordinates.* In a broader sense, it can also include external stakeholders, including but not limited to customers and suppliers (Ellis & Hopkinson, 2010). However, Managerial Communication is considered an applied and essential discipline that continues to engage scholars in research and has become one of the most important elements of concern within the context of global management.

Nevertheless, the goal of ethical communication within the global business context is comprehensive in that it intends to develop and disseminate relevant knowledge, which will increase the effectiveness and efficiency of managers and employees, especially in the contemporary multicultural and diverse business environment, by acting ethically. Although much has been written about and practiced in actual managerial situations, ethical communication is still in the developmental stage today. We are continuously experiencing new approaches in terms of political correctness, whistle blowers’ activities, legal disputes “he said I said”, and more. The scope, however, is to integrate it within the area of managerial communication, which already expands beyond the walls of the global organization. It involves interaction between two or more diverse individuals who must communicate in a business situation, whether it is Manager to Employee (M2E), Business to Business (B2B), Business to Customer/Guest (B2CG), or in a “non-verbal” and “impersonal setting” such as social media across the globe (MIT, 2009; Monash University, 2010; Cornell University, 2011). Indeed, good communication practices in the working environment are developed over time through experience and education. Too often, miscommunication can lead to create conflict, business disruption, personal negative consequences as result of personal attacks. It is important, therefore, that firms not only have communication training and manuals at their disposal, but also that they master the art of “ethical managerial communication, especially in the global business landscape.”

In an ideal world, a message sender could easily predict how others will perceive his or her message. In such a world, television commercials would be optimally placed, and no one would be offended by an inter-office email. In such a world, there would be no language barriers, no political, religious, gender, or cultural constraints. Unfortunately, the business world does not deal with such utopias, it does not operate In a vacuum, and consequently business leaders must be organized and prepared with well-formulated communication policies in place to avoid possible pitfalls.

Communicating strategically involves several basic elements: Purpose, Message Sender (Encoder), Message Configuration, Message Receiver (Decoder), Channel of Communication, and Expected Outcome. When properly applied, communication should be an easy task to accomplish. However, all too frequently, we hear that a company's major hurdle to success is communication. Consequently, talented managers with expertise in their field often fail in their duties simply because they lack the ability to communicate effectively. They also run the risk of delegating ineffectively because of their own inability to communicate effectively. A marketing manager who has innovative ideas about how to capture more customers, for instance, will be passed over if he/she is unable to make his/her suggestions clear and compelling. Many strategic plans may never be implemented if there is lack of communication ability (Thatam, 2008). Having a well-defined policy is, therefore, key. Such a plan will have one goal in mind: to communicate a request, an idea, accomplishment, event, or even a failure. In other words, effective communication is neither a function of trial and error nor is it a matter of doing what comes naturally. Effectiveness in managerial communication requires managers to establish clear goals and then apply principles and insights to make wise choices about language and behavior in the communication process.

This paper describes general ethical communication with real-life examples on how prominent companies have a communications policy in place, and how they use the results to raise awareness about the criticality of communication issues within organizational settings, especially during this current era of dynamic interconnectivity due to IT evolution. It also addresses the responsibility of executives who manage complex international businesses, and have a need to communicate effectively with diverse cultures in foreign lands. Therefore, the focus is on the importance of effective and ethical communication, both oral and written, while emphasizing the criticality of culture and cultures in business communication. Overall, it explores ways in which intrapersonal, interpersonal, intercultural, group, and organizational communication is experienced within both companies and cultures.

From a practitioner's perspective, the International Association of Business Communicators has established very clear and concise standards in their communication's policies (IABC, 2015):

The Global standard is defined by communication professionals around the world embracing a shared career purpose and six core Principles as the building blocks of their work. Informed by a passion for engaging audiences with strategic communication, the purpose and Principles focus our work and form a global standard.

Their organization's six principles are *Ethics, Consistency, Context, Analysis, Strategy, and Engagement.* Their members' day-to-day communication includes cultural values, compliance with the law, and truthful, fair and accurate representation of the organization, and mutual respect and understanding. They communicate ethically with sensitivity to cultural values and beliefs, act without deception and in accordance with the law, represent the organization truthfully, fairly and accurately, enable mutual understanding and respect, and adhere to the "IABC Code of Ethics for Professional Communicators and the Code of Ethics for Communication Professionals" (IABC, 2015).

However, a review of current academic and trade's literature shows that catalyst for violating these principles is the current political and business landscape where everything unethical is fair game. Since everyone can be self-designated journalist through blogs and membership in social media platforms, reaching an audience of millions of followers, journalists are compelled to do the impossible in order to stand out as trustworthy reporters. In fact, using an example of political reporting, it appears as there are no limits to what a journalist can do when investigating a politician and report what was never possible "Before Social Media (BSM). Directly related is the concerning trend which originated through the use of social media where online based digital and non-verbal communication platforms have given tools to anyone to communicate freely and even incognito. The platforms, unless the ownership decides otherwise, allow members to communicate and disseminate specific content whether it is trusted, real, verified, obscene, insulting, misleading, coercive, and much more. What is more disheartening is the breach of confidentiality and leaks to the various media which is then transmitted by machines to anyone around the globe (OECD, 2012). Most concerning is the speed and the intensity of communication and the impossible immediate measurements as to how to interpret, validate and accept what is being communicated. In addition, it appears as the agility to use semantic to quickly convey a message that did not gain acceptance or rather, created controversy, may allow the decoder to accept even the most unethical message because it may be expressed differently. To use an analogy derived from the political arena, players involved in the much-heated discussion about "global warming" realized that the way the message was being communicated to the audience found significant acceptance variations by both believers and non- believers. However, when the message morphed to "Climate Change", the number of believers increased significantly (Kahan, 2014a; Kahan, 2014b). Further examples are highlighted by, Kahan (2015) who argues that "advocacy groups regularly report polls that paint a very different picture. "A new study," their press releases announce, show that "an overwhelming majority of Americans" "Blue State and Red ones alike," enough "to swing" an upcoming presidential election etc.— "support taking action" immediately to combat global warming. The producers of such polls do not always release information about the survey's wording or the (mysteriously characterized) methods used to analyze them (e.g., Koch, 2013). But when they do, researchers note that the questions posed were likely to confuse, mislead, or herd the survey respondents toward desired answers (Kohut, 2010)." Hence, these communications' strategies are proof of potentially unethical behavior to represent a personal or a group agenda not every stakeholder may agree-disagree with. Also, considering a purely political and fiscal misrepresentation, members of the British Parliament once argued that the national debt in Britain was not increasing under their leadership, in fact an increase in deficit was defined as "Deficit Surplus" (HCI, 1961). Is this an unethical way to communicate a factual and rather negative fiscal situation? Certainly, this question is arguable, depending on what the stakeholders believe. Accordingly, what can managers learn from these strategies? What are the implications? Is it fair game if managers behave unethically and communicate untrue or misleading messages to their audience? Johannesen (1996) posits that one must be careful not to stretch the facts, or assemble them only to prove him/ herself, and instead prove the argument on its own merits. Deception, coercion, intentional bias, manipulation and bribery should have no place in a speech intended to ethically communicate a persuasive message, (Johannesen, 1996). In his book *Ethics in Human Communication* Johannesen (1996), offers valuable insights in verbal communication' interaction and in attempting to persuade an audience. Rather to offer advise as to what to do/ say in communication, he proposes what not to do. Specifically, "Do Not:

- Use false, fabricated, misrepresented, distorted or irrelevant evidence to support arguments or claims.
- Intentionally use unsupported, misleading, or illogical reasoning.
- Represent yourself as informed or an "expert" on a subject when you are not.
- Use irrelevant appeals to divert attention from the issue at hand.
- Ask your audience to link your idea or proposal to emotion-laden values, motives, or goals to which it is actually not related.
- Deceive your audience by concealing your real purpose, by concealing self-interest, by concealing the group you represent, or by concealing your position as an advocate of a viewpoint.
- Distort, hide, or misrepresent the number, scope, intensity, or undesirable features of consequences or effects.
- Use "emotional appeals" that lack a supporting basis of evidence or reasoning.
- Oversimplify complex, gradation-laden situations into simplistic, two-valued, either-or, polar views or choices.
- Pretend certainty where tentativeness and degrees of probability would be more accurate.
- Advocate something which you yourself do not believe in.

Finally, Johannesen (1996) points on the importance of avoiding fallacies. "Fallacies are another way of saying false logic. These rhetorical tricks deceive your audience with their style, drama, or pattern, but add little to your speech in terms of substance and can actually detract from your effectiveness" (Johannesen, 1996).

Past, Present, and Future Applicability of Ethical Managerial Communication

Interest has been shown in the art of communication since the classical age. The Greeks developed specific communication methods and techniques that conferred it the status of a science. In the contemporary age, the communication theory has experienced an impressive growth, becoming a major preoccupation for many specialists in extremely different domains (psychology, philosophy, marketing and public relations, management, etc.). Managerial communication today has a special status, derived from an organizational framework simply known as *business communications* in which it is performed, from its goals, purpose and role (Gheorghe et al., 2009). For example, Carlson's (1951) classic study was based upon nine senior Scandinavian managers recording the details of each activity they engaged in. Subsequent researchers have empirically documented the volume, hierarchical direction, and purposes of managerial communication (Landsberger, 1961; Kelly, 1964; Horne & Lupton, 1965; Stinchcombe, 1974). Lawrence and Lorsch (1967) found that managerial communications and influence from lower and middle levels of management increased the quality of the decision-making process. Also, Vroom and Yetten (1973) have investigated managerial communication and decision-making among managers, and their impact on the quality of decision making and implementation. Vroom (1964), in his studies of both autocratic and participative decisions, found that communication amongst diverse work groups required a greater investment of time, but produced a higher acceptance of decisions and increased the probability that the decision would be executed efficiently. Astley and Zammuto (1992) more explicitly centralize managerial communication in the sense-making processes that both create and disseminate managerial knowledge, thereby making and shaping communities and organizations. For them, "managers espouse their own theories about the way their world works, and the conceptual language they use establishes a context within which organizational life is constructed and reconstructed."

Weick (1995) argues that the basis of managerial action is not the world as objectively given but rather the world as people understand it to be. Rejecting traditional approaches to management scholarship that assume objectivity and rationality as human characteristics, Weick (1995) considers interpretation of communication in general as the underpinning of human nature. Several empirical studies of communication during mergers have provided support for the positive effects of managerial communication on employee attitudes and behaviours, especially in relationship with diverse work groups (Covin et al., 1996; Schraeder, 2001; Zorn et al., 2000).

Other researchers have provided empirical support for the positive effects of communication on organizational performance. For example, Miller, Johnson, and Grau (1994) found that communication was a significant factor in reducing employees' anxiety and increasing their willingness to participate in planned activities. Similarly, Wanberg and Banas (2000) examined the role of communication in a longitudinal study of government reorganization. They found that employees who received adequate information about the organization plan demonstrated more positive attitudes toward the organization. More recent organizational researchers have suggested that communication is particularly important in organizational change processes (Zorn et al., 2000; Armenakis & Harris, 2002).

The role of organizational communication in a change context is generally defined as a process through which companies announce, explain, or prepare employees for change (Armenakis & Harris, 2002). This process perspective suggests that when employees receive sufficient and appropriate communication in a change context (i.e., appropriate justification for, and information about, the change and timely feedback), they will have more favourable attitudes towards the change which, in turn, should result in positive organizational outcomes (Goodman & Truss, 2004).

Effective communication within an organization has also been identified as a significant factor in helping employees understand the need for change, as well as the personal effects of a proposed change (Armenakis & Harris, 2002). This becomes even more critical in a global organization operating in any given host country. Increasing employees' understanding of the change process may also reduce the level of uncertainty and resistance toward the change and, thus, help promote employees' involvement in and acceptance of the change (Goodman & Truss, 2004). The importance of effective communication is noted also by Weick, Sutcliffe and Obstfeld (2005) who argue that it is talk that brackets action and thus gives meaning. Harvard Busines School focused on the meaning and application of effective communication, and emphasized that "Face-to-Face Communication" be used for clarity and impact by the "Results-Driven Manager" (HBS, 2004).

However, over time, the concept of managerial communication and specifically Ethical Managerial Communication has been ascribed numerous and varied meanings. Its exact meaning is still intensely debated. There are several definitions of managerial communication: 1) it is an applied, interdisciplinary field focusing on language and behavior within an organizational context (Brownell, 2003); 2) it focuses on cross-cultural communication across various contexts: interpersonal, group, organizational and, in some instances, mediated (Kraut et al., 1982; Kraut et al., 2002); 3) it includes all relevant forms and channels of communication that managers may select in accomplishing their purposes, including written, oral, nonverbal, and mediated (Cornelissen, 2004); and 4) its research supplies the principles and insights that help practitioners to apply knowledge derived from all other disciplines as they seek to increase their effectiveness (Clampitt, 2005).

In an organizational approach, ethical managerial communication represents the decisive means by which the manager fulfils his/her tasks and duties, and employs the competences and skills pertaining to his/her role in the company and in relation to business partners (Gheorghe et al., 2009) - all interactions within an appropriate and ethical manner. The manager sends information to the members of an organization and its business partners, and their response influences his/her subsequent decisions and behavior. The quality of communication channels depends on the functionality of the communication system. This system needs to be conceived as a dynamic organism, capable of adapting to the information needs of the company at any moment, at any level, responding to any problems that may influence and condition its normal functioning (Johansson & Heide, 2008; Gheorghe et al., 2009).

Within a company, the individual and the group performance of the employees largely depends on the quality and ethical delivery of managerial communication. The manager communicates for the purpose of sending and receiving information, triggering adequate answers, and implicitly, influencing the receptors' decisions and their response to the transmitted messages. The efficient and ethical management of communication is a weighty responsibility for any manager, and the way he/she fulfils it is fundamental to business success. Managers need to inform all employees of company missions and goals, and related costs and targets. However, a manager is also interested in conveying information on task fulfilment, and suggestions and opinions on the well-being of the company, as seen by employees; hence, micro aggression of any kind must be avoided to achieve optimal success. At the same time, the members of the managerial team must also exchange information with regard to any technical, economic, and social problems affecting the company in a mutually ethical manner. Within the global business framework and the scope of this chapter, managerial communication becomes an important element of the interaction between all players. Thus, a system of reciprocal cooperation is created, facilitating the fundamental objectives of the company.

Published literature (Dance, 1970; Campbell & Level Dale, 1985; Clampitt, 2005; Stefanescu & Popa, 2008) emphasizes many modes of communication. However, two modes stand out as the most important: formal and informal. Formal communication can be defined as a set of rules that all stakeholders in the organization strictly adhere to. It is a structured flow of information formally conveyed to members within and outside the organization. The structure enables the flow of communication in a way that guarantees the transfer of a specific knowledge effectively, effortlessly, precisely, timely, and confidentially. In other words, the structure is the only formal channel of communication. Formal communication within the organization includes but is not limited to: departmental meetings, conferences, telephone calls, emails, text messages, company news releases, media interviews and specialist publications.

Informal communication cannot be as readily defined since its content is derived from unplanned events that may occur under specific circumstances. Informal communication is based on the realization that individuals or group members cannot be effective without personal interaction amongst its members. Therefore, informal communication is personal, unofficial, and mostly verbal. While it is unplanned for, past experience shapes informal communication. Accordingly, it is mostly through *informal communication* that unethical communication behaviour may occur. Because managers may be unprepared for what is not planned, and because the communication may be sudden and spontaneously, the necessity to communicate in any way or means available may cause the message to lose its meaning, while unethical components may carry more weight and micro aggression toward employees may become inevitable.

When formal communication is non-existent, informal communication occurs organically between individuals and within a team. When a crisis occurs, key players who have not been trained in communication develop and sporadically implement an immediate communication plan based on successful past experiences. When emergencies happen, a manager is able to promptly begin communicative interactions, fostering effective crisis management (McKinney et al., 2005).

Managerial communication acts as an integrated relationship with those inside the company as well as those outside the company. Competitive companies have understood this, and have promoted communicative ethical competence as a philosophy assumed by management and the organization as a whole. In many companies, communication is considered to be, and is used as, one of the most valuable instruments of strategic management. Conversely, the defective transmission of information, communication breakdowns, and lack of transparency and honesty frequently account for business failures.

Examples of the criticality of using managerial communication are prevalent in the international political arena. The online version of The Hill Times, a Canadian weekly newspaper, reports that the current Prime Minister of Canada, Stephen Harper, has taken communiqués to a new level. The Hill Times reports that Mr. Harper's office and departments employ approximately 1,500 communications staffers (Ryckewaert, 2011). Quite a high number considering that Canada's population is about one tenth of that of the USA.

Approaches to Managerial Communication

Over time, multiple approaches to communication have been built. According to literature (Dance, 1970; Campbell & Level Dale, 1985; Clampitt, 2005; Copley, 2004; Stefanescu & Popa, 2008), there are four approaches that are the most significant and prevalent in managerial practice: the one-way communication model, the circuit communication model, the interactive communication model, and the behavioural model.

The one-way communication approach is a classic model (Schramm, 1955; Campbell & Dale Level, 1985). Managers who choose this approach (from transmitter to receptor or from encoder to decoder), which Clampitt (2005) called "the arrow approach" (p. 1), start from the presupposition that the receptor's feedback is not needed as long as the information and decisions transmitted were clearly formulated, in a language that is adequate and unambiguous. This idea relies on the belief that if the message is clear for the transmitter, it must be equally clear to the receptor. The latter will act in complete accordance with the content of the message received. By adopting this type of communication, the manager considers that, by using a clear and precise language, the decision he/she transmits will be correctly understood and complied with by the receiver, without any feedback required. This type of communication is a model that proves defective, as it generates problems at the organizational level. Employees often complain about the lack of information or about the fact that the information reaches them distortedly. In the absence of a response, this sort of information can no longer be corrected. The inadequate distribution of the information from the upper level of management to the lower levels was critiqued by Peter Drucker (1993) - when taking up the one-way communication model, a manager invariably ignores the receptor.

Communication is incomplete if information is misunderstood. Many theorists consider that we may speak of communication only when the receiver gives feedback. Under the conditions of the ever-increasing complexity of company activities, the efficiency of managerial communication process is not fully sustained by adopting a one-way communication model. Organizational practice has shown that efficient managerial communication relies on a plurality of factors. Among them, employee feedback to messages received from management attests to communication comprehension and makes possible the adaptation of employee behavior to managerial expectations. Overlooking employee responses can have negative effects upon the success of the communication process and, consequently, upon the company in general.

Another approach of managerial communication is circuit communication, which supposes the existence, in all cases, of the receptor's response (reaction) to the received message. Unlike the *arrow approach*, this type of communication starts from the presupposition that the manager must know all problems facing subordinates are facing in fulfilling assigned tasks, and all their opinions and views on activities they carry within the company. The success of this type of managerial approach depends on the manager's skills in psychology and of his/her ability to stimulate the employee devotion towards the company. The disadvantage of approaching this sort of communication comes from the large amount of time spent in discussions and debates, which may negatively reflect on the effectiveness and efficacy of the company.

Interactive communication is yet another way of approaching communication. Interactive communication supposes an exchange of ideas between those who communicate, each having in turn, the role of receptor and transmitter. This model of communication is particularly characteristic of organizations in which employees' creative skills are appreciated and their participation in problem solving is stimulated. Interactive communication relies on group creativity, the valorisation of proposals, and suggestions and ideas expressed by members of the organization. Its aim is to identify solutions generated by the exchange of ideas. The effectiveness of this type of communication is conditioned by the compatibility of those who communicate their shared level of knowledge, experience, values, and behaviours.

In 1985, Campbell and Level proposed a more complex model of communication – the behavioural model. The two researchers analyzed the managerial communication process by studying transmitter expectations of receptor reactions to a message. The anticipation of likely employee responses to a message helps the manager structure and adapt the message in order to illicit a positive response. The determination of the receiver's behavior subsequent to the communication must be, in the two researchers' view, the transmitter's first goal. He/she should also consider the outside interferences that might occur and prejudice the communication process.

Although companies have gone through massive changes with respect to the way they approach managerial communication, none of the models presented above are remotely close to perfection. Each has, as shown, both advantages and disadvantages. In essence, any communication must be approached in a manner that best suits the set purpose and the communication competence of all concerned. He/she must ensure the smooth transit of the communication process through all channels, both formal and informal, and both inside and outside the company.

Development of the Managerial Communication Competence

Although communication may at first glance appear simple and uncomplicated, it is in fact a complex undertaking. Clampitt (2005) argues that communication within the firm is an important skill for all managers, irrespective of their seniority. Effective communication requires training and development. Often, organizations do not invest sufficient money, time, and effort in developing effective communication skills that in turn results in communication failure.

Many researchers have placed communicational competence at the very core of managerial success. Reflecting on the qualities that underpin managerial success, Maxwell (2002) ranks the manager's ability to communicate efficiently first in importance, with a rating of 38% (p. 101). It is notable that Maxwell gives other components a markedly lower grade: creativity – 31%, management knowledge – 19%, relationships – 12% (2002). In turn, Drucker (1977) urges managers to improve their communicative competence, so that they may be noted for their "ability to communicate with people and to introduce to them their own thoughts and ideas in such a way as to get them to understand and be persuaded" (p. 262). Furthermore, "this ability to express oneself may be the most important aptitude one can have" (Drucker, 1977).

A manager's ability to constantly improve his/her communication skills is fundamental to the operation of any company. In the process, the true understanding of *managerial communication* and its application becomes most critical for any manager. The result is a positive-communicative aptitude that fosters a climate of open mindedness and trust and repels conflict and tension. Additionally, the ability to convey unpleasant news or information with diplomacy, to divert conflict tactfully, and to solve problems with authority is a key aspect of effective communication.

Published literature (Johansson & Heide, 2008; Gheorghe et al., 2009) shows that too often communication by managers fail because of lack of proper training, lack of follow-up and follow through, and lack of consequence for those who do not perceive the communication to be relevant or important. Accordingly, managers often abdicate the responsibility for communicating effectively with their internal communication department and lack the confidence to facilitate discussion within their teams (Clampitt, 2005). Communication is far from simple, and experienced communicators recognize, therefore, the need to be persistent until their messages have been clearly received, understood, and dealt with accordingly. The results of an investigation into persistent and redundant communication revealed that clarity in messaging was not the goal for redundant communication (Girard, 2011). Even if a powerful manager is clear and direct with an employee-team member, it is still the redundancy that counts in order to get the core of the message delivered as intended.

Strategic communication, policy-making, and guidance for consistent information activity, both internally and externally, are of increased interest to researchers. It is key that sensitive information be safeguarded effectively. E.g. computer hackers are now able to use social media to gain competitive advantage. WikiLeaks (Johnson, 2011) provides a vivid example of a seemingly weaker social media stakeholder empowered to compel concessions from an apparently stronger adversary (Castells, 2007). Certainly, companies ignore the power of social media within the context of communication at their peril. Top management, however, should be rather concerned that leaks can be detrimental to any company, and therefore the need to be prepared should be a priority.

The Role of Information Technology in Contemporary Communication Practice

Advances in information technology are allowing organizations to: (1) distribute information at increased rates of speed; (2) make more information available than ever before; (3) allow broader and more immediate access to this information; (4) encourage participation in the sharing and use of information; and (5) integrate systems and functions in unprecedented ways.

The political tumult since 2011 in the Middle East has illustrated the key role of social media. Similarly, global corporations are using social media to disseminate all manner of information, whether marketing related or human resources related (Shah, et al. 2005). The most popular social media outlets such as Facebook, Twitter, and various other Web 2.0 technologies, are being used to communicate with individuals internally and externally across the globe.

Although using social media to communicate can be challenging, executives often use it effectively to stay in touch with all concerned in a timely and effective fashion (Lenhart & Fox, 2006). Oracle's CEO Jonathan Benoit, http://blogs.oracle.com/jonathan (Oracle, 2011), Bill Marriott Chairman & CEO of Marriott International http://www.blogs.marriott.com/, and John Mackey Whole Foods CEO http://www2.wholefoodsmarket.com/blogs/jmackey/ use internal and external blogs. The phenomenon delivers measurable benefits to all stakeholders (Drezner & Farrell, 2004). Internal blogs can, for example, facilitate the collation of workplace data. This information can be used to aid performance evaluations and many other applications. Data collected on external parties such as guests/customers can be used in the application of competitive analytics, Customer Relations Management (CRM), Customer Experience Management (CEM), and other marketing related applications. With unparalleled access to stakeholders, IT communication must avoid any breach of privacy and unlawful collection of personal information.

New Developments in Ethical Communication

With the evolution of social media, there has been an increased interest by people in launching blogs, becoming members of online platforms that profile business people, and having personal websites as a tool for personal branding. This evolution has allowed business people to be positively exposed yet also criticized. Accordingly, anything said can be voice or video recorded, and can be used against the person being put in the spotlight. Therefore, communicating ethically in this ever-increasing interconnected and overexposed world has become one the most feared factor for many managers.

In 2007, Alex Brigham, an expert in the field of ethics and compliance, founded the Ethisphere Institute with a website and magazine. Its scope is to explore, examine, and circulate best practices through Ethisphere's proprietary research and rating system (Ethisphere, 2018). The Institute publishes a yearly report ranking the 100 most ethical global companies, 100 most influential - ethical business people, and a report on lawyers that matter. Ethisphere is not unique in rating and exposing the best ethical people and companies. Similarly, the Dow Jones Sustainability Indices publishes a yearly review of the most globally sustainable companies (DJ, 2015). A company that is publicly traded having a low DJ sustainability index score may not be attractive to investors; therefore, the manager must make any effort in ensuring that the index score's high. How the manager communicates this strategic goal and inspires all stakeholders to buy into it becomes a highly ethical and challenging task. This is to demonstrate that businesses and business leaders around the world are being watched, closely evaluated, and criticized (whether negatively of positively) around the clock. Therefore, the business landscape has and continues to transition into a new era of self-policing and carefully dealing in all business-related endeavors in order to stay ethically – business viable. Accordingly, the way managers communicate, what they communicate, and how they use communication, has become an integral component in business strategy and in striving to achieve competitive advantage. As a result, companies and management are compelled not only to participate but also anticipate and prevent what could be detrimental to the company's future success. By saying even one wrong word, not only the going concern of the business may be in jeopardy but also the lives of all stakeholders involved could change forever. In sum, considering that we now live in the era of hi-tech evolution with no point of return, communicating in the best ethical way will be one of the most important key success factors for business managers and the companies they work with.

Use of Effective Communication to Create Competitive Advantage

Earlier in the paper we discussed that when researching competitive advantage, some major research questions come to mind: why are some competitors more successful than others? Why do some executives consistently make the right decisions while others invariably fail? Studies in the field of managerial communication reveal that failure to effectively communicate leads to lower productivity, lower profitability, and short-term survivorship. In response to continuous failure, Fortune 500 companies have been hiring experts in the field of corporate communication in order to gain competitive advantage. A global search for job opportunities in *Corporate Communication* revealed that most job descriptions include some common themes: "Identifying, anticipating, and prioritizing communication needs; providing strategic insight and direction for organizational communication within the organization; developing a concerted stakeholder engagement effort, especially among business leaders - complete with metrics and aligned with the company's *change management* program; partnering with the company's leadership team at a strategic level - coaching and counselling them; influencing leadership thinking in communication outreach; developing executive communications strategies for members of the company's leadership team; leading, developing, and executing internal organizational and employee communication programs to engage employees and heighten their level of commitment to the new operating model's goals and objectives; and managing issues and crisis situations that may arise, in coordination with senior management" (Johnson & Johnson, 2011).

Even the most talented managers, who attempt to lead an organization without effective communication especially without the concept of managerial communication, will ultimately fail while their more communicatively astute counterparts succeed. Many strategic plans may never be implemented due to lack of communication from managers. Increased managerial communication effectiveness enables practitioners at all management levels to realize the benefits of proper communication (Munter, 2011). In response to companies' demand for improved communication, institutions are now incorporating new disciplines into executive training on the topic of communication. One such discipline is *Emotional Intelligence* (EI) to improve communication (UC Berkeley, 2015). Through the concept of EI, managers can reflect on their own behaviour in order to improve their communication, thus acting ethically and successfully. Key components/ factors in such executive training include:

- Reading own emotional state and understanding how it affects the ability to improve interactions with co-workers and management.
- Interpreting co-workers' emotions and the situations that could result in different emotions, feelings and moods.
- Comprehending the importance of effective co-worker relationships that consider all parties' emotions.
- Understanding the positive and negative impacts that emotions can have on management and leadership.

A QUALITATIVE FIELD INVESTIGATION ON MANAGERIAL COMMUNICATION

Methodology of the Study

In support of the criticality of managerial communication discussed earlier in the paper, we present and discuss the findings of a qualitative study on the topic of communication in general. The study uses philosophical and ethnographic research methodology to investigate and assess the status-quo of contemporary managerial communication policy implementation within firms. The study applies qualitative methodology using interpretative techniques to analyze the non-intrusive collection of data. This data is obtained from a convenience sample of companies across industries listed in the Fortune 500 directory, and from companies that provide communication related services.

The methodology uses the techniques of coding and frequency, and trend and pattern analysis. Coding is an analytical process in which data is categorized to facilitate the detailed analysis of critical variables which have variety, richness, and individual character. Coding is also used to distinguish between a set of variables followed by an additional in-depth interpretive coding in which more specific trends and patterns can be interpreted. Thus, coding allows for summarizing the prevalence and relevance of codes, discussing similarities and differences among them. In addition, it uses recursive abstraction, a methodology where datasets are summarized. Those summaries are then further summarized until a subset of useful data is obtained (Denzin & Lincoln, 2005; Loseke & Cahil, 2007; Holliday, 2007).

Data Collection

Data from previous studies was extrapolated principally from published scholarly literature and partially from practitioners' trade literature. The qualitative data was obtained from companies' websites, financial reporting, and other publicly available documents. Information was assessed accurately and consistently.

About 100 firms representing America's largest and most successful corporations listed in the Fortune 500 directory were selected to be investigated in the study (CNN, 2017). We specifically selected companies based on their success, which in turn infers competitive advantage, and that *communication* in general may be an integral part of their strategic planning. We determined that a convenience sample of 100 firms was appropriate for this exploratory study. From the sample however, we found that only 27 firms had data readily available. We particularly searched for company data that included communications' policy, the policy content, and to what extent the policy was implemented - for example, at the corporate level or at other levels of the organization chart; whether a communications plan was effectively implemented; and if they had information they could freely provide.

RESULTS

Summary From Published Literature

The synthesis of the findings from published literature revealed that firms across industries cannot neglect the importance of a well formulated and implemented communication policy when operating in this century of high-tech evolution. A well-executed communication policy has a direct correlation with a company's success. Furthermore, the implementation of a managerial communication plan allows for maximum efficiency of information dissemination as well as the protection of confidential and highly sensitive data, which is vital to maintaining advantage over a competitor. Also, of key importance is the methodology in which data is disseminated, and the degree of confidentiality as to who should receive the information and what to do with it. For example, using company blogs, Facebook, intranet, internet mail, written internal memorandum, etc. Table 1 shows the factors a firm should consider in the formulation of a managerial communication plan identified in an earlier study on Managerial Communication for an industry specific investigation (Camillo & Di Pietro, 2011).

Once the factors to be considered in the formulation of a communication plan have been identified, a logistics of the critical components must be developed (see Table 2).

Much debate pervades the education sector on managerial communication. Since it was first introduced in the classroom, academicians have argued about whether the subject should be catalogued and taught as a discipline, or be part of the social sciences, or simply regarded as an integral tool for the practitioner in the field. In addition, scholars and practitioners in the field have yet to agree on a convention about the definition, distinction, meaning, and application of various terms used almost interchangeably within the context of managerial communication (see introduction section in this paper for additional highlights). Nevertheless, top business schools today offer communication classes, both general and specific, as a requisite for those majoring in journalism or mass communication, and as an elective for those students enrolled in MBA programs.

Regardless of prevailing managerial communication debates, published literature and events (including that of the WikiLeaks release of sensitive U.S. Department of Defence documents) (Johnson, 2011). In addition, the series of events over the years 2017 and 2018 that involved the leaking or whistleblowing of confidential/ classified information from various U.S. Government branches/ agencies, (USDOJ, 2018;

Table 1. Factors a firm should consider in the formulation of a managerial communications plan

Factors (Not rank specific)
Good communication skills and proper etiquette by managers are essential
The value of learning about culture and cultures
Effectively practicing Managerial Communication
Must have a communication plan in place
Defining the scope and the goal of the plan
Deciding on the critical components of the communication plan
Who should be in charge of disseminating what information
Who should receive the information
What should the content of the information include
The criticality of the timing on when information should be released
What methodology should be used to relay the information
Determining how to store, track, retrieve, and if necessary delete the disseminated information
Planning for unintended consequences and how to deal with them
Implementing an effective control mechanism that can monitor all company information to avoid distortion, tempering, and manipulation of the original information by intruders
Clear the Managerial Communication initiative with legal department before implementing the final plan.

Table 2. Critical components and logistics of a communication plan

Who is responsible for the plan and dissemination of information?	What should the plan include?	When should the plan be implemented?	How should the plan be developed?	Where – through which channel should the information be disseminated?	Who are the stakeholders?
Management-appointed spokes person	Policy and plan type of communication: internal-external, how much and level of confidentiality	At inception or by timely adoption, specific timing, frequency, ongoing	Self developed, hiring an expert, adoption from parent company, research	At specified location, either with public access or private, at all designated physical locations and in cyber space, directly via memo, email, presentation, or indirectly accessible on intranet, website, or personal by relaying to others in person, or in writing - electronically, voice and video recording, or by other means such as witness observation and taking notes	All management, employees and customers, all persons as appointed by management

OSC, 2018) as well as the leaking or whistleblowing of sexual misconduct of public figures in national-international media and entertainment (Cheung, 2018), offer compelling evidence that not only is there a need for companies to implement an effective communication policy support by a dynamically updated training plan, but there is also a need to formulate a policy that is effective in protecting confidential data.

Summary From Structured Interviews

Data obtained from companies' websites was transcribed, coded, and analyzed for frequency and pattern. Results were synthesized applying recursive abstraction, then summarized, tabulated, and are presented below. The first information we tried to find was: does the company have a communication department? If it did, does it have a communication policy in place? What are the most important factors included in the communication policy? Does the policy cover internal and external communication? We also looked for examples if any, about internal and external communication policy, e.g. a meeting (internal) or a press release (external), was available? Table 3 lists the most essential elements we found and believe a firm should consider in policy creation.

Communication policies require efficient practicality and compelled adherence by all stakeholders. Not only must everything be recorded at any time for any given situation, but the rules must be followed without exception. Table 4 shows the outline of an actual meeting agenda that highlights the importance of producing a record about anything concerning an important company meeting. In this scenario a financial matter is discussed. A lot is at stake before the final financial results can be communicated to all stakeholders: the company stock value, the effect of the financial performance results will have on

Table 3. Essential elements to consider when creating a communication policy

Essential Elements of Communication
1. Purpose
2. Message Sender (Encoder)
3. Message Configuration (timing, content, level of confidentiality)
4. Message Receiver (Decoder)
5. Channel of Communication (electronic, type written, in person)
6. Expected Outcome

customers, employees, and business associates outside the company. (In order to protect the identity of the company and the identity of the meeting participants the names have been omitted).

We also determined and summarized several internal factors that are critical to management in the formulation and implementation of a communication policy and plan (see Table 5). The results in table 5 concur with the industry specific factors determined in previous study. See Table 1.

Summary of the Results

In this era of rattling technological advances, managers must understand the complexity of ethical managerial communication, and must decide to what extent a communication policy should be implemented. In the case of a company that operates globally, there is a need to change and adapt the communication policy to reflect the diversity and local culture and of the stakeholders' country of origin. Hence, education and continuous training programs have to be in place, especially if firms operate as multinationals or conglomerates. One must also consult with legal experts to ensure that no potential legal infringements exist. In the case of an international or multinational company, both countries' host and home-countries' legal aspects must be considered before a policy can be freely implemented. The findings from companies that have a communication policy in place reveal six common elements they value the most before a plan is implemented (see Table 4). These elements revolve around the information that needs to be disseminated as highlighted below:

Purpose: define the purpose of the policy and determine whether messages disseminated based on this policy will be clearly understood by all stakeholders. Assess the decoder's perception about the creditability of your company and the validity of the message being sent.

Message Sender (Encoder): Encoding means translating information into a message in the form of symbols that represent ideas or concepts into the coded message that will be communicated. Encoding involves the use of specific language, types of words, and graphic, visual or auditory representations. Thus, encoding translates ideas into messages that others can interpret and understand. When encoding a message, the sender decides what to transmit based on what he/she believes about the receiver's (decoder's) knowledge and assumptions, along with additional information he/she wants the receiver (decoder) to have. It is important for the sender to use symbols that are familiar to the intended receiver. The sender should always create a scenario to mentally visualize the communication from the receiver's point of view (Munter, 2011).

Table 4. Sample communication meeting schedule regarding quarterly performance results

Q1-Quarterly Meeting – North America Division
▪ **Purpose:** quarterly performance results and strategic planning review
▪ **Date and Time:** April 16st. 20xx
▪ **Venue:** Head Office Executive Boardroom
▪ **Present:** VP Finance, Divisional Managers
▪ **Participants excused:** (List all absentees)
▪ **In attendance:** (List all attendees)
▪ **Agenda items**:
1. Approval of previous meeting minutes
2. Discussion of matters pending or arising from previous meeting
3. Discussion of agenda items in order of priority:
a. As planned by the meeting chair
b. As submitted by meeting attendees
c. As submitted by absentees
d. Items from the Board of Directors, Shareholders, other Executives/Stakeholders
4. Financial performance review
5. Sales and Marketing Strategies feedback
6. New Business Development
7. Divisional Activities at regional and Strategic Business Unit (SBU) Level
8. Production – Inventory – Backlog, etc…
9. Logistics and Distribution
10. Quality Assurance Report
11. New Projects – R&D report
12. Ethics report
13. CSR (Corporate Social Responsibility) Report
14. Human Resources Issues
15. Union Issues (if applicable)
16. Communications and Media Relations report
17. Other Business Issues
18. Date of next meeting and deadline for submitting new agenda items
19. Time meeting was adjourned
20. Signed: Minutes taken by…

Table 5. Factors a firm should consider in the formulation of a managerial communications policy

Factors
• Management responsible for the policy must possess good communication skills
• Effective practicing of managerial communication
• Understand the demographics of the stakeholders: different cultures and beliefs, diversity…
• Understand for whom the policy is being developed: employees, customers…
• Demonstrate good ethics
• Must have an effective and well formulated communications policy and plan in place
• Decide who should be in charge of developing and implementing the policy and plan
• Define the scope and the goal of the policy and plan
• Determine what the policy and plan should include
• Decide who should be in charge of disseminating what information
• Determine who the stakeholders are
• When should be the information disseminated
• What is the information about and what should the information include
• What channel of communication should be used
• How should the information be filed, stored, tracked, retrieved, classified, or deleted
• Have a contingency plan for unexpected response or action against the firm
• Have an effective monitoring system in place for accurate feed-back and corrective action if necessary
• Be ready to
• Prepare to counter negative criticism and take action for "Damage Control"
• Always consult with the legal representative before implementing a policy, a plan or before responding to negative criticism or action by stakeholders.

Message Configuration: strategic formulation of the message being disseminated. What is the message? Is it negative, positive, informative, persuasive, or reinforcing? Does it raise awareness about something new or something to be concerned about? Does the message carry a further message to a sub-audience? Does the encoder require feedback? What is the level of confidentiality? Is this the right timing?

Channel of Communication: A communication channel is the means used to convey a message. Channels can be oral, written, visual, auditory, electronic, internal or external mail distribution, or via telephone. Various media such as television, websites, blogs, radio, etc. also exist. The effectiveness of each channel fluctuates depending on the characteristics of the communication. For example, when immediate feedback is necessary, oral communication channels are more effective because any uncertainties can be corrected instantaneously. In a situation where the message must be delivered to a wider audience, other channels should be considered.

Message Receiver (Decoder): The receiver is the individual (or individuals) by whom the message is intended to be received. Once the message is received, examined, and interpreted, the decoder assigns some type of meaning to it. Successful communication takes place when the receiver correctly decodes and interprets the sender's message. The extent to which the decoder comprehends the message will depend on several factors: familiarity with the topic, the creditability of the sender, validity of the message based on prior relationship, and trust. The receiver's interpretation of the message is influenced by his/her experiences, attitude, knowledge, skills, perception, and culture. It is, in a way, the reverse of what the encoder attempts to determine before a message is disseminated.

Expected Outcome, Feedback: These are important components of the communication process. Feedback and expected outcome are crucial in the evaluation of the effectiveness of the message. Feedback provides an opportunity for the sender to determine if the message correctly served its purpose. Did it produce the expected outcome and does corrective action need to be taken to reduce or eliminate confusion? Misunderstandings and eventual failure to ethically and effectively communicate is caused by several factors: inappropriate channel of communication, incorrect grammar, offensive language, micro aggression, words that may be misconstrued, miss-translation, etc. Regardless of the policy in place, communication within an organization can only be successful and effective if the communication process is flawlessly implemented and carried out. Ineffective communication can be averted if the organization thinks of communication as a process of continuous improvement. The results of this qualitative investigation offer useful insights into the criticality of having a communications policy and plan in effect at all levels of the organizational chart. The section below highlights this study's findings, and proposes useful recommendations for the practitioner in the field, for educators who wish to include the critical components of a managerial communications policy into their curriculum, and for graduating business major students about to join the workforce.

SOLUTIONS AND RECOMMENDATIONS

Strategic and Ethical Managerial Communication is a vast field of study, which affects every individual who works within the organization. Despite its unstable or non-standardized position in the academic world, research in the field of communication is of great importance. The need for a solid communication infrastructure within an organization is key at every level. Having a communication department contributes to the overall competitive strategy of the company. Not only is good managerial communication dependent on the communication skilfulness of individual managers, it also pivots on the response of subordinates. However, the problem will continue to persist until an agreement for a solution can be mitigated in regards to the criticality and complexity of ethical communication in general. Specifically, scholars and practitioners in the field should agree whether the subject should be catalogued and taught as a discipline, be part of the social sciences, or simply regarded as an integral tool for the practitioner in the field. Furthermore, the definition, distinction, meaning, and application of various terms used almost interchangeably within the context of managerial communication must be discussed and agreed upon "conventionally" in order to have common understanding of the application across the board (see introduction section in this paper for additional highlights). The results will be mutually beneficial to all stakeholders. In this way, a communication plan will be taught, learned in the classroom, and applied in the field the same as a budget or any other component of the strategic planning. Therefore, a communication plan can be described as a tool that helps an individual, such as a manager, decide how he/she intends to have the organization understand the team's plans, strategies, and operations objectives. In an era of advanced technological innovation, we can relay a message in person, by email, by texting, over social network sites such as Facebook and Twitter, or simply indirectly through gossip. Too often messages reach unintended audiences. Consequences derived from miscommunication can be detrimental to an entire organization, especially in the international arena. Yet, incidents such as this do happen on a regular basis. It is also worth noting that once electronic messages have been sent, they can be stored by anyone in perpetuity. In sum, future studies should audit the effectiveness of communication policies by applying measurement matrices, surveys, and focus groups especially in relationship to evolution of information technology. The development of a model for global standardization of corporate communication would be beneficial to the entire international business community. Business schools should require that managerial communication be included in their curriculum at undergraduate and graduate levels, in required disciplines such as journalism, and in related disciplines such as marketing, accounting, finance, management, and leadership.

LIMITATIONS OF THE STUDY

To conduct this study, about 100 companies listed in the Fortune 500 directory on CNN.com (CNN, 2017) were contacted. There were several challenges. Ironically, as the study was about communication, the main challenge was finding the right department or person who could confirm if the company had a communication policy in place. Although we had contacted several firms' communications and external relations offices if they would agree to provide their policies and other materials, they declined our request due to company's internal-corporate proprietary-confidentiality policies. Nevertheless, we were able to determine that about 27 companies had a communication link or sub-page on their corporate website, dedicated to various audiences. E.g. shareholders, employees, customers, etc. Usually this was established through public relations departments. Although several attempts were made to communicate with the persons in charge using electronic mail, no personalized reply was ever received; instead, only automated email responses were received. This confirms that the complexity and criticality of communication in the modern era will remain a hot topic for discussion. Company information can be received (pushed) as deemed worthy and necessary; however, it cannot be received (pulled) by simply contacting a communication's department or individual. Clearly this is an area companies can improve upon.

CONCLUSION

An extensive review of the literature and data obtained from selected companies provided valuable information about the status-quo of contemporary communication. In sum, effective and ethical managerial communication is a vital skill for everyone in business today, especially for managers at all levels of global companies. Great communicators have a key advantage in building managerial influence especially while starting their careers. Knowing how to communicate ethically and effectively in every business situation is not only strategically important but critical to business success. From sensitively articulated employee feedback to persuasive announcements to customers, today's executive must be a frontline communicator.

In order to master the art of communication, a manager has to apply the following proficiencies:

- Understand the optimal 'medium' to present information.
- Learn the best timing to deliver key messages.
- Master the art of self-editing.

Grasping the best timing for *bad news* is paramount in the business world, especially during economic downturns when employees face job loss. Knowing when to communicate forthcoming layoffs is a tricky task. With a comprehensive communication policy in place, many scenarios can be planned for making it easier for management to deliver grave tidings. Most importantly, always think of strategic decisions and not only tactical ones, companies have long-term goals and communicating tactical decisions only may be counterproductive in the long-run.

This study is a subsequent study of an industry specific one (Camillo & Di Pietro, 2011), which investigates managerial communication cross-nationally and across-industries, and contributes to extant business research by raising awareness about the criticality of managerial communication. It illustrates the need for further study of this discipline in business schools, and provides useful insights regarding the factors and logistics needed to create and implement a communication policy and plan.

REFERENCES

Abbe, A., Gulick, L. M. V., & Herman, J. L. (2007). *Cross-cultural competence in Army leaders: A conceptual and empirical foundation*. Washington, DC: U.S. Army Research Institute. doi:10.21236/ADA475798

Ali, M. (2011). *Chartis Launches ReputationGuard®, Reputational Risk Insurance*. Retrieved from http://www.chartisinsurance.com/searchresults/search_295_195443.html

Allen, J. (2011). $16 muffins, $8 coffee served in Justice Audit. *Reuters Online Edition*. Retrieved from http://www.reuters.com/article/2011/09/21/us-usa-justice-muffins-idUSTRE78J7B020110921

Arasaratnam, L. A., & Doerfel, M. L. (2005). Intercultural communication competence: Identifying key components from multicultural perspectives. *International Journal of Intercultural Relations, 29*(2), 137–163. doi:10.1016/j.ijintrel.2004.04.001

Armenakis, A., & Harris, S. (2002). Crafting a change message to create transformational readiness. *Journal of Organizational Change Management, 1*(2), 169–183. doi:10.1108/09534810210423080

Astley, W. G., & Zammuto, R. F. (1992). Organization science, managers and language games. *Organization Science, 3*(4), 443–460. doi:10.1287/orsc.3.4.443

Brownell, J. (2003). Applied Research in Managerial Communication. *The Cornell Hotel and Restaurant Administration Quarterly, 44*(2), 39–49. doi:10.1016/S0010-8804(03)90017-6

Calhoun, C. (2011). Communication as Social Science (and More). *International Journal of Communication, 5*, 1479–1496.

Camillo, A. A., & Di Pietro, L. (2011). The Importance of Managerial Communication for Hospitality Organizational Settings in the Era of High-Tech Evolution. *Hosteur, 20*(2), 19–27.

Campbell, D. P., & Level Dale, A. (1985). A Black Box Model of Communication. *Journal of Business Communication, 22*(3), 37–47. doi:10.1177/002194368502200304

Carlson, S. (1951). *Executive Behavior*. Stockholm: Strombergs.

Castells, M. (2007). Communication, power and counter-power in the network society. *International Journal of Communication*, *1*(1), 238–266.

Chen, G. M., & Starosta, W. J. (1998). *Foundations of Intercultural Communication*. Boston: Allyn and Bacon.

Cheung, S. (2018). *#MeToo: Speaking Out Against Sexual Misconduct; Timeline: Sexual Misconduct Allegations Against Public Figures*. Retrieved October 10, 2018 from: https://www.nbcphiladelphia.com/entertainment/entertainmentnews/Sexual-Misconduct-Accusations-490592161.html

Clampitt, P. (2005). *Communicating for Managerial Effectiveness*. New York: Sage Publications.

CNN. (2017). *Money, Annual Ranking of America's Largest Corporations. Fortune 500 companies*. Available from the Web site: http://money.cnn.com/magazines/fortune/fortune500/2017/full_list/

Copley, P. (2004). *Marketing Communications Management. Concepts and Theories, Cases and Practices*. Oxford, UK: Elsevier.

Cornelissen, J. (2004). *Corporate communications. Theory and Practice*. London: Sage Publications Ltd.

Cornell University. (2011). *Managerial Communication. An introduction to key library resources for Hotel Administration.* Available from the Web site: http://guides.library.cornell.edu/HADM3365

Covin, T., Sightler, K., Kolenko, T., & Tudor, R. (1996). An investigation of post-acquisition satisfaction with the merger. *The Journal of Applied Behavioral Science*, *32*(2), 125–141. doi:10.1177/0021886396322001

Cushner, K., & Brislin, R. W. (1996). *Intercultural interactions: A practical guide*. Thousand Oaks, CA: Sage.

Dance, F. (1970). The concept of communication. *Journal of Communication*, *20*(2), 201–210. doi:10.1111/j.1460-2466.1970.tb00877.x

Denzin, N. K., & Lincoln, Y. S. (2005). *The Sage Handbook of Qualitative Research*. Thousand Oaks, CA: Sage.

DJ. (2015). *Dow Jones Sustainability Indices*. Accesses June 24, 2015 at http://www.sustainability-indices.com/review/industry-group-leaders-2014.jsp

Drezner, D., & Farrell, H. (2004). *The power and politics of blogs*. Paper presented at the American Political Science Association Conference, Chicago, IL.

Drucker, P. (1977). *People and Performance*. New York: Harper`s College Press.

Drucker, P. (1993). *Inovatia si sistemul antreprenorial*. Editura Enciclopedica, Bucaresti.

Earley, P. C., & Ang, S. (2003). *Cultural intelligence: Individual interactions across cultures*. Stanford, CA: Stanford University Press.

Ellis, N., & Hopkinson, G. (2010). The construction of managerial knowledge in business networks: Managers' theories about communication. *Industrial Marketing Management*, *39*(3), 413–424. doi:10.1016/j.indmarman.2007.08.011

Ethisphere. (2018). Research, rating and certification of corporate and institutional ethics, anti-corruption and sustainability. *The Ethisphere Institute History*. Retrieved October 19, 2018 from https://ethisphere.com/about-updated/

Gheorghe, P., Gardan, D., & Geangu, P. (2009). *The Importance of Managerial Communication in Establishing the Company Marketing Communication.* Paper presented at the International Conference on Administration and Business, ICEA – FAA, Faculty of Business and Administration, University of Bucharest.

Girard, K. (2011). *It's Not Nagging-Why Persistent, Redundant Communication Works.* Paper presented at the Research and Ideas, Working Knowledge Conference, Harvard Business School, UK.

Goodman, J., & Truss, C. (2004). The medium and the message: Communicating effectively during a major change initiative. *Journal of Change Management*, *4*(3), 217–229. doi:10.1080/1469701042000255392

Gross, L. (2011). Communication as the Discipline of the 21st Century. *International Journal of Communication*, *5*, 1497–1498.

Hall Edward, T. (1959). *The Silent Language*. New York: Doubleday.

HBS. (2004). *Face-to-Face Communications for Clarity and Impact by the Results-Driven Manager*. Boston: Harvard Business School Press.

HCI (House of Commons Intervention). (1961). *Budget Resolutions and Economic Situation. In Speeches, Interviews & Other Statements.* Archives of Margaret Thatcher Foundation. Accessed October 19, 2018, at https://www.margaretthatcher.org/document/101096

Henderson, L. S. (1986). Unraveling the Meaning of Managerial Communication: A Conceptual Explication and Model for Guiding Future Research. *Academy Of Management Best Papers Proceedings*, 219-223.

Holliday, A. R. (2007). *Doing and Writing Qualitative Research.* London, UK: Sage Publications. doi:10.4135/9781446287958

Horne, J., & Lupton, T. (1965). The work activities of middle managers: An exploratory study. *Journal of Management Studies*, *1*(21), 14–33. doi:10.1111/j.1467-6486.1965.tb00563.x

IABC. (2015). *The six principles of the profession. The Global Standard of the Profession*. International Association of Business Communicators. Retrieved June 24, 2015 from https://www.iabc.com/global-standard-2/

Johannesen, R. (1996). *Ethics in human communication* (4th ed.). Prospect Heights, IL: Waveland Press.

Johansson, C., & Heide, M. (2008). Speaking of change: Three communication approaches in studies of organizational change. *Corporate Communications*, *13*(3), 288–305.

Johnson, C. (2011, August). Case Against Wiki Leaks Part Of Broader Campaign. *NPR News*. Accessed from the Web site: http://www.npr.org/2011/05/11/136173262/case-against-wikileaks-part-of-broader-campaign

Johnson & Johnson. (2011, December). *Director, Corporate Communications Job*. Health Care Systems Inc. Accessed from the Web site: http://www.careers.jnj.com/region

Kahan, D. M. (2014a). *"Ordinary science intelligence": A science comprehension measure for use in the study of risk perception and science communication*. Cultural Cognition Project Working Paper No. 112.

Kahan, D. M. (2014b). Making climate-science communication evidence-based—all the way down. In M. Boykoff & D. Crow (Eds.), Culture, politics and climate change (pp. 203-220). New York, NY: Routledge Press.

Kahan, D. M. (2015). Climate-Science Communication and the Measurement Problem. *Advances in Pol. Psych., 36*, 1-43. Available at SSRN:https://ssrn.com/abstract=2459057

Kelly, J. (1964). The study of executive behavior by activity sampling. *Human Relations, 17*(3), 277–287. doi:10.1177/001872676401700310

Koch, W. (2013, November 13). Americans back greenhouse gas cuts from power plants. *USA Today.* Retrieved from http://www.usatoday.com/story/news/nation/2013/11/13/americans-greenhouse-gas-cuts-power-plants/3508001/

Kohut, A. (2010, June 13). Views on climate change: What the polls show. *New York Times*, p. A22. Retrieved from http://www.nytimes.com/2010/06/14/opinion/l14climate.html?_r=0

Kraut, R. E., Egido, C., & Galegher, J. (2002). Patterns of contact and communication in scientific research collaboration. In J. Galegher & R. Kraut (Eds.), *Intellectual Teamwork: Social and technological foundations of group work*. Hillsdale, NJ: Lawrence Erlbaum Associates.

Kraut, R. E., Lewis, S. H., & Swezey, L. W. (1982). Listener responsiveness and the coordination of conversation. *Journal of Personality and Social Psychology, 43*(4), 718–731. doi:10.1037/0022-3514.43.4.718

Landsberger, H. (1961). Horizontal Dimension in Bureaucracy. *Administrative Science Quarterly, 6*(3), 299–322. doi:10.2307/2390705

Lawrence, P. R., & Lorsch, J. W. (1967). *Organization and Environment: Managing Differentiation and Integration*. Cambridge, MA: Harvard University Press.

Leeds-Hurwitz, W. (1990). Notes in the History of Intercultural Communication: The Foreign Service Institute and the Mandate for Intercultural Training. *The Quarterly Journal of Speech, 76*(3), 262–281. doi:10.1080/00335639009383919

Lenhart, A., & Fox, S. (2006). *Bloggers: A portrait of the Internet's new story tellers*. Washington, DC: Pew Internet & American Life Project.

Loseke, D. R., & Cahil, S. E. (2007). Publishing qualitative manuscripts: Lessons learned. In C. Seale, G. Gobo, J. F. Gubrium, & D. Silverman (Eds.), *Qualitative Research Practice: Concise Paperback Edition* (pp. 491–506). London: Sage.

Lustig, M. W., & Koester, J. (2010). *Intercultural competence: interpersonal communication across cultures*. Boston: Pearson/Allyn & Bacon.

Makau, J. (2009). Ethical and unethical communication. In W. Eadie (Ed.), 21st century communication: A reference handbook. (pp. 435-444). Thousand Oaks, CA: SAGE Publications, Inc. doi:10.4135/9781412964005.n48

Maxwell, J. C. (2002). *Cele 21 de legi supreme ale liderului*. Editura Amaltea, Bucaresti.

Mckinney, E. H. Jr, Barker, J. R., Davis, K. J., & Smith, D. (2005). How Swift Starting Action Teams Get off the Ground: What United Flight 232 and Airline Flight Crews Can Tell Us About Team Communication. *Management Communication Quarterly*, *19*(2), 198–237. doi:10.1177/0893318905278539

Miller, V., Johnson, J., & Grau, J. (1994). Antecedents to willingness to participate in a planned organizational change. *Journal of Applied Communication Research*, *22*(1), 59–80. doi:10.1080/00909889409365387

MIT Massachusetts Institute of Technology. (2009, August). *Advanced Managerial Communication*. Accessed from the Web: http://ocw.mit.edu/courses/sloan-school-of-management/

Monash University. (2010, January). *Managerial Communication*. Retrieved from http://www.monash.edu.au/

Munter, M. (2011). *Guide to Managerial Communication* (8th ed.). Prentice Hall Publisher.

OECD. (2012). *Machine-to-Machine Communications: Connecting Billions of Devices*. OECD Digital Economy Papers, No. 192. OECD Publishing. Retrieved from http://www.oecd-ilibrary.org/science-andtechnology/machine-to-machine-communications_5k9gsh2gp043-en

Oracle. (2011, August). *Oracle CEO Blog*. Retrieved from http://blogs.oracle.com/jonathan/

Ortiz, F. (2012). In *Encyclopædia Britannica*. Retrieved June 27, 2012 from: http://www.britannica.com/EBchecked/topic/848801/Fernando-Ortiz

OSC. (2018). *Latest News. U.S. Office of the Special Counsel*. Accessed October 10, 2018 at: https://osc.gov/Pages/News.aspx

Rogers, E. M., Hart, W. B., & Miike, Y. (2002). Edward T. Hall and the History of Intercultural Communication: The United States and Japan. *Keio Communication Review*, *24*, 1–5.

Rogers Everett, M., & Steinfatt Thomas, M. (1999). *Intercultural Communication*. Prospect Heights, IL: Waveland Press.

Ryckewaert, L. (2011, November). PM Harper takes communications strategy to new level. *Hill Times News Online*. Retrieved from http://www.hilltimes.com/news/2011/11/21/pm-harper-takes-communications-strategy-to-new-level/28868

Schraeder, M. (2001). Identifying employee resistance during the threat of a merger: An analysis of employee perceptions and commitment to an organization in a pre-merger context. *The Mid-Atlantic Journal of Business*, *37*(4), 191–204.

Schramm, W. (1955). *The Process and Effects of Mass Communication*. Urbana, IL: University of Illinois Press.

Shah, D. V., Cho, J., Eveland, W. P. Jr, & Kwak, N. (2005). Information and expression in a digital age: Modelling Internet effects on civic participation. *Communication Research, 32*(5), 531–565. doi:10.1177/0093650205279209

Starbucks. (2011, November). *Starbucks to Present at Morgan Stanley Global Consumer Conference*. Starbucks Coffee Company Investor Relations. Retrieved from http://investor.starbucks.com/phoenix.zhtml?c=99518&p=irol-irhome

Stefanescu, C., & Popa, L. (2008, February). *Managerial Communication, Paper No. 7172*. Retrieved from http://mpra.ub.uni-muenchen.de/7172/

Stevens, B. (2005). What communication skills do employers want? Silicon Valley recruiters respond. *Journal of Employment Counseling, 42*(1), 2–9. doi:10.1002/j.2161-1920.2005.tb00893.x

Stinchcombe, A. L. (1974). *Creating Efficient Industrial Administration*. New York: Academic Press.

Thatam, S. A. (2008). *Strategic Communication: A Primer*. Advanced Research and Assessment Group.

Ting-Toomey, S. (1999). *Communicating across cultures*. New York: Guilford.

UC Berkeley. (2015). *Using Emotional Intelligence to Improve Communication*. UC Berkeley Extension. Retrieved June 25, 2015 from http://extension.berkeley.edu/search/publicCourseSearchDetails.do?method=load&courseId=8939289&gclid=CI2akq7Cq8YCFUGTfgod5lwAdw

UNESCO. (2010). *Transcultural Communication in the Digital Age*. Retrieved from http://www.unesco.org/en/university-twinning-and-networking/access-by-region/europe-and-north-america/austria/unesco-chair-in-multilingual-transcultural-communication-in-the-digital-age-902/

USDOJ. (2018). *All News*. U.S. Department of Justice Office of the Inspector General.

Vicini, J. (2011), Government did not pay $16 for muffins after all. *Reuters Online Edition*. Retrieved from http://www.reuters.com/article/2011/09/30/us-usa-justice-muffins-idUSTRE78T54220110930

Vroom, V. H. (1964). *Work and Motivation*. Willey New York.

Vroom, V. H., & Yetton, P. W. (1973). *Leadership and decision making*. Pittsburgh, PA: University of Pittsburgh Press. doi:10.2307/j.ctt6wrc8r

Wanberg, C. R., & Banas, J. T. (2000). Predictors and outcomes of openness to changes in a reorganizing workplace. *The Journal of Applied Psychology, 85*(1), 132–142. doi:10.1037/0021-9010.85.1.132 PMID:10740964

Weick, K. (1995). *Sensemaking in organizations*, Sage, London: Weick, K., Sutcliffe, K. M., & Obstfeld, D. (2005), Organizing and the process of sensemaking. *Organization Science, 16*(4), 409–421. doi:10.1287/orsc.1050.0133

Whiting, J. W. M. (1986). George Peter Murdock (1897–1985). *American Anthropologist*, *88*(3), 682–686. doi:10.1525/aa.1986.88.3.02a00120

Wholefoods. (2011, August). *John Mackey's Blog*. Retrieved from http://www2.wholefoodsmarket.com/blogs/jmackey/

Wing, D. W. (2010). Microaggressions in Everyday Life: Race, Gender, and Sexual Orientation. Hoboken, NJ: John Wiley & Sons.

Zorn, T., Page, D., & Cheney, G. (2000). Nuts about change: Multiple perspectives on change-oriented communication in a public sector organization. *Management Communication Quarterly*, *13*(4), 515–566. doi:10.1177/0893318900134001

ADDITIONAL READING

Edfelt, R. B. (2010). *Global comparative management: A functional approach*. Thousand Oaks, CA: Sage.

Hamlin, S. B. (1989). The Art of Q & A. In *How to Talk So People Listen: The Real Key to Job Success*. New York, NY: Harper Paperbacks.

Hattersley, M., & McJannet, L. J. (1996). Giving and Receiving Feedback. In *Management Communication: Principles and Practice*. New York, NY: McGraw-Hill.

Mclean, S. (2010). *Business communication for success*. Flatworld Knowledge Publishing.

Munter, M. (1995). Consult/Join Meetings. In *Guide to Managerial Communication: Effective Business Writing and Speaking* (5th ed.). Upper Saddle River, NJ: Prentice Hall.

Schein, E. (1988). *The Process of Building and Maintaining a Group*. Upper Saddle River, NJ: Prentice Hall.

KEY TERMS AND DEFINITIONS

Communication: The use of available resources to convey information, to move, to inspire, to persuade, to enlighten, to connect is an inherently ethical undertaking. Regardless of context, communication involves choice, reflects values, and has consequences. These three key elements of communication form the basis of its ethical makeup.

Communication Plan: The art and science of reaching target audiences using marketing communication channels such as advertising, public relations, experiences, or direct mail, for example. It is concerned with deciding who to target, when, with what message, and how. The communication plan serves as a guide to the communication efforts throughout the duration of the project. It is a living and working document, and is updated periodically as audience needs change.

Communication Policy: Strategic information dissemination and a protection of transmission of confidential data.

Electronic Communication: Communication by advanced technologies.

Ethics: The study of values, of what is more or less important, of the "good," of behavioral guidelines and norms. Ethics provides frameworks and tools for recognizing and assessing available options and for differentiating between more or less morally justified pathways in any given situation. Ethics is a choice. An individual or group has options available in any given situation while being morally responsible.

Information Technology: A term that encompasses all forms of technology used to create, store, exchange, and use information in its various forms (business data, voice conversations, still images, motion pictures, multimedia presentations, and other forms, including those not yet conceived). It's a convenient term for including both telephony and computer technology in the same word.

Managerial Communication: Decisive means by which the manager fulfils his/her tasks and duties, and employs the competences and skills pertaining to his/her role in the company and in relation to business partners. The manager sends information to the members of an organization and its business partners, and their response influences his/her subsequent decisions and behavior.

Section 5
Collaboration and Improved Engagement

Chapter 19
Dataveillance in the Workplace:
Moving Beyond Divergent Perspectives

Regina Connolly
Dublin City University, Ireland

Cliona McParland
Dublin City University, Ireland

ABSTRACT

The many obvious benefits that accompany digital technology have been matched by some less welcome and more contentious impacts. One of these is the steady erosion of employee privacy. Whilst employee performance has frequently been the object of scrutiny, the increasing number of organizations that monitor employees through advanced digital technologies has added a dystopian edge to existing employee privacy concerns, particularly as many employees are unable to exercise choice in relation to use of these technologies. If unaddressed, their concerns have potential to impact the psychological contract between employee and employer, resulting in loss of employee trust, negative attitudes, and counterproductive work behaviors. This chapter outlines some of the emerging issues relating to use of employee monitoring technologies. It summarizes both management rationale for monitoring as well as employee privacy concerns and proposes an ethical framework that is useful for balancing these differing perspectives.

INTRODUCTION

Organisations and employees exist within a rapidly changing business context. The changing contours of global economics and shifting market pressures have resulted in a work environment that is now characterized by less job security and where the nature of work has become more intense, cognitively complex, team-based and frequently distributed. Many employers feel that they must satisfy a market imperative that is constantly pushing for greater productivity if their organizations are to remain competitive. Attempts to satisfy that imperative have resulted in a relentless drive for efficiency and a focus on rigorous performance quotas, which in turn have become key determinants of employment and promotion.

DOI: 10.4018/978-1-5225-8516-9.ch019

Technological advancements have facilitated the achievement of those efficiencies and in particular have enabled employers to gain more detailed insights into employee performance, including insights as to the use of technology both during and after work hours. This however, has generated understandable privacy concerns for employees. For example employees are becoming increasingly aware of the ways in which management can employ such technologies to track their location, monitor their email communications and computer interactions, measure their performance and even monitor their health and social media activity – all to an unprecedented level. Moreover, the volume and frequency of the data collection, how it is managed and the ways in which it will be employed is rarely disclosed and this opacity creates an asymmetric power balance that can negatively impact employee productivity and motivation as well reduce trust in employers and consequent commitment to the organisation.

As profit driven organizations strive to manage their business in an efficient and productive manner, it is perhaps unrealistic to expect that organizations would not avail of the obvious empowering benefits that digital technologies, including communication, location and activity tracking applications afford them. Furthermore, it can be argued that they may in fact have legitimate reasons to monitor employee actions. However, for an employee, knowing that their performance is being monitored and that there is increased potential for that information to be used against them as part of performance assessment or promotion evaluation exercises inevitably changes their perspective of the parameters of the employment relationship.

This unequal balance of power resulting from workplace surveillance raises a number of questions, in particular those relating to the ethical nature of managements' ability to monitor employees' technology-enabled interactions. The aim of this chapter therefore is to outline some of the major issues relating to workplace surveillance. It starts by discussing dataveillance and related privacy concerns from the employee perspective. The potential impact of workplace surveillance on employee trust and how this may manifest is described. The motivation behind managements' decision to employ monitoring technologies in the workplace is also outlined. Following this, an ethical framework that may assist when considering how to balance the needs of both parties is detailed.

DATAVEILLANCE

Technology has enabled an invasion of employee privacy on a hitherto unimagined scale, but it is important to note that many monitoring techniques have a long established presence in the offline world also. In fact, one of the earliest known examples relates to an observation unit known as the Panopticon, which was designed to house prison inmates in the 18th century. The unit was designed to allow an observer to observe undetected so that prison inmates were seamlessly individualised, were made constantly visible, but could never see themselves (Foucault, 1977). In this way they provided a constant source of information, but were subsequently unable to communicate in the existing relationship. The basic principles of this observation system played on the fundamental vulnerability of human nature, turning visibility into a trap and ensuring that a covert presence held the power. Examples of modern day computer-mediated surveillance techniques rely heavily on these basic principles. Clarke (1988) coined the term 'dataveillance' to describe the systematic monitoring of the actions or communications of individuals. The pervasive nature of modern technologies, including Internet of Things and wearable technologies, provides the opportunity for constant observation and continuous data collection as well as ensuring that surveillance is employed 'through' an individual, rather than simply 'over them' as would be case with video surveillance. In fact, the monitoring of employees' computer-related interactions has previously been described as an 'electronic whip' used unfairly by management (Tavani, 2004). In this way employees are now facing an electronic form of panopticism whereby they can be observed by an electronic supervisor who never leaves the office (Wen *et al.,* 2007). As individual privacy is compromised in a digital work environment, it is worth exploring what such privacy comprises.

INFORMATION PRIVACY

Privacy is a complex construct and one that remains beset by conceptual and operational confusion. It is an ambiguous concept in the sense that it is difficult to either define or understand as for every definition of privacy sourced from the literature, a counter example can be easily produced (Introna, 1996). This conceptual confusion has been exacerbated by the multiplicity of perspectives that have been applied to examinations of the construct, resulting in a highly fragmented set of concepts, definitions and relationships. For example, privacy is often examined as a psychological state, a form of power, an inherent right or an aspect of freedom (Parker, 1974; Acquisti, 2002; Rust, Kannan, & Peng, 2002). Many overlapping concepts such as confidentiality, anonymity, secrecy and ethics have added to the confusion that surrounds the construct (Margulis, 2003). One consequence of this is that our understanding of privacy concerns remains fragmented, as in being defined by the field and focus of each researcher, the concepts that are examined and the ways in which they are validated remain inconsistent and therefore are of limited generalizability. As Solove (2006: 479) notes, 'privacy seems to be about everything and therefore is about nothing'. Unsurprisingly therefore, it has been described as a concept that is 'in disarray' (Solove 2006: 477) due to the fact that there is no consensus regarding how it should be defined or conceptualized (Margulis 2003).

The imperative for greater clarity stems from the fact that information privacy is an issue of increasing concern to many stakeholders, including consumers, employers, privacy activists, researchers and policy makers. To a great extent, these concerns relate directly to the exponential growth of Internet-based technologies. Whilst the benefits bestowed by such technologies is undisputed, it is an undeniable fact that they have generated considerable concern regarding the way in which they can be used to collate and use information on individuals without their prior permission. For example, the recent surge of pervasive technologies into society has generated privacy concerns amongst employees as they have become increasingly aware of the ways in which management can also employ such technologies to monitor their work product development, their location, physical location and activity as well as email and computer interactions in the workplace.

In an attempt to reduce this confusion, Clarke (1999) identified four dimensions of privacy: privacy of a person, personal behaviour privacy, personal communication privacy, and personal data privacy. Information privacy (as opposed to physical privacy) is a multidimensional concept (Xu et al., 2011) and many overlapping concepts such as secrecy and anonymity have been linked to it, consequently adding to the confusion that surrounds the construct. However, progress is being made in this regard. As the majority of communications today are digitised and stored, Bélanger and Crossler (2011) contend that personal communication privacy and data privacy can be merged into the construct of information privacy. The distinction between information privacy as opposed to physical privacy is easily identifiable. The latter concerns physical access to an individual and the individual's surroundings and private space, whilst the former concerns access to individually identifiable personal information (Smith, Dinev,

& Xu, 2011). In terms of historical development, attention was initially paid to the concept of physical privacy, but more recently with the increasing pervasiveness of communication technologies, the concept of information privacy has acquired greater significance. As far back as 1986, Mason predicted that four major concerns would result from the increased use of information and communication technologies - privacy, accuracy, property and accessibility. This prediction has proved to be correct and particularly so in relation to concerns regarding information privacy. Examinations of information privacy are based on the assumption that the ultimate target of review is information as opposed to physical privacy. Because information privacy is part of general privacy research, many of the early privacy concepts have been applied to information privacy, although it is also true that information-specific privacy concepts exist. For example, Smith, Milberg, and Burke (1996) propose four dimensions of information privacy: collection, unauthorized secondary use, improper access, and errors.

Central to our understanding of the privacy construct is the issue of control, specifically the individual's need to have control over their personal information. Control has been defined as "*the power of directing command, the power of restraining*" (Oxford, 1996, p. 291) and is consistently proposed in the literature as a key factor in relation to understanding individual privacy concerns. The concept of privacy as control can be traced back to Westin's (1967) and Altman's (1975) general privacy theories. Altman described general privacy as the selective control of access to the self (1975, p. 24). This emphasis on control was subsequently developed by Altman (1975), Culnan (1993), and Smith *et al.* (1996). However, Dinev & Hart (2006) have shown that while control influences privacy concerns, it does not in itself equate to privacy. Consequently, definitions of 'privacy as control' have evolved into privacy as '*ability* to control,' a distinction that has been emphasised by Smith *et al.* (2011). Thus, Dinev et al., (2013) assert that there is a need to integrate the different perspectives acquired from different fields in order to build a more rigorous, empirically testable framework of privacy and its closely associated correlates, which have often been confused with or built into definitions of privacy. Personal control is important as it relates to the interest of individuals to control or significantly influence the handling of personal data (Clarke, 1988). Practitioner reports confirm the importance that individuals attribute to being able to control their personal information particularly in relation to the use of Internet-based systems. This desire to control personal information has remained consistent throughout the past 20 years. For example, as far back as 1999, a Harris poll indicated that 70% of online users felt uncomfortable disclosing personal information, whilst a 2003 Harris poll of 1010 adults also found that 69% of those surveyed described their ability to control the collection of personal information as being 'exceptionally important.' Similarly, a 2007 Pew Internet survey showed that 85% of adults considered it to be very important that they should be able to control access to their personal information (Madden, Fox, Smith, & Vitak, 2007). A more recent (2014) Pew Research Centre survey has shown that users remain highly concerned about their privacy and the collection and use of their personal information. This is particularly important in light of the fact that research has shown that information privacy concerns negatively influence consumer attitudes such as their willingness to use online transaction environments (Bélanger, Hiller, & Smith, 2002; Pavlou, Liang, & Xue, 2007) and result in a greater reluctance to provide personal information (Dinev & Hart, 2006)

This issue of control and privacy may not always be as clear-cut as it at first seems however. In fact, it can be argued that not every loss or gain or control necessarily constitutes a loss or gain of privacy (Parker, 1974). For example, a user of an Internet-based technology who voluntarily provides personal information in the course of their interaction may not necessarily view this as a loss of control and consequently a loss of privacy. Even if the knowledge that each of their computer-based interactions leaves behind a detailed trail of information regarding who they are, their behaviour and habits and other potentially sensitive information about themselves – it may not necessarily constitute a lack of control or loss of privacy in their eyes. Once again it becomes apparent that the definition and scope of privacy concern dependent upon the context in question, as well as the attitudes and perceptions of those involved. Privacy concerns in an employment context therefore deserved specific examination.

SURVEILLANCE: EMPLOYEE CONCERNS

Legally companies do have the right to monitor their employees and such monitoring is on the increase. A 2017 study of 1627 firms completed by the American Management Association found that 78% of major companies monitor the Internet usage, phone and email of their employees. This represents a steep increase over the past 20 years (from a figure of 35% in 1997). The figure is even higher for companies within the financial sector with over 92.1 per cent of firms within that category participating in some form of surveillance. Email is a fundamental means of communication and the contents of emails sent by employees in a work context are of interest to employers for a variety of reasons including ensuring that company policies are being adhered to, to ensure that employee communication with colleagues and customers is appropriate and to ensure that disgruntled employees do not steal company data or engage in other questionable behaviours. In a drive to reduce costs and improve efficiency, companies are employing an increasing array of tracking and monitoring technology to allow them to view what their employees are doing at all times. Productivity can be monitored through company mobile phones and laptops that already have Xnspy monitor application installed which tracks employee Internet usage, emails, browsing history, number of phone calls and text messages sent during work hours. Similarly, keystroke-logging applications can inform employers when a keyboard has been unused for more than 15 minutes, whilst location trackers enable monitoring of employees using GPS. Company wellness schemes provide health and activity information, whilst sensor and heat-based sensors can indicate the length of time an employee is at the work desk.

Companies such as StealthGenie specialise in monitoring employees' mobile phones, Inland Empire requires its employees to carry scanning devices that show how quickly they are moving boxes and the outcomes of such tracking is subject to performance reviews, whilst employees at Amazon and Unified Grocers warehouses wear headsets which tell them what to do and how much time they have to do it. Such tracking is used extensively in call centres with companies such as Paychez tracking the duration of phone calls and time between phone calls at their call centre. However, tracking has also pervaded the health service delivery industry with nurses at Mills-Peninsula Health services hospital in California having to wear tracking devices so that the hospital can see where they are at all times. One common issue characterises all of these situations, which is that employees have no control over how the collected data will be used. Whilst such metrics may increase compliance and productivity, they come at a cost to employees. As Connolly (2013) (in Semuels; 2013) notes, the technology is being used to satisfy the needs of the employer, but is being leveraged against the employee. It provides employers with an increasing array of data to use to justify changes in the workplace and tilts the playing field in favour of the industry against the employee. The information extracted from that data can be used to justify pay cuts, to pay people piecemeal or to fire people outrights. For example, the AMA 2017 report found that 26% of employers had fired employees for misuse of the Internet, 25% had terminated employees for email misuse and 6% had fired employees for misuse of office phones.

A more indirect and nuanced cost relates to actual the employee-employer relationship, which is typically perceived as being a two-way exchange, with the focus squarely upon the perceptions of reciprocal promises and obligations of both parties (Guest, 2004). These perceived obligations form a psychological contract that has been described as an individual employees' "belief in mutual obligations between that person and another party such as an employer" (Rousseau and Tijoriwala, 1998: 679). In short, employees have implicit and sometimes unvoiced expectations regarding employee contributions, in terms of effort, loyalty and ability for organizational inducements such as pay, promotion and job security (Morrison and Robinson, 1997; Conway and Briner, 2002). However, the monitoring of performance represents a threat to that previously accepted contract and indeed can be perceived as a breach of employee expectations, which in turn can lead to feelings of injustice or betrayal (Morrison and Robinson, 1997). In short, as workplace privacy becomes comprised by technology, the knowledge power dynamic shifts in favour of the employer and this has potential to break the psychological trust contract between employee and employer. For example, many studies indicate that the implementation of surveillance by organisations can be interpreted as a sign the employee is untrustworthy (Smith & Tabak, 2009; Zureik, 2003), they are underperforming in their role (Douthitt & Aiello, 2001; Martin et al., 2016) or they are not committed to the organisation (Jensen & Raver, 2012). The impact of such a trust breach is likely to manifest in significant negative outcomes. Many social exchange theory (SET) researchers (Holland et al., 2015; Gould Williams, 2003; Stanton and Stam, 2003) have shown that a lack of trust within the relationship can negatively impact an employees' behaviours, actions or willingness to share or disclose their information in the workplace. From or HR perspective, it has been linked closely to employee commitment (Searle et al., 2011; Nichlos et al., 2009; Kepes & Delery, 2007), employee wellbeing (Biljsma & Koopman, 2003) and employee turnover (Connell et al., 2003) with research showing that perceived psychological contract violation negatively impacts organizational commitment (Lemire and Rouillard, 2005), work satisfaction (Sutton and Griffin, 2003), job security (Kramer *et al.* 2005) and motivation (Lester *et al.* 2001), as well as increasing employee stress levels (Gakovic & Tetrick, 2003).

These outcomes are likely to apply in the context of workplace surveillance and lack of trustworthiness that it implies. For example, trust has been shown to be a critical component in the relationship between management and employees particularly within the computer-mediated or knowledge based organisations (Dietz & Fortin, 2007; Holland et al., 2015; Mayer et al., 1995; Boxall and Purcell, 2011; Searle et al., 2011). More specifically, a small but growing body of evidence shows that surveillance in the workplace can negatively influence employee stress levels, work attitudes and trust in management (Holland, Cooper, & Hecker, 2015). Recent research (Martin et al., 2016) conducted in Australia has shown that attitudes towards surveillance in the workplace play an important role in determining whether surveillance systems and practices result in counterproductive work behaviours. These many include, but are not limited to, manipulating the surveillance system (Taylor & Bain, 1999), avoiding monitored areas (Nussbaum & diRivage, 1986; Stanton, 2002; Stanton & Weiss, 2000) and deliberately falsifying the amount of work they are completing (Taylor & Bain, 1999). It may also manifest in absenteeism, lateness and lack of productivity (Martin et al., 2016) as well as other deliberate violations of company regulations. Thus, what companies gain in productivity may be lost in engagement, empowerment and trust, particularly if there is a lack of transparency regarding the monitoring behaviour and how the collected data is used.

A number of theories in the literature can help provide an understanding of how employees react or adjust their behaviour once they become aware that they are being monitored in the workplace. Protection motivation theory for example, suggests that employees protect their sensitive information by analysing the threats to their privacy, the likelihood their information will be breached, the severity of an attack and their ability to cope should it occur (Rodgers, 1975; Li, 2012). In this way, protection motivation theory suggests that employees will adjust their behavioural response in order to cope with or avoid what they deem to be a threat to their privacy. Similarly, psychological reactance theory suggests that employees may engage in counterproductive behaviours if they believe their freedom or ability to control a situation is under threat in any way (Jensen & Raver, 2012; Graupmann et al., 2012). Communication privacy management (CPM) theory is also an important focus in research on electronic surveillance and related workplace attitudes and behaviours. For example CPM suggests that individuals manage the boundaries around their personal information in order to determine what information they chose to disclose and what information they wish to protect (Petronio, 2002). When applied to the computer-mediated workplace environment however, this theory posits that employees make the decision to disclose or conceal their personal information based on the expected use of the information and perhaps more significantly their relationship with the organisation (Stanton & Stam, 2003).

As workplace surveillance is unlikely to decrease and may in fact become a more widely embedded condition of employment, the question will move from asking whether it is acceptable, to how it can be more effectively managed so as to avoid counter productive work behaviours and negative organisational impacts. The answer to that may lie in part with the issue of empowerment. This draws from the literature where many social analysts have suggested that the implementation of employee empowerment programmes can provide a plausible solution to improve employee attitudes, behaviours and increase trust in management. For example, numerous studies indicate that employees who are empowered in the workplace are more satisfied (Lauitizi et al., 2009; Wong & Laschinger, 2013; Beaulieu et al., 1997), committed (Beaulieu et al., 1997; Laschinger et al., 2001) and are accountable for their actions (Laschinger et al., 1999) leading to higher productivity and profitability for the organisation. Moreover, a strong positive link has been identified between employee empowerment and trust in management (Wager et al., 2010; Laschinger et al., 2000; Sarmiento et al., 2004) thus suggesting employees who are empowered by their organization are more likely to display positive behavioural tendencies in the employee management relationship than those who are not. Based on Kanter's (1977; 1995) Theory of Structural Power it is further evident that it is the characteristics of the organisation that determine empowerment within the workplace structure (Laschinger et al., 2001, 2004; Bradbury-Jones et al., 2007; Krebs et al., 2008; Wagner et al., 2010). A work environment that provides employees with access to information, resources, support and allows them opportunities to learn and develop is empowering, and for Laschinger et al., (2001) encourages them to accomplish their work more successfully and achieve their goals effectively and efficiently in comparison with those who are not empowered by their organisation. Similarly for Nelson and Quick (2012) empowerment provides employees with a sense of belongingness to the organisation and high levels of job enrichment, whereby they take responsibility over their own tasks in the workplace. Thus, when the characteristics of the organisation are structured so that employees feel empowered, they respond accordingly by improving their attitude, increasing their commitment to their job and rising to any challenges management place before them, benefiting management and those in power through increased organisational effectiveness. The value of this discussion lies in the fact that this brings our attention back to the question of how employers can manage the data monitoring process in such a way as to ensure that employees perceive the process as fair and empowering. Answering that question may be more complex, but in the first instance it provides an interesting avenue for further exploration. It will required identification of the specific factors and variables that positively influence employee empowerment and engagement in the workplace (Saif and Saleh, 2013) within the context of the existing unique information privacy and power balance concerns related to usage of employee monitoring technology.

SURVEILLANCE: MANAGEMENT'S MOTIVATION

Workplace surveillance clearly raises many ethical and social issues. However in order to adequately address many of these issues we must first consider the motivations behind managements decision to employ monitoring technologies in the first place. While many reports emphasis the risks faced by the employee, it is reasonable to assume that in some instances management may have legitimate reasons to monitor their employee's actions. For example, profit driven organisations aim to manage their business in an efficient and productive manner and as such it may be unreasonable to expect that such companies would not avail of methods or employ technologies to ensure that their employees are completing the job they are being paid to do. Furthermore and perhaps more notably, organisations continually face the risk of adverse publicity resulting from offensive or explicit material circulating within the company and as such many employ monitoring technologies to protect themselves from costly litigation claims (Laudon & Laudon, 2001). The Internet has increased the possible threat of hostile work environment claims by pro- viding access to inappropriate jokes or images that can be transmitted internally or externally at the click of a button (Lane, 2003). In fact, a study carried out in 2000 concluded that 70% of the traffic on pornographic Websites occurs during office hours, with ComScore networks reporting 37% of such visits actually taking place in the office environment (Alder, Noel, & Ambrose, 2006). .

Whilst the need to improve productivity is a common rationale for employee monitoring, other motivations such as minimising theft and preventing workplace litigation can be considered equally justifiable in the eyes of management seeking to protect the interests of the organisation. The former motivation is particularly understandable as research shows that employees stole over 15 billion dollars in inventory from their employers in the year 2001 alone (Lane, 2003). In addition, the seamless integration of technology into the workplace has increased the threat of internal attacks with Lane (2003) noting the ease at which sensitive corporate data and trade secrets can be down- loaded, transmitted, copied or posted onto a Web page by an aggrieved employee. Internal attacks typically target specific exploitable information, causing significant amounts of damage to an organisation (IBM, 2006). Management need to ensure that their employees use their working time productively and are therefore benefiting the organisation as a whole (Nord, McCubbins, & Horn Nord, 2006). It is apparent however, that tensions will remain constant between both parties unless some form of harmony or balance between the interests of both the employer and employee is achieved.

In order to balance this conflict of interests however it is vital that clearly defined rules and disciplinary offences are implemented into the workplace (Craver, 2006). The need for structure becomes all the more apparent when one considers the differing views and tolerance levels certain managers may hold (Selmi, 2006). For example, if an employee is hired to work, then technically they should refrain from sending personal emails or shopping online during working hours. However, as a general rule, most management will overlook these misdemeanours as good practice or in order to boost worker morale. The situation becomes more serious however when the abuse of Internet privileges threatens to affect the company itself, be it through loss of profits or adverse publicity for the company. Furthermore, the problem increases as boundaries in the modern workplace begin to blur and confusion between formal and informal working conditions arise (Evans, 2007). For example by allowing an employee to take a company laptop into the privacy of their own home, management could be sending out a message that the computer can be used for personal use which may lead to the employee storing personal data on management's property. Legally, the employer would have claims over all of the data stored on the computer and could use it to discipline or even terminate an employee. In fact, it is this apparent lack of natural limit in regards what is acceptable or indeed unacceptable relating to workplace privacy which makes the task of defining appropriate principles all the more difficult to comprehend (Godfrey, 2001).

AN ISSUE OF JUSTICE AND FAIRNESS

The recent surge in the use of communication monitoring technologies within the computer-mediated work environment has further brought the issues of justice and fairness centre stage in the literature. In fact, justice and fairness are often cited as key drivers in managing the ethical and privacy concerns of employees who are subjected to monitoring practices within the computer-mediated work environment (Stan- ton, 2000a, 2000b; Zweig & Webster, 2002). Organisational justice is an overarching term used to describe individuals' perceptions of what is fair and just within the workplace. For researchers such as Stanton (2000b) justice theories thus provide researchers with a solid framework to help predict the perceived fairness of specific organisational procedures, outcomes and actions.

Justice perceptions for the main are separated into three specific forms notably (1) procedural justice, (2) distributive justice, and (3) interactional justice. The first of these antecedents, procedural justice centres around an individuals' perception that the organisational decision-making process will produce fair and just outcomes (Barrett-Howard & Tyler, 1986; Stanton, 2000b; Hauenstein, McGonigle, & Flinder, 2001). In this way, procedural justice act as a critical factor for understanding the relations between the supervisors' social power and the employees' subsequent reactions to it whereby they perceive positive outcomes in a more favourable light (Mossholder, Bennett, Kemery, & Wesolowski, 1998). Distributive justice refers to the distribution of outcomes, measuring the extent to which employees feel recognised and therefore appropriately rewarded for their efforts within the workplace (Stanton, 2000b; Cohen-Charash & Spector, 2001; Hauenstein *et al.,* 2001). In this way manage- ment are required to treat employees who are similar in respect to a certain outcome in the same manner, as opposed to basing decisions on arbitrary characteristics (Daft, 2000). According to Cohen-Charash and Spector (2001) if a distributive injustice is perceived, it will affect an employee's emotions, cognitions and their overall behaviour. The final facet of organisational justice, interactional justice, stems from the interpersonal communications of the workplace, examining the quality of the interpersonal treatment employees experience at the hands of the company power-holders (Bies & Moag, 1986; Cohen-Charash & Spector, 2001). More specifically it examines the extent to which employees' believe they have been treated with dignity, sincerity and respect during the distribution of outcomes as well as the process undertaken to achieve them by company decision-makers (Stanton, 2000b; Helne, 2005). Consequently if an employee perceives interpersonal injustice they are more likely to act negatively towards their direct supervisor as opposed to the organisation or the injustice in question (Cohen-Charash & Spector, 2001). Organisational justice theories have been linked to research on performance monitoring – specifically electronic performance monitoring (EPM) in the literature (Stanton & Barnes- Farrell, 1991; Stanton, 2000a, 2000b). EPM differs from traditional (non-electronic) forms of monitoring in that it can be carried out on a continuous, large-scale basis recording multiple dimensions of a single workers performance (Stanton, 2000a).

The ubiquitous nature of these monitoring technologies contributes to the employees' ethical concerns relating to loss of personal privacy in the workplace.

Furthermore it is apparent that risk perceptions can affect how an individual makes specific decisions, subsequently influencing their behaviour. In fact studies show that when an employee is aware they are under surveillance, they modify their behaviour accordingly. For example, a study carried out by SHRM in 2005 found that as many as 75% of employees display a certain degree of caution in relation to what they write in emails due to possible monitoring by the organisation. Similarly, the study showed that 47% are equally cautious in relation to telephone conversations while in the workplace environment. Studies show however that the degree of risk perceived by an individual can be reduced if trust exists in a particular situation (So & Sculli, 2002). In this way the significance of trust within studies on risk perception cannot be understated. In fact, an individuals' need to trust often relates directly to the risks involved in a given situation and consequently the pervasive nature of communication-monitoring practices within the computer-mediated organisation hold risks that are unique to that context (Mayer *et al.,* 1995). In order for trust to be engendered however, employees must feel confident that the boundaries between what is acceptable and unacceptable in relation to information monitoring are clearly and openly stated. Those companies that are successful at building that trust and managing the uncertainty associated with communication monitoring practices will benefit from increased employee confidence.

It is becoming increasingly apparent that there is a significant disparity between management and employee perspectives on the issue of workplace surveillance. The uncertainty and lack of control related to the use of these communication monitoring technologies in the workplace reflects the significant asymmetry that exists in terms of what they mean to management versus the employee. While it is apparent that technology has created better, faster and cheaper ways for individuals to satisfy their own needs, the capability to leverage this technology is far higher for companies than for the employee. Because unequal forces, leading to asymmetric information availability, tilt the playing field significantly in favour of industry, such technologies do not create market benefit to all parties in an equitable manner (Prakhaber, 2000). As such one of the major tasks facing the computer-mediated organisation is that of identifying the factors to improve employees' attitudes and behavioural reactions towards surveillance in the workplace. There is a distinct need for clear measures that govern the effective and fair use of communication technologies in the workplace allowing management to monitor their staff in a reasonable and rational manner. Management should consider the ethical and social impacts that surveillance techniques may have within the workplace and employ specific policies which may both minimise the negative implications associated with the use of such technology as well as helping to improve employee receptive- ness overall.

Organisations looking for ways in which to balance this conflict of interest between management and employees are focusing towards the use of workplace policies, many of which are framed on established or predefined codes of ethics. For example, Marx and Sherizen (1991) argue that employees should be made aware in advance of any monitoring practices conducted in the workplace before it actually occurs. In this way the individual can electively decide whether or not he or she wishes to work for that particular organisation. Furthermore the authors suggest that the employee should have the right to both view information collated on them and challenge inaccurate information before it can be used against them. This idea of 'transparency' in relation to surveillance methods is commonly supported by privacy advocates. Management need to have clearly defined sanctions in place within the organisation informing employees of the depth and detail of monitoring practices in the company whilst deterring them from abusing workplace systems.

Other ethical strategies focus solely on how management use the information collated on employees in the workplace. Again we can note that the scope of surveillance is generally divided into two main components - one relating to the actual act of monitoring or surveillance itself, the second relating to how the collated information can be used. In some cases it is reasonable to assume that employees may not fear the act of surveillance but more so how the information could be used and whether or not employers will make subsequent judgments about them (Introna, 2001). For example, McParland and Connolly (2009) found that 33% of employees they surveyed were concerned that their employers would react negatively to their use of personal email in the workplace however 24% still thought it was reasonable to use work email to chat freely with their friends and col- leagues. Once again the lines regarding what are acceptable or indeed unacceptable forms of behaviour begin to blur.

In order to alleviate much of this confusion other researchers such as Turban, King, Lee, Liang, and Turban (2010) apply the basic ethical principles to information collected in an online environment. It is apparent however that these basic ethical principles can also be applied to the use of communication-monitoring technologies in the workplace environment thus providing a solid framework to guide management in their efforts to monitor employees in a fair and effective manner. The basic principles include the following;

- **Notice or Awareness:** Employees should be made aware of the extent and detail of monitoring techniques, prior to the collection or use of personal information.
- **Choice or Consent:** Employees should be made aware of how the collated in- formation can be used and consent must be granted by the employee by signing a workplace policy or notification which out- lines the companies monitoring practices.
- **Access or Participation:** Employees should be able to access certain information on them and challenge the validity of the data.
- **Integration or Security:** Employees should be assured that their personal information is kept secure within the organisation and cannot be used in a way that was not intended.
- **Enforcement or Redress:** Employees must be made aware of organisational sanctions set in place such that a misuse of workplace systems will be detected and punished by management. Otherwise there is no deterrent or indeed enforceability to protect privacy. Effective workplace policies need to protect the interests of all parties involved, ergo a code needs to be developed that protects the interests of both the employee and the employer.

Legitimacy is similar to that of necessity in so far as data can only be obtained for a justifiable purpose and must not contravene an employee's fundamental or inherent right to privacy. Organisations must also comply with the notion of proportionality, using the most non-intrusive or least excessive action in order to obtain the desired information. For example the monitoring of emails should if possible focus on the general information such as the time and transmission as opposed to the content if the situation permits. If however viewing of the email content is deemed necessary then the law presides that the privacy of those outside of the organisation should also be taken into account and that reasonable efforts be made to inform the outside world of any monitoring practices. Any data that is collated on an employee must only be retained for as long as is necessary under European law and data that is no longer needed should then be deleted. Management should specify a particular retention period based on their business needs so as employees are constantly aware of the on-going process. Furthermore, provisions should be set in place to ensure that any data that is held by the employer will remain secure and safe from any form of intrusion or disturbance.

FUTURE RESEARCH

Although there is evidence that workplace tracking and surveillance is increasing, the lines regarding what are correct and moral forms of behaviour continually blur thus limiting our overall understanding of the main issues involved as well as the ways in which to target them. In fact, the use of Internet-based technologies in the workplace presents businesses and employees with opportunities to engage in behaviours for which comprehensive under- standings or rules have not yet been established. As such it is imperative that future research aims to alleviate this confusion by addressing these issues from both a rigorous and relevant perspective. The themes identified in this paper have implications for future academic work in the area of workplace surveillance In order to examine and understand the factors that inhibit and amplify workplace surveillance issues future researchers must begin by exploring these issues directly with those that face them. There is significant scope for a large-scale detailed study to be conducted that addresses some if not all of these issues from both an employee and employer perspective. A study conducted in such a manner could not only identify the frequent concerns that exist in response to workplace surveillance techniques but could further explore what technologies IS departments employ to monitor activities and perhaps more importantly why. Only then can we try to establish some form of balance or harmony between both parties in the computer-mediated workplace environment. Further research into the main issues of workplace surveillance will be of great significance and interest to practitioners also. Employees are the lifeblood of any organisation and only by understanding the behavioural outcomes of such individuals can we begin to understand the factors that predict the perceptions, attitudes and beliefs that are generated through the implementation of communication monitoring techniques in the workplace. Consequently future research into some of these major issues will have significant and important consequences for the businesses that employ these growing and developing technologies.

CONCLUSION

Technology-enabled surveillance and tracking of employees in increasing both in terms of pervasiveness and sophistication. The primary objective of this chapter was to address the issue of electronic monitoring in the computer-mediated work environment. It explored the ethical impact of monitoring in the computer-mediated work environment, addressing whether managements ability to monitor employee actions in workplace represents good business practice or constitutes an invasion of privacy. While it is apparent that management may have legitimate reasons to monitor employees' actions in the workplace, the privacy rights of the employee cannot be ignored. In this way it is paramount that some form of harmony or balance between the interests of the employer and the employee is achieved. Whilst much colloquial discussion of work- place surveillance exists, empirical studies on this issue are in short supply. A greater awareness of increased surveillance and the corresponding acuteness of information privacy concerns point to the need for research on this issue. Consequently, our understanding of these issues and the ways in which employee privacy concerns could be diminished, thus positively impacting productivity and morale, provide a fruitful avenue for future privacy research.

REFERENCES

Acquisti, A. (2002). *Protecting privacy with economic: Economic incentives for preventive technologies in ubiquitous computing environment*. Paper presented at the Workshop on Socially-informed Design of Privacy-enhancing Solutions in Ubiquitous Computing, New York, NY.

Alder, G. S., Noel, T. W., & Ambrose, M. L. (2006). Clarifying the effects of Internet monitoring on job attitudes: The mediating role of employee trust. *Information & Management*, *43*(7), 894–903. doi:10.1016/j.im.2006.08.008

Altman, I. (1975). *The environment and social behaviour: Privacy, personal space, territory, and crowding*. Monterey, CA: Brooks/Cole.

AMA Survey. (2001). *Workplace monitoring and surveillance*. Retrieved from http://www.amanet. org/research/pdfs/ems_short2001.pdf

AMA Survey. (2003). *Email rules, policies and practices survey*. Retrieved from http://www. amanet. org/research/pdfs/email_policies_practices.pdf

AMA Survey. (2005). *Electronic monitoring and surveillance survey*. Retrieved from http://www. amanet. org/research/pdfs/ems_summary05.pdf

Barrett-Howard, E., & Tyler, T. R. (1986). Procedural justice as a criterion in allocation decisions. *Journal of Personality and Social Psychology*, *50*(2), 296–304. doi:10.1037/0022-3514.50.2.296

Beaulieu, R., Shamian, J., Donner, G., & Pringle, D. (1997). Empowerment and commitment of nurses in long term care. *Nursing Economics*, *15*(1), 32–41.

Bélanger, F., & Crossler, R. E. (2011). Privacy in the digital age: A review of information privacy research in information systems. *Management Information Systems Quarterly*, *35*(4), 1017–1041. doi:10.2307/41409971

Bélanger, F., Hiller, J. S., & Smith, W. J. (2002). Trustworthiness in electronic commerce: The role of privacy, security, and site attributes. *The Journal of Strategic Information Systems*, *11*(3-4), 245–270. doi:10.1016/S0963-8687(02)00018-5

Bies, R. J., & Moag, J. F. (1986). Interactional justice: Communication criteria of fairness. In R. J. Lewicki, B. H. Sheppard, & M. H. Bazerman (Eds.), *Research on negotiations in organisations* (Vol. 1, pp. 43–55). Greenwich, CT: JAI Press.

Boxall, P., & Purcell, J. (2011). *Strategy and Human Resource Management* (3rd ed.). Basingstoke, UK: Palgrave Macmillan.

Clarke, R. (1999). Internet privacy con- cerns confirm the case for intervention. *Communications of the ACM*, *42*(2), 60–67. doi:10.1145/293411.293475

Clarke, R. A. (1988). Information technology and dataveillance. *Communications of the ACM*, *31*(5), 498–512. doi:10.1145/42411.42413

Cohen-Charash, Y., & Spector, P. E. (2001). The role of justice in organizations: A meta- analysis. *Organizational Behavior and Human Decision Processes*, *86*(2), 278–321. doi:10.1006/obhd.2001.2958

Connell, J., Ferres, N., & Travalione, T. (2003). Engendering trust in manager-subordinate relationships. *Personnel Review*, *32*(5), 569–587. doi:10.1108/00483480310488342

Craver, C. B. (2006). Privacy issues affecting employers, employees and labour organizations. *Louisiana Law Review*, *66*, 1057–1078.

Culnan, M. J. (1993). How did they get my name? An exploratory investigation of consumer attitudes toward secondary information use. *Management Information Systems Quarterly*, *17*(3), 341–364. doi:10.2307/249775

D'Urso, S. C. (2006). Who's watching us at work? Toward a structural-perceptual model of electronic monitoring and surveillance in organisations. *Communication Theory*, *16*(3), 281–303. doi:10.1111/j.1468-2885.2006.00271.x

Daft, R. L. (2000). *Management* (5th ed.). Hinsdale, IL: The Dryden Press.

Dietz, G., & Fortin, M. (2007). Trust and justice in the formation of joint consultation committees. *Journal of International Human Resource Management*, *18*(7), 1159–1181. doi:10.1080/09585190701391867

Dinev, T., & Hart, P. (2006). An extended privacy calculus model for e-commerce transactions. *Information Systems Research*, *17*(1), 61–80. doi:10.1287/isre.1060.0080

Dinev, T., Xu, H., Smith, J. H., & Hart, P. (2013). Information privacy and correlates: An empirical attempt to bridge and distinguish privacy-related concepts. *European Journal of Information Systems*, *22*(3), 295–316. doi:10.1057/ejis.2012.23

Dirks, K., & Ferrin, D. L. (2002). Trust in leadership: Meta-analytic findings and implications for research and practice. *The Journal of Applied Psychology*, *87*(4), 611–628. doi:10.1037/0021-9010.87.4.611

Douthitt, E. A., & Aiello, J. R. (2001). The role of participation and control in the effects of computer monitoring on fairness perceptions, task satisfaction, and performance. *The Journal of Applied Psychology*, *86*(5), 867–874. doi:10.1037/0021-9010.86.5.867

Elgesem, D. (1999). The structure of rights in directive 95/46/EC on the protection of individuals with regard to the processing of personal data and the free movement of such data. *Ethics and Information Technology*, *1*(4), 283–293. doi:10.1023/A:1010076422893

European Union. (2002). *Directive 95/46/EC: Article 29 WP55*. Retrieved from http://ec.europa. eu/justice_home/fsj/privacy/docs/wpdocs/2002/ wpss_en.pdf

Evans, L. (2007). Monitoring technology in the American workplace: Would adopting English privacy standards better balance employee privacy and productivity? *California Law Review*, *95*, 1115–1149.

Ferrin, D. L., & Dirks, K. T. (2003). The use of rewards to increase and decrease trust: Mediating processes and differential effects. *Organization Science*, *14*(1), 18–31. doi:10.1287/orsc.14.1.18.12809

Foucault, M. (1977). *Discipline and punish: The birth of the prison*. London, UK: Penguin Books.

Ghosh, A. P. (1998). *E-commerce security – Weak links, best defences*. Hoboken, NJ: John Wiley & Sons.

Godfrey, B. (2001). Electronic work monitoring: An ethical model. In *Selected papers from the second Australian institute conference on computer ethics* (pp. 18-21). Academic Press.

Gould-Williams, J. (2003). The importance of HR practices and workplace trust in achieving superior performance: A study of public-sector organizations. *International Journal of Human Resource Management, 14*(1), 28–54. doi:10.1080/09585190210158501

Graupmann, V., Jonas, E., Meier, E., Hawelka, S., & Aichhorn, M. (2012). Reactance, the self, and its group: When threats to freedom come from the ingroup versus the outgroup. *European Journal of Social Psychology, 42*(2), 164–173. doi:10.1002/ejsp.857

Greenberg, L., & Barling, J. (1999). Predicting employee aggression against coworkers, subordi- nates and supervisors: The roles of person behaviors and perceived workplace factors. *Journal of Organizational Behavior, 20*(6), 897–913. doi:10.1002/(SICI)1099-1379(199911)20:6<897::AID-JOB975>3.0.CO;2-Z

Harris Interactive. (2003). *Poll*. Retrieved from http://www.harrisinteractive.com/harris_poll/ index.asp?PID=365

Hauenstein, N. M. A., McGonigle, T., & Flinder, S. W. (2001). A meta-analysis of the relationship between procedural justice and distributive justice: Implications for justice research. *Employee Responsibilities and Rights Journal, 13*(1), 39–56. doi:10.1023/A:1014482124497

Helne, C. A. (2005). Predicting workplace deviance from the interaction between organizational justice and personality. *Journal of Managerial Issues, 17*(2), 247–263.

Holland, P. J., Cooper, B., & Hecker, R. (2015). Electronic monitoring and surveillance in the workplace: The effects on trust in management, and the moderating role of occupational type. *Personnel Review, 44*(1), 161–175. doi:10.1108/PR-11-2013-0211

IBM. (2006). *Stopping insider attacks: How organizations can protect their sensitive information*. Retrieved from http://www-935.ibm.com/ services/us/imc/pdf/gsw00316-usen-00-insider- threats-wp.pdf

Introna, L. D. (1996). Privacy and the computer: Why we need privacy in the information society. *Metaphilosophy, 28*(3), 259–275. doi:10.1111/1467-9973.00055

Introna, L. D. (2001). Workplace surveillance, privacy and distributive justice. In R. A. Spinello & H. T. Tavani (Eds.), *Readings in cyberethics* (pp. 519–532). Sudbury, MA: Jones and Barlett.

Jackson, T., Dawson, R., & Wilson, D. (2001). *The cost of email interruption (Item No. 2134/495)*. Loughborough, UK: Loughborough University Institutional Repository.

Jensen, J. M., & Raver, J. L. (2012). When self-management and surveillance collide: Conse- quences for employees' trust, autonomy, and discretionary behaviors. *Group & Organization Management, 37*(3), 308–346. doi:10.1177/1059601112445804

Kanter, R. (1977). *Men and Women of the Corporation*. New York, NY: Basic Books.

Kanter, R. (1993). *Men and Women of the Corporation* (2nd ed.). New York, NY: Basic Books.

Kepes, S., & Delery, J. E. (2007). HRM systems and the problem of internal fit. In P. Boxall, J. Purcell, & P. Wright (Eds.), *The Oxford Handbook of Human Resource Management* (pp. 385–404). New York, NY: Oxford University Press.

Krebs, J., Madigan, E., & Tullai-McGuiness, S. (2008). The rural nurse work environment and structural empowerment. *Policy, Politics & Nursing Practice*, *9*(1), 28–39. doi:10.1177/1527154408316255

Lane, F. S. (2003). *The naked employee: How technology is compromising workplace privacy*. New York, NY: AMACOM.

Laschinger, H. K., Finegan, J., Shamian, J., & Wilk, P. (2001). Impact of structural and psychological empowerment on job strain in nursing work settings: Expanding Kanter's model. *JONA: The Journal of Nursing Administration*, *31*(5), 260–272. doi:10.1097/00005110-200105000-00006

Laschinger, H. K., Finegan, J. E., Shamian, J., & Wilk, P. (2004). A longitudinal analysis of the impact of workplace empowerment on work satisfaction. *Journal of Organizational Behavior*, *25*(4), 527–545. doi:10.1002/job.256

Laschinger, H. K., Wong, C., & Grau, A. (2013). Authentic leadership, empowerment and burnout: A comparison in new graduates and experienced nurses. *Journal of Nursing Management*, *21*(3), 541–552. doi:10.1111/j.1365-2834.2012.01375.x

Laschinger, H. K. S., Finegan, J., Shamian, J., & Casier, S. (2000). Organizational trust and empowerment in restructured healthcare settings: Effects on staff nurse commitment. *The Journal of Nursing Administration*, *30*(9), 413–425. doi:10.1097/00005110-200009000-00008

Laschinger, H. K. S., Wong, C., McMahon, L., & Kaufmann, C. (1999). Leader behaviour impact on staff nurse empowerment, job tension and work effectiveness. *The Journal of Nursing Administration*, *29*(5), 28–39. doi:10.1097/00005110-199905000-00005

Laudon, K. C., & Laudon, J. P. (2001). *Essentials of management information systems: Organisation and technology in the networked enterprise* (4th ed.). Upper Saddle River, NJ: Prentice Hall.

Laudon, K. C., & Laudon, J. P. (2002). *Management information systems: Managing the digital firm* (7th ed.). Upper Saddle River, NJ: Prentice Hall.

Laudon, K. C., & Traver, C. G. (2010). *E-commerce 2010 – Business technology society* (6th ed.). Upper Saddle River, NJ: Prentice Hall.

Lautizi, M., Laschinger, H. K., & Ravazzolo, S. (2009). Workplace empowerment, job satisfaction and job stress among Italian mental health nurses: An exploratory study. *Journal of Nursing Management*, *17*(4), 446–452. doi:10.1111/j.1365-2834.2009.00984.x

Lawrence, T. B., & Robinson, S. L. (2007). Ain't misbehavin: Workplace deviance as organizational resistance. *Journal of Management*, *33*(3), 378–394. doi:10.1177/0149206307300816

Li, Y. (2012). Theories in online information privacy research: A critical view and an integrated framework. *Decision Support Systems*, *54*(1), 471–481. doi:10.1016/j.dss.2012.06.010

Louis Harris and Associates. (1999). *Poll.* Retrieved from http://www.natlconsumersleague.org/FNLSUM1.PDF

Madden, M., Fox, S., Smith, A., & Vitak, J. (2007). *Digital footprints: Online identity management and search in the age of transparency*. Retrieved July 29, 2018, from http://pewresearch. org/pubs/663/digital-footprints

Margulis, S. T. (2003). On the status and contribution of Westin's and Altman's theories of privacy. *The Journal of Social Issues*, *59*(2), 411–429. doi:10.1111/1540-4560.00071

Martin, A. J., Wellen, J. M., & Grimmer, M. R. (2016). An eye on your work: How empowerment affects the relationship between electronic surveillance and counterproductive work behaviours. *International Journal of Human Resource Management*, *27*(21), 2635–2651. doi:10.1080/09585192.2016.1225313

Marx, G., & Sherizen, S. (1991). Monitoring on the job: How to protect privacy as well as property. In T. Forester (Ed.), *Computers in the human context: Information technology, productivity, and people* (pp. 397–406). Cambridge, MA: MIT Press.

Mason, R. (1986). Four ethical issues of the information age. *Management Information Systems Quarterly*, *10*(1), 4–12. doi:10.2307/248873

Mayer, R. C., Davis, J. D., & Schoorman, F. D. (1995). An integrative model of organisational trust. *Academy of Management Review*, *20*(3), 709–734. doi:10.5465/amr.1995.9508080335

McParland, C., & Connolly, R. (2009). *The role of dataveillance in the organsiation: Some emerging trends*. Paper presented at the Irish Academy of Management Conference, Galway, UK.

Mossholder, K. W., Bennett, N., Kemery, E. R., & Wesolowski, M. A. (1998). Relationships between bases of power and work reactions: The mediational role of procedural justice. *Journal of Management*, *24*(4), 533–552. doi:10.1177/014920639802400404

Nelson, D., & Quick, J. (2012). *Principles of Organizational Behavior: Realities and Challenges*. South Western.

Nichols, T., Danford, A., & Tasiran, A. (2009). Trust, employer exposure and the employment relations. *Economic and Industrial Democracy*, *30*(2), 241–265. doi:10.1177/0143831X09102429

Nord, G. D., McCubbins, T. F., & Horn Nord, J. (2006). Email monitoring in the workplace: Privacy, legislation, and surveillance software. *Communications of the ACM*, *49*(8), 73–77.

Nussbaum, K., & duRivage, V. (1986). Computer monitoring: Mismanagement by remote control. *Business and Society Review*, (56): 16–29.

Parker, R. B. (1974). A definition of privacy. *Rutgers Law Review*, *27*(1), 275.

Pavlou, P. A., Liang, H., & Xue, Y. (2007). Understanding and mitigating uncertainty in online exchange relationships: A principal–agent perspective. *Management Information Systems Quarterly*, *31*(1), 105–136. doi:10.2307/25148783

Petronio, S. (2002). *Boundaries of Privacy: Dialectics of Disclosure*. Albany, NY: State University of New York Press.

Pew Research Center. (2014). *Public Perceptions of Prvacy and Security in the Post-Snowden Era*. Pew Research Center.

Prakhaber, P. R. (2000). Who owns the online consumer? *Journal of Consumer Marketing, 17*(2), 158–171. doi:10.1108/07363760010317213

Robinson, S. L., & Bennett, R. J. (1997). *Workplace deviance: Its definition, its manifestations, and its causes*. Greenwich, CT: JAI Press.

Robinson, S. L., & Rousseau, D. M. (1994). Violating the psychological contract: Not the exception but the norm. *Journal of Organizational Behavior, 15*(3), 245–259. doi:10.1002/job.4030150306

Rodgers, R. (1975). A Protection Motivation Theory of Fear Appeals and Attitude Change. *The Journal of Psychology – Interdisiplinary and Applied, 91*(1), 93 – 114.

Rousseau, D., Sitkin, S., Burt, R., & Camerer, C. (1998). Not so different after all: A cross- discipline view of trust. *Academy of Management Review, 23*(3), 393–404. doi:10.5465/amr.1998.926617

Rust, R. T., Kannan, P. K., & Peng, N. (2002). The customer economics of internet privacy. *Journal of the Academy of Marketing Science, 30*(4), 455–464. doi:10.1177/009207002236917

Safire, W. (2002). The great unwatched. *The New York Times*. Retrieved from http://query.nytimes. com/gst/fullpage.html?res=9A03E7DB1E3FF93BA25751C0A9649C8B63

Saif, N., & Saleh, A. (2013). Psychological empowerment and job satisfaction in Jordanian hospitals. *International Journal of Humanities and Social Science, 3*(16), 250–257.

Sarmiento, T. P., Laschinger, H. K. S., & Iwasiw, C. (2004). Nurse educators workplace empowerment, burnout, and job satisfaction: Testing Kanters theory. *Journal of Advanced Nursing, 46*(2), 134–143. doi:10.1111/j.1365-2648.2003.02973.x

Searle, R., Den Hartog, D. N., Weibel, A., Gillespie, N., Six, F., Hatzakis, T., & Skinner, D. (2011). Trust in the employer: The role of high-involvement work practices and procedural justice in European organizations. *International Journal of Human Resource Management, 22*(5), 1069–1092. doi:10.1080/09585192.2011.556782

Selmi, M. (2006). Privacy for the working class: Public work and private lives. *Louisiana Law Review, 66*, 1035–1056.

Semuels, A. (2013, April 8). Monitoring up-ends balance of power at workplace some say. *Los Angeles Times*. Retrieved from http:// www.latimes.com/business/money/la-fi-mo-monitoring-upends-balance-of-power-at-work- place-20130408,0,7425573.story

SHRM. (2005). *Workplace privacy – Poll findings: A study by the society for human resource management and careerjournal.com*. Retrieved from http://www.shrm.org/Research/Survey- Findings/Documents/Workplace%20Privacy%20Poll%20Findings%20-%20A%20Study%20by%20SHRM%20and%20CareerJournal.com.pdf

Siegall, M., & Gardner, S. (2000). Contextual factors of psychological empowerment. *Personnel Review, 29*(6), 703–722. doi:10.1108/00483480010296474

Smith, H. J., Dinev, T., & Xu, H. (2011). Informa- tion privacy research: An interdisciplinary review. *Management Information Systems Quarterly*, *35*(4), 989–1015. doi:10.2307/41409970

Smith, H. J., Milberg, J. S., & Burke, J. S. (1996). Information privacy: Measuring individuals' concerns about organizational practices. *Management Information Systems Quarterly*, *20*(2), 167–196. doi:10.2307/249477

Smith, W. P., & Tabak, F. (2009). Monitoring employee e-mails: Is there any room for privacy? *The Academy of Management Perspectives*, *23*(4), 33–48. doi:10.5465/amp.23.4.33

So, M. W. C., & Sculli, D. (2002). Theroleoftrust, quality, value and risk in conducting e-business. *Industrial Management & Data Systems*, *102*(9), 503–512. doi:10.1108/02635570210450181

Solove, D. J. (2006). A taxonomy of privacy. *University of Pennsylvania Law Review*, *154*(3), 477–564. doi:10.2307/40041279

Stanton, J., & Stam, K. (2003). Information Technology, Privacy and Power within Organizations: A View from Boundary Theory and Social Exchange Perspectives. *Surveillance & Society*, *1*(2), 152–190. doi:10.24908s.v1i2.3351

Stanton, J. M. (2000a). Reactions to employee performance monitoring: Framework, review, and research directions. *Human Performance*, *13*(1), 85–113. doi:10.1207/S15327043HUP1301_4

Stanton, J. M. (2000b). Traditional and electronic monitoring from an organizational justice perspec- tive. *Journal of Business and Psychology*, *15*(1), 129–147. doi:10.1023/A:1007775020214

Stanton, J. M., & Barnes-Farrell, J. L. (1996). Effects of electronic performance-monitoring on personal control, satisfaction and performance. *The Journal of Applied Psychology*, *81*(6), 738–745. doi:10.1037/0021-9010.81.6.738

Stanton, J. M., & Weiss, E. M. (2000). Electronic monitoring in their own words: An exploratory study of employees' experiences with new types of surveillance. *Computers in Human Behavior*, *16*(4), 423–440. doi:10.1016/S0747-5632(00)00018-2

Tavani, H. T. (2004). *Ethics and technology: Ethical issues in an age of information and communication technology*. Chichester, UK: John Wiley & Sons.

Taylor, P., & Bain, P. (1999). 'An assembly line in the head': Work and employee relations in the call centre. *Industrial Relations Journal,* (30), 101–117.

Thomas, K. W., & Velthouse, B. S. (1990). Cognitive elements of empowerment: An 'interpretative' model of intrinsic task motivation. *Academy of Management Review*, (19): 312–330.

Turban, E., King, D., Lee, J., Liang, T. P., & Turban, D. (2010). *Electronic commerce 2010: A managerial perspective* (6th ed.). Upper Saddle River, NJ: Pearson.

Turban, E., Leidner, D., McClean, E., & Wetherbe, J. (2006). *Information technology for management – Transforming organisations in the digital economy* (5th ed.). New York, NY: John Wiley & Sons.

Turow, J., Feldman, L., & Metlzer, K. (2005). *Open to exploitation: American shoppers online and offline*. Philadelphia, PA: Annenberg Public Policy Centre, University of Pennsylvania.

Tyler, T. (2003). Trust within organisations. *Personnel Review*, *32*(5), 556–568. doi:10.1108/00483480310488333

Wagner, J., Cummings, G., Smith, D., Olson, J., Anderson, L., & Warren, S. (2010). The Relationship between structural empowerment and psychological empowerment for nurses – a systematic view. *Journal of Nursing Management*, *18*(4), 448–462. doi:10.1111/j.1365-2834.2010.01088.x

Wang, H., Lee, M. K. O., & Wang, C. (1998). Consumer privacy concerns about internet marketing. *Communications of the ACM*, *41*(3), 63–70. doi:10.1145/272287.272299

Wen, H. J., Schwieger, D., & Gershuny, P. (2007). Internet usage monitoring in the workplace: Its legal challenges and implementation strategies. *Information Systems Management*, *24*(2), 185–196. doi:10.1080/10580530701221072

Wong, C. A., & Laschinger, H. K. (2013). Authentic leadership, performance, and job satisfaction: The mediating role of empowerment. *Journal of Advanced Nursing*, *69*(4), 947–959. doi:10.1111/j.1365-2648.2012.06089.x

Xu, H., Dinev, T., Smith, J. H., & Hart, P. (2011). Information privacy concerns: Linking individual perceptions with institutional privacy assurances. *Journal of the Association for Information Systems*, *12*(12), 798–824. doi:10.17705/1jais.00281

Zureik, E. (2003). Theorizing surveillance: the case of the workplace. In D. Lyon (Ed.), *Surveillance as Social Sorting* (pp. 31–56). Oxford, UK: Routledge.

Zweig, D., & Webster, J. (2002). Where is the line between benign and invasive? An examination of psychological barriers to the acceptance of awareness monitoring system. *Journal of Organizational Behavior*, *23*(5), 605–633. doi:10.1002/job.157

Chapter 20
Improving Virtual Team Effectiveness

Edward T. Chen
University of Massachusetts – Lowell, USA

ABSTRACT

Virtual teams are vastly more effective now than they were in the past. This chapter explores published articles and cases that highlight the usage of virtual teams on virtual projects. The authors will analyze a successful case with a struggle at the beginning and then an unsuccessful case with a strong start. The chapter will address the virtual workplace and then move on to the topic of teleworking. They authors will introduce the communication systems that are on the rise to make virtual teams more effective. Performance of virtual teams will be explained, followed by how to enhance the virtual team effectiveness.

INTRODUCTION

The use of virtual teams is more common in society now. This was not always the case two decades ago. There have been studies as well as cases in which virtual teams are used. In some cases, they work and have been effective, and the opposite can be said when they do not work. In order to fully explore the importance of virtual teams in today's age, many factors need to be accounted for. This paper will explore the effectiveness of virtual teams today compared to the use of them in years prior. Along with this analysis, this paper will explain factors that lead to their success and downfall. Followed by the general use of them in companies, and how certain companies have difficulties implementing them.

Information systems and the growth of high speed Internet across the globe have enabled companies to implement a global virtual team structure (Piccoli, Powell, & Ives, 2004). Companies implementing virtual teams have seen a reduction in costs, greater utilization, increased access to new markets, and a larger pool of resources with a greater variation in skill sets (Olson, Appunn, McAllister, Walters, & Grinnell, 2014). However, working virtually does come with challenges. Virtual teams need to navigate communication difficulties, the effects of culturally diverse membership, and the technical difficulties involved in linking regions across large distances (Chang, Hung, & Hsieh, 2014; Grosse, 2002; Jarvenpaa & Leidner, 1999; Jones, 2009; Lisak & Erez, 2015). In order to maximize the benefits and minimize

DOI: 10.4018/978-1-5225-8516-9.ch020

the weaknesses from virtual teams, managers need to be more involved than they are with local teams. Virtual teams require the manager to establish and closely monitor organizational design within the team, with an eye toward encouraging an environment of trust and open, effective communication (Henderson & Lee, 1992; Gaan, 2012; Krebs, Hobman, & Bordia, 2006; Morgan, Paucar-caceres, & Wright, 2014; Zolin & Hinds, 2004). A manager must also mitigate conflict that arises. He or she must function in multiple roles, including administrator, coach, and advisor, throughout the lifespan of the team. The objective of this chapter is to explore the challenges of virtual teams and identify how to manage them in order to maximize performance (Brunelle, 2012).

Research for this chapter is comprised of several journal articles, corporate white papers, and trade magazines that revealed overlapping coverage of reasons to build virtual teams, limitations, challenges that team members encounter, managerial tactics, and the future outlook for virtual teams in a variety of settings. These articles contained empirical evidence of claims; however, to date it appears more research is needed to support virtual team best practices. Thus, this chapter is written for both IS researchers and IT practitioners.

VIRTUAL TEAMS

In recent years, there have been unprecedented technological advancements, which have made virtual teams more viable than ever before. Businesses sometimes prefer virtual teams for numerous organizational advantages, as they look to expand beyond their traditional boundaries. This expansion can allow companies to access a vast pool of previously unattainable resources (Eissa, Fox, Webster, & Kim, 2012). In addition to the enhanced skills of these personnel, many companies find benefits in reduced cost and increased utilization (Horwitz, Bravington & Silvis 2006). Although there are many benefits to virtual teams, there are weaknesses to address. The major challenge of virtual teams is ensuring proper communication. The lack of face-to-face communication limits the effectiveness, due to the inability to pick up on important nonverbal cues (Kayworth & Leidener, 2002). There are methods and techniques used by managers of virtual teams to minimize these weaknesses and provide an environment suited for maximizing success and performance (Morgan, Paucar-caceres, & Wright, 2014).

Virtual teams are defined as groups of employees with unique skills, situated in distant locations, whose members must collaborate using technology across space and time to accomplish important organizational tasks (Lipnack & Stamps, 2000). Modern virtual teams are assembled with individuals from all areas of the world based on their expertise and fit with the virtual team being assembled. Coupled with their unique talents, they can bring experiences and perspectives to complement other team members. More importantly, when configured and managed appropriately, virtual teams can be more productive than traditional face-to-face teams (Siebdrat, Hoegl & Ernst, 2009).

Any individual on this virtual team can work in any location. This is done through the use of the Internet and technology that focus on communication. Virtual teams are complex and require no face-to-face interactions. Work is submitted to each member on the team, and the team can meet remotely. There are many challenges that a virtual team goes through, and through an article by Gina Abudi (2010a & 2010b), some of these challenges will be highlighted.

The Effective Case

In the case written by Abudi (2010a & 2010b), the project was to implement a knowledge management database company-wide for an IT services organization. Th team consisted of seven people, in which one was the project manager (PM). Only three of the team members have had the chance to work together in the past before working on what was considered a major project for the company. Abudi (2010a) mentions that this project was having a lot of difficulties from the start of the project timeline. Members would miss meetings, work would not get done, and there would be multiple complaints between the PM and the team members. Abudi (2010b) highlights that the team may have had some issues with what was mentioned, but not with cultural differences. This was because a company that worked globally and frequently worked with others of diverse backgrounds.

The case follows a lot of mistakes that occurred towards the beginning of the project. These mistakes had really disrupted the project and the virtual team for moving forward. Once these issues were highlight, there was a stakeholder meeting for the team and decisions were being made. The stakeholders did not want to simply cancel the project as it was part of a five-year plan and wanted to ensure its success. They realized that the PM was having a tough time controlling the direction and the virtual team. Along with this decision, the stakeholders realized that the team seemed to be too thin for the work that they were doing. The decision they made was to add another PM and a few more team members. Along with this they issued more meetings and a schedule for receiving updates. Abudi (2010b) summarizes the case by looking at the challenges they faced and how to overcome them. The project ended in success, and they were able to implement this database for tracking project resources. This case study highlights a virtual team that has been effective and using some references from Meredith. Shafer, and Mantel (2018), the factors that make it effective will be further analyzed.

The virtual team used in the case study by Abudi (2010a) met many challenges. As team members were across the globe, they worked to fulfill the project needs. Members were in Asia, Europe, and across the US. They were not able to meet face-to-face and because of that a virtual team was necessary. Working effectively with the diverse backgrounds was not the issue here. They were able to work quite well with each other's cultural differences, but they lacked the direction. This was a key component later down the line, as this helped them effectively get the work done. Another component that led to the virtual team's success was their use of communication in the organization. Stakeholders and the project sponsor were kept up to date continuously. They were aware that the virtual team were running into quite a few problems. They considered the comments made by everyone, and then decided that it was time to do something about it. Meredith et al. (2018) mention that projects need active planning, monitoring and controlling in the cycle of the project. Things that need to continuously be monitored and controlled would be time, cost, and the scope. The three items that are essential to any project. The stakeholders had their meetings and realized that they were off track with time and cost. Somewhere in all of this, the scope was being buried under the constant issues and they were losing their direction. This relayed into changes in staff but become a core piece to ensuring the project's success (Chang, Hung, & Hsieh, 2014).

These were core elements to the success of the project's success, but to ensure something like this would not happen again, processes were put in place. Using the case from Abudi (2010a & 2010b) and using Meredith et al. (2018) as sources for virtual team analyses, issues can be brought to light along with the path this company took to resolve it. The PM of the project in this case worked with the team and the co–PM to identify issues in the project. There were three issues that they were able to identify: team members not working well together, issues with project time and scope, and being able to capture the requirements of the project. The stakeholders introduced the changes and with the increase in team members, they needed to get to know one another. Virtual teams are more successful with there is a chance to learn more about each other. This will help them collaborate, brainstorm, and draw inspiration (Meredith et al., 2018). This kick-off event to get to know each other was a great step forward to building a stronger team. The next issue of the project plan was handled with starting the project from scratch. The stakeholders did not want to remove anyone from the team, but simply wanted to reboot it. This time around they had a better-defined scope and timeline, along with the project sponsor playing an active part in the project. This would lead to the constant monitoring mentioned (Meredith et al., 2018). As any issues arise, they can quickly be dealt with. The final mentioned issue would be handled by an additional source. They acquired a business analyst to develop the requirements needed to ensure the project's success. Once these requirements were clearly laid out, the business would be pulled away from the project.

All these issues were handled properly and worked well with this organization. Issues were addressed and were followed by procedures that can be used in other projects. This led to the success of this project and the virtual team was able to prove to be effective. They were able to complete status reporting and were able to comfortable work well with one another. Abudi (2010b) states that the team felt as if they were part of something great for the organization. This meant that morale alone was much better than it was before. Team members no longer felt as if they were lost on the direction of the project. They can see end goal of the project and what it meant for the company. This was a case on an effective virtual team.

The Non-Effective Case

Not every virtual team will be effective. In a small case study, "Virtual Team Successes and Stresses – A Case Study" (TMC, 2016), involving a virtual team composed of members across the globe, this virtual team was not able to be successful. The project started off with the PM requiring that everyone fill out a Cultural Orientations Indicator. The PM created a message board, and due to not being to do a face-to-face kick-off meeting they used more time to introduce themselves. Ground rules were set at the end of the meeting, and then they went on their own ways until work was required. When the time came to when the PM needed to get their sales reports, the PM was not able to get that from everyone. The PM then used humor in meetings to lighten up the mood in case anyone was nervous. After a while some of the team members decided to not speak or would just not attend the meetings. This virtual team was no longer effective.

To address the whole case study, the PM started strong and ended poorly. Starting off with the beginning of the case study, the PM focus on building the team. Virtual teams do well when they are able to have access to something that allows them to get to know one another. This is the one aspect of this case study that went well. The PM heavily focused on this and is essential to a team's success. The PM also showed the awareness of the virtual team. As it is difficult to grasp the mood of the group without being able to have that face-to-face interaction, the PM realized that something was wrong. The PM then tried their own way of getting what they needed from the group members using humor.

Using humor was one of the biggest issues that led to the ineffectiveness of the virtual team. As humor is a great way to lighten to mood, it is also very hard to assume that everyone understands it, especially when this group was composed of members from Japan, Mexico, Germany, Korea, and the US. Establishing virtual workplaces take a lot of setup and maintenance costs (Cascio, 2000). There are normal issues of trust in every team, and with it being virtual, it has an even higher issue of trust. In this case study, the PM uses humor and does not realize that it can be seen as distasteful in some cultures or just not understood. The mistake helped create a gap in understanding between the team members and the PM which help led to the team's downfall. In a virtual team, the most important concept to understand is that there are differences. Most prominently, cultural differences, as this is something that a project team needs to be able to do if it is to be a virtual team. The case study comes with some suggestions, such as an individual talk with each of the team members to establish a relationship. This would have been very effective, as this would help the PM understand more of the cultural differences that they were working with. The member who was not giving reports was the Japanese team member. This team member was under strict laws in Japan in terms of data protection and felt that they could not trust their PM. This is an oversight of their PM as this communication between them is vital to getting work done (Kayworth & Leidner, 2002; Chang, Hung, & Hsieh, 2014).

Communication is very important for a virtual team, as such for any team. In a virtual team they are met with no nonverbal cues, so they are troubled with understanding exactly what someone is trying to say. This team became ineffective when cultural difference was not addressed as the project went on. The PM did a great job establishing these differences at the beginning of the project, but then started to fall apart when they did not know how to handle the situation of not getting required tasks of the team members. There are many cases in which virtual teams are ineffective, but much like the first case introduced, there are cases in which they start off poorly and execute a strong finish (Chang, Hung, & Hsieh, 2014; Jarvenpaa & Leidner, 1999).

The Virtual Workplace

It is important to understand that every project is different. These differences need to be established to understand whether or not a virtual team can be deemed as effective. Companies need to identify a lot of things before setting a virtual team up. Cascio (2000) mentions that the first step to creating a virtual team is based on whether or not a virtual workplace is needed for a project. Not every company can implement a virtual workplace, let alone have the appropriate project for a virtual workplace. If the employee needs to be reached immediately at multiple points during the project and is not the PM, then a virtual workplace is not ideal. Cascio (2000) points out that jobs in sales, marketing, project engineering, and consulting are best for a virtual workplace. This is because any job that is focused on being serviced or knowledge oriented using some form of computer system can be done virtually anywhere. Especially, if this is done over the Internet or over the phone. Cascio (2000) recommends that no new employees are placed in a virtual workplace or in a virtual team. This is because that employee would need to learn essential business skills and to learn the position.

Now if a virtual workplace can be done, it raises the question of which employees should be incorporated into this workplace, and if this would be more effective than having them at a physical location. Staying on topic of these jobs being revolved around projects, identifying employees would be difficult. This employee would need to have a certain set of characteristics as suggested by Cascio (2000). These characteristics include being open minded with a positive attitude, having a results management style, and possessing effective communication skills, and having the ability to delegate effectively. If an employee can have these skills, and if every employee put into a virtual team has these characteristics, workflow would be much smoother than if they did not. Now after an employee has been viewed as applicable to be used in a virtual team and workplace. There is a problem of identifying the project as more effective in a virtual team. There are pros and cons to a virtual team. A virtual team can save time, reduce expenses, and provide easier access. Employees in this virtual team are able to balance their own personal and professional lives much easier. For the final pro, since communication and reports are done online, there is a constant documentation of milestones and activities. If there is ever a need to go over something, there is access to it.

The cons of using a virtual team usually lies in the dynamic of the team. It is a problem of whether they will work well together. Virtual teams do not meet face-to-face and are often met with language barriers if composed of employees from different regions of the world. On top of this, if an employee starts to become out of touch, there is the need to wait on that employee to respond themselves instead of waiting for them to come into work. In a virtual team, there is also the constant need of keeping everyone in a positive mood, so that they continue to brainstorm and participate in any discussions. The final con is the large amount of mistrust. Since most of the time span in a virtual team is spent working and submitting work to fellow team members online, there is little room for building a relationship. Cascio (2000) says that the lack of trust in a group leads to a lower group productivity. Having a distant and not participative team member lowers the effectiveness of the group. If all of this can be taken into consideration and a virtual workplace is viewed as effective to the company, then it can be done.

Once a company can move to the phase in which a virtual team can be used, proper training is needed to enhance the effectiveness of the virtual team. A PM needs to be trained to handle information coming from people of different backgrounds. General team members need to be trained to handle different social environments and social protocols (Cascio, 2000). After training, there is the idea of having employees to do teleworking. Teleworking has been growing more and more, and this is because it adds more time and flexibility to an employee's life. They are able to work from any location and preform just as well as they would if they were at the office. Teleworking has been up on the rise to accommodate a lot of employees (Sánchez, Pérez, de Luis Carnicer, Jiménez, 2007).

Teleworking, Workplace Flexibility, and Firm Performance

Teleworking has given organizations high workplace flexibility. Since virtual teams have members teleworking when working on a project, adopting this practice for more than just virtual teams makes sense. Sánchez et al. (2007) researched teleworking adoption, workplace flexibility, and the firm performance. Teleworking as defined by Sánchez et al. (2007) is a combination of characteristics of several types of flexibility that a workplace practice. Teleworking is simply allowing employees to work from remote locations. From the article, it is mentioned that teleworking has proven to help building space, support facilities, and help manage costs on equipment. Teleworking enables employees to manage their own time and spatial flexibility. Employees may be able to work around notable events or meetings that come up, while maintaining the access to work on a project. Teleworking has employees more involved in their job. Sánchez et al. (2007) suggests that employees that are more involved in their job design are more satisfied with their work and more productive. Employees find it easier to be productive on their own time that they set. The article also suggests that this supports teamwork because it generates more qualitative information. The reason as to which they are more able to telework is because they have the knowledge of what they need to be doing and can keep themselves organized. Sánchez et al. (2007) expects to find a positive relationship between teleworking adoption and workplace flexibility. Meaning that teleworking and workplace flexibility are highly correlated when looking at an organization that seems adaptable to any situation.

Sánchez et al. (2007) have used research to finalize their findings in the relationship between workplace flexibility and firm performance, and teleworking and firm performance. All their results suggest that both workplace flexibility and teleworking have a positive impact on firm performance. Relating teleworking to virtual teams, it seems that there is a positive impact with the use of virtual teams. Teleworking in a virtual team is very closely related. In a virtual team and working on a virtual project, it is said that, that employee is technically teleworking on that project. This does not mean that the employee is teleworking from the company they are working out of. It just simply means that they are working on this project from a remote location. An employee can be working on a virtual project from their desk at the office working on other assignments, while apart of this virtual team. The flexibility teleworking has for an employee is extremely high. This allows for multitasking if a project is important while managing day-to-day tasks. As teleworking is more common for managers and knowledge employees, stated by Sánchez et al. (2007).

Communication Technology

Technology has given virtual teams a place in the organization. Even if an employee is not teleworking, organization still provides access to these systems so that employees feel as if they can send a quick message to someone. Though there are consequences to using such systems, Cameron & Webster (2005) have found that once employees have access to these systems, they are more reluctant to get up and have a face-to-face conversation. Mentioned earlier about formality, people have deemed it more convenient to send a message without having to call or walk up to their office. This constant informality has made it difficult for organizations to perceive tasks are important. Many organizations have run into the issue of sending formal messages over IM systems. This has become an issue because there is no 'paper trail" over IM systems stated by Cameron & Webster (2005). It is recommended to use traceable formats for formal communication. This is where virtual teams usually fall short of keeping such formality. A lot of tasks in today's environment are assigned over these systems. Another problem that organizations face using IM systems is with the casual use of them. Much like catching some browsing the Internet or sitting on Facebook, employees with messaging close coworkers instead of working. This reduces the effectiveness of employees, but it is hard to say if it is more detrimental than the good it does for an organization. Overall, technology has opened avenues of communication for virtual teams.

BUILDING VIRTUAL TEAMS

In 2009, the Economist Intelligence Unit conducted a survey of 407 participants from $100m plus annual companies in various industries. With 318 respondents, the survey found that virtual teams range from five to twenty people. Designed primarily for project-based work, respondents indicated that they spend nearly 50% of the total time on off-site virtual team projects. 16% of the respondents indicated they spent more than 80% of their time on virtual team projects. The report also indicated that only 14% of managers use face-to-face interviews and only 7% use technologies such as video conferencing to conduct remote interviews (*Economist*, 2009). Therefore, managers are faced with the challenge of assembling a team of members who can work together, virtually, to meet the project goals.

Ironically, face-to-face meetings can serve as a litmus test for how knowledgeable and comfortable potential team members are with the technologies they may be using in the virtual team. However, Furst's research indicated that although technology savvy team members are valuable assets for communication and collaboration, interpersonal and teamwork skills may be of higher importance (Furst, Reeves, Benson, & Blackburn, 2004). Furthermore, Kirkman, et al. (2004) state that extrinsic motivators are often absent in virtual teams, therefore, building a team with a high level of intrinsic motivation is also key to high virtual team performance (Fan, Chen, Wang, & Chen, 2014; Klein, Noe & Wang, 2006).

Virtual teams are strong with an open line of communication. As appealing as they are for many organizations, in 2001 they fell short of their goals 82% of the time based on an article written by Ferrazzi (2015). In 2009 a new report came out that noted virtual teams to increase organization gains by up to 43% (Ferrazzi, 2015). This was only done with an effective virtual team, so the question now is how to create such a virtual team. There are many tips out there for creating and managing a virtual team, but this does not guarantee an effective team. Ferrazzi (2015) wrote about how to create that right team for an organization. One of the most important pieces to establish is having enough people for the task. Placing too many tasks on one or two individuals can lead to a stressful environment. Identifying the correct people and the correct size for the tasks that need to be completed is essential to an effective virtual team. Ferrazzi (2015) claims that once this is made, the next essential step is finding the right leadership. Having that go to leader that team members can trust provide a strong chance for success. Tips that have been around for any virtual team is to create a strong trust between everyone in the team, keeping an open line of communication, and keeping a clear sense of responsibilities. If all of these stay true throughout the course of a virtual project, then the chances of success are even higher. Further into the article, Ferrazzi (2015) mentions on identifying key forms of communication and finding ways to highlight progress. Communication has already been mentioned through the form of IM systems. Ways to highlight progress can be done in many ways.

In Meredith et al.'s book (2018), highlighting progress is done in a couple of ways. This is seen most commonly through the types of controls. These control processes are more than just waiting for something to just go wrong. They are also used to track progress of a project. In doing so, milestones are a way to say that they have made it to a part of the project that no longer needs to be looked at. Milestones are also a way to motivate a virtual team. These milestones as Ferrazzi (2015) claims are a celebration for the virtual team. This is meant to help team members feel more connected and engaged and help them feel as if they contributed to something. Similar to the first case study mentioned by Abudi (2010b). They were successful and throughout the project, the team was met with constant reports, but they felt as if they are contributing to something great. Motivation for a virtual team is not something easily attained. PM's must find what motivates the team, and the individuals that make up the team (Klein, Noe & Wang, 2006).

Challenges of Performance

Compared to traditional face-to-face teams, virtual teams present some unique challenges for companies, team managers, and members. Stemming from vast differences in culture and communication, diversity is evident and often the most significant challenge for virtual teams (Pearlson, Saunders, & Galletta, 2016; Staples & Zhao, 2006). Also, the degree of virtualization, say 25% versus 100% dispersion, dictates the severity of challenges that virtual teams may face (Schlenkrich & Upfold, 2009).

To gain a better understanding of these challenges, managers must look at the different components of virtual team diversity to include culture, communication, technology, and logistics. If a virtual team is comprised of members from multiple countries such as the U.S., China, India, and Germany, cultural differences will inevitably exist. Differences can include varying expectations, biases, and communication skills and habits (Iles & Hayers, 1997). When communicating via email, phone, or even video, important intricacies such as facial expressions, vocal modulations, verbal signals, and body gestures can be altered or lost in translation. As a medium to facilitate communication amongst the virtual team, the very technologies used can also present several challenges. For example, team members may be afraid of or lack skills necessary to operate technologies such as video teleconferencing equipment. Furthermore, some virtual team members may have a strong preference for one technology over another, say email versus phone. Lastly, logistical challenges exist for team members spread across multiple time zones. While this enables teams to work around the clock and follow-the-sun, shift overlap may be necessary for day-to-day communication and team meetings (Kayworth & Leidner, 2002).

Ferrazzi (2015) includes excellent tips on creating that ideal effective virtual team. Virtual teams are common and have been becoming more important in today's business environment. Reasons as to which they have become more important revolves around the productiveness of employees. As virtual teams are becoming more attractive to organizations, there are still some problems with adopting them. Training requires a lot of time and finding the optimized team for a project has proven to be difficult. Along with taking a lot of time, the training needs to be diverse, as a PM will meet and deal with many diverse team members. The PM has the most important role in the success of the project. The problem they often face is developing that motivation for everyone. A PM is responsible for making every individual feel as if they are important as mentioned in an article by Dube and Marnewick (2016). In a virtual team, there are many individuals, and if a PM can get to everyone to make them feel as if they are doing great work. Individuals in turn will pursue improving themselves in striving to correcting their shortcomings (Fan, et al., 2014; Klein, Noe & Wang, 2006).

Dube and Marnewick (2016) also talks about a team's performance. If the PM of the virtual team can continuously outline the team's goals and objectives, the team can perform well. Communication comes up again, as it is a key factor in which a virtual team does well. Communication among team members helps identify who is responsible for what. It is always for collaboration to occur and for help to be sought out without lengthy delays. Dube & Marnewick (2016) go in depth about a project team performance. In virtual teams, most individuals are assigned with tasks that come together with one or two other individuals working on the project to make up a team. A project team that is explained by Dube & Marnewick (2016) is the collection of all the teams in a project. A project is made up of many temporary teams and teams are made up of individuals that are assigned with tasks that come together with other individuals in that temporary team. Once the team itself is done with its goal, the team is abolished and reformed with new tasks and new individuals. Performance is measured by the activities completed by the virtual team over the course of time allotted to complete the project. This is where the bigger milestones are labelled, while each time a team completes their task a milestone is also reached. Performance for the virtual team is measured by all three prior components. The individual, the team, and the project. The collection of performances makes up the measure in which a virtual team can be assessed.

Enhancers of Virtual Teams

Virtual teams can perform well, but there are ways to ensure they can be great. In an article written by Derven (2016), it ensures that a competent virtual team has a good mix of functional, cross-functional, and technical skills. While group members should have these set of skills, they come together under an inclusive leader. This is because most virtual teams have a diverse setup. They include team members from all over the world. An inclusive leader will surely help the group feel that their ideas are heard and treated appropriately. As it may be demanding with a diverse group, an inclusive leader can act as a catalyst to new innovative ideas.

Derven (2016) mentions that every virtual team should have a clearly outlined purpose. The article claims that the purpose should be; explicit, achievable, measurable, refreshing as circumstance change, and a key driver for milestones. With an explicit purpose, team members to can strive to achieve it without confusion. If the purpose is measurable then team members can view how well they are doing. The purpose of it being refreshing as circumstance change is to ensure no stagnation in the team. As a situation can drastically change, as long as the purpose changes with it and is clear, the virtual team should be able to handle it. It should be clear that the team is adaptable. The purpose should not be the overall end goal for the project, the purpose should be attainable in a brief time frame. This will keep motivation up and move the virtual team in a forward manner.

The next enhancer for virtual teams is the people involved. Keeping the group diverse with the essential skills to reach each purpose is very important. Derven (2016) includes stages of team development. The stages are Forming, Storming, Norming, and Performing. Forming is defining task. Storming is the stage in which scope is established. Norming is about communication. Lastly, Performing is all about working together to do well. Derven (2016) also mentions that there should be performance goals as to align the team with a shared interest to avoid conflicts.

Process is the last enhancer that plays a role with the organization itself. Process focuses on making sure that the virtual team is staying on time, budget, and fitting the appropriate scope. This is the point in which the virtual team is monitored and controlled by the sponsor and stakeholders. A PM cannot handle everything that the stakeholders want the project to be, and because of this, constant reports sent to stakeholders help keep them in the loop. With every milestone that may be reached by the virtual team, there could be a change in scope from the stakeholders. This is where the virtual team needs to be adaptable, as the original goal can be vastly different than the ending results of the project (Orlikowski, 2000).

The four enhancers that Derven (2016) uses to help create a more effective virtual team is ideal for any project. There should be a strong sense of diversity and inclusion from management. A purpose needs to be outlined so that the team can fulfill the goals of the project. People are essential to completing the tasks, and as motivation is kept high between everyone, the team will perform well. Finally, the process in which the virtual team is monitored and controlled is important. Having the constant monitoring helps handle problems as they arise. A control process helps with conflict management and can help keep the virtual team on track in terms of time, cost, and scope.

Due to the nature of virtual teams, it appears that team empowerment is more critical to success than it is in traditional collocated teams. Theories suggest that this is vitally important for day-to-day operations as well as the end goal of customer satisfaction (Curseu, Schalk, & Wessel, 2008; and Piccoli, Powell, & Ives, 2004). Process improvement for virtual teams includes high levels of planning, collaboration, resource distribution, and performance improvements. Virtual teams are significantly involved in these areas. It is believed that high levels of potency, meaningfulness, autonomy, and impact will have positive impacts on virtual team process improvement.

Additionally, virtual teams must meet or exceed the goals of internal stakeholders and external customers. Studies indicate that if the four dimensions of empowerment are high, virtual teams will be able to satisfy customers. This assumption is based on the study that intrinsically motivated, self-sufficient, and knowledgeable team members are positively positioned to promptly handle a variety of customer concerns, regardless of the level of dispersion from team members or the organization (Fan, et al., 2014; Kirkman et al., 2004).

CONCLUSION

Virtual teams are used in many organizations and they have had their good moments and their bad ones. They are rapidly growing in use for many organizations. As they adopt the use of virtual teams, they build new process to ensure the successfulness of the virtual team. Many organizations are developing ways for their employees to find some intrinsic value that assists them to keep working. Organizations use teleworking, and in doing so, it results in some employees working in virtual teams. Factors that needed to be accounted for in virtual teams involved being diverse, keeping an open line of communication with everyone involved, and identifying the goals for the virtual project team. Virtual teams today have processes that have been built over in prior years and are being refined to suit the organization and the type of project. Not every organization will be able to implement them, but many are already on the path to adopting them.

Virtual teams are going to continue to rise in popularity in the global economy and today's leaders must ensure that they have the skill set to lead these teams. There are several challenges to virtual teams but they are not insurmountable and the benefits outweigh the challenges. Conventional wisdom suggests that performance of team's decreases as the level of dispersion increases, causing management to view virtual teams as a risk to delivering success. However, the use of virtual teams is becoming more of a commonality rather than a rarity in our existing global, competitive corporate environments. With the rapid innovations of the Internet and various computer-mediated communication systems companies are quickly hopping on the virtual team band wagon. Virtual teams give companies the ability to work globally, gain entrance into new markets and address staffing needs while promoting corporate social responsibility. Recent studies show that that if the appropriate tools and leadership are in place, and executed properly, virtual teams can actually outperform teams that are co-located if they are set up and managed properly.

Virtual teams present a unique opportunity for businesses to respond to market needs. By tapping into the global talent pool and dispersing team members, companies can improve their position to provide quality, cost effective, and valuable products and services in a timely manner. Key to this process is the successful construction and management of virtual teams. Understanding the difference between traditional and virtual teams is the first step, followed by a deeper understanding of how diversity creates challenges for virtual teams. With proper structure and planning, managers can use various tactics to sustain a highly functional level of communication and collaboration among dispersed team members. Furthermore, by utilizing communication and collaboration products, virtual teams can increase their productivity resulting in greater competitive advantage.

Managers shall set up a plan to gradually build the virtual team from infrastructure layer, to tactical layer, to strategic layer. Once the team structure is constructed, managers can follow Tuckman's four-step model to develop a robust and productive virtual team. As mentioned earlier, the future of human achievement will be driven by the leverage of talented groups of people, not individuals. If utilized properly, virtual teams can significantly contribute to this achievement on a global scale.

In conclusion, virtual teams can provide great corporate strategic benefits. These benefits include reducing costs, enhancing team perspective through diversity, entering new global markets, and increasing productivity. These benefits are not gained by just setting up virtual teams. The organization, as a whole, needs to be designed such that it provides a framework that integrates virtual teams. Managers need to be cognizant of the effects of distance and culture to team performance. Building trust and ensuring open communication among the team members should be high priorities. The manager also needs to be a leader to the team; encapsulating the administrator, coach, and advisor functions. In the end, managing virtual teams is more challenging than local teams and requires constant interaction in order to maximize effectiveness.

REFERENCES

Abudi, G. (2010a). *A Virtual Global Team in Trouble: A Case Study - Part I.* Retrieved August 15, 2018 from https://www.ginaabudi.com/a-virtual-global-team-in-trouble-a-case-study-part-i/

Abudi, G. (2010b). *A Virtual Global Team in Trouble: A Case Study - Part II: Now What?* Retrieved August 15, 2018 from https://www.ginaabudi.com/a-virtual-global-team-in-trouble-a-case-study-part-ii-now-what/

Brunelle, E. (2012). Virtuality in work arrangements and affective organizational commitment. *International Journal of Business and Social Science*, *3*(2), 56–62.

Cameron, A. F., & Webster, J. (2005). Unintended consequences of emerging communication technologies: Instant messaging in the workplace. *Computers in Human Behavior*, *21*(1), 85–103. doi:10.1016/j.chb.2003.12.001

Cascio, W. F. (2000). Managing a virtual workplace. *The Academy of Management Perspectives*, *14*(3), 1–10. doi:10.5465/ame.2000.4468068

Chang, H. H., Hung, C. J., & Hsieh, H. W. (2014). Virtual teams: Cultural adaptation, communication quality, and interpersonal trust. *Total Quality Management & Business Excellence*, *25*(11/12), 1318–1335. doi:10.1080/14783363.2012.704274

Curseu, P. L., Schalk, R., & Wessel, I. (2008). How do virtual teams process information? A literature review and implications for management. *Journal of Managerial Psychology*, *23*(6), 628–652. doi:10.1108/02683940810894729

Dervén, M. (2016). Four drivers to enhance global virtual teams. *Industrial and Commercial Training*, *48*(1), 1–8. doi:10.1108/ICT-08-2015-0056

Dube, S., & Marnewick, C. (2016). A conceptual model to improve performance in virtual teams. *South African Journal of Information Management, 18*(1), 1-10. http://dx.doi.org.umasslowell.idm.oclc.org/10.4102/sajim.v18i1.674

Economist Intelligence Unit. (2009). Managing virtual team: Taking a more strategic approach. *The Economist*. Retrieved September 15, 2012 from http://graphics.eiu.com/upload/eb/NEC_Managing_virtual_teams_WEB.pdf

Eissa, G., Fox, C., Webster, B. D., & Kim, J. (2012). A framework for leader effectiveness in virtual teams. *Journal of Leadership, Accountability and Ethics*, *9*(2), 11–22.

Fan, K. T., Chen, Y. H., Wang, C. W., & Chen, M. (2014). E-leadership effectiveness in virtual teams: Motivating language perspective. *Industrial Management & Data Systems*, *114*(3), 421–437. doi:10.1108/IMDS-07-2013-0294

Ferrazzi, K. (2014). Getting virtual teams right. *Harvard Business Review*. Retrieved September 1, 2018 from https://hbr.org/2014/12/getting-virtual-teams-right

Furst, S. A., Reeves, M., Benson, R., & Blackburn, R. S. (2004). Managing the life cycle of virtual teams. *The Academy of Management Perspectives*, *18*(2), 6–20. doi:10.5465/ame.2004.13837468

Gaan, N. (2012). Collaborative tools and virtual team effectiveness: An inductively derived approach in India's software sector. *Decision (Washington, D.C.)*, *39*(1), 5–27.

Grosse, C. U. (2002). Managing communication within virtual intercultural teams. *Business Communication Quarterly*, *65*(4), 22–38. doi:10.1177/108056990206500404

Henderson, J. C., & Lee, S. (1992). Managing I/S design teams: A control theories perspective. *Management Science*, *38*(6), 757–777. doi:10.1287/mnsc.38.6.757

Horwitz, F. M., Bravington, D., & Silvis, U. (2006). The promise of virtual teams: Identifying key factors in effectiveness and failure. *Journal of European Industrial Training*, *30*(6), 472–494. doi:10.1108/03090590610688843

Iles, P., & Hayers, P. K. (1997). Managing diversity in transnational project teams: A tentative model and case study. *Journal of Managerial Psychology*, *12*(2), 95–117. doi:10.1108/02683949710164190

Jarvenpaa, S. L., & Leidner, L. E. (1999). Communication and trust in global virtual teams. *Organization Science*, *10*(6), 791–815. doi:10.1287/orsc.10.6.791

Jones, T. L. (2009). *Virtual team communication and collaboration in Army and corporate applications*. Retrieved September 15, 2012 from http://www.dtic.mil/cgi-bin/GetTRDoc?AD=ADA502091

Kankanhalli, A., Tan, B. C. Y., & Wei, K.-K. (2007). Conflict and performance in global virtual teams. *Journal of Management Information Systems*, *23*(3), 237–274. doi:10.2753/MIS0742-1222230309

Kayworth, T. R., & Leidner, D. E. (2002). Leadership effectiveness in global virtual teams. *Journal of Management Information Systems*, *18*(3), 7–40. doi:10.1080/07421222.2002.11045697

Kirkman, B. L., Rosen, B., Tesluk, P. E., & Gibson, C. B. (2004). The impact of team empowerment on virtual team performance: The moderating role of face-to-face interaction. *Academy of Management Journal*, *47*(2), 175–192.

Klein, H. J., Noe, R., & Wang, C. (2006). Motivation to learn and course outcomes: The impact of delivery mode, learning goal orientation, and perceived barriers and enablers. *Personnel Psychology*, *59*(3), 665–702. doi:10.1111/j.1744-6570.2006.00050.x

Krebs, S. A., Hobman, E. V., & Bordia, P. (2006). Virtual teams and group member dissimilarity: Consequences for the development of trust. *Small Group Research*, *37*(6), 721–741. doi:10.1177/1046496406294886

Lipnack, J., & Stamps, J. (2000). *Virtual teams: People working across boundaries with technology* (2nd ed.). New York: Wiley.

Lisak, A., & Erez, M. (2015). Leadership emergence in multicultural teams: The power of global characteristics. *Journal of World Business*, *50*(1), 3–14. doi:10.1016/j.jwb.2014.01.002

Meredith, J. R., Shafer, S. M., & Mantel, S. J. Jr. (2018). *Project Management: A Strategic Managerial Approach* (10th ed.). Hoboken, NJ: Wiley.

Morgan, L., Paucar-caceres, A., & Wright, G. (2014). Leading effective global virtual teams: The consequences of methods of communication. *Systemic Practice and Action Research*, *27*(6), 607–624. doi:10.100711213-014-9315-2

Olson, J. D., Appunn, F. D., McAllister, C. A., Walters, K. K., & Grinnell, L. (2014). Webcams and virtual teams: An impact model. *Team Performance Management*, *20*(3/4), 148–177. doi:10.1108/TPM-05-2013-0013

Orlikowski, W. J. (2000). Using technology and constituting structures: A practice lens for studying technology in organizations. *Organization Science*, *11*(4), 404–428. doi:10.1287/orsc.11.4.404.14600

Pearlson, K. E., Saunders, C. S., & Galletta, D. F. (2016). *Managing and Using Information Systems: a strategic approach* (6th ed.). Hoboken, NJ: John Wiley & Sons, Inc.

Piccoli, G., Powell, A., & Ives, B. (2004). Virtual teams: Team control structure, work processes, and team effectiveness. *Information Technology & People*, *17*(4), 359–379. doi:10.1108/09593840410570258

Sánchez, A. M., Pérez, M. P., de Luis Carnicer, P., & Jiménez, M. J. V. (2007). Teleworking and workplace flexibility: A study of impact on firm performance. *Personnel Review*, *36*(1), 42–64. doi:10.1108/00483480710716713

Schlenkrich, L., & Upfold, C. (2009). A guideline for virtual team managers: The key to effective social interaction and communication. *The Electronic Journal of Information Systems Evaluation*, *12*(1), 109–118.

Siebdrat, F., Hoegl, M., & Ernst, H. (2009). How to manage virtual teams. *MIT Sloan Management Review*, *50*(4), 63–68.

Staples, D. S., & Zhao, L. (2006). The effects of cultural diversity in virtual teams versus face-to-face teams. *Group Decision and Negotiation*, *15*(4), 389–406. doi:10.100710726-006-9042-x

TMC. (2016). *Virtual team successes and stresses – a case study*. Retrieved August 20, 2018 from http://www.tmcorp.com/Perspectives/Global-Advice/Global-Advice/80/vobid--787/

Zivick, J. (2012). Mapping global virtual team leadership actions to organizational roles. *Business Review (Federal Reserve Bank of Philadelphia)*, *19*(2), 18–25.

Zolin, R., Hinds, P. J., Fruchter, R., & Levitt, R. E. (2004). Interpersonal trust in cross-functional, geographically distributed work: A longitudinal study. *Information and Organization*, *14*(1), 1–26. doi:10.1016/j.infoandorg.2003.09.002

Chapter 21
Collaborative Learning Strategies in Organizations

Sandra Sanz Martos
Universitat Oberta de Catalunya, Spain

Mario Pérez-Montoro
University of Barcelona, Spain

ABSTRACT

Among the different types of innovative learning initiatives, organizations have been implementing communities of practice as a collaborative learning strategy. However, in many cases, one finds the term community of practice attributed to other types of communities or work groups. This chapter aims to define, identify, and characterize communities of practice and differentiate them from other organizational structures which are not such communities. It establishes a comparison among them and observes the benefits obtained from each structure, indicating which strategy to apply depending on the goal or challenge. Finally, a number of conclusions and guidelines on the future development of communities of practice are presented.

INTRODUCTION

In recent years, there has been a gradual introduction of the knowledge-sharing culture in organizations. Gone are the old dynamics based on poorly understood competition, where institutions thought lack of collaboration between colleagues could lead to better performance, since the person sitting at the neighboring desk would be considered a rival, and employees avoided helping each other with problems or explaining work tasks, as they saw their colleagues as threats that could put possible promotion at risk.

The current trend is in the opposite direction: encouraging and facilitating knowledge exchange and mutual help. This fosters training through collaborative learning and work and places greater value than ever on learning from colleagues who share the same professional tasks or responsibilities. Gone is the need to use weighty, impersonal volumes or training materials. Even in training new employees, the strategy of using the most senior colleagues, who have been doing the work of the new recruits for years, as trainers is being adopted.

DOI: 10.4018/978-1-5225-8516-9.ch021

A growing number of public and private institutions are looking to implement new, innovative training techniques based on collaborative learning and work. In some, but not all, cases, these initiatives are integrated into a broader strategy of knowledge management. Numerous companies and public institutions have seen the need for their members to exchange experiences and know-how. Among other things, this leads to multiple intangible benefits, such as avoiding duplication of processes, preventing talent flight and increasing the climate of trust and feeling of belonging. In short: more competitive organizations.

Collaborative learning has different applications (Jenkins, 2015). These range from informal and face-to-face situations in the organization itself, to online networks and finally to cohesive, mutually committed groups that form communities. Virtual communities of practice are usually the most fruitful, as they produce a greater volume of interaction and continuity. Furthermore, the tacit commitment acquired by members increases participation even further. Among such communities, those that stand out are the ones that provide value to organizations. These are communities of interest, learning and practice. It is the latter, the communities of practice, that are probably growing most steadily, and which organizations see as having the greatest potential for increasing knowledge in the organization.

The words of Richard McDermott, "the key to driving change towards sharing knowledge probably lies in communities of practice" (McDermott 1999), have somehow become the magic key for many business people, who see communities of practice as the solution to many of their problems. This has led to somewhat uncontrolled expansion, which has largely contributed to use of the term to refer to work groups and other communities that are not communities of practice.

One of the aims of this study is to sort out this confusion and identify and characterize communities of practice compared to other work teams or groups, and other types of communities, such as communities of learning or interest. At the same time, it does not lose sight of the fact that different goals require different strategies. In some cases, the organization should turn to project teams to solve a problem or improve a process; in other situations, such as learning how to use a new computer tool, it should turn to a community of learning. Thus, each need should be covered by one organizational strategy or another.

The chapter ends with a number of conclusions and future lines of research that raise certain unresolved issues, such as managing return on investment (ROI) and the application of big data management techniques to identify new contributions and ideas.

COMMUNITIES OF PRACTICE

No one now doubts that the subject of communities of practice arouses increasingly more interest in the academic field and in that of professional consultancy. Also, this subject is related to the emergent field of social knowledge (Gallo & Yan, 2015; Gurteen, 2012).

However, this widespread interest is simultaneously bringing about a curious and, to some extent, perverse phenomenon. As occurred with the term "information" in the 1980s and 1990s, in recent years the expression "Community of Practice" has become a clear example of a buzzword. In other words, it has become an expression that more and more people are using but which, sadly, very few people know exactly what they are referring to when they use it. Endless companies, consultants, e-learning specialists, Human Resources department managers, among many others, state that they are currently working with this type of strategy. None of them, each with their particular focus, has the slightest hesitation in declaring their unconditional submission to this new enterprise when, often regrettably, they are not at all certain of what it consists or the extent of this type of community.

Amid this sea of confusion, the term Communities of Practice ends up being continuously applied to other types of groups or communities or even work activities that very often have nothing to do with them. Probably one of the reasons that led Wenger and Snyder, two of the most prestigious authors who have theorized about the universe of this special type of community, to write their article "Communities of practice: the organizational frontier" (Wenger and Snyder, 2000) was the desire to try to put an end to this. However, the confusion and the application of the concept continues to rise. The more known the term becomes, the worse the use that is made of it in the non-specialist environments.

Despite the fact that in the scientific literature, the authors coincide in defining communities of practice in very similar terms (although always with small nuances), when transferred to organizational environments or seminars, and even more so to the Internet, we have been able to detect that the application of the concept of community of practice is very often incorrect. In this sense, it should be no surprise that, for example, in many of the workshops on communities of practice that are given to those in charge of knowledge management in companies, cases that are very far from being CoPs may be presented as examples to illustrate the sessions. Or that in talks or lectures, participants can hurry to identify initiatives for the creation of working groups of a different nature in their companies as genuine Communities of Practice. Or that texts appear on the Internet on supposed experiences that are christened as CoPs without they really being so.

Yet, what really is a community of practice? Ever since Etienne Wenger coined the term in the book published with Jane Lave entitled *Situated learning. Legitimate peripheral participation* (Cambridge University Press, 1991), many authors have defined the concept.

Consequently, for example, Wenger himself, along with Snyder (2000), later defined it as "a group of people who meet informally to share their experience and passion for a common enterprise." In 2002, he extended and improved this definition in the book that he published with McDermott and Snyder (*Cultivating Communities of practice*) as follows: "groups of people that share a concern, a set of problems, or a passion about a topic, and who deepen their knowledge and expertise in this area by interacting on an ongoing basis." According to Sergio Vásquez (2002) "a community of practice is a group of people linked by a common, recurring and stable practice whereby they learn in this common practice." Also, Lesser and Storck (2003) defined it as follows: "a community of practice is a group whose members regularly engage in sharing and learning, based on their common interests." While John Seely Brown (2003) in the 5th Annual Braintrust Knowledge Management Summit in San Francisco defined CoPs as "a group of people with different functions and viewpoints, committed to joint work over a significant period of time during which they construct objects, solve problems, learn, invent and negotiate meanings and develop a way of reading mutually."

We could extend this list of definitions and ascertain that they can reach considerable dimensions. In any event, it is clear that two defining aspects concur in all of them: commitment and common interest. In short, communities of practice are a group of people who carry out the same professional activity or responsibility and who, concerned with a common problem or moved by a common interest, expand their knowledge and expertise in this matter through ongoing interaction (Sanz, 2008).

However, despite the best efforts of these authors to offer a comprehensive definition of them, it is clear that CoPs continue to be confused with other types of communities such as learning communities (Hydle at al., 2014) or interest and with other organisation-related groups such as formal or informal groups and working teams: problem-solving, multidisciplinary or virtual.

OTHER ORGANISATIONAL STRUCTURES

In the context of organisations, it is often the custom to create and develop small groups or communities (in short, organisational structures) to improve internal operations and so meet the desired aims more adequately.

Communities of Practice constitute a special type of these organisational structures. However, if we put this type of community to one side and take another look at the different strategies commonly implemented in organisations, we can identify three large types of groupings or organisational structures: groups, working groups and communities.

Broadly speaking, and in intuitive terms and for any context, communities can be defined as sets, groupings or congregations of people who live together under certain constitutions and rules. However, if we are talking about groups and teams, we need to understand them as groups of people brought together for specific research or a specific service.

The element that certainly most clearly differentiates groups and teams from communities is that the former work to achieve an aim, which is what binds them together and is their *raison d'être*. However, in communities the fact of sharing is what defines them. They share things: zones, services or interests. For example, in the case of a community of owners, this is the common use of the shared building; and in an educational community, the services and interests of the training centre. There is no specific aim other than that they form part of something that is common to others or that is of interest to everyone. You may be chosen to become part of a group or team, but not to become part of a community. You will be part of a community simply by being in it, by sharing things with it, by being governed by its more or less explicit rules.

If we now turn our attention to the context of organisations, we can identify a series of different types of groups, working teams and communities. Among the main group types, we can identify formal and informal working groups. Among the working teams, we can identify problem-solving working teams, self-managed teams, multidisciplinary teams and virtual teams. However, for communities we can identify communities of interest, learning communities and communities of practice.

Groups

In most cases, communities of practice develop at the very heart of the organisation. It is not difficult therefore to confuse them with the groups that are deployed within this context.

In the context of organisations, groups should be seen as organisational structures that comprise two or more individuals, who interact, are inter-dependent and who have combined to meet specific aims.

In this type of context, groups are usually allocated a series of functions and are used to carry out certain organisational strategies. As a result, they are particularly suited to modifying behaviour, attitudes and values and to disciplining their members. They can in fact be used to exert pressure on members who fail to comply with the rules to make them do so. In addition to this, they are also useful in decision-making and negotiation. Members with different backgrounds can contribute different perspectives to the decision-making process. However, this does not mean that group decisions are always better than individual decisions.

There is a nucleus of common characteristics that, in part at least, define the groups in organisational contexts. These include the fact that they tend to present certain internal communication patterns. This communication can be channelled through a key member or flow freely among all the members of a group. On the other hand, another typical characteristic is that when group interactions are efficient they can influence motivation. If, for example, the members of a group take part in establishing objectives, they will probably make a greater commitment to meeting group goals. Leadership also plays an important role in the context of group processes. Understanding the concepts that refer to groups helps understand the interactions between leaders and followers and also the interactions between all group members. Finally, groups also offer clear advantages to the individuals that comprise them. They offer social satisfaction to their members, the same as a sense of belonging and support for the needs of individuals, they promote communication and they provide security.

We should stress that a wide variety of groups, whose composition, functions and other properties differ significantly, coexist within the organisational context. In this sense, groups in organisational contexts can be classified in many ways and according to different criteria. The general criteria (that are not exclusive in nature) that are most commonly used to classify them are temporality, purpose, hierarchy and activity.

According to the time criterion, two different types of groups can be identified based on the type of stability in the relationships that bind their members together: permanent and temporary groups. Permanent groups are seen as being stable in time and are responsible for the everyday operating and maintenance tasks of the organisation. The time permanency of these groups does not prevent changes being made to their composition. A good example of this is the different departments that make up a company. However, temporary groups (created *ad hoc*) are designed to carry out transitory tasks, projects or activities. The group has a limited duration and breaks up once its function is complete or it has achieved its aim. This could be a research and development group, a study commission, an advisory committee, etc.

In addition, according to the purpose criterion, and based on the aims to be achieved, four different types of groups can be identified in these contexts: production groups, problem-solving groups, conflict-resolution groups and organisational change and development groups. In production groups, their members undertake specific work together. These are the departments and units of the organisation. Problem-solving groups focus on specific problems of the organisation. Quality circles or project study groups are clear examples of these types of groups. Conflict-resolution groups tackle situations of confrontation between the different parts of the organisation or the organisation with the outside world. Essentially, they are negotiation groups. Finally, organisational change and development groups include different groups and group techniques. These include training groups, team development groups and awareness groups.

According to a hierarchical criterion, two different types of groups can also be identified based on the location within the organisational structure: vertical differentiation and horizontal differentiation groups. Vertical differentiation groups comprise members, who, in turn, belong to different organisation structures ranging from senior management ("strategic apex"), through middle management groups ("middle line") to non-managerial groups ("operating core"). Horizontal differentiation groups, however, coincide with the different functional groups. These are groups that provide specialist services (in terms of production, research, etc.), based on specific skills, and temporary committees, created with different missions, which are essentially to advise and take decisions.

Finally, according to the activity, two different types of working groups can be identified: group activity groups and individual activity groups. Group activity groups are team groups with interdependent tasks, group aims and incentives, stable relationships, etc. However, individual activity groups are dominated by individual activity and values. Members are linked together by little more than sharing a space, a task, professional speciality or reporting to the same boss. A "sales team" in which, among other conditions, individual commissions are awarded (which generates competition among its members), could be seen as a clear example of this final type.

Putting these general criteria of temporality, purpose, hierarchy and activities to one side, the specialist literature contains a certain consensus for accepting and arranging organisational groups according to the degree of formality that characterises them. This classification has been suggested by Robbins (2008) and also coincides with the classification also suggested by authors Hellriegel & Slocum (2008). According to this classification, groups can be arranged by two large categories: formal and informal groups.

Formal groups are defined by the organisational structure, with a number of work allocations designed that establish tasks. In these groups, the behaviour that members should commit to is stipulated by and aimed at organisational goals. The six members of a flight crew are an example of a formal group. These groups are defined and planned to achieve the aims of the organisation. Departments or commissions, for example, irrespective of other criteria, share their formal character. Command and task groups are stipulated in these departments or commissions. Command groups are determined by the company organisation chart. This comprises subordinates who report directly to an appointed manager. Task groups are also determined by the organisation and represent employees who carry out specific types of work. These are also known as functional groups.

In contrast, informal groups are presented as alliances that are not formally structured, nor are they determined by the organisation. These groups are natural formations within the work environment that appear in response to the need for social contact. Three employees from different departments who almost always have lunch together are an example of an informal group. Spontaneous relationships occur between the members of the organisation and are geared towards meeting the personal and social needs of its components. Groups that are created through friendship or attraction, groups of people who share the same problem, can be examples of this type. Interest groups and friends groups can be identified in informal groups. Interest groups are members of the organisation who may join together to achieve a specific aim of common interest (such as exchanging holidays or improving their salary conditions). In friends groups, however, their members share specific characteristics, such as similar age or origins, and they frequently go beyond the work context.

Working Teams

Stephen P. Robbins (2004) places special interest on differentiating working teams from working groups. According to this author, a working group is one where its members primarily interrelate to share information and to take decisions in such a way as to be able to help each member to develop in their area of responsibility. Its performance is merely the sum of the contribution of each member of the group. There is not the necessary positive synergy to create a general level of performance greater than that of the sum of its contributions. However, in the case of teams, this positive synergy is created through a coordinated effort, whereby the sum of its individual efforts is greater. Management seeks this positive synergy that will enable their organisations to increase performance. The extensive use of teams creates the potential for an organisation to generate greater results without an increase in contributions.

Teams can be classed on the basis of their objectives. The three most common forms of team that are found in an organisation are problem-solving teams, self-managed teams and multidisciplinary teams.

In problem-solving teams, members share ideas or offer suggestions on how to improve work processes and methods. Rarely, however, do they have the authority to put any of their suggested actions into practice. One example of problem-solving teams are quality circles. Self-managed teams, in contrast, are groups of employees (normally between 10 and 15) who take on the responsibilities of their former supervisors. Generally speaking, this includes work planning and scheduling, collective control over work pace, taking operational decisions and the execution of the actions on the problems. Completely self-managed working teams even select their own members and make them assess each other's performance. Finally, multidisciplinary teams are made up of employees of the same hierarchical level but from different work divisions, who meet to carry out a task. Multidisciplinary teams are an efficient means of allowing people from different divisions in an organisation (or even between organisations) to exchange information, develop new ideas and solve problems, and coordinate complex projects.

It is also important to point out that Robbins (2004) distinguishes a fourth a kind of team that he calls virtual teams, which use computational technology to bring together physically dispersed members with the aim of achieving a common objective. These teams may do the same as the other teams, such as exchange information, take decisions, complete tasks and also include other members from the same organisation or connect them with employees from other organisations, e.g. suppliers or partners. They may meet for a few days to solve a problem, for a few months to complete a project or they may exist permanently.

Communities

As we mentioned, communities can be identified as the third type of organisational structure, along with working groups and working teams, which are usually developed to improve the correct operation of organisations. If we leave communities of practice to one side, we can distinguish two large types of community: learning communities and communities of interest.

We will begin by describing learning communities. Learning communities are contexts in which the students learn thanks to their participation and involvement, in collaboration with other students, the teacher and other adults, in genuine processes of research and collective construction of knowledge on personal and socially relevant questions (Onrubia 2004, González-Patiño 2018).

The premise on which the idea of classrooms as learning communities is based is the consideration that individual learning is, to a large extent, inseparable from the collective construction of knowledge, and that this collective construction constitutes the context, the platform and the basic support so that each student can advance in their own knowledge. In line with this, the activity of the classrooms that are structured as learning communities is not organised, as in traditional classrooms, around the teacher conveying specific pre-established content, but around research processes on specific subjects previously agreed between teacher and students, and which teacher and students tackle jointly and collaboratively.

These processes can take diverse specific forms, such as the creation of projects, case analysis, situation-problem solving or preparing products which will be presented in public. The true and relevant nature of the situations, activities and tasks based on collaborative knowledge-construction processes that are carried out in the classrooms that are structured as learning communities are specified in a whole series of traits that radically define the traits that typically characterise the activity in traditional classrooms (Onrubia 2004, González-Patiño, 2018). Consequently, in a classroom organised as a learning community, teacher and students commonly tackle global and complex tasks, the resolution of which demands the combined use of knowledge and skills of various types. Considering within this framework the diversity of the students as an essential resource for favouring learning and benefitting somewhat, traditional teaching could never enable students to acquire the same knowledge in the same way and at the same time.

This way, for example, students in a subject such as physics learn to resolve the exercises together and share the way of understanding the concepts in such a way that the ones who find it more difficult to reason and understand the process of how to solve a problem can solve them by listening to their classmates. And this way, they all learn at the same time.

Within this educational context, it is also important to note that it is not possible to obviate the influence of e-learning on the growing interest in communities. In training platform classrooms conceived by some large companies or on the forums of some intranets it is relatively frequent to share the process of assimilation of new skills or new knowledge. In the sphere of secondary education, the use of learning communities as a training resource is becoming increasingly more frequent.

To conclude this characterisation, we should make it clear that learning communities are not reserved exclusively for teaching classrooms and education but can clearly be exported to organisational contexts. However, we should not forget that in these contexts too, the knowledge that is conveyed continues to be linked to concepts or subjects and not to "ways of doing". For example, the case may arise that a learning community emerges around a new IT tool that an organisation has acquired, and that a number of colleagues decide to help each other to learn how it works more quickly. It is clear that we are not speaking of communities of practice because there is not the desire to share experience or to tackle or solve some task or other, but the process of learning how to use new software. The learning community will end when all the members know how to use the new tool. If we remember the Wenger and Snyder article (2000), communities of practice are not bound to the end of a project or specific objective.

We will now go on to describe communities of interest. Just as the learning communities are largely linked to e-learning, the communities of interest are part of the heart of the Internet. Scientists were the first to use the Internet to share data, cooperate in research and exchange information. However, as of the second half of the 1990s, this use has extended to other interests. Certainly, without looking any further, the "fan" phenomenon has also been one of its greatest driving forces: rock fans, film buffs, avid readers, and so on. Today, the casuistries are infinite. From cancer patients who share how to face the effects of chemotherapy (the Hospital Clínico in Barcelona, Spain) is running an initiative that is as brilliant as it is valuable in this sense) to mothers' groups who share breastfeeding and ante-natal preparation techniques or information about nurseries and schools (as is the case, for example, on the forum of the *Crianza Natural Spanish* website), besides being able to buy childcare, breastfeeding, etc. products online.

Communities of interest share a common interest or passion. The interests may be as varied as the hobbies or casuistries of people. However, the common interest is not the professional practice and although they share techniques or ways of doing things, the common focus does not revolve around learning a specific aspect. Another of their distinctive characteristics, as defended by Amstrong, A. & Hagel, J. (2000), is the mutual lack of acquaintance between their members. Although face-to-face meetings of small groups between members belonging to the community are relatively frequent, it is more common for a member not to know the majority of their colleagues personally. It is even highly probable that they do not know any of them.

COMMUNITIES OF PRACTICE COMPARED WITH OTHER ORGANISATIONAL STRUCTURES

Up to now, we have introduced a general and intuitive definition of communities of practice and we have made a characterisation of some of the principal structures or groups, besides communities of practice, that are used by organisations to improve their strategies when meeting the objectives that they are pursuing. We will now make a comparative analysis between some of these organisational structures and communities of practice.

However, we are not going to make a comparative analysis between every single one of the structures described and communities of practice, but we are going to limit ourselves to comparing only those groups that, due to their special nature, may be confused with communities of practice: formal task groups, problem-solving teams, multidisciplinary teams, virtual teams, learning communities and communities of interest.

In order to complete this analysis, we are first going to extract a series of characterisation elements that will allow us to make a synthetic characterisation of all the organisational structures chosen and then present, in a more experiential form, a comparative analysis.

The characterisation elements that we will be using can be classed in two large general groups or categories: organisational elements (type of leadership, connection with the organisation's processes and cohesion factor) and practical implementation elements (size, virtuality, calendar of meetings, time limitation). All of these elements, with the occasional aid of some illustrative cases, will allow us later to identify clearly the differences and similarities between each one and so complete our comparative analysis.

Synthetic Characterization of Some Organizational Structures

We will begin by defining the formal group. These groups need conventional, recognised and active leadership. The task to be carried out is what keeps them together. It is one of the most numerous of the working groups, with between 13 and 16 people, because it is felt that the more members the better and the quicker they can complete the task if each member specialises in one thing. Virtuality is minimal in these groups and the pace of meetings is frequent. The groups will be kept together until the next company reorganisation.

On the other hand, the problem-solving team works more autonomously, and the leader delegates in the team or a team member. The team works until the problem is solved. To ensure its ability to solve and its agility, it is a good idea for these groups not to exceed 12 people, although 10 or fewer members is advised. Virtuality may be partial, yet at the same time it will be necessary to meet frequently, at least twice a week.

In the multidisciplinary team, as in the case of the problem-solving team, leadership is delegated in the actual team. The desirable number of members should be around 10 people. They can work virtually although they will need the face-to-face characteristic to meet frequently. And the achievement of the proposed objective, to solve a process, will be the end of the team.

On the other hand, in the virtual team, the project commissioned is the cohesion factor of its members, which they themselves lead. Virtuality enables communication with a larger number of people, overcoming space-time limitations, so virtual teams are usually bigger. Although it is probable that they need to meet from time to time, they can operate almost exclusively virtually. Its members will be affected by the next reorganisation, although virtuality fosters long-lasting work relationships.

For a learning community to work, by contrast, it is suitable to have the figure of an animator or moderator, as in the case of the communities of practice (Rubin, J. At al., 2014). What keeps its members together is the learning object and this disappears when they have learned what they were seeking to learn. The ideal number of members is between 20 and 25, which ensures that the contents are assimilated at more or less the same pace. It is not necessary to meet, as the community can work perfectly without the need for meetings

By contrast, communities of interest do not need any type of leadership, as it is the interest that moves their members. Each one gets out what they have come looking for, exchanges information, acquires the articles they need, etc. Moderation/animation makes no sense in this context. This type of community is very big in terms of number of members, they work entirely virtually and their members are a part of it for as long as they find a reason to be connected with it.

Finally, within this same synthetic layout, in communities of practice the role of the moderator/animator is vital to ensure their success. It is necessary for a member respected by the rest to control the interventions and the subjects proposed and to urge all the members to participate. In addition, in virtual communities of practice, moderators have an even more valuable role as they are responsible for organising the knowledge that is exchanged, saving the files that have been provided, summarising the contributions made, etc. It is a very similar mission to that of the moderator of learning communities. The cohesion factor is the desire to share professional practice, share their experience with other colleagues and benefit from the expertise of the others. This interest can last a lifetime because there will always be new things to learn and share, and the commitment of their members is too strong a bond. In order for the exchange of knowledge to be sufficiently rich, it is desirable for the number of participants to be considerable, between a minimum of 50 and a maximum of 80. Neither is it desirable for the number to be too big as it would then become an unmanageable community. If the CoPs are virtual, and it is desirable for them to be so – although we should not forget that there are also face-to-face communities of practice that are absolutely valid – they do not need face-to-face meetings at all.

Comparative Analysis

Once the synthetic characterisation of the organisational structures is complete, we are going to offer a comparative analysis of all of them and the communities of practice.

We will start with the similarities and differences between the formal task group and the communities of practice. As we have already said, these groups have an assigned fixed, highly specific task that they have to carry out. For example, a company's Human Resources Department will probably have more than one formal task group in operation: selection, hiring, payrolls, risk prevention, training. This very specific factor which may probably lead to a high level of specialisation is at the heart of a possible confusion between these groups and communities of practice, perhaps due to the level of skill that they may achieve. But not even these teams' own synergy, which will perhaps lead to confusion that is more difficult to untangle with regard to CoPs, occurs in this type of groups. This is because they are simply a group of people who work together every day on a set of continuous and interdependent tasks. Their duration as a team is totally dependent on the coming reorganisation and there is no commitment among them.

We will now compare problem-solving groups with communities of practice. One of the most common applications for problem-solving teams during the 1980s was quality circles. These are teams of 8 to 10 employees and supervisors who have a shared area of responsibility and who meet regularly to discuss problems, recommend solutions and take corrective actions. Described like this, many would consider this a CoP, as their respective definitions seem to coincide. But that is not the case. There are a number of clear characteristics, which we have described above that at first glance would not fit in: they have fewer members than CoPs, there is no clear leader which, unlike the communities of practice, these teams do not need and the time limitation that depends on problems being solved. However, the clearest element that sets them apart is the cohesion factor: the aim of the team is to solve one or more problems, in short, to achieve their aim. To do this, they meet as many times as necessary, but there is no desire to share their expertise nor is there any commitment with regard to other members of the group. The group's purpose is to solve the problem posed to them and once solved they will not maintain contact nor will they exchange information until there is a new problem to solve.

We will now look at the comparison between multidisciplinary teams and communities of practice. Many companies have used horizontal teams without frontiers for decades. For example, IBM created a huge temporary multidisciplinary team in the 1960s, which included employees from the different departments in the company to develop its highly successful *360 System*. Similarly, committees made up of members from all departmental lines are another example of a multidisciplinary team. These teams are clearly distinguished from communities of practice – as well as from the key factor of being a team they are motivated by a specific aim – in that their members do not belong to the same area of speciality. This makes it impossible to share their professional practice and, therefore in this sense, for an exchange of expertise to occur (Bashouri and Duncan, 2014).

The similarities and differences between learning communities and communities of practice, although fewer, are also clear. The frontier between communities of practice and learning communities is diffuse, but we feel that there is a factor that distinguishes them clearly. The former occur and are understood in the context of organisations or professions. In other words, they belong to everyday work, to everyday professional practice, hence the name community of practice. However, learning communities are confined to the teaching profession and the process of assimilating concepts and subjects, but there are a number of additional features that help us differentiate between them. As a result, for example, the difference in the number of members in learning communities is less than for CoPs and also, unlike communities of practice, learning communities come to an end when the target knowledge of the learning process has been acquired. Besides this, they coincide fully in the possibility of a total virtuality should there be a preference for face-to-face and also the need for a moderator/animator. As in the case of CoPs, this figure is vitally important to ensure the functioning of learning communities.

We will conclude this analysis by comparing communities of interest and communities of practice. Communities of interest share information and experiences and these may or may not be connected with professional practice. For example, at http://cnx.org professionals associated with education collaborate to share open educational resources and share news information concerning these resources. Also, http://eprints.reclis.org contains the first open content repository, specifically for libraries. These two examples are closely associated with the profession, but at no point do they go deeply into its knowledge or skill, but they do share information, news and resources. As we said above, communities of interest are clearly an Internet-derived product. This type of community only exists in a virtual sense and what usually occurs is that a members does not personally know the majority of their colleagues. It is even highly likely that they do not know any of them. This is in contrast to learning communities and communities of practice, where their members do know each other prior to the start of the community. However, one characteristic that communities of interest and communities of practice have in common is that the time limitation of these two types of community constitutes the end of the interest. Although these characteristics are long-lasting in the case of communities of interest, and interest is renewed. When one member stops connecting, it is very easy for a new member to appear.

SOME ILLUSTRATIVE CASES

Our exposition would be incomplete were we not to offer some cases that illustrate the ideas set out so far. To meet this objective, we are going to give a brief presentation of two Spanish cases that we feel to be paradigmatic with regard to the promotion and development of a community of practice: the cases of *La Caixa* and of *Repsol YPF*.

As we will see below, the case of "La Caixa" and the case of Repsol YPF are very different. In one, CoPs appear completely spontaneously from a good melting pot while in the other they are implemented in a much more guided way under a controlled system of objectives and associated incentives. It is clear that both cases are a success as we are speaking of two of the most powerful companies in Spain. However, in the case of Repsol YPF, we run the risk that by working by objectives we are losing sight of one of the principles that define communities of practice. What happens when these objectives have been attained? Does the CoP disappear? Should this be the case, we would surely no longer be speaking of a community of practice. It would be something else, perfectly valid and useful – just look at the results – but if we take into account all of the arguments that we have been defending throughout this chapter, the examples of communities shown by Repsol YPF are on a rather diffuse border.

La Caixa

The "Caixa d'Estalvis i Pensions de Barcelona" bank, known as "La Caixa", has undergone exponential growth over the last ten years, making it Spain's third largest bank.

In 2000, this bank found itself in the position of having to train a large number of employees to replace workers who had retired and to ensure expansion.

To carry out this training, it commissioned an expert e-learning company to create a virtual training platform. As a result, *VirtaulaCaixa* began offering training, with two trial virtual classrooms and 25 new employees. The model proved so successful that in 2004 more than 5,800 recent employees had received training through this new e-learning model.

As well as pedagogical innovation and participatory design methods, a determining factor of the success of the VirtaulaCaixa was the student support system, which was implemented using different media that had been specifically designed for the different communities taking part in VirtaulaCaixa: new employees, service managers, trainers and many more.

Students are, in fact, arranged into communities. New employees have two levels of participation in the community: their virtual classroom and the total community of new employees. In their virtual classroom, they have the support of two trainers, who are in charge of guiding them through the learning process. These new employees, however, also participate socially in VirtaulaCaixa enabling them to communicate with other work colleagues at the bank who are in the same situation (e.g. they have recently joined) and to share problems, opportunities and worries. In other words, participation in VirtaulaCaixa creates a community of new employees.

On many occasions, this community of new employees functions as a learning community depending on which point in the training they have reached. This outstanding custom of sharing the learning process, and overcoming difficulties together, creates an excellent melting pot from where future communities of practice can originate. By this, we do not mean that these learning communities become CoPs once these new employees are working to full capacity. Nowadays, this is impossible because once they have completed their training, they stop being part of the community of new employees and their reference framework becomes the area of business to which they belong. However, they retain that spirit of sharing and of community which favoured the growth of incipient communities of practice, as we shall explain below.

VirtaulaCaixa currently comprises four communities: Virtaula (the permanent training community for all "la Caixa" employees), New Employees (the online training environment for first-year employees), Trainers (the community of practice and learning for all "la Caixa" trainers) and Financial Services Manager (the training environment associated with the professional development programme for Financial Services Advisors).

The first community, Virtaula, is divided into different DANs (Business Area Management). Each DAN brings together a group of branches that belong to the same zone (county, district, neighbourhood, etc.). In each DAN there may be between 60 and 80 workers. Each business area manager has available the training actions that their employees receive. These actions are carried out through a forum where the different topics for discussion are proposed. A number of initiatives are created here by the area managers – in this particular case, women managers – who choose to promote and encourage employees to share their experiences. This is the case of the Hortaleza-Canillas DAN and the Aljarafe I DAN, where, under the slogan "we all learn from everyone", incipient CoPs have come into being.

Alongside the DANs are the E-groups. These are groups that do not correspond directly to a DAN and where knowledge about specialist subjects is exchanged. Both the DAN and the e-groups comment and discuss concepts related to professional banking practice. These concepts originate from small deliveries of teaching material called "pills" which are specific doses of training content. All employees have access to these pills through the library. This is a highly useful formula that is closer to the learning community than the community of practice. Whatever shape it takes, what is clear is that the spirit of mixing with others and of sharing, so creating a true social fabric of knowledge, flows through the Virtaula.

Repsol YPF

Repsol YPF is an oil company that is on the list of the world's 100 biggest companies. After the two original companies, Repsol and YPF, merged, its growth and expansion has been unstoppable, which has led to an exponential increase in workers who need to be trained and integrated. A lot of employees working on the same things on opposite sides of the world.

The oil company also has an award that is hard to achieve: that of recognition of the transparency of its website. For the third year running, the Repsol YPF website, www.repsolypf.com, has been the most valued of the Spanish Ibex-35 companies thanks to its transparency in the management of the contents of its European corporate website. It is evident that this points to a clear desire to systematise and standardise processes to the utmost. On it, one can find a huge amount of information about the company's structure, organisation and results.

Part of this desire to systematise and standardise is shown in the Knowledge Management model with the aim of knowing who does what and how they do it. Benefitting from the experience of so many employees and sharing it with the others. Combining both efforts and criteria. All of this is achieved through the communities of practice that they implement.

The Knowledge Management Model has two basic components: the human and organisational component (introduction of new organisational structures such as the Communities of Practice where objectives, indicators, Knowledge Maps, etc. are associated) and the processes / technology component (introduction of processes and technology that aid collaboration, enabling knowledge management).

The Knowledge Management programme is based on the operation of Communities of Practice. The main objective of the Communities of Practice is to generate mechanisms to share and collaborate in the acquisition, publication, search, retrieval and reuse of knowledge, improving the company's operating and general results.

Each of these communities brings together the specialists and people interested in a specific subject, based on a site in the company intranet, where they have information about the subjects relating to their activity (Canavan, Scott and Mangematin, 2013).

The Communities of Practice belonging to this knowledge management system are: Geosciences, Acquisition, quality control and log evaluation. (E-log), Safety and Environment (SyMA), Drilling and workover (Drilling), Well Stimulation (EP), Surface facilities (ISUP), Production, Maintenance of facilities (Maintenance) and Reservoirs

Each community is coordinated by a Manager, who is responsible for the community being formed, developing and continuing. They would be the equivalent of the moderator/animator. They lead the definition of objectives and organise and lead the general activities. Working with them is a Motor Team (which would be the equivalent of what we call animator/moderator), which helps the manager in defining the objectives and plans, and assumes the leadership in various functions of the community: communication, organisation of workshops, updating the site, leading teams in specific subjects or initiatives, etc. The remaining members participate as the Active Community, contributing their knowledge and reusing that of the others. The sponsor of the community is a management-level person, who keeps the community's initiatives in line with the interest of the business.

They also have face-to-face activities in the form of workshops, which bring together the active community, the motor group and the managers with the aim of sharing experiences, knowledge, problems solved and good practices, based on a predetermined subject area / problem.

There is a team in the Systems Department devoted exclusively to the requirements of the managers of the Communities of Practice and of the Knowledge Management Team. The Knowledge Management Team is interdisciplinary in nature, comprised of technology, humanistic careers and specific business professionals (Borzillo, Schmitt, Antino, 2012).

Besides this, Repsol YPF has a programme called Management by Commitment, which regulates the commitments undertaken by the employees, monitors their fulfilment and awards recognition. Knowledge Management is integrated with the Management by Commitment Programme, annually defining objectives related to knowledge management. This integration offers the opportunity to the people in charge of the communities of practice of being able to devote more time to them, empowering the results currently obtained.

The members of the communities (motors and managers) take part and undertake commitments with their day-to-day work voluntarily, becoming clear benchmarks of the behaviours of collaboration, cooperation, proactivity and excellence fostered and rewarded by Repsol YPF through Management by Commitment. They even receive recommendations on the percentage of time to devote to the CoP (15%) and to the motor teams (10%).

Participation and collaboration in the knowledge management initiatives are rewarded by the management through its Annual Recognitions Plan. In this plan, the behaviours that are rewarded are as follows: 1) Active participation in the community. 2) The contribution of experts and benchmarks. 3) Innovation and excellence in professional practice.

Actions to communicate the recognition to the whole of the company are carried out through letters to directors, publications on the intranet, newsletters and Technical Information Newsletter. The prizes range from attendance at congresses or on courses, suitcases up to objects of tangible value.

CONCLUSION

This study achieves two major objectives: firstly, it defines and characterizes communities of practice and, secondly, it establishes a comparison with other types of communities and organizational strategies that are often confused with the former. As previously stated, these strategies are absolutely valid and contribute to improving the operation of organizations.

"Communities of practice are a group of people who share the same activity or professional responsibility and, concerned about a shared problem or motivated by a common interest, heighten their knowledge and expertise in this field through ongoing interaction"[1] (Sanz-Martos 2010). Two elements distinguish communities of practice from other communities and work groups. Firstly, in order to share daily practice, members of the community must "share the same activity or professional responsibility"; secondly the interest (not the goal, given that we are talking about communities and not project groups or teams) is "to heighten knowledge or expertise through ongoing interaction".

The third conclusion is that the appropriate strategy to be applied or fostered depends on the organization's goal or interest. If the aim is to improve a process or solve a problem, then project teams should be used, as these are goal oriented and provide solutions to such issues. However, if the aim is, for instance, to learn how to use a new computer tool then a learning community should be developed to help members of the organization to work with the tool in a faster, more reliable way. And, finally, if the aim is to create greater cohesion in an organization, whereby members improve their daily practice, avoid duplicating processes and increase competitiveness, we should look to a community of practice.

Involvement of the HR department is crucial for the consolidation of communities of practice. Alignment of the community's interests with those of the organization is essential if the community of practice is to feel legitimized and that its activity is being recognized. If not, participation will be harmed and the community's continuity put at risk. This is where the change in organizational culture becomes so important. Only in this way, by boosting knowledge-sharing culture, will collaborative learning-based models be successfully adopted.

In this context, one of the challenges facing us is the need to progress in an area that still needs tackling: establishing the tangible benefits (the intangible ones are better known, as indicated throughout this study) provided by communities of practice to the organization, i.e. the return on investment (ROI). The little reticence that remains with regard to adopting this type of strategy in organizations would undoubtedly disappear if there were rigorous studies showing objective results for the ROI.

Finally, another issue topic for future study is the potential use of big data management techniques in organizations that have several communities of practice working at once. This would help detect almost automatically all new contributions and ideas that arise from the different communities. This very attractive way of accessing information at a given moment could be valuable, or even decisive.

These two aspects, added to the benefits described here, could accelerate the already growing trend of fostering communities of practice in both public and private institutions.

REFERENCES

Amstrong, A., & Hagel, J. (2000). The real value of online communities. In E. L. Lesser & M. Fontaine (Eds.), *Knowledge and communities* (pp. 85–98). Boston: Butterworth-Heinemann. doi:10.1016/B978-0-7506-7293-1.50009-3

Bashouri, J., & Duncan, G. (2014). Communities of practice: Linking knowledge management and strategy in creative firms. *The Journal of Business Strategy*, *35*(6), 49–57. doi:10.1108/JBS-08-2013-0072

Bond, M. A., & Lockee, B. B. (2014). *Building communities of practice for distance educators*. New York: Springer. doi:10.1007/978-3-319-03626-7

Borzillo, S., Schmitt, A., & Antino, M. (2012). Coomunities of practice: keeping the company agile. *Journal of Business Strategy*, *33*(6), 22-30.

Bronfman, V. S. (2002). Comunidades de práctica. Workshop. GEC S.A., Barcelona, Spain.

Brown, J. S., & Duguid, P. (1991). Organizational learning and communities of practice: Towards a Unified View of working, learning and innovation. *Organization Science*, *2*(1), 40–57. doi:10.1287/orsc.2.1.40

Canavan, D., Scott, P. S., & Mangematin, V. (2013). Creative professional service firms: Aligning strategy and talent. *The Journal of Business Strategy*, *34*(3), 24–32. doi:10.1108/JBS-10-2012-0058

Coll, C. (2001). Las comunidades de aprendizaje y el futuro de la educación: el punto de vista del forum universal de las culturas. Simposio Internacional Sobre Comunidades de Aprendizaje.

Coll, C. (2004). Una experiencia educativa con futuro. *Trabajadores de la enseñanza, 249*, 12-13. Retrieved February 2, 2009, from http://www.fe.ccoo.es/publicaciones/TE/249/249pdf

Else, S. (2003). Practicing Knowledge Communities. *Knowledge Management*. Retrieved February 2, 2009, from http://www.destinationkm.com/articles/default.asp?ArticleID=1044

Fisher, G. (2001). Communities of interest: learning through the Interaction of Multiple Knowledge Systems. In *Proceedings of the 24thIRIS Conference*. Ulvik, Departament of Information Science.

Gallo, G., & Yan, Ch. (2015). The Effects of Reputational and Social Knowledge on Cooperation. *Proceedings of the National Academy of Sciences of the United States of America*, *112*(12), 3647–3652. PMID:25775544

Glueck, M. (Ed.). (2006). *Work the Net: a Management Guide for Formal Networks*. New Delhi: GTZ.

González-Patiño, J. (2018). Learn, Teach and Share, Participation in Expanded Educational Communities: Madrid Pikler Seminar as a Practice of Continuing Education between Childhood Professionals. *Digital Education Review, 33.*

Gurteen, D. (2012). *Leading Issues in Social Knowledge Management. A collection of important Social Knowledge Management papers*. Academic Publishing International.

Hellriegel, D., & Slocum, J. W. (2008). Organizational Behavior (12th ed.). Cincinnati, OH: South-Western College Publishing (Thomson Learning).

Homana, G. (n.d.). Youth Political Engagement in Australia and the United States: Student Councils and Volunteer Organizations as Communities of Practice. *Journal of Social Science Education, 17*(1).

Hydle, K., Kvalshaugen, R., & Breuning, K. (2014). Transnational practices in communities of task and communities learning. *Management Learning*, *45*(5), 609–629. doi:10.1177/1350507613500881

Jenkins, H., Ito, M., & boyd, d. (2015). *Participatory culture in a networked era: A conversation on youth, learning, commerce, and politics*. Cambridge, MA: Polity Press.

Lave, J., & Wenger, E. (1991). *Situated Learning: Legitime Peripheral Participation*. Cambridge, UK: Cambridge University Press. doi:10.1017/CBO9780511815355

Lesser, E. L., & Storck, J. (2001). Communities of practice and organizational performance. *IBM Systems Journal, 40*(4). Retrieved February 2, 2009, from http://www.research.ibm.com/journal/sj/404lesser.html

Mc Dermott, R. (1999). Nurturing Three Dimensional communities of Practice: How to get the most out of human networks. *Knowledge management Review*. Retrieved February 2, 2009, from http://www.co-i-l.com/coil/knowledge-garden/cop/dimensional.shtml

McDermott, R. (1999). Why Information Technology Inspired But Cannot Deliver Knowledge Management. *California Management Review*, *41*(3), 103–117. doi:10.2307/41166012

Onrubia, J. (2004). Las aulas como comunidades de aprendizaje. *Trabajadores de la enseñanza, 249*, 14-15. Retrieved February 2, 2009, from http://www.fe.ccoo.es/publicaciones/TE/249/249pdf

Robbins, S. P. (2008). *Organizational Behavior* (13th ed.). Prentice Hall.

Rubin, J. (2014). The learning strategy prism: Perspectives of learning strategy experts. *System*, *43*(1).

Sanz, S. (2009). *Comunitats de pràctica o l'aprenentatge compartit*. Revista Guix.

Webber, E. (2018). *Building Successful Communities of Practice*. London: Tacit.

Wenger, E. (1998). *Communities of practice: Learning, meaning, and identity*. Cambridge, UK: Cambridge University Press. doi:10.1017/CBO9780511803932

Wenger, E., White, N., & Smith, J. D. (2009). *Digital Habitats: stewarding technology for communities*. Portland, OR: CPsquare.

Wenger, E., McDemortt, R., & Snyder, W. (2002). Cultivating Communities of practice. Boston: Harvard Business Scholl Press.

Wenger, E., & Snyder, W. (2000, January). Communities of practice: The organizational frontier. *Harvard Business Review*, 139–145.

KEY TERMS AND DEFINITIONS

Communities of Interest: Group of people who share a common interest or passion and exchange information, news and products with regard to it.

Communities of Practice: Group of people who perform the same professional activity or responsibility who, concerned with a common problem or moved by a common interest, expand their knowledge and expertise in this subject through ongoing interaction.

Formal Task Group: Group formed by workers responsible for a specific work task.

Learning Communities: Contexts in which the students learn thanks to their participation and involvement, in collaboration with other students, the teacher and other adults, in genuine processes of research and collective construction of knowledge on personal and socially relevant questions.

Multidisciplinary Team: Organizational structure formed by employees of the same hierarchical level but from different work divisions, who meet to carry out a task.

Problem-Solving Team: Organizational structure formed by workers who share ideas or offer suggestions on how to improve working processes and methods.

Virtual Team: Organizational structure formed by employees who use computational technology to bring together physically dispersed members with the aim of achieving a common objective.

ENDNOTE

1 Author's translation of "Las comunidades de práctica son un grupo de personas que desempeñan la misma actividad o responsabilidad profesional que preocupados por un problema común o movidos por un interés común profundizan en su conocimiento y pericia en este asunto a través de una interacción continuada".

APPENDIX

Table 1.

	Type of leadership	Cohesion factor	Size	Virtuality	Calendar of meetings	Time limitation
Formal Task Group (or functional team)	Formal	Task to carry out	13-16 per.	Minimal	Frequent	Until the next reorganisation
Problem-Solving Team	Delegated	Problem to solve	8-12 per.	Partial	Very frequent	Until the problem is solved
Multidisciplinary Team	Delegated	Processes to improve	8-12 per.	Partial	Very frequent	Until the process is improved
Virtual Team	Delegated	Task to carry out	15-30 per.	Total	Practically non-existent	Until the next reorganisation
Learning Community	Moderator/ animator	Learning	20- 25 per.	Total	Non-existent	Until the knowledge has been acquired
Community of Interest	________	Interest	100-500 per.	Total	Non-existent	While the interest lasts
Community of Practice	Moderator/ animator	Sharing professional practice	50-80 per.	Total	Non-existent	While the interest and the commitment of its members last

Chapter 22
Using Innovative Internal Communication to Enhance Employee Engagement

Karen Mishra
Campbell University, USA

Aneil K. Mishra
East Carolina University, USA

Khaner Walker
Lenovo, USA

ABSTRACT

This chapter examines the innovative internal communication practices of Lenovo, a $45 billion Fortune Global 500 technology company. In particular, this study examines how this company uses internal communication to promote collaboration and engagement across dispersed employees' teams. Internal communications (or internal marketing) is generally led by marketing or PR professionals with expertise in human resources, public relations, marketing, social media, and/or employee engagement. One new way that companies are extending internal communication is by extending its use of digital communication. Lenovo has been a leader in the use of social media at work and is now innovating its communications to include a mobile app. This chapter describes how Lenovo has developed both its intranet and its new mobile app and how innovative internal communication can promote engagement and collaboration.

INTRODUCTION

This chapter examines the internal communication practices of a Lenovo, a $45 billion multinational technology company. Lenovo has been a pioneer in building a digital workplace to maintain engagement with its workforce around the world. In 2012, Lenovo hired an internal communication executive, Nancy Liang, away from Cummins to create a company intranet to bridge its "east meets west" workforce. As a "born-global" company, Lenovo sought a way to communicate from the top to all of its employees simultaneously around the world.

DOI: 10.4018/978-1-5225-8516-9.ch022

This case study examines some of the challenges associated with internal communication in a global firm include geographic and cultural barriers, and cross-functional collaboration (Neill & Jiang, 2017). Liang worked to bridge those barriers by creating messaging in both English and Mandarin that originated from the top executive, and CEO Yang Yuanqing, known as "YY" by employees. This is important in today's global context as firms aim to interact and communicate with their home employees as well as those in their host countries where they operate (Molleda, 2009; Neill & Jiang, 2017).

The intranet that Nancy and her team created was built in partnership with Human Resources so that each person who used the internal messaging system was connected to the HR system, highlighting their title, location, contact information and connection to others in the corporate structure. This made it easier for their peers to keep track of where they were located and whom they were connected to. As Lenovo is an "employer of choice" this also helped employees keep track of colleagues who might have been poached by other employers, especially in China.

With many employees now working away from their desks, Lenovo is seeking a way to connect and communicate with them quickly and efficiently. Research by Konica (2017) shows that according to employees, one barrier to productivity is accessing data when away from their desks. Lenovo is attempting to remove the barriers of communication by creating a mobile app to disseminate company information for employees on the go. After having success with its global intranet, Khaner Walker, the new Director Global Internal & External Communications at Lenovo, wants to find a way to reach all employees, regardless of where they work. He believes that the mobile app will improve both connectivity and productivity.

Despite attempts to create a digital workplace, functional silos still appear to be a barrier to effective implementation of integrated marketing communication (Kitchen, Spickett Jones, & Grimes, 2007; Ots & Nyilasy, 2015). This is especially true of internal and external communication (i.e. marketing and corporate communication) as well as human resources. (Neill & Jiang, 2017). In addition, enterprises of the future will rely more on the virtual organization in which communication spans multiple boundaries: Trust is crucial in order for that digital communication to be well received (Te'eni, 2001). This article will highlight the internal communication (internal comms) strategies of Lenovo and explore how they can build employee engagement, collaboration and trust.

LITERATURE REVIEW

The Role of Internal Communication

As integrated marketing communications has been developed and accepted (Schultz, Tennenbaum & Lauterborn, 1992), there has been debate about whether or not IMC should be the primary responsibility of advertising, marketing, or public relations (Smith, 2013). As IMC continues to flourish and gain acceptance, one piece of the IMC puzzle is rarely discussed: internal communications (e.g., internal public relations, internal marketing).

Lauterborn (2004) defined inward marketing as a focus on employees, stating that organizations must consider their employees as their first stakeholders when preparing this integrated plan. Internal public relations (or internal communications) recognize that employees are an important and distinct public (Mishra, Boynton & Mishra, 2014). By including employees as a distinct public or stakeholder in a marketing communications plan, an organization will build trust with employees through open and honest communications as well as harness their enthusiasm and commitment to the organization with other stakeholders (Mishra, 2007). Gronstedt (2000) found that firms that integrate communications are better able to communicate their values and brand promises to customers, which in turn ultimately improves the reputation of those firms.

The final piece of the IMC puzzle, internal public relations (or internal communications), is quickly becoming a priority due to the growth of company intranets (Mishra, Mishra & Walker, 2016). The practice of internal communication can enhance an organizational culture by promoting employee engagement through open communication (Cahill, 1995; Deloitte, 2013; Harrison, 2013; Men & Stacks, 2014). Research has consistently argued for and empirically found that greater sharing of information by the organization serves to enhance employee empowerment, including a greater sense of impact on the organization and a greater sense of meaning (Mishra, & Spreitzer, 1998; Spreitzer & Mishra, 1999; Siegall & Gardner, 2000; Mills & Ungson 2003). Similar arguments and findings exist for the positive effect of communication within an organization on employee engagement (Kress, 2006; Saks, 2006; Rockland, 2014). In fact, a recent survey by PWC found that 20% of engagement by employees occurs as a result of the company's internal communications (Rockland, 2014). Welch & Jackson (2007) also identified internal communication as crucial for achieving employee engagement. A 2007/2008 Watson Wyatt study found that "Firms that communicate effectively are four times as likely to report high levels of employee engagement as firms that communicate less effectively." Most recently, a Deloitte culture survey (2013) found that 50% of employees feel that "regular and candid communication" leads to a "culture of meaningful purpose."

The Role of Leadership Communication

Leaders play an important role in communicating the brand promise to all stakeholders, including employees (Vallaster & de Chernatony, 2002). Recent research confirms that authentic and transparent leadership communication leads to employee engagement, trust, and collaboration (Men & Stacks, 2014). A Watson Wyatt (2008-2009) study found that those strategies that engage employees include communication from managers, leadership communication, and a focus on internal communication. In fact, the most effective brand building efforts emphasize the importance of employees in transmitting information from company leadership to external stakeholders (Vallaster & de Chernatony, 2002). D'Aprix (2009) concluded that organizational leaders have lost credibility with external stakeholders because they have not been truthful with employees about a variety of issues that impact the company and its customers. However, employees are more willing to take on the role of brand ambassador when they understand and trust brand information from the top (Vallaster & de Chernatony, 2002).

The Role of Trust

Effective internal communication can improve the trust between employees and management within an organization (DeBussy, Ewing & Pitt, 2003; Gavin & Mayer, 2005; Zeffane, Tipu, & Ryan, 2011) by widely sharing information, and by building engagement and commitment. In one study (Robson & Tourish, 2005), employees identified a need for more internal communications, including face-to-face meetings, more openness, greater listening, improved email communication, more appreciation, an improved newsletter, and communications training in order to empower and engage employees. Often, however, top managers feel that communication with external constituents is more important than communication with internal ones (Therkelsen & Fiebich, 2003). A more recent study of retail employees (Mishra & Boynton, 2009) found that those managers that take time for face-to-face meetings, to listen, and to provide feedback for employees on a regular basis, build strong trusting relationships with those employees who in turn have feelings of loyalty to both the local retail establishment and the larger corporate entity, as well.

Employee Engagement

Employee engagement is defined as "the degree to which an individual is attentive and absorbed in the performance of his or her role (Saks, 2006, p. 602)". In the management literature, this "discretionary effort" is also known as organizational citizenship behavior (OCB), behavior that is both non-rewarded and discretionary, or above and beyond what is expected of the employee (Yankelovich & Immerwahr, 1983; Organ, 1988). A recent study found that employee engagement is positively impacted by employer branding, leading to greater employee discretionary effort (Piyachat, Chanongkorn & Panisa, 2014). In fact, a greater emphasis on internal branding can lead to creating highly engaged employees, or brand ambassadors within a company (Asha & Jyothi, 2013). To ensure maximum success in the organization, the values of both the organization and the employee should match (Asha & Jyothi, 2013). In fact, 72.5% of discretionary effort was explained by such a match (Asha & Jyothi, 2013). Engaged employees as brand ambassadors can positively influence the reputation of the company through their use of social media (Dreher, 2014). Customers trust that employees are credible and authentic spokesmen (and women) of their companies, which allows their messages to gain traction (Dreher, 2014). Employees increasingly rely on digital communication both inside and outside of the organization to understand and share their firm's brand promise.

The Digital Workplace

With over one-third of employees working remotely (Pendell & Dvorak, 2018), it is critical for companies to figure out how to maintain a culture of open communication with their employees, regardless of where they work. It is crucial for companies to create an effective digital workplace culture (Pendell & Dvorak, 2018) in order to ensure all employees are receiving the most timely and accurate information about their companies.

Research in the use of digital technology at work has found that mobile technology is the driving force behind what is now being referred to as the "Digital Workplace" (Corbin, 2016). This makes it easier for internal comms professionals to reach employees in new ways and in new places. Mobile technology that is within an arm's reach of us and that is accessible 24/7 not only enables internal comms professionals to access employees who may not always be sitting at their desks, but it may also foster communication that fosters greater collaboration as well.

In addition to employees' use of social media to interact with customers, companies can use it to promote collaboration among employees. A recent study examined how social media can enhance the way companies build an engaged workforce (Towers Watson, 2013). It found that only 56% of companies are using social media to build a sense of community with its workforce, such as sharing information with employees about culture, teambuilding or innovation (Towers Watson, 2013). The Towers Watson study also found that only 23% of organizations are effective at building a shared experience with their remote workforce (Towers Watson, 2013). Web 2.0 technologies, such as an intranet, allow a firm to connect employees, customers, and partners (Lee, 2011). Only 45% of companies surveyed actually use such a site and of those, just less than 35% found them effective (Towers Watson, 2013). Increasingly, companies are developing intranets and other types of internal social media in order to keep employees apprised of the internal communications of the organization (Nakata, Zhu & Izberk-Bilgin, 2011).

The Role of a Company's Internal Communications

One benefit of an internal communications effort, such as a company intranet, is to allow for two-way communication with employees (Lipiainen, Karjaluoto & Nevalainen, 2014), such as getting and giving feedback and ideas. In addition, a global company has the added challenge of communicating with employees regardless of their location (Lipiainen, Karjaluoto & Nevalainen, 2014) in a way that respects not only corporate culture, but also ethnic culture. One reason global communications fail is that managers are not aware of "local sensitivities" (Mounter, 2003: p. 268). Khaner Walker, Director of Global Internal and External Communications at Lenovo, noted that in the eastern part of the world, an employee values community and leadership, so they want updates from their direct manager in order to show respect and ensure full alignment, but some managers aren't equipped to deliver updates. This is where the intranet can help augment a manager's ability to share information across the organization (Lee, 2011).

Ruppel & Harrington (2002) found that "intranet implementation is facilitated by a culture that emphasizes an atmosphere of trust and concern for other people (ethical culture), flexibility and innovation (developmental culture), and policies, procedures and information management (hierarchical culture)". Effective internal comms can also engage employee to share company information as brand ambassadors.

Employees as Brand Ambassadors

Finally, a focus on internal comms signals that employees are important stakeholders with equal access to information. A study of consultants by Su & Contractor (2011) found that "the organizational intranets contained both tacit (e.g., skill learning, sales and marketing) as well as explicit (e.g., articles, deliverables, and policies) information." When employees are encouraged to participate in that communication, they are more committed to their brand (Gelb & Rangarajan, 2014). Those networks build trust, which in turn build trust and credibility for the brand (Gelb & Rangarajan, 2014). The Towers Watson study (2013) concurred, finding that "remote workers are looking for clear communication, integrity and coaching from their managers."

In addition to improving information sharing, intranets and other internal comms efforts are also ways to improve social capital as well. One recent study found that intranets are especially important for socializing new employees into an organization as well as serving as an organizational knowledge tool to retain employees (Chu & Chu, 2011). Specifically, Chu & Chu (2011) found that "the newcomers' adoption of intranet techniques has significant effects on socialization regarding how well they master their job, define their role, learn about their organization's culture and goals, and become socially integrated (p. 1175)." Radick (2011) noted a change in the use of intranets, "Whereas the intranet used to be focused on connecting people to information, it's now about connecting people to people."

Heather noted that their internal communications efforts, both electronic and face-to-face, should be transparent and trustworthy:

People can see through corporate BS. If it's got that tone, (then) they're not really saying what they mean, – so it's just important to be as plainspoken as you can and to be as transparent as you can. I know a lot of organizations try to hold information back and think 'oh, we're not ready to say that', but to the extent that you can give away as much as you know, it will go a long way towards creating that climate of trust.

In addition, it is not just Heather's team that has this responsibility, but the executive leadership, such as Chairman Yang Yuanqing (or YY, as he is called) at Lenovo that has this responsibility: "That's how you gain trust: your leaders go out there face-to-face, and be as visible and as open to taking questions as they can. They should provide as much information as they feel they can without compromising the business (H. Lowe, personal communication, May 5, 2013)."

Finally, when employees feel committed to the brand, they are more likely to positively engage with customers, which also builds brand equity (Gelb & Rangarajan, 2014). Employees have a wide reach beyond customers, however, and can positively impact prospective customers, prospective employees, and the general public (Gelb & Rangarajan, 2014) through open communication and positive collaboration.

RESEARCH QUESTION

This exploratory study of internal communication professionals and their internal customers seeks to understand the role of internal communications in a multinational technology company with locations around the globe. This study focuses on the role of the company intranet and mobile app in its internal communications strategy to share information, foster employee engagement and collaboration, and facilitate brand ambassadorship for Lenovo. This study used exploratory, semi-structured interviews conducted with managers responsible for public relations and/or internal communication at their firm (see interview questions in Appendix I), as well as employees who utilize the company intranet on a daily basis (see interview questions in Appendix II).

METHOD

The first and second author and a research assistant conducted all interviews in person. Each conversation was recorded, transcribed, and analyzed to understand how and what executives think about internal communications at Lenovo. Eight Lenovo executives participated in this study. Four of the participants work in internal communications for Lenovo at the headquarters in Morrisville, North Carolina. Five executives, also located at the North American headquarters in Morrisville, North Carolina, use the intranet on a daily basis; two from the accounting department and two from inside sales, and one from business insights. A snowball technique was used in obtaining interview subjects for this study. One of the accountants is an MBA student of the first author and referred the first author to the second accountant. The inside sales executives were both alumni of the first author's university. Another Lenovo executive introduced the business insights executive to the second author. This was appropriate for this study because some degree of trust is helpful between the researcher and the interviewee to understand their role in internal communication (Atkinson & Flint, 2001).

The interview questions for the internal communications staff specifically asked how they execute internal communications at Lenovo (see Appendix 1). The interview questions for the other executives asked how they feel internal communications are accessible and useful to them at Lenovo (see Appendix 2).

The interviews were conducted asking about internal communications in general, to understand Lenovo's best practices.

INTERVIEW FINDINGS

The internal communication executives interviewed for this study are:

1. Nancy Liang, Executive Director - *Global Corporate Strategy & Planning*
2. Khaner Walker, Director Global Internal & External Communications
3. Kelly Reid, Senior Global Communications & Content Strategist
4. Heather Lowe, Senior Communications Manager

The other executives interviewed for this study are:

1. Kim Marut, North America Balance Sheet Lead Accountant
2. Marian Lakin, Monetization Controller
3. Joanna Still, Inside Sales Rep
4. Stephanie Mack, Inside Account Manager
5. Susan Moore, Web Operations/Business Insights

The primary theme that emerged from these interviews is how internal communications practices impacts employee engagement, trust and collaboration.

RESULTS

Lenovo's Success With Its Internal Communications

Khaner Walker is the Director of Global Internal and External Communications at Lenovo in Raleigh, North Carolina. One of his primary roles is to support many different departments via the internal communications function. Through his extensive background, MBA from UNC's Kenan-Flagler School of Business, and work experience in journalism and public relations, Khaner has a unique vision for how *Lenovo Central* as well as other internal comms efforts can provide timely, accurate, and critical content for employees across the globe. His goal is "to grow *Lenovo Central's* reach and usefulness for employees, along with enabling more interaction with employees (social postings on their own "wall," creating their own image galleries, etc.)." He has found that the more *Lenovo Central* grows, the more competitive and creative each department head becomes in getting out the most interesting content on their particular site within *Lenovo Central*. Khaner's previous work experience has proven to be an extremely effective preparation for seeking out important information for Lenovo employees to know about and then translate that information in a way that is timely, accurate, and compelling (K. Walker, personal communication, January 18, 2013; March 30, 2018).

Nancy Liang, *Executive Director - Global Corporate Strategy & Planning* at Lenovo (N. Liang, personal communication, June 28, 2013), was previously Khaner's boss. She came to Lenovo with a Harvard MBA and six years of experience at Cummins, where she was Director of Internal Communications. At the time of the study, she lead the team of six employees for the $39 billion company, who do most of the work in communicating news to all Lenovo employees around the globe, including *Lenovo Central.* Nancy has since been promoted recently to the Strategy & Planning team at Lenovo. Her personal philosophy for internal communications at Lenovo is PCPC: People, Content, Process, Channel. She set the path that internal comms still follows.

In terms of *People,* it is important to Nancy that 1) messages are sent to the right set of stakeholders; and that 2) messages are sent from the correct manager. When it has been decided that a message will come directly from the top, Nancy is insistent that decisions are deliberately made to send messages from either Chairman and CEO Yang Yuanqing's company email or his personal email, depending on the message and the target audience. This is critical, as research has found that CEOs believe that communication coming directly from the top positively influence "employees' feelings towards work and the organization's bottom line (Pincus, Rayfield & Cozzens, 1991, p. 27)." Recent research by the Edelman Trust Barometer (2014) confirms that "trust in the person leading the company is inextricably linked with trust in the company itself."

Nancy confirmed that this is true for Lenovo and for Chairman and CEO Yang Yuanqing, as well. When speaking to a class of MBA students at Meredith College in Raleigh, North Carolina (N. Liang, personal communication, October 28, 2013), she remarked that "YY", as she calls him, "reads everything that is on *Lenovo Central*". She said that this confirms for her and for her team that what they do is of utmost importance for the company. In addition, any new information or announcement coming from one of his senior vice presidents, YY wants on *Lenovo Central* within 24 hours of them speaking or writing about it (N. Liang, personal communication, October 28, 2013).

One of her team members, Kelly Reid, was senior manager of global internal communications. Kelly's job was to manage and curate content for *Lenovo Central* (K. Reid, personal communication, May 5, 2013). As far as *Content*, Kelly said that, "we know who our audience is for the most part. It's the 30,000 Lenovo employees around the world." Nancy feels, however, that it is important to craft the message in just the right way for the audience it is intended for. For instance, it is critical to know your audience and whether the message should be in English or Mandarin or both. Kelly agreed, saying that "the most effective way to communicate a message to people of many languages is by combining art and copy, so it's in a poster form." Kelly added that, "I think the biggest challenge because it's the most important challenge is asking the question 'why are we sending this. Why are we communicating this to the audience?'"

When Nancy is strategizing about *Process*, her team gathers, curates, writes, produces, and monitors the information that is posted on *Lenovo Central.* This includes financial information, interviews, photos from events, links to articles written about Lenovo, and monitoring the mechanism to encourage employees to co-create content, as well. Her team also works with each department at Lenovo to make sure that their own portals are up-to-date and useful for their own teams. Khaner mentioned that he is finding that department heads are becoming more competitive with each other in the content that they publish, wanting to make sure that they are putting forth their best effort.

The most important *Channel* her team communicates through is *Lenovo Central*, where information is available 24/7. This channel comes complete with a new news banner that changes each day, a photo gallery, a video gallery from around the world, and a place on *Lenovo Central* for events, such as a recent London fashion show or the Chairman's CCTV award. There is also a spot on the front page of *Lenovo Central* where employees can co-create content by updating news themselves and share it with fellow employees. This is critical for helping employees feel like they are an important part of creating and building the Lenovo culture. Heather, Senior Manager Internal Communications mentioned that ideally, they are looking for employees to contribute more to this social media presence: "We're moving towards a social media-based system, where no one person has the burden of creating content. It's crowd-sourced, meaning everybody is feeding in his or her view of the organization into one central hub. It's built piece by piece instead of a team of five or seven people churning out masses of content for the rest." Kelly also stressed the importance of adding content to *Lenovo Central* for employees:

The most effective way to create a lasting message is by putting it on Lenovo Central, which has the news section and the community section, and having the person go and find it and read it. Because they discovered it on their own…we're trying to move away from email communications and start to build a sense of discovery on Lenovo Central.

This social media aspect of *Lenovo Central* allows employees to share information internally. They can post to their "wall" and share news and updates, which also helps fellow employees see how users are connected back to the up-to-date HR directory so that everyone can see who they are, whom they work for, and where they work in the organization.

One other important channel Lenovo uses is its *annual Kickoff event* in April where Chairman and CEO Yang lays out the strategic plan for the year so that employees are kept informed on the mission and vision of the company. Chairman and CEO Yang and his top executives meet with employees in three places around the world to make sure that everyone has an opportunity to be involved. Top managers share messages about the strategic plan, the Lenovo brand, and the new Lenovo products.

The newest channel introduced by the internal comms teams is a new mobile app, LC Lite, which is available on the Google Play Store. As employees are more dispersed in their work, companies need to keep up with them by offering timely communications where they are. A recent Gallup study found that 31% of employees say that they work remotely 80-100% of the time (Dvorak & Pendell, 2018). This is problematic for firms who rely on face-to-face or paper communication. Khaner created the mobile app to address this issue. In addition, he is hoping it will reduce the number of unnecessary emails employees end up ignoring and help them focus on what is important to them.

We definitely realized people have gone mobile,– that was our next evolution. So we don't care really where you access it (company information). Whether it's on the web or on the mobile app. I think it will also just help us stop sending so many emails. When you log into the app you can subscribe to a specific newsfeed. So if I'm a North America PCSD PC person I can sign up for A, North America news, and I can sign up for B, PC news. So it can be much more specific and individualized to you. You know, John Doe in finance. Sally Mae in H.R. If you get more focused then that means I think it would cut away at least 30% of the emails that I send or just the Comms team sends. That means there will (also) be more focus when we do have an email from YY.

Figure 1. Screenshot of Lenovo Central homepage
Note. Screenshot from "Lenovo Central". Copyright 2018 by Copyright Holder. Reprinted with permission.

Figure 2. Screenshot of Lenovo Central employee wall
Note. Screenshot from "Lenovo Central". Copyright 2018 by Copyright Holder. Reprinted with permission.

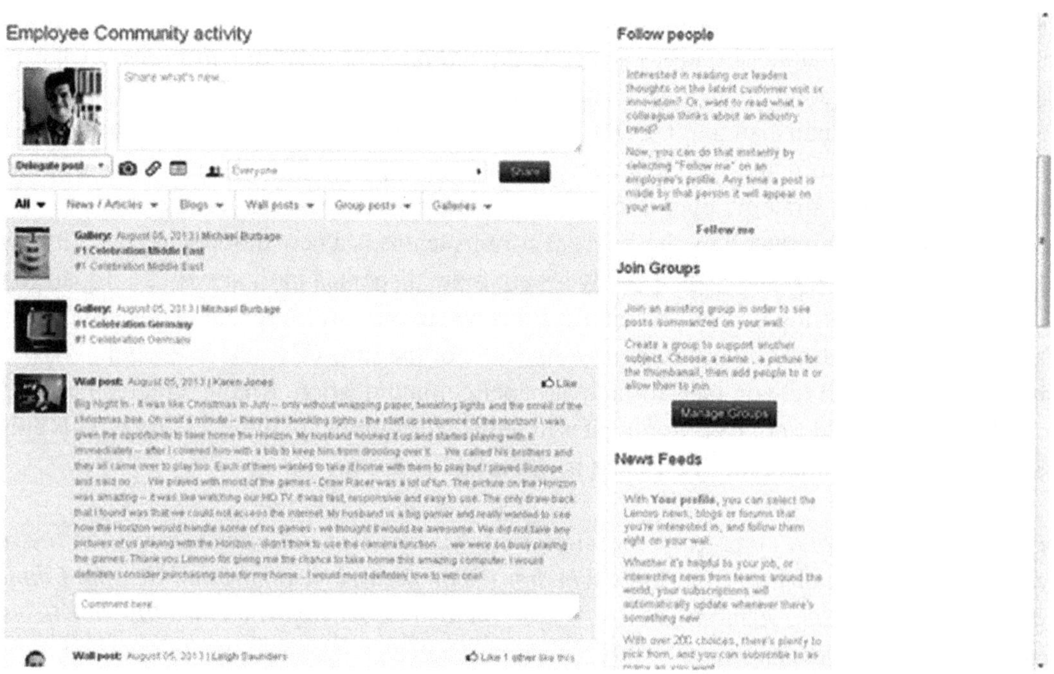

It is important to understand how all internal comms efforts impact its intended audience, as well. For example, the accounting employees use *Lenovo Central* to get up-to-date information they need on employees from all over the world. When Kim, an accounting manager, needs an organizational chart for a group in China, she knows she can count on *Lenovo Central* to have the most current information (K. Marut, personal communication, February 26, 2013). This was particularly critical for her during a restructuring when people were moving to new positions, or especially in China, where people frequently leave the company for new positions. Toni, an accounting manager, also noted that this is critical because then she can rely on *Lenovo Central* to give her the most up-to-date information rather than rely on rumors, which are not necessarily accurate (A. Lakin, personal communication, March 15, 2013). Toni noted that *Lenovo Central* is also very good at keeping her apprised of senior level changes in the organization. The one thing Toni would change about *Lenovo Central* would be for it to keep better track of lower-level moves, as her department regularly deals with folks from all levels of the organization, all over the world.

The sales function also values *Lenovo Central*. Joanna and Stephanie are both inside sales reps at Lenovo. They value this as something that helps keep them "in-the-loop". They find it up-to-date and organized. While they don't know who is behind *Lenovo Central*, they are impressed nonetheless at how timely the information is that they can rely on. This is especially important for them because their bosses are not always available on-site to provide them with this timely information in a face-to-face manner. They know that they have access to company information regardless of whether or not they are able to meet with their supervisor on a regular basis to get company and employee information directly (J. Still, personal communication, March 15, 2013; S. Mack personal communication, March 20, 2013).

Challenges With Internal Communications

Some of the employees noted that while they appreciate Lenovo Central, they have no idea who is in charge of it or any of the internal communications they receive. This might be a problem if those employees need to utilize the intranet to share information themselves throughout the company and don't know the official channels and/or people to go through to share that information. While the internal communications staff works hard behind the scenes, there might be an opportunity to be more visible to the employees whom they are there to help.

Susan Moore shared that there is an opportunity to improve internal communications overall at Lenovo. She wondered, "How can we communicate better with one another? Many times we hear from people after the fact saying, "Oh, I was not aware of this." And it just creates kind of a bit of a churn. I absolutely feel that, with the size of our organization and that we're not all geographically located in one location, we find a better communication path so that we can keep people apprised of things and engaged. Because you can push out information; but you need to make certain you've got that closed loop."

Another challenge is communicating ethnic and/or cultural teachings through internal communications efforts. A couple of the employees interviewed expressed a desire for more exposure and communication around global culture to help them better understand how different cultures operate in the locations where Lenovo operates. They noted that since people are the core of the company, working all over the globe, it is important to understand those cultures because of who they are and where they're from.

The Larger Role of Internal Communications at Lenovo

Khaner Walker, Global Director of Internal and External Communications, summed up what he thinks is the role that *Internal Comms* ultimately plays within Lenovo and in evangelizing the Lenovo brand. He also articulated his new vision for a mobile workforce including his new mobile app.

I think our Intranet has had a key role in Lenovo's transformation from a PC company, to what we call a PC+ company (tablets, smartphones, data centers, etc.). This has been a major, substantive shift for Lenovo, considering our deep legacy in PCs from both Lenovo and IBM PC, and how our employees have enjoyed a considerable amount of success just from Lenovo's growing PC business.

We use the Intranet, LC Lite, digital displays, and more to go beyond the strategy Yuanqing (our CEO) lays out on a PowerPoint slide – we bring it to life in a way employees can understand, see for themselves, and ultimately embrace.

The company's continued, successful transformation from a one business / PC business model to a multi-business model, relies on an engaged, motivated, and supportive employees. Internal Communications plays a critical role in aligning the company on this strategy, in boosting employee morale, and so much more. Our focus continues to be on finding the right channels and the right types of content that will engage our employees the most.

Our move to a digital-first strategy for the stories we draft and videos and podcasts we produce, is being underpinned by analytics that inform what types of content we create, for which situations, and which channels. Our goal for Internal Communications at Lenovo is to create an Employee Engagement score and dashboard that each of our teams can access and use, and in doing so be among a handful of companies leading EX (employee experience).

DISCUSSION AND CONTRIBUTIONS

Lenovo is a global company: is it possible for other multi-national corporations to incorporate its best practices in internal communication, engagement and collaboration? There are some key takeaways.

1. **Make Daily Communication a Priority:** Even though top executives are busy, lower level employees crave information about the company, the strategy, and their fellow employees. Making information available (such as on a company intranet) prevents rumors and false information from taking over. Even when you as the manager don't have time to spend in daily face-to-face conversations with employees, an intranet can help fill in the information gaps. In addition, the more positive information employees have at their disposal, the better brand ambassadors they can be for the company when friends and neighbors ask about your brands and services.
2. Establish one global language for the company to use so that everyone knows what to expect and how to receive internal communication messages. This helps to create a consistent message and

Figure 3. Lenovo Mobile app screenshot
Note. Screenshot from "Lenovo Mobile app". Copyright 2018 by Copyright Holder. Reprinted with permission

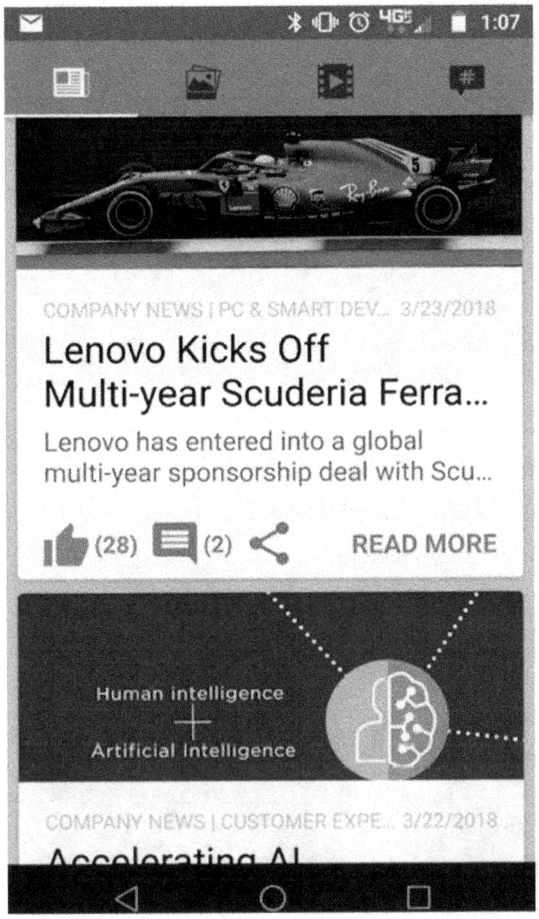

delivery, as well. However, organizations should be flexible in their use of language, and consider incorporating a second key language, to keep all employees engaged in other parts of the world to avoid any major misunderstandings

3. **Share Cultural Information as Well as Company Information**: As organizations become more global in its employees and operations, it should find ways to help employees learn about what is culturally important and relevant about all employees in order to them in order to increase their personal understanding of each other. This will help employees learn to appreciate the background and experience of fellow team members who work in other locations.
4. **Create a Dynamic Communications Vehicle:** (Such as a company intranet or daily email digest) to disseminate messages in a timely and interesting way to all employees. Make sure that this is a two-way communications vehicle, not just a one-way tool. Employees will feel more engaged if they have the opportunity to participate in and co-create communication efforts. If this is a two-way communications vehicle, employees will be more likely to remain engaged and utilize this as much as or more than email.

Figure 4. Lenovo Mobile app screenshot
Note. Screenshot from "Lenovo Mobile app". Copyright 2018 by Copyright Holder. Reprinted with permission

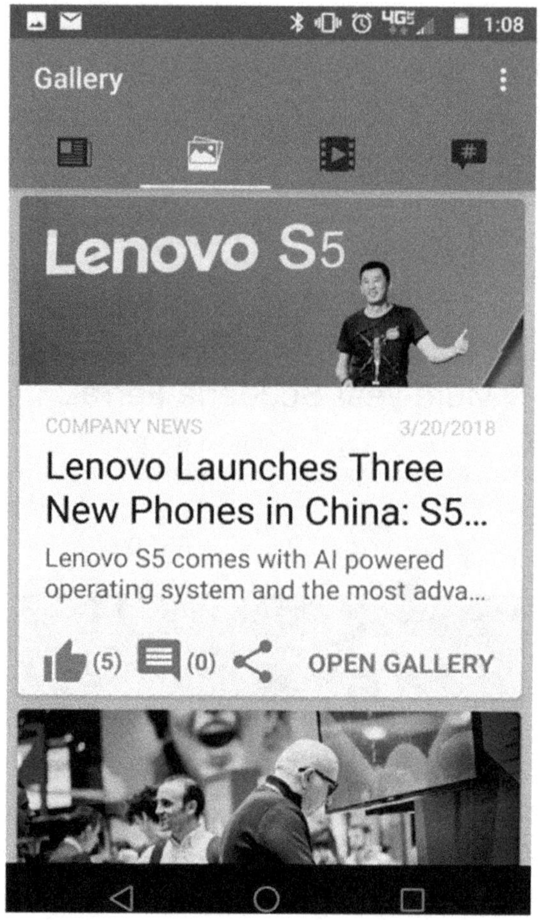

5. Partner with HR to make sure that the HR directory is up-to-date and is tied into the communications system. This can help facilitate the exchange of timely and accurate information among a directory of global employees, as well as help build important relationships across cultural and country boundaries.
6. Let employees know who the internal communications team is. The team should be accessible to all employees so that they know who they can go to for up-to-date information as well as who can help them share new information with their colleagues.
7. **Share Brand Strategy:** By sharing strategic information with your employees, you can engage them in the vision of the company, its products, and the future direction of the company so that they become brand ambassadors for your company. Year after year, the Edelman Trust Barometer (2013; 2014) finds that consumers trust information from "someone like me" more than they trust information from traditional advertising. If your employees share brand information that they learn from the intranet, it will be much more powerful than any advertising campaign.

Figure 5. Lenovo Mobile app screenshot
Note. Screenshot from "Lenovo Mobile app". Copyright 2018 by Copyright Holder. Reprinted with permission

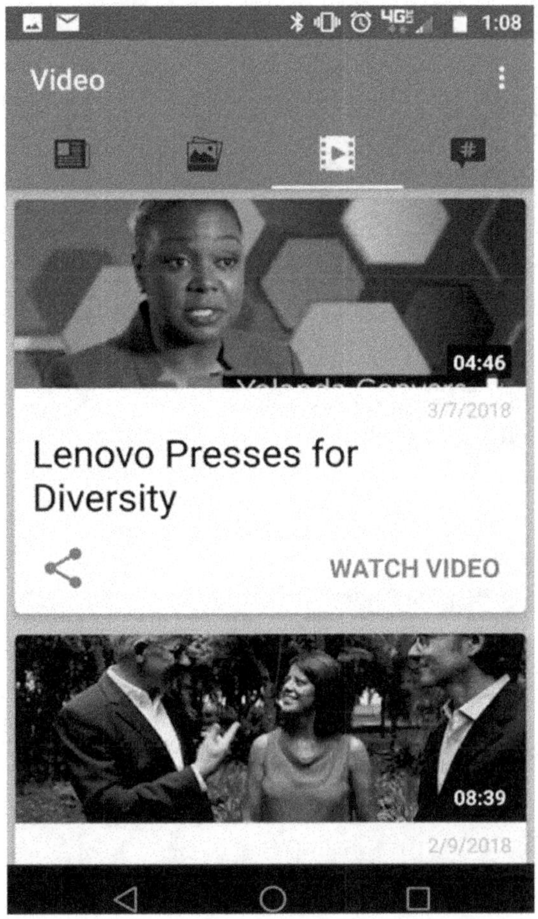

8. **Continually Innovate:** Now that employees are working remotely more often and travel just as much, you need to have a communications strategy that travels with your employees. Lenovo's new mobile app is one way for employees to take Lenovo news and updates along with them wherever they are (Gallup, 2018). Khaner's idea for a new podcast series is another innovation to keep employees educated as they travel (Figure 7).

FUTURE RESEARCH DIRECTIONS

Companies like Lenovo represent a "best practice" in internal communications. Future research should study how many other Fortune Global 500 companies are actually using internal communications such as an intranet or mobile app in their own firms to allow employees to be kept up-to-date on all internal and external matters about their firm. In addition, future research should consider whether colleges are preparing future executives for this role in companies. Internal communications is a relatively new role in corporate communications, which may be why there are relatively few executives suited to take on

Figure 6. Lenovo Mobile app screenshot
Note. Screenshot from "Lenovo Mobile app". Copyright 2018 by Copyright Holder. Reprinted with permission

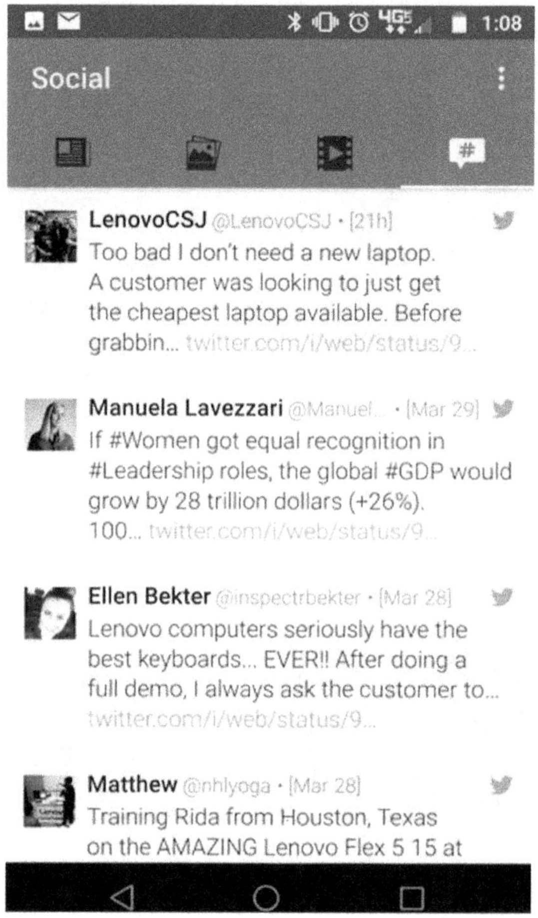

this new challenge. Finally, future research should address whether or not Fortune Global 500 internal comms are doing what Lenovo is doing, sharing its internal communications in two languages, when this company has headquarters in both Beijing and North Carolina. The former Director of Global Internal Communications, who is now *Executive Director - Executive Assistant to Chairman & CEO*, speaks both Mandarin and English, which makes her uniquely qualified to manage internal comms in both languages. How many other companies are thinking globally when they are developing their internal communications department? Or is English the dominant language of business?

CONCLUSION

As a global technology leader, Lenovo is also leading the way in developing world-class employee communications. Designed to bridge cultures and languages, Lenovo internal communications strategies ensures that employees get up-to-date information about their colleagues and their company. Lenovo also

Figure 7. Lenovo Podcast screenshot
Note. Screenshot from "Lenovo Podcast". Copyright 2018 by Copyright Holder. Reprinted with permission

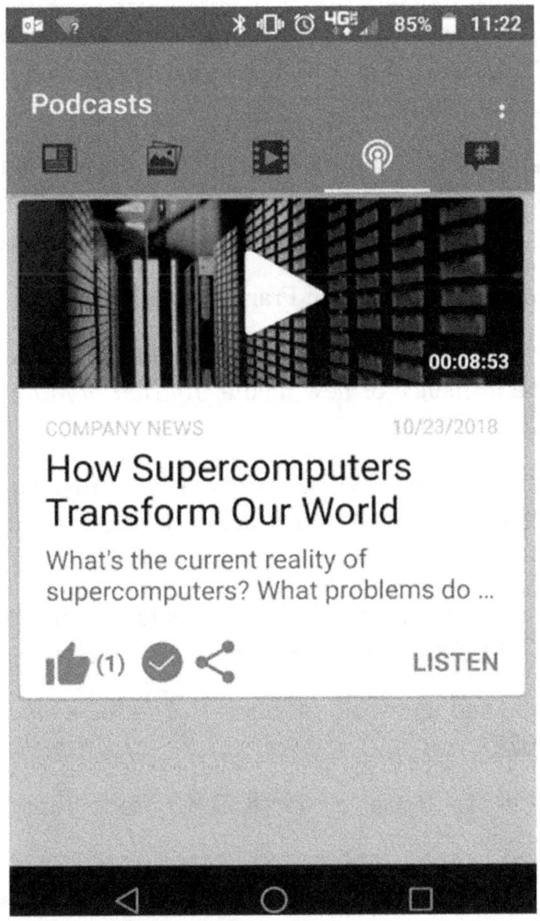

uses its internal communications efforts engage its employees with information about the company, to instill a sense of pride about the Lenovo brand, and to foster brand ambassadorship among its employees.

As companies grow and become more global in scope, internal communications in all forms will be critical for crossing both geographic and socio-cultural boundaries, as well as engaging employees in acting as brand ambassadors, and sharing critical information about their company to their customers, neighbors, colleagues, and friends.

REFERENCES

Asha, C. S., & Jyothi, P. (2013). Internal branding: A determining element of organizational citizenship behavior. *The Journal of Contemporary Management Research*, *7*(1), 37–57.

Atkinson, R., & Flint, J. (2001). Accessing hidden and hard-to-reach populations: Snowball research strategies. *Social Research Update*, *33*. Retrieved from http://sru.soc.surrey.ac.uk/SRU33.pdf

Cahill, D. (1995). The managerial implications of the learning organization: A new tool for internal marketing. *Journal of Services Marketing*, *9*(4), 43–51. doi:10.1108/08876049510094513

Chu, A., & Chu, R. (2011). The intranet's role in newcomer socialization in the hotel industry in Taiwan – technology acceptance model analysis. *International Journal of Human Resource Management*, *22*(5), 1163–1179. doi:10.1080/09585192.2011.556795

Corbin, J. (2016). What it takes to succeed in the digital workplace: A better understanding of mobile technology. *Technology Enabled Learning Excellence Essentials*. Retrieved on November 26 from https://search-proquest-com.proxy.campbell.edu/docview/1955028382?accountid=146941

D'Aprix, R. (2009). *The Credible Company*. San Francisco: Jossey-Bass.

DeBussy, N., Ewing, M., & Pitt, L. (2004). Stakeholder theory and internal marketing communications: A framework for analyzing the influence of new media. *Journal of Marketing Communications*, *9*(3), 147–161. doi:10.1080/1352726032000129890

Deloitte Core Beliefs and Culture Survey. (2013). Retrieved on August 6 from http://www.deloitte.com/assets/Dcom-UnitedStates/Local%20Assets/Documents/us_leadership_2013corebeliefs&culturesurvey_051613.pdf

Dolphin, R. R. (2005). Internal communications: Today's strategic imperative. *Journal of Marketing Communications*, *11*(3), 171–190. doi:10.1080/1352726042000315414

Dreher, S. (2014). Social media and the world of work. *Corporate Communications*, *19*(4), 344–356. doi:10.1108/CCIJ-10-2013-0087

Edelman Trust Barometer. (2013). Retrieved on 8/21/13 from http://www.edelman.com/insights/intellectual-property/trust-2013/

Edelman Trust Barometer. (2014). Retrieved on 1/22/14 from http://www.edelman.com/insights/intellectual-property/2014-edelman-trust-barometer/

Gelb, B. D., & Rengarajan, D. (2014). Employee contributions to brand equity. *California Management Review*, *56*(2), 95–112. doi:10.1525/cmr.2014.56.2.95

Gronstedt, A. (2000). *The customer century: Lessons from world-class companies in integrated marketing communication*. New York: Routledge.

Harrison, A. G. (2013). Engagement Ring: Building connections between employees and strategy. *Public Relations Tactics*, *20*(5), 16.

Kalla, H. K. (2005). Integrated internal communications: A multidisciplinary perspective. *Corporate Communications*, *10*(4), 302–314. doi:10.1108/13563280510630106

Kitchen, P. J., Spickett-Jones, J. G., & Grimes, T. (2007). Inhibition of Brand Integration amid Changing Agency Structures. *Journal of Marketing Communications*, *13*(2), 149–168. doi:10.1080/13527260601009803

Konica Minolta Releases Results of its New Report, "the Digital Workplace Initiative." (2017). *Entertainment Close - Up*. Retrieved from https://search-proquest-com.proxy.campbell.edu/docview/1897303332?accountid=146941

Kress, N. (2005). Engaging your employees through the power of communication. *Workspan*, *48*(5), 26–36.

Lee, I. (2011). Overview of emerging Web 2.0-based business models and web 2.0 applications in business: An ecological perspective. *International Journal of E-Business Research*, *7*(4), 1–16. doi:10.4018/jebr.2011100101

Lipiainen, H., Karjaluoto, H., & Nevalainen, M. (2014). Digital channels in the internal communication of a multinational corporation. *Corporate Communications*, *19*(3), 275–286. doi:10.1108/CCIJ-07-2012-0050

Mangold, W. G., & Faulds, D. J. (2009). Social media: The new hybrid element of the promotion mix. *Business Horizons*, *52*(4), 357–365. doi:10.1016/j.bushor.2009.03.002

Men, L. R., & Stacks, D. (2014). The effects of authentic leadership on strategic internal communication and employee-organization relationships. *Journal of Public Relations Research*, *26*(4), 301–324. doi: 10.1080/1062726X.2014.908720

Mills, P. K., & Ungson, G. (2003). Reassessing the limits of structural empowerment: Organizational constitution and trust as controls. *Academy of Management Review*, *28*(1), 143–153. doi:10.5465/amr.2003.8925254

Mishra, A. K. (1996). Organizational responses to crisis: The centrality of trust. In R. Kramer & T. Tyler (Eds.), *Trust in organizations* (pp. 261–287). Newbury Park, CA: Sage. doi:10.4135/9781452243610.n13

Mishra, A. K., & Mishra, K. E. (1994). The role of mutual trust in effective downsizing strategies. *Human Resource Management*, *33*(2), 261–279. doi:10.1002/hrm.3930330207

Mishra, A. K., & Mishra, K. E. (2013). *Becoming a Trustworthy Leader: Psychology & Practice*. Routledge Press.

Mishra, K. E. (2007). *Organizational communication and its role in building trust, commitment, and a positive reputation through relationship management with employees*. Dissertation.

Mishra, K. E., & Boynton, L. (2009). *Talk-the-Talk: Using Internal Communication to Build Trust with Employees*. International Public Relations Research Conference, Miami, FL.

Mishra, K. E., Boynton, L., & Mishra, A. K. (2014). Driving Employee Engagement: The Expanded Role of Internal Communications. *Journal of Business Communication*, *51*(2), 183–202. doi:10.1177/2329488414525399

Mishra, K. E., Schwarz, G. M., & Mishra, A. K. (2011). The Evolution of Trust and Control as Seen through an Organization's Human Resources Practices. In R. Searle (Ed.), Trust and Human Resource Management. Cheltenham, UK: Edward Elgar.

Mishra, K. E., Walker, K., & Mishra, A. K. (2014). Employee Use of Social Media in the Workplace: How "Lenovo Central" brings employees together. In I. Lee (Ed.), Integrating Social Media into Business Practice, Applications, Management, and Models. Academic Press.

Mishra, A. K., & Spreitzer, G. M. (1998). Explaining How Survivors Respond to Downsizing: The Roles of Trust, Empowerment, Justice and Work Redesign. *Academy of Management Review*, *23*(3), 567-588.

Molleda, J.-C. (2009). Construct and Dimensions of Authenticity in Strategic Communication Research. *Anagramas Rumbos y Sentidos de la Comunicacion*, *8*(15), 85–97. doi:10.22395/angr.v8n15a6

Mounter, P. (2003). Global internal communication: A model. *Journal of Communication Management*, *7*(3), 3. doi:10.1108/13632540310807412

Nakata, C., Zhu, Z., & Izberk-Bilgin, E. (2011). Integrating marketing and information services functions: A complementarity and competence perspective. *Journal of the Academy of Marketing Science*, *39*(5), 700–716. doi:10.100711747-010-0236-z

Neill, M.S., & Jiang, H. (2017). Functional silos, integration & encroachment in internal communication. *Public Relations Review*, *43*, 850-962.

Organ, D. W. (1988). *Organizational citizenship behavior: The good soldier syndrome*. Lexington, MA: Lexington Books.

Ots, M., & Nyilasy, G. (2015). Integrated Marketing Communications (IMC): Why Does It Fail? *Journal of Advertising Research*, *55*(2), 132–145. doi:10.2501/JAR-55-2-132-145

Pendell, R., & Dvorak, N. (2018). Digitizing Culture: Are You Doing It Wrong? *Gallup Business Journal*. Retrieved on 6/13/18 from http://news.gallup.com/businessjournal/234425/digitizing-culture-doing-wrong.aspx?utm_source=alert&utm_medium=email&utm_content=morelink&utm_campaign=syndication

Pincus, D. J., Rayfield, R. E., & Cozzens, M. D. (1991). The Chief Executive Officer's internal communications role: A benchmark program of research. In L. A. Grunig & J. E. Grunig (Eds.), *Public Relations Research Annual* (Vol. 3, pp. 1–36). Hillsdale, NJ: Lawrence Earlbaum Associates.

Pincus, J. D., Rayfield, R. E., & Cozzens, M. D. (1991). The chief executive officer's internal communication role: A benchmark program of research. *Journal of Public Relations Research*, *3*(1-4), 1–35. doi:10.12071532754xjprr0301-4_1

Piyachat, B., Chanongkorn, K., & Panisa, M. (2014). The mediate effect of employee engagement on the relationship between perceived employer branding and discretionary effort. *DLSU Business & Economics Review*, *24*(1), 59–72.

Quirke, B. (2008). *Making the connections: Using internal communication to turn strategy into action*. Burlington, VT: Gower.

Radick, S. (2011). *The power of social networks: Reviving the intranet*. Public Relations Tactics.

Robson, P., & Tourish, D. (2005). Managing internal communication: An organizational case study. *Corporate Communications*, *10*(3), 213–222. doi:10.1108/13563280510614474

Rockland, D. B. (2014). *Why internal communications is a business driver*. Tactics.

Ruppel, C. P., & Harrington, S. J. (2001). Sharing knowledge through intranets: A study of organizational culture and intranet implementation. *Professional Communication*, *44*(1), 37–52. doi:10.1109/47.911131

Saks, A. M. (2006). Antecedents and consequences of employee engagement. *Journal of Managerial Psychology, 21*(7), 600–619. doi:10.1108/02683940610690169

Schultz, D. E., Tannenbaum, S. I., & Lauterborn, R. F. (1993). *Integrated marketing communication: Pulling it together and making it work.* Lincolnwood, IL: NTC Publishing Group.

Siegall, M., & Gardner, S. (2000). Contextual factors of psychological empowerment. *Personnel Review, 29*(6), 703–722. doi:10.1108/00483480010296474

Smith, B. G. (2013). The public relations contribution to IMC: Deriving opportunities from threats and solidifying public relations' future. *Public Relations Review, 39*(5), 507–513. doi:10.1016/j.pubrev.2013.09.012

Spreitzer, G. M., & Mishra, A. K. (1999). Giving Up Control Without Losing Control: Trust and Its Substitutes' Effects on Managers' Involving Employees in Decision Making. *Group & Organization Management, 14*(2), 155–187. doi:10.1177/1059601199242003

Su, C., & Contractor, N. (2011). A Multidimensional Network Approach to Studying Team Members' Information Seeking From Human and Digital Knowledge Sources in Consulting Firms. *Journal of the American Society for Information Science and Technology, 62*(7), 1257–1275. doi:10.1002/asi.21526

Te′eni, D. (2001). A Cognitive-Affective Model of Organizational Communication for Designing IT. *MIS Quarterly, 25*(2), 251-312. Retrieved on June 13, 2018 from http://www.jstor.org/stable/3250931

Therkelsen, D. J., & Fiebich, C. L. (2003). The supervisor: The linchpin of employee relations. *Journal of Communication Management, 8*(2), 120–129. doi:10.1108/13632540410807592

Towers Watson Study. (2013). Retrieved from http://www.towerswatson.com/en/Insights/IC-Types/Survey-Research-Results/2013/05/Infographic-2013-Change-and-Communication-ROI-Study

Vallaster, C., & deChernatony, L. (2004). Internal brand building and structuration: The role of leadership. *European Journal of Marketing, 40*(7/8), 761–784. doi:10.1108/03090560610669982

Watson Wyatt White Paper. (2008/2009). *Driving business results through continuous engagement.* Retrieved on 29 August from http://www.watsonwyatt.com/research/pdfs/2008-US-0232.pdf

Welch, M., & Jackson, P. R. (2007). Rethinking internal communication: A stakeholder approach. *Corporate Communications, 12*(2), 177–198. doi:10.1108/13563280710744847

Yankelovich, D., & Immerwahr, J. (1983). *Putting the work ethic to work.* New York: Public Agenda Foundation.

Zeffane, R., Tipu, S. A., & Ryan, J. C. (2011). Communication, Commitment & Trust: Exploring the Triad. *International Journal of Business and Management, 6*(6), 77–87. doi:10.5539/ijbm.v6n6p77

ADDITIONAL READING

Brown, B., Sikes, J., & Willmott, P. (2013). *Bullish on digital: McKinsey Global Survey Results*. McKinsey & Company.

Burgess, C. (2013). *The Social Employee: How Great Companies Make Social Media Work*. McGraw-Hill.

KEY TERMS AND DEFINITIONS

Lenovo: Lenovo is not just another technology company. We make the technology that powers the world's best ideas. We design tools for those who are driven by accomplishment. We are the company that powers the people who Do. The engine that helps them Do more. Do better. Do what's never been done. And we are united in the quest to help our users defy the impossible.

Lenovo Central: The company intranet for Lenovo.

APPENDIX 1: INTERVIEW QUESTIONS FOR INTERNAL COMMUNICATION EXECUTIVES

1. Tell me about your role in communications at Lenovo.
2. What is your biggest challenge in developing relevant and timely communications in a global company?
3. What is the most effective way to share one message to people in different places?
4. What is the most effective way to share one message to people who speak different languages?
5. How does Lenovo's culture affect the way you choose to communicate across departmental or business borders?
6. How do marketing, communications and public relations work together to create organizational messages?
7. How do your organizational messages mesh with your external advertising messages?
8. Which come first, the external brand messages or the internal ones?
9. What role does the internet play in the way you communicate with employees?
10. What role does face-to-face communication play in the way you share messages about the company and the brand with employees?
11. What role does the immediate supervisor play in disseminating your messages?
12. If you could design an ideal communications system, what would it look like?
13. If you could design a new undergraduate communications class, what would it include?
14. What is the role does trust play in building open and transparent communications systems?
15. What is the role of the leader in building open and transparent communication systems?
16. As a recipient of those messages, what do you like about the communication process?
17. Is there anything you would change, if you could? Please elaborate.
18. Is there anything else you would like to share about this process?

APPENDIX 2: INTERVIEW QUESTIONS FOR LENOVO EMPLOYEES

1. Tell me about how internal communications work at Lenovo.
2. How does Lenovo's culture affect the way you see that messages work across departmental or business borders?
3. Do you feel that your organizational messages mesh with your external advertising messages?
4. What role does the internet play in the way the organization communicates with employees?
5. What role does face-to-face communication play in the way your manager shares messages about the company and the brand with employees?
6. If you could design an ideal communications system, what would it look like?
7. What is the role does trust play in building open and transparent communications systems?
8. What is the role of the leader in building open and transparent communication systems?
9. As a recipient of those messages, what do you like about the communication process?
10. Is there anything you would change, if you could? Please elaborate.
11. Is there anything else you would like to share about this process?

Compilation of References

(1992). Hidden Conflict. InKolb, D., & Bartunek, J. M. (Eds.), *Organizations: Uncovering Behind-The-Scenes Disputes*. Newbury Park, CA: Sage.

Aalgaard, J. (2015). *Communicating Across the Generations*. Retrieved from http://gettingsmart.com/2015/01/communicating-across-generations/

Abbe, A., Gulick, L. M. V., & Herman, J. L. (2007). *Cross-cultural competence in Army leaders: A conceptual and empirical foundation*. Washington, DC: U.S. Army Research Institute. doi:10.21236/ADA475798

Abowd, G. D., Dey, A. K., Brown, P. J., Davies, N., Smith, M., & Steggles, P. (1999). Towards a Better Understanding of Context and Context-Awareness. *Proceedings of the 1st international symposium on Handheld and Ubiquitous Computing*. 10.1007/3-540-48157-5_29

Abudi, G. (2010a). *A Virtual Global Team in Trouble: A Case Study - Part I*. Retrieved August 15, 2018 from https://www.ginaabudi.com/a-virtual-global-team-in-trouble-a-case-study-part-i/

Abudi, G. (2010b). *A Virtual Global Team in Trouble: A Case Study - Part II: Now What?* Retrieved August 15, 2018 from https://www.ginaabudi.com/a-virtual-global-team-in-trouble-a-case-study-part-ii-now-what/

Acquisti, A. (2002). *Protecting privacy with economic: Economic incentives for preventive technologies in ubiquitous computing environment*. Paper presented at the Workshop on Socially-informed Design of Privacy-enhancing Solutions in Ubiquitous Computing, New York, NY.

Acuff, R. D., Fagan, L. M., Rindfleisch, T. C., Levitt, B. J., & Ford, P. M. (1997). *Lightweight, Mobile E-Mail for Intra-Clinic Communication*. Paper presented at the 1997 AMIA Annual Fall Symposium, Nashville, TN.

Adams, D., Acedo, C., & Popa, S. (2012). In Search of Quality Education. In C. Acedo, D. Adams, & S. Popa (Eds.), *Quality and Qualities: Tensions in Higher Education* (pp. 1–22). Rotterdam: Sense Publishers.

Adams, G., & Schilit, T., & Want. (1993). An infrared network for mobile computers. *Proceedings USENIX Symposium on Mobile & Location-Independent Computing,* 10.

Adomavicius & Tuzhilin. (2011). Context-aware recommender systems. In *Recommender systems handbook* (pp. 217–253). Springer. doi:10.1007/978-0-387-85820-3_7

ADR Options A Spectrum Of Processes. (2018). Retrieved From Https://Www.Cadreworks.Org/Resources/Cadre-Materials/Adr-Options

Aerts, D. (2009). Quantum structure in cognition. *Journal of Mathematical Psychology*, *53*(5), 314–348. doi:10.1016/j.jmp.2009.04.005

Aerts, D., Broekaert, J., & Smets, S. (1999). The Liar-paradox in a Quantum Mechanical Perspective. *Foundations of Science*, *4*(2), 115–132. doi:10.1023/A:1009610326206

Aerts, D., & de Bianchi, M. (2014). The extended Bloch repre- sentation of quantum mechanics and the hidden-measurement so- lution to the measurement problem. *Annals of Physics*, *351*, 975–1025. doi:10.1016/j.aop.2014.09.020

Ahmad, A., Francis, A., & Zairi, M. (2007). Business process reengineering: Critical success factors in higher education. *Business Process Management Journal*, *13*(3), 451–469. doi:10.1108/14637150710752344

Ah-Teck, J. C., & Starr, K. (2013). Principals' perceptions of "quality" in Mauritian schools using the Baldrige framework. *Journal of Educational Administration*, *51*(5), 680–704. doi:10.1108/JEA-02-2012-0022

Akcigit, U. (2009). *Firm Size, Innovation Dynamics and Growth. In 2009 Meeting Papers (No. 1267)*. Society for Economic Dynamics.

Alder, G. S., Noel, T. W., & Ambrose, M. L. (2006). Clarifying the effects of Internet monitoring on job attitudes: The mediating role of employee trust. *Information & Management*, *43*(7), 894–903. doi:10.1016/j.im.2006.08.008

Ali, M. (2011). *Chartis Launches ReputationGuard®, Reputational Risk Insurance*. Retrieved from http://www.chartisinsurance.com/searchresults/search_295_195443.html

Allen, J. (2011). $16 muffins, $8 coffee served in Justice Audit. *Reuters Online Edition*. Retrieved from http://www.reuters.com/article/2011/09/21/us-usa-justice-muffins-idUSTRE78J7B020110921

Allen, N., & Meyer, P. (1990). Organizational socialization tactics: A longitudinal analysis of links to newcomers' commitment and role orientation. *Academy of Management Journal*, *33*(4), 1–18.

Alonso, O., Gertz, M., & Baeza-Yates, R. (2007). On the value of temporal information in information retrieval. *SIGIR Forum*, *41*(2), 35-41. 10.1145/1328964.1328968

Altaian, I., & Taylor, D. A. (1983). *Social penetration: The development of interpersonal relationships*. New York: Holt, Rhinehart, and Wilson.

Altman, I. (1975). *The environment and social behaviour: Privacy, personal space, territory, and crowding*. Monterey, CA: Brooks/Cole.

AMA Survey. (2001). *Workplace monitoring and surveillance*. Retrieved from http://www.amanet. org/research/pdfs/ems_short2001.pdf

AMA Survey. (2003). *Email rules, policies and practices survey*. Retrieved from http://www. amanet.org/research/pdfs/email_policies_practices.pdf

AMA Survey. (2005). *Electronic monitoring and surveillance survey*. Retrieved from http://www. amanet.org/research/pdfs/ems_summary05.pdf

American Management Association. (2015). *Leading the Four Generations at Work*. Retrieved from http://www.amanet.org/training/articles/Leading-the-Four-Generations-at-Work.aspx

American National Standard ANSI/ASQC A3-1978. (1978). *Quality Systems Terminology*. Milwaukee, WI: American Society for Quality Control.

Amstrong, A., & Hagel, J. (2000). The real value of online communities. In E. L. Lesser & M. Fontaine (Eds.), *Knowledge and communities* (pp. 85–98). Boston: Butterworth-Heinemann. doi:10.1016/B978-0-7506-7293-1.50009-3

Anastasi, A. (1988). *Psychological testing* (6th ed.). New York, NY: Macmillan Publishing.

Anderson, T., Gisborne, K. D., & Holliday, P. N. (2012). Every officer is a leader: Coaching leadership, learning, and performance in justice, public safety, and security organizations. Trafford Publishing. Retrieved from www.trafford.com

Anderson, J. G. (1993). *Evaluating Health Care Information Systems: Methods and Applications*. Sage Publications, Inc.

Anderson, R. (2002). Reforming science teaching: What research says about inquiry. *Journal of Science Teacher Education*, *13*(1), 1–12. doi:10.1023/A:1015171124982

Anderson, T. K., Geisborne, K., & Halliday, P. (2017). *Every officer is a leader: Coaching leadership, learning and performance in justice, public safety and security organizations*. Holly Spring, NC: International Academy of Public Safety.

Antoci, A., & Sabatini, F. (2018). Online networks, social interaction ans segregation: An evolutionary approach. *Journal of Evolutionary Economics*, *28*(4), 859–883. doi:10.100700191-018-0556-6

Arasaratnam, L. A., & Doerfel, M. L. (2005). Intercultural communication competence: Identifying key components from multicultural perspectives. *International Journal of Intercultural Relations*, *29*(2), 137–163. doi:10.1016/j.ijintrel.2004.04.001

Ardichvili, A., & Manderscheid, S. V. (2008). Emerging practices in leadership development. *Advances in Developing Human Resources*, *10*(5), 619–631. doi:10.1177/1523422308321718

Armenakis, A., & Harris, S. (2002). Crafting a change message to create transformational readiness. *Journal of Organizational Change Management*, *1*(2), 169–183. doi:10.1108/09534810210423080

Armstrong, A., & Thornton, N. (2012). Incorporating Brookfield's discussion techniques synchronously into asynchronous online courses. *The Quarterly Review of Distance Education*, *13*(1), 1–9.

Ary, D., Jacobs, L. C., & Razavieh, A. (2002). *Introduction to research in education*. Wadsworth, Thomson Learning.

Asha, C. S., & Jyothi, P. (2013). Internal branding: A determining element of organizational citizenship behavior. *The Journal of Contemporary Management Research*, *7*(1), 37–57.

Ashkanasy, N., & Rush, S. (2004). Emotional rescue: A conversation with Neal M. Ashkanasy. *Leadership in Action*, *24*(4), 15–18. doi:10.1002/lia.1078

Associated Press. (2011a, April 19). A timeline of Tressel's NCAA troubles. *USA Today*. Retrieved August 28, 2015 from http://usatoday30.usatoday.com/sports/college/football/2011-04-19-2215755358_x.htm

Associated Press. (2011b, May 30). Jim Tressel resigns as Ohio State's coach. *CBS News*. Retrieved August 28, 2015 from http://www.cbsnews.com/news/jim-tressel-resigns-as-ohio-states-coach/

Astley, W. G., & Zammuto, R. F. (1992). Organization science, managers and language games. *Organization Science*, *3*(4), 443–460. doi:10.1287/orsc.3.4.443

Asunda, P. (2010). Productivity, social networks and net communities in the workplace. *Techniques - American Vocational Association*, *85*(5), 38–41.

Atkinson, R., & Flint, J. (2001). Accessing hidden and hard-to-reach populations: Snowball research strategies. *Social Research Update*, *33*. Retrieved from http://sru.soc.surrey.ac.uk/SRU33.pdf

Atmanspacher, H., Filk, T., & Römer, H. (2004). Quantum Zeno features of bistable perception. *Biological Cybernetics*, *90*(1), 33–40. doi:10.100700422-003-0436-4 PMID:14762722

Austin, J. (2010). *The collaboration challenge: How nonprofits and businesses succeed through strategic alliances*. San Francisco, CA: Jossey-bass.

Avolio, B. J. (1999). *Full leadership development: Building the vital forces in organizations*. Thousand Oaks, CA: Sage Publications.

Avolio, B. J., & Bass, B. M. (2002). *Developing potential across a full range of leadership*. Mahwah, NJ: Erlbaum.

Avrahami, D., Gergle, D., Hudson, S. E., & Kiesler, S. (2007). Improving the match between callers and receivers: A study on the effect of contextual information on cell phone interruptions. *Behaviour & Information Technology*, *26*(3), 247–259. doi:10.1080/01449290500402338

Aziz, O., Panesar, S., Netuveli, G., Paraskeva, P., Sheikh, A., & Darzi, A. (2005). Handheld computers and the 21st century surgical team: A pilot study. *BMC Medical Informatics and Decision Making*, *5*(1), 28. doi:10.1186/1472-6947-5-28 PMID:16109177

Baciu, A. (2016). *Artificial intelligence is more artificial than intelligent*. Retrieved November 12, 2018 at https://www.wired.com/2016/12/artificial-intelligence-artificial-intelligent/

Baker, T. (2000). *Effective police leadership*. New York, NY: Looseleaf Law Publications, INC.

Bakker, M., Leenders, R. T. A. J., Gabbay, S. M., Kratzer, J., & Van Engelen, J. M. L. (2006). Is trust really social capital? Knowledge sharing in product development projects. *The Learning Organization*, *13*(6), 594–605. doi:10.1108/09696470610705479

Bakshy, E., Rosenn, I., Marlow, C., & Adamic, L. (2012). The Role of Social Networks in Information Diffusion. *International World Wide Web Conference*, Lyon, France. 10.1145/2187836.2187907

Banathy, B. H., & Jenks, C. L. (1990, April). *The transformation of education: By design*. Paper presented at the Annual Meeting of the American Educational Research Association, Boston, MA. Retrieved from http://files.eric.ed.gov/fulltext/ED323660.pdf

Banathy, B. H. (1991). *Systems Design of Education: A Journey to Create the Future*. Englewood Cliffs, NJ: Educational Technology Publications.

Banilower, E. R., Smith, P. S., Weiss, I. R., Malzahn, K. A., Campbell, K. M., & Weis, A. M. (2013). *Report of the 2012 national survey of science and mathematics education*. Chapel Hill, NC: Horizon Research, Inc.

Barbuto, J., & Burbach, M. E. (2006). The emotional intelligence of transformational leaders: A field study of elected officials. *The Journal of Social Psychology*, *146*(1), 51–64. doi:10.3200/SOCP.146.1.51-64 PMID:16480121

Bardram, J. E., & Hansen, T. R. (2004). The AWARE architecture: supporting context-mediated social awareness in mobile cooperation. *Proceedings of the 2004 ACM conference on Computer supported cooperative work*. 10.1145/1031607.1031639

Bardram, J. E., & Hansen, T. R. (2010). Context-Based Workplace Awareness. *Computer Supported Cooperative Work*, *19*(2), 105–138. doi:10.100710606-010-9110-2

Bardram, J. E., Hansen, T. R., & Soegaard, M. (2006). AwareMedia: A shared interactive display supporting social, temporal, and spatial awareness in surgery. *Proceedings of the 2006 20th anniversary conference on Computer supported cooperative work*. 10.1145/1180875.1180892

Barnard, C. (1938). *The functions of the executive* (2nd ed.). Harvard University Press.

Barnatt, C. (2008). Higher Education 2.0. *International Journal of Management Education*, *7*(3), 47–56. doi:10.3794/ijme.73.250

Bar-On, R. (1988). *The development of a concept of psychological well-being* (Doctoral dissertation). Grahamstown, South Africa: Rhodes University.

Bar-On, R. (2006b). The Bar-On model of emotional-social intelligence. *Psicothema, 18,* 13-25.

Bar-On, R., Handley, R., & Fund., S. (2006). The impact of emotional intelligence on performance. In V.U. Druskat, F. Sala, & G. Mont (Eds.), *Linking emotional intelligence and performance at work.* Mahwah, NJ: Lawrence Erlbaum Associates.

Bar-On, R. (1997). *Bar-On Emotional Quotient Inventory: Technical manual.* Toronto, Canada: Multi-Health Systems.

Bar-On, R. (1997). *The Bar-On Emotional Quotient Inventory (EQ-i): Technical manual.* Toronto, Canada: Multi-Health Systems.

Bar-On, R. (2006). The Bar-On model of emotional-social intelligence (ESI). *Psicothema, 18,* 13–25. PMID:17295953

Bar-On, R. (2006a). *EQ-i leadership user's guide.* Toronto, Canada: Multi-Health Systems.

Bar-On, R. (2016). Beyond IQ & EQ: The Bar-On Multifactor Model of Performance. In U. Kumar (Ed.), *The Wiley handbook of personality assessment* (pp. 104–118). London, UK: John Wiley & Sons. doi:10.1002/9781119173489.ch8

Bar-On, R. (2016). *Beyond IQ and EI: The Bar-On Multifactor Model of Performance.* In U. Kumar (Ed.), *Personality Assessment: The Way Forward.* London: Wiley.

Bar-On, R. (2018). The Multifactor Measure of Performance: Its development, norming, and validation. *Frontiers in Psychology, 9*(140), 1–16. PMID:29515479

Barrett-Howard, E., & Tyler, T. R. (1986). Procedural justice as a criterion in allocation decisions. *Journal of Personality and Social Psychology, 50*(2), 296–304. doi:10.1037/0022-3514.50.2.296

Barrow, L. H. (2006). A brief history of inquiry: From dewey to standards. *Journal of Science Teacher Education, 17*(3), 265–278. doi:10.100710972-006-9008-5

Barton, C., Fromm, J., & Egan, C. (2012). *The millennial consumer-debunking stereotypes.* BCG.

Bashouri, J., & Duncan, G. (2014). Communities of practice: Linking knowledge management and strategy in creative firms. *The Journal of Business Strategy, 35*(6), 49–57. doi:10.1108/JBS-08-2013-0072

Bass, B. M. (1985). *Leadership and performance beyond expectations.* New York: Free Press.

Bass, B. M., & Avolio, B. J. (1994). *Improving organizational effectiveness through transformational leadership.* Thousand Oaks, CA: Sage Publications.

Bass, B. M., & Avolio, B. J. (2004). *Multifactor leadership questionnaire: Manual and sample set* (3rd ed.). Redwood City, CA: Mind Garden, Inc.

Bateman, T., & Organ, D. (1983). Job satisfaction and the good soldier: The relationship between affect and employee "citizenship". *Academy of Management Journal, 26*(4), 587–595.

Bauman, T., & Williams, R. (2004). *The Business Of Process: Research Issues In Managing Indigenous Decison-Making And Disputes In Land.* AIATSIS Research Disucssion Paper No. 13.

Bavelas, J. B., Chovil, N., & Roe, L. (1995). Gestures specialized for dialogue. *Personality and Social Psychology, 21*(4), 394–405. doi:. doi:10.1177/0146167295214010

Bayley, D. H. (1996). *Police for the Future.* Oxford, UK: Oxford University Press.

BBC News. (2017, April 4). *Nivea removes 'white is purity' deodorant advert branded 'racist.'* Retrieved from https://www.bbc.com/news/world-europe-39489967

BBC News. (2018, May 22). *Urban Outfitters removes vases 'ripped-off' from Bristol artist*. Retrieved from https://www.bbc.com/news/uk-england-bristol-44189267

Beattie, G., & Shovelton, H. (1999). Iconic hand gestures that accompany spontaneous speech. *Journal of Language and Social Psychology*, *18*(4), 438–463. doi:10.1177/0261927X99018004005

Beaulieu, R., Shamian, J., Donner, G., & Pringle, D. (1997). Empowerment and commitment of nurses in long term care. *Nursing Economics*, *15*(1), 32–41.

Bélanger, F., & Crossler, R. E. (2011). Privacy in the digital age: A review of information privacy research in information systems. *Management Information Systems Quarterly*, *35*(4), 1017–1041. doi:10.2307/41409971

Bélanger, F., Hiller, J. S., & Smith, W. J. (2002). Trustworthiness in electronic commerce: The role of privacy, security, and site attributes. *The Journal of Strategic Information Systems*, *11*(3-4), 245–270. doi:10.1016/S0963-8687(02)00018-5

Belderbos, R., & Somers, D. (2015). Do Technology Leaders Deter Inward R&D Investments? Evidence from regional R & D location Decisions in Europe.2015-02. Regional Studies.

Bennett, M., Hughes, S., & Hermann, M.S.G. (1999). The Art of mediation. Boulder, CO: NITA.

Bennett, S., Bishop, A., Dalgarno, B., Waycott, J., & Kennedy, G. (2012). Implementing Web 2.0 technologies in higher education: A collective case study. *Computers & Education*, *59*(2), 524–534. doi:10.1016/j.compedu.2011.12.022

Benoit, W. (1995). *Accounts, excuses, and apologies: A theory of image restoration*. State University of New York Press.

Benoit, W. (2015). *Accounts, excuses, and apologies: Image repair theory and research*. State University of New York Press.

Benson, V., Filippaios, F., & Morgan, S. (2010). Online social networks: Changing the face of business education and career planning. *International Journal of Business and Management*, *4*(1), 20–33.

Bergmo, T. S., Johnsen, E., Johansen, M. A., & Solvoll, T. (2016). Evaluation of a context spesific communcation system based on smartphone. In *eTELEMED 2016, The Eight International Conference on eHealth, Telemedicine, and Social Medicine*. International Academy, Research and Industry Association (IARIA).

Berkowitz, S. (2013, May 2). NCAA had record $71 million surplus in fiscal 2012. *USA Today*. Retrieved March 17, 2014 from http://www.usatoday.com/story/sports/college/2013/05/02/ncaa-financial-statement-surplus/2128431/

Berk, R. (2013). Face-to-face versus online course evaluations: A 'consumer's guide' to seven strategies. *Journal of Online Teaching and Learning*, *9*(1), 140–148.

Berman, M., & Lowery, W. (2018, March 30). Baton Rouge police release video showing fatal shooting of Alton Sterling, plan to fire one officer. *The Washington Post*. Retrieved from https://www.washingtonpost.com/news/post-nation/wp/2018/03/30/baton-rouge-police-will-fire-officer-who-shot-and-killed-alton-sterling/?utm_term=.f817ac12c1fd

Bernhardt, V. (2013). *Translating data into information to improve teaching and learning*. New York: Routledge. doi:10.4324/9781315853758

Bernstein, A., Vorburger, P., & Egger, P. (2005). *Direct Interruptablity Prediction and Scenario-based Evaluation of Wearable Devices: Towards Reliable Interruptability Predictions*. Paper presented at the First International Workshop on Managing Context Information in Mobile and Pervasive Environments MCMP-05.

Berry, G. (1997). Leadership and the development of quality culture in schools. *International Journal of Educational Management*, *11*(2), 52–65. doi:10.1108/09513549710163943

Betts, F. (1992, November). How Systems Thinking Applies to Education. *Educational Leadership*, *50*(3), 38–41. Retrieved from http://search.proquest.com/docview/224857527?accountid=12528

Bien, L. (2014, November). A complete timeline of the Ray Rice assault case. *SB Nation*. Retrieved from http://www.sbnation.com/nfl/2014/5/23/5744964/ray-rice-arrest-assault-statement-apology-ravens

Bies, R. J., & Moag, J. F. (1986). Interactional justice: Communication criteria of fairness. In R. J. Lewicki, B. H. Sheppard, & M. H. Bazerman (Eds.), *Research on negotiations in organisations* (Vol. 1, pp. 43–55). Greenwich, CT: JAI Press.

Bilandzic, A. (2018). Social and Spatial Precursors to Innovation: The Diversity Advantage of the Creative Fringe. *The Journal of Community Informatics*, *14*(1). Retrieved from http://ci-journal.org/index.php/ciej/article/view/1455

Bilich, F., & Neto, A. A. (1997). Strategic total quality management. *Total Quality Management*, *8*(2-3), 88–89. doi:10.1080/0954412979767

Bisgaard, J. J., Heise, M., & Steffensen, C. (2004). *How is Context and Context-awareness Defined and Applied? A Survey of Context-awareness*. Department of Computer Science, Aalborg University.

Blake, R. R., & Mouton, J. S. (1964). *The Managerial Grid*. Houston, TX: Gulf Publishing Company.

Blaney, J. R., Lippert, L. R., & Smith, J. S. (2013). Repairing the athlete's image. Lanham, MD: Lexington Books (Rowman & Littlefield).

Blank, W. (2001). *The 108 skills of natural born leaders*. New York, NY: American Management Association.

Blavin, J. H., & Cohen, L. G. (2002). Gore, Gibson, And Goldsmith: The Evolution Of Internet Metaphors In Law And Commentary. *Harvard Journal of Law & Technology*, 16.

Blinder, A. (2017, May 2). Ex-officer who shot Walter Scott pleads guilty in Charleston, *NY Times*. Retrieved from https://www.nytimes.com/2017/05/02/us/michael-slager-walter-scott-north-charleston-shooting.html

Block, F. E. III, & Block, F. E. Jr. (2016). Understanding Caregiver Workflows: A Proposal for Alarm Condition Priorities. *Biomedical Instrumentation & Technology*, *50*(2), 114–116. doi:10.2345/0899-8205-50.2.114 PMID:27046686

Blum, N. J., & Lieu, T. A. (1992). Interrupted care. The effects of paging on pediatric resident activities. *American Journal of Diseases of Children*, *146*(7), 806–808. doi:10.1001/archpedi.1992.02160190038016 PMID:1496947

Bogliacino, F., Piva, M., & Vivarelli, M. (2012). R&D and Employment: An application of the LSDVC Estimator using European Microdata. *Economics Letters*, *116*(1), 56–59. doi:10.1016/j.econlet.2012.01.010

Bolden, R. (2007). Trends and perspectives in management and leadership development. *Business Leadership Review*, *4*, 1-13. Retrieved from http://www.mbaworld.com/bss/blr

Bond, M. A., & Lockee, B. B. (2014). *Building communities of practice for distance educators*. New York: Springer. doi:10.1007/978-3-319-03626-7

Bone, D., & Normore, A. H. (2014). Progressive law enforcement leaders effectively manage departmental risk. *Law Enforcement Today (LET): The Law Enforcement Community*. Retrieved from http://www.lawenforcementtoday.com/2014/07/13/striving-for-educational-excellence-in-law-enforcement-leadership-the-case-of-jefferson-parish-sheriffs-office/

Bone, D. (1996). Quality management is collegiate management: Improving practice in a special school. In P. Lomax (Ed.), *Quality Management in education: Sustaining the vision through Action Research* (pp. 19–46). London: Routledge and Hyde Publications.

Bone, D., Normore, A. H., & Javidi, M. (2015). *Human factors: police leaders improving safety while developing meaningful public trust. FBI Law Enforcement Journal.*

Bonstingl, J. J. (1992). The quality revolution in education. *Educational Leadership*, *50*(3), 4–9.

Bonstingl, J. J. (1993). The quality movement: What's it really about? *Educational Leadership*, *51*(1), 66–70.

Boren, C. (2011, July 15). Report: Ohio State's Jim Tressel had history of compliance violations. *The Washington Post.* Retrieved October 18, 2015 from https://www.washingtonpost.com/blogs/early-lead/post/report-ohio-states-jim-tressel-had-history-of-compliance-violations/2011/07/15/gIQAJjbFGI_blog.html

Borges, N. J., Kirkham, K., Deardorff, A. S., & Moore, J. A. (2012). Development of emotional intelligence in a team-based learning internal medicine clerkship. *Medical Teacher*, *34*(10), 802–806. doi:10.3109/0142159X.2012.687121 PMID:23009257

Borko, H. (2004). Professional development and teacher learning: Mapping the terrain. *Educational Researcher*, *33*(8), 3–15. doi:10.3102/0013189X033008003

Borzillo, S., Schmitt, A., & Antino, M. (2012). Coomunities of practice: keeping the company agile. *Journal of Business Strategy*, *33*(6), 22-30.

Botan, C. (1993). A human nature approach to image and ethics in international public relations. *Journal of Public Relations Research*, *5*(2), 71–81. doi:10.12071532754xjprr0502_02

Botan, C. (1997). Ethics in strategic communication campaigns: The case for a new approach to public relations. *Journal of Business Communication*, *34*(2), 188–202. doi:10.1177/002194369703400205

Botsis, T., Solvoll, T., Scholl, J., Hasvold, P., & Hartvigsen, G. (2007). Context-aware systems for mobile communication in healthcare - A user oriented approach. *Proceedings of the 7th Wseas International Conference on Applied Informatics and Communications*, 69-74.

Boulos, M. N., & Wheeler, S. (2007). The emerging Web 2.0 social software: An enabling suite of sociable technologies in health and health care education. *Health Information and Libraries Journal*, *24*(1), 2–23. doi:10.1111/j.1471-1842.2007.00701.x PMID:17331140

Bourdieu. (1987). *In Other Words: Essays toward a Reflective Sociology*. Stanford.

Bourdieu, P. (1990). *In other Words: Essays Towards a Reflexive Sociology*. Stanford, CA: Stanford University Press.

Bouygues, U. K. (1999). *Ltd V*. Dahl Jensen UK Ltd.

Bowers, C. P. (1996). Courts, Contracts, And The Appropriate Discount Rate: A Quick Fix For The Legal Lottery. *The University of Chicago Law Review. University of Chicago. Law School*, *63*(3), 1099–1137. doi:10.2307/1600250

Boxall, P., & Purcell, J. (2011). *Strategy and Human Resource Management* (3rd ed.). Basingstoke, UK: Palgrave Macmillan.

boyd, d. m., & Ellison, N. B. (2007). Social network sites: Definition, history, and scholarship. *Journal of Computer-Mediated Communication, 13*(1), 210-230.

Boyd, D. R., Bee, H. L., & Johnson, P. A. (2011). *Lifespan development*. Toronto: CA Pearson Canada.

Braaten, M., & Windschitl, M. (2011). Working toward a stronger conceptualization of scientific explanation for science education. *Science Education*, *95*(4), 639–669. doi:10.1002ce.20449

Brackett, M. A., Rivers, S. E., & Salovey, P. (2011). Emotional Intelligence: Implications for Personal, Social, Academic, and Workplace Success. *Social and Personality Psychology Compass*, *5*(1), 88–103. doi:10.1111/j.1751-9004.2010.00334.x

Braddock, R., Mahony, P., & Taylor, P. (2006). Globalisation, commercialism, managerialism and internationalisation. *International Journal of Learning*, *13*(8), 61–67.

Bradner, E., Kellogg, W. A., & Erickson, T. (1999). The adoption and use of \“BABBLE\” a field study of chat in the workplace. *Proceedings of the Sixth European conference on Computer supported cooperative work.*

Brandt, R. (2003). Is this school a learning organization? 10 ways to tell. *Journal of Staff Development*, *24*(1), 10–16. Retrieved from http://search.proquest.com/docview/211520094?accountid=12528

Brazeal, L. M. (2008). The image repair strategies of Terrell Owens. *Public Relations Review*, *34*(2), 145–150. doi:10.1016/j.pubrev.2008.03.021

Brinson, S. L., & Benoit, W. L. (1999). The tarnished star: Restoring Texaco's damaged public image. *Management Communication Quarterly*, *12*(4), 483–519. doi:10.1177/0893318999124001

Bristow, D., & Vasilopoulous, R. (1995). The New CCDC 2: Facilitating Dispute Resolution Of Construction Projects. *Constitutional Law Journal (Newark, N.J.)*, *11*(2), 95–117.

Bronfman, V. S. (2002). Comunidades de práctica. Workshop. GEC S.A., Barcelona, Spain.

Brooks, R. (2013, November 7). Is Urban Outfitters stealing work from independent designers AGAIN? *The Village Voice*. Retrieved from https://www.villagevoice.com/2013/11/07/is-urban-outfitters-stealing-work-from-independent-designers-again/

Brooks, J., & Normore, A. (2010). Educational leadership and globalization: Literacy for a glocal perspective. *Educational Policy*, *24*(1), 52–82. doi:10.1177/0895904809354070

Brownell, J. (2003). Applied Research in Managerial Communication. *The Cornell Hotel and Restaurant Administration Quarterly*, *44*(2), 39–49. doi:10.1016/S0010-8804(03)90017-6

Brown, J. F., & Marshall, B. L. (2008). Continuous quality improvement: An effective strategy for improvement of program outcomes in a higher education setting. *Nursing Education Perspectives*, *29*(4), 205–211. PMID:18770948

Brown, J. S., & Duguid, P. (1991). Organizational learning and communities of practice: Towards a Unified View of working, learning and innovation. *Organization Science*, *2*(1), 40–57. doi:10.1287/orsc.2.1.40

Brown, S., & Kappes, L. (2012). *Implementing the Common Core State Standards: A Primer on "Close Reading of Text"*. Washington, DC: Kaplan Institute.

Bruce, T., & Tini, T. (2008). Unique crisis response strategies in sports public relations: Rugby league and the case for *diversion. Public Relations Review*, *34*(2), 108–115. doi:10.1016/j.pubrev.2008.03.015

Brunelle, E. (2012). Virtuality in work arrangements and affective organizational commitment. *International Journal of Business and Social Science*, *3*(2), 56–62.

Bruza, P., Kitto, K., Nelson, D., & McEvoy, C. (2009). Is there some- thing quantum-like about the human mental lexicon? *Journal of Mathematical Psychology*, *53*, 362-377. doi:10.1016/j.jmp.2009.04.00

Bryman, A. (1992). *Charisma and leadership in organizations*. London: Sage Publications.

Bryman, A. (2013). *Leadership and organizations*. London, UK: Routledge.

Buckholz, S., Lashbrook, W., & Wenburg, J. (1976). *Toward the measurement and processing of social styles*. Paper presented at the International Communication Association, Portland, OR.

Buckingham, M., & Coffman, C. (1999). *First, break all the rules: What the world's greatest managers do differently*. New York, NY: Simon & Schuster.

Buczynski, S., & Hansen, C. B. (2010). Impact of professional development on teacher practice: Uncovering connections. *Teaching and Teacher Education*, *26*(3), 599–607. doi:10.1016/j.tate.2009.09.006

Bühring-Uhle, C., Kirchhoff, L., & Scherer, G. (2006). Arbitration And Mediation. In *International Business*. New York: Kluwer Law International.

Burgoon, J. K., Byuller, D. B., Hale, J. L., & deTurck, M. A. (1984). Relational message associated with nonverbal behaviors. *Human Communication Research*, *10*(3), 351–378. doi:10.1111/j.1468-2958.1984.tb00023.x

Burns, J. (1978). *Leadership*. New York: Open Road Integrated Media.

Burton, J. W. (1993). Conflict Resolution As Political Philosophy. In H. Van Der Merwe & D. J. Sandole (Eds.), Conflict Resolution Theory And Practice: Integration And Application (pp. 55-64). Manchester, UK: Manchester University Press.

Burton, J. W. (1990). *Conflict Resolution And Prevention*. New York: St. Martin's Press.

Burton, J. W. (1997). *Violence Explained: The Sources Of Conflict, Violence And Crime And Their Prevention*. Manchester, UK: Manchester University Press.

Burton, J. W. (1998). Conflict Resolution: The Human Dimension. *International Journal of Peace Studies*, *3*(1), 4.

Buscaglia, E. (1996). Corruption And Judicial Reform In Latin America. *Policy Studies*, *17*(4), 273–285. doi:10.1080/01442879608423713

Buscaglia, E., & Stephan, P. B. (2005). An Empirical Assessment Of The Impact Of Formal Versus Informal Dispute Resolution On Poverty: A Governance-Based Approach. *International Review of Law and Economics*, *25*(1), 89–106. doi:10.1016/j.irle.2004.06.004

Busemeyer, J., Matthew, M., & Wang, Z. (2006). A quantum in- formation processing theory explanation of disjunction effects. In R. Sun & N. Miyake (Eds.), Proceedings of 28th annual confer- ence of the cognitive science society & the 5th international conference of cognitive science (pp. 131–135). Academic Press.

Busemeyer, J., Wang, Z., & Lambert-Mogiliansky, A. (2009). Empirical comparison of markov and quantum models of decision making. *Journal of Mathematical Psychology, 53*(5), 423 – 433. doi: .2009.03.002 doi:10.1016/ j.jmp

Busemeyer, J., & Bruza, P. (2012). *Quantum Models of Cognition and Decision*. Cambridge University Press. doi:10.1017/CBO9780511997716

Cahill, D. (1995). The managerial implications of the learning organization: A new tool for internal marketing. *Journal of Services Marketing*, *9*(4), 43–51. doi:10.1108/08876049510094513

Caldwell, B. (2005). *School-based management. Education Policy Series. International Academy of Education and International Institute for Educational Planning*. UNESCO.

Caldwell, B. (2007). *Self managing schools and improved learning outcomes*. Canberra: Department of Employment, Education, Training and Youth Affairs.

Calhoun, C. (2011). Communication as Social Science (and More). *International Journal of Communication*, *5*, 1479–1496.

Cameron, A. F., & Webster, J. (2005). Unintended consequences of emerging communication technologies: Instant messaging in the workplace. *Computers in Human Behavior*, *21*(1), 85–103. doi:10.1016/j.chb.2003.12.001

Camillo, A. A., & Di Pietro, L. (2011). The Importance of Managerial Communication for Hospitality Organizational Settings in the Era of High-Tech Evolution. *Hosteur*, *20*(2), 19–27.

Campbell, D. P., & Level Dale, A. (1985). A Black Box Model of Communication. *Journal of Business Communication*, *22*(3), 37–47. doi:10.1177/002194368502200304

Campbell, J. P., McHenry, J. J., & Lauress, W. L. (1990). Modeling Job performance in a population of jobs. *Personnel Psychology*, *43*(2), 313–333. doi:10.1111/j.1744-6570.1990.tb01561.x

Canavan, D., Scott, P. S., & Mangematin, V. (2013). Creative professional service firms: Aligning strategy and talent. *The Journal of Business Strategy*, *34*(3), 24–32. doi:10.1108/JBS-10-2012-0058

Carayannis, E. G., & Campbell, D. F. J. (2009). 'Mode 3' and 'Quadruple Helix': Toward a 21st century fractal innovation ecosystem. *International Journal of Technology Management*, *46*(3/4), 201–234. doi:10.1504/IJTM.2009.023374

CareerBuilder. (2010). *More than four-in-ten workers over the age of 35 currently work for a younger boss, finds new CareerBuilder survey*. Retrieved from http://www.careerbuilder.com/share/aboutus/pressreleasesdetail.aspx?id=pr554&sd=2/17/2010&ed=12/31/2010&siteid=cbpr&sc_cmp1=cb_pr554

Carlson, J. F., Geisinger, K. F., & Jonson, J. L. (2017). *The Twentieth Mental Measurements Yearbook*. Lincoln, NE: Buros Center for Testing.

Carlson, S. (1951). *Executive Behavior*. Stockholm: Strombergs.

Carnegie, D. A. Inc. (1993). The leader in you. New York, NY: Pocket Books.

Carnegie, D. (1936). *How to win friends and influence people*. New York, NY: Simon and Schuster.

Carnevale, P. J., & Pruitt, D. G. (1992). Negotiation And Mediation. *Annual Review of Psychology*, *43*(1), 531–582. doi:10.1146/annurev.ps.43.020192.002531

Caruso, D. R. (1999). *Applying the ability model of emotional intelligence to the world of work*. Retrieved from cjwolfe.com/article.doc

Cascio, W. F. (2000). Managing a virtual workplace. *The Academy of Management Perspectives*, *14*(3), 1–10. doi:10.5465/ame.2000.4468068

Castells, M. (2007). Communication, power and counter-power in the network society. *International Journal of Communication*, *1*(1), 238–266.

Castilla, E. J. (2005). Social networks and employee performance in a call center. *American Journal of Sociology*, *110*(5), 1243–1283. doi:10.1086/427319

Chang, C.-S., & Chang, H.-H. (2007). Effects of internal marketing on nurse job satisfaction and organizational commitment: Example of medical centers in southern Taiwan. *The Journal of Nursing Research*, *15*(4), 265–274. doi:10.1097/01.JNR.0000387623.02931.a3 PMID:18080971

Chang, H. H., Hung, C. J., & Hsieh, H. W. (2014). Virtual teams: Cultural adaptation, communication quality, and interpersonal trust. *Total Quality Management & Business Excellence*, *25*(11/12), 1318–1335. doi:10.1080/14783363.2012.704274

Chau, P. (2010). Online higher education commodity. *Journal of Computing in Higher Education*, *22*(3), 177–191. doi:10.100712528-010-9039-y

Chen & Kotz. (2000). *A survey of context-aware mobile computing research*. Technical report, Technical Report TR2000-381, Dept. of Computer Science, Dartmouth College.

Chen, G. M., & Starosta, W. J. (1998). *Foundations of Intercultural Communication*. Boston: Allyn and Bacon.

Cheng, E. W. L., Li, H., & Fox, P. (2007). Job performance dimensions for improving final project outcomes. *Journal of Construction Engineering and Management*, *133*(8), 592–599. doi:10.1061/(ASCE)0733-9364(2007)133:8(592)

Cheng, Y. C. (2003). Quality assurance in education: Internal, interface, and future. *Quality Assurance in Education*, *11*(4), 202–213. doi:10.1108/09684880310501386

Cheng, Y. C., & Tam, W. M. (1997). Multi-models of quality in education. *Quality Assurance in Education*, *5*(1), 22–31. doi:10.1108/09684889710156558

Cherniss, C., & Goleman, D. (2001). *The emotionally intelligent workplace*. San Francisco, CA: Jossey-Bass.

Cheung, S. (2018). *#MeToo: Speaking Out Against Sexual Misconduct; Timeline: Sexual Misconduct Allegations Against Public Figures*. Retrieved October 10, 2018 from: https://www.nbcphiladelphia.com/entertainment/entertainmentnews/Sexual-Misconduct-Accusations-490592161.html

Cheung, M. K. C., Chiu, P.-Y., & Lee, M. K. O. (2011). Online social networks: Why do students use facebook? *Computers in Human Behavior*, *27*(4), 1337–1343. doi:10.1016/j.chb.2010.07.028

Cheung, S. O., Suen, H. C., & Lam, T. I. (2002). Fundamentals Of Alternative Dispute Resolution Processes In Construction. *Journal of Construction Engineering and Management*, *128*(5), 409–417. doi:10.1061/(ASCE)0733-9364(2002)128:5(409)

Chickering, A. W., & Potter, D. (1993). TQM and quality education: Fast food or fitness center. *The Educational Record*, *74*(2), 35–36.

Chihani, B., Bertin, E., Jeanne, F., & Crespi, N. (2011). Context-aware systems: a case study. In Digital Information and Communication Technology and Its Applications (pp. 718-732). Springer. doi:10.1007/978-3-642-22027-2_60

Chin, W., Marcolin, B., & Newsted, P. (2003). A partial least squares latent variable modeling approach for measuring interaction effects: Results from a Monte Carlo simulation study and an electronic-mail emotion/adoption study. *Information Systems Research*, *14*(2), 189–217. doi:10.1287/isre.14.2.189.16018

Chizmar, J. F. (2000). Total quality management of teaching and learning. *Journal of Economic Education*, *25*(2), 1–8. doi:10.1080/00220485.1994.10844828

Chu, A., & Chu, R. (2011). The intranet's role in newcomer socialization in the hotel industry in Taiwan – technology acceptance model analysis. *International Journal of Human Resource Management*, *22*(5), 1163–1179. doi:10.1080/09585192.2011.556795

Chughtai, Buckley, & Finian. (2008). *Work engagement and its relationship with state and trait trust: A conceptual analysis*. Retrieved from, http://findarticles.com/p/articles/mi_qa5335/is_200809/ai_n29493978/?tag=content;col1

Church, A. H. (1997). Managerial self-awareness in high-performing individuals in organizations. *The Journal of Applied Psychology*, *82*(2), 281–292. doi:10.1037/0021-9010.82.2.281 PMID:9109286

Cicero, M. (1971). *Selected works* (M. Grant, Trans.). Middlesex, UK: Penguin Books.

Cicero, M. (2012). *On living and dying well* (T. Habinek, Trans.). London, UK: Penguin Books.

Cincera, M., & Veugelers, R. (2012). Young leading innovators and the EU's R&D intensity gap. *Economics of Innovation and New Technology*, 1-22.

Ciriaci, D., Moncada-Paternò-Castello, P., & Voigt, P. (2013). *Innovation and Employment: A sustainable relation?* IPTS Working Papers on Corporate R&D and Innovation series - European Commission – No. 01/2013 – EUR 25807 EN.

Ciribelli, M. (2003). *Como realizar uma dissertação de mestrado através da pesquisa científica*. Rio de Janeiro: Viveiros de Castro Editora.

Civil Evidence Act, (1995).

Clampitt, P. (2005). *Communicating for Managerial Effectiveness*. New York: Sage Publications.

Clark, C., Werth, L., & Ahten, S. (2012). Cyberbullying and incivility in the online learning environment, Part I: Addressing faculty and student perceptions. *Nurse Educator*, *37*(4), 150–156. doi:10.1097/NNE.0b013e31825a87e5 PMID:22688872

Clarke, N. (2010). Emotional intelligence and its relationship to transformational leadership and key project manager competences. *Project Management Journal*, *41*(2), 5–20. doi:10.1002/pmj.20162

Clarke, R. (1999). Internet privacy con- cerns confirm the case for intervention. *Communications of the ACM*, *42*(2), 60–67. doi:10.1145/293411.293475

Clarke, R. A. (1988). Information technology and dataveillance. *Communications of the ACM*, *31*(5), 498–512. doi:10.1145/42411.42413

Clayton, M. (1995). Encouraging the kaizen approach to quality in a university. *Total Quality Management*, *6*(5/6), 593–601. doi:10.1080/09544129550035242

Cloke, K., & Goldsmith, J. (2011). *Resolving conflicts at work: Ten strategies for everyone on the job* (3rd ed.). San Francisco: Jossey-Bass.

CNN. (2017). *Money, Annual Ranking of America's Largest Corporations. Fortune 500 companies*. Available from the Web site: http://money.cnn.com/magazines/fortune/fortune500/2017/full_list/

Coad, A., & Hölzl, W. (2010). *Firm growth: empirical analysis* (No. 1002). Papers on economics and evolution.

Coakes, E., Smith, P. A. C., & Alwiss, D. (2011). Sustainable innovation and right to market. *Information Systems Management*, *28*(1), 30–42. doi:10.1080/10580530.2011.536110

Coate, L. E. (1990). TQM on campus: Implementing total quality management in a university setting. *Business Officer*, *24*(5), 26–35.

Cockburn, T. (2005). Communities of Commitment: Leadership, Learning Spirals, Teamwork and Emotional Regimes on an MBA, 1997-1999. Available from ProQuest and from the library of the University of Wales, Cardiff, UK.

Cockburn, T. (2006). *A complexity-based typology of emotional regimes in teams*. ITPNZ conference – Research that Counts, Napier, New Zealand.

Cockburn, T. (2010). Employee Commitment and the development of Corruption: A Case Study. In A. Stachowicz-Stanusch (Ed.), *Organizational Immunity to Corruption: Building Theoretical and Research Foundations*. Warsaw: Polish Academy of Sciences.

Cockburn, T., Jahdi, K. S., & Wilson, E. (2012). Ethical capital and the culture of integrity: 3 cases in UK and NZ. In W. Amann & A. Stachowicz-Stanusch (Eds.), *Business Integrity in Practice – insights from international case Studies*. New York, NY: Business Expert Press.

Cockburn, T., Jahdi, K., & Wilson, E. (Eds.). (2015). *Responsible governance: International perspectives for the new era*. New York, NY: Business Expert Press.

Cockburn, T., & Smith, P. A. C. (2018). Vuca and the Power of Emergence Teams. In D. Dalcher (Ed.), *The Evolution of Project Management Practice*. Routledge.

Cockburn, T., Smith, P. A. C., Martins, B., & Valles, R. S. (2016). Conflict of interest or Community of collaboration? Leadership, Dialectics and Dialog issues in community renewal and SME collaboration process. In A. Normore, L. Long, & M. Javidi (Eds.), *Handbook of Effective Communication, Leadership and Conflict Resolution*. IGI Global. doi:10.4018/978-1-4666-9970-0.ch012

Cocklin, B. (1999). Gumly Gumly Public School as a learning community. In J. Retallick, B. Cocklin, & K. Coombe (Eds.), *Learning Communities in Education* (pp. 265–286). London: Routledge.

Cohen-Charash, Y., & Spector, P. E. (2001). The role of justice in organizations: A meta- analysis. *Organizational Behavior and Human Decision Processes*, *86*(2), 278–321. doi:10.1006/obhd.2001.2958

Coiera, E. (2000). When Conversation Is Better Than Computation. *Journal of the American Medical Informatics Association*, *7*(3), 277–286. doi:10.1136/jamia.2000.0070277 PMID:10833164

Coiera, E., & Tombs, V. (1998). Communication behaviours in a hospital setting: An observational study. *BMJ (Clinical Research Ed.)*, *316*(7132), 673–676. doi:10.1136/bmj.316.7132.673 PMID:9522794

Coll, C. (2001). Las comunidades de aprendizaje y el futuro de la educación: el punto de vista del forum universal de las culturas. Simposio Internacional Sobre Comunidades de Aprendizaje.

Coll, C. (2004). Una experiencia educativa con futuro. *Trabajadores de la enseñanza, 249*, 12-13. Retrieved February 2, 2009, from http://www.fe.ccoo.es/publicaciones/TE/249/249pdf

Combe, I., & Bostchen, G. (2004). Strategy paradigms for the management of quality: Dealing with complexity. *European Journal of Marketing*, *38*(5), 500–523. doi:10.1108/03090560410529187

Commonwealth of Australia. (2008). *Quality education: The case for an education revolution in our schools*. Retrieved from http://apo.org.au/files/Resource/deewar_quality-education_2008.pdf

Conlin, J., Langford, D., & Kennedy, P. (1996). *The Relationship Between Construciton Procurement Strategies And Construction Contract Disputes*. Paper Presented At The CIB W92 North Meets South, Durban, South Africa.

Connell, J., Ferres, N., & Travalione, T. (2003). Engendering trust in manager-subordinate relationships. *Personnel Review*, *32*(5), 569–587. doi:10.1108/00483480310488342

Conroy, R. J. (2017). *Beyond emotional intelligence: A correlational study of multifactor measures of performance and law enforcement leadership styles* (Doctoral dissertation). Dallas Baptist University.

Conroy, R. J. (2017). *Beyond emotional intelligence: A correlational study of multifactor measures of performance and law enforcement leadership styles (Order No. 10643144)*. ProQuest Dissertations & Theses Global.

Conte, E., Todarello, O., Federici, A., Vitiello, F., Lopane, M., Khrennikov, A., & Zbilut, J. P. (2007). Some remarks on an experiment suggesting quantum-like behavior of cognitive entities and formulation of an abstract quantum mechanical formalism to describe cognitive entity and its dynamics. *Chaos, Solitons, and Fractals*, *31*(5), 1076–1088. doi:10.1016/j.chaos.2005.09.061

Contruction And Regeneration Act, (1996).

Cook, J., & Wall, T. (1980). New work attitude measures of trust, organizational commitment and personal need non-fulfillment. *Journal of Occupational Psychology*, *53*(1), 39–52. doi:10.1111/j.2044-8325.1980.tb00005.x

Coombs, W. T. (1995). Choosing the right words: The development of guidelines for the selection of "appropriate" crisis response strategies. *Management Communication Quarterly*, *8*(4), 447–476. doi:10.1177/0893318995008004003

Coombs, W. T. (2015). *Ongoing crisis communication: Planning, managing, and responding*. Los Angeles, CA: Sage.

Cooper, R. K., & Sawaf, A. (1997). *Executive EI: Emotional intelligence in leadership & organizations*. New York, NY: Grosset/Putnam Inc.

Copley, P. (2004). *Marketing Communications Management. Concepts and Theories, Cases and Practices*. Oxford, UK: Elsevier.

Corbin, J. (2016). What it takes to succeed in the digital workplace: A better understanding of mobile technology. *Technology Enabled Learning Excellence Essentials*. Retrieved on November 26 from https://search-proquest-com.proxy.campbell.edu/docview/1955028382?accountid=146941

Cornelissen, J. (2004). *Corporate communications. Theory and Practice*. London: Sage Publications Ltd.

Cornell University. (2011). *Managerial Communication. An introduction to key library resources for Hotel Administration*. Available from the Web site: http://guides.library.cornell.edu/HADM3365

Costa, A. L., & Garmston, R. J. (2002). *Cognitive coaching: A foundation for renaissance schools*. Norwood, MA: Christopher-Gordon.

Costa, A. L., & Garmston, R. J. (2015). *Cognitive coaching: Developing self-directed learners and leaders*. Lanham, MD: The Rowan & Littlefield Publishing Group, Inc.

Costa, P. T. Jr, & McCrae, R. R. (1992). *Revised NEO Personality Inventory (NEO–PI–R) and NEO Five-Factor Inventory (NEO–FFI) professional manual*. Odessa, FL: Psychological Assessment Resources.

Cousins, S. B., & Kahn, M. G. (1991). The visual display of temporal information. *Artificial Intelligence in Medicine*, *3*(6), 341–357. doi:10.1016/0933-3657(91)90005-V

Covin, T., Sightler, K., Kolenko, T., & Tudor, R. (1996). An investigation of post-acquisition satisfaction with the merger. *The Journal of Applied Behavioral Science*, *32*(2), 125–141. doi:10.1177/0021886396322001

Coy, D., & Kovacs-Long, J. (2005). Maslow and Miller: An exploration of gender and affiliation in the journey to competence. *Journal of Counseling and Development*, *83*(2), 138–145. doi:10.1002/j.1556-6678.2005.tb00590.x

Cranston, N. (2000). The impact of school-based management on primary school principals: An Australian Perspective. *Journal of School Leadership*, *10*(3), 214–232.

Cranston, N. C. (2001). Collaborative decision-making and school-based management: Challenges, rhetoric and reality. *Journal of Educational Enquiry*, *2*(2), 1–26.

Craver, C. B. (2006). Privacy issues affecting employers, employees and labour organizations. *Louisiana Law Review*, *66*, 1057–1078.

Crawford, L. E. D., & Shutler, P. (1999). Total quality management in education: Problems and issues for the classroom teacher. *International Journal of Educational Management*, *13*(2), 67–72. doi:10.1108/09513549910261122

Creede, C., Fisher-Yoshida, B., & Gallegos, P. (Eds.). (2012). *The reflective, facilitative, and interpretive practices of the coordinated management of meaning: making lives, making meanings*. Teaneck, NJ: Fairleigh Dickinson Press.

Creswell, J. W. (2013). *Qualitative inquiry & research design: Choosing among five approaches* (3rd ed.). Thousand Oaks, CA: Sage.

Crossan, M. M., Lane, R. E., & White, R. E. (1999). An organizational learning framework: From intuition to institution. *Academy of Management Review*, *24*(3), 522–537. doi:10.5465/amr.1999.2202135

Culnan, M. J. (1993). How did they get my name? An exploratory investigation of consumer attitudes toward secondary information use. *Management Information Systems Quarterly*, *17*(3), 341–364. doi:10.2307/249775

Cummings, H. W., Long, L., & Lewis, M. (1986). *Managing communication in organizations*. Scottsdale, AZ: Gorsuch-Scarisbrick.

Currie, W. (1999). Revisiting management innovation and change programmes: Strategic vision or tunnel vision? *Omega*, *27*(6), 647–660. doi:10.1016/S0305-0483(99)00023-7

Curseu, P. L., Schalk, R., & Wessel, I. (2008). How do virtual teams process information? A literature review and implications for management. *Journal of Managerial Psychology*, *23*(6), 628–652. doi:10.1108/02683940810894729

Cushner, K., & Brislin, R. W. (1996). *Intercultural interactions: A practical guide*. Thousand Oaks, CA: Sage.

Czarnitzki, D., & Delanote, J. (2013). Young innovative companies: The new high-growth firms? *Industrial and Corporate Change*, *22*(5), 1315–1340. doi:10.1093/icc/dts039

D'Aprix, R. (2009). *The Credible Company*. San Francisco: Jossey-Bass.

D'Urso, S. C. (2006). Who's watching us at work? Toward a structural-perceptual model of electronic monitoring and surveillance in organisations. *Communication Theory*, *16*(3), 281–303. doi:10.1111/j.1468-2885.2006.00271.x

Daft, R. L. (2000). *Management* (5th ed.). Hinsdale, IL: The Dryden Press.

Dahlgaard, J. J., Kristensen, K., & Kanji, G. K. (1995). Total quality management and education. *Total Quality Management*, *6*(5), 445–456. doi:10.1080/09544129550035116

Dai, D., Frank, J., & Sun, I. (2011). Procedural justice during police-citizen encounters: The effects of process-based policing on citizen compliance and demeanor. *Journal of Criminal Justice*, *39*(2), 159–168. doi:10.1016/j.jcrimjus.2011.01.004

Dalton, M., & Hollenbeck, G. P. (1996). *How to design an effective system for developing managers and executives*. Greensboro, NC: Center for Creative Leadership.

Dance, F. (1970). The concept of communication. *Journal of Communication*, *20*(2), 201–210. doi:10.1111/j.1460-2466.1970.tb00877.x

Daniels, H., & Warmington, P. (2007). Analyzing third generation activity systems: Labour power, subject, position and personal transformation. *Journal of Workplace Learning*, *19*(6), 377–391. doi:10.1108/13665620710777110

Darling-Hammond, L. (2010). Teacher education and the American future. *Journal of Teacher Education*, *61*(1-2), 35–47. doi:10.1177/0022487109348024

Darling-Hammond, L., & Berry, B. (2006). Highly qualified teachers for all. *Educational Leadership*, *64*(3), 14.

Davis, C. H. F. III, Deil-Amen, R., Rios-Aguilar, C., & Canche, M. S. G. (2001). Voluntary turnover, social capital and organizational performance. *Academy of Management Review*, *26*(3), 446–456. doi:10.5465/amr.2001.4845830

Davis, E. A., & Smithey, J. (2009). Beginning teachers moving toward effective elementary science teaching. *Science Education*, *93*(4), 745–770. doi:10.1002ce.20311

Dawnays Ltd v FG Minter Ltd (2 All ER 1389; [1971] 1 WLR 1205 1971).

De Cremer, D., & Tyler, T. R. (2005). Managing group behavior: The interplay between procedural justice, sense of self, and cooperation. *Advances in Experimental Social Psychology, 37*, 151–218. doi:10.1016/S0065-2601(05)37003-1

De Grauwe, A. (2005). Improving quality of education through school-based management: Learning from international experiences. *International Review of Education, 51*(4), 269–287. doi:10.100711159-005-7733-1

Debecker, G. (1997). *The gift of fear: Survival signals that protect us from violence*. New York, NY: Dell Books.

DeBussy, N., Ewing, M., & Pitt, L. (2004). Stakeholder theory and internal marketing communications: A framework for analyzing the influence of new media. *Journal of Marketing Communications, 9*(3), 147–161. doi:10.1080/1352726032000129890

DeCosta, M., Berquist, E., & Holbeck, R. (2015). A desire for growth: Online full-time faculty's perception of evaluation processes. *The Journal of Educators Online, 13*(2), 73–102.

Dellar, G. B. (1998). School Climate, School Improvement and Site-based Management. *Learning Environments Research, 1*(3), 353–367. doi:10.1023/A:1009970210393

Deloitte Core Beliefs and Culture Survey. (2013). Retrieved on August 6 from http://www.deloitte.com/assets/Dcom-UnitedStates/Local%20Assets/Documents/us_leadership_2013corebeliefs&culturesurvey_051613.pdf

Deloitte plc. (2017). *Technology Industry Outlook 2017 In-depth insight on growth opportunities and challenges in technology*. Retrieved from https://www2.deloitte.com/tr/en/pages/technology-media-and-telecommunications/ articles/technology-industry-outlook-2017.html

Denzin, N. K., & Lincoln, Y. S. (2005). *The Sage Handbook of Qualitative Research*. Thousand Oaks, CA: Sage.

Derven, M. (2016). Four drivers to enhance global virtual teams. *Industrial and Commercial Training, 48*(1), 1–8. doi:10.1108/ICT 08 2015 0056

Desjardins, C., & Obara, Y. (1993). From Québec to Tokyo: Perspectives on TQM. *Educational Leadership, 51*(1), 68–69.

Dewey, J. (1934). *Art as experience*. New York: Minton, Malach, and Co.

Dewing, J., Hancock, S., Brooks, J., Pedder, L., Adams, L., Riddaway, L., & O'Connor, P. (2004). An account of 360° review as part of a practice development strategy. *Practice Development in Health Care, 3*(4), 193–209. doi:10.1002/pdh.156

Dickson, D. (1999). Barriers to communication. In *Interaction for practice in community nursing* (pp. 84–132). London: Palgrave. doi:10.1007/978-1-349-14757-1_5

Diddams, M., & Chang, G. C. (2012). Only human: Exploring the nature of weakness in authentic leadership. *The Leadership Quarterly, 23*(3), 593–603. doi:10.1016/j.leaqua.2011.12.010

Diekmann, J., Girard, M., & Abdul-Hadi, N. (1994). *Disputes Potential Index: A Study Into The Predictability Of Contract Disputes*. Academic Press.

Dietz, G., & Fortin, M. (2007). Trust and justice in the formation of joint consultation committees. *Journal of International Human Resource Management, 18*(7), 1159–1181. doi:10.1080/09585190701391867

Diggins, P. B. (1997). Reflections on leadership characteristics necessary to develop and sustain learning school communities. *School Leadership & Management, 17*(3), 413–425. doi:10.1080/13632439769953

Dinev, T., & Hart, P. (2006). An extended privacy calculus model for e-commerce transactions. *Information Systems Research, 17*(1), 61–80. doi:10.1287/isre.1060.0080

Dinev, T., Xu, H., Smith, J. H., & Hart, P. (2013). Information privacy and correlates: An empirical attempt to bridge and distinguish privacy-related concepts. *European Journal of Information Systems*, *22*(3), 295–316. doi:10.1057/ejis.2012.23

DiPietro, R. A. (1993). TQM: Evolution, scope and strategic significance for management development. *Journal of Management Development*, *12*(7), 11–18. doi:10.1108/02621719310044910

Dirks, K., & Ferrin, D. L. (2002). Trust in leadership: Meta-analytic findings and implications for research and practice. *The Journal of Applied Psychology*, *87*(4), 611–628. doi:10.1037/0021-9010.87.4.611

Dishman, L. (2017). *This is the State of Small Business Failure in the US*. Retrieved November 11th,2018 from https://www.fastcompany.com/40435072/this-is-the-state-of-small-business-failure-in-the-u-s

DJ. (2015). *Dow Jones Sustainability Indices*. Accesses June 24, 2015 at http://www.sustainability-indices.com/review/industry-group-leaders-2014.jsp

Dobbins, K. (2009). Feeding innovation with learning lunches: Contextualising academic innovation in higher education. *Journal of Further and Higher Education*, *33*(4), 411–422. doi:10.1080/03098770903272495

Doherty, G. D. (1993). Towards total quality management in higher education: A case study of the University of Wolverhampton. *Higher Education*, *25*(3), 321–339. doi:10.1007/BF01383857

Dohrmann, G., & Epstein, D. (2011, May 30). SI investigation reveals eight-year pattern of violations under Tressel. *Sportsillustrated.com.* Retrieved June 14, 2011 from http://www.si.com/more-sports/2011/05/30/jim-tressel

Dolphin, R. R. (2005). Internal communications: Today's strategic imperative. *Journal of Marketing Communications*, *11*(3), 171–190. doi:10.1080/1352726042000315414

Donaldson, E., Ensher, E. A., & Grant-Vallone, E. J. (2000). Longitudinal examination of mentoring relationships on organizational commitment and citizenship behavior. *Journal of Career Development*, *26*(4), 233–248. doi:10.1177/089484530002600401

Donavan, D., Brown, T., & Mowen, J. (2004). Internal benefits of service-worker customer orientation: Job satisfaction, commitment and organizational citizenship behaviors. *Journal of Marketing*, *68*(1), 128–146. doi:10.1509/jmkg.68.1.128.24034

Donnithorne, L. R. (1994). *The west point way of leadership: From learning principled leadership to practicing it*. New York, NY: Doubleday.

Douthitt, E. A., & Aiello, J. R. (2001). The role of participation and control in the effects of computer monitoring on fairness perceptions, task satisfaction, and performance. *The Journal of Applied Psychology*, *86*(5), 867–874. doi:10.1037/0021-9010.86.5.867

Doyle, M., & Straus, D. (1976). *How to make meetings work*. New York, NY: Berkeley Publishing Group.

Dreher, S. (2014). Social media and the world of work. *Corporate Communications*, *19*(4), 344–356. doi:10.1108/CCIJ-10-2013-0087

Drezner, D., & Farrell, H. (2004). *The power and politics of blogs*. Paper presented at the American Political Science Association Conference, Chicago, IL.

Drucker, P. (1977). *People and Performance*. New York: Harper`s College Press.

Drucker, P. (1993). *Inovatia si sistemul antreprenorial*. Editura Enciclopedica, Bucaresti.

Drysdale, L., Goode, H., & Gurr, D. (2009). An Australian model of successful school leadership. *Journal of Educational Administration, 47*(6), 697–708. doi:10.1108/09578230910993087

Dube, S., & Marnewick, C. (2016). A conceptual model to improve performance in virtual teams. *South African Journal of Information Management, 18*(1), 1-10. http://dx.doi.org.umasslowell.idm.oclc.org/10.4102/sajim.v18i1.674

Duquette, C. (2015). Relating Historical Consciousness to Historical Thinking Through Assessment. In *New Directions in Assessing Historical Thinking*. New York: Routledge.

Duschl, R. A., Schweingruber, H. A., & Shouse, A. W. (2007). *Taking science to school. Learning and teaching science in grades K-8*. Washington, DC: National Academies Press.

Dussault, M., Frenette, E., & Fernet, C. (2013). Leadership: Validation of a self-report scale. *Psychological Reports, 112*(2), 419–436. doi:10.2466/01.08.PR0.112.2.419-436 PMID:23833872

Eagle, L., & Brennan, R. (2007). Are students customers? TQM and marketing perspectives. *Quality Assurance in Education, 15*(1), 44–60. doi:10.1108/09684880710723025

Earley, P. C., & Ang, S. (2003). *Cultural intelligence: Individual interactions across cultures*. Stanford, CA: Stanford University Press.

Economist Intelligence Unit. (2009). Managing virtual team: Taking a more strategic approach. *The Economist*. Retrieved September 15, 2012 from http://graphics.eiu.com/upload/eb/NEC_Managing_virtual_teams_WEB.pdf

Edelman Trust Barometer. (2013). Retrieved on 8/21/13 from http://www.edelman.com/insights/intellectual-property/trust-2013/

Edelman Trust Barometer. (2014). Retrieved on 1/22/14 from http://www.edelman.com/insights/intellectual-property/2014-edelman-trust barometer/

Eisenstadt, S. A., Wagner, M. M., Hogan, W. R., Pankaskie, M. C., Tsui, F. C., & Wilbright, W. (1998). Mobile workers in healthcare and their information needs: Are 2-way pagers the answer? *Proc AMIA Symp., 1998*, 135–139. PMID:9929197

Eissa, G., Fox, C., Webster, B. D., & Kim, J. (2012). A framework for leader effectiveness in virtual teams. *Journal of Leadership, Accountability and Ethics, 9*(2), 11–22.

Eker, M., Eker, S., & Pala, F. (2008). The effects of job satisfaction on organizational commitment among Turkish health care staff: An empirical study. *Journal of Academic Studies, 10*(36), 46–68.

Elgesem, D. (1999). The structure of rights in directive 95/46/EC on the protection of individuals with regard to the processing of personal data and the free movement of such data. *Ethics and Information Technology, 1*(4), 283–293. doi:10.1023/A:1010076422893

Ellis, B., & Normore, A. H. (2014). Police leadership: Connecting with communities through a partnership initiative. *Peace Officers Research Association of California Law Enforcement*. Retrieved from http://porac.org/

Ellis, B., Javidi, M., & Normore, A. H. (2018). The toxicity of the spiteful leader. *Law Enforcement Today*. Retrieved from, https://www.lawenforcementtoday.com/toxicity-spiteful-leader/

Ellis, B., Normore, A. H., & Javidi, M. (2018a). Getting left of boom: Troubleshooting poor outcomes. *Law Enforcement Today*. Retrieved from, https://www.lawenforcementtoday.com/getting-left-boom-troubleshooting-poor-outcomes/

Ellis, B., Normore, A. H., & Javidi, M. (2018b). Auftragstaktik': Building organizational leadership through mission control. *The Tactical Edge (National Tactical Officers Association), 2018*, 82-86. Retrieved from, http://public.ntoa.org/default.asp?action=issue&year=2018&season=3%20-%20Summer&pub=Tactical%20Edge

Ellis, B., Normore, A. H., & Javidi, M. (2018c). How leadership training is an effective tool against civil liability. *Police Chief Magazine*. Retrieved from, http://www.policechiefmagazine.org/police-leadership-training-effective-tool-against-civil-liability/

Ellis, G., & Normore, A. H. (2015). Performance management strategies for effective leadership in law enforcement: An accountability process. *FBI Law Enforcement Bulletin*. Retrieved from http://leb.fbi.gov/2015/february/performance-management-strategies-for-effective-leadership-an-accountability-process

Ellis, B., & Normore, A. H. (2016). Effective engagement and communication between first-line police supervisors and police officers. In *The handbook of effective communication, leadership, and conflict resolution (pp. 479 – 493)*. Hershey, PA: IGI Global Publishers. doi:10.4018/978-1-4666-9970-0.ch025

Ellis, N., & Hopkinson, G. (2010). The construction of managerial knowledge in business networks: Managers' theories about communication. *Industrial Marketing Management*, *39*(3), 413–424. doi:10.1016/j.indmarman.2007.08.011

Else, S. (2003). Practicing Knowledge Communities. *Knowledge Management*. Retrieved February 2, 2009, from http://www.destinationkm.com/articles/default.asp?ArticleID=1044

Emstad, A. B. (2011). The principal's role in the post-evaluation process. How does the principal engage in the work carried out after the schools self-evaluation? *Educational Assessment, Evaluation and Accountability*, *23*(4), 271–288. doi:10.100711092-011-9128-0

Engel, R. (2003). *How police supervisory styles influence patrol officer behavior*. Washington, DC: US Department of Justice. Retrieved from https://www.ncjrs.gov/pdffiles1/nij/194078.pdf

Engel, R. S. (2005). Citizens' perceptions of distributive and procedural injustice during traffic stops with police. *Journal of Research in Crime and Delinquency*, *42*(4), 445–481. doi:10.1177/0022427804272725

Engeström, Y. (2001). Expansive learning at work: Toward an activity theoretical reconceptualization. *Journal of Education and Work*, *14*(1), 133–156. doi:10.1080/13639080020028747

Engeström, Y., & Glaveanu, V. (2012). On third generation activity theory: Interview with Yrjö Engeström. *Europe's Journal of Psychology*, *8*(4), 515–518. doi:10.5964/ejop.v8i4.555

Enter, J. (2006). *Challenging the law enforcement organization: The road to effective leadership*. Dacula, GA: Narrow Road Press.

Epictetus. (1995). *The art of living: The classical manual on virtue, happiness, and effectiveness, (Interpreted by Sharon Lebell)*. New York, NY: HarperCollins.

Epstein, D., & Miller, R. T. (2011). Slow off the mark: Elementary school teachers and the crisis in science, technology, engineering, and math education. *Science Progress*. Retrieved from www.americanpress.org

Erbe, N. (2011). *Negotiation alchemy: global skills inspiring and transforming diverging worlds*. Berkeley, CA: Public Policy Press.

Erbe, N. (2014). *Approaches to managing organizational diversity and innovation*. Hershey, PA: IGI Global Press. doi:10.4018/978-1-4666-6006-9

Erbe, N., & Normore, A. H. (2015). *Cross-cultural collaboration and leadership in modern organizations*. Hershey, PA: IGI Global Publishers.

Erickson, M. L., Gibbs, J. P., & Jensen, G. F. (1977). The deterrence doctrine and the perceived certainty of legal punishments. *American Sociological Review*, *42*(2), 305–317. doi:10.2307/2094607 PMID:860865

Ethisphere. (2018). Research, rating and certification of corporate and institutional ethics, anti-corruption and sustainability. *The Ethisphere Institute History*. Retrieved October 19, 2018 from https://ethisphere.com/about-updated/

European Union. (2002). *Directive 95/46/EC: Article 29 WP55*. Retrieved from http://ec.europa. eu/justice_home/fsj/privacy/docs/wpdocs/2002/ wpss_en.pdf

Evans, L. (2007). Monitoring technology in the American workplace: Would adopting English privacy standards better balance employee privacy and productivity? *California Law Review*, *95*, 1115–1149.

Ewen, S. (1988). *All consuming images: The politics of style in contemporary culture*. New York: Basic Books.

Fan, K. T., Chen, Y. H., Wang, C. W., & Chen, M. (2014). E-leadership effectiveness in virtual teams: Motivating language perspective. *Industrial Management & Data Systems*, *114*(3), 421–437. doi:10.1108/IMDS-07-2013-0294

Farrey, T. (2011, May 30). Timeline: Jim Tressel's fall. *ESPN.com.* Retrieved July 19, 2011 from http://sports.espn.go.com/ncf/news/story?id=6607982

Fehr, E. & Gaechter, S. (2000). *Fairness and Retaliation: The economics of reciprocity*. Academic Press.

Feldman, J. (2014, May 28). Urban Outfitters accused of ripping off artist's design, sparks Tumblr fury. *Life*. Retrieved from https://www.huffpost.com/entry/urban-outfitters-spires-copyright-infringement_n_5403244

Felstiner, W. L., Abel, R. L., & Sarat, A. (1980). The Emergence And Transformation Of Disputes: Naming, Blaming, Claiming.... *Law & Society Review*, *15*(3/4), 631. doi:10.2307/3053505

Fenn, P. (2006). Conflict Management And Dispute Resolution. In D. Lowe & R. Leiringer (Eds.), *Commercial Management Of Projects: Defining The Discipline* (pp. 234–269). Blackwell Publishing. doi:10.1002/9780470759509.ch11

Fenn, P., Lowe, D., & Speck, C. (1997). Conflict And Dispute In Construction. *Construction Management and Economics*, *15*(6), 513–518. doi:10.1080/014461997372719

Ferguson, J., & Tryjankowski, A. (2009). Online versus face to face learning: Looking at modes of instruction in Master's level courses. *Journal of Further and Higher Education*, *33*(3), 219–228. doi:10.1080/03098770903026149

Fernandes, V. M. (2013) *The Effectiveness of Total Quality Management as a School Improvement Process* (Doctoral dissertation). Monash University, Melbourne, Australia. Retrieved from http://arrow.monash.edu.au/hdl/1959.1/871750

Fernandes, V. (2016). Reframing Continuous School Improvement in Australian Schools. In A. Normore, L. Long, & M. Javidi (Eds.), *Handbook of Research on Effective Communication, Leadership, and Conflict Resolution* (pp. 98–124). Hershey, PA: Information Science Reference. doi:10.4018/978-1-4666-9970-0.ch006

Fernandes, V. (2019a). Glocalising Educational Leadership Development in the Asia-Pacific Region. In V. Fernandes & P. W. K. Chan (Eds.), *Asia Pacific Education: Leadership, Governance and Administration*. Hershey, PA: Information Age Publishing.

Fernandes, V. (2019b). Disrupting the Norm? Implementing Educational Business Improvement Models in Pakistani Public-Private School Partnerships. In V. Fernandes & P. W. K. Chan (Eds.), *Asia Pacific Education: Leadership, Governance and Administration*. Hershey, PA: Information Age Publishing.

Ferrazzi, K. (2014). Getting virtual teams right. *Harvard Business Review*. Retrieved September 1, 2018 from https://hbr.org/2014/12/getting-virtual-teams-right

Ferrin, D. L., & Dirks, K. T. (2003). The use of rewards to increase and decrease trust: Mediating processes and differential effects. *Organization Science*, *14*(1), 18–31. doi:10.1287/orsc.14.1.18.12809

Fisher, G. (2001). Communities of interest: learning through the Interaction of Multiple Knowledge Systems. In *Proceedings of the 24thIRIS Conference.* Ulvik, Departament of Information Science.

Fisher, G. (1980). *International negotiation: A cross cultural perspective.* Yarmouth, ME: Intercultural Press.

Fisher, G. (1988). *Mindsets.* Yarmouth, ME: Intercultural Press.

Fisher, R., & Ury, W. (1986). *Getting to yes: Negotiating agreement without giving in.* Bergenfield, NJ: Penguin.

Fisher, R., Ury, W., & Patton, B. (1981). *Getting to Yes: Negotiating Agreement Without Giving In.* New York: Penguin Books.

Fishman, B. J., Penuel, W. R., Allen, A. R., Cheng, B. H., & Sabelli, N. O. R. A. (2013). Design-based implementation research: An emerging model for transforming the relationship of research and practice. *National Society for the Study of Education, 112*(2), 136-156.

Flaherty, J. (2010 October/November). Bridging the digital divide: A non-technical approach to the use of new technology in post-secondary teaching and learning. *Academic Matters Journal of Higher Education*, 21-26.

Flick, U. (2004). Design and process in qualitative research. In U. Flick, E. von Kardorff, & I. Steinke (Eds.), *A companion to qualitative research* (pp. 146–152). Thousand Oaks, CA: Sage.

Florica, T., Mozelius, P., Shabalina, O., Balan, O., Malliarakis, C., Miller, C., & Jones, P. (2013). An international approach to creative pedagogy and students' preferences of interactive media. *Proceedings of the International Conference on E-Learning*, 479-487.

Fogarty, J., Hudson, S. E., Atkeson, C. G., Avrahami, D., Forlizzi, J., Kiesler, S., ... Yang, J. (2005). Predicting human interruptibility with sensors. *ACM Transactions on Computer-Human Interaction, 12*(1), 119–146. doi:10.1145/1057237.1057243

Fogarty, J., Lai, J., & Christensen, J. (2004). Presence versus availability: The design and evaluation of a context-aware communication client. *International Journal of Human-Computer Studies, 61*(3), 299–317. doi:10.1016/j.ijhcs.2003.12.016

Folger, R., Konovsky, M. A., & Cropanzano, R. (1992). A due process metaphor for performance appraisal. *Research in Organizational Behavior, 14*, 129–129.

Fonseca, F. (2012, February). Navajo nation sues Urban Outfitters over goods. *Associated Press.* Retrieved from http://www.nbcnews.com/id/46574519/ns/business-retail/t/navajo-nation-sues-urban-outfitters-over-goods/#.Vd-wTLS_uTA

Forde, P. (2011, May 30). Tressel's end fits with saga's pattern. *ESPN.com.* Retrieved June 14, 2011 from http://espn.go.com/espn/print?id=6607408&type=story

Forkosh-Baruch, A., & Hershkovitz, A. (2012). A Case Study of Israeli Higher-Education Institutes Sharing Scholarly Information with the Community via Social Networks. *The Internet and Higher education, 15*(1), 56–68. doi:10.1016/j.iheduc.2011.08.003

Forst, B. (1984). Overburdened Courts And Underutilized Information Technology: A Modern Prescription For A Chronic Disorder. *Judicature, 68*, 30.

Fortunato, J. A. (2008). Restoring a reputation: The Duke University lacrosse scandal. *Public Relations Review, 34*(2), 116–123. doi:10.1016/j.pubrev.2008.03.006

Foster, M. K., Francescucci, A., & West, B. C. (2010). Why users participate in online social networks. *International Journal of Business and Management, 4*(1), 3–19.

Foucault, M. (1977). *Discipline and punish: The birth of the prison.* London, UK: Penguin Books.

Fox, A. (2011). Mixing it up. *Society of Human Resource Management*, *56*(5). Retrieved from http://www.shrm.org/Publications/hrmagazine/EditorialContent/2011/0511/Pages/0511fox.aspx

Franco, R. (2007). *Quantum mechanics, Bayes' theorem and the conjunction fallacy.* arXiv preprint quant-ph/0703222

Franklin, B. (1950). *The autobiography of Benjamin Franklin and selections from his other writings*. New York, NY: Random House, Inc.

Friend, T. (2011, May). Maurice Clarett tells his side. *ESPN.com.* Retrieved October 24, 2015 from http://sports.espn.go.com/ncf/news/story?id=1919246

Furst, S. A., Reeves, M., Benson, R., & Blackburn, R. S. (2004). Managing the life cycle of virtual teams. *The Academy of Management Perspectives*, *18*(2), 6–20. doi:10.5465/ame.2004.13837468

Gaan, N. (2012). Collaborative tools and virtual team effectiveness: An inductively derived approach in India's software sector. *Decision (Washington, D.C.)*, *39*(1), 5–27.

Gallo, G., & Yan, Ch. (2015). The Effects of Reputational and Social Knowledge on Cooperation. *Proceedings of the National Academy of Sciences of the United States of America*, *112*(12), 3647–3652. PMID:25775544

Gallup, Inc. (2010). *The state of the global workplace: A worldwide study of employee engagement and wellbeing.* Retrieved from http://www.gallup.com

Gammage, D. T. (2008). Three decades of implementation of school-based management in the Australian Capital Territory and Victoria in Australia. *International Journal of Educational Management*, *22*(7), 664–675. doi:10.1108/09513540810908575

GAO / US Government Accountability Office. (1998). *Military Recruiting: The Department of Defense Could Improve Its Recruiter Selection and Incentive Systems.* A United States Congressional Report Submitted to the Committee on Armed Services in the United States Senate on the 30th of January, 1988 (GAO/NSIAD – 98 – 58).

Garbutt, S. (1996). The transfer of TQM from industry to education. *Education + Training*, *38*(7), 16–22. doi:10.1108/00400919610130736

Garmston, R., & Wellman, B. (1998). *The adaptive schools sourcebook.* Norwood, MA: Christopher- Gordon.

Garrison, D., Anderson, T., & Archer, W. (2000). Critical inquiry in a text-based environment: Computer conferencing in higher education. *The Internet and Higher Education*, *2*(2-3), 87–105. doi:10.1016/S1096-7516(00)00016-6

Garrison, D., Anderson, T., & Archer, W. (2010). The first decade of the community of inquiry framework: A retrospective. *Internet and Higher Education*, *13*(1/2), 5–9. doi:10.1016/j.iheduc.2009.10.003

Garrity, C. B., & Baris, M. A. (1994). *Caught in the middle: Protecting the children of high-conflict divorce*. New York: Lexington Books.

Gatto, T. (2018, August 24). Urban Meyer and Zach Smith: A timeline of key events in abuse scandal. *The Sporting News*. Retrieved from http://www.sportingnews.com/us/ncaa-football/news/zach-smith-urban-meyer-timeline-domestic-violence-allegations-ohio-state-florida-courtney-smith-ex-wife/qdgwf1d3j9n41skbguxgqsql0

Gee, C. (2014). The Role of Emotional Intuitions in Moral Judgments and Decisions. *Journal of Cognition and Neuroethics*, *2*(1), 161–171.

Gelb, B. D., & Rengarajan, D. (2014). Employee contributions to brand equity. *California Management Review*, *56*(2), 95–112. doi:10.1525/cmr.2014.56.2.95

Gheorghe, P., Gardan, D., & Geangu, P. (2009). *The Importance of Managerial Communication in Establishing the Company Marketing Communication.* Paper presented at the International Conference on Administration and Business, ICEA – FAA, Faculty of Business and Administration, University of Bucharest.

Ghosh, A. P. (1998). *E-commerce security – Weak links, best defences.* Hoboken, NJ: John Wiley & Sons.

Gibbons, M., Limoges, C., Nowotny, H., Schwartzman, S., Scott, P., & Trow, M. (1994). *The New production of Knowledge-The dynamics of science and research in contemporary societies.* London: Sage.

Gibson, J., Ivancevich, J., Donnelly, J., & Konopaske, R. (2011). *Organizations: Behaviors, structures, and processes* (14th ed.). New York, NC: McGraw-Hill Education.

Gilligan, C. (1982). *In a different voice: Psychological theory and women's development.* Cambridge, MA: Harvard University Press.

Girard, K. (2011). *It's Not Nagging-Why Persistent, Redundant Communication Works.* Paper presented at the Research and Ideas, Working Knowledge Conference, Harvard Business School, UK.

Gladwell, M. (2008). *Outliers: The story of success.* New York, NY: Little, Brown & Company.

Glueck, M. (Ed.). (2006). *Work the Net: a Management Guide for Formal Networks.* New Delhi: GTZ.

Glynn, M. A. (1996). Innovative genius: A framework for relating individual and organizational intelligences to innovation. *Academy of Management Review, 21*(4), 1081–1111. doi:10.5465/amr.1996.9704071864

Godfrey, B. (2001). Electronic work monitoring: An ethical model. In *Selected papers from the second Australian institute conference on computer ethics* (pp. 18-21). Academic Press.

Goetsch, D. L., & Davis, S. B. (2000). *Quality management: Introduction to total quality management for production, processing and services* (3rd ed.). Prentice-Hall International Inc.

Goldin-Meadow, S. (1997). When gestures and words speak differently. *Current Directions in Psychological Science, 6*(5), 138–143. doi:10.1111/1467-8721.ep10772905

Goldin-Meadow, S. (2002). *Hearing gestures: How our hands help us think.* Cambridge, MA: Belknap Press.

Goldin-Meadow, S., Kim, S., & Singer, M. (1999). What the teacher's hands tell the student's mind about math. *Journal of Educational Psychology, 91*(4), 720–730. doi:10.1037/0022-0663.91.4.720

Goleman, D. (1998, November). What makes a leader? *Harvard Business Review*, 92-102.

Goleman, D. (1995). *Emotional intelligence: Why it can matter more than IQ.* New York: Bantam Books.

Goleman, D. (1996). *Emotional intelligence.* New York, NY: Bantam Books.

Goleman, D. (1998). *Working with emotional intelligence.* New York, NY: Bantam Books.

Goleman, D. (2000). Leadership that gets results. *Harvard Business Review, 78*(2), 78–90.

Goleman, D. (2006). *Social intelligence.* New York, NY: Bantam Books.

Goleman, D., Boyatzis, R., & McKee, A. (2002). *Primal leadership: Realizing the power of emotional intelligence.* Boston: Harvard Business School Press.

González, J., & Garazo, T. (2006). Structural relationships between organizational service orientation, contact employee job satisfaction and citizenship behavior. *International Journal of Service Industry Management, 17*(1), 23–50. doi:10.1108/09564230610651561

González-Patiño, J. (2018). Learn, Teach and Share, Participation in Expanded Educational Communities: Madrid Pikler Seminar as a Practice of Continuing Education between Childhood Professionals. *Digital Education Review, 33.*

Goodard, J. T. (2010). Toward Glocality: Facilitating leadership in an age of diversity. *Journal of School Leadership, 20*, 37–56.

Goodman, J., & Truss, C. (2004). The medium and the message: Communicating effectively during a major change initiative. *Journal of Change Management, 4*(3), 217–229. doi:10.1080/1469701042000255392

Gould-Williams, J. (2003). The importance of HR practices and workplace trust in achieving superior performance: A study of public-sector organizations. *International Journal of Human Resource Management, 14*(1), 28–54. doi:10.1080/09585190210158501

Grabner-Kraeuter, S. & Waiguny, M. (2011). *Why users stay in online social networks: perceptions of value, trust, subjective norm and the moderating influence of duration of use.* American Marketing Association.

Graham-Harrison, E. (2016, May 28). Black man is washed whiter in China's racist detergent advert. *The Guardian.* Retrieved from https://www.theguardian.com/world/2016/may/28/china-racist-detergent-advert-outrage

Graham, J. (1991). An essay on organizational citizenship behavior. *Employee Responsibilities and Rights Journal, 4*(4), 249–270. doi:10.1007/BF01385031

Granovetter, M., & McGuire, P. (1998). The Making of an Industry: Electricity in the United States. In M. Callon (Ed.), *The Laws of the Markets* (pp. 147–173). Blackwell. doi:10.1111/j.1467-954X.1998.tb03473.x

Granshaw, L. (2014, May 24). Did Urban Outfitters sell an artist's work without permission – again? *The Daily Dot.* Retrieved from https://www.dailydot.com/business/urban-outfitters-steal-artists-work/

Gratch, J., Wang, N., Gerten, J., Fast, E., & Duff, R. (2007). Creating Rapport with Virtual Agents. *International Conference on Intelligent Virtual Agents*, Paris, France. 10.1007/978-3-540-74997-4_12

Gratton, L., & Truss, C. (2003). The three-dimensional people strategy: Putting human resources policies into action. *The Academy of Management Executive, 17*(3), 74–86.

Graupmann, V., Jonas, E., Meier, E., Hawelka, S., & Aichhorn, M. (2012). Reactance, the self, and its group: When threats to freedom come from the ingroup versus the outgroup. *European Journal of Social Psychology, 42*(2), 164–173. doi:10.1002/ejsp.857

Greenberg, L., & Barling, J. (1999). Predicting employee aggression against coworkers, subordi- nates and supervisors: The roles of person behaviors and perceived workplace factors. *Journal of Organizational Behavior, 20*(6), 897–913. doi:10.1002/(SICI)1099-1379(199911)20:6<897::AID-JOB975>3.0.CO;2-Z

Greenhow, C. (2011). Online social networks and learning. *On the Horizon, 19*(1), 4–12. doi:10.1108/10748121111107663

Greenwood, M. S., & Gaunt, H. J. (1994). *Total quality management for schools.* London: Cassell.

Grensing-Pophal, L. (2018). *How to handle 5 generations in the workplace.* Academic Press.

Grinder, M. (2008). *The elusive obvious.* Battle Ground, WA: Michael Grinder and Associates.

Gronstedt, A. (2000). *The customer century: Lessons from world-class companies in integrated marketing communication*. New York: Routledge.

Grosse, C. U. (2002). Managing communication within virtual intercultural teams. *Business Communication Quarterly, 65*(4), 22–38. doi:10.1177/108056990206500404

Gross, L. (2011). Communication as the Discipline of the 21st Century. *International Journal of Communication, 5*, 1497–1498.

Gross, S. R., & Syverud, K. D. (1992). Getting To No: A Study Of Settlement Negotiations And The Selection Of Cases For Trial. *Michigan Law Review, 90*, 323–373. PMID:10115793

Grudin, J. (1994). Groupware and social dynamics: Eight challenges for developers. *Communications of the ACM, 37*(1), 92–105. doi:10.1145/175222.175230

Grumdahl, C. R. (2010). *How schools can effectively plan to meet the goal of improving student learning* (Doctoral dissertation). University of Minnesota. Retrieved from:https://conservancy.umn.edu/bitstream/handle/11299/59567/Grumdahl_umn_0130E_10969.pdf?sequence=1

Gudykunst, W. B., & Kim, Y. Y. (1992). *Communicating with strangers: An approach to intercultural communication* (2nd ed.). New York: McGraw-Hill.

Guille, A., Hacid, H., Favre, C., & Zighed, D. A. (2013). Information Difusion in Online Social Networks: A Survey. *Association for Computing Machinery, 42*(2), 17–28.

Gurteen, D. (2012). *Leading Issues in Social Knowledge Management. A collection of important Social Knowledge Management papers*. Academic Publishing International.

Guskey, T., & Yoon, K. (2009). What works in professional development. *Phi Delta Kappan, 90*(7), 495–500. doi:10.1177/003172170909000709

Hackett, J. (2000). *Construction Claims: Current Practice And Case Management*. London: LLP Professional Publishing.

Hackman, M., & Johnson, C. (2013). *Leadership: A communication perspective* (6th ed.). Long Grove, IL: Wave Land Press.

Hackman, R., & Oldham, G. (1975). Development of the Job Diagnostic Survey. *The Journal of Applied Psychology, 60*(2), 150–170. doi:10.1037/h0076546

Hackman, R., & Oldham, G. (1976). Motivation through the design of work: A test of a theory. *Organizational Behavior and Human Performance, 16*(2), 250–279. doi:10.1016/0030-5073(76)90016-7

Haidt, J. (2001). The emotional dog and its rational tail: A social intuitionist approach to moral judgment. *Psychological Review, 108*(4), 814–834. doi:10.1037/0033-295X.108.4.814 PMID:11699120

Håkansson, H. (1987). Product development in networks. In H. Håkansson (Ed.), *Technological development: A network approach* (pp. 84–128). New York: Croom Helm.

Halbesleben, J. R. B., & Wheeler, A. R. (2008). The relative roles of engagement and embeddedness in predicting job performance and intention to leave. *Work and Stress, 22*(3), 242–256. doi:10.1080/02678370802383962

Hale, R., & Whitlam, P. (1997). *Towards the virtual organization*. London: The McGraw-Hill Co.

Hall Edward, T. (1959). *The Silent Language*. New York: Doubleday.

Hallinger, P., & Heck, R. H. (2011). Exploring the journey of school improvement: Classifying and analyzing patterns of change in school improvement processes and learning outcomes. *School Effectiveness and School Improvement*, *22*(1), 1–27. doi:10.1080/09243453.2010.536322

Hall, J. (1973). Communication revisited. *California Management Review*, *15*(3), 177. doi:10.2307/41164439

Hammill, G. (2015). Mixing and matching four generations of generations of employees. *FDU Magazine Online*. Retrieved from: http://www.fdu.edu/newspubs/magazine/05ws/generations.htm

Hams, B. (2012). *Ownership thinking: How to end entitlement and create a culture of accountability, purpose, and profit*. New York, NY: McGraw Hill.

Handley, R. (1997, April). AFRS rates emotional intelligence. *Air Force Recruiter News*.

Hardy, C., & Phillips, N. (1998). Strategies of Engagement: Lessons from the Critical Examination of Collaboration and Conflict in an Interorganizational Domain. *Organization Science*, *9*(2), 217–230. doi:10.1287/orsc.9.2.217

Hargadon, A. (2003). *How Breakthroughs Happen*. Boston, MA: Harvard Business School Press.

Harris Interactive. (2003). *Poll*. Retrieved from http://www.harrisinteractive.com/harris_poll/ index.asp?PID=365

Harris, A., & Spillane, J. (2008). Distributed leadership through the looking glass. *Management in Education*, *22*(1), 31–34. doi:10.1177/0892020607085623

Harrison, A. G. (2013). Engagement Ring: Building connections between employees and strategy. *Public Relations Tactics*, *20*(5), 16.

Harrisson, T. R. (2003). Victims, Targets, Protectors, And Destroyers: Using Disputant Accounts To Develop A Grounded Taxonomy Of Disputant Orientations. *Conflict Resolution Quarterly*, *20*(3), 307–329. doi:10.1002/crq.27

Harter, A., & Hopper, A. (1994). A distributed location system for the active office. *IEEE Network*, *8*(1), 62–70. doi:10.1109/65.260080

Harter, J., Schmidt, F., & Hayes, T. (2002). Business-united-level relationship between employees satisfaction. *The Journal of Applied Psychology*, *87*(2), 268–279. doi:10.1037/0021-9010.87.2.268 PMID:12002955

Hauenstein, N. M. A., McGonigle, T., & Flinder, S. W. (2001). A meta-analysis of the relationship between procedural justice and distributive justice: Implications for justice research. *Employee Responsibilities and Rights Journal*, *13*(1), 39–56. doi:10.1023/A:1014482124497

Hauser, R., Paul, R., Bradley, J., & Jeffrey, L. (2012). Computer self-efficacy, anxiety and learning in online versus face to face medium. *Journal of Information Technology Education*, *11*, 141–154. doi:10.28945/1633

Hayes, D., Christie, P., Mills, M., & Lingard, B. (2004). Productive leaders and productive leadership: Schools as learning organisations. *Journal of Educational Administration*, *42*(4/5), 520–538. doi:10.1108/09578230410554043

Hazelton, V., & Long, L. (1988). Concepts for public relations education, research, and practice: A communication point of view. *Central States Speech Journal*, *39*(2), 77–87. doi:10.1080/10510978809363239

HBS. (2004). *Face-to-Face Communications for Clarity and Impact by the Results-Driven Manager*. Boston: Harvard Business School Press.

HCI (House of Commons Intervention). (1961). *Budget Resolutions and Economic Situation. In Speeches, Interviews & Other Statements*. Archives of Margaret Thatcher Foundation. Accessed October 19, 2018, at https://www.margaretthatcher.org/document/101096

Hearn, S., & White, N. (2009). *Communitites of Practice:Linking, knowledge.policy and practice*. London: Overseas Development Institute.

Heath, B., Hills, B., & Berry, M. (1994). *The Origin Of Conflict Within The Construction Process*. Paper Presented At The First Plenary Meeting Of TG15, The Netherlands.

Heidemann, J., Klier, M., & Probst, F. (2012). Online social networks: A survey of a global phenomenon. *Computer Networks*, *56*(18), 3866–3878. doi:10.1016/j.comnet.2012.08.009

Hellriegel, D., & Slocum, J. W. (2008). Organizational Behavior (12th ed.). Cincinnati, OH: South-Western College Publishing (Thomson Learning).

Helne, C. A. (2005). Predicting workplace deviance from the interaction between organizational justice and personality. *Journal of Managerial Issues*, *17*(2), 247–263.

Henderson, L. S. (1986). Unraveling the Meaning of Managerial Communication: A Conceptual Explication and Model for Guiding Future Research. *Academy Of Management Best Papers Proceedings*, 219-223.

Henderson, J. C., & Lee, S. (1992). Managing I/S design teams: A control theories perspective. *Management Science*, *38*(6), 757–777. doi:10.1287/mnsc.38.6.757

Hermelin, E., Lievens, F., & Robertson, I. T. (2007). The validity of assessment centres for predicting supervisory performance ratings: A meta-analysis. *International Journal of Selection and Assessment*, *15*(4), 405–411. doi:10.1111/j.1468-2389.2007.00399.x

Hernandez, J. R., Jr. (2001). *Total quality management in education: The application of TQM in a Texas school district* (Unpublished doctoral dissertation). University of Texas, Austin, TX. Retrieved November 3, 2008, from Dissertations & Theses: Full Text. (Publication No. AAT 3034546)

Hersh, W., Helfand, M., Wallace, J., Kraemer, D., Patterson, P., Shapiro, S., & Greenlick, M. (2002). A systematic review of the efficacy of telemedicine for making diagnostic and management decisions. *Journal of Telemedicine and Telecare*, *8*(4), 197–209. doi:10.1258/135763302320272167 PMID:12217102

Hibbert, K., & Rich, S. (2006). Virtual communities of practice. In J. Weiss, J. Hunsinger, & J. Trifonas (Eds.), *The international handbook of virtual learning environments* (pp. 563–579). Springer. doi:10.1007/978-1-4020-3803-7_22

Hill, A., Melon, L., Laker, B., & Goddard, J. (2016, October 20). *The one type of leader who can turn around a failing school*. Retrieved on October, 30 2018, from https://hbr.org/2016/10/the-one-type-of-leader-who-can-turn-around-a-failing-school

Hill, L. B., Long, L. W., & Javidi, M. (1994). Principled Negotiation: Achieving Intercultural Effectiveness. In N. Honna, L. Hill, B. Hoffer, & Y. Tokeshita (Eds.), Organizational behaviors in cross-cultural settings. Vol. II, Intercultural Understanding and Communication. Tokyo: Sanshuusha Publishers.

Hill, P. W., Rowe, K. J., Holmes-Smith, P., & Russell, V. J. (1996). The Victorian Quality Schools Project: A study of school and teacher effectiveness (Report, Volume 1). Centre for Applied Educational Research: University of Melbourne.

Hodgkinson, M., & Brown, G. (2003). Enhancing the quality of education: A case study and some emerging principles. *Higher Education*, *45*(3), 337–352. doi:10.1023/A:1022680504729

Hodgkinson, M., & Kelly, M. (2007). Quality management and enhancement processes in UK business schools: A review. *Quality Assurance in Education*, *15*(1), 77–91. doi:10.1108/09684880710723043

Hofstede, G. (2001). *Culture's Consequences: comparing values, behaviors, institutions, and organizations across nations* (2nd ed.). Thousand Oaks, CA: Sage.

Hogan, R. (2002). What is Personality? *Advantage Hiring Newsletter.* Retrieved on November 2015 at http:// www.Advantagehiring.com/newsletter/1100/n1100_2.htm

Hogan, R., & Hogan, J. (2001). Assessing Leadership: A View from the Dark Side. *International Journal of Selection and Assessment*, *9*(1/2), 40–51. doi:10.1111/1468-2389.00162

Holland, P. J., Cooper, B., & Hecker, R. (2015). Electronic monitoring and surveillance in the workplace: The effects on trust in management, and the moderating role of occupational type. *Personnel Review*, *44*(1), 161–175. doi:10.1108/PR-11-2013-0211

Holleran, K., Pappas, J., Lou, H., Rubalcaba, P., Lee, R., & Clay, S. (2003). Mobile Technology in a Clinical Setting. *AMIA ... Annual Symposium Proceedings - AMIA Symposium. AMIA Symposium*, 2003. PMID:14728368

Holliday, A. R. (2007). *Doing and Writing Qualitative Research.* London, UK: Sage Publications. doi:10.4135/9781446287958

Holness, G. V. R. (2001). Achieving quality using TQM and ISO. *ASHRAE Journal*, *43*(1), 195–199.

Holt, M. (1993a). Dr. Deming and the improvement of schooling: No instant pudding. *Journal of Curriculum and Supervision*, *9*(1), 6–23.

Holt, M. (1993b). The educational consequences of W. Edwards Deming. *Phi Delta Kappan*, *74*(5), 382–388.

Homana, G. (n.d.). Youth Political Engagement in Australia and the United States: Student Councils and Volunteer Organizations as Communities of Practice. *Journal of Social Science Education, 17*(1).

Hong & Landay. (2004). An architecture for privacy-sensitive ubiquitous computing. *Proceedings of the 2nd international conference on Mobile systems, applications, and services*, 177-189.

Horne, J., & Lupton, T. (1965). The work activities of middle managers: An exploratory study. *Journal of Management Studies*, *1*(21), 14–33. doi:10.1111/j.1467-6486.1965.tb00563.x

Horvitz, E., & Apacible, J. (2003). Learning and reasoning about interruption. *Proceedings of the 5th international conference on Multimodal interfaces.*

Horvitz, E., Koch, P., Kadie, C. M., & Jacobs, A. (2002). Coordinate: Probabilistic forecasting of presence and availability. *Proceedings of the 18th Conference in Uncertainty in Artificial Intelligence (UAI'02)*, 224-233.

Horwitz, F. M., Bravington, D., & Silvis, U. (2006). The promise of virtual teams: Identifying key factors in effectiveness and failure. *Journal of European Industrial Training*, *30*(6), 472–494. doi:10.1108/03090590610688843

Hovland, C., Janis, I., & Kelley, H. (1953). *Communication and persuasion.* New Haven, CT: Yale University Press.

Howell, J. P., & Costley, D. L. (2006). *Understanding behaviors for effective leadership* (2nd ed.). Upper Saddle River, NJ: Prentice Hall.

Hristova, A. (2008). *Conceptualization and Design of a Context-aware platform for user centric Applications. Master of Science in Communication Technology Master*. Trondheim: Norwegian University of Science and Technology.

Hubbard, S., & Menzel, S. (1995). Mt. Edgecumbe High School case study report. In S. Hubbard & S. Menzel (Eds.), *The Study of School-to-Work Reform Initiatives. Volume II: Case Studies* (pp.5-55). Studies of Education Reform Series. Academy for Educational Development, Washington, DC. National Inst. for Work and Learning. Retrieved from http://files.eric.ed.gov/fulltext/ED397551.pdf

Huddleston, T. (2014, November). Urban Outfitters' profits and shares tumble. *Fortune*. Retrieved from http://fortune.com/2014/11/17/urban-outfitters-shares-dip-as-namesake-brand-weighs-down-same-store-sales/

Hughes, P. (Ed.). (1988). *The challenge of identifying and marketing quality in education*. Sydney, Australia: The Australian Association of Senior Educational Administrators.

Hurlbert, J. S. (2001). Social networks, social circles and job satisfaction. *Work and Occupations*, *18*(4), 415–430. doi:10.1177/0730888491018004003

Hydle, K., Kvalshaugen, R., & Breuning, K. (2014). Transnational practices in communities of task and communities learning. *Management Learning*, *45*(5), 609–629. doi:10.1177/1350507613500881

Hylton, K. N. (1990). The Influence Of Litigation Costs On Deterrence Under Strict Liability And Under Negligence. *International Review of Law and Economics*, *10*(2), 161–171. doi:10.1016/0144-8188(90)90021-K

IABC. (2015). *The six principles of the profession. The Global Standard of the Profession*. International Association of Business Communicators. Retrieved June 24, 2015 from https://www.iabc.com/global-standard-2/

IBM. (2006). *Stopping insider attacks: How organizations can protect their sensitive information*. Retrieved from http://www-935.ibm.com/ services/us/imc/pdf/gsw00316-usen-00-insider- threats-wp.pdf

Idrus, N. (1995). Empowerment as a manifestation of total quality: A study in three countries. *Total Quality Management*, *6*(5 & 6), 603–612. doi:10.1080/09544129550035251

Idrus, N. (1996). Towards total quality management in academia. *Quality Assurance in Education*, *4*(3), 34–40. doi:10.1108/09684889610125850

Iles, P., & Hayers, P. K. (1997). Managing diversity in transnational project teams: A tentative model and case study. *Journal of Managerial Psychology*, *12*(2), 95–117. doi:10.1108/02683949710164190

INITIATIVEONE. (2018). *Are generational differences that important to workplace culture?* Retrieved from: https://www.initiative-one.com/insights/blog/generational-differences-in-the-workplace/

Innes, J. E., & Booher, D. E. (1999). Consensus building and complex adaptive systems: A framework for evaluating collaborative planning. *Journal of the American Planning Association*, *65*(4), 412–423. doi:10.1080/01944369908976071

Introna, L. D. (1996). Privacy and the computer: Why we need privacy in the information society. *Metaphilosophy*, *28*(3), 259–275. doi:10.1111/1467-9973.00055

Introna, L. D. (2001). Workplace surveillance, privacy and distributive justice. In R. A. Spinello & H. T. Tavani (Eds.), *Readings in cyberethics* (pp. 519–532). Sudbury, MA: Jones and Barlett.

Jackman, J. & Stober, M. (2003, April). Fear of feedback. *Harvard Business Review*.

Jackson, D. S. (2000). The School Improvement Journey: Perspectives on leadership. *School Leadership & Management Development*, *20*(1), 61–78. doi:10.1080/13632430068888

Jackson, T., Dawson, R., & Wilson, D. (2001). *The cost of email interruption (Item No. 2134/495)*. Loughborough, UK: Loughborough University Institutional Repository.

Jamali, H. R., Russell, B., Nicholas, D., & Watkinson, A. (2014). Do online communities support research collaboration? *Journal of International Management*, *66*(6), 603–622.

Janesick, V. J. (2011). *Stretching exercises for qualitative researchers* (3rd ed.). Thousand Oaks, CA: Sage. doi:10.1177/136078041101600402

Janoff, S. (1991). The influence of legal education on moral reasoning Process. *Minnesota Law Review*, *76*, 193–238.

Jarvenpaa, S. L., & Leidner, L. E. (1999). Communication and trust in global virtual teams. *Organization Science*, *10*(6), 791–815. doi:10.1287/orsc.10.6.791

Javidi, M., Nash, R., Normore, Hoina, C., Valenti, V., Scott, W., … Javidi, A. (2016). *Magnanimous officers.* The International Academy of Public Safety. Retrieved from, http://leicld.com/magnus/

Jehn, K. A. (1994). Enhancing Effectivenes: An Investigation Of Advantages And Disadvantages Of Value-Based Intragroup Conflict. *International Journal of Conflict Management*, *5*(3), 223–238. doi:10.1108/eb022744

Jehn, K. A., & Mannix, E. A. (2001). The Dynamic Nature Of Conflict: A Longitudinal Study Of Intragroup Conflict And Group Performance. *Academy of Management Journal*, *44*(2), 238–251.

Jenkins, H., Ito, M., & boyd, d. (2015). *Participatory culture in a networked era: A conversation on youth, learning, commerce, and politics*. Cambridge, MA: Polity Press.

Jenkins, S. (2013, January 20). NCAA touts amateurism rules over open market, but which is more corrupt. *The Washington Post.* Retrieved January 22, 2014 from http://www.washingtonpost.com/sports/colleges/ncaa-touts-amateurism-rules-over-open-market-but-which-is-more-corrupt/2013/09/20/511e18ea-2204-11e3-a358-1144dee636dd_story.html

Jensen, J. M., & Raver, J. L. (2012). When self-management and surveillance collide: Conse- quences for employees' trust, autonomy, and discretionary behaviors. *Group & Organization Management*, *37*(3), 308–346. doi:10.1177/1059601112445804

Jerome, A. M. (2008). Toward prescription: Testing the rhetoric of atonement's applicability in the athletic arena. *Public Relations Review*, *34*(2), 124–134. doi:10.1016/j.pubrev.2008.03.007

Johannesen, R. (1996). *Ethics in human communication* (4th ed.). Prospect Heights, IL: Waveland Press.

Johansson, C., & Heide, M. (2008). Speaking of change: Three communication approaches in studies of organizational change. *Corporate Communications*, *13*(3), 288–305.

John, L., & Johnson, M. (2010). *Getting the most from an age-diverse workforce.* Retrieved from http://www.generationsincbook.com

Johnsen, E., Bergmo, T., Johansen, M., & Solvoll, T. (2016). Evaluation of a Context Specific Communcation System Based on Smartphone. Nurses Use and Experiences. *Proceedings from The 14th Scandinavian Conference on Health Informatics 2016.*

Johnson & Johnson. (2011, December). *Director, Corporate Communications Job.* Health Care Systems Inc. Accessed from the Web site: http://www.careers.jnj.com/region

Johnson, C. (2011, August). Case Against Wiki Leaks Part Of Broader Campaign. *NPR News*. Accessed from the Web site: http://www.npr.org/2011/05/11/136173262/case-against-wikileaks-part-of-broader-campaign

Johnson, R., Stewart, C., & Bachman, C. (2015). What drives students to complete online courses? What drives faculty to teach online? Validating a measure of motivation orientation in university students and faculty. *Interactive Learning Environments*, *23*(4), 528–543. doi:10.1080/10494820.2013.788037

Jones, T. L. (2009). *Virtual team communication and collaboration in Army and corporate applications*. Retrieved September 15, 2012 from http://www.dtic.mil/cgi-bin/GetTRDoc?AD=ADA502091

Jones, J. P., & Seraphim, D. (2008). TQM implementation and change management in an unfavourable environment. *Journal of Management Development*, *27*(3), 291–306. doi:10.1108/02621710810858614

Jones, M. (2006). Which is a better predictor of job performance: Job satisfaction or life satisfaction? *Journal of Behavioral and Applied Management*, *8*(1), 20–42.

Judge, T., Parker, S., Colbert, A., Heller, D., & Remus, I. (2001). Job satisfaction: a cross-cultural review. In N. Anderson, D. Ones, H. Sinangil, & C. Viswesvaran (Eds.), *Handbook of Industrial, Work and Organizational Psychology* (Vol. 2, pp. 25–52). London: Sage Publications.

Jules, C. (2009). Feedback as a unit of work: A data-driven approach to organizational coaching. *OD Practitioner*, *41*(3), 8–12.

Kahan, D. M. (2014a). *"Ordinary science intelligence": A science comprehension measure for use in the study of risk perception and science communication.* Cultural Cognition Project Working Paper No. 112.

Kahan, D. M. (2014b). Making climate-science communication evidence-based—all the way down. In M. Boykoff & D. Crow (Eds.), Culture, politics and climate change (pp. 203-220). New York, NY: Routledge Press.

Kahan, D. M. (2015). Climate-Science Communication and the Measurement Problem. *Advances in Pol. Psych., 36*, 1-43. Available at SSRN:https://ssrn.com/abstract=2459057

Kahn, R. L. (1964). Introduction. In R. L. Kahn & E. Boulding (Eds.), *Power And Conflict In Organizations* (pp. 1–7). Basic Books.

Kahn, W. A. (1990). Psychological conditions of personal engagement and disengagement at work. *Academy of Management Journal*, *33*(4), 692–724.

Kalla, H. K. (2005). Integrated internal communications: A multidisciplinary perspective. *Corporate Communications*, *10*(4), 302–314. doi:10.1108/13563280510630106

Kamer, F. (2010, May 27). Are Brooklyn fashion designers being ripped off by Urban Outfitters? *The Village Voice*. Retrieved from https://www.villagevoice.com/2010/05/27/are-brooklyn-fashion-designers-being-ripped-off-by-urban-outfitters/

Kankanhalli, A., Tan, B. C. Y., & Wei, K.-K. (2007). Conflict and performance in global virtual teams. *Journal of Management Information Systems*, *23*(3), 237–274. doi:10.2753/MIS0742-1222230309

Kanter, R. (1977). *Men and Women of the Corporation*. New York, NY: Basic Books.

Kaplan, S. (2014, September). #WhyIStayed: She saw herself in Ray Rice's wife, Janay, and tweeted about it. So did thousands of others. *The Washington Post*. Retrieved from http://www.washingtonpost.com/news/morning-mix/wp/2014/09/09/whyistayed-she-saw-herself-in-ray-rices-wife-janay-and-tweeted-about-it-so-did-thousands-of-others/

Kaplan, A. M., & Haenlein, M. (2011). The early bird catches the news: Nine things you should know about micro-blogging. *Business Horizons*, *54*(2), 105–113. doi:10.1016/j.bushor.2010.09.004

Kasper-Fuehrer, E. C., & Ashkanasy, N. M. (2001). Communicating trustworthiness and building trust in interorganisational virtual organization. *Journal of Management*, *27*(3), 235–254. doi:10.1016/S0149-2063(01)00090-3

Katz, D., & Kahn, R. L. (1978). *The Social Psychology of Organizations* (2nd ed.). New York: Wiley.

Katz, M. H., & Schroeder, S. A. (1988). The sounds of the hospital. Paging patterns in three teaching hospitals. *The New England Journal of Medicine*, *319*(24), 1585–1589. doi:10.1056/NEJM198812153192406 PMID:3200267

Kayworth, T. R., & Leidner, D. E. (2002). Leadership effectiveness in global virtual teams. *Journal of Management Information Systems*, *18*(3), 7–40. doi:10.1080/07421222.2002.11045697

Keis, K., & Javidi, M. (2014). *Deliberate leadership: Creating success through personal style*. Vancouver: CRG Publishing.

Kelly, J. (1964). The study of executive behavior by activity sampling. *Human Relations*, *17*(3), 277–287. doi:10.1177/001872676401700310

Kendon, A. (1997). Gesture. *American Review of Anthropology*, *26*, 109–128.

Kendon, A. (2004). *Gesture: Visible action as utterance*. Cambridge, UK: Cambridge University Press; doi:10.1017/CBO9780511807572

Kepes, S., & Delery, J. E. (2007). HRM systems and the problem of internal fit. In P. Boxall, J. Purcell, & P. Wright (Eds.), *The Oxford Handbook of Human Resource Management* (pp. 385–404). New York, NY: Oxford University Press.

Khalil, A., & Connelly, K. (2005). Improving Cell Phone Awareness by Using Calendar Information. Human-Computer Interaction - INTERACT 2005, 588-600.

Khalil, A., & Connelly, K. (2006). *Context-aware Telephony: Privacy Preferences and Sharing Patterns.* Paper presented at the CSCW'06, Banff, Alberta, Canada. 10.1145/1180875.1180947

Khrennikov, A. (1999). Classical and quantum mechanics on in- formation spaces with applications to cognitive, psychological, social, and anomalous phenomena. *Foundations of Physics*, *29*(7), 1065–1098. doi:10.1023/A:1018885632116

Khrennikov, A. (2008). Bell-Boole inequality: Nonlocality or probabilistic incompatibility of random variables? *Entropy (Basel, Switzerland)*, *10*(2).

Kidd, A. G., Sharratt, C., & Coleman, J. (2004). Mobile communication regulations updated: how safely are doctors' telephones used? *Qual Saf Health Care, 13*(6), 478. doi:10.1136/qhc.13.6.478

Kirkman, B. L., Rosen, B., Tesluk, P. E., & Gibson, C. B. (2004). The impact of team empowerment on virtual team performance: The moderating role of face-to-face interaction. *Academy of Management Journal*, *47*(2), 175–192.

Kitchen, P. J., Spickett-Jones, J. G., & Grimes, T. (2007). Inhibition of Brand Integration amid Changing Agency Structures. *Journal of Marketing Communications*, *13*(2), 149–168. doi:10.1080/13527260601009803

Klein, H. J., Noe, R., & Wang, C. (2006). Motivation to learn and course outcomes: The impact of delivery mode, learning goal orientation, and perceived barriers and enablers. *Personnel Psychology*, *59*(3), 665–702. doi:10.1111/j.1744-6570.2006.00050.x

Koch, W. (2013, November 13). Americans back greenhouse gas cuts from power plants. *USA Today*. Retrieved from http://www.usatoday.com/story/news/nation/2013/11/13/americans-greenhouse-gas-cuts-power-plants/3508001/

Kodama, M. (2005). New knowledge creation through dialectical leadership: A case of IT and multimedia business in Japan. *European Journal of Innovation Management*, *8*(1), 31–55. doi:10.1108/14601060510578565

Koerber, D., & Zabara, N. (2017). Preventing damage: The psychology of crisis communication buffers in organized sports. *Public Relations Review*, *43*(1), 193–200. doi:10.1016/j.pubrev.2016.12.002

Kohlberg, L. (1964). *Development of moral character and moral ideology*. New York, NY: Russell Sage Foundation.

Kohlberg, L. (1975). The Cognitive-Developmental Approach to Moral Education. *Phi Delta Kappan*, *56*(10), 670–677.

Kohlberg, L. (1981). *The philosophy of moral development: essays on moral development*. New York, NY: Harper and Row.

Kohlberg, L., & Elfenbein, D. (1975). The development of moral judgement concerning capital punishment. *The American Journal of Orthopsychiatry*, *54*(4), 614–640. doi:10.1111/j.1939-0025.1975.tb01191.x PMID:1180344

Kohn, A. (1993). Turning learning into a business: Concerns about total quality management. *Educational Leadership*, *51*(1), 58–61.

Kohut, A. (2010, June 13). Views on climate change: What the polls show. *New York Times*, p. A22. Retrieved from http://www.nytimes.com/2010/06/14/opinion/l14climate.html?_r=0

Kolb, D. M., & Williams, J. (2003). *Everyday negotiation: Navigating the hidden agendas in bargaining*. San Francisco: Jossey-Bass.

Konica Minolta Releases Results of its New Report, "the Digital Workplace Initiative." (2017). *Entertainment Close - Up*. Retrieved from https://search-proquest-com.proxy.campbell.edu/docview/1897303332?accountid=146941

Konovsky, M., & Organ, D. (1996). Dispositional and contextual determinants of organizational citizenship behavior. *Journal of Organizational Behavior*, *17*(3), 253–266. doi:10.1002/(SICI)1099-1379(199605)17:3<253::AID-JOB747>3.0.CO;2-Q

Koper, C. S. (1995). Just enough police presence: Reducing crime and disorderly behavior by optimizing patrol time in crime hot spots. *Justice Quarterly*, *12*(4), 649–672. doi:10.1080/07418829500096231

Kop, R. (2011). The challenges to connectivist learning on open online networks: Learning experiences during a massive open online course. *International Review of Research in Open and Distance Learning*, *12*(3), 19–37. doi:10.19173/irrodl.v12i3.882

Kostopoulos, K. C., Spanos, Y. E., & Prastacos, G. P. (2013). Structure and Function of Team Learning Emergence: A Multilevel Empirical Validation. *Journal of Management*, *39*(6), 1430–1461. doi:10.1177/0149206311419366

Koudal, P., & Coleman, G. C. (2005). coordinating operations to enhance innovation in the global corporation. *Strategy and Leadership*, *33*(4), 20–32. doi:10.1108/10878570510608013

Kouzes, J. M., & Posner, B. Z. (2008). *A Leader's Legacy*. San Francisco, CA: Jossey-Bass.

Kovacs, J., & King, M. (2005). *Studying the Impact of the Quality in Schools and Quality and Improvement in Schools and Preschools Initiatives: 1997-2003*. Quality Learning and Improvement in Schools and Preschools Summary Report, November 2005 [Electronic Version]. Melbourne: Quality Learning Australia Pty Ltd. Retrieved from http://www.qla.com.au/pathtoitems/QLA_QISP_Report.pdf

Kovacs, J. (2009). *Facilitating Change in Australian Schools: Applying a Business Quality Improvement Model. Unpublished Doctoral dissertation*. Melbourne, Australia: Swinburne University of Technology. Retrieved from http://researchbank.swinburne.edu.au/vital/access/manager/Repository/swin:14100

Krajcik, J. S., Blumenfeld, P. C., Marx, R. W., & Soloway, E. (1994). A collaborative model for helping middle grade science teachers learn project-based instruction. *The Elementary School Journal*, *94*(5), 483–497. doi:10.1086/461779

Kraut, R. E., Egido, C., & Galegher, J. (2002). Patterns of contact and communication in scientific research collaboration. In J. Galegher & R. Kraut (Eds.), *Intellectual Teamwork: Social and technological foundations of group work*. Hillsdale, NJ: Lawrence Erlbaum Associates.

Kraut, R. E., Lewis, S. H., & Swezey, L. W. (1982). Listener responsiveness and the coordination of conversation. *Journal of Personality and Social Psychology*, *43*(4), 718–731. doi:10.1037/0022-3514.43.4.718

Krebs, J., Madigan, E., & Tullai-McGuiness, S. (2008). The rural nurse work environment and structural empowerment. *Policy, Politics & Nursing Practice*, *9*(1), 28–39. doi:10.1177/1527154408316255

Krebs, S. A., Hobman, E. V., & Bordia, P. (2006). Virtual teams and group member dissimilarity: Consequences for the development of trust. *Small Group Research*, *37*(6), 721–741. doi:10.1177/1046496406294886

Kress, N. (2005). Engaging your employees through the power of communication. *Workspan, 48*(5), 26–36.

Kriesberg, L. (1998). *Constructive conflicts: From escalation to resolution.* Lanham, MD: Rowman and Littlefield.

Kritek, P. B. (1994). *Negotiating at an uneven table: Developing moral courage in resolving our conflicts.* San Francisco: Jossey-Bass Publishers.

Kritzer, H. M., Sarat, A., Trubek, D. M., Bumiller, K., & Mcnichol, E. (1984). Understanding The Costs Of Litigation: The Case Of The Hourly-Fee Lawyer. *Law & Social Inquiry, 9*(3), 559–581. doi:10.1111/j.1747-4469.1984.tb00020.x

Krug, D., & Oakley, E. (1994). *Enlightened leadership: Getting to the heart of change.* New York, NY: Simon & Schuster.

Kruse, N. W. (1981). Apologia in team sport. *The Quarterly Journal of Speech, 67*(3), 270–283. doi:10.1080/00335638109383572

Kukulska-Hulme, A. (2012). How should the higher education workforce adapt to advancements in technology for teaching and learning? *The Internet and Higher Education, 15*(4), 247–254. doi:10.1016/j.iheduc.2011.12.002

Kumaraswamy, M. M. (1997). Conflicts, Claims And Disputes In Construction. *Engineering, Construction, and Architectural Management, 4*(2), 95–111. doi:10.1108/eb021042

Kumar, S., Kumar, P., & Bhasker, B. (2018). Interplay trust, information privacy concerns and behavioural intention of users on online social networks. *Behaviour & Information Technology, 37*(6), 622–633. doi:10.1080/0144929X.2018.1470671

Kwan, P. Y. K. (1996). Application of total quality management in education: Retrospect and prospect. *International Journal of Educational Management, 10*(5), 25–35. doi:10.1108/09513549610146114

Lakshmi, K. (2012). Employee engagement- A corporate boon. 10 ways for effective engagement. *Advances in Management Journal, 5*(2), 64–65.

Landsberger, H. (1961). Horizontal Dimension in Bureaucracy. *Administrative Science Quarterly, 6*(3), 299–322. doi:10.2307/2390705

Landy, F. J. (2005). Some historical and scientific issues related to research on emotional intelligence. *Journal of Organizational Behavior, 26*(4), 412. doi:10.1002/job.317

Lane, F. S. (2003). *The naked employee: How technology is compromising workplace privacy.* New York, NY: AMACOM.

Langhorn, S. (2004a). *The role of emotions in service encounters* (Doctoral dissertation). University of Luton.

Langhorn, S. (2004b). How emotional intelligence can improve management performance. *International Journal of Hospitality Management, 16*(4), 220–230. doi:10.1108/09596110410537379

Laschinger, H. K. S., Finegan, J., Shamian, J., & Casier, S. (2000). Organizational trust and empowerment in restructured healthcare settings: Effects on staff nurse commitment. *The Journal of Nursing Administration, 30*(9), 413–425. doi:10.1097/00005110-200009000-00008

Laschinger, H. K. S., Wong, C., McMahon, L., & Kaufmann, C. (1999). Leader behaviour impact on staff nurse empowerment, job tension and work effectiveness. *The Journal of Nursing Administration, 29*(5), 28–39. doi:10.1097/00005110-199905000-00005

Laschinger, H. K., Finegan, J. E., Shamian, J., & Wilk, P. (2004). A longitudinal analysis of the impact of workplace empowerment on work satisfaction. *Journal of Organizational Behavior, 25*(4), 527–545. doi:10.1002/job.256

Laschinger, H. K., Finegan, J., Shamian, J., & Wilk, P. (2001). Impact of structural and psychological empowerment on job strain in nursing work settings: Expanding Kanter's model. *JONA: The Journal of Nursing Administration*, *31*(5), 260–272. doi:10.1097/00005110-200105000-00006

Laschinger, H. K., Wong, C., & Grau, A. (2013). Authentic leadership, empowerment and burnout: A comparison in new graduates and experienced nurses. *Journal of Nursing Management*, *21*(3), 541–552. doi:10.1111/j.1365-2834.2012.01375.x

Laudon, K. C., & Laudon, J. P. (2001). *Essentials of management information systems: Organisation and technology in the networked enterprise* (4th ed.). Upper Saddle River, NJ: Prentice Hall.

Laudon, K. C., & Laudon, J. P. (2002). *Management information systems: Managing the digital firm* (7th ed.). Upper Saddle River, NJ: Prentice Hall.

Laudon, K. C., & Traver, C. G. (2010). *E-commerce 2010 – Business technology society* (6th ed.). Upper Saddle River, NJ: Prentice Hall.

Lautizi, M., Laschinger, H. K., & Ravazzolo, S. (2009). Workplace empowerment, job satisfaction and job stress among Italian mental health nurses: An exploratory study. *Journal of Nursing Management*, *17*(4), 446–452. doi:10.1111/j.1365-2834.2009.00984.x

Lave, J., & Wenger, E. (1991). *Situated Learning: Legitime Peripheral Participation*. Cambridge, UK: Cambridge University Press. doi:10.1017/CBO9780511815355

Lavelle, J., Brockner, J., Konovsky, M., Price, K., Henley, A., Taneja, A., & Vinekar, V. (2008). Commitment, procedural fairness, and organizational citizenship behavior: A multifoci analysis. *Journal of Organizational Behavior*, *30*(3), 337–357. doi:10.1002/job.518

Lawrence, K. (2013). *Developing Leaders in a VUCA environment*. UNC-Kenan-Flagler Business School whitepaper.

Lawrence, P. R., & Lorsch, J. W. (1967). *Organization and Environment: Managing Differentiation and Integration*. Cambridge, MA: Harvard University Press.

Lawrence, T. B., & Robinson, S. L. (2007). Ain't misbehavin: Workplace deviance as organizational resistance. *Journal of Management*, *33*(3), 378–394. doi:10.1177/0149206307300816

Lax, D., & Sebenius, J. (1986). *The Manager As Negotiator*. New York: Free Press.

Leeds-Hurwitz, W. (1990). Notes in the History of Intercultural Communication: The Foreign Service Institute and the Mandate for Intercultural Training. *The Quarterly Journal of Speech*, *76*(3), 262–281. doi:10.1080/00335639009383919

Lee, I. (2011). Overview of emerging Web 2.0-based business models and web 2.0 applications in business: An ecological perspective. *International Journal of E-Business Research*, *7*(4), 1–16. doi:10.4018/jebr.2011100101

Lee, Y. R., & Lazarus, H. (1993). Uses and criticisms of total quality management. *Journal of Management Development*, *12*(7), 5–10. doi:10.1108/02621719310044901

Leithwood, K. (1994). Leadership for school restructuring. *Educational Administration Quarterly*, *30*(4), 498–518. doi:10.1177/0013161X94030004006

Leithwood, K., & Menzies, T. (1998). A review of research concerning the implementation of site-based management. *School Effectiveness and School Improvement*, *9*(3), 233–285. doi:10.1080/0924345980090301

Lenhart, A., & Fox, S. (2006). *Bloggers: A portrait of the Internet's new story tellers*. Washington, DC: Pew Internet & American Life Project.

Lennick, D., & Kiel, F. (2005). *Moral intelligence: Enhancing business performance & leadership success*. Upper Saddle River, NJ: Wharton School Publishing.

Len-Rios, M. E. (2010). Image repair strategies, local news portrayals and crisis stage: A case study of Duke University's lacrosse team crisis. *International Journal of Strategic Communication*, *4*(4), 267–287. doi:10.1080/1553118X.2010.515534

Leonard-Barton, D., & Sensiper, S. (1998). The role of tacit knowledge in group innovation. *California Management Review*, *40*(3), 112–132. doi:10.2307/41165946

Leonard, D., & McAdam, R. (2003). An evaluative framework for TQM dynamics in organisations. *International Journal of Operations & Production Management*, *23*(5/6), 652–677. doi:10.1108/01443570310476663

Leonardi, P. M., & Vaast, E. (2017). Social media and ther affordances for organizing: A review and agenda for research. *The Academy of Management Annals*, *11*(1), 150–188. doi:10.5465/annals.2015.0144

Leonard, P., & Rintoul, H. (2010). An international collaboration: Examining graduate educational leadership in Louisiana and Ontario. In A. Normore (Ed.), *Advances in educational administration, 11. Global perspectives on educational leadership reform: The development and preparation of leaders of learning and learners of leadership* (pp. 301–321). Emerald Group Publishing Limited. doi:10.1108/S1479-3660(2010)0000011018

Lesh, B. (2011). "Why won't you just tell us the Answer?" Teaching historical thinking in grades 7-12, Portland, OR: Stenhouse Publishers.

Lesmerises, D. (2011, June 7). Ohio State President Gordon Gee: "Flurry of activity" led to Jim Tressel resignation. *Cleveland.com.* Retrieved October 27 from http://www.cleveland.com/osu/index.ssf/2011/06/ohio_state_president_gordon_ge.html

Lesmerises, D. (2014a, June 3). Gordon Gee: 'I think everyone won'-closing the book on the Ohio State tattoo scandal. *Cleveland.com.* Retrieved October 27 from http://www.cleveland.com/osu/index.ssf/2014/06/gordon_gee_i_think_everyone_wo.html

Lesmerises, D. (2014b, June 5). Urban Meyer: 'I can tell you there is nothing behind door no. 2'-Closing the book on the Ohio State football scandal. *Cleveland.com.* Retrieved October 28, 2015, 2015 http://www.cleveland.com/osu/index.ssf/2014/06/urban_meyer_i_can_tell_you_the.html

Lesmerises, D. (2014c, June 11). Gene Smith: 'We moved forward a long time ago"- Closing the book on the Ohio State football scandal. *Cleveland.com.* Retrieved October 27 from http://www.cleveland.com/osu/index.ssf/2014/06/gene_smith_our_kids_are_much_f.html

Lesser, E. L., & Storck, J. (2001). Communities of practice and organizational performance. *IBM Systems Journal, 40*(4). Retrieved February 2, 2009, from http://www.research.ibm.com/journal/sj/404lesser.html

Levi, D. (2011). *Group Dynamics for Teams*. Thousand Oaks, CA: Sage.

Lewicki, R. J., Saunders, D. M., & Barry, B. (2006). *Negotiation* (5th ed.). Boston: McGraw-Hill Irwin.

Lieberman, H., & Selker, T. (2000). Out of context: Computer systems that adapt to, and learn from, context. *IBM Systems Journal*, *39*(3-4), 617 - 632. doi:10.1147j.393.0617

Lind, E. A., Kanfer, R., & Earley, P. C. (1990). Voice, control, and procedural justice: Instrumental and noninstrumental concerns in fairness judgments. *Journal of Personality and Social Psychology*, *59*(5), 952–959. doi:10.1037/0022-3514.59.5.952

Lindsay, P. (2018). *The craft of university teaching*. Toronto: University of Toronto Press.

Linkins, J. (2011, May 26). Urban Outfitters continues their grand tradition of ripping off designers. *Life*. Retrieved from https://www.huffpost.com/entry/urban-outfitters-steal_n_867604

Lipiainen, H., Karjaluoto, H., & Nevalainen, M. (2014). Digital channels in the internal communication of a multinational corporation. *Corporate Communications*, *19*(3), 275–286. doi:10.1108/CCIJ-07-2012-0050

Lipnack, J., & Stamps, J. (2000). *Virtual teams: People working across boundaries with technology* (2nd ed.). New York: Wiley.

Lipschultz, A. (2014). The complexity of clinical alarm systems. *Biomedical Instrumentation & Technology*, *48*(3), 204–210. doi:10.2345/0899-8205-48.3.204 PMID:24847931

Li, Q. (2009). Knowledge building in an online environment: A design-based research study. *Journal of Educational Technology Systems*, *37*(2), 195–216. doi:10.2190/ET.37.2.f

Lisak, A., & Erez, M. (2015). Leadership emergence in multicultural teams: The power of global characteristics. *Journal of World Business*, *50*(1), 3–14. doi:10.1016/j.jwb.2014.01.002

Little, J. W. (1988). Seductive images and organizational realities in professional development. In A. Lieberman (Ed.), *Rethinking school improvement*. New York, NY: Teachers College Press.

Little, L. (2005). Leadership Communication and the Johari Window. *Administrator*, *24*(3), 4.

Li, Y. (2012). Theories in online information privacy research: A critical view and an integrated framework. *Decision Support Systems*, *54*(1), 471–481. doi:10.1016/j.dss.2012.06.010

Locke, E. A. (1990). The nature and causes of Job satisfaction. In M. D. Dunnette & L. M. Hough (Eds.), Handbook of Industrial and Organizational Psychology (pp. 1297–1349). Palo Alto, CA: Consulting Psychologists Press.

Locke, E. A. (1968). *What is Job satisfaction?* Washington, DC: American Psychology Association.

Locke, E., Latham, G., & Erez, M. (1988). The determinants of goal commitment. *Academy of Management Review*, *13*(1), 23–39. doi:10.5465/amr.1988.4306771

Lo, M.-C., & Ramayah, T. (2009). Dimensionality of organizational citizenship behavior (OCB) in a multicultural society: The case of Malaysia. *International Business Research*, *2*(1), 48–55. doi:10.5539/ibr.v2n1p48

London, M., & Tornow, W. (1998). 360-degree feedback - more than a tool. In W. Tornow, M. London, & C. Associates (Eds.), *Maximizing the value of 360-degree feedback* (pp. 1–8). San Francisco, CA: Jossey Bass.

Long, L., & Hazelton, V. (1984). Assessing communication behavior: An application within the public relations profession. Journal of Applied Communication.

Long, L. W. (2003). Mapping Organizational Culture: An Integration of Communication and Organizational Design. *Intercultural Communication Studies*, *12*(2), 127–142.

Long, S., Aust, D., Abowd, G., & Atkeson, C. (1996). Cyberguide: Prototyping context-aware mobile applications. In *Conference Companion on Human Factors in Computing Systems, CHI '96* (pp. 293–294). New York: ACM.

Lord Woolf. (1998). *Access To Justice: Interim And Final Reports By Lord Woolf To The Lord Chancellor*. Academic Press.

Loseke, D. R., & Cahil, S. E. (2007). Publishing qualitative manuscripts: Lessons learned. In C. Seale, G. Gobo, J. F. Gubrium, & D. Silverman (Eds.), *Qualitative Research Practice: Concise Paperback Edition* (pp. 491–506). London: Sage.

Louis Harris and Associates. (1999). *Poll*. Retrieved from http://www.natlconsumersleague.org/FNLSUM1.PDF

Luft, J., & Ingham, H. (1955). The Johari window, a graphic model of interpersonal awareness. In *Proceedings of the western training laboratory in group development*. Los Angeles, CA: UCLA.

Lundvall, B.-Å. (1992). *National Systems of Innovation: Towards a Theory of Innovation and Interactive Learning*. London: Pinter.

Lustig, M. W., & Koester, J. (2010). *Intercultural competence: interpersonal communication across cultures*. Boston: Pearson/Allyn & Bacon.

Macey, W., & Schneider, B. (2008). The meaning of employee engagement. *Industrial and Organizational Psychology: Perspectives on Science and Practice*, *1*(01), 3–30. doi:10.1111/j.1754-9434.2007.0002.x

Madden, M., Fox, S., Smith, A., & Vitak, J. (2007). *Digital footprints: Online identity management and search in the age of transparency*. Retrieved July 29, 2018, from http://pewresearch. org/pubs/663/digital-footprints

Madjeski, M., Johnson, M., & Bellovin, S. M. (2011). *The Failure of Online Social Network Privacy Settings*. Columbia University Computer Science Technical Reports.

Madu, C. N., Aheto, J., Kuei, C., & Winokur, D. (1994). Adoption of strategic total quality management philosophies: Multi-criteria decision analysis model. *International Journal of Quality & Reliability Management*, *13*(3), 57–72. doi:10.1108/02656719610116081

Madu, C. N., & Kuei, C. (1993). Dimensions of quality teaching in higher institutions. *Total Quality Management*, *4*(3), 325–338. doi:10.1080/09544129300000046

Major, W. (2014). Contagion in the classroom: The need for physical and emotional connectedness for deep learning classrooms offering social experience. *Liberal Education*, *100*(4), 66–69.

Makau, J. (2009). Ethical and unethical communication. In W. Eadie (Ed.), 21st century communication: A reference handbook. (pp. 435-444). Thousand Oaks, CA: SAGE Publications, Inc. doi:10.4135/9781412964005.n48

Malamed, C. (2009). *10 ways to organize instructional content*. E-Learning podcast 2.0.

Malik, M., Nawab, S., Naeem, B., & Danish, R. Q. (2010). Job satisfaction and organizational commitment of University teachers in public sector of Pakistan. *International Journal of Business and Management*, *5*(6), 17–26. doi:10.5539/ijbm.v5n6p17

Malone, T. W., Grant, K. R., Lai, K.-Y., Rao, R., & Rosenblitt, D. (1987). Semistructured messages are surprisingly useful for computer-supported coordination. *ACM Transactions on Information Systems*, *5*(2), 115–131. doi:10.1145/27636.27637

Manacapilli, T., Matthies, C. F., Miller, L. W., Howe, P., Perez, P. J., Hardison, C. M., & Sims, C. S. (2012). *Reducing attrition in selected Air Force training pipelines*. Santa Monica, CA: RAND Corporation.

Management, N. Z. (2012). A conversation across the generations. *New Zealand Management*, *59*(6), 21.

Mangold, W. G., & Faulds, D. J. (2009). Social media: The new hybrid element of the promotion mix. *Business Horizons*, *52*(4), 357–365. doi:10.1016/j.bushor.2009.03.002

Manso, J. (1996). *Estatística descritiva e previsão* (2nd ed.). Covilhã: Universidade da Beira Interior.

Margulis, S. T. (2003). On the status and contribution of Westin's and Altman's theories of privacy. *The Journal of Social Issues*, *59*(2), 411–429. doi:10.1111/1540-4560.00071

Markos, S., & Sridevi, M. S. (2010). Employee engagement: The key to improving performance. *International Journal of Business and Management*, *5*(12), 89–96.

Marks, H. M., & Printy, S. M. (2003). Principal leadership and school performance: An Integration of Transformational and Instructional Leadership. *Educational Administration Quarterly, 39*(3), 370–397. doi:10.1177/0013161X03253412

Marmasse, N., Schmandt, C., & Spectre, D. (2004). WatchMe: Communication and Awareness Between Members of a Closely-Knit Group. UbiComp 2004: Ubiquitous Computing, 214-231.

Maroco, J. (2007). *Análise Estatística com utilização do SPSS* (3rd ed.). Lisboa: Edições Sílabo.

Marshall, A. (2011, March 8). Ohio State football coach Jim Tressel suspended 2 games, fined $250,000 in aftermath of Yahoo report. *Cleveland.com.* Retrieved June 14, 2011 from http://www.cleveland.com/osu/index.ssf/2011/03/post_36.html

Marshall, B., Choi, J., El-Shinnaway, M. M., North, M., Svensson, L., Wang, S., ... Valenzuala, J. P. (2009). Online and offline social ties of social network website users: An exploratory study in eleven societies. *Journal of Computer Information Systems, 50*(1), 54–64.

Marshall, J. C., Smart, J., & Horton, R. M. (2010). The design and validation of equip: An instrument to assess inquiry-based instruction. *International Journal of Science and Mathematics Education, 8*(2), 299–321. doi:10.100710763-009-9174-y

Marsh, S., & Briggs, P. (2009). Examining trust, forgiveness and regret as computational concepts. In *Computing with social trust* (pp. 9–43). London: Springer.

Martin, A. J., Wellen, J. M., & Grimmer, M. R. (2016). An eye on your work: How empowerment affects the relationship between electronic surveillance and counterproductive work behaviours. *International Journal of Human Resource Management, 27*(21), 2635–2651. doi:10.1080/09585192.2016.1225313

Martin, J., & Nakayama, T. (2008). *Experiencing intercultural communication: An introduction* (3rd ed.). Boston: McGraw-Hill.

Marx, G., & Sherizen, S. (1991). Monitoring on the job: How to protect privacy as well as property. In T. Forester (Ed.), *Computers in the human context: Information technology, productivity, and people* (pp. 397–406). Cambridge, MA: MIT Press.

Mason, R. (1986). Four ethical issues of the information age. *Management Information Systems Quarterly, 10*(1), 4–12. doi:10.2307/248873

Massaguer, D., Hore, B., Diallo, M. H., Mehrotra, S., & Venkatasubramanian, N. (2009) Middleware for pervasive spaces: Balancing privacy and utility. In *Proceedings of the 10th ACM/I- FIP/USENIX International Conference on Middleware, Middleware '09* (pp. 13:1-13:20). New York, NY: Springer-Verlag. 10.1007/978-3-642-10445-9_13

Masters, G. N. (2010). *Teaching and learning school improvement framework. Melbourne: Australian Council for Educational Research (ACER).* Brisbane: Department of Education and Training.

Mastrofski, S. D., Snipes, J. B., & Supina, A. E. (1996). Compliance on demand: The public's response to specific police requests. *Journal of Research in Crime and Delinquency, 33*(3), 269–305. doi:10.1177/0022427896033003001

Masuch, M. (1985). Vicious Circles in Organizations. *Administrative Science Quarterly, 30*(1), 14-33.

Matsumoto, D., Keltner, D., Shiota, M. N., & O'Sullivan, F. M. (2008). Facial expressions of emotion. Handbook of emotions, 211-234.

Maxwell, J. C. (2002). *Cele 21 de legi supreme ale liderului.* Editura Amaltea, Bucaresti.

Mayer, R. C., Davis, J. D., & Schoorman, F. D. (1995). An integrative model of organisational trust. *Academy of Management Review, 20*(3), 709–734. doi:10.5465/amr.1995.9508080335

Maylett, T. M., & Riboldi, J. (2007). Using 360° Feedback to Predict Performance. *Training & Development*, (September): 48–52.

Mazerolle, L., Sargeant, E., Cherney, A., Bennett, S., & Murphy, K. (2014). Procedural Justice and Police Legitimacy in Policing. Academic Press.

Mazerolle, L., Antrobus, E., Bennett, S., & Tyler, T. R. (2012b). Shaping citizens perceptions of police legitimacy: A randomized field trial of procedural justice. *Criminology*, *51*(1), 33–64. doi:10.1111/j.1745-9125.2012.00289.x

Mazerolle, L., Bennett, S., Antrobus, E., & Eggins, E. (2012a). Procedural Justice, routine encounters, and citizen perceptions of police: Main findings from the Queensland Community Engagement Trial (QCET). *Journal of Experimental Criminology*, *8*(4), 343–367. doi:10.100711292-012-9160-1

Mc Dermott, R. (1999). Nurturing Three Dimensional communities of Practice: How to get the most out of human networks. *Knowledge management Review*. Retrieved February 2, 2009, from http://www.co-i-l.com/coil/knowledge-garden/cop/dimensional.shtml

McAdam, R., Leonard, D., Henderson, J., & Hazlett, S. A. (2006). A grounded theory research approach to building and testing TQM theory in operations management. *International Journal of Management Sciences*, *36*, 825–837. doi:10.1016/j.omega.2006.04.005

McCluskey, J. D. (2003). *Police requests for compliance: Coercive and procedurally just tactics*. LFB Scholarly Pub.

McCroskey, J. & Young, T. (1981). Ethos and credibility: the construct and its measurement after three decades. *Central States Speech Journal, 32*(981), 24-34.

McDermott, R. (1999). Why Information Technology Inspired But Cannot Deliver Knowledge Management. *California Management Review*, *41*(3), 103–117. doi:10.2307/41166012

Mcgovern, F. E. (1996). Beyond Efficiency: A Bevy Of ADR Justifications (An Unfootnoted Summary). *Dispute Resolution Magazine, 3*.

McKimm, J. (2003). Assuring quality and standards in teaching. In H. Fry, S. M. Ketteridge, & S. Marshall (Eds.), *A Handbook for Teaching and Learning in Higher Education* (2nd ed.; pp. 182–199). London: Kogan Page.

Mckinney, E. H. Jr, Barker, J. R., Davis, K. J., & Smith, D. (2005). How Swift Starting Action Teams Get off the Ground: What United Flight 232 and Airline Flight Crews Can Tell Us About Team Communication. *Management Communication Quarterly*, *19*(2), 198–237. doi:10.1177/0893318905278539

McNeill, D. (1992). Hand and mind: What gestures reveal about thought (1st ed.). Chicago, IL: Chicago University Press.

McParland, C., & Connolly, R. (2009). *The role of dataveillance in the organsiation: Some emerging trends*. Paper presented at the Irish Academy of Management Conference, Galway, UK.

Mehra, S., & Ranganathan, S. (2008). Implementing total quality management with a focus on enhancing customer satisfaction. *International Journal of Quality & Reliability Management, 25*(9), 913-927. doi: 02656710810908070

Mehra, S., Hoffman, J., & Sirias, D. (2001). TQM as a management strategy for the next millenia. *International Journal of Operations & Production Management*, *21*(6), 855–877. doi:10.1108/01443570110390534

Meisel, Z., & Oldham, J. (2011, May 24). Ray Small tells all: Ex-Buckeye says he sold memorabilia, some players don't 'think about' rules. *The Lantern*. Retrieved October 14, 2015 from http://thelantern.com/2011/05/ray-small-tells-all-ex-buckeye-says-he-sold-memorabilia-some-players-dont-think-about-rules/

Meister, J. C., & Willyerd, K. (2010). Mentoring millennials. *Harvard Business Review*, (May): 1–5. PMID:20429252

MeMarco, M. (2018). *The multigenerational workforce: How communication styles impact office culture*. Retrieved from: https://www.staffmanagement.com/blog- multigenerational-workforce-communication-styles/

Mendonca, E. A., Chen, E. S., Stetson, P. D., McKnight, L. K., Lei, J., & Cimino, J. J. (2004). Approach to mobile information and communication for health care. *International Journal of Medical Informatics*, *73*(7), 631–638. doi:10.1016/j.ijmedinf.2004.04.013 PMID:15246044

Men, L. R., & Stacks, D. (2014). The effects of authentic leadership on strategic internal communication and employee-organization relationships. *Journal of Public Relations Research*, *26*(4), 301–324. doi:10.1080/1062726X.2014.908720

Merchant, G. (2012). Unravelling the social network: Theory and research. *Learning, Media and Technology*, *37*(1), 4–19. doi:10.1080/17439884.2011.567992

Meredith, J. R., Shafer, S. M., & Mantel, S. J. Jr. (2018). *Project Management: A Strategic Managerial Approach* (10th ed.). Hoboken, NJ: Wiley.

Metcalfe, A., Fisher, D., Gingras, Y., Jones, G., Rubenson, K., & Snee, I. (2010, October/November). How influential are faculty today? Responses from the Canadian Professorate. *Academic Matters Journal of Higher Education*, 16-20.

Meyer, J., & Herscovitch, L. (2001). Commitment in the workplace: Toward a general model. *Human Resource Management Review*, *11*(3), 299–326. doi:10.1016/S1053-4822(00)00053-X

Meyer, P., Stanley, D., Herscovitch, L., & Topolnytsky, L. (2002). Affective, continuance, and normative commitment to theorganization: A meta-analysis of antecedents, correlates, and consequences. *Journal of Vocational Behavior*, *61*(1), 20–52. doi:10.1006/jvbe.2001.1842

Meyerson, D., Weick, K. E., & Kramer, R. M. (1996). Swift Trust and Temporary Groups. In Trust in Organizations. Sage.

Milewski, A., & Smith, T. (2000). Providing presence cues to telephone users. *CSCW '00: Proceedings of the 2000 ACM conference on Computer supported cooperative work*. 10.1145/358916.358978

Milgram, R. M., Dunn, R., & Price, G. E. (Eds.). (1993). *Teaching and counseling gifted and talented adolescents: An international learning style perspective*. Westport, CT: Praeger.

Milia, L., Rogers, N., &Akerstedt, T. (2012). *Sleepiness, long distance commuting and night work as predictors of driving performance*. /journal.pone.0045856 doi:10.137/1

Miller, H., Watkins, R., & Webb, D. (2009). The use of psychological testing to evaluate law enforcement leadership competencies and development. *Police Practice and Research*, *10*(1), 49–60. doi:10.1080/15614260802128575

Miller, V., Johnson, J., & Grau, J. (1994). Antecedents to willingness to participate in a planned organizational change. *Journal of Applied Communication Research*, *22*(1), 59–80. doi:10.1080/00909889409365387

Mills, P. K., & Ungson, G. (2003). Reassessing the limits of structural empowerment: Organizational constitution and trust as controls. *Academy of Management Review*, *28*(1), 143–153. doi:10.5465/amr.2003.8925254

Minnick, A., Pischke-Winn, K., & Sterk, M. B. (1994). Introducing a two-way wireless communication system. *Nursing Management*, *25*(7), 42–47. doi:10.1097/00006247-199407000-00011 PMID:8044475

Mishra, A. K., & Spreitzer, G. M. (1998). Explaining How Survivors Respond to Downsizing: The Roles of Trust, Empowerment, Justice and Work Redesign. *Academy of Management Review*, *23*(3), 567-588.

Mishra, K. E. (2007). *Organizational communication and its role in building trust, commitment, and a positive reputation through relationship management with employees*. Dissertation.

Mishra, K. E., & Boynton, L. (2009). *Talk-the-Talk: Using Internal Communication to Build Trust with Employees.* International Public Relations Research Conference, Miami, FL.

Mishra, K. E., Schwarz, G. M., & Mishra, A. K. (2011). The Evolution of Trust and Control as Seen through an Organization's Human Resources Practices. In R. Searle (Ed.), Trust and Human Resource Management. Cheltenham, UK: Edward Elgar.

Mishra, K. E., Walker, K., & Mishra, A. K. (2014). Employee Use of Social Media in the Workplace: How "Lenovo Central" brings employees together. In I. Lee (Ed.), Integrating Social Media into Business Practice, Applications, Management, and Models. Academic Press.

Mishra, A. K. (1996). Organizational responses to crisis: The centrality of trust. In R. Kramer & T. Tyler (Eds.), *Trust in organizations* (pp. 261–287). Newbury Park, CA: Sage. doi:10.4135/9781452243610.n13

Mishra, A. K., & Mishra, K. E. (1994). The role of mutual trust in effective downsizing strategies. *Human Resource Management, 33*(2), 261–279. doi:10.1002/hrm.3930330207

Mishra, A. K., & Mishra, K. E. (2013). *Becoming a Trustworthy Leader: Psychology & Practice.* Routledge Press.

Mishra, K. E., Boynton, L., & Mishra, A. K. (2014). Driving Employee Engagement: The Expanded Role of Internal Communications. *Journal of Business Communication, 51*(2), 183–202. doi:10.1177/2329488414525399

MIT Massachusetts Institute of Technology. (2009, August). *Advanced Managerial Communication.* Accessed from the Web: http://ocw.mit.edu/courses/sloan-school-of-management/

Mitchell, S., Spiteri, M. D., Bates, J., & Coulouris, G. (2000). Context-aware multimedia computing in the intelligent hospital. *Proceedings of the 9th workshop on ACM SIGOPS European workshop: beyond the PC: new challenges for the operating system.* 10.1145/566726.566730

Mitka, M. (2013). Joint commission warns of alarm fatigue: Multitude of alarms from monitoring devices problematic. *Journal of the American Medical Association, 309*(22), 2315–2316. doi:10.1001/jama.2013.6032 PMID:23757063

Mitroff, I. I. (1998). *Smart thinking for crazy times: The art of solving the right problems.* San Francisco: Berrett-Koehler.

Mizzaro, S., Nazzi, E., & Vassena, L. (2008). Retrieval of context-aware applications on mobile devices: how to evaluate? *Proceedings of the second international symposium on Information interaction in context.* 10.1145/1414694.1414710

Mnookin, R. H., & Susskind, L. E. (Eds.). (1999). Negotiating on Behalf of Others: Advice to Lawyers, Business Executives, Sports Agents, Diplomats, Politicians, and Everybody Else. Thousand Oaks, CA: Sage Publications.

Modell, S. (2009). Bundling management control innovations: A field study of organisational experimenting with total quality management and the balanced scorecard. *Accounting, Auditing & Accountability Journal, 22*(1), 59-90. doi: 09513570910923015

Moffitt, M. L., & Bordone, R. C. (Eds.). (2005). *The Handbook Of Dispute Resolution.* San Francisco, CA: Jossey-Bass.

Molleda, J.-C. (2009). Construct and Dimensions of Authenticity in Strategic Communication Research. *Anagramas Rumbos y Sentidos de la Comunicacion, 8*(15), 85–97. doi:10.22395/angr.v8n15a6

Monash University. (2010, January). *Managerial Communication.* Retrieved from http://www.monash.edu.au/

Moncada-Paternò-Castello, P. (2011). The growth of companies in the EU: the case for a more sophisticated research and innovation policy. IPTS Policy Briefs series – November 2011.

Moncada-Paternò-Castello, P., & Voigt, P. (2013). *The effect of innovative SMEs' growth to the structural renewal of the EU economy-a projection to 2020*. Academic Press.

Moncada-Paternò-Castello, P., Ciupagea, C., Smith, K., Tübke, A., & Tubbs, M. (2010, April). Does Europe perform too little corporate R&D? A comparison of EU and non-EU corporate R&D performance. *Research Policy*, *39*(4), 523–536. doi:10.1016/j.respol.2010.02.012

Mone, E., & London, M. (2009). *Employee engagement: Through effective performance management*. New York, NY: Taylor-Francis Group.

Montecinos, C., Madrid, R., Fernández, M. B., & Ahumada, L. (2014). A goal orientation analysis of teachers' motivations to participate in the school self-assessment processes of a quality assurance system in Chile. *Educational Assessment, Evaluation and Accountability*, *26*(3), 241–261. doi:10.100711092-014-9190-5

Moore, C. (1986). *The mediation process*. New York, NY: Jossey Bass.

Moore, C. (1989). *The Mediation Process*. San Francisco: Jossey Bass.

Moore, C. W. (2014). *The Mediation Process: Practical Strategies For Resolving Conflict*. New York, NY: John Wiley & Sons.

Moore, J., & Schleppegrell, M. (2014). Using a functional linguistics metalanguage to support academic language development in the English Language Arts. *Linguistics and Education*, *26*, 92–105. doi:10.1016/j.linged.2014.01.002

Moran, M., Seaman, J., & Tinti-Kane, H. (2011). *Teaching, Learning, and Sharing: How Today's Higher Education*. Boston: Pearson Learning Solutions.

Morgan, L., Paucar-caceres, A., & Wright, G. (2014). Leading effective global virtual teams: The consequences of methods of communication. *Systemic Practice and Action Research*, *27*(6), 607–624. doi:10.100711213-014-9315-2

Morgeson, F. P., Campion, M. A., Dipboye, R. L., Hollenbeck, J. R., Murphy, K., & Schmitt, N. (2007). Reconsidering the use of personality tests in personnel selection contexts. *Personnel Psychology*, *60*(3), 683–729. doi:10.1111/j.1744-6570.2007.00089.x

Morton, J., & Alireza, A. (2018). *Open strategy intermediaries? a framework for understanding the role of facilitators in open strategy-making*. Paper presented at Twenty-Sixth European Conference on Information Systems (ECIS2018), Portsmouth, UK.

Moss, D. (2017). *5 generations + 7 values = endless opportunities*. Retrieved from: https://www.shrm.org/hr-today/news/hr-news/conference-today/pages/2017/5-generations-7-values-endless-opportunities.aspx

Mossholder, K. W., Bennett, N., Kemery, E. R., & Wesolowski, M. A. (1998). Relationships between bases of power and work reactions: The mediational role of procedural justice. *Journal of Management*, *24*(4), 533–552. doi:10.1177/014920639802400404

Moten, J., Fitterer, A., Brazier, E., Leonard, J., & Brown, A. (2013). Examining online college cyber cheating methods and preventative measures. *The Electronic Journal of E-Learning*, *11*(2), 139–146.

Motowidlo, S. J., Borman, W. C., & Schmit, M. J. (1997). A theory of individual differences in Task and Contextual performance. *Human Performance*, *10*(2), 71–83. doi:10.120715327043hup1002_1

Moulaert, F., & Nussbaumer, J. (2005). Beyond the Learning Region: The Dialectics of Innovation and Culture in Territorial Development. In R. A. Boschma & R. C. Kloosterman (Eds.), *Learning from Clusters: A Critical Assessment* (pp. 89–109). Springer. doi:10.1007/1-4020-3679-5_5

Mounter, P. (2003). Global internal communication: A model. *Journal of Communication Management*, *7*(3), 3. doi:10.1108/13632540310807412

Mowlana, H. (1986). *Global information and world communication*. White Plains, NY: Longman.

Mulford, B. (2008) The leadership challenge improving learning in schools. Australian Education Review. Melbourne: Australian Council for Educational Research (ACER).

Multi-Health Systems. (2011). MHS: 2011 catalog. Ontario, Canada: Academic Press.

Munoz, M. A., Rodriguez, M., Favela, J., Martinez-Garcia, A. I., & Gonzalez, V. M. (2003). Context-aware mobile communication in hospitals. *Computer*, *36*(9), 38–46. doi:10.1109/MC.2003.1231193

Munter, M. (2011). *Guide to Managerial Communication* (8th ed.). Prentice Hall Publisher.

Murgatroyd, S., & Morgan, C. (1993). *Total quality management and the school*. Buckingham, UK: Open University Press.

Murphy, J. H. (2018). *A quantitative study of key indicators of effective management leadership* (Doctoral dissertation). Piedmont International University.

Murray, R. (2017). *Communication among different generations*. Retrieved from: http://robert-murray.com/communication-among-different-generations/

Musashi, M. (1974). *A book of five rings* (V. Harris, Trans.). Woodstock, NY: The Overlook Press.

Muyia, H. (2009). Approaches to and instruments for measuring emotional intelligence: A review of selected literature. *Advances in Developing Human Resources*, *11*(6), 690–702. doi:10.1177/1523422309360843

Myerson, S. G., & Mitchell, A. R. J. (2003). Mobile phones in hospitals. *BMJ (Clinical Research Ed.)*, *326*(7387), 460–461. doi:10.1136/bmj.326.7387.460 PMID:12609917

Nagin, D. S. (1998). Criminal deterrence research at the outset of the twenty-first century. *Crime and Justice*, *23*, 1–42. doi:10.1086/449268

Nakata, C., Zhu, Z., & Izberk-Bilgin, E. (2011). Integrating marketing and information services functions: A complementarity and competence perspective. *Journal of the Academy of Marketing Science*, *39*(5), 700–716. doi:10.100711747-010-0236-z

National Communication Association. (2015). *What is communication?* Retrieved from https://www.natcom.org/discipline/

National Governors Association Center for Best Practices and Council of Chief State School Officers. (2010). *Common core state standards for English language arts and Literacy in history/social studies, science, and technical subjects*. Washington, DC: Authors.

National Research Council. (2000). *Inquiry and the National Science Education Standards*. Washington, DC: National Academy Press.

National Research Council. (2007). *Taking science to school: Learning and teaching science kindergarten to eighth grade*. Washington, DC: National Academy Press.

National Research Council. Committee on Conceptual Framework for the New K-12 Science Education Standards. (2011). A framework for K-12 science education: Practices, crosscutting concepts, and core ideas. Washington, DC: National Academy Press.

Navaratnam, K. K. (1997). Quality management in education must be a never-ending journey. In K. Watson & S. Modgol (Eds.), *Educational dilemma: Debate and diversity; VI: Quality in education*. London: Cassell.

NCAA. (2010, December 23). *NCAA Requires Loss of Contests for Six Ohio State Football Student-Athletes*. Retrieved August 29, 2015 from http://www.dispatch.com/content/stories/sports/2010/12/23/text-of-ncaa-press-release.html?sid=101

Neill, M.S., & Jiang, H. (2017). Functional silos, integration & encroachment in internal communication. *Public Relations Review*, *43*, 850-962.

Nelson, D., & Quick, J. (2012). *Principles of Organizational Behavior: Realities and Challenges*. South Western.

Nelson, L., Bly, S., & Sokoler, T. (2001). Quiet calls: talking silently on mobile phones. *CHI '01: Proceedings of the SIGCHI conference on Human factors in computing systems*. 10.1145/365024.365094

NGSS Lead States. (2013). *Next Generation Science Standards: For States, by States*. Washington, DC: The National Academies Press.

Ngware, M. W., Wamukuru, D. K., & Odebero, S. O. (2006). Total quality management in secondary schools in Kenya: Extent of practice. *Quality Assurance in Education*, *14*(4), 339–362. doi:10.1108/09684880610703947

Nichols, T., Danford, A., & Tasiran, A. (2009). Trust, employer exposure and the employment relations. *Economic and Industrial Democracy*, *30*(2), 241–265. doi:10.1177/0143831X09102429

Nicol, D., Minty, I., & Sinclair, C. (2003). The social dimensions of online learning. *Innovations in Education and Teaching International*, *40*(3), 270–280. doi:10.1080/1470329032000103807

Nilsen, T. R. (1974). *Ethics of speech communication* (2nd ed.). Indianapolis, IN: Bobbs-Merrill.

Noddings, N. (2012). *Philosophy of education* (3rd ed.). Boulder, CO: Westview Press.

Nonaka, I. (1994). A Dynamic Theory of Organizational Knowledge Creation. *Organization Science*, *5*(1).

Nonaka, I. (1995). *The Knowledge-Creating Company*. Paper delivered at Theseus Institute, Conference on The Emergent Corporation, Sophia Antipolis, France.

Nonaka, I., & Teece, D. (Eds.). (2001). *Managing Industrial Knowledge*. London: Sage.

Nord, G. D., McCubbins, T. F., & Horn Nord, J. (2006). Email monitoring in the workplace: Privacy, legislation, and surveillance software. *Communications of the ACM*, *49*(8), 73–77.

Normore, A. H. (2009). Culturally relevant leadership for social justice: Honoring the integrity of First Nations communities in Northeast Canada. In J. Collard & A. H. Normore (Eds.), *Leadership and intercultural dynamics* (pp. 47–68). Charlotte, NC: Information Age Publishing.

Normore, A. H. (2017). Prologue: Police leadership from a futurist viewpoint. In T. Anderson, K. Geisborne, & P. Halliday (Eds.), *Every officer is a leader: Coaching leadership, learning and performance in justice, public safety and security organizations* (pp. 459–464). Holly Spring, NC: International Academy of Public Safety.

Normore, A. H., & Brooks, J. S. (2014). *Educational leadership for social justice: Views from the social sciences*. Charlotte, NC: Information Age Publishing.

Normore, A. H., Javidi, M., Anderson, T., Normand, N., Hoina, C., & Scott, W. (2014). *Moral compass for law enforcement professionals*. Holly Springs, NC: International Academy of Public Safety.

Normore, A., & Erbe, N. (2013). *Collective efficacy: interdisciplinary perspectives on international leadership*. Bingley, UK: Emerald Group Publishing. doi:10.1108/S1479-3660(2013)20

Northouse, P. (2013). *Leadership: Theory and practice* (6th ed.). Thousand Oaks, CA: Sage Publishing.

Northouse, P. (2013). *Leadership: theory and practice* (6th ed.). Thousand Oaks, CA: Sage.

Not enough students to fill university campuses, expert says. (2016). Retrieved from https:// www.cbc.ca/news/canada/sudbury/laurentian-university-barrie-campus

Nussbaum, K., & duRivage, V. (1986). Computer monitoring: Mismanagement by remote control. *Business and Society Review*, (56): 16–29.

O'Kane, C. (2017, September 13). Viral photo of Florida "hot cops" leads to calendar fundraiser for Irma. *CBS News*. Retrieved from https://www.cbsnews.com/news/hot-cops-gainesville-florida-viral-photo-hurricane-irma-calendar-fundraiser/

OECD. (2012). *Machine-to-Machine Communications: Connecting Billions of Devices*. OECD Digital Economy Papers, No. 192. OECD Publishing. Retrieved from http://www.oecd-ilibrary.org/science-andtechnology/machine-to-machine-communications_5k9gsh2gp043-en

Oetzel & Ting-Toomey, S. (2013). The handbook of communication. Thousand Oaks, CA: Sage.

Ohio State Buckeyes-2014 NCAA Football Champions. (2014). Retrieved July 29, 2015 from http://www.ohiostatebuckeyes.com/sports/m-footbl/2014-championship.html

Ohio State football players sanctioned. (2010, December 26). *ESPN.com News Service*. Retrieved August 29, 2015 from http://sports.espn.go.com/ncf/news/story?id=5950873

Ohio State players, alums stand behind Tressel. (2011, May 31). *Sportsillustrated.com*. Retrieved June 1, 2011 http://sportsillustrated.cnn.com/2011/football/ncaa/05/30/tressel-reaction.ap/index.html

Olaniran, B. A., Scholl, J. C., Williams, D. E., & Boyer, L. (2012). Johnson and Johnson phantom recall: A fall from grace or a re-visit of the ghost of the past. *Public Relations Review*, *38*(1), 153–155. doi:10.1016/j.pubrev.2011.08.001

Olaniran, B., & Williams, D. (2001). Anticipatory model of crisis management. In R. Heath (Ed.), *Handbook of public relations* (pp. 487–500). Thousand Oaks, CA: Sage. doi:10.4135/9781452220727.n41

Olson, J. D., Appunn, F. D., McAllister, C. A., Walters, K. K., & Grinnell, L. (2014). Webcams and virtual teams: An impact model. *Team Performance Management*, *20*(3/4), 148–177. doi:10.1108/TPM-05-2013-0013

Onrubia, J. (2004). Las aulas como comunidades de aprendizaje. *Trabajadores de la enseñanza, 249*, 14-15. Retrieved February 2, 2009, from http://www.fe.ccoo.es/publicaciones/TE/249/249pdf

Oracle. (2011, August). *Oracle CEO Blog*. Retrieved from http://blogs.oracle.com/jonathan/

Organ, D. (1977). A reappraisal and reinterpretation of the satisfaction-causes-performance hypothesis. *Academy of Management Review*, *2*(1), 46–53. doi:10.5465/amr.1977.4409162

Organ, D. W. (1988). *Organizational citizenship behavior: The good soldier syndrome*. Lexington, MA: Lexington Books.

Organ, D. W., & Moorman, R. (1993). Fairness and Organizational citizenship behavior: What are the connections? *Social Justice Research*, *6*(1), 5–18. doi:10.1007/BF01048730

Organ, D., & Lingl, A. (1995). Personality, satisfaction and organizational citizenship behaviors. *The Journal of Social Psychology*, *135*(3), 339–250. doi:10.1080/00224545.1995.9713963

Orlikowski, W. J. (2000). Using technology and constituting structures: A practice lens for studying technology in organizations. *Organization Science*, *11*(4), 404–428. doi:10.1287/orsc.11.4.404.14600

Ortega-Argilés, R., & Brandsma, A. (2010). EU-US differences in the size of R&D intensive firms: Do they explain the overall R&D intensity gap? *Science & Public Policy*, *37*(6), 429–441. doi:10.3152/030234210X508633

Orth, J. V. (2003). *Due process of law: A brief history*. University Press of Kansas.

Ortiz, F. (2012). In *Encyclopædia Britannica*. Retrieved June 27, 2012 from: http://www.britannica.com/EBchecked/topic/848801/Fernando-Ortiz

OSC. (2018). *Latest News. U.S. Office of the Special Counsel*. Accessed October 10, 2018 at: https://osc.gov/Pages/News.aspx

OSU athletic director Gene Smith on timeline of events. (2010, December 23). *WEWSNewsChannel5*. Retrieved August 29, 2015 from https://www.youtube.com/watch?v=aJ3z7_oM5W0

OSU coach Jim Tressel on Suspensions. (2010, December 23). *WEWSNewsChannel5*. Retrieved August 29, 2015 from https://www.youtube.com/watch?v=OuqH3PVQJAg

Ots, M., & Nyilasy, G. (2015). Integrated Marketing Communications (IMC): Why Does It Fail? *Journal of Advertising Research*, *55*(2), 132–145. doi:10.2501/JAR-55-2-132-145

Palmer, P. (1998). *The courage to teach*. San Francisco, CA: Jossey-Bass.

Parker, J., & Coiera, E. (2000). Improving Clinical Communication: A View from Psychology. *Journal of the American Medical Informatics Association*, *7*(5), 453–461. doi:10.1136/jamia.2000.0070453 PMID:10984464

Parker, P. A., & Sorensen, J. (2008). Emotional intelligence and leadership skills among NHS managers: An empirical investigation. *International Journal of Clinical Leadership*, *16*(3), 137–142. Retrieved from http://www.radcliffe-oxford.com /journals/J24_The_International_Journal_of_Clinical_Leadership/default.htm

Parker, R. B. (1974). A definition of privacy. *Rutgers Law Review*, *27*(1), 275.

Park, H., & Reber, B. (2008). Relationship building and the use of Websites: How Fortune 500 companies use their Websites to build relationships. *Public Relations Review*, *34*(4), 409–411. doi:10.1016/j.pubrev.2008.06.006

Park, S., Na, E., & Kim, E. (2014). The relationship between online activities, netiquette and cyberbullying. *Children and Youth Services Review*, *42*, 74–81. doi:10.1016/j.childyouth.2014.04.002

Parks, S. D. (2005). *Leadership can be taught: A bold approach for a complex world*. Boston, MA: Harvard Business Review Press.

Parry, M. (2010). Tomorrow's college. *Chronicle of Higher Learning*, *57*(11), 84–86.

Partnership for assessment of readiness for college and careers (PARCC). (2011). *PARCC model content frameworks for ELA-literacy*. Author.

Paternoster, R., Brame, R., Bachman, R., & Sherman, L. W. (1997). Do fair procedures matter? The effect of procedural justice on spouse assault. *Law & Society Review*, *31*(1), 163–204. doi:10.2307/3054098

Paul, J. A., Baker, H. M., & Cochran, J. D. (2012). Effect of online social networking on student academic performance. *Computers in Human Behavior*, *28*(6), 2117–2127. doi:10.1016/j.chb.2012.06.016

Paupp, T. (2014). *Redefining human rights in the struggle for peace and development*. New York: Cambridge University Press.

Pavlou, P. A., Liang, H., & Xue, Y. (2007). Understanding and mitigating uncertainty in online exchange relationships: A principal–agent perspective. *Management Information Systems Quarterly*, *31*(1), 105–136. doi:10.2307/25148783

Payne, W. (1985). *A Study of Emotion: Developing Emotional Intelligence; Self-Integration; Relating to Fear, Pain and Desire (Theory, Structure of Reality, Problem-Solving, Contraction/Expansion, Tuning In/Coming Out/Letting Go)* (Doctoral dissertation). Available from Worldcat Dissertations. (437626710)

Pearce, B. (2007). *Making social worlds: a communication perspective*. London: Blackwell.

Pearce, B., & Pearce, K. (2000). Extending the theory of the coordinated management of meaning ("CMM") through a community dialogue process. *Communication Theory*, *4*(4), 405–423. doi:10.1111/j.1468-2885.2000.tb00200.x

Pearlson, K. E., Saunders, C. S., & Galletta, D. F. (2016). *Managing and Using Information Systems: a strategic approach* (6th ed.). Hoboken, NJ: John Wiley & Sons, Inc.

Pedersen, E. R. (2001). Calls.calm: enabling caller and callee to collaborate. *CHI '01 extended abstracts on Human factors in computing systems*. 10.1145/634067.634207

Pendell, R., & Dvorak, N. (2018). Digitizing Culture: Are You Doing It Wrong? *Gallup Business Journal*. Retrieved on 6/13/18 from http://news.gallup.com/businessjournal/234425/digitizing-culture-doing-wrong.aspx?utm_source=alert&utm_medium=email&utm_content=morelink&utm_campaign=syndication

Pendlebury, S., & Enslin, P. (2000). Lifelong learning for a new society. In J. Field & M. Leicester (Eds.), *Lifelong learning: Education across the lifespan* (pp. 149–157). New York: Routledge Falmer.

Penuel, W. R., Fishman, B. J., Haugan Cheng, B., & Sabelli, N. (2011). Organizing research and development at the intersection of learning, implementation, and design. *Educational Researcher*, *40*(7), 331–337. doi:10.3102/0013189X11421826

Petronio, S. (2002). *Boundaries of Privacy: Dialectics of Disclosure*. Albany, NY: State University of New York Press.

Pew Research Center. (2014). *Public Perceptions of Prvacy and Security in the Post-Snowden Era*. Pew Research Center.

Pfeffer, N., & Coote, A. (1991). Is Quality Good for You? A Critical Review of Quality Assurance. In *Welfare Services. Social Policy Paper No. 5*. London: Institute for Public Policy Research.

Pfeiffer, W. (1994). *Basic communication model*. Pfeiffer & Company library of theories and models: management. Retrieved from, http://home.snu.edu/~jsmith/library/body/v25.pdf

Piaget, J. (1932). *The moral judgement of the child*. New York, NY: Free Press.

Piaget, J. (1952). *The origins of intelligence in children*. New York, NY: International Universities Press. doi:10.1037/11494-000

Piaget, J. (1977). *Development of thought: equilibration of cognitive structures*. New York, NY: Viking Press.

Piccoli, G., Powell, A., & Ives, B. (2004). Virtual teams: Team control structure, work processes, and team effectiveness. *Information Technology & People*, *17*(4), 359–379. doi:10.1108/09593840410570258

Pickavance, K. (2007). *Construction Law And Management*. London: Routledge.

Pincus, D. J., Rayfield, R. E., & Cozzens, M. D. (1991). The Chief Executive Officer's internal communications role: A benchmark program of research. In L. A. Grunig & J. E. Grunig (Eds.), *Public Relations Research Annual* (Vol. 3, pp. 1–36). Hillsdale, NJ: Lawrence Earlbaum Associates.

Pincus, J. D., Rayfield, R. E., & Cozzens, M. D. (1991). The chief executive officer's internal communication role: A benchmark program of research. *Journal of Public Relations Research*, *3*(1-4), 1–35. doi:10.12071532754xjprr0301-4_1

Piyachat, B., Chanongkorn, K., & Panisa, M. (2014). The mediate effect of employee engagement on the relationship between perceived employer branding and discretionary effort. *DLSU Business & Economics Review*, *24*(1), 59–72.

Podsakoff, P., & MacKenzie, S. (1993). Citizenship behavior and fairness in organizations: Issues and directions for future research. *Employee Responsibilities and Rights Journal*, *6*(3), 257–269. doi:10.1007/BF01419449

Podsakoff, P., & MacKenzie, S. (1997). Impact of organizational citizenship behavior on organizational performance: A review and suggestions for future research. *Human Performance*, *10*(2), 133–151. doi:10.120715327043hup1002_5

Podsakoff, P., MacKenzie, S., Paine, J., & Bachrach, D. (2000). Organizational citizenship behaviors: A critical review of the theoretical and empirical literature and suggestions for future research. *Journal of Management*, *26*(3), 513–563. doi:10.1177/014920630002600307

Ponte, L. M. (2001). Broadening Traditional ADR Notions Of Disclosure: Special Considerations For Posting Conflict Resolution Policies And Programs On E-Business Web Sites. *Ohio State Journal Of Dispute Resolution*, *17*, 321.

Porter, C., Neal, S., & Medina, A. (2000, October). Leadership development at the executive level. *The Police Chief*, 179 - 187.

Power, M., & Vaughan, N. (2010). Redesigning online learning for international graduate seminar delivery. *Journal of Distance Education*, *24*(2), 19–38.

Poyatos, F. (2002a). *Nonverbal communication across disciplines* (Vol. 1). Philadelphia, PA: John Benjamins.

Poyatos, F. (2002b). *Nonverbal communication across disciplines. Paralanguage, kinesics, si- lence, personal and environmental interaction* (Vol. 2). Philadelphia, PA: John Benjamins. doi:10.1075/z.ncad2

Prakhaber, P. R. (2000). Who owns the online consumer? *Journal of Consumer Marketing*, *17*(2), 158–171. doi:10.1108/07363760010317213

Prensky, M. (2006). Listen to the natives. *Educational Leadership*, *63*(4), 8–13.

Prensky, M. (2011). In the 21st century university, let's ban (paper) books. *The Chronicle of Higher Education*, *58*(13), 309.

Prensky, M. (2014). Innovation experimentation and courage in the education of students for the future. *Educational Technology*, *54*(1), 64.

Price Waterhouse Coopers. (2013). Corporate Choices. In *International Arbitration*. Academic Press.

Priest, G. L., & Klein, B. (1984). The Selection Of Disputes For Litigation. *The Journal of Legal Studies*, *12*(1), 1–55. doi:10.1086/467732

Priest, H., Stagl, K., Klein, C., & Salas, E. (2006). Virtual teams: Creating context for distributed teamwork. In C. Bowers, E. Salas, & F. Jentsch (Eds.), *Creating high-tech teams* (pp. 185–211). Washington, DC: American Psychological Association. doi:10.1037/11263-009

Printy, S. M., Marks, H. M., & Bowers, A. J. (2009). Integrated Leadership: How Principals and Teachers Share Transformational and Instructional Influence. *Journal of School Leadership*, *19*(5), 504–532.

Pruett, M., & Thomas, H. (1996). Thinking About Quality and its Links with Strategic Management. *European Management Journal*, *14*(1), 37–46. doi:10.1016/0263-2373(95)00045-3

Pruitt, D., & Kim, S. (2004). *Social conflict: escalation, stalemate and settlement*. New York: McGraw-Hill.

Purdum, T. S. (1994, February 24). Bradley rebukes Clinton on Japan. *The New York Times*, p. C1-C2.

Pyle, E., & Ludlow, R. (2011, July 16). *Ohio State football: Tressel had early history of warnings*. Retrieved October 14, 2015 from http://www.dispatch.com/content/stories/local/2011/07/16/tressel-had-early-history-of-warnings.html

Quirke, B. (2008). *Making the connections: Using internal communication to turn strategy into action*. Burlington, VT: Gower.

Rabin, M. (1993). Incorporating fairness into game theory and economics. *The American Economic Review*, 1281–1302.

Radick, S. (2011). *The power of social networks: Reviving the intranet*. Public Relations Tactics.

Rafi, Y. (2017). *Productivity secrets of high-performance employees at Google & Apple*. Retrieved from https://blog.taskque.com/productivity-secrets-high-performance-employees-google-apple/

Rahim, M. A. (1986). Managing Conflict. In *Organizations*. New York, NY: Praeger.

Rahim, M. A. (2002). Toward a theory of managing organizational conflict. *International Journal of Conflict Management, 13*(3), 206–235. doi:10.1108/eb022874

Raines, C. (2015). *4GenR8tns: Succeeding with colleagues, cohorts & customers*. Retrieved from http://www.generationsatwork.com/articles_succeeding.php

Rampa, S. H. (2005). *The Relationship between Total Quality Management and School Improvement. Unpublished doctoral dissertation*. Pretoria, South Africa: University of Pretoria. Retrieved from http://repository.up.ac.za/bitstream/handle/2263/23595/Complete.pdf?sequence=5

Rampton, J. (2017). Different motivations for different generations of workers: Boomers, *Gen X, Millennials, and Gen Z*. Retrieved from: https://www.inc.com/john-rampton/different-motivations-for-different-generations-of-workers-boomers-gen-x-millennials-gen-z.html

Rands, M., Levinger, G., & Mellinger, G. D. (1981). Patterns Of Conflict Resolution And Marital Satisfaction. *Journal of Family Issues, 2*(3), 297–321. doi:10.1177/0192513X8100200303

Rawlins, B. (2006). Prioritizing stakeholders for public relations. *Institute for Public Relations*. Retrieved October 18, 2015 from http://pdfcast.org/pdf/prioritizing-stakeholders-for-public-relations

Raykov, T., & Grayson, D. (2003). A test for change of composite reliability in scale development. *Multivariate Behavioral Research, 38*(2), 143–159. doi:10.1207/S15327906MBR3802_1

Ready, K. (2013). *In Search of Japan's Missing Startups*. Retrieved October 2017 at https:// www. forbes.com/sites/kevinready/2013/05/17/in-search-of-japans-missing-startups/#709c868b6f06

Reddy, S. (2007). *SCHOOL QUALITY: Perspectives from the Developed and Developing Countries*. Azim Premji Foundation. Retrieved from http://www.azimpremjifoundation.org/pdf/ConsolidatedSchoolQualityreport.pdf

Redmond, R., Curtis, E., Noone, T., & Keenan, P. (2008). Quality in higher education: The contribution of Edward Deming's principles. *International Journal of Educational Management, 22*(5), 432–441. doi:10.1108/09513540810883168

Rego, A., Ribeiro, N., & Cunha, M. P. (2010). Perceptions of Organizational virtuousness and happiness as predictors of Organizational citizenship behaviors. *Journal of Business Ethics, 93*(2), 215–235. doi:10.100710551-009-0197-7

Reid, A., Cranston, N., Keating, J., & Mulford, B. (2010). *Exploring the Public Purposes of Education in Australian Primary Schools*. Report on an ARC-Linkage Project conducted in partnership with the Australian Government Primary Principals Association (AGPPA); and the Foundation for Young Australians. Retrieved from: http://www.agppa.asn.au/index.php?option=com_content&view=article&id=28&Itemid=18

Reisig, M. D., Bratton, J., & Gertiz, M. G. (2007). The construct validity and refinement of process-based policing measures. *Criminal Justice and Behavior, 34*(8), 1005–1028. doi:10.1177/0093854807301275

Rhys Jones, S. (1994). How Constructive Is Construction Law? *Constitutional Law Journal (Newark, N.J.)*, *10*(1), 28–38.

Richards, R. (n.d.). *Command presence: Feeding your own self confidence*. Retrieved from the internet August 30, 2015, http://www.withthecommand.com/2004-May/PA-Richards-commandpresence.html

Richardson, J. (2012). Face to face versus online tuition: Preference, performance and pass rates in White and ethnic minority students. *British Journal of Educational Technology*, *43*(1), 17–27. doi:10.1111/j.1467-8535.2010.01147.x

Rich, B. L., Lepine, J. A., & Crawford, E. R. (2010). Job engagement: Antecedents and effects on job performance. *Academy of Management Journal*, *53*(3), 617–635. doi:10.5465/amj.2010.51468988

Richmond, S. L., Rollin, P. F., & Brown, J. M. (2004). *What makes a successful leader*. Retrieved from http://ideashape.com/leadership-research.htm

Rickards, T. (2000). Creativity and the management of change. *Australian Journal of Communication*, *27*(3), 163–164.

Riggio, R. E., & Carney, D. (2003). *Manual for the Social Skills Inventory* (2nd ed.). Redwood City, CA: Mind Garden.

Rintoul, H. (2011). *Transforming educational practices. The online graduate experience: Concerns, challenges and dilemmas*. Paper presented at the annual meeting of the Center for the Study of Leadership and Ethics in Education, Victoria, Canada.

Robbins, S. P. (2008). *Organizational Behavior* (13th ed.). Prentice Hall.

Robinson, B. M. (1996). *Total quality management in education: The empowerment of a school community* (Unpublished doctoral dissertation). University of Nebraska, Lincoln, NE.

Robinson, W. (2002). The Effects Of The Human Rights Act 1998 On Arbitration. *Amicus Curiae,* (42).

Robinson, S. L., & Bennett, R. J. (1997). *Workplace deviance: Its definition, its manifestations, and its causes*. Greenwich, CT: JAI Press.

Robinson, S. L., & Rousseau, D. M. (1994). Violating the psychological contract: Not the exception but the norm. *Journal of Organizational Behavior*, *15*(3), 245–259. doi:10.1002/job.4030150306

Robson, P., & Tourish, D. (2005). Managing internal communication: An organizational case study. *Corporate Communications*, *10*(3), 213–222. doi:10.1108/13563280510614474

Rockland, D. B. (2014). *Why internal communications is a business driver*. Tactics.

Rodgers, R. (1975). A Protection Motivation Theory of Fear Appeals and Attitude Change. *The Journal of Psychology – Interdisiplinary and Applied, 91*(1), 93 – 114.

Rogers Everett, M., & Steinfatt Thomas, M. (1999). *Intercultural Communication*. Prospect Heights, IL: Waveland Press.

Rogers, P. (2004, June 10-11). *Trends in conflict 2010-2030*. Centre for Humanitarian Dialogue Mediators Retreat, Oslo, Norway.

Rogers, E. M., Hart, W. B., & Miike, Y. (2002). Edward T. Hall and the History of Intercultural Communication: The United States and Japan. *Keio Communication Review*, *24*, 1–5.

Rosenberg, M. (2003). Redefining e-learning. *Performance Improvement*, *42*(3), 38–41. doi:10.1002/pfi.4930420307

Rousseau, D. (2004). Psychological Contracts in the Workplace: Understanding the Ties That Motivate. *Academy of Management Executive, 18*(1), 120-127.

Rousseau, D. M. (1995). *Psychological Contracts in Organizations: Understanding Written and Unwritten Agreements*. Sage.

Rousseau, D., Sitkin, S., Burt, R., & Camerer, C. (1998). Not so different after all: A cross- discipline view of trust. *Academy of Management Review*, *23*(3), 393–404. doi:10.5465/amr.1998.926617

Rowland, R. C., & Jerome, A. M. (2004). On organizational apologia: A reconceptualization. *Communication Theory*, *14*(3), 191–211. doi:10.1111/j.1468-2885.2004.tb00311.x

Rubin, J. (2014). The learning strategy prism: Perspectives of learning strategy experts. *System*, *43*(1).

Ruppel, C. P., & Harrington, S. J. (2001). Sharing knowledge through intranets: A study of organizational culture and intranet implementation. *Professional Communication*, *44*(1), 37–52. doi:10.1109/47.911131

Russell, J. L., Jackson, K., Krumm, A. E., & Frank, K. A. (2013). Theories and research methodologies for design-based implementation research: Examples from four cases. *Yearbook of the National Society for the Study of Education*, *112*(2), 157–191.

Rust, R. T., Kannan, P. K., & Peng, N. (2002). The customer economics of internet privacy. *Journal of the Academy of Marketing Science*, *30*(4), 455–464. doi:10.1177/009207002236917

Ryckewaert, L. (2011, November). PM Harper takes communications strategy to new level. *Hill Times News Online*. Retrieved from http://www.hilltimes.com/news/2011/11/21/pm-harper-takes-communications-strategy-to-new-level/28868

Saari, L. M., & Judge, T. A. (2004). Employee Attitudes and Job satisfaction. *Human Resource Management*, *43*(4), 395–407. doi:10.1002/hrm.20032

Safire, W. (2002). The great unwatched. *The New York Times*. Retrieved from http://query.nytimes. com/gst/fullpage.html?res=9A03E7DB1E3FF93BA25751C0A9649C8B63

Saif, N., & Saleh, A. (2013). Psychological empowerment and job satisfaction in Jordanian hospitals. *International Journal of Humanities and Social Science*, *3*(16), 250–257.

Saks, A. M. (2006). Antecedents and consequences of employee engagement. *Journal of Managerial Psychology*, *21*(7), 600–619. doi:10.1108/02683940610690169

Sala, F. (2001). *It's lonely at the top: Executives' emotional intelligence self (mis) perceptions*. Retrieved from http://www.eiconsortium.org

Sallis, E. (1993). *Total quality management in education*. London: Kogan Page Ltd. doi:10.4324/9780203417010

Salovey, P., & Mayer, J. D. (1988). Emotional Intelligence. *Imagination, Cognition and Personality*, *9*(3), 185–211. doi:10.2190/DUGG-P24E-52WK-6CDG

Samad, S. (2005). Unraveling the organizational commitment and job performance relationship: Exploring the moderating effect of job satisfaction. *Business Review (Federal Reserve Bank of Philadelphia)*, *4*(2), 79–84.

Sammon, M. J., Karmin, L. S. B., Peebles, E., & Seligmann, D. D. (2006). *MACCS: Enabling communications for mobile workers within healthcare environments*. Paper presented at the MobileHCI'06.

Sánchez, A. M., Pérez, M. P., de Luis Carnicer, P., & Jiménez, M. J. V. (2007). Teleworking and workplace flexibility: A study of impact on firm performance. *Personnel Review*, *36*(1), 42–64. doi:10.1108/00483480710716713

Sandbank, T., Schmueli-scheueur, M., Konopnicki, D., Herzig, J., Richards, J., & Piorkowski, D. (2017), *Detecting Egregious Conversations between Customers and Virtual Agents*. ArXiv: 1711:05780v1

Sandman, P. (2012). *Responding to community outrage: Strategies for effective risk communication*. American Industrial Hygiene Association.

Sanz, S. (2009). *Comunitats de pràctica o l'aprenentatge compartit*. Revista Guix.

Saraph, J. V., & Sebastian, R. J. (1993). Developing a quality culture. *Quality Progress*, *26*(9), 73–78.

Sarmiento, T. P., Laschinger, H. K. S., & Iwasiw, C. (2004). Nurse educators workplace empowerment, burnout, and job satisfaction: Testing Kanters theory. *Journal of Advanced Nursing*, *46*(2), 134–143. doi:10.1111/j.1365-2648.2003.02973.x

Sarver, M. B. (2008). *Leadership and effectiveness: An examination of the leadership styles of Texas police chiefs and the correlates of the most effective leaders* (Doctoral dissertation). Available from ProQuest Dissertations and Theses database. (UMI No. 3311989)

Saturday Night Live. (2017, April 9). Pepsi Commercial – SNL. *YouTube video*. Retrieved from https://www.youtube.com/watch?v=Pn8pwoNWseM

Sauner-Leroy, J. B. (2004). Managers and productive investment decisions: The impact of uncertainty and risk aversion. *Journal of Small Business Management*, *42*(1), 1–18. doi:10.1111/j.1540-627X.2004.00094.x

Sawhney, N., & Schmandt, C. (2000). Nomadic radio: Speech and audio interaction for contextual messaging in nomadic environments. *ACM Transactions on Computer-Human Interaction*, *7*(3), 353–383. doi:10.1145/355324.355327

Sayeed, O. B., & Shanker, M. (2009). Emotionally intelligent managers & transformational leadership styles. *Indian Journal of Industrial Relations*, *44*, 593–610. Retrieved from http://www.srcirhr.com/ijir.php

Scheel, C. (2007). Why the Latin American region has not succeeded in building world-class industrial clusters. In *KGCM proceedings*. Winter Garden, FL: International Institute of Informatics and Systems.

Schelling, T. C. (1957). Bargaining, Communication, And Limited War. *The Journal of Conflict Resolution*, *1*(1), 19–36. doi:10.1177/002200275700100104

Schilit & Theimer. (1994). Disseminating active map information to mobile hosts. *Network, IEEE*, *8*(5), 22-32.

Schilit, B., Adams, N., & Want, R. (1994). *Context-aware computing applications*. Paper presented at the Mobile Computing Systems and Applications. 10.1109/WMCSA.1994.16

Schilit, Hilbert, & Trevor. (2002) Context-aware communication. *Wireless Communications, IEEE*, *9*(5), 46–54.

Schlenkrich, L., & Upfold, C. (2009). A guideline for virtual team managers: The key to effective social interaction and communication. *The Electronic Journal of Information Systems Evaluation*, *12*(1), 109–118.

Schmidt, A., Aidoo, K. A., Takaluoma, A., Tuomela, U., Van Laerhoven, K., & Van de Velde, W. (1999). Advanced interaction in context. In *Handheld and ubiquitous computing* (pp. 89–101). Springer. doi:10.1007/3-540-48157-5_10

Schmidt, A., Takaluoma, A., & Mäntyjärvi, J. (2000). Context-Aware telephony over WAP. *Personal and Ubiquitous Computing*, *4*(4), 225–229.

Schmoker, M., & Wilson, R. B. (1993). Adapting total quality doesn't mean "turning learning into a business". *Educational Leadership*, *51*(1), 62–63.

Scholl, J., Hasvold, P., Henriksen, E., & Ellingsen, G. (2007). *Managing Communication Availability and Interruptions: A Study of Mobile Communication in an Oncology Department*. Pervasive Computing.

Schraeder, M. (2001). Identifying employee resistance during the threat of a merger: An analysis of employee perceptions and commitment to an organization in a pre-merger context. *The Mid-Atlantic Journal of Business*, *37*(4), 191–204.

Schramm, W. (1955). *The Process and Effects of Mass Communication.* Urbana, IL: University of Illinois Press.

Schultz, D. E., Tannenbaum, S. I., & Lauterborn, R. F. (1993). *Integrated marketing communication: Pulling it together and making it work.* Lincolnwood, IL: NTC Publishing Group.

Schultz, J. R. (2014). *Four-cornered Leadership: A Framework for Making Decisions.* CRC Press, Taylor & Francis Group.

Schumpeter, J. A. (1942). Capitalism, Socialism and Democracy. Harper & Brothers.

Scott, P., & Mouza, C. (2007). The impact of professional development on teacher learning, practice and leadership skills: A study on the integration of technology in the teaching of writing. *Journal of Educational Computing Research, 37*(3), 229–266. doi:10.2190/EC.37.3.b

Searle, R., Den Hartog, D. N., Weibel, A., Gillespie, N., Six, F., Hatzakis, T., & Skinner, D. (2011). Trust in the employer: The role of high-involvement work practices and procedural justice in European organizations. *International Journal of Human Resource Management, 22*(5), 1069–1092. doi:10.1080/09585192.2011.556782

Seeger, M. W. (2006). Best practices in crisis communication: An expert panel process. *Journal of Applied Communication Research, 34*(3), 232–244. doi:10.1080/00909880600769944

Seixas, P., & Morton, T. (2013). *The Big six: Historical thinking concepts.* Boston: Cengage Learning.

Seligman, M., & Csikszentmihalyi, M. (2000). Positive psychology: An introduction. *The American Psychologist, 55*(1), 5–14. doi:10.1037/0003-066X.55.1.5 PMID:11392865

Selmi, M. (2006). Privacy for the working class: Public work and private lives. *Louisiana Law Review, 66,* 1035–1056.

Selwyn, N. (2012). Social Media in Higher Education. In *The Europa World of Learning* (62nd ed.). Routledge.

Semple, C., Hartman, F., & Jergas, G. (1994). Construction Claims And Disputes: Causes And Cost/Time Overruns. *Journal of Construction Engineering and Management, 120*(4), 785–795. doi:10.1061/(ASCE)0733-9364(1994)120:4(785)

Semuels, A. (2013, April 8). Monitoring up-ends balance of power at workplace some say. *Los Angeles Times.* Retrieved from http:// www.latimes.com/business/money/la-fi-mo-monitoring-upends-balance-of-power-at-workplace-20130408,0,7425573.story

Senge, P. (n.d.). Transforming the Practice of Managemen. *HRD Quarterly, 4*(1), 5-32.

Senge, P. (1990). *The Fifth Discipline: The Art and Practice of the Learning Organisation.* New York: Doubleday.

Senge, P. (1990). *The Fifth Discipline: The Art and practice of the Learning organization.* New York: Doubleday.

Senge, P. M. (1994). *The fifth discipline: The art & practice of the learning organization.* New York, NY: Doubleday.

Shah, D. V., Cho, J., Eveland, W. P. Jr, & Kwak, N. (2005). Information and expression in a digital age: Modelling Internet effects on civic participation. *Communication Research, 32*(5), 531–565. doi:10.1177/0093650205279209

Shaw, B. (2001, March 9). What, Gee worry? OSU president's lack of concern over the Tressel scandal will likely raise some with the NCAA: Bud Shaw's sports spin. *Cleveland.com.* Retrieved October 27, 2015 from http://www.cleveland.com/budshaw/index.ssf/2011/03/what_gee_worry_osu_presidents.html

Sherman, L. W. (1990). Police crackdowns: Initial and residual deterrence. *Crime and Justice, 12,* 1–48. doi:10.1086/449163

Shewart, W. A. (1931). *Economic Control of Quality of Manufactured Product.* New York: Van Nostrand.

Shipper, F., & Wilson, C. (1991). *The impact of managerial behaviors on group performance, stress, and commitment.* Paper presented at The Impact of Leadership Conference, Center for Creative Leadership, Colorado Springs, CO.

Shortell, D. (2016, April 18). 'Basketball cop' turns noise complaint into national project. *CNN.* Retrieved from https://www.cnn.com/2016/04/18/us/beyond-the-call-of-duty-basketball-cop/index.html

SHRM. (2005). *Workplace privacy – Poll findings: A study by the society for human resource management and career-journal.com.* Retrieved from http://www.shrm.org/Research/Survey- Findings/Documents/Workplace%20Privacy%20Poll%20Findings%20-%20A%20Study%20 by%20SHRM%20and%20CareerJournal.com.pdf

Siebdrat, F., Hoegl, M., & Ernst, H. (2009). How to manage virtual teams. *MIT Sloan Management Review, 50*(4), 63–68.

Siegall, M., & Gardner, S. (2000). Contextual factors of psychological empowerment. *Personnel Review, 29*(6), 703–722. doi:10.1108/00483480010296474

Siegel, P. (2000). Using Baldridge to improve education: A rationale based on results. *Training & Development, 54*(2), 66–67.

Siewiorek, D., Smailagic, A., Furukawa, J., Krause, A., Moraveji, N., & Reiger, K. (2003). SenSay: a context-aware mobile phone. *Wearable Computers, 2003. Proceedings. Seventh IEEE International Symposium on.* 10.1109/ISWC.2003.1241422

Silins, H. (1994). Leadership Characteristics and School Improvement. *Australian Journal of Education, 38*(3), 268–281. doi:10.1177/000494419403800306

Silins, H., & Mulford, B. (2002). Schools as learning organisations: The case for system, teacher and student learning. *Journal of Educational Administration, 40*(5), 425–446. doi:10.1108/09578230210440285

Silins, H., Mulford, B., Zarins, S., & Bishop, P. (2000). Leadership for Organizational Learning in Australian Secondary Schools. In K. Leithwood (Ed.), *Understanding Schools as Intelligent Systems* (pp. 267–291). Stamford, CT: JAI Press. doi:10.1080/03057640302041

Silins, H., Zarins, S., & Mulford, B. (2002). What characteristics and processes define a school as a learning organisation? Is this a useful concept to apply to schools? *International Education Journal, 3*(1), 24–32.

Sim, K. L., & Rogers, J. W. (2009). Implementing lean production systems: Barriers to change. *Management Research News, 32*(1), 37–49. doi:10.1108/01409170910922014

Simpson, M., Cockburn-Wootten, C., & Cockburn, T. (2005). Resistance; the unexpected consequences of implementing change. In *International Conference on Case Study teaching and learning*. University of Auckland.

Sir Robert Peel's Principles of Law Enforcement. (n.d.). Retrieved on October 12, 2015 from https://www.durham.police.uk/AboutUs/Documents/Peels_Principles_Of_Law_Enforcement.pdf

Sisler, H. E. (2015). Crisis of man to crisis of men: Ray Rice and the NFL's transition from crisis of image to crisis of ethics. *TopSCHOLAR.* Retrieved October 18, 2015 from http://digitalcommons.wku.edu/theses/1520/

Skov, B., & Høegh, T. (2006). Supporting information access in a hospital ward by a context-aware mobile electronic patient record. *Personal and Ubiquitous Computing, 10*(4), 205–214. doi:10.100700779-005-0049-0

Slawson, N. (2017, October 8). Dove apologises for ad showing black woman turning into white one. *The Guardian.* Retrieved from https://www.theguardian.com/world/2017/oct/08/dove-apologises-for-ad-showing-black-woman-turning-into-white-one

Sledgianowski, D., & Kulviwat, S. (2009). Using social network sites: The effects of playfulness, critical mass and trust in a hedonic context. *Journal of Computer Information Systems, 49*(4), 74–83.

Smith, E. (2011, December 20). Ohio State hit with bowl ban, Tressel gets show-cause penalty. *USA Today.*

Smith: Tressel's speech to team "eloquent." (2011, May 30). *USA Today.* Retrieved August 28, 2015 from http://usatoday30.usatoday.com/sports/college/football/2011-05-30-4107396395_x.htm

Smith, B. G. (2013). The public relations contribution to IMC: Deriving opportunities from threats and solidifying public relations' future. *Public Relations Review, 39*(5), 507–513. doi:10.1016/j.pubrev.2013.09.012

Smith, G., Sorensen, C., Gump, A., Heindel, A., Caris, M., & Martinez, C. (2011, March). Over-coming student resistance to group work: Online versus face to face. *Internet and Higher Education, 14*(2), 121–128. doi:10.1016/j.iheduc.2010.09.005

Smith, H. J., Dinev, T., & Xu, H. (2011). Informa- tion privacy research: An interdisciplinary review. *Management Information Systems Quarterly, 35*(4), 989–1015. doi:10.2307/41409970

Smith, H. J., Milberg, J. S., & Burke, J. S. (1996). Information privacy: Measuring individuals' con- cerns about organizational practices. *Management Information Systems Quarterly, 20*(2), 167–196. doi:10.2307/249477

Smith, P., & Cockburn, T. (2013). *Dynamic Leadership Models for Global Business: Enhancing Digitally Connected Environments.* IGI Global. doi:10.4018/978-1-4666-2836-6

Smith, P., & Cockburn, T. (Eds.). (2014). *Impact of Emerging Digital Technologies on Leadership in Global Business.* IGI Global. doi:10.4018/978-1-4666-6134-9

Smith, R. A. (1962). Question Of Arbitrability-The Role Of The Arbitrator, The Court, And The Parties. *Southwestern Law Journal, 16*(1).

Smith, W. P., & Tabak, F. (2009). Monitoring employee e-mails: Is there any room for privacy? *The Academy of Management Perspectives, 23*(4), 33–48. doi:10.5465/amp.23.4.33

Snarey, J. R. (1985). A Cross-cultural Universality of Social-moral Development: A Critical Review of Kohlbergian Research. *Psychological Bulletin, 97*(2), 202–232. doi:10.1037/0033-2909.97.2.202 PMID:3983300

Snarey, J., Reimer, J., & Kohlberg, L. (1985). The kibbutz as a model for moral education: A longitudinal cross-cultural study. *Journal of Applied Developmental Psychology, 6*(2-3), 151–172. doi:10.1016/0193-3973(85)90057-7

Snowden, D. J. (2012). Retrieved June 6, 2012, from http://en.wikipedia.org/wiki/Dave_Snowden

Solomon, J. (2013, August 6). Jay Bilas uses NCAA store to highlight Johnny Manziel scandal. *AL.com.* Retrieved September 16, 2014 from www.al.com

Solove, D. J. (2006). A taxonomy of privacy. *University of Pennsylvania Law Review, 154*(3), 477–564. doi:10.2307/40041279

Solvoll, T. (2013b). *From being interrupted by mobile devices to CallMeSmart - a context-sensitive communication system for mobile communication in hospitals.* UiT The Arctic University of Norway.

Solvoll, T., Arntsen, H., & Hartvigsen, G. (2017). Alarm Fatigue vs User Expectations Regarding Context-Aware Alarm Handling in Hospital Environments Using CallMeSmart. *Stud Health Technol Inform, 241*, 159-164.

Solvoll, T., Fasani, S., Ravuri, A. B., Tiemersma, A., & Hartvigsen, G. (2010). *Evaluation of an Ascom/trixbox system for context sensitive communication in hospitals.* Paper presented at the 8th Scandinavian Conference on Health Informatics, Copenhagen, Denmark.

Solvoll, T., Gironi, L., & Hartvigsen, G. (2013). *CallMeSmart: An Ascom/Trixbox Based Prototype for Context Controlled Mobile Communication in Hospitals.* Paper presented at the Information Science and Applications (ICISA), 2013 International Conference on Information Science and Applications. 10.1109/ICISA.2013.6579344

Solvoll, T., Gironi, L., Giordanengo, A., & Hartvigsen, G. (2013). CallMeSmart: A VoIP Softphone on Android Based Mobile Devices Using SIP. In *eTELEMED 2013, The Fifth International Conference on eHealth, Telemedicine, and Social Medicine* (Vol. 15, pp. 198-203). International Academy, Research and Industry Association (IARIA).

Solvoll, T., Hanssen, B., Aring, R.D., Giordanengo, A., & Hartvigsen, G. (2015). CallMeSmart: Location Tracking Using BLE Beacons. *Proceedings from The 13th Scandinavien Conference on Health Informatics.*

Solvoll, T., Tiemersma, A., Kerbage, E., Fasani, S., Ravuri, A. B., & Hartvigsen, G. (2011). Context-sensitive Communication in Hospitals: A User Interface Evaluation and Redesign of Ascom Wireless IP-DECT Phones. *eTELEMED 2011, The Third International Conference on eHealth, Telemedicine, and Social Medicine*, 37 – 46.

Solvoll, T. (2013a). Mobile Communication in Hospitals: What is the Problem? In C. Rückemann (Ed.), *Integrated Information and Computing Systems for Natural, Spatial, and Social Sciences* (pp. 287–301). Hershey, PA: Information Science Reference. doi:10.4018/978-1-4666-2190-9.ch014

Solvoll, T. (2016). *Mobile Communication in Hospitals: Is It Still a Problem? In Handbook of Research on Effective Communication, Leadership, and Conflict Resolution* (pp. 545–564). Hershey, PA: IGI Global. doi:10.4018/978-1-4666-9970-0.ch029

Solvoll, T., & Scholl, J. (2008). Strategies to reduce interruptions from mobile communication systems in surgical wards. *Journal of Telemedicine and Telecare*, *14*(7), 389–392. doi:10.1258/jtt.2008.007015 PMID:18852324

Solvoll, T., Scholl, J., & Hartvigsen, G. (2010). Physicians interrupted by mobile devices relations between devices, roles and duties. *Studies in Health Technology and Informatics*, *160*, 1365.

Solvoll, T., Scholl, J., & Hartvigsen, G. (2013). Physicians Interrupted by Mobile Devices in Hospitals: Understanding the Interaction Between Devices, Roles, and Duties. *Journal of Medical Internet Research*, *15*(3), e56. doi:10.2196/jmir.2473 PMID:23470528

So, M. W. C., & Sculli, D. (2002). Theroleoftrust, quality, value and risk in conducting e-business. *Industrial Management & Data Systems*, *102*(9), 503–512. doi:10.1108/02635570210450181

Sones, E. (2009, October). 360 assessment, an easier pill to swallow: Implementation of peer assessment for captain's career course students and staff. *U.S. Army Medical Department Journal,* 59-63.

Sonnentag, S., & Frese, M. (2002). Performance concepts. In S. Sonnentag (Ed.), *Psychological Management of Individual Performance: A Handbook in the Psychology of Management in Organizations* (pp. 3–25). West Sussex, UK: John Wiley & Sons. doi:10.1002/0470013419

Sosa, E. (2010). *The Epistemology Of Disagreement.* His Armchair Philosophy.

Sousa, R. (2003). Linking Quality Management to Manufacturing Strategy: An Empirical Investigation of Customer Focus Practices. *Journal of Operations Management*, *21*(1), 1–18. doi:10.1016/S0272-6963(02)00055-4

Sousa, R., & Voss, C. (2002). Quality Management Re-visited: A Reflective Review and Agenda for Future Research. *Journal of Operations Management*, *20*(1), 91–109. doi:10.1016/S0272-6963(01)00088-2

Spanbauer, S. J. (1989). *Measuring and Costing Quality in Education.* Appleton, WI: Fox Valley Technical College Foundation.

Spreitzer, G. M., & Mishra, A. K. (1999). Giving Up Control Without Losing Control: Trust and Its Substitutes' Effects on Managers' Involving Employees in Decision Making. *Group & Organization Management*, *14*(2), 155–187. doi:10.1177/1059601199242003

Spurck, P. A., Mohr, M. L., Seroka, A. M., & Stoner, M. (1995). The impact of a wireless telecommunication system on time efficiency. *The Journal of Nursing Administration*, *25*(6), 21–26. doi:10.1097/00005110-199506000-00007 PMID:7776003

Stacey, R. D. (2001). *Complex Responsive Processes in Organizations*. London: Routledge.

Stanton, J. M. (2000a). Reactions to employee performance monitoring: Framework, review, and research directions. *Human Performance*, *13*(1), 85–113. doi:10.1207/S15327043HUP1301_4

Stanton, J. M. (2000b). Traditional and electronic monitoring from an organizational justice perspec- tive. *Journal of Business and Psychology*, *15*(1), 129–147. doi:10.1023/A:1007775020214

Stanton, J. M., & Barnes-Farrell, J. L. (1996). Effects of electronic performance-monitoring on personal control, satisfaction and performance. *The Journal of Applied Psychology*, *81*(6), 738–745. doi:10.1037/0021-9010.81.6.738

Stanton, J. M., & Weiss, E. M. (2000). Electronic monitoring in their own words: An exploratory study of employees' experiences with new types of surveillance. *Computers in Human Behavior*, *16*(4), 423–440. doi:10.1016/S0747-5632(00)00018-2

Stanton, J., & Stam, K. (2003). Information Technology, Privacy and Power within Organizations: A View from Boundary Theory and Social Exchange Perspectives. *Surveillance & Society*, *1*(2), 152–190. doi:10.24908s.v1i2.3351

Staples, A. (2011, May 30). Tressel tries to take brunt of NCAA wrath with Ohio State resignation. *Sportsillustrated.com*. Retrieved June 1, 2011 from http://sportsillustrated.cnn.com/2011/writers/andy_staples/05/30/Jim.Tressel.OSU/index.html

Staples, D. S., & Zhao, L. (2006). The effects of cultural diversity in virtual teams versus face-to-face teams. *Group Decision and Negotiation*, *15*(4), 389–406. doi:10.100710726-006-9042-x

Starbucks. (2011, November). *Starbucks to Present at Morgan Stanley Global Consumer Conference*. Starbucks Coffee Company Investor Relations. Retrieved from http://investor.starbucks.com/phoenix.zhtml?c=99518&p=irol-irhome

Starratt, R. (2005). Cultivating the moral character of learning and teaching: A neglected dimensions of educational leadership. *School Leadership & Management*, *25*(4), 399–411. doi:10.1080/13634230500197272

Staub, R. E. I. (1996). *The heart of leadership: 12 practices of courageous leaders*. Provo, UT: Publishers Press.

Staw, B. (1986). Organizational psychology and the pursuit of the happy/productive worker. *California Management Review*, *28*(4), 40–53. doi:10.2307/41165214

Stefanescu, C., & Popa, L. (2008, February). *Managerial Communication, Paper No. 7172*. Retrieved from http://mpra.ub.uni-muenchen.de/7172/

Stein, S. J., & Book, H. (2010). *The EQ edge: Emotional intelligence and your success*. Ontario, Canada: John Wiley & Sons.

Stevens, B. (2005). What communication skills do employers want? Silicon Valley recruiters respond. *Journal of Employment Counseling*, *42*(1), 2–9. doi:10.1002/j.2161-1920.2005.tb00893.x

Steyn, G. M. (2000). Applying Principles of TQM to a learning process: a case study. *SAJHE/SATHO, 14*(1), 11-14. Retrieved from: http://hdl.handle.net/10500/242

Stinchcombe, A. L. (1974). *Creating Efficient Industrial Administration*. New York: Academic Press.

Stogdill, R. (1974). Handbook of leadership. New York: The Free Press: A Division of McMillan Publishing.

Stone, D., Patton, B., & Heen, S. (1999). *Difficult conversations: How to discuss what matters most*. New York, NY: Viking.

Su, C., & Contractor, N. (2011). A Multidimensional Network Approach to Studying Team Members' Information Seeking From Human and Digital Knowledge Sources in Consulting Firms. *Journal of the American Society for Information Science and Technology*, *62*(7), 1257–1275. doi:10.1002/asi.21526

Sunshine, J., & Tyler, T. (2003a). Moral solidarity, identification with the community, and the importance of procedural justice: The police as prototypical representatives of a group's moral values. *Social Psychology Quarterly*, *66*(2), 153–165. doi:10.2307/1519845

Sunshine, J., & Tyler, T. R. (2003b). The role of procedural justice and legitimacy in shaping public support in policing. *Law & Society Review*, *37*(3), 513–548. doi:10.1111/1540-5893.3703002

Supovitz, J. (2013). Situated research design and methodological choices in formative program evaluation. *National Society for the Study of Education Yearbook*, *112*(2), 372–399.

Svensson, M., & Klefsjö, B. (2006). TQM-based self-assessment in the education sector: Experiences from a Swedish Upper Secondary School Project. *Quality Assurance in Education*, *14*(4), 299–323. doi:10.1108/09684880610703929

Sykes, J. (1996). Claims And Disputes In Construction. *Constitutional Law Journal (Newark, N.J.)*, *12*(1), 3–13.

Sykes, R. E., & Clark, J. P. (1975). A theory of deference exchange in police-civilian encounters. *American Journal of Sociology*, *81*(3), 584–600. doi:10.1086/226109

Sztajn, P. (1992). A matter of metaphors: Education as a handmade process. *Educational Leadership*, *50*(3), 35–37.

Tabachnick, B. G., & Fidell, L. S. (2001). *Using multivariate statistics* (4th ed.). Needham Heights, MA: Allyn & Bacon.

Talaei-Khoei, A., Solvoll, T., Ray, P., & Parameshwaran, N. (2011). Policy-based Awareness Management (PAM): Case study of a wireless communication system at a hospital. *Journal of Systems and Software*, *84*(10), 1791–1805. doi:10.1016/j.jss.2011.05.024

Talaei-Khoei, A., Solvoll, T., Ray, P., & Parameshwaran, N. (2012). Maintaining awareness using policies; Enabling agents to identify relevance of information. *Journal of Computer and System Sciences*, *78*(1), 370–391. doi:10.1016/j.jcss.2011.05.013

Tang, J. C., Yankelovich, N., Begole, J., Kleek, M. V., Li, F., & Bhalodia, J. (2001). ConNexus to awarenex: extending awareness to mobile users. *Proceedings of the SIGCHI conference on Human factors in computing systems*. 10.1145/365024.365105

Tankebe, J., & Liebling, A. (2013). *Legitimacy and criminal justice: An international exploration*. OUP Oxford. doi:10.1093/acprof:oso/9780198701996.001.0001

Tate, T. P., Collins, P., Xu, Y., Yau, J. C., Krishnan, J., Prado, Y., & Warschauer, M. (2019). Visual-Syntactic Text Format: Improving Adolescent Literacy. *Scientific Studies of Reading*, 1–18.

Tavani, H. T. (2004). *Ethics and technology: Ethical issues in an age of information and communication technology*. Chichester, UK: John Wiley & Sons.

Taylor, P., & Bain, P. (1999). 'An assembly line in the head': Work and employee relations in the call centre. *Industrial Relations Journal,* (30), 101–117.

Taylor, E. W. (2001). Transformative learning theory: A neurobiological perspective of the role of emotions and unconscious ways of knowing. *International Journal of Lifelong Education*, *20*(3), 218–236. doi:10.1080/02601370110036064

Te'eni, D. (2001). A Cognitive-Affective Model of Organizational Communication for Designing IT. *MIS Quarterly*, *25*(2), 251-312. Retrieved on June 13, 2018 from http://www.jstor.org/stable/3250931

Temponi, C. (2005). Continuous improvement framework: Implications for academia. *Quality Assurance in Education, 13*(1), 17–36. doi:10.1108/09684880510578632

Temtime, Z. T. (2003). The Moderating Impacts of Business Planning and Firm Size on the Total Quality Management Practices. *The TQM Magazine, 15*(1), 52–60. doi:10.1108/09544780310454457

Terry, P. M. (1996). *Using Total Quality Management Principles to Implement School-Based Management.* Paper presented at the 14th Annual International Conference of the International Association of Management, Toronto, Ontario, Canada. Retrieved from: http://files.eric.ed.gov/fulltext/ED412590.pdf

Tess, P. A. (2013). The role of social media in higher education classes (real and virtual) – A literature review. *Computers in Human Behavior, 29*(5), A60–A68. doi:10.1016/j.chb.2012.12.032

Thatam, S. A. (2008). *Strategic Communication: A Primer.* Advanced Research and Assessment Group.

The Channel Tunnel Group Ltd v. Balfour Beatty Construction Ltd. (1993).

The Ohio State University. (2011, December 20). *Statement on NCAA sanctions.* Retrieved August 28, 2015 from http://www.ohiostatebuckeyes.com/genrel/122011aab.html

The Ohio State University. (2018a). *Gene Smith.* Retrieved from http://ohiostatebuckeyes.com/staff/gene-smith/

The Ohio State University. (2018b). *Urban Meyer.* Retrieved from http://ohiostatebuckeyes.com/coach/urban-meyer/

The Problem. (1997). In J. H. Steyn (Ed.), *Alternative Dispute Resolution, Issue Paper 8 (Project 94).* Pretoria: South African Law Commission.

The Weather Network. (2018). Retrieved from www.theweathernetwork.com

Therkelsen, D. J., & Fiebich, C. L. (2003). The supervisor: The linchpin of employee relations. *Journal of Communication Management, 8*(2), 120–129. doi:10.1108/13632540410807592

Thibaut, J., Walker, L., LaTour, S., & Houlden, P. (1973). Procedural justice as fairness. *Stanford Law Review, 26*(6), 1271. doi:10.2307/1227990

Thomas, M., Hawkins, A., Christian, F., Merlene, M., & de Meyrick, C. (2011). *Independent Review of the School Based Management Report.* Summary Report (October 2011). Department of Education and Communities, NSW: ARTD Consultants. Retrieved from: https://www.det.nsw.edu.au/media/downloads/about-us/statistics-and-research/key-statistics-and-reports/irsb-management-pilot-sr.pdf

Thomas, K. W., & Velthouse, B. S. (1990). Cognitive elements of empowerment: An 'interpretative' model of intrinsic task motivation. *Academy of Management Review*, (19): 312–330.

Thorndike, E. L. (1920). Intelligence and its use. *Harper's Magazine, 140,* 227-235.

Thorndike, R. L., & Stein, S. (1937). An eval- uation of the attempts to measure social intelligence. *Psychological Bulletin, 34*(5), 275–285. doi:10.1037/h0053850

Tidd, J. (2001). Innovation management in context: Environment, organization and performance. *International Journal of Management Reviews, 3*(3), 169–183. doi:10.1111/1468-2370.00062

Ting-Toomey, S. (1999). *Communicating across cultures.* New York: Guilford.

Tjosvold, D. (2008). The conflict-positive organization: It depends upon us. *Journal of Organizational Behavior, 29*(1), 19–28. doi:10.1002/job.473

TMC. (2016). *Virtual team successes and stresses – a case study*. Retrieved August 20, 2018 from http://www.tmcorp.com/Perspectives/Global-Advice/Global-Advice/80/vobid--787/

Tomlinson, G. (2010). Building a culture of high employee engagement. *Strategic HR Review*, *9*(3), 25–31. doi:10.1108/14754391011040046

Tompkins, T. C. (1995). Role of diffusion in collective learning. *The International Journal of Organizational Analysis*, *3*(1), 69–85. doi:10.1108/eb028824

Topper, A. (2007). Are they the same? Comparing the instructional quality of online and face-to-face graduate education courses. *Assessment & Evaluation in Higher Education*, *32*(6), 681–691. doi:10.1080/02602930601117233

Torres, C. A., & Antikainen, A. (2003). Introduction to a sociology of education: Old dilemmas in a new century? In C. A. Torres & A. Antikainen (Eds.), *The International Handbook on the Sociology of Education: An International Assessment of New Research and Theory* (pp. 1–18). Lanham, MD: Rowman & Littlefield.

Towers Watson Study. (2013). Retrieved from http://www.towerswatson.com/en/Insights/IC-Types/Survey-Research-Results/2013/05/Infographic-2013-Change-and-Communication-ROI-Study

Treem, J. W., & Leonardi, P. M. (2012). Social Media Use in Organizations: Exploring the Affordances of Visibility, Editability, Persistence, and Association. *Communication Yearbook*, *36*(1), 143–189.

Tressel resignation: A timeline of quotes (2011, May 30). *The Columbus Dispatch*. Retrieved August 28, 2015 from http://www.dispatch.com/content/stories/sports/2011/05/30/timeline-in-quotes.html

Tressel, J. (2011, March 8). Jim Tressel press conference 3/8/11. *Eleven Warriors*. Retrieved from http://www.youtube.com/watch?v=_wyQwtXvCC4

Trochim, W. M., & Donnelly, J. P. (2014). *Estimates of statistics for the behavioral sciences* (8th ed.). Belmont, CA: Wadsworth.

Trompenaars, F., & Hampden-Turner, C. (2012). *Riding the waves of culture*. New York: McGraw Hill.

Tully, E. (2002, May). The slippery slope. *National Executive Institute Associates, Major Cities Chiefs Association and Major County Sheriff's Association Leadership Bulletin,* 1-11.

Turban, E., King, D., Lee, J., Liang, T. P., & Turban, D. (2010). *Electronic commerce 2010: A managerial perspective* (6th ed.). Upper Saddle River, NJ: Pearson.

Turban, E., Leidner, D., McClean, E., & Wetherbe, J. (2006). *Information technology for management – Transforming organisations in the digital economy* (5th ed.). New York, NY: John Wiley & Sons.

Turner, T. W. (2006). *Identifying emotional intelligence competencies differentiating FBI national academy graduates from other law enforcement leaders* (Doctoral dissertation). University of Virginia.

Turner, T. W. (2006). *Identifying emotional intelligence competencies differentiating FBI national academy graduates from other law enforcement leaders*. ProQuest Dissertations & Theses Global. (304965891)

Turner, D. (2004). Perceiving The World Differently. In C. Bell & D. Kahane (Eds.), *Intercultural Dispute Resolution In Aboriginal Contexts*.

Turow, J., Feldman, L., & Metlzer, K. (2005). *Open to exploitation: American shoppers online and offline*. Philadelphia, PA: Annenberg Public Policy Centre, University of Pennsylvania.

Twedt, C. (2017, September 20). 'Hot cop' in hot water as anti-Semitic posts surface. *Ragan's PR Daily*. Retrieved from https://www.prdaily.com/crisiscommunications/Articles/Hot_cop_in_hot_water_as_antiSemitic_posts_surface_23267.aspx

Tyler, T. (2003). Trust within organisations. *Personnel Review*, *32*(5), 556–568. doi:10.1108/00483480310488333

Tyler, T. R. (1988). What is procedural justice?: Criteria used by citizens to assess the fairness of legal procedures. *Law & Society Review*, *22*(1), 103–135. doi:10.2307/3053563

Tyler, T. R. (1990). *Why people obey the law*. Princeton University Press.

Tyler, T. R. (2003). Procedural justice, legitimacy, and the effective rule of law. In M. Tonry (Ed.), *Crime and justice: A review of research* (Vol. 30, pp. 431–505). Chicago: University of Chicago Press.

Tyler, T. R. (2004). Enhancing police legitimacy. *The Annals of the American Academy of Political and Social Science*, *593*(1), 84–99. doi:10.1177/0002716203262627

Tyler, T. R. (2010). *Why people cooperate: The role of social motivations*. Princeton University Press. doi:10.1515/9781400836666

Tyler, T. R., & Huo, Y. (2002). *Trust in the law: encouraging public cooperation with the police and courts through*. Russell Sage Foundation.

U. (2007). *United Nations Declaration On The Rights Of Indigenous People* (A/RES/61/295). New York, NY: United Nations. Retrieved From Https://Www.Un.Org/Development/Desa/Indigenouspeoples/Declaration-On-The-Rights-Of-Indigenous-Peoples.Html

UC Berkeley. (2015). *Using Emotional Intelligence to Improve Communication*. UC Berkeley Extension. Retrieved June 25, 2015 from http://extension.berkeley.edu/search/publicCourseSearchDetails.do?method=load&courseId=8939289&gclid=CI2akq7Cq8YCFUGTfgod5lwAdw

Ullrich, C., Tan, X., Borau, K., Shen, L., Luo, H., & Shen, R. (2008). Why Web 2.0 is good for learning and for research: principles and prototypes. *Proceedings of the 17 th International World Wide Web Conference*, 705-714. 10.1145/1367497.1367593

Ulmer, R. R., Seeger, M. W., & Sellnow, T. L. (2007). Post-crisis communication and renewal: Expanding the parameters of post-crisis discourse. *Public Relations Review*, *33*(2), 130–134. doi:10.1016/j.pubrev.2006.11.015

Ulmer, R. R., Sellnow, T. L., & Seeger, M. W. (2009). Post-crisis communication and renewal: Understanding the potential for positive outcomes in crisis communication. In R. L. Heath & D. H. O'Hair (Eds.), *Handbook of Risk and Crisis Communication*. New York: Routledge.

Ulmer, R. R., Sellnow, T. L., & Seeger, M. W. (2019). *Effective crisis communication: Moving from crisis to opportunity* (4th ed.). Thousand Oaks, CA: Sage.

UNESCO. (2010). *Transcultural Communication in the Digital Age*. Retrieved from http://www.unesco.org/en/university-twinning-and-networking/access-by-region/europe-and-north-america/austria/unesco-chair-in-multilingual-transcultural-communication-in-the-digital-age-902/

United Nations Commission On International Trade Law. (2015). *UNCITRAL Model Law On International Commercial Arbitration*. Retrieved from Http://Www.Uncitral.Org/Uncitral/En/Uncitral_Texts/Arbitration/1985Model_Arbitration_Status.Html

United States Army. (2017). *Army profession and leadership policy*. Regulation 600-10. Department of the Army. Retrieved from, http://data.cape.army.mil/web/repository/doctrine/ar600-100.pdf

University of Guelph closing 2 satellite campuses. (2015). Retrieved from www.thestar.com/news/queenspark/2015

University of Windsor closing its centre for studies in social justice. (2013). Retrieved from Nationalpost.com/…to-join-ghostly…haunting-university-campuses

Ury, W., Brett, J. M., & Goldberg, S. B. (1988). *Getting disputes resolved: Designing systems to cut the costs of conflict*. San Francisco: Jossey-Bass.

USDOJ. (2018). *All News*. U.S. Department of Justice Office of the Inspector General.

Uselac, S. (1993). *Zen Leadership: The Human Side of Total Quality Team Management*. Loudonville, OH: Mohican.

Valdesolo, P., & DeSteno, D. (2011). Synchrony and the social tuning of compassion. *Emotion (Washington, D.C.)*, *11*(2), 262–266. doi:10.1037/a0021302 PMID:21500895

Valenti, J. (2017, September 24). Zoe Quinn: after Gamergate, don't 'cede the internet to whoever screams the loudest. *The Guardian*. Retrieved from https://www.theguardian.com/technology/2017/sep/24/zoe-quinn-gamergate-online-abuse

Vallaster, C., & deChernatony, L. (2004). Internal brand building and structuration: The role of leadership. *European Journal of Marketing*, *40*(7/8), 761–784. doi:10.1108/03090560610669982

Van Dyne, L., Graham, J., & Dienesch, R. (1994). Organizational citizenship behavior: Construct redefinition, measurement and validation. *Academy of Management Journal*, *37*(4), 765–802.

van Lieshout, E., van der Veer, S., Hensbroek, R., Korevaar, J., Vroom, M., & Schultz, M. (2007). Interference by new-generation mobile phones on critical care medical equipment. *Critical Care (London, England)*, *11*(5), R98. doi:10.1186/cc6115 PMID:17822524

Van Maanen, J. (1973). *Working the street: A developmental view of police behavior*. Retrieved from https://dspace.mit.edu/bitstream/handle/1721.1/1873/SWP-0681-14451100.pdf

Van Vught, F. A., & Westerheijden, D. F. (1992). *Quality Management and Quality Assurance in European Higher Education: Methods and Mechanics*. Center for Higher Education Policy Studies, University of Twente.

van Zee, E. (2000). Analysis of a student-generated inquiry discussion. *International Journal of Science Education, 22*, 115–142.

Veletsianos, G. (2011). Higher education scholars' participation and practices on Twitter. *Journal of Computer Assisted Learning*, *28*(4), 336–349. doi:10.1111/j.1365-2729.2011.00449.x

Veliz, C. (2018). *Common Sense for A.I. Is a Great Idea But it's harder than it sounds*. Retrieved on 12th November 2018 at https://slate.com/technology/2018/03/paul-allens-plan-to-teach-artificial-intelligence-common-sense.html

Vicini, J. (2011), Government did not pay $16 for muffins after all. *Reuters Online Edition*. Retrieved from http://www.reuters.com/article/2011/09/30/us-usa-justice-muffins-idUSTRE78T54220110930

Victor, D. (2017, April 5). Pepsi pulls ad accused of trivializing Black Lives Matter. *NY Times*. Retrieved from https://www.nytimes.com/2017/04/05/business/kendall-jenner-pepsi-ad.html

Viswesvaran, C. (2001). Assessment of individual job performance: a review of the past century and a look ahead. In N. Anderson, D. Ones, H. Sinangil, & C. Viswesvaran (Eds.), *Handbook of Industrial, Work and Organizational Psychology* (Vol. 1, pp. 110–126). London: SAGE Publications. doi:10.4135/9781848608320.n7

Von Hippel, E. (1988). *The Sources of Innovation.* New York: Oxford University Press.

Von Neumann, J. (1933). Mathematische Grundlagen der Quantenmechanik. *Monatshefte Für Mathematik, 40*(1), A31.

Voss, C., & Raz, T. (2016). *Never split the difference: Negotiating as if your life depended on it* (1st ed.). New York, NY: Harper Business, an imprint of HarperCollins Publishers.

Vroom, V. H. (1964). *Work and Motivation.* Willey New York.

Vroom, V. H., & Yetton, P. W. (1973). *Leadership and decision making.* Pittsburgh, PA: University of Pittsburgh Press. doi:10.2307/j.ctt6wrc8r

Wagner, J., Cummings, G., Smith, D., Olson, J., Anderson, L., & Warren, S. (2010). The Relationship between structural empowerment and psychological empowerment for nurses – a systematic view. *Journal of Nursing Management, 18*(4), 448–462. doi:10.1111/j.1365-2834.2010.01088.x

Walker, D. (2010, December 23). Ohio State Buckeyes: Why Terrelle Pryor and others should sit out the Sugar Bowl. *The Bleacher Report.* Retrieved October 27, 2015 from http://bleacherreport.com/articles/551973-bad-buckeyes-why-terrell-pryor-and-others-should-sit-out-the-sugar-bowl

Walker, L.J. (1989). A Longitudinal Study of Moral Reasoning. *Child Development, 60,* 157-160.

Walker, L.J. (1987). Moral Stages and Moral Orientations in Real-life and Hypothetical Dilemmas. *Developmental Psychology, 58,* 842–858.

Walpole, M., & Noeth, R. J. (2002). *The Promise of Baldrige for K-12 Education.* ACT Policy Report: ACT Policy Research Inc. Retrieved from https://www.act.org/research/policymakers/pdf/baldrige.pdf

Wanberg, C. R., & Banas, J. T. (2000). Predictors and outcomes of openness to changes in a reorganizing workplace. *The Journal of Applied Psychology, 85*(1), 132–142. doi:10.1037/0021-9010.85.1.132 PMID:10740964

Wang, B., Song, D., Wang, B., Zhang, P., Li, J., Song, D., & Shang, Z. (2018a). Exploration of Quantum Interference in Doc- ument Relevance Judgement Discrepancy. *Entropy (Basel, Switzerland), 18*(4), 144. doi:10.3390/e18040144

Wang, H., Lee, M. K. O., & Wang, C. (1998). Consumer privacy concerns about internet marketing. *Communications of the ACM, 41*(3), 63–70. doi:10.1145/272287.272299

Wang, S. K., Hsu, H. Y., Reeves, T. C., & Coster, D. C. (2014). Professional development to enhance teachers' practices in using information and communication technologies (ICTs) as cognitive tools: Lessons learned from a design-based research study. *Computers & Education, 79,* 101–115. doi:10.1016/j.compedu.2014.07.006

Wang, Z., & Busemeyer, J. (2013). A Quantum Question Order Model Supported by Empirical Tests of an A Priori and Precise Prediction. *Topics in Cognitive Science, 5*(4), 689–710. doi:10.1111/tops.12040 PMID:24027203

Want, Schilit, Adams, Gold, Petersen, Goldberg, … Weiser. (1995) An overview of the parctab ubiquitous computing experiment. Personal Communications, IEEE, 2(6), 28 43.

Want, R., Hopper, A., Falcao, V., & Gibbons, J. (1992). The active badge location system. *ACM Transactions on Information Systems, 10*(1), 91–102. doi:10.1145/128756.128759

Wark, G. R., & Krebs, D. L. (1996). Gender and Dilemma Differences in Real-Life Moral Judgment 32. *Developmental Psychology, 32*(2), 220–230. doi:10.1037/0012-1649.32.2.220

Washington State Office Of Administrative Hearings. (2015). *Glossary For Administrative Hearings.* Author.

Waters, M. (2004). The leadership role of the first-line supervisor in police operations. *Florida Police Chief Magazine*. Retrieved from, http://www.clearwaterpolice.org/articles/waters.asp

Watkins, M. (2002). *Breakthrough business negotiation*. San Francisco: Jossey-Bass.

Watson Wyatt White Paper. (2008/2009). *Driving business results through continuous engagement*. Retrieved on 29 August from http://www.watsonwyatt.com/research/pdfs/2008-US-0232.pdf

Waxman, O. B. (2014, December 15). 10 times social media made the world better in 2014. *TIME*. Retrieved from http://time.com/3633786/heartwarming-stories-2014/

Webber, E. (2018). *Building Successful Communities of Practice*. London: Tacit.

WEF. (2015). *Collaborative Innovation Transforming Business, Driving Growth*. Geneva: World Economic Forum.

Weick, K. (1995). *Sensemaking in organizations*, Sage, London: Weick, K., Sutcliffe, K. M., & Obstfeld, D. (2005), Organizing and the process of sensemaking. *Organization Science*, *16*(4), 409–421. doi:10.1287/orsc.1050.0133

Weick, K. E. (2000). Quality Improvement: A Sensemaking Perspective. In R. E. Cole & W. R. Scott (Eds.), *The Quality Movement & Organization Theory* (pp. 155–172). Thousand Oaks, CA: Sage Publications Inc.

Weiser, M. (1991). The computer for the 21st century. *Scientific American*, *265*(3), 94–104. doi:10.1038cientificamerican0991-94 PMID:1675486

Weiser, M., Gold, R., & Brown, J. S. (1999). The origins of ubiquitous computing research at parc in the late 1980s. *IBM Systems Journal*, *38*(4), 693–696. doi:10.1147j.384.0693

Welch, M., & Jackson, P. R. (2007). Rethinking internal communication: A stakeholder approach. *Corporate Communications*, *12*(2), 177–198. doi:10.1108/13563280710744847

Weller, L. D. (1998). Unlocking the culture for quality schools: Reengineering. *International Journal of Educational Management*, *12*(6), 250–259. doi:10.1108/09513549810237959

Welsh-Huggins, A. (2013, June 5). Ohio State President Gordon Gee resigns. *The Boston Globe*. Retrieved October 25, 2015 from https://www.bostonglobe.com/sports/2013/06/05/ohio-president-gee-resigns/ifaooLYgKU6YAiqkjzOaSK/story.html

Wenger, E., McDemortt, R., & Snyder, W. (2002). Cultivating Communities of practice. Boston: Harvard Business Scholl Press.

Wenger, E., White, N., & Smith, J. D. (2009). *Digital Habitats: stewarding technology for communities*. Portland, OR: CPsquare.

Wenger, E. (1998). *Communities of Practice: Learning, Meaning, and Identity*. Cambridge, UK: Cambridge University Press. doi:10.1017/CBO9780511803932

Wenger, E., & Snyder, W. (2000, January). Communities of practice: The organizational frontier. *Harvard Business Review*, 139–145.

Wen, H. J., Schwieger, D., & Gershuny, P. (2007). Internet usage monitoring in the workplace: Its legal challenges and implementation strategies. *Information Systems Management*, *24*(2), 185–196. doi:10.1080/10580530701221072

Wenying, W. (2005). Role Of Conciliation In Resolving Disputes: A PRC Perspective. *The Ohio State Journal On Dispute Resolution, 20*(421).

Westbrook, Woods, Rob, Dunsmuir, & Day. (2011). Association of interruptions with an increased risk and severity of medication administration errors. *Archives of Internal Medicine, 170*(8), 683-690.

Westerman, J. W., & Rosse, J. G. (1997). Reducing the threat of rater nonparticipation in 360-degree feedback systems: An exploratory examination of antecedents to participation in upward ratings. *Group & Organization Management, 22*(2), 288–309. doi:10.1177/1059601197222008

Whiting, J. W. M. (1986). George Peter Murdock (1897–1985). *American Anthropologist, 88*(3), 682–686. doi:10.1525/aa.1986.88.3.02a00120

Wholefoods. (2011, August). *John Mackey's Blog*. Retrieved from http://www2.wholefoodsmarket.com/blogs/jmackey/

Wilkinson, A., Dundon, T., & Grugulis, I. (2007). Information but not consultation: Exploring employee involvement in SMEs. *International Journal of Human Resource Management, 18*(7), 1279–1297. doi:10.1080/09585190701393798

Williams, F. P., & McShane, M. D. (1998). Criminology Theory: Selected Classic Readings (2nd ed.). Cincinnati, OH: Anderson Publishing Co.

Williams, L., & Anderson, S. (1991). Job satisfaction and organizational commitment as predictors of organizational citizenship and in-role behaviors. *Journal of Management, 17*(3), 601–617. doi:10.1177/014920639101700305

Wilson, M. (2014, September). Urban Outfitters CEO to employees: Kent State sweatshirt sale an 'unfortunate occurrence'. *PR Daily*. Retrieved from http://www.prdaily.com/Main/Articles/Urban_Outfitters_CEO_to_employees_Kent_State_sweat_17280.aspx

Wilson, S. M. (2013). Professional development for science teachers. *Science, 340*(6130), 310–313. doi:10.1126cience.1230725 PMID:23599481

Winchcl, B. (2014, September). Urban Outfitters offends with red-stained 'vintage' Kent State sweatshirt. *PR Daily*. Retrieved from http://www.prdaily.com/Main/Articles/17261.aspx

Windschitl, M., Thompson, J., Braaten, M., & Stroupe, D. (2012). Proposing a core set of instructional practices and tools for teachers of science. *Science Education, 96*(5), 878–903. doi:10.1002ce.21027

Wineburg, S. (2001). *Historical thinking and other unnatural Acts: Charting the future of teaching the past*. Philadelphia: Temple University Press.

Wing, D. W. (2010). Microaggressions in Everyday Life: Race, Gender, and Sexual Orientation. Hoboken, NJ: John Wiley & Sons.

Winslade, J., & Monk, G. (2000). *Narrative Mediation: A New Approach To Conflict Resolution*. San Francisco: Jossey-Bass Publishers.

Wisdom, J., Chor, K., Hoagwood, K., & Howitz, S. (2014). *Innovation Adoption: A Review of Theories and Constructs, Adm policy Ment Health*. Springer.

Wong, C. A., & Laschinger, H. K. (2013). Authentic leadership, performance, and job satisfaction: The mediating role of empowerment. *Journal of Advanced Nursing, 69*(4), 947–959. doi:10.1111/j.1365-2648.2012.06089.x

Woolf, N. (2016, November 18). Urban Outfitters settles with Navajo Nation after illegally using tribe's name. *The Guardian*. Retrieved from https://www.theguardian.com/us-news/2016/nov/18/urban-outfitters-navajo-nation-settlement

Wren, J. (2006). A quest for a grand theory of leadership. In G. Goethals & G. Sorenson (Eds.), *The quest for a general theory of leadership* (pp. 1–38). Cheltenham, UK: Edward Elgar Publishing. doi:10.4337/9781847202932.00008

Wu, R., Rossos, P., Quan, S., Reeves, S., Lo, V., Wong, B., ... Morra, D. (2011). An evaluation of the use of smartphones to communicate between clinicians: A mixed-methods study. *Journal of Medical Internet Research*, *13*(3), e59. doi:10.2196/jmir.1655 PMID:21875849

Xiaowei, L. (2006). A test on the systematic fuzzy measures of the key degree for the core employees' performance traits. *Canadian Social Science*, *2*(5), 38–43.

Xu, H., Dinev, T., Smith, J. H., & Hart, P. (2011). Information privacy concerns: Linking individual perceptions with institutional privacy assurances. *Journal of the Association for Information Systems*, *12*(12), 798–824. doi:10.17705/1jais.00281

Yankelovich, D., & Immerwahr, J. (1983). *Putting the work ethic to work.* New York: Public Agenda Foundation.

Yazzie, R. (2004). Navajo Peacemaking And Intercultural Dispute Resolution. In C. Bell & D. Kahane (Eds.), Intercultural Dispute Resolution In Aboriginal Contexts. Academic Press.

Yin, R. K. (2014). *Case study research: Design and methods* (5th ed.). Thousand Oaks, CA: Sage.

Yoshino, M. (1968). *Japan's managerial system: Tradition and innovation.* Cambridge, MA: MIT Press.

Young, K. (2011). Social ties, social networks and the Facebook experience. *International Journal of Emerging Technologies and Society*, *9*(1), 20–34.

Yukalov, V., & Sornette, D. (2011). Decision Theory with Prospect Interference and Entanglement. *Theory And Decision: An International Journal For Methods And Models In The Social And Decision. The Sciences*, *70*(3), 283–328.

Yulk, G., & Becker, W. (2006). Effective empowerment in organizations. *Organizational Management Journal*, *3*(3), 210–231. doi:10.1057/omj.2006.20

Zeffane, R., Tipu, S. A., & Ryan, J. C. (2011). Communication, Commitment & Trust: Exploring the Triad. *International Journal of Business and Management*, *6*(6), 77–87. doi:10.5539/ijbm.v6n6p77

Zinger, D., Naranjo, A., Gilbertson, N., Amador, I., & Warschauer, M. (2017). A design-based research approach to improving professional development of the Smithsonian Learning Lab. *Contemporary Issues in Technology & Teacher Education*, *17*(3).

Zivick, J. (2012). Mapping global virtual team leadership actions to organizational roles. *Business Review (Federal Reserve Bank of Philadelphia)*, *19*(2), 18–25.

Zolin, R., Hinds, P. J., Fruchter, R., & Levitt, R. E. (2004). Interpersonal trust in cross-functional, geographically distributed work: A longitudinal study. *Information and Organization*, *14*(1), 1–26. doi:10.1016/j.infoandorg.2003.09.002

Zoller, K. (2015). The Philosophy of Communicative Intelligence. In Cross-Cultural Collaboration and Leadership in Modern Organizations. IGI Global.

Zoller, K. (2008). Nonverbal patterns of teachers from 5 countries: Results from the TIMSS-R video study. *Dissertation Abstracts International. A, The Humanities and Social Sciences*, *68*(9-A), 154.

Zoller, K., & Landry, C. (2010). *The choreography of presenting: the 7 essential abilities of effective presenters.* Thousand Oaks, CA: Corwin Press.

Zorn, T., Page, D., & Cheney, G. (2000). Nuts about change: Multiple perspectives on change-oriented communication in a public sector organization. *Management Communication Quarterly*, *13*(4), 515–566. doi:10.1177/0893318900134001

Zureik, E. (2003). Theorizing surveillance: the case of the workplace. In D. Lyon (Ed.), *Surveillance as Social Sorting* (pp. 31–56). Oxford, UK: Routledge.

Zweig, D., & Webster, J. (2002). Where is the line between benign and invasive? An examination of psychological barriers to the acceptance of awareness monitoring system. *Journal of Organizational Behavior*, *23*(5), 605–633. doi:10.1002/job.157

About the Contributors

Anthony H. Normore, Ph.D, is professor of educational leadership, and department chair of Graduate Education at California State University Dominguez Hills, located in metropolitan Los Angeles. Dr. Normore obtained his Ph.D from the Ontario Institute for the Studies in Education (OISE) at the University of Toronto. His multi-pronged research focusses on (a) the (mis)-interpretation and (mis)-use of leadership and management in higher education, and (b) leadership development of urban school leaders in the context of ethics and social justice. He is the author of 20+ books including: Leading against the grain: Lessons from visionaries for creating just and equitable schools (2018, Teachers College Press), Foundations of educational leadership: The key to developing excellent and equitable schools (2017, Routledge), Restorative practice meets social justice: Un-silencing the voices of at-promise students (2017, IAP), and; Handbook of research on communication, leadership, and conflict resolution (2016, IGI Global publishers). He worked as a teacher, school and district administrator in Canadian schools for 20+ years and then moved to Higher Education where he spent 15+ years. As a professor, he has published 200+ book chapters, research reviews, monographs, and peer-reviewed articles in professional educational leadership journals (e.g., Journal of Educational Administration, Journal of School Leadership, Alberta Journal of Educational Leadership, Educational Administration Quarterly, etc.), law enforcement journals (e.g., Police Chief, FBI law Enforcement Bulletin, International Policing Journal, Law Enforcement Today, etc.), and 300+ regional, national and international professional conference presentations, symposia, and invited keynote addresses. Dr. Normore serves on various editorial review board. He is the recipient of the AERA 2013 Bridge People Award for Leadership for Social Justice SIG, and the 2015 Willower Award of Excellence in Research awarded by UCEA Consortium for the Study of Leadership and Ethics in Education.

Mitch Javidi holds a Ph.D from University of Oklahoma. Mitch is an envisioneer with over 30 years of practical and hands-on Leadership Development experience in diverse industries including Academia, Military, Law Enforcement, Government, and Technology. As a globally recognized leader, he is the founder of the National Command & Staff College, Institute for Credible Leadership Development and the Criminal Justice Commission for Credible Leadership Development. He has trained at the Joint Special Operations Command "JSOC" and the US Army Special Operations Command "USASOC." He was awarded the honorary member of the United States Army Special Operations Command in 1999 and honorary Sheriff by the National Sheriffs' Association in 2016. He served as a tenured Associate Professor at NC State University for 16 years before taking an early retirement but continues to serve as an Adjunct professor without pay (by choice) at both NC State and Illinois State Universities. He is a member of the "Academy of Outstanding Teachers and Scholars" at NC State University and the Distinguished 2004 Alumni of the University of Oklahoma. Mitch is the developer of "MAGNUS," a general theory of Leadership. He has published scholar with over 890+ conference presentations worldwide to include presentations for Fortune 500 companies as well as top Public Safety organizations including FBI NAA, HAPCOA, HIDTA, National Tactical officers Association, California Police Chiefs Associations, National Sheriffs Association, WLLE, and may other national and state associations. His most recent co-authored article was published in the Police Chief Magazine. His most recent books include "Deliberate Leadership: Achieving Success Through Personal Styles," "Handbook of Research on Effective Communication, Leadership, and Conflict Resolution", and "Moral Compass for the Law Enforcement Professionals". His coauthored article entitled "Human Factors: Police Leaders Improving Safety While Developing Meaningful Public Trust" coauthored with Dr. Anthony Normore and Lt. Darius Bone was recently published by the FBI Law Enforcement Bulletin. Click here for publications. Dr. Javidi was the recipient of prestigious "Person of the Year" award by the National Society of Accountants ~ Senator William Victor "Bill" Roth, Jr. "Roth IRA" received the award in the following year

Larry W. Long holds a Ph.D in Communication from the University of Oklahoma and is Professor and Director Emeritus of the School of Communication at Illinois State University. Currently, he serves as Provost, National Command & Staff College. Dr. Long is a retired artillery and infantry officer who completed 21 years of honorable service with the Army National Guard and is an honorary member of the U.S. Army Special Forces, Fort Bragg, North Carolina. He received numerous decorations including the Army Commendation Medal and the Oklahoma Army National Guard Commendation Medal. He has experience overseeing international programs in France and Korea and has served as visiting professor for Novancia Grande école de commerce in Paris, France. In addition, he received the honor of being named as the 1998-99 "Person of the Year" by the National Society of Accountants for his work in developing their strategic plan and process decision making systems. Dr. Long has been qualified as an expert witness in product liability litigation, particularly in the areas of warning label efficacy and research methodology. He has published over 40 books, book chapters and articles in national and international journals. He has presented over 100 research reports at national and international meetings. He has received special recognition and awards for teaching, service, and scholarship from the College of Humanities and Social Sciences at North Carolina State University, Illinois State University, Central States Communication Association, and the National Communication Association.

* * *

Reuven Bar-On is acknowledged as one of the leading pioneers, researchers and practitioners in emotional intelligence, and he coined the term "EQ" and developed the Bar-On EQ-i to assess this construct. He has developed 11 other assessment instruments including the Bar-On Multifactor Measure of Performance to assess a wider range of contributors to human behavior, performance and well-being. Dr. Bar-On has authored or co-authored more than 50 publications, and his work has been cited in more than 12,000 publications to date. He has held adjunct professorships in three universities and has been affiliated with other academic institutes. Dr. Bar-On has served on the editorial boards of four journals and presently serves as an Associate Editor at Frontiers in Psychology. His firm, Bar-On Test Developers, is currently partnering with a software company to develop a VR simulator to assess and develop emergency management, which is funded by the NIH.

Olaf Cames, MSc(Dist) is a visiting researcher in quantum cognition science (US/UK campuses). He holds a doctor of business administration and an MSc with distinction from the University of Liverpool (UK). He is for 34 years in Information Technology and CEO in US/EU startups transforming quantum information sciences research into patents and engineered blueprints. His research is on quantum cognition models for describing human decision making in different applications as models for measuring, forecasting and visualising humanoid mental statuses. His patents and inventions relate to quantum mechanical decision support system apparatuses capable of predicting future state believes, desires, intentions, worldview and logical structures that an individual is likely to expose while moving forward in time. Olaf Cames is a registered researcher on IBM's quantum computer with 24/7 access to quantum computing hardware. His quantum decision models execute on IBM Q quantum computers experimental verify that clinical research in quantum decision science transforms in scale, scope and speed meeting demands in industry, finance, higher education and the executive branch of the government. Predicting future state of mind an individual is likely to expose while moving forward in time has found practical applications in Dr Olaf Cames patents for preventing crime by forecasting intentions to act, establishing election security by quantum-resistant identity theft and reducing operational risk/costs by hiring process optimisation.

Angelo A. Camillo, Ph.D, teaches capstone courses Strategic Management and Business Policy in the School of Business and Economics at Sonoma State University, California, USA . He has over 35 years of international hospitality industry management experience and has worked and lived in ten countries and four continents. He holds a degree from Heidelberg Hotel Management School Germany, a MBA from San Francisco State University, and a PhD from Oklahoma State University. He specializes in Strategic Management, Global Enterprise Management, Management Consulting and Design Thinking, Hospitality Entrepreneurship and Business Development, Wine Education, Wine List and Menu Engineering, Nutritional Analysis and Food Products Labeling. He is also hospitality business consultant to American and international clients.

Isabell Camillo is a Ph.D Candidate at Niagara University, NY. Her dissertation work centres around the strategic positioning of First Follower within leadership & followership dynamics/management & subordinate tensions. Her interdisciplinary research agenda focuses on interpersonal perception, negotiation, decision-making, social innovation & human side of strategy, design thinking & co-creation, and online research methodologies related to global organizational leadership and policy implications. She received a BA in modern languages, a certificate in adult education teaching ESL, and an MA in linguistics from Brock University, and holds certificates in international trade, business management, and leadership from Niagara College Canada.

Vera Silva Carlos has a PhD in Management. She lectured several Curricular Units at UBI between 2012 and 2015, namely Marketing, E-Commerce and Web Marketing and Distribution and Merchandising. She currently lectures Introduction to Marketing, Organizational Behavior, New Business Forms and New Product Development, as Assistant Professor at the University of Aveiro, and is a collaborator of the Center for Research in Business Sciences (NECE-UBI). Among other publications, she has two chapters published in books and an article indexed to SCOPUS in the area of Digital Marketing.

Edward T. Chen is a professor of Management Information Systems of Operations and Information Systems Department in the Manning School of Business at University of Massachusetts Lowell. Dr. Chen has published numerous refereed research articles in scholarly journals and refereed chapters in reference books. Dr. Chen has served as vice-president, board director, track chair, and session chair of many IS/IT professional associations and conferences. Professor Chen has also served as journal editor and editorial reviewer for many academic journals.

Gordon Cockburn is a senior consultant, owner GA Consulting ltd and independent researcher. Studied System Engineering and management of Complexity at UAE, UK. Gordon specialises in transport logistics and systems. He has consulted for and been a director of major international transport corporations as well as advisor to S.M.E.s in UK and overseas for over 30 years. Currently lives in Spain.

Regina Connolly is Professor of Information Systems at Dublin City University, Ireland. She specialises in the intersection of digital innovation with behavioural science. Her work has been published in top Information System and eGovernment journals and she is also the recipient of several international

Richard Conroy, PhD has served as a Director of Police at the university level, an Assistant Chief of Police at the municipal level, and a Special Agent in Charge at the state level. He is a graduate of the FBI National Academy and a life-member of the International Association of Chiefs of Police (IACP). Dr. Conroy is a member of the National Sheriffs' Association (NSA) and holds a Ph.D. in Leadership Studies from Dallas Baptist University. His doctoral research is in the area of emotional intelligence and performance measurement and included using the Multifactor Measure of Performance™ instrument to predict leadership styles in sheriffs' and chief deputies throughout the United States. He is a certified practitioner/consultant in emotional intelligence using the EQ-i 2.0 and the EQ360 assessments. Dr. Conroy is an assistant professor of criminal justice at Dallas Baptist University and a faculty member at the National Command & Staff College and the Caruth Police Institute.

Kara Dellacioppa is Director of the Faculty Development Center at CSU Dominguez Hills. She is Professor of Sociology and author of This Bridge Called Zapatismo (2009) and co-editor of Culture, Politics and Resistance in the 21st Century (2012). She has published peer reviewed articles in Latin American Perspectives, New Political Science, Social Justice, Latino Studies, and International Review of Modern Sociology. Her current research focuses on Women and Academic Leadership.

Brian Ellis is a 20-year veteran of the Sacramento Police Department. Lieutenant Ellis has worked in a number of specialized assignments including with the Problem Oriented Policing Unit, Parole Intervention and Career Criminal Apprehension Teams, Narcotics and Robbery/Burglary divisions. He is currently the SWAT commander and oversees the Metro Division's Special Operations section. Brian earned his undergraduate degree in Criminal Justice from California State, Sacramento and has a MS in Organizational Leadership from National University. Brian is a life-long student of leadership, and passionate about helping others. He has written articles for several publications, including Law Enforcement Today, Police Chief Online, Peace Officers Research Association of California, Police One, The Oxford University Press, The Journal of California Law Enforcement; and has contributed to chapters in IGI Global Publishing textbooks. Please follow him on Twitter @BrianEllis10.

Venesser Fernandes works as an Educational Leadership Lecturer in the Faculty of Education, Monash University, Australia. Her areas of teaching and research interest include: Leadership and Organisational Development Studies; School Leadership; School Accountability and Improvement Systems, Data-Driven Decision-making Processes; Evidence-based School Improvement Systems; Effects of Globalisation; and Social Justice Issues in Education. Dr. Fernandes is currently involved in a Principal Preparation Program running in partnership with Monash University, the Department of Education & Training, Victoria and Bastow Institute of Educational Leadership. This program focuses on the leadership development of aspiring principals within state schools around Victoria, Australia. She has previously worked as a School Reviewer for the Department of Education & Training, Victoria and actively researches in this space. Dr. Fernandes works as an educational consultant with schools and school systems focusing on whole school continuous improvement systems. She is currently engaged in qualitative case-study research within schools that investigates the effectiveness of data-informed decision-making processes being used in Victoria across public, independent and Catholic school systems and focuses upon the leadership function that facilitates these processes.

Nicole Gilbertson is the Site Director of the University of California, Irvine History Project. She directs professional development for history teachers through state and federal grant programs, fee-for-service contracts, and open workshops. Dr. Gilbertson received a Ph.D. in history from the University of California, Irvine while at the same time earning a teaching credential in secondary history-social science. She has authored journal articles on historical thinking, a history curriculum, Humanities Out There, and portions of the proposed California History-Social Science Framework.

Saleem Gul is an Assistant Professor of Project Management at the Institute of Management Sciences, Peshawar. Dr. Gul has over 17 years of teaching experience at the university level. He specializes in teaching: project management, management, research methodology, writing a literature review, qualitative techniques, and complexity. Dr. Gul is a certified trainer and has been conducting training on project management, specifically focusing on the PMI's BoK. Dr. Gul, is an Alumnus of the University of Southampton, where he completed his PhD in the management of complex projects.

Kate Harris is a National Board Certified teacher who teaches Social Studies at Pittsburgh CAPA 6-12, in Pittsburgh, PA. She has also mentored new and pre-service teachers through the Duke University MAT program, of which she is a graduate and currently mentors teachers in the University of Pittsburgh's MAT program. She also has incorporated content-based professional development throughout her career, including authoring a chapter for Bringing the Great War Home, a 2014 American Battle Monuments Commission project, a U.S. Fulbright Summer Seminar abroad for teachers in 2011, and participation in additional seminars sponsored by Gilder-Lehrman, the National Humanities Center, and College Board.

Brian Jarrett, JD, LL.M., Ph.D., is Director of the Program on Negotiation, Conflict Resolution, and Peace-building at California State University Dominguez Hills. He is a lawyer, mediator, and sociologist. He teaches mediation, law, arbitration, dispute-management systems, and restorative practices. He publishes on a host of dispute resolution topics including best practices in mediation, restorative justice, and dispute-systems design.

Alexander Javidi joined the National Command & Staff College (NC&SC) as an intern 6 years ago and worked his way up to his current position working closely with the board commissioners to set standards, and develop and implement training to ensure that minimum standards are maintained. He is responsible for identifying appropriate training providers (including interviews, briefing, appointment letters) and initiating training. He worked closely with the National tactical Officers Association to complete curriculum and help launch the NTOA Command College. He was also instrumental in build up and the launch of the California Tactical Officers Association's on-line academy. Alexander lead the team to complete a comprehensive college credit at the Columbia Southern University. He is a 4-Star certified Credible Leader awarded by the Criminal Justice Commission for Credible Leadership development (CJC-CLD). Alexander is a co-author of the "MAGNUS – Describing the Magnanimous Officer" article published in 2016 by the International Academy of Public Safety. He holds a BA degree in Homeland Security from the American Military University, 2017.

Angela M. Jerome, Ph.D., is a professor of communication at Western Kentucky University. Dr. Jerome obtained her Ph.D. from University of Kansas. Her research focuses on organizational rhetoric, image repair, and sport communication.

James Klopovic holds a Doctor of Public Policy from Charles Sturt University, Sydney Australia, with concentration on service project capacity building at the organizational and community levels focusing on community policing, delinquency prevention, reducing recidivism and reducing prison populations. He has served as a senior staffer on The North Carolina Governor's Crime Commission for 24 years and he is retired from the United States Air Force where he served in multiple locales including South East Asia and the Middle East in numerous capacities including as a logistics line officer, training detachment commander, Department of Défense Advisor (from 1977-78) to the Imperial Iranian Air Force, Area Recruiter for the ROTC and Air Force Academy and Associate Professor, Arizona State University. James has 45 years of experience in the public sector providing leadership at federal, state and local levels with subject matter expertise in strategic planning, municipal governance, financial development, federal granting, community and organizational development, implementation and evaluation. James developed numerous programs one of which was detailing the processes and procedures for School Resource Officers which led to a $10M bill from the NC General Assembly and nearly a decade of sustained granting from the NC Governor's Crime Commission to fund SROs state-wide. SROs grew from 200 in 1995 to over 800 officers in 2012 - and growing - resulting in safer learning environments state-wide. James has served as the principal investigator/project director on a series of research projects to analyse and propose model local projects which led to granting initiatives for dozens of municipal and state initiatives. His technical support to numerous local government entities created and enhanced services ideas such as delinquency prevention, re-entry and decriminalizing the mentally ill. He has broad experience in logistics, training and education as well as project and program design, implementation, management and building program and organizational permanency. He has authored or collaborated on numerous publications on community policing, community development and effective/efficient delivery of public services. His books include: Effective Program Practices for At-Risk Youth: A Continuum of Community Based Programs, Civic Research Institute, Inc., 2003. http://www.civicresearchinstitute.com/epy.html . From the Bottom-Up – Reforming the Criminal Justice System with Capacity Building, Re-entry and a Movement (working title). Civic Research Institute, Inc., Expected release, summer 2019.

Jenell Krishnan is a doctoral candidate at the University of California, Irvine School of Education. She has published work in the Journal of Adolescent and Adult Literacy and the Journal of Child Language. Her research interests focus on research practice partnerships and formative assessment in the technology-enhanced classroom. She received her M.S. in Curriculum and Instruction from the State University of New York at Fredonia and taught English Language Arts at the secondary level for six years at a Title 1 public school in New York State.

Cliona McParland is a Doctoral research scholar at Dublin City University. Her research focuses on the organisational impact of digital innovation, particularly how it influences employee outcomes. She also works as an independent consultant to industry bodies.

Aneil Mishra is the Tom Arthur Professor of Leadership at the East Carolina University College of Business in Greenville, NC.

Karen Mishra is a visiting associate professor of business at the Lundy-Fetterman School of Business at Campbell University in Buies Creek, NC.

Renée J. Mitchell has served in the Sacramento Police Department for twenty-one years and is currently a Police Sergeant. She holds a Bachelor of Science in Psychology from the University of California, Davis, a Master of Arts in Counseling Psychology from the University of San Francisco, a Master of Business Administration from the California State University, Sacramento, a Juris Doctorate from the University of the Pacific, McGeorge School of Law and a Ph.D. from the University of Cambridge. She was a 2009/2010 Fulbright Police Research Fellow, a National Police Foundation Fellow, and an Evidence-Based Policing Hall of Famer.

Mario Pérez-Montoro is a Professor in the Department of Information Science and Media Studies at the University of Barcelona. Working on Interaction Design and Information Visualization Graduate in Organization of Systems of Documentation in the Company by the Polytechnic University of Catalonia, is Doctor in Philosophy and Sciences of the Education by the University of Barcelona. Within his academic trajectory it is possible to emphasize that he has carried out postgraduate studies in the Institute of Discipline of the Community of Bologna (Italy), and has been visiting professor (Center of Studies of Language and Information)) of the University of Stanford (California, USA) and the Information School of UC Berkeley (California, USA). His scientific career focuses on some aspects of the various aspects (conceptual, semantic, epistemological and pragmatic) related to the topic of information theory and knowledge management. The phenomena of information (Scarecrow Press, 2007) and knowledge management in organizations (Trea, 2008). He is currently a professor at the Faculty of Library and Information Science of the University of Barcelona and participates as a consultant in various Information and Knowledge Management projects in the business environment and public administration. Specialties: Planning and implementation of Information and Knowledge Management projects in organizations

Andrew S. Pyle is an Assistant Professor in the Department of Communication. He completed his PhD in Communication at George Mason University, and his MA in Applied Communication from the University of Arkansas at Little Rock. His research focuses on the intersection of crisis communication and intercultural communication. He is also interested in the ways that organizations employ social media to manage crisis communication. He also studies the scholarship of teaching and learning, seeking methods for enhancing the classroom experience for students and faculty alike. Dr. Pyle is teaching courses in the areas of Public Relations and Crisis Communication.

Heather M. Rintoul is Associate Professor in the Schulich School of Education, Nipissing University, Ontario, Canada. Dr. Rintoul holds a Ph.D. from the University of Toronto, specializing in Educational Administration. Her graduate teaching (doctoral and masters), writing, and research focuses on values, ethics and ethical decision-making, leadership, reflective practice, organizational management and social justice. She is the Executive Director International of the Consortium for the Study of Leadership and Ethics in Education, Director of Nipissing University Center for the Study of Leadership and Ethics (NUCSLE), one of 10 centers worldwide of CSLEE part of the umbrella organization UCEA International, and the Editor-in-Chief of the Journal of Authentic Leadership in Education. Heather is a recent recipient of the Authentic Leadership Award. She has published in periodicals: Educational Management, Administration & Leadership (EMAL); Values, Ethics, and Educational Administration (VEEA); Journal of Authentic Leadership in Education (JALE). Examples of her writing and research can also be found in books: Global perspectives on educational leadership reform, Emerald; Examining the assistant principalship, IAP; Pathways to excellence, Emerald; Handbook of research on effective communication, leadership, and conflict resolution, IGI Books.

Ricardo Gouveia Rodrigues has a Ph.D. in Business and lectures Marketing Research, Entrepreneurial Marketing and Data Analysis to undergraduate, master and doctoral students at the University of Beira Interior, Portugal. He is also a researcher and deputy director at the Research Centre for Enterprise Science (NECE – Núcleo de Estudos em Ciências Empresariais). His main research interests are Entrepreneurial Marketing and Entrepreneurship Education, but he's also interested in studying the impact of marketing efforts on themes such as physical activity, children behaviour and happiness. Ricardo Gouveia Rodrigues has published several books and book chapters, as well as peer reviewed papers in international journals.

Sandra Sanz Martos is a PhD in Information and Knowledge Society (2010) by the UOC. Degree in Documentation from the University of Granada (1998) and in Hispanic Philology from the University of Barcelona (1995) Since September 1999, she is a full professor at the Information and Communication Sciences Department of the Open University of Catalonia. During these years she has been director of the program of the Degree in Documentation in the periods 2001-2003 and 2005-2007. He currently directs the specialization "Digital communication for social transformation UOC-SETEM." Her doctoral thesis work is the first in Spanish on the conceptualization and characteristics of the communities of practice. And it presents, in addition, a model of success factors of this type of communities. This work is entitled: Communities of practice: fundamentals, characteristics and behavior. Two years later, she published an adaptation with a manual format in the UOC publishing house as it appears in the list of scientific publications. As a researcher she has been working for fifteen years around collaborative learning, learning and practice communities -the subject of her doctoral thesis- collaborative work and knowledge exchange through social networks. She is a member of the research group GAME (Learning, Media and Entertainment Research Group) recognized as a group consolidated by the AGAUR in 2017. Where he participates -among others- in the R & D project Playful culture, digital competence and learning. Since 2013 she has been a member of the European research network Communities and culture Network + (2013 -) as a result of his postdoctoral stay at the School of Media, Film and Music at the University of Sussex between July and October 2013. Where she started to research about learning communities and social activism. She is also a member of the ThinkEPI Group and a regular contributor to the ThinkEPI Yearbook. Analysis of trends in information and communication (2011-).

Peter Smith is President and CEO of The Leadership Alliance Inc. (TLA), a global consortium of authorities in various disciplines. Peter himself maintains a worldwide consulting practice assisting leading public and private sector organizations enhance performance by optimizing activities related to complexity leadership and critical sustainability drivers such as Interactive Planning, knowledge management, organizational learning, and innovation. He is Director, Center Strategy for the Center for Dynamic Leadership Models in Global Business. Through his research and practice in Dynamic Complexity, Network Visualization & Analysis, Social Network Analysis, Complex Adaptive Systems, and other emerging paradigms, Peter has developed unique in-depth expertise in cross-organizational leadership, organizational learning, digitally-facilitated knowledge sharing, teamwork, collaborative community development, and the identification of Opinion Leaders and Innovation Champions – keys to enhancing Social Capital and successfully implementing any significant systemic organizational undertaking such as Triple Bottom Line Sustainability. Peter has designed and led a number of leadership programs for blue ribbon organizations in UK and N. America. The breadth of Peter's practical hands-on management experience has proven invaluable in ensuring that he can relate to the problems and pressures faced by organizations in today's complex and ambiguous global environments, and it is fundamental to framing his research interests which include Triple Bottom Line Sustainability and related emerging paradigms. Prior to establishing his consulting practice Peter held various senior positions with Exxon in New York and across North America in I/T, HR, R&D, Operations, and Mathematics. In 1990 as an Exxon representative he was one of the founding associates of Peter Senge's Organizational Learning Center (OLC) at MIT, and during the period 1990-94, first as an Exxon representative and later as an independent consultant for TLA, he participated in various systems thinking, microcomputer simulation, and system dynamics activities and projects through the OLC. During this period he also became a TLA associate of Interact, the Philadelphia-based consultancy headed by Dr. Russel Ackoff, and participated in various Interactive Planning projects. Peter has served as Professor of Management Learning Processes with the Canadian School of Management, as Executive Director of The International Foundation for Action Learning- Canada, and as Chair of the International Community of Action Learners. He is Managing Editor of the Journal of Knowledge Management Practice, and Consulting and Special Issues Editor of The Learning Organization. He is also Associate Editor (Practitioners) for IGI's International Journal of Sociotechnology & Knowledge Management. Peter has had published more than sixty academic papers on a broad range of topics related to leadership and performance enhancement, including chapters in "The Handbook of Business Strategy", and IGI's "The Encyclopedia of Communities of Practice in Information & Knowledge Management" and ""Handbook of Research on Socio-Technical Design And Social Networking Systems". He is co-author of "Dynamic Leadership Models for Global Business: Enhancing Digitally Connected Environments" published by IGI Global in January 2013, and co-editor of:"Impact Of Emerging Digital Technologies On Leadership In Global Business". Peter is in demand internationally as a speaker, workshop leader and conference chair.

Terje Solvoll started his career as a researcher in Telenor R&D early in 2001 as a Cand. Scient within computer science. Here he worked mainly with mobile phones and mobile technology. He managed projects developing interactive real time multiplayer games for mobile phones using PDA's and WiFi to simulate smartphones and UMTS/3G networks before 3G was available. In this project, he collaborated with Compaq R&D department in Huston USA. He worked further with tracking within WiFi, Bluetooth, GSM and low frequency radio networks, sending positions from sheep's and signals from medical sensors attached to the animal to the farmer, using GSM networks. In this project, he collaborated with MIT Media lab in Boston Massachusetts USA, center for Things That Think. In 2003, Terje Solvoll left Telenor and started to work with in the commercial industry and satellite communications. He worked as a Systems Supervisor for Dualog AS, which delivers ship-shore IT services to the ships and electronic reporting systems to fishing vessels through satellite communication. He worked here until 2006, and after several hospital stays, he decided to go back to research, and mainly research within telemedicine and e-health. In April 2006, he started at Norwegian Centre for Telemedicine as a project manager for an eczema-counselling project, where parents of children suffering of atopic eczema could have counselling using Internet to communicate with dermatologist to treat the patients, and avoid hospitalization. In 2007, he started to work with his PhD, within mobile communication for hospitals, which he finished in 2013. During this time and until today, he has been supervising more than 20 students on master level within Informatics/Computer science, Telemedicine/E-Health, Industrial design, Business Creation and Entrepreneurship, and one PhD Candidate within Telemedicine/E-health in Italy, Rome. He has also been involved in several other projects, which involves professional networks for dentists, stroke diagnosing and treatment in rural areas using High Definition video conferencing systems through dedicated networks guaranteeing quality, decision-making systems, medical sensors, and more. In October 2015 he started the spinoff company CallMeSmart AS.

Carolyn N. Stevenson is a Full-Time Faculty member at Purdue University Global. She has over 18 years teaching and administrative experience in higher education. She holds a Master of Arts degree in Communication, Master of Business Administration, and Doctor of Education with an emphasis in Higher Education. Prior to pursuing a career in higher education, she worked in the publishing field and served as a technical writing consultant. She currently serves as Associate Editor for the International Journal of Technologies and Educational Marketing (IJTEM), published by IGI-Global; Editorial Board Member and Reviewer for the Journal of Education and Learning published by the Canadian Center of Science and Education. Publications include: Technical Writing: A Comprehensive Resource for Technical Writers at all Levels, (Martinez, Hannigan, Wells, Peterson and Stevenson) Revised and Updated Edition, Kaplan Publishing, Building Online Communities in Higher Education Institutions: Creating Collaborative Experience (with Joanna Bauer), published by IGI Global, and Promoting Climate Change Awareness through Environmental Education (with Lynn Wilson), published by IGI Global.

Timothy W. Turner, EdD, retired as a Supervisory Special Agent after serving 22 years with the with the Federal Bureau of Investigation. His last assignment was as a Program Manager for the Leadership Development Institute of the FBI Academy, at Quantico, Virginia. Dr. Turner most recently served as Dean of the School of Public Service and Administration at Anderson University (South Carolina).

Khaner Walker is the Director of Global Internal & External Communications at Lenovo, based in Morrisville, N.C.

Doron Zinger, Ph.D., is the Director of the University of California, Irvine, CalTeach math and science teacher preparation program. In this role he oversees and instructs in the blended program which prepares STEM majors to teach math and science. Prior to taking on this role Doron was a high school science teacher and administrator, working in historically underrepresented communities to improve learning opportunities in K-12 settings. Doron's research interests include teacher preparation and learning, especially in science and in urban settings. Doron has taught a number of courses at the undergraduate and graduate levels, including teacher preparation courses. Additionally, Doron conducts and researches professional development across a broad range of settings. Doron has published peer reviewed articles and chapters on both teacher preparation and ongoing teacher professional development.

Kendall Zoller (Ed.D.) is an author, researcher, educator, and global speaker. He co-authored The Choreography of Presenting (Corwin-Press, 2010) and has over forty peer reviewed articles and chapters on education and leadership. He has worked with schools in China, India, Malaysia, Indonesia, Europe, Canada and The United States. He was a guest author in Bob Garmston's Presenter's Fieldguide. As president of Sierra Training Associates, Inc., he provides seminars and keynotes on communicative intelligence, adaptive leadership, and facilitation/presentation skills to schools, districts, universities, state agencies, and corporations across the United States and internationally. His international research focuses on identifying nonverbal patterns in the learning environment and their influences on thinking, memory, and learning. He introduced Nonverbal Communicative Intelligence (2007) and Communicative Intelligence (2014). His extensive experience includes training corporate executive level, sales teams, senior managers, university faculty and staff, law enforcement leaders, administrators, and teachers. He is a Cohort I Fellow and mentor to the National Academy for Science and Mathematics Education Leadership.

Index

D

E

F

G

H

I

J

K

L

M

N

O

P

Q

R

S

T

U

V

W

www.ingramcontent.com/pod-product-compliance
Lightning Source LLC
LaVergne TN
LVHW080405011026
849161LV00009B/2350